THE
JEWISH STATE

THE
JEWISH STATE

THE STRUGGLE FOR
ISRAEL'S SOUL

Yoram Hazony

A NEW REPUBLIC BOOK

BASIC
BOOKS

MEMBER OF THE
PERSEUS BOOKS GROUP

Published by Basic Books,
A Member of the Perseus Books Group

Designed by Amy Evans McClure

Library of Congress Cataloging-in-Publication Data
Hazony, Yoram.
The jewish state: the struggle for Israel's soul / Yoram Hazony.
p. cm.
Includes index.
ISBN 0-465-02901-9
1. Post-Zionism.   2. Zionism—History—20th century.
3. Jews—Israel—Identity.   4. Israel—Politics and government—20th century.
I. Title.
DS113.4 .H39 2000
320.54'095694—dc21
00-21814
FIRST EDITON

00 01 02 03 04 / 10 9 8 7 6 5 4 3 2 1

Contents

Acknowledgments

THE PROBLEMS TREATED IN this book have been central to my research and thinking since 1994. Throughout this period, I have been at the Shalem Center, a research and educational institute in Jerusalem, and this book has benefited to a great degree from the environment that Shalem has provided me. It was in conversation and seminars at the center that most of the ideas presented here were first advanced, often by individuals other than myself. It is at the center, too, that these ideas have undergone a process of refinement of a kind only possible in a learning community of scholars and students whose strengths are in diverse disciplines. And it is the center that has, for the past five years, afforded me the resources without which I could not have pursued a work of this scope. This book is therefore the product of efforts by no small number of individuals, all of whom deserve thanks for their unique contributions to it. I will restrict myself to naming those whose contributions were central to the project as a whole.

First among these are the members of the Shalem Center's senior management, Ofir Haivry, Daniel Polisar, Joshua Weinstein, and Yishai Haetzni, who have been my close collaborators for five years. Each of them has had a direct hand in providing me with an intellectual environment that made this work possible. In particular, Ofir Haivry has from the outset served as a tireless partner in the exploration of every corner of Israeli culture and history, offering me his own ideas on the subject and serving as my main sounding board for most of my own innovations in these areas. I am especially grateful for the assistance of Dan Polisar, who has by this point read the book in several drafts and who has made crucial editorial suggestions on a humbling number of occasions. I would also like to thank Hillel Fradkin, David Hazony, Michael Oren, Joshua Weinstein, and Ken Weinstein, who read the entire manuscript and offered significant criticism.

In addition, a special contribution was made in 1995 by William Kristol and John Podhoretz of the *Weekly Standard* and in 1996 by Neal Kozodoy of *Commentary*, who devoted precious time and advice to bringing the first versions of the materials in this book into print.

This book has required research spanning three continents and several languages, which was feasible only due to the assistance of an exceptionally capable research staff. Dina Blank signed on with me as a research assistant more than four years ago, bringing to the book an arsenal of research talents and unmatched enthusiasm. Her resourcefulness and devotion have left their imprint on every page of the book, and on everyone who has worked on the project. Evelyne Geurtz headed my research team for three years, applying her superb critical abilities and judgment to sorting through mountains of raw historical data, as well as recruiting and supervising the research assistants working on the project. Lior Ya'akobi, head of the Shalem Center's research services, has been the team's ace archival researcher, consistently unearthing historical data in an astonishing array of hardly known archives, long-defunct publications, and books and manuscripts that are supposed not to exist anymore. Among the others who contributed their time and expertise to the research effort, special thanks go to Menucha Brand, Miryam Brand, Liat Hartman-Jachman, Avraham Levitt, Aryeh Mendelovitch, Akiva Mevurach, and Julie Zimmerman. My assistant Wendy Kagan brought all this together, fighting unimagined logistical and administrative battles, spending late nights in transatlantic phone calls, and handling the demands of the outside world so that I could devote the necessary time to completing the book.

In addition, I would like to thank members of the Shalem community who have permitted me to make use in this work of research that they conducted under their own auspices: Dina Blank permitted me to use primary source material from her senior thesis and from a second unpublished paper written at Columbia, both of them on the role of intellectuals in Israeli politics. Avraham Levitt allowed me to draw from sections of his paper on the history of Israeli art, which he wrote as a Shalem Graduate Fellow in 1997–1998, a scaled-down version of which was published later in the center's periodical, *Azure*. And Dan Polisar shared with me materials from his research on the Israeli educational system, which was sponsored by the Avi Chai Foundation from 1997 to 1999.

I also owe a debt of gratitude to individuals who have worked to make sure that this book was all it could be in a market that "everyone" said could not tolerate another book on Israel. Martin Peretz, publisher of the *New Republic* and New Republic Books, chose to take an unknown author under his wing out of a deep love for Zionism and a conviction that the Jewish people could stand to hear something different from the views that have come to dominate the last generation of scholarship about Israel. Tim Bartlett of Basic Books has provided me with trenchant, sometimes breathtaking criticism of the book, in so doing improving it dramatically. He has not only been a first-rate editor but a true gentleman, and I am thankful to have entered my first commercial publishing enterprise with such a partner. In addition to successfully bringing the book to publication, my agents Glen Hartley and Lynn Chu have given me much in the way of self-confidence and wisdom about the book business that I desperately needed. Ken Weinstein invested substantial efforts in bringing the book to the attention of the publishing world. Finally, I owe special thanks to Leonard Polisar, who placed at my disposal not only his legal expertise but also his generosity, patience, and humor, all of which were more than needed in my efforts to make sense of the New York publishing business.

Throughout, I had the gracious support of the board of trustees of the Shalem Foundation: Ronald S. Lauder, Roger Hertog, Barry Klein, William Kristol, Allen Roth, and Jacob Schuster. All of them have given generously of their time and experience in assisting me with this project, I am especially thankful for the help of Ronald S. Lauder, chairman of the Shalem Foundation, who has offered me boundless encouragement since the first days of my work on this project. I owe a particular debt of thanks to Roger Hertog, who has read and reread the manuscript and offered numerous important suggestions on how to better project its central points, in addition to dedicating much care and thought to a broad range of subjects related to the publication of the book.

Above all, Zalman Chaim Bernstein, may his memory be blessed, shared with me his warmth, wisdom, and love of inspired action, as well as his profound belief in the eternity of Israel. I only wish he had been able to see this project through to its completion.

Lastly, I wish to thank my wife, Yael, who has given me all I ever wanted: A literary critic who has no concern for politics but only for the truth and the dictates of decency. A friend who goes with me to the mountaintops and valleys, sometimes carrying me back. And a home full of children who gather around the table on Friday nights, talking about the Jewish state.

Yoram Hazony
Eli, Israel
November 1, 1999

Note on the Text and Sources

M Y INTENTION IN THIS BOOK has been to maintain academic standards of scholarship, while at the same time producing a book from which readers with little or no background in Zionist history can nevertheless benefit. For this reason, I have made every effort to render this edition user-friendly to the English reader. This means, in particular, that I have cited English editions of various works originally in Hebrew or German wherever these were available, except in situations where the English translation was inadequate; and in these cases, too, I have tried to provide an English source for the sake of comparison. Similarly, I have attempted to reduce the confusion introduced by the fact that many Zionist and Israeli organizations have frequently merged and split and changed their names, by referring to them only under one, easily understandable name. Thus, the Zionist Organization (ZO) does not become the World Zionist Organization (WZO) after World War I, and the present Israeli Labor party is referred to by this name rather than by its original name, the Workers of the Land of Israel party (Mapai), which was in use until about thirty years ago. By the same token, individuals who hebraized their names are referred to only by the names under which they were later known, so that Golda Myerson is always Golda Meir, and Moshe Shertok is always Moshe Sharett. Although this necessarily introduces some semantic anachronism into the book, I believe that this method adds much in terms of the clarity of the history and its accessibility to a broad range of readers.

For the same reason, I have in two instances deviated from the usual conventions for citation of sources. The first case is that of news stories from the

Israeli press up to and including the 1960s, which very frequently printed direct quotations from public figures without enclosing them in quotation marks. This practice was common even when entire spoken paragraphs were being transcribed in the press verbatim, so that it is not possible today to know with certainty when a given quote was in fact a paraphrase. All quotations of this type should therefore be treated as though the reporter may have been paraphrasing.

A similar difficulty presents itself in the case of Maurice Friedman's exhaustive three-volume biography of Martin Buber. This is an extremely idiosyncratic work, which musters a vast amount of material from Buber's writings and speeches but without any footnotes and often without quotation marks. Despite this unorthodox method, I have found that Friedman's "paraphrases" are usually reliable direct quotations. Where I have been unable to locate his primary sources, I have therefore treated them in the text in the same manner as the rest of his quotations, while indicating which ones are Friedman's paraphrases in the notes at the back of the book.

Introduction:
The Jewish State Doesn't
Live Here Anymore

M Y PARENTS, BOTH OF THEM born in Israel, came to the United States in 1965—the same year that David Ben-Gurion, founding father of the Jewish state and former prime minister, was handed the resounding electoral defeat that marked the end of his influence over the country. At the time, two facts were obscured from their view. First, neither of my parents suspected that they would be in America for good. My father was a young nuclear physicist who had conducted research at Israel's first nuclear facility at Nahal Sorek. He had been a supporter of Ben-Gurion and a Labor Zionist from his youth, serving as a youth movement counselor in Labor's Noar Oved ("Working Youth") organization in the days when Shimon Peres was among its national stars. And he was, in a sense, a fulfill-ment of all that David Ben-Gurion had come to stand for: The application of ever-increasing know-how to the construction of a physically and militar-ily ever more powerful Israel. But like many other physical scientists who left Israel at the time to deepen their knowledge and experience abroad, he could not know that Israel would soon reach the limits of its breathtaking early growth and that there would be little hope of finding employment as a physicist by the time he was ready to go back.

The second fact that was obscured from my parents' view was that the Israel they had left was soon to be altered beyond recognition. Even before their departure, there had already been much talk about the great generational divide that had opened up between the ideologically committed Labor Zionist founders, who had literally built the country with a plow in one hand and rifle in the other—and their sons, university-trained authors, academics, journalists, professionals, and businessmen, whom the novelist S. Yizhar called "the espresso generation." This generation of the sons certainly paid its dues in military service, but its members' failure to ignite like their fathers had for the cause of the Jewish state was gradually to become an open scandal, perhaps *the* open scandal of the years after Ben-Gurion had been expunged from public life. My father knew little about any of this. He was, after all, a physicist, with little interest in authors, journalists, and businessmen, and even less in espresso. And unlike so many others of his generation, he grew up believing in the cause of his own parents, who had emigrated to Palestine from Kiev in 1924, when there were fewer than 95,000 Jews in the country. It had always been clear to his parents that "it was going to be bad" if they stayed in Europe, and the Jewish state-in-the-making was for them, as for the rest of Ben-Gurion's followers, nothing short of salvation. And in this they were right. Within twenty-five years, virtually all of the family and friends whom they had left behind had perished.

I never knew my grandfather, who died the year after I was born. But I knew he had joined the Labor movement's first cooperative settlement, Nahalal, and had even served as a Labor party representative in the Tel Aviv workers' council, taking Moshe Sharett's seat when Sharett, who later became Israel's second prime minister, went on to bigger and better things. And since I also had no difficulty sympathizing with the things my parents believed to be important, I was able, somehow, to grow up a Ben-Gurionist as my grandfather had been, even in America. From my childhood, I believed that it was only because of Zion that my parents had lived and I had been born and that it was in Israel, where I would learn to fight as a Jew and to create as a Jew, that I would find my salvation. My father's home was, as it turned out, something of a time capsule, in which I was able to grow up with such thoughts, safe in the illusion that these were things that all Israeli children my age believed. And when, after high school, I went back to Israel and to my uncle's house, I saw no evidence to the contrary. My cousins were religious children, growing up in a time capsule of their own—something that neither they nor I understood at the time—a West Bank settlement called Kedumim, the first modern Jewish community in the heart of Samaria. And they, like me, continued to believe that the Jewish state would be the expression of their visions and their dreams in times of well-being and their strength and shield in times of suffering. No one in Kedumim ever mentioned to me that there were Jews in Israel who did not believe in the Jewish state. Immersed in their own historical missions and adventures, I doubt my cousins had even noticed.

It was only when my fiancée and I returned to Israel in 1986 with the intention of building our lives there—we were married the following year—that I gradually began to get wind of the tragedy that had taken place in this land. I say gradually, because those were years when Yitzhak Shamir was usually prime minister, and more often than not, Yitzhak Rabin was responsible for the country's defense. These two men, dour and advanced in years but nonetheless remarkably energetic, represented the last of the generation of the founders. Although they had originated on opposite ends of the political spectrum—Shamir had led the rightist underground organization Lehi (the "Stern group"), while Rabin had risen through the ranks of the kibbutz-movement dominated military force, the Palmah—both had been commanders during the struggle for independence forty years earlier, fighting more or less side by side to bring the Jewish state into being. Here, leading the country every day, were the very same Zionists who had been at the helm, as it seemed, forever. And I do not believe that we were much different from most Israelis in feeling this way. It was as though the Jewish state were not only invincible and eternal but also led by great men who had themselves somehow been frozen in time, destined to remain upright at the helm, defending the Jewish people against all danger, forever.

This was ridiculous, of course, and it did not last long. A few years later, I was already serving regularly in the army reserves, and there my views of the Jewish state underwent a brisk readjustment. The Israeli army is still, as it has been since the founding of the state, composed of most of the adult male population, and in one or two months of service a year, one quickly catches sight of virtually everything taking place within Israeli society. Perched atop a rooftop in Hebron with a Netanya businessman for a twelve-hour watch; or guarding a communications relay on a mountain peak for days on end with a newly immigrated Russian poet; or on patrol in an Arab village with a kibbutznik officer in command of the jeep—during one stint or the next, you gradually get to see and hear everything.

And the "everything" was something rather shocking, but also unambiguous: The Jews of Israel are an exhausted people, confused and without direction. This is not to say that they are unwilling to fight. Israelis still agree that they will carry on their struggle if they must. But in no end of discussions, it was made clear to me that there was a vast gulf between their *willingness* to fight and sacrifice and their ability to understand *why* they should do so. Certainly, they all knew that we were at war—including those who believed we could and should get out of it—but as soon as the discussion skidded close to the reasons that it might be worth being in this fight, the screen went blank. Of what value is the Jewish people? What can it contribute to mankind? What is to be gained by joining in its struggle? Why should one sacrifice on its behalf? Why should the Jewish state exist at all?

These are questions that you do not expect to hear answered at too high a level by every soldier in the Israel Defense Forces (IDF). But, on the other hand, without *some* answer as to what this was all about—this people, its country, and the seemingly endless war—no army can possibly keep fighting for very long.

And I learned more: There was the intelligent young officer to whom I pointed out Tel Shiloh as we drove by in our jeep, the ruins of what had for nearly four centuries been the "capital" of the confederated Jewish tribes before the establishment of the kingdom. "What kingdom?" he asked, in all seriousness. From him I understood that even the educated in Israel do not necessarily know what Shiloh was, or who King David was, or what he achieved for his people. Then there was the Passover I spent with a company on intifada duty in Ramallah. The IDF rabbinate had provided every conceivable ritual object and ornament for the traditional service; the observant among the soldiers were familiar enough with the seder to read the story verbatim from the text provided by the chaplaincy; and a few more soldiers knew some traditional melodies. But most sat on their hands in boredom as the ancient text was muttered without explanation or comment, filing out sheepishly when they finally lost patience. From this I learned that almost an entire army base could voluntarily show up at a religious-historical commemoration in search of a connection with their people and their past, and yet without a single person present knowing how to achieve it. And then there was the pudgy young officer, days before finishing out his four-year tour of duty, who objected when I inadvertently referred to him as a Jew. "Don't say that to me," he said huskily, putting his hand up like a traffic cop. "If you want, you can talk to me as a human being. But don't talk to me as a Jew. That doesn't speak to me." From him I understood that one had to be careful whom one implicated in being a Jew in the Jewish state.

I certainly never met anyone in those days who referred to himself as "post-Zionist" or "post-Jewish." But these terms, if unspoken, were already implicit in everything around me. Was this really the armed forces of the Jewish state? Were these members of the Jewish nation, defending their people, their tradition, and their ancestral homeland? Or were they someone else, here almost by accident, trying to get by in a story whose meaning they could not understand?

These thoughts were only sharpened when, beginning in 1991, I became an aide to then Deputy Foreign Minister Benjamin Netanyahu and began to attend closed-door deliberations in the Knesset, Israel's parliament. Here, I had the opportunity to see at close range the last of the generation of the founders—men such as Ezer Weizman and Yitzhak Rabin, Yitzhak Shamir and Ariel Sharon, men made of rock and wire and gold, whose voices still shook in describing their land, whose eyes still filled with barely restrained tears in discussing events, and whose minds were still nimble with reasons and strategies and arguments for how to advance the cause of the Jews, as they had done without reservation their entire lives. And I had the opportunity to compare them to most of the younger parliamentarians, educated, glossy, and shallow: people who never display emotion other than feigned good-naturedness, or else genuine anger over some personal affront or other; and who would evidence no embarrassment considering a proposed policy exclusively on its value for generating headlines about themselves; and who have long since become guarded about using expressions such as "the interests of the Jewish people"—or even just "the Jewish people"—which might leave someone feeling uncomfortable. And here, too, I found myself wondering: Is this really the Jewish state? Do these men and women really believe themselves to be heirs to the pre-state Zionist congresses and the early parliaments of Ben-Gurion's time, which deliberated in all seriousness and with all their hearts over the survival or destruction of the Jewish nation?

In 1994, I left politics to establish a research institute intended to inject some ideas into the barren contests of ego and mediacraft of which so much of Israeli public life consists. The aim of this institute, the Shalem Center in Jerusalem, was to focus on public issues that had been neglected: education, constitutional and electoral reform, economics and health care, religion-state questions, and public culture. Israelis of all persuasions had for a generation spent themselves in endless disputations over the PLO and West Bank settlements—so that virtually anything else qualified as a neglected issue.

Yet the moment I began paying serious attention to what was taking place outside the confines of Israel's traditional foreign-policy conundrums, I collided once again with the problem of the "post-Jewish" state. But this time it was on a far greater scale: In the Education Ministry, the chairman of a committee revising the public-school history curriculum announced that the Jewish people would be included in the new curriculum, "but certainly not as a subject of primary importance"; in the Defense Ministry, an official code of values and principles was approved for training Israeli soldiers in which the Jewish people and the Jewish state are not even mentioned; on the Supreme Court, the chief justice had devised a new constitutional doctrine whereby the "Jewish" character of the state had to be interpreted "at the highest level of abstraction" so that it became identical with the universal dictates of what is acceptable in any generic democracy; prominent officials and public figures had begun to talk of changing the Israeli national anthem (to remove the words "Jewish soul") and repealing the Law of Return (so that Diaspora Jews would no longer have a right to immigrate to Israel)—and so on.[1]

In a word, lack of Jewish purpose and meaning was no longer someone's personal problem. The "post-Jewish" condition had become a matter of national policy—to the point that one could easily imagine the Jewish state, for which such a fantastic price had been paid in sweat and blood, actually being dismantled in favor of a *non*-Jewish state: a political state for which the ideals and memories, traditions and interests of the Jews would be— simply irrelevant.[2]

In 1995, I began to study this issue in earnest, and this book represents the result of five years of my attempting to understand the riddle of "the Jewish state"—what was originally meant by this concept and how it came to its present condition of decay. Of course, not everyone will be troubled by what I am describing; some may even take pleasure in it. But for those who find the prospect of the dissolution of the Jewish state to be a painful one, I also hope to provide some clues as to what must be done to effect its restoration.

Not too long ago, few Jews—or Christians, for that matter—would have had difficulty justifying the existence of a Jewish state. The destruction of European Jewry left a profound impression on the generation that witnessed it, a fact reflected in the sweeping political alignments that brought about Jewish independence in Palestine on May 14, 1948: The declaration of Israel's independence was signed by every Jewish political party in Palestine, from the Communists to Agudat Israel (the "ultra-Orthodox"), and the consensus among American Jews was nearly as impressive; the previous year, both the United States and the Soviet Union had supported the creation of the Jewish state at the United Nations; and both the Democratic and Republican parties had included pro-Zionist planks in their platforms during the previous American presidential election. This is not to say that sympathy for Jewish losses during the war was the sole factor that created these political constellations. But without the emotions stirred by the Holocaust, it is nonetheless doubtful whether such a consensus would have been possible in any of these arenas.

The fifty-two years that have elapsed since the founding of the state of Israel have not been all glory, to say the least. And although the idea of the Jewish state remains a powerful one, it is obvious that many people of good- will—especially those who came of age after the cause of the Palestinian Arabs began to attract attention in the early 1970s—can no longer say for certain whether the Jewish state was *really* such a noble dream, or whether it was worth the costs involved in its realization. For this reason, it may be worth revisiting the case for the Jewish state, which not so long ago seemed so self-evident.

The idea of restoring the Jews to political independence in Zion is of course no new idea. Jews and others have contemplated such a possibility since antiquity. But the Zionist Organization (ZO) founded in Basel, Switzerland, in 1897 with the aim of securing Jewish independence in Palestine differed from all previous efforts to hasten the return of the Jews to their land in one crucial respect: This was a movement whose leaders were formerly assimilated Jews, individuals who had "returned to their people" (as they put it) with a sufficient understanding of statecraft—that is, of how political states are actually created and maintained—to have a chance of seeing the project through.

The greatest of these Zionist leaders was the Viennese journalist Theodor Herzl, the founder of the Zionist Organization, about whom I will have more to say later. Herzl had already reached acclaim throughout Europe as a man of letters, when, at age thirty-five, he decided he would devote his remaining days to securing a political state for the Jewish people. He offered two reasons that such a state was a desperate necessity, which continue to comprise the rational justification for maintaining and building up the Jewish state, even to this day.

First, Herzl believed that personal security and liberty for the Jews was an aim inextricably bound up with Jewish political power. Although Herzl was in many respects a good liberal Jew, four years in Paris covering the intrigues of the French capital—including the rising tide of anti-Semitism in this seat of enlightenment—had persuaded him that legal enactments alone could not guarantee the position of the Jews in any state. "It was erroneous . . . to believe that men can be made equal by publishing an edict in the Imperial Gazette,"[3] he wrote. And in fact, even where Jews had been granted formal equality, nowhere did this promise translate into a status comparable to that enjoyed by the national majority. And for good reason: "Like everything else in relations between peoples, this is a matter of power";[4] and since the Jews were everywhere a small minority and powerless, no fundamental change in their condition would be possible. In most countries, social and economic circumstances would throw the liberalizers out of power sooner or later. And when this happened, whatever gains the Jews had made would only be challenged again. Then, whatever the Jews did not have the political power to protect would be destroyed:

> What form this [destruction] will take, I cannot surmise. Will it be a revolutionary expropriation from below or a reactionary confiscation from above? Will they drive us out? Will they kill us? . . . [In] France there will come a social revolution whose first victims will be the big bankers and the Jews. . . . In Russia there will simply be a confiscation from above. In Germany they will make emergency laws . . . In Austria people will let themselves be intimidated by the Viennese rabble . . . There, you see, the mob can achieve anything.[5]

Not many Jews were willing to accept such arguments at the end of the last century. But they were wrong, and Herzl was right. A few years later, the Germans and Austrians, as well as many other European peoples, participated in the wholesale slaughter of the Jewish communities that had lived among them for centuries. And while Jews in England and the United States were spared this fate, it is also true that these nations did virtually nothing on behalf of the Jews of Europe: They refused to open their gates to Jewish refugees when the opportunity arose and passed up on military intervention in the Holocaust as well. Although all of the leading Zionist figures greatly admired the United States and Britain, there was never any question that these countries could be a substitute for a strong *Jewish* political and military power, which alone could guarantee the Jews as a people security and freedom. And such a Jewish political and military power could only come with the creation of a Jewish state. I believe that no one has expressed this sentiment more clearly in recent years than Israeli prime minister Ehud Barak, who visited Auschwitz in 1992 when he was still chief of staff of the Israeli armed forces. Israelis are not likely soon to forget the expression on his features, as captured by the reporters' cameras. "We came fifty years too late," he said.[6]

But the effects of Jewish weakness did not end with physical insecurity or even with social discrimination. And this was Herzl's second argument: For even where Jews *did* achieve something approaching political and social equality, this achievement was of necessity at the expense of the Jews' character as Jews. A Jew whose aim was to succeed in his chosen profession had no choice but to accommodate himself—whether consciously or unconsciously—to the expectations and ideas of the national majority. Thus, it is the desire of the weak to please the powerful that dominates the life of emancipated Jews, and the result is a servile imitation of prevailing gentile norms. On the one hand, he discards his own national past, ignobly jettisoning all that was precious to his forefathers in order not to appear different from the majority; on the other hand, it is precisely this fear of making oneself different that destroys any prospect that the Jews as a people will ever create a profound and important modern civilization of their own. Thus, the Jewish empowerment entailed in creating a Jewish state was not merely a matter of guaranteeing external, physical security of the Jews. Ultimately, its aim is to provide an *internal* security of the soul, which is the indispensable precondition for the emergence of a noble, uniquely Jewish character and civilization.

In Herzl's view, the Jews had once possessed such inner security, not only in ancient times but even in medieval Europe, where their spiritual and intellectual inheritance had succeeded in imparting to them—in the midst of persecution—a "great strength, an inner unity which we have lost. A generation which has grown apart from Judaism does not have this [inner] unity; it can neither rely upon our past nor look to our future." The Jews could not very well recreate the environment of the medieval ghetto, living a despised existence on the margins of society. But an independent Jewish state could solve this dilemma: There, and only there, could the Jews participate fully in every aspect of the society and the state, while at the same time recovering their ability to be of independent mind and ideals, as their forefathers had been. In returning to their own national life, Herzl believed, "We shall thereby regain our lost inner wholeness, and along with it a little character—our own character. Not a Marrano-like, borrowed, untruthful character, but our own."[7]

The case for the Jewish state is frequently presented as a matter of "rights." The Jews, it is said, have a "right" to physical security, or to political self-determination, or to cultural self-expression, and so on. This is in keeping with the manner in which virtually all normative public discourse has been conducted since the French Revolution, and there is nothing wrong with this. But it bears keeping in mind that no one is actually moved to do anything by such an assertion of rights. Herzl did not establish the Zionist Organization because the Jews had a "right" to anything, nor did Jews return to Palestine and establish a state there because they had a "right" to do so. Rather, all these things were done because certain Jews and Christians believed that there *should* be a Jewish state and that this aim was noble, important, and worth making great sacrifices to achieve. No one during the 1890s believed that the Jews did not have an in-principle right to continue living in peace in Germany; rather, the claim made by Zionists was that this right would be impossible to realize under conditions of chronic political weakness. The same is true for all other Jewish interests (i.e., the rights to life, liberty, and property) and ideals (i.e., the right to pursue high Jewish character and civilization). One could make a great show of seeking and obtaining all of these "rights" on paper, the Zionists argued. But anyone for whom it makes a great deal of difference whether Jewish interests and ideals have a chance of being realized *in reality* will eventually have to concede the need for Jewish political power on a scale that can exist only in an independent Jewish state.

And herein resides the essential meaning of Israel's declaration of independence, which asserts "the right of the Jewish people to be masters of their own fate, like all other nations, in their own sovereign state."[8]

Not surprisingly, the political leaders of the various Arab movements and states that have competed with the Jews for influence in Palestine since World War I have always rejected these arguments out of hand, claiming (1) that whatever may have been the experiences of the Jews historically, they did not have the right to become a majority in Palestine over the objections of the country's Arab population; and (2) that even with a demographic majority, the Jews still do not have the right to maintain a "Jewish state" over the objections of Israel's Arab citizens. For various reasons, I believe the first argument—that the Jewish majority came into being illegitimately—to be mistaken. Errors and injustices were, of course, committed in the process of bringing the state of Israel into existence, and I think there is much value in coming to terms with this fact. Yet all the new historical work done in recent years has not, in my opinion, succeeded in establishing that, in general, the means used to settle Jews in Palestine and create a Jewish majority there were illegitimate. However, I will neither defend this view here nor criticize those who disagree with me, for the simple reason that both sides of the argument have been debated endlessly in every possible forum and I do not believe I could add much that has not already been said.

By contrast, the second claim, that a specifically Jewish state is *intrinsically* illegitimate, is one that was almost entirely neglected until recently, despite the fact that it has always been a subject of immense importance. Certain theories, now widely accepted, concerning what constitutes a legitimate regime are indeed incompatible with the concept of a Jewish state (no matter how this term is defined)—an issue that was raised in 1975 when the United Nations equated Zionism (i.e., the existence of a Jewish state) with racism. At the time, this declaration was dismissed in the free world as a hypocritical maneuver on the part of the Communist and Arab dictatorships to defame a democratic country and the West in general. And, indeed, this is what it was. But the fact that anti-Zionism has since World War II turned into the court philosophy of despots and terrorists cannot erase the fact that historically, anti-Zionism has had adherents of the highest intellectual integrity—people who believed that a Jewish state, *any* Jewish state, is necessarily an unjust regime. And this is an argument that those who wish the Jewish state well must be able to answer and to answer well, if only for themselves. For without a satisfactory answer to the charge that the Jewish state is inherently illegitimate, it can only be a matter of time until the political constellation on which this state is predicated begins to collapse.

Few today remember that when the idea of establishing a sovereign state for the Jewish people was made the goal of the Zionist Organization, it was greeted by many leading Jewish intellectuals as an abomination. Thinkers such as Hermann Cohen and Franz Rosenzweig—and later on Martin Buber, Gershom Scholem, Hannah Arendt, Albert Einstein, and Hans Kohn—all opposed the idea of a Jewish state.[9] And for much the same reason. All of them argued that the Jewish people was in its essence an achievement of the "spirit," which would be degraded and corrupted ("like all other nations") the moment it was harnessed to tanks and explosives, politics and intrigue, bureaucracy and capital—in short, to the massive worldly power of the state. This did not, of course, mean that no Jew should be involved in politics, but rather that no *state* should be a Jewish one, so that the Jewish people as a whole (or Judaism as a faith) could itself be retained in its perfect purity as an ideal. In practice, this point of view engendered a politics that held that the Jews should *not* strive to become a majority in Palestine and that that country should be established constitutionally on a "binational" basis—meaning that it would become a "non-Jewish" state in which the Jews as a people would have no special status and in which the mechanisms of state power could not be used to advance Jewish interests or ideals that were not acceptable to the country's Arab population.

This binationalist view was almost completely discredited among Jews after World War II because of its association with the catastrophe of the Holocaust. In the years immediately prior to the war, Palestine was being governed by the British on what was effectively a binational basis: Jews trying to escape Europe were permitted to enter the country, but only in numbers that the British believed the Arabs would tolerate. When the demand for immigration certificates grew too great and the Arabs reacted with violence, the British cut back on the number of Jews permitted to enter the country, deporting illegal Jewish immigrants by force. By war's end, it had become clear that even a weak Jewish regime in Palestine, in the years immediately before and during the war, would have been able to rescue hundreds of thousands of Jews who had perished, perhaps even millions. For the next forty years, virtually no one in Israel or the West could respectably oppose the idea of a Jewish state, and anti-Zionism, as I have said, became an intellectual truncheon in the hands of despots and terrorists who were not overly troubled by what had happened in World War II.

Today, however, the intellectual climate has changed, in no small part because with the demise of the Soviet Union, and one can now give voice to anti-Zionist ideas without immediately associating oneself with totalitarianism. This is true throughout the West, but it is most evident among Israeli Jewish intellectuals, whose political and moral concepts have deep roots in German-Jewish anti-Zionist philosophy. In countless books and articles and works of art, and, in recent years, in public policy as well, the drift of Israeli political culture has been toward what in Israel is called a "state of its citizens"—a regime that not only seeks a "separation" between Jewish religion and state but which also seeks a separation between Jewish *nationality* and state. According to this principle, there is no room for the state to display particularist characteristics and missions. And indeed, the capstone of the post-Zionist project, being declared with increasing frequency, is the abrogation of the Law of Return (which recognizes the right of all Jews to immigrate to Israel), creating a state of perfect equality in which Arabs and Jews will have identical standing and "foreign" Jews—the Jews of the Diaspora—

will have none at all. In this way, Israel is to become something very similar to what the early anti-Zionist thinkers had always demanded: A "non-Jewish" regime with no special relationship with the Jews as a people, either within its boundaries or in the Diaspora.

This does not mean that Israelis have begun to describe themselves as anti-Zionists (or even as "post-Zionists"); on the contrary, there are still very few Israeli political or cultural leaders who are willing to pay the rhetorical price of publicly associating themselves with such revolutionary terms. But this fact seems to be doing nothing to prevent the spread of ever more daring criticisms of Israel's character as the state of the Jewish people. Indeed, in the last twenty years, and especially after 1993, respected public figures have made it their business to demand not only the repeal of the Law of Return but the dejudaization of the Israeli flag and the national anthem, as well as the downgrading of the Jewish-national content in the public-school curriculum, the Israel Defense Forces, and the country's constitution as interpreted by the Supreme Court. And what cannot be dejudaized by government fiat has been attacked publicly: the legitimacy of the concept of Jewish sovereignty; the legitimacy of the academic discipline of Jewish history; every national hero from Herzl to Golda Meir, from the pioneer Joseph Trumpeldor to the fighter-poetess Hannah Senesh; the justice of Israel's actions during every one its wars, as well as in its operations on behalf of Holocaust survivors and Sephardi Jewry; the place in national life of the city of Jerusalem, the Western Wall, and the Passover seder. Even the idea that medieval Jews were innocent victims of persecution is being challenged by Hebrew University historians claiming that Jews were at least partially responsible for Christian hatred of them.

When one considers all of these examples and others, it is impossible to escape the conclusion that Israel's public culture is undergoing a massive shift away from the ideas and norms that characterized it as a Jewish state— a very broad phenomenon that in the last few years has received the name "post-Zionism." And yet I cannot emphasize strongly enough that those who today explicitly refer to themselves as post-Zionists (and who accept virtually all of these as reasonable developments) are a minority, even within Israeli academic and literary circles. Were it only for this minority, it would hardly be worth a book. The real subject of the pages that follow is the mainstream of Jewish cultural figures in Israel—those who appear constantly on television as commentators on subjects of national importance, whose books are best-sellers and are taught in the public schools, who attend parties in the homes of Israel's leading politicians, and who serve on government committees regardless of whether Labor or Likud is in power. I recognize that these are in many cases people who call themselves Zionists and are proud to be Israelis, and who will not particularly enjoy appearing

in a book on post-Zionism. But I think that by the time a prominent professor, novelist, or politician is calling for the addition of an Arab symbol on
the Israeli flag (Eliezer Schweid),[10] for European courts to be given the authority to overturn Israeli law (Amnon Rubinstein),[11] or for Israeli Jews to
convert to Christianity or Islam so as to make Israel a more "normal" state
(A. B. Yehoshua),[12] it seems to me that the time has come to point out that
they, too, are an important part of the problem.

In my view, it is these establishment cultural figures, even more than the
circles of self-professed post-Zionists, who are today paving the way to the
ruin of everything Herzl and the other leading Zionists sought to achieve.
Indeed, they are pushing us toward the dismantling of Israel's character as
the Jewish state.

This book seeks to achieve two aims. First, I hope to persuade the reader
that the idea of the Jewish state is under systematic attack from its own cultural and intellectual establishment. I am not, of course, speaking of an effort directed against Israel's physical existence but rather of one leveled
against Israel's legal, political, and moral status as the state of the Jewish
people. Second, I trace the history of the struggle over the idea of the Jewish
state, with the hope that this will offer some clues as to how we have arrived
at this juncture and where we can go from here.

With this in mind, I have divided the book into four sections. Part 1 is a
survey of the ideas and personalities that now constitute Israel's increasingly
"post-Zionist" cultural and political mainstream. In this section, I look at the
works of leading authors, academics, and artists, as well as at their copious utterances in media interviews, to try to offer a sense of the growing opposition
to the traditional idea of the Jewish state. In the area of government, I have
similarly attempted to touch on central aspects of educational policy, foreign
affairs and defense policy, and the developing Israeli constitution, in order to
offer an understanding of how this opposition has in recent years been translating itself into actual decisions of Israel's government.

The rest of the book is devoted to seeking an explanation for how all of
this came to be. In Part 2, I retell the story of the founding of the Zionist
Organization, so that it is possible to compare the original Zionist idea with
what took place after Herzl's death. In this my aim is to demonstrate what
was once clearly understood: that Herzl's movement was a reaction *against*
the failure of the emancipation, which had never actually succeeded in providing the Jews with safety and well-being through their participation in the
social-contract state. As such, political Zionism was from the outset concerned with the accumulation of power in the hands of a Jewish guardian-

organization—and later a Jewish guardian-state—whose aim would be to transform the Jewish people into a substantial force in international affairs in the interest of securing the life and dignity of Jews everywhere. It is this state that was the goal of David Ben-Gurion, Berl Katznelson, and the other leaders of the dominant stream of Labor Zionism, who in the wake of the Holocaust succeeded in uniting the Jewish people around this idea and around the Jewish War of Independence in Palestine, which actually brought the state into being.

As I have said, outside of academic circles it is hardly remembered today that the idea of the Jewish state was once opposed by a majority of Jewish intellectuals and civic leaders in Western Europe, who believed it to be an immoral departure from what they saw as the Jewish ideal of national disempowerment and statelessness. Even less known is how these overtly anti-Zionist ideals came to be imported into the Zionist movement. I therefore end Part 2 with the story of how Herzl's most gifted follower, a German-Jewish student named Martin Buber, editor of the Zionist Organization newspaper, left the ZO after a bitter quarrel with the great leader, within a few years returning to become the foremost theoretician of the opposition to a Jewish state. It was Buber who adjusted Hermann Cohen's overtly anti-Zionist theories to fit a world in which Zionism was rapidly gaining steam, and who, basing himself on his works on Hasidism and the philosophy of *I and Thou*, can today be understood as the most important Jewish interpreter of the view that the movement for a Jewish state was based on morally questionable premises.[13]

In Parts 3 and 4, I describe the process by which the dream of the Jewish state, as conceived by Herzl and Ben-Gurion, became discredited among large segments of the cultural-political leadership of that very state after it was founded. These chapters retell the story of David Ben-Gurion's lifelong struggle to bring the Jewish state into being. But at the same time, they also refocus the historical spotlight on a group that has thus far received relatively little attention: The intellectuals of Jewish Palestine, many of whom were immigrants from Germany who considered themselves to be disciples or allies of Martin Buber. It was this community of German-Jewish intellectuals in Jerusalem that became the backbone of the Hebrew University of Jerusalem, founded in 1925 as the only university in Palestine—and whose humanities and social science faculties were to a large degree responsible for the establishment of every other academic institution in these fields in Israel. And it was these same individuals who were also at the center of the political opposition to the Jewish state within the Jewish community in Palestine.[14]

Naturally, not all intellectuals from German Central Europe were uniform in their ideas, much less active opponents of the Jewish state as a polit-

ical aim. Nevertheless, on the whole it was this community that gave the detractors of the Jewish state the intellectual and institutional base from which
to alter the course of Israeli history. Thus, this movement was often coordinated from the office of the Hebrew University's first chancellor, Judah
Magnes. It was supported by many of the university's most important professors, including Buber himself. And it was endorsed by the university's
leading financial backer, the New York banker Felix Warburg, also a prominent opponent of the Jewish state. This association between the Hebrew
University and the increasingly desperate political efforts to prevent the
founding of a Jewish state continued even after the Holocaust, even after
the UN decision in 1947 to support the creation of a Jewish state, and even
after the declaration of the Jewish state in May 1948 and the attack on it by
the armed forces of the neighboring Arab regimes.[15]

The opposition of many of Jewish Palestine's leading intellectuals to the
establishment of a Jewish state rarely receives more than a mention in books
dealing with Israel's founding, and its effects on the development of Israel's
subsequent culture have hardly been explored; indeed, when they are discussed at all, the politics of intellectual leaders such as Buber and Magnes
are treated as though they simply dissipated with the founding of the state.
But this was not the case. To understand what actually happened, I look at
the activities of Buber and his most important followers after the founding
of the state of Israel—both on the cultural level, in which leading figures at
the Hebrew University continued to refine the very same historical and
philosophical theories that had constituted the conceptual undercarriage of
Jewish anti-Zionism; and on the political level, in which Buber, his associates, and his heirs resumed their campaign to discredit Ben-Gurion and his
Jewish state as a false Messianism, a totalitarianism, or even an imitation of
fascism.[16] I seek to show that this decades-long work of delegitimizing
mainstream Labor Zionism, particularly among children from Labor
Zionist homes studying at the Hebrew University, reached its climax in the
overt attack that Buber and dozens of other Hebrew University professors,
along with hundreds of their students, leveled against the prime minister
during the Lavon Affair in 1961—an attack at once cultural and political,
and which was so successful that it effectively ended Ben-Gurion's career in
both arenas.

Finally, I seek to return the reader to the present state of Israel, described
at the beginning of the book. Here it is my contention that the conceptual
and cultural vacuum left after Ben-Gurion's disappearance was filled by the
idea of Israel as an essentially "neutral" state, as advocated by the leading
lights at the Hebrew University and their students. It was this often unwit-
ting adoption of the anti-Zionist theories of Hermann Cohen in the very
heart of Israel's cultural mainstream in post-Ben-Gurion Israel that was

largely responsible for the phenomenon that we are now seeing under the name of "post-Zionism." Indeed, one would not be far off the mark in saying that today's highly successful movement to do away with virtually everything that distinguishes Israel as a Jewish state is little more than Martin Buber's revenge for a wound inflicted on him by Theodor Herzl nearly a century ago. And today there exists the possibility that Buber's ideological children are on the verge of transforming Israel into precisely that which the early dreamers of Zionism had fought to escape: A state devoid of any Jewish purpose and meaning, one that can neither inspire the Jews nor save them in distress.

There is no point in retelling all of this merely as a protracted eulogy for a cause that once meant a great deal to us. If my criticism is at points harsh, my intention is not to bury the Jewish state but to contribute to the awakening that is so critical if it is to be restored. Despite the confusion that reigns in Israel—and increasingly among the Jews of the Diaspora—over the question of the Jewish character of the state, the great majority of Israel's Jews are by no means committed to post-Zionist ideals. For this majority, the possible dissolution of the Jewish state is still a personal matter that touches the innermost recesses of the soul. If Israelis today are largely silent before the victories of post-Zionism, it is because real resistance requires counter-ideas, an alternative vision that can restore the purpose and meaning that has been lost in their own lives and in that of their nation. In the closing pages of the book, I therefore turn to the subject of creating this alternative vision, in the hope of leaving the reader with a better understanding of what must be done if Israel is to begin along the path toward Jewish national restoration.

PART

CHAPTER I

The Culture Makers Renounce the Idea of the Jewish State

The Israeli Urge to Suicide

In the summer of 1994, the Israeli daily *Ha'aretz* published a lengthy polemic by Aharon Meged entitled "The Israeli Urge to Suicide," in which the well-known novelist—a thoroughly acceptable and otherwise noncontroversial member of the small clique that constitutes Israel's cultural establishment—accused the nation's intellectual leadership, almost to a man, of conspiring to destroy the moral and historical basis for the Jewish state's existence, and with it the Jewish state itself.

"For two or three decades now," Meged wrote,

> a few hundred of our "society's best," men of the pen and of the spirit—academics, authors, and journalists, and to these one must add artists and photographers and actors as well—have been working determinedly and without respite to preach and prove that our cause is not just: Not only that it has been unjust since the Six Day War [in 1967] and the "occupation," which is supposed to be unjust by its very nature; and not only since the founding of the state in 1948, a birth which was itself "conceived in sin" . . . —but since the beginnings of Zionist settlement at the end of the last century.

Like overt anti-Zionists of the past, Israel's intellectuals had long ago abandoned the view that Zionism, while engendering rare acts of injustice, was a fundamentally just cause. Instead, they had come to believe that the cause of the Jewish state was wrong *in principle*, and the result was an entire culture of hatred against the Jewish state. But a single example was the cultural leaders' habit of identifying the IDF with the Nazis—a trend which had ballooned to include "thousands of articles . . . hundreds of poems, songs, and satires, tens of documentary and dramatic films, exhibitions and paintings and photographs." Taken as a whole, these and other works like them "constitute a monstrous indictment against Israel," an indictment in the face of which sympathy for the Jewish state was fast becoming untenable.[1]

Meged's essay was no ordinary piece of cultural punditry. It marked the beginning of a volcanic outpouring of accusation, justification, rationalization, and counter-accusation that continued to appear in all the media in the years that followed, under headlines emphasizing and reemphasizing the term "post-Zionism"—which was used to describe a new period in Israeli history, either already begun or else on the threshold, in which the idea of a Jewish state was recognized as being effectively dead. An attempt to gather the articles from the Israeli press on the subject quickly produced a volume almost six hundred pages long, and the debate has continued to flare up again every few months, seemingly without possibility of exhaustion.[2]

Yet Meged's accusations, in and of themselves, could not have triggered such a furor; little of what he had to say was much of a surprise to anyone familiar with Israeli culture. Israeli society is small and its intellectual world is smaller. It only *has* a few hundred men of the pen and of the spirit, and these form a tight-packed and intellectually monochromatic clique whose cynicism with regard to the idea of the Jewish state has been a fixture of public discourse for decades. Who could have missed them? They *are* Israel's intellectual and cultural establishment—their works stocking Israel's three major theaters and its two main art museums, their ideas politically correct in its tiny cartel of universities and on Israel's two television stations, their constant comment filling the opinion pages, literary section, and weekend supplement of the only prestige newspaper, *Ha'aretz.* They are the ones who, together with North Tel Aviv's high society of business stars and yuppie-politicos with whom they socialize, are referred to by everyday Israel as "the *branja*"—a Yiddish word meaning "the experts" or "the guild." They're the people running the show. Why, then, the carrying on?

What allowed Meged's piece to draw blood was in part the identity of the author himself. A lifelong member of Israel's literary establishment and a political dove (who had long supported the establishment of a Palestinian state), Meged was as true an insider among Israeli culture-makers as one could have, so that when he spoke of the "emotional and moral identification" of hundreds of "society's best" with the enemies of Zionism, he was describing individuals nearly all of whom he had known well for years—a defection that ensured the piece would gain at least a certain notoriety.

More important, however, was the timing of the article, written at a political juncture that allowed it to draw unprecedented attention to the question of where Israel's leading academics, authors, and artists were trying to take the country. Israel is a country that concerns itself with war and party politics—*tachles,* as Israelis like to say, "the bottom line," "the action-item"—and the doings of the literati, despite their nightly appearances on talk shows, had long been regarded as irrelevant. A clear example of the disregard with which the political leaders of both major parties, Labor and Likud, had rejected the ideas of the culture makers was their long-standing dismissal of the idea that Israel should seek peace with Yasser Arafat by granting him an independent Palestinian Arab state in the West Bank, Gaza, and eastern Jerusalem. The *branja* had been widely known to support such a radical step for decades, but before 1993, no one had taken this option too seriously. Opinion polls had shown no real support for this scheme among Israeli Jews, and both parties had therefore remained adamant that Arafat was the kingpin of international terrorism, with neither the moral nor the political standing to negotiate with Israel about anything.

Yet with the signing of the Oslo agreement between Arafat and the Labor government in September 1993, the perennial theory of the political impotence of Israel's intellectuals began sickeningly to totter. Published less than nine months after the signing of the accords, "The Israeli Urge to Suicide" focused attention on the undeniable fact that the ideology of the intellectuals, which had been considered so irrelevant for so long, had in the end succeeded in undermining—and then reversing—the worldview of the political leadership. And if the opinions of the intellectuals could, apparently without warning, bring about so vast a political change in the country's foreign and security policy, was it not merely a matter of time before the rest of their ideas would become the policy of the state as well?

There was no waiting for the answer. The atmosphere of emotional liberation of those heady days gave intellectuals the confidence they needed to say out loud what previously had only been said in whispers, and it rapidly became clear that although the Oslo agreement may have been the *branja*'s most spectacular political achievement, it was in fact only the tip of an iceberg. Suddenly, Israel opened its newspapers and found itself seriously discussing virtually any idea or policy that could be devised for undermining the legal and moral basis for the existence of Israel as a Jewish state—from discarding the national flag to placing the city of Jerusalem under UN authority to repealing the Law of Return.

"Is Zionism nearing its end?" Aharon Meged asked in "The Israeli Urge to Suicide." And in the years that followed, what had long been evident to insiders in Israel's cultural establishment gradually became obvious to all: that the idea of the Jewish state had grown so dubious and confused among educated Israelis that one could seriously question such a state would continue to exist.

The pages that follow survey the ideas of Israel's culture makers as they relate to the Jewish state; in Chapter 2 I will trace the influence of post-Zionist ideas on the institutions of the state of Israel and the threat that this influence poses to Israel's existence as a Jewish state. Obviously, a cultural threat of this kind cannot be described as precisely as a military threat, where one can count tanks and missile launchers. Any effort to understand which way the winds are blowing in a civilization is necessarily impressionistic and subject to all the weaknesses that such impressionism entails. Nevertheless, I think that when one begins to look at Israel's few hundred "men of the spirit" and at what they permit themselves to say and write about the cause of the Jewish state, the picture that emerges is clear. The hope of the early Zionists that the return of the Jews to their land would produce a civilization compatible with their persistence as an independent nation, has, it seems, proved to have been in vain.

Academia

For well over a century, Jewish intellectuals—and especially those German-Jewish academics who constituted the mainstream of Jewish philosophy in the last century—have had serious doubts concerning the legitimacy and desirability of harnessing the interests of the Jewish people to the worldly power of a political state. Only the Holocaust, the most extreme demonstration of the evil of Jewish powerlessness imaginable, succeeded in turning the objections of the intellectuals to the Jewish state into an embarrassment, for the most part driving their opposition underground.[3] Yet Jewish intellectuals, even in Israel, never became fully reconciled to the empowerment of the Jewish people entailed in the creation of a Jewish state. For example, Martin Buber, then living in Jerusalem, argued in 1958 that the belief in the efficacy of power embraced by so many Jews in his generation had been learned from Hitler.[4] And with time, this manner of discussing the Jewish national power—which had been a staple of Jewish anti-Zionist rhetoric prior to the Holocaust—began to regain its previous legitimacy. Thus, Israel's most influential philosopher, Yeshayahu Leibowitz of the Hebrew University, had no difficulty calling the Israeli armed forces "Judeo-Nazis," and declared that Israel would soon be engaging in the "mass expulsion and slaughter of the Arab population" and "setting up concentration camps."[5] Similarly,

Jacob Talmon of the Hebrew University, Israel's most respected historian, asserted that "there is no longer any aim or achievement that can justify . . . twentieth-century battle," arguing that Israeli leaders who justified warfare on the grounds of national interest or historical rights were a throwback to the "Devil's accomplices in the last two generations . . . [who] warped the soul of millions and all but exterminated the Jewish people."[6]

By the 1970s, Israel's universities and newspapers had become home to a new generation of intellectuals—the students of Leibowitz and Talmon—for whom the enormities of World War II were not even a memory. This generation of intellectuals inherited a distaste for the Zionist quest for Jewish national power from their teachers. But unlike their teachers, they lived in a world in which Zionism had been branded an illegitimate political movement by the General Assembly of the United Nations and in which the stigma against devastating academic treatment of Zionism was rapidly eroding.[7] These "new" Israeli academics found themselves able to find academic positions and funding, whether in Israel or abroad, to write books that were for the most part "scientific" elaborations of the same accusations against the Jewish state that earlier scholars had generally dared to express only as "opinions."

For years, discussions of post-Zionism within Israel have tended to give undue prominence to a group of researchers known as "the new historians"—a pattern that has recently spread to the United States, where extensive attention has been paid to two "new histories" of the Arab-Israeli conflict: *Righteous Victims: A History of the Arab-Israeli Conflict, 1881–1999* by Benny Morris of Ben-Gurion University (1999) and *The Iron Wall: Israel and the Arab World* by Israeli-born Avi Shlaim of Oxford (2000). On the whole, these and similar works that began appearing as early as twenty years ago are "new" not because of the recently declassified archival sources they utilize but due to their orientation, which emphasizes the morally questionable nature of Jewish actions to a degree previously found only among anti-Zionist (generally non-Jewish) historians. Shlaim's *Iron Wall,* for example, presents merciless portraits of a long line of Zionist leaders previously considered heroes by the Israeli mainstream: Thus David Ben-Gurion becomes a "power-hungry" Israeli "strongman" who led an Israel "more intransigent than the Arab states"; Chief of Staff Moshe Dayan is described as "aggressive and ruthless," more "power-hungry" even than Ben-Gurion, dragging the IDF into one "unprovoked act of aggression" after another; and Golda Meir is said to have been systematically "intransigent" and to have "ruled . . . her country with an iron rod." At one point, Shlaim even asserts that the entire state of Israel has been gripped by "collective psychosis."[8]

Readers of a book of this kind naturally emerge feeling that Israel's policies were far less admirable than they may previously have believed. Yet, the kind of history Shlaim presents is essentially a long series of disconnected—if unappealing—events, which leave the impression that had Israel been led by more moderate individuals, it might actually have developed a foreign policy marked by decency and fairness. The same cannot be said, however, for the far more sophisticated and intelligent work of Benny Morris, whose aim is no less than to present a new historiographic framework for understanding all of Israeli history. In *Righteous Victims,* Morris contends that Zionism was from the outset "a colonizing and expansionist ideology and movement" that was infected by "the European colonist's mental obliteration of the 'natives,'" which reduced the Arabs to "objects to be utilized when necessary." As such, the entire Zionist enterprise tended toward the dispossession of the Arabs—an effort that was from the outset "tainted by a measure of moral dubiousness."[9] And once one is writing history on the basis of such premises, the rest of the picture falls easily into place: The physical expulsion, or transfer, of at least large segments of the Arab population in Palestine is said to have become a matter of "virtual consensus" among Zionist leaders—a consensus that "without doubt contributed" to Jewish actions in Palestine during the War of Independence. The result was, as Morris has written, that the Jewish forces "committed far more atrocities in 1948 than did Arab forces," and what they did can be described as "a variety of ethnic cleansing."[10]

While these and similar books dealing with Zionist policy toward the Arabs[11] have received much attention, the truth is that this entire genre of what may be called "original sin" books is relatively pedestrian in comparison with other trends in the universities that have received significantly less publicity. At least as damaging has been an entire tradition of research demonstrating that the policies of the Zionist founders toward the Jews—whom they were ostensibly saving—suffered from a "taint of moral dubiousness" as well. This tradition was pioneered by Tel Aviv University sociologist Yonathan Shapiro (d. 1997), according to whom the state of Israel is only a "formal democracy," which has since its founding functioned as an essentially authoritarian regime—an insight being applied by his students in a range of studies that argue, for example, that the IDF was used by the Labor government as a tool in preventing the social advancement of Sephardi Jews.[12] The prominent Hebrew University political scientist Ze'ev Sternhell similarly argues in *The Founding Myths of Israel* (1986) that the Labor Zionist leaders systematically betrayed the humanist ideals to which it paid lip service, in order to create a militarist and chauvinist state whose Jewish national character remains "highly problematic" to this day.[13] And Yehuda Shenhav, head of the sociology department at Tel Aviv University, has joined the ongoing academic efforts to bring out the dark side of Israeli operations to bring Jews from Arab countries to

Israel during the 1950s; according to Shenhav, the Israeli government conspired to force Iraqi Jews to leave their possessions in Baghdad, possibly for fear that if they were not impoverished, they might use their wealth to oppose its policies or return to Iraq.[14]

Equally damning is the new set of history books describing the perfidies committed by Labor Zionism in its dealings with the Holocaust and its survivors. Of these, the most successful has been *The Seventh Million* by journalist-historian Tom Segev (1991), which won extensive attention for its claim that Zionist leaders had "deep contempt" and "disgust" for their relatives in the Diaspora and that this, combined with an ideological fixation on establishing a Jewish state, contributed to their failure to pursue options for saving European Jewry during the Holocaust.[15] Even more virulent is the historian Idith Zertal, who teaches social thought and Holocaust studies at Hebrew University and the Interdisciplinary Center in Herzlia, whose book *The Gold of the Jews* (1996) compares the absorption of Holocaust refugees into Jewish Palestine to rape, arguing that in using the survivors to build their Jewish state, the Zionists turned them into "appropriated objects" who were then "defiled" and "violated" twice: first by the Nazis, and then again by the Jews.[16]

Each of these books can be said to be microhistorical, seeking to depict the crimes and errors of the Zionist movement or the state of Israel only with regard to a particular historical period or a given issue. To be sure, each of these books constitutes an additional brick in the wall of the new history of the Jewish state—a history in which one gets the impression that the actions of the Zionists were always execrable. But there are other, more efficient ways to destroy the history of a nation. To see how, one need only consider the macrohistorical work of Israel's leading academic historiographers, who seek a revision of Jewish history *in its entirety*.

The broad strokes of argument made by the new historiographers is as follows: The idea of a unitary Jewish people or nationality, with a common identity and a common history of past persecution in the lands of the dispersion, is a myth. Jews in the Diaspora were not a nationality at all but rather a large number of unconnected religious communities, each with its own past, problems, and experiences, without any grand common denominator. In fact, the concept of a Jewish people or nationality with which we are familiar was at least partially *invented* in the late nineteenth century by Zionist politicians. As the prominent Hebrew University sociologist Baruch Kimmerling explains, the Zionist leaders created this "partially reconstructed and partially invented past" with the intention of establishing "a direct linkage between the 'Jewish past' . . . and the contemporary situation of Zionist colonization." In other words, the story of a unitary and tormented Jewish people returning to its ancestral home was manufactured to provide legitimacy for an otherwise sordid movement to disinherit and exploit Palestine's indigenous inhabitants. The supposed national history of the Jewish people was thus nothing more than "a weapon . . . in the struggle of Zionism against other streams in Judaism, and in the struggle against the Arabs."[17]

It goes without saying that if the Zionists were able to use the weapon of Jewish national history to such great effect, then someone has to take this weapon away from them. And this is precisely what Baruch Kimmerling and his colleagues have set about doing. Thus, the history of Zionism is re-told by Kimmerling as though it were any other nineteenth-century colonialist enterprise: A small number of European whites come to Palestine to construct a settlement whose prospects for success—like those of all other colonial enterprises—rest on the twin assumptions of dispossession of the native people and their continued suppression by means of a draconian military regime built along racialist lines. And these characteristics, as we are told, remain the basis of today's Jewish state.[18]

Academics hostile to the "invented national narrative" are teaching at all of Israel's leading universities.[19] But none of them has laid out the new historiographic "agenda" as explicitly as the historian Moshe Zimmermann of the Hebrew University. Zimmermann argues that the entire premise of Jewish history as a unity describing the history of a single Jewish nationality was laid down by Zionist historians responding to the needs of a particular group of "consumers" in their own day. But with the changes taking place in Israeli society—which, he says, is now coming to accept the "slaughter" of various "holy cows" of Zionism—the premise underlying the old narrative of the Jewish people, as we have known it, has also now "expired":

> For if the ground has been swept away, not only from under the feet of Zionism but also from under the entire interpretation that orthodox Zionism gave to Jewish history, then all of Jewish history is in need of a new interpretation.

Fortunately, Zimmermann has a "new" version of Jewish history to propose: one in which the unity that had been artificially imposed by the "problematic" idea of a Jewish "nationality" will no longer be assumed.

> Methodologically, the point of departure is no longer . . . the a priori distinctness of Jewish history, but rather that of "universal history" . . . From the moment that the premise of Jewish or Israeli distinctness is no longer axiomatic . . . all of history looks different.

Indeed, it does. For once the discipline of Jewish history as we know it— in which the Jewish people is a unitary and distinct actor—is dissolved into the new "universal history," each Jewish community is divorced from the overall framework of the traditional Jewish historic narrative and becomes the product of a local, non-Jewish milieu. In such a fragmented history, the concepts and values and aspirations of the Jews as a distinct people naturally dissipate,[20] being replaced by greater empathy for the communities in which the Jews lived. Zimmermann assembles lists of historical conclusions that he believes may arise from studying "universal history" in place of the traditional "Jewish history," including:

1. Not every accusation leveled against the Jews of the Middle Ages was without justification.[21]
2. "Assimilation" . . . kept Judaism alive no less than it has undermined it.
3. Zionism "imported" anti-Semitism into the Middle East.
4. Zionism used the refugees from the Holocaust as a lever to advance aims of its own.
5. Zionism is not the optimal solution . . . to what is known as "the Jewish problem."

Moreover, says Zimmermann, given the experience of the national-states of Europe, which are now on the road to "post-sovereignty," the perspective of "universal history" will permit a "reconsideration of the Israeli fixation regarding sovereignty" and of the "blatantly ethnocentric" concept of the Jewish state.[22]

Thus far I have focused on Israeli academics whose research deals directly with Jewish and Israeli history. But while historians and political sociologists have naturally been on the cutting edge of the "new" research trends, they have received crucial support from professors in other fields—especially philosophy—whose public pronouncements and writings have contributed much to the post-Zionist atmosphere in the media and often reveal a great deal about what is taking place in university classrooms as well.

In certain cases, influential academics helped these trends along by openly challenging Zionism or the concept of a Jewish state. These include scholars such as Menahem Brinker of the Hebrew University, one of Israel's leading scholars of Hebrew literature, who told the press not long ago that "Zionism is not a metaphysical thing. It's a rather totalitarian one which has outlived its usefulness and will ebb away in time";[23] and Amos Elon, one of Israel's best-known journalist-historians (and author of a biography of Herzl), who has decried what he calls the "tragic tendency of large parts of Israeli society to reinterpret its tradition in the harsh terms of an integralist or religious state ideology still known under the old name 'Zionism.'"[24] Others manage to devote their academic work to taking such positions, a case in point being Yosef Agasy of the Tel Aviv University philosophy department, whose recent book *Who Is an Israeli?* (1991) explains that the present Israeli state resembles Nazi Germany or the Soviet Union, in that its interests are those of a nonexistent "phantom nation" (in Israel's case, the Jewish people), which is used as a pretext to justify an "anti-democratic" regime and policies of subversion abroad.[25] Also in this category is the Tel Aviv University philosophy department's Adi Ophir, who has for the last ten years been editor of a highbrow journal called *Theory and Criticism,* published by the Van Leer Institute with the financial support of the Education Ministry, whose aim is the cultivation of the "new history" and other similar trends within Israeli academia.[26] Ophir's own writings include a recent article in which he describes Israel as "the garbage heap of Europe," a "site of experiments . . . in ethnic cleansing," "a regime that produces and distributes evil systematically." He then identifies the cause of all this—Israel's identity as a Jewish state:

> They keep on telling us about the return of the Jews to history as a political and military power . . . and about the Jewish military strength that enables us to defend Jews wherever they may be . . . [But] Jewish sovereignty . . . has turned out to be the biggest danger to Jewish cultural and moral existence . . . They tell us that the only question left open, the only real question, is how to get "peace." . . . They fail to realize that the real question lies in the very idea of national sovereignty. . . . We envision a state that will not be a [Jewish] nation-state.[27]

While there are plenty of academics of this type, the real danger to the Jewish state does not come from its self-professed opponents, who are still a clear minority. Rather, it lies in that large section of Israeli academia that does not necessarily see itself as "post-Zionist" but that has with time moved inexorably away from what was once the mainstream Labor-Zionist consensus regarding even the most basic aspects of maintaining a Jewish state. No one better represents the influence of post-Zionist ideas on mainstream thinkers than Eliezer Schweid of Hebrew University's department of Jewish philosophy. Schweid was for many years the great hope of ideological Labor Zionism, and today he is one of Israel's only remaining Zionist thinkers. It is therefore all the more painful to recognize that even Schweid's Zionism has begun to gravitate toward what he himself describes as a "universal Zionism"—a principle that seeks to resolve the most embarrassing dilemmas of Zionist particularism by giving them up. Thus, he proposes altering the Israeli flag and national anthem in keeping with a "universal Zionism" that is equally representative of both Jews and non-Jews:

> The only way to solve the problem is to add to the Zionist flag [i.e., the present Israeli flag] a symbol that will represent the participation of the Arab mi-

nority, and to compose an anthem . . . that will express the Zionist purpose on a *universal* level: Loyalty to the land of Israel, to Jerusalem, and to the state of Israel as symbols which express the hope of redemption, brotherhood, and peace for all who are called by the name Israel and among all peoples. Such an anthem could unite all the citizens of the state, even though each one of them would use it to express his own national or religious identity, and the substance of his own special connection to the land of Israel, Jerusalem, and the state of Israel.[28]

Now, one does not have to be too much of a philosopher to recognize that "universal Zionism" is identical in content to the generic, universalist patriotism that has always been advocated by anti-Zionist intellectuals. Moreover, it seems obvious that a proposal such as Schweid's can contribute nothing to the problem of shoring up the collapsing idea of the Jewish state. Indeed, particularistic Jewish legislation such as the Law of Return, which Schweid wants to retain, would not last six months after the addition of a crescent moon to the Israeli flag. Whether one calls this "Universal Zionism" or post–Zionism, the fact is that such proposals can do no more than to wreak confusion among those who still believe in the Jewish state, while demonstrating that there is hardly a corner of Israeli academia that is not in retreat before the inevitable.

And for years now, other leading academics have been bombarding the Israeli public with their own political and cultural proposals, to much the same effect. Thus, Avishai Margalit and Moshe Halbertal, both of the Hebrew University philosophy department, have argued that the state of Israel is morally obligated to offer Arabs "special rights" for the protection of their culture and to maintain an Arab majority in those parts of the country where Arabs are concentrated; Israel must be "neutral," on the other hand, toward the Jews, since they constitute the "dominant culture," which can "take care of itself."[29] A related proposal by Hebrew University anthropologist Danny Rabinovitch would have the government publicly confess to "the original sin of Israel" by establishing an official day of mourning to "mark the suffering of the Palestinians during the rise of Israel."[30] And Tel Aviv University historian Yehuda Elkana has opposed Holocaust-awareness programs, which focus attention on collective victimization in the past in a manner that is reminiscent of fascist regimes. His own belief is that Israeli leaders must make every effort to "uproot the rule of historical remembrance from our lives."[31] Along the same lines, Yaron Ezrahi, a noted professor of political science at the Hebrew University, has written a book called *Rubber Bullets* (1997), in which he objects to raising children on myths of national heroism, which he considers "poisonous milk on which fathers often nurse their sons." In place of these, he hopes for the development of a more "moderate, humanly accommodating vision of communal existence," such as the one he found in a Dutch tourist booklet, which looked forward with resignation to a time when Holland will "disappear from history."[32]

One hopes for relief from Yael Tamir of the Tel Aviv University philosophy department (appointed absorption minister in the Barak government in 1999), who showed much courage in publishing her book *Liberal Nationalism* (1993), in which she defends nationalist particularism against the prevailing antinationalist ideas. And yet even here, where a self-professed Zionist intellectual dares to defend nationalism in principle, she ends up stripping it down so far that what remains is the hope of a world "in which traditional nation-states wither away, surrendering their power to make strategic, economic, and ecological decisions to regional organizations, and their power to structure cultural policies to local national communities." In short, Tamir, too, proposes a political ideal that gives the impression of denying the ultimate legitimacy of a sovereign Jewish state.[33]

This then, is the achievement of post-Zionism in Israeli academia. A systematic struggle is being conducted by Israeli scholars against the idea of the Jewish state, its historic narrative, institution, and symbols. Of course, there are elements of truth in *some* of the claims being advanced by Israeli academics against what was once the Labor Zionist consensus on these subjects. But so overwhelming is the assault that it is unclear whether any aspect of this former consensus can remain standing; and such is the state of confusion and conceptual decay among those who still feel loyal to the old ideal of the Jewish state that they themselves are often found advancing ideas that are at the heart of the post–Zionist agenda.

Against this onslaught, the response has been limited. The resistance to the new ideas has included some of Israel's foremost academics, including the political philosopher Shlomo Avineri, the historians Anita Shapira, Shabtai Teveth, Mordechai Bar-On, and Yosef Gorny, the sociologist Moshe Lissak, and a handful of others. Former education minister Amnon Rubinstein's writings on the new historians are also significant.[34] But this rearguard is heavily outgunned, in part because of the sheer volume of post-Zionist academic output—a single issue of *Theory and Criticism* in 1999 amassed no fewer than *fifty* original academic articles seeking to establish the "new" view of Israeli history.[35] Moreover, one cannot help but notice that nearly all of the leading scholars who have made serious contributions to the efforts to fend off the post-Zionist tide are in their sixties and seventies, while their opponents are for the most part significantly younger. What this might mean for the future of Israel's universities and for the future of intellectual life in the Jewish state, one can only begin to imagine.

Literature

The term *anshei ruah* ("men of the spirit") is a common Hebrew expression used to refer to intellectuals and artists in general. But at the same time, these words also carry the clear connotation that such culture makers are in fact the "spiritual leaders" of their readers. And in fact, Israel's most prominent intellectuals—especially authors of fiction such as Amos Oz, A. B. Yehoshua, David Grossman, and Meir Shalev—are often treated as though they *are* the country's spiritual leaders. Not only are their works taught in the public school system and in the universities as the highest expression of a resurrected Hebrew civilization (and therefore as the pinnacle of Zionist achievement), but they are also usually the best-selling books in the country as well, each one a cultural "event" with which educated Israelis are expected to be conversant. Between books, such authors are the object of incessant attention in the media, which are insatiably interested in their views on literature and culture, morals and religion, social policy and foreign policy—in short, on everything. And to add to all this, they frequently teach literature at Israel's universities as well. For this reason, the influence of post-Zionist ideas on Israeli writers is a subject of especial importance for understanding which way the winds are blowing across Israel's cultural landscape.

Tracing the effect of post-Zionist ideas in literature, however, is substantially more complicated than doing so in academia, where there are always a decent number of professors willing to be explicit about the "meaning" of their research. Writers of fiction are notoriously uninterested in offering explicit explanations of the "message" of their works, and without such assistance, it is all too easy to fall into the trap offering overly simplistic interpretations of symbols and scenes and characters whose role may not necessarily be clear-cut. In well-written novels, characters do not necessarily represent unequivocal ideological positions, and even when they do, they may or may not be expressing the views of the author when they speak; moreover, the ideas of a given character may also develop over the course of the book. An additional problem is the fact that many of Israel's leading authors (including those who refer to themselves as Zionists) are great devotees of satire—a technique that allows them to level barbs of the most devastating variety against everything others hold sacred, while being in a position to deflect criticism "lacking in humor."

Yet even with all this said, Israel's leading novelists deal with Zionism and the Jewish state incessantly in their works. And even if they do not like to comment on their own books, they *do* appear frequently in the media to express their views on Israeli political culture. As a consequence, Israel's authors are often individuals whose views exert a definite pressure on Israeli society to move in a given direction: toward a state that has discarded many of the ideals once embraced by its founders.

There is probably no more obvious example than Meir Shalev, the son of Yitzhak Shalev, a one-time Labor Zionist (he later joined Menachem Begin's Irgun) who was in the years after the Holocaust one of Israel's better-known poets. The younger Shalev was catapulted to literary stardom in 1988 with the publication of *A Russian Romance*, one of the most successful works of fiction ever published in Israel (it sold over 100,000 copies in Israel and also became a best-seller in Germany and Austria).[36] It may also be the most merciless parody ever written on the subject of the Labor Zionists who were at the forefront of the struggle for a Jewish state. Because the book largely escaped any taint of "post-Zionism" and because it is so typical of the way Zionism is treated in current Israeli literature, it is worth dwelling on it to get a sense of just what is being parodied and in what manner.

Shalev's novel tells the story of three men and a woman, young Zionist firebrands from Russia who pour their entire lives into the establishment of an impoverished commune in the Galilee, which they eventually succeed in building into a thriving agricultural cooperative. One of the settlement's founding fathers, we are told, never ceases to love a Russian whore back in the old country, but he nevertheless marries the commune's female cook after losing in a lottery to determine who will be saddled with her. Another of the founders, the descendant of "the only Jew in Russia to rape Cossacks," spends the entire book building a monstrous hoard of weaponry and ammunition, but he is in the end blown up along with his cache; his comrades cry little at the loss of their friend, but they do grieve "for so many good weapons gone forever." Another one of the "founders" is a mule that the others discuss as if it were a human being and which they eulogize, upon its death, as "one of the monumental figures of the Movement." But the Zionist pioneers' devotion to guns and mules only underscores their utter contempt for human life. Throughout the book, wars are vaguely mentioned, but no one bothers to refer to names or dates. People in the community die, but no one cares. A couple is murdered by Arabs, and all the founders can do is praise themselves for it, boasting with pleasure that there has been no family in the village that has not sacrificed to bullets, malaria, suicides. "May our determination be redoubled by our grief," they tell one another. "We have chosen life and we shall surely live."[37]

Unlike the real-life Zionist pioneers, however, Shalev's Zionists live a life bereft of any political or historical motives that could give meaning to their sacrifices. His characters know virtually nothing of the ideals that filled the actual Jewish settlers' lives, letters, and memoirs: They have nothing to say about redeeming their people from persecution or restoring their dignity through national independence. Much of the story takes place during the

Holocaust, but it hardly earns a mention. At one point, one of the founders makes reference to it in the village newsletter: "In the Diaspora, too, the Jewish people spills its blood," he writes, "yet their Jewish blood is pointless in death as in life." Then everyone goes back to talking about improving their citrus-growing techniques. When Efraim, the son of one of the farmers, becomes anguished over what is happening in Europe and determines to enlist to fight the Nazis, his father responds with contempt: "A boy your age can make his contribution right here. You're not going off to any war."[38]

Efraim runs away from home and serves with a British commando unit in Tunisia, where he performs deeds of remarkable heroism before being horribly disfigured in a battle. Shalev's characters nowhere make the connection between Efraim's cause and their own lives, and when he returns to the village after an absence of two years, the Jews of the village show him no trace of gratitude or compassion. All they feel is revulsion, which Shalev paints in vivid detail:

> Efraim was home. Wearing the soft yellow desert boots and winged-dagger insignia of a commando, and his ribbons, decorations, and sergeant's stripes . . . Efraim stepped out of the car and smiled at the villagers gathered there. . . . Mouths opened wide, retching with horror and consternation. Men came running from the green fields, from the leafing orchards, from the cowsheds and the chicken coops to stand before Efraim and howl. . . . [The teacher] emerged from the schoolhouse and loped heavily towards his former pupil. . . . Shutting his eyes, he bellowed like a slaughtered ox. . . . The crowd pressed together in fear, a whole village stood shrieking.[39]

In a few sentences, all of Labor Zionism is revealed in its shallowness, hypocrisy, and callous villainy. For the Zionist founders, every sacrifice, no matter how extreme, is worthwhile in the name of their movement. But a decorated Jewish soldier, tragically wounded in the fight to save the lives of Europe's Jews, is for them nothing but a horror.

Nor does his treatment at the hands of the Zionists improve. After Efraim's homecoming, the Jewish farmers only shun him and despise him. In stark contrast, it is the *British* officers stationed in Palestine—preserved in Israeli memory as a hard-hearted oppressor—who display the only nobility and humanity in the book. It is they who love Efraim dearly for what he has done, including "the lame Major Stoves, two lean, quiet Scottish commando officers who gave Efraim an embrace, and an Indian quartermaster whose heart thumped loudly at the sight of the medals on my uncle's chest." It is they, and not the Zionist idealists, who try to help the wounded Jewish soldier rebuild his life, building him a small structure in which he can live and coming to drink beer with him. Similarly, it is the men of his unit who chip in to buy him a pedigreed bull so that he can earn a livelihood. Shalev spells out the meaning for any reader who might have missed it: "The British know how to honor their heroes."[40]

In the end, Efraim is forced to flee the village because of the Zionists' revulsion for him, and now the pettiness, vindictiveness, and sexual vandalism that had characterized the Zionist settlers' meaningless existence is turned to a purpose: The rest of the novel chronicles the campaign of vengeance by means of which Efraim's family successfully destroys the lives of the Zionist settlement's founding fathers. Efraim's grandfather strikes back at his former friends by leaving the fruit in his orchards to drop from the trees and rot. And one of Efraim's nephews sleeps with "every last one" of the founders' married daughters and granddaughters in turn, calling out their relationships to the founders ("I'm screwing Liberson's granddaughter!" "I'm screwing Ya'akovi's wife!") from the top of the water tower as his campaign progresses. Another nephew transforms his grandfather's farm into a cemetery for members of the founders' generation ("the traitors") who left Palestine for America and made vast fortunes there. The dead capitalists are returned to the village in coffins, having paid tremendous sums before dying to be buried in a graveyard for *halutzim*—the vaunted Hebrew term for "pioneers." Those Jews who attained success in America are in this way awarded the same posthumous glory as those who devoted their lives to backbreaking labor in the wastes of Palestine. And the Zionist founders are thus robbed of the only thing that ever mattered to them: the sanctimonious myth of their own moral superiority.

Toward the end of the book, as he is surveying the wreckage of his life's work, the settlement's old schoolteacher Ya'akov Pinness undergoes a conversion experience ("at the age of ninety-five, Pinness looked up to discover that . . . fresh breezes blew over the earth") and defects to the side of the destroyers. Suddenly, we find him taking up his pen and writing in the village newsletter that the effort for which they had sacrificed their entire lives had been mistaken. "We were wrong," he wrote, "Wrong educationally. Wrong politically. Wrong in how we thought about the future. We are like the blind beasts that perish, up to their necks in mire." In the pages that follow, Pinness elaborates, explaining to anyone who will listen that the Jews had been fools for having sought redemption in a reunion with the soil of ancient Israel, which they had vainly imagined to be somehow related to them, somehow their own:

> "This vulgar earth must have split its sides laughing at the sight of us pioneers kissing and watering it with our tears of thanksgiving," [said Pinness.] . . . He now understood how easily the earth shook off whatever trivial images men cloaked it in. "Why, it's nothing but a tissue of poor fictions anyway, the earth!" he exclaimed. "A thin crust beneath which is nothing but pure selfishness."[41]

Shalev's book is a satire, of course. And it is so successful because Shalev's caricature really does build in part on weaknesses of the old Labor Zionism that deserve to be brought out. (His critique of the movement's crass materialism, for example, is a crucial point that is unfamiliar to most Israeli readers.) But what makes Shalev's novel a classic of contemporary post-Zionist literature is not the fact that it pokes fun at what was once sacrosanct. Rather, it is the manner in which virtually every aspect of Zionism is made to appear invidious, its every ideal repugnant and its every adherent loathsome—while those cast in a favorable light are inevitably those who revolted against the Zionists (Efraim, Ya'akov Pinness) or else those who historically opposed them (the British). In fact, so successful is *A Russian Romance* that it is impossible to detect *anything* in the Jewish return to Palestine that might have once been worthy of our identification or admiration. Shalev is not involved here in the kind of satire that destroys a rickety wall or two so we can build another. He is razing the house.

Needless to say, Israeli literature did not begin this way. Early Jewish nationalist authors and poets such as S. Y. Agnon, Haim Nahman Bialik, Shaul Tchernikovsky, Nathan Alterman, and Uri Tzvi Greenberg produced a literature imbued with a love for the Jewish people and for the resurrection of this people in its land, and were felt to be the moving spirit uplifting the settlers of Jewish Palestine and instilling in them the strength for great deeds. The next generation of writers, including Aharon Meged, Moshe Shamir, and the poet Haim Guri, were individuals who came of age during the struggle for Jewish independence. Although their novels, short stories, and plays more realistically reflected the actual Jewish state being constructed in Israel, their works similarly conveyed a belief in the importance and justice of the Zionist cause. Typical of these was Moshe Shamir's runaway best-seller *He Walked in the Fields* (1947). Shamir's novel told the story of Uri, a young leader in the Jewish underground organization Palmah, who is torn between the duties of command and his pregnant girlfriend. In the end, Uri dies in a training accident, throwing himself on a live grenade to save his friends. The tragedy was given even greater poignancy by the fact that Shamir's own real-life brother was killed during the War of Independence, not long after the novel was published, and Israelis continued to flock to hear the story retold in major stage and screen productions well into the 1960s. (In the film version, Uri was played by Asi Dayan, the son of former chief of staff Moshe Dayan.)[42]

But the days of this kind of Zionist literature were numbered, and in the years following the establishment of the state, certain Israeli writers had already begun to use their writings to question the meaning and justice of the war that had resulted from the Jewish struggle for independence.[43] Most important among them was S. Yizhar (Yizhar Smilansky), probably Israel's most influential author, of whom the leading novelist Amos Oz has justly observed, "There is some Yizhar in every writer who has come after him."[44] In 1949, only months after the guns had fallen silent, Yizhar stunned the newborn state by publishing a series of short stories savaging the Jewish use of military power during the war. Among these was "The Prisoner," in which he told the story of a group of Israeli soldiers who capture an innocent Arab shepherd, steal his livestock, and take immense pleasure beating and torturing him, before packing him off to be imprisoned. Even the story's Jewish protagonist, although troubled by the injustice, also fails to release the prisoner when the opportunity presents itself.

In another story, "Hirbet Hiza," Yizhar likewise portrays the Jewish soldiers in the war as arbitrarily cruel. Not only are the soldiers assigned to expel Arab civilians from their village, but Yizhar goes out of his way to emphasize that these young Jews were morally repugnant even *before* getting the order: They swap stories about the donkeys they have been shooting for fun. They beg to get the machine gun so they can try to gun down the unarmed Arabs fleeing the village. When one Arab tries to leave the village with a camel bearing his possessions, they tell him if he does not leave the camel, they will kill him. "They're like animals," the Jewish soldiers keep telling one another. Here, too, the protagonist feels pangs of remorse, and when another soldier tries to cheer him by mentioning the homeless Jewish immigrants who may yet live there, he seethes with anger:

> Why hadn't I thought of that? . . . We'll house and absorb immigrants.
> . . . We'll open a grocery, build a school, maybe even a synagogue. . . . Fields
> will be plowed and sown and reaped, and great deeds will be done.
> . . . Who'll even remember that there was once some Hirbet Hiza here, which
> we drove out and inherited. We came, we shot, we burned, we detonated, we
> exiled. What the hell are we doing here?[45]

In these stories, too, the Jewish soldier is presented stripped of any context that may explain or mitigate his behavior, so that the wrongs he commits seem to be absolute: The reader has no reason to believe that the soldiers have acted in anger or in anguish or out of understandable miscalculation, so that what is depicted can be interpreted only as evil in its pure form. And for this reason, Yizhar's stories leave the reader little choice but to question whether the war could possibly have been worth the costs involved. And in fact, it is this that his soldiers are chronically asking themselves. Thus, in "Before Zero Hour," one of Yizhar's soldiers suspects that the young Jews going off to battle are merely being swindled and that the war in which they are fighting is no more than nonsense. ("How foolish war is . . . Shots are being fired all the time . . . Then, suddenly, a funeral . . . And someone may recite one of those nice verses you say before dying, instead of yelling: 'You asses! You're being cheated! Don't go! What fatherland? You'll be killed.'") Similarly, in his novel *Days of Ziklag* (1958), the narrator is so far from understanding what the war is about that he sees himself as the biblical Isaac being sacrificed on the altar of his father's ideological lunacy: "I hate our father Abraham," he writes. "What right does he have to sacrifice Isaac? Let him sacrifice himself. I hate the God that sent him . . . To slaughter sons as a proof of love! . . . Scoundrels, what do the sons have to die for?"[46]

Obviously, such a degree of alienation from the perspective of the Jewish efforts to establish the state were bound to cause Yizhar trouble with some in the Zionist literary establishment, and in fact it did. But his writings were received with enthusiasm by at least one literature professor at the Hebrew University, Shimon Halkin, who was then working to teach his students— in the words of one Israeli literary historian—the difference between "tendentious-Zionist-preaching literature" and "skeptical, non-ideational literature."[47] Yizhar's works were obviously of the latter type, and these became a model not only for student writers at the university but also for a literary journal founded by recent university graduates called *Achshav* ("Now"), which worked to lionize Yizhar and to deprecate more traditional Labor Zionist writers such as Nathan Alterman, and the culture of mainstream Labor Zionism in general.[48] It was these circles close to Halkin and *Achshav* that produced most of the leading Israeli writers familiar to us today, including most of the recipients of the coveted Israel Prize in Literature in the last two decades: The novelists Amos Oz, A. B. Yehoshua, and Aharon Appelfeld, the poets Yehuda Amichai, Nathan Zach, and Dalia Rabikovitch, and the playwright Nissim Aloni.[49] And it is these authors, too, who have worked so hard to demonstrate the truth of Amos Oz's observation that there is some Yizhar "in every writer who has come after him."

Consider Oz himself, for instance. Oz is an exceptionally gifted novelist, who is perhaps the undisputed spokesman for Israel's literature, if not for all of Israeli culture. Yet Oz's works are characterized by a grim ambivalence toward the Jewish state, its symbols and historical triumphs. For example, Oz has long harbored a kind of aversion toward Jerusalem, the preeminent symbol of Jewish redemption, both national and religious, which he views as a "city of lunacy," "a city surrounded by forces desiring my death."[50] This sentiment is powerfully expressed in his novel *My Michael* (1968), which presents the Jewish capital as a city of brooding insanity and illness that his famous protagonist, Hanna Gonen, longs to see destroyed ("Perhaps she [i.e., Jerusalem] had been conquered in the meantime . . . Perhaps she had

finally crumbled to dust. As she deserved").[51] And indeed, the book ends
with Hanna sending the imaginary Arab terrorists at her command to attack
the city. In *Black Box* (1987), Oz's neo-hippie protagonist refers to the
struggle for the Jewish state as "these wars and all the bullshit" and, in a crucial act of downsizing, redefines Zionism to be "wanting everyone to be
okay. And for everyone to do just a little for the country, even something really tiny."[52] In *Fima* (1991), Oz focuses his attention on a middle-aged man
who spends his time fantasizing about founding a new Israeli political
movement. As it turns out, Fima too has difficulties adjusting to the reality
of a Jewish state, so he likes to compare the Jews of Israel to the Cossacks.
He also likes to compare the idea that the Jews are a nation to fascism: "The
time has come to stop feeling like a nation . . . Let's cut that crap. . . . These
are semi-fascist motifs. . . . We really aren't a nation anyway." And when
Fima sees Jews walk around Jerusalem with guns in their belts, he wonders
when it was that the Jews became "scum": "Was the sickness implicit in the
Zionist idea from the outset? Is there no way for the Jews to get back onto
the stage of history except by becoming scum? . . . And weren't we already
scum before we got back onto the stage of history?"[53]

Themes such as these in Oz's fiction are backed up by his frequent media
appearances, which likewise send a message of carefully controlled disdain
for Jewish nationalism. As a student in the early 1960s, for example, Oz says
that he poured his efforts into the search for an Israeli literature that would
permit an "escape from the claws of Zionism" and "create a spiritual distance of thousands of miles from the land of Israel."[54] And his description of
his present views is not so far from this: Today he is Israel's most eloquent
advocate of the idea that rather than taking pride in the Jewish flag or the
Jewish state, one should consider these aims of Herzl's Zionism to be a
"curse":

> I would be more than happy to live in a world composed of dozens of civi-
> lizations . . . without any one emerging as a nation-state: No flag, no em-
> blem, no passports, no anthem. No nothing. Only spiritual civilizations tied
> somehow to their lands, without the tools of statehood. . . . To take pride in
> these tools of statehood? . . . Not I. . . . Nationalism itself is, in my eyes, the
> curse of mankind.

Despite seeing nationalism as "the curse of mankind" and despite his contempt for so much of what in fact comprises the Jewish state, Oz says that the
experience of the Holocaust has caused him to "accept" Jewish nationalism, at
least "up to a point."[55] There is no reason to doubt him when he says this—in
fact, he has suffered being considered a reactionary on the literary scene for
defending Zionism this strongly. And perhaps Oz can live this way, considering the central triumphs of the Jewish people in his lifetime to be a curse,

while at the same time accepting them up to a point. But it is obvious that the great majority of Israeli Jews *cannot* live this way. For once *they* have come to think of the struggles and achievements of the IDF as "these wars and all the bullshit" and Jerusalem as "a city of lunacy" and the national flag as representing "the curse of mankind" and Jews bearing arms as "scum"—that is, once other educated Israelis have come to see things through the looking glass of Oz's writings—it is a safe bet that the number of those willing to sacrifice for the existence of the Jewish state will be small indeed.

Perhaps Israel's second most prominent writer is A. B. Yehoshua, who is likewise known as a frequent and sincere defender of Zionism. Yet in Yehoshua, too, one finds an almost obsessive need to take a hammer to the Zionist narrative and the idea of the Jewish state. Yehoshua first made a name for himself with a story called "Facing the Forests" (1963), about a student from the university who takes a job as a watchman in a Jewish National Fund forest. As the student reads his books, the Jewish hikers in the forest begin to look to him "like a procession of Crusaders" (in real life, Arab propaganda had often compared the Jewish return to Israel to the brutal and transient Crusader kingdom in Palestine during the Middle Ages). Moreover, he becomes aware that the forest itself, the pride of Zionism, has been planted on the ruins of an Arab village. The longer he watches over the forest, the more he sympathizes with the Arabs, to the point that when an Arab comes to set fire to the forest, the student turns a blind eye, letting him burn it to the ground. (For those for whom this is too subtle, Yehoshua ends the story by having the student physically beaten by the Zionist who gave him the job.)[56]

Yehoshua's novel *The Lover* (1977) is one of the most successful literary works ever written in Israel and the novel most frequently taught in Israeli public schools.[57] Like Shalev's *A Russian Romance,* Yehoshua's book is also a satire in which reasonable youngsters are pitted against Zionist types of their parents' generation. Here, too, the characters identified with traditional Zionism are portrayed in exclusively negative terms: Asya, a high-school teacher of Zionist history, is too caught up in her work and her cause to care for her family; Asya's father, one of the founders of the state, has been cast aside and ostracized by the vindictive Zionist political machine; Schwartzy, the high-school principal, is a Zionist hypocrite who is constantly preaching ideals of community and self-sacrifice but is incapable of applying them to himself; and the unnamed IDF officer inducting recruits during the Yom Kippur War is a malicious lunatic who purposely sends one of the protagonists to the front with a weapon he does not know how to use to get him killed. The sympathetic figures, on the other hand, are those who are oppressed by the Zionist characters and in one way or another stand up to them: Gabriel, who had left Israel ten years earlier and, now that he has returned, deserts from the IDF in mid-battle; Asya's fifteen-year-old daughter

Dafi, who riddles her mother with questions about whether the establishment of Israel was really worth it but never gets any answers; and Na'im, an
Arab boy employed in Dafi's father's garage, who cares for a dying Jewish
woman even though she dislikes Arabs.

The conflict between the generations comes to a head in a scene in which
Asya, substituting in Dafi's high-school history class, presents the history of
Labor Zionism to her daughter. The bell has already rung at the end of the
lesson, when Dafi suddenly comes awake and begins interrogating her
mother in front of the entire class:

> "I don't understand," I said, "why you say that they were right, I mean the
> people of the Second Aliya [i.e. Labor Zionism], thinking that [settlement in
> Palestine] was the only choice after so much suffering? How can you say that
> there wasn't another choice? And that was the only choice?" I could see that
> she didn't understand.
> "Whose suffering?"
> "Our suffering, all of us."
> "In what sense?"
> "All this suffering around us . . . wars . . . people getting killed . . . suffer-
> ing in general . . . Why was that the only choice?. . . " It seemed nobody un-
> derstood what I meant.
> Mommy smiled and dodged the question: "That is really a philosophical
> question. We have tried to understand their thinking, but now the bell has
> rung, and we won't be able to solve that question during recess, I'm afraid."
> The class laughed. I wanted to bury myself. Idiots.[58]

Asya is apparently unable to answer even the most obvious criticism of
the Zionism she spends her life justifying, and she escapes only by using her
authority over the class to belittle her daughter's questions and declare them
out of bounds. Having thus been humiliated by her mother, Dafi resolves
her clash with her noxious Zionist elders by going to bed with Na'im.

Yehoshua's books and stories are accompanied by a steady stream of media interviews and lectures, in which he has done as much as anyone to den-
igrate the ideas and symbols underpinning the Jewish state. Thus, Yehoshua
has, for example, announced that Israel has outgrown its political alliance
with the Jews of the Diaspora ("We don't need you anymore . . . We do not
need the money . . . except to buy ourselves candies . . . We do not need the
political support"). He has announced that most Israelis no longer want
greater Jewish immigration ("The majority of the public here is telling you
this explicitly . . . It also doesn't want more Jewish immigration. It is
crowded enough here").[59] He has announced his distaste for Jerusalem ("In
recent years I have been building up my anti-Jerusalem ideology a bit") and
his contempt for the Western Wall as a Jewish symbol ("It broadcasts absur-

dity and frustration"). He has announced that conditions should be placed on the right of Diaspora Jews to receive Israeli citizenship ("No longer should citizenship be granted [to immigrant Jews] automatically, but rather it should be suspended for a few years, up until the new Jewish immigrant can prove his belonging to the Israeli identity").[60] And recently he has argued that it would be best if Israeli Jews would convert to Christianity and Islam because this would serve to "normalize" Israel:

[I realize] . . . this looks crazy, unrealistic now, but perhaps in another one hundred, two hundred years it will be possible. . . . We have to turn this people into a people without a [distinctive] religion . . . Let the members of the Jewish people be Christians, Moslems . . . Religiously, there should be a number of different options so that our people can belong to various religions.[61]

It is difficult to imagine where Yehoshua believes he is going with his dream of a Christian and Muslim "Jewish" people in Israel. But one thing is certain. To the degree that Israelis internalize the lessons Yehoshua is trying to teach, the idea of the Jewish state as we have known it will simply cease to exist.

Amos Oz and A. B. Yehoshua are authors who frequently speak out on public affairs, and as a consequence, the Israeli media have devoted significant attention to their views on subjects touching on Zionism. Less commented upon are the messages regarding the Jewish state being advanced by Aharon Appelfeld, Israel's most important writer on the Holocaust. Appelfeld is himself a survivor, whose novel *The Searing Light* (1980) has been widely discussed for its implication that Holocaust refugees arriving in Israel after independence were received in conditions that reminded them of the Nazi concentration camps.[62] Recently, however, Appelfeld has repeated this chilling accusation in a more explicit form in "Looking Up Close," an essay that also appears in his autobiography *Life Story* (1999), in which he explicitly claims, "I had known suffering in the ghetto and in the camp, but now [in the Israeli army] it was not the suffering of hunger and thirst I experienced, but distress of the soul."

His explanation, as far as I can understand it, is as follows. Appelfeld seems to believe that his experiences in the Israeli army was in a sense a continuation of his experience during the Holocaust, "except that now the faces changed": In place of the fear he felt as a child on the verge of being murdered by the Nazis, he was now subjected to "the fear of the sergeant tyrannizing you day and night." Yet in one decisive respect, the Israeli army in Appelfeld's telling of it can be understood as if it were *worse* than the Holocaust. For during his years in the concentration camp and as a fugitive hiding in the forests, Appelfeld had taught himself to sit for hours gazing at the vegetation or at moving water. And it was the modicum of "happiness" he found in these hours that allowed him to suppress both fear and hunger and that "protected me from spiritual annihilation." Only in the Israeli army did he for the first time find himself robbed of the ability to defend himself in this manner. "In the army, this secret experience was taken from me," he says. "I did not have even an hour to myself." Thus, if we are to accept what Appelfeld seems to be saying at face value, it was not during the Holocaust, in which he lost both of his parents, that he learned the meaning of "suffering of the soul" and stood without protection before the threat of "spiritual annihilation." This happened to him only in 1950, two years after Israel's independence, when he was called to be trained as a Jewish soldier.

Now, one cannot argue with these kinds of emotions, and Appelfeld may well have experienced them precisely as he describes them. But what is important here is not the personal experiences of a traumatized Jewish child. It is the *ideological* inferences that one of Israel's leading writers draws from these experiences. And Appelfeld's ideological conclusions are, in Israeli terms, revolutionary. For in complete opposition to the lesson that most Jews learned from the Holocaust, Appelfeld argues that what saved him was *weakness:* "I survived the war, not because I was strong or because I fought for my life. I was like a tiny animal that found momentary refuge in incidental grace, living off what the minute brings it. This danger made me a child attentive to my surroundings and to myself, *but not a strong child.*"

According to Appelfeld, it was the fact that he was endangered and weak that gave him the uncanny gift of being "attentive to his surroundings." And it was this gift that helped him evade physical threats and that permitted him to find bits of happiness that brought him spiritual salvation—the "hidden happiness of the weak."

Aharon Appelfeld is not only one of Israel's most prominent writers. He is probably the Jewish state's foremost spokesman on the Holocaust. Yet in his capacity as witness, he speaks of how the suffering he experienced during the Holocaust was a lesser suffering, in a sense, than that inflicted upon him in the army of the Jewish state; and when he speaks of what a Jew needed in order to survive the inferno, he speaks not of the strength that the Jewish state and its army provide, but of the weakness that the Jews of Europe already had in quantity. And once one comes to conceive of Jewish power (such as that in the hands of an IDF sergeant) as being little more than an opening for cruelty and terror, and of Jewish weakness as a possible key to salvation (even from the Holocaust), the central Zionist premise on which the Jewish state was built begins to crumble. For if it is weakness, not strength, that saves, then what really was the point of establishing a Jewish armed forces and a Jewish state? The very premise of the state's existence is quietly called into question.[63]

In this regard it is also worth mentioning David Grossman, perhaps the most respected of Israel's younger writers other than Meir Shalev. Grossman gained national attention with his *The Yellow Wind* (1987), a collection of essays on the Israeli administration of the West Bank that drew controversy, among other reasons, for comparing Palestinian Arabs to the Jews of the exile. (The Arabs, he writes, repeat "the ancient Jewish strategy of exile. . . . They close their eyes . . . they fabricate their Promised Land. 'Next year in Jerusalem,' said the Jews . . . and the meaning was that they were not willing to compromise. . . . And here also, again and again, that absolute demand: Everything.")[64] Grossman had preceded this with a novelized version of the same themes called *The Smile of the Lamb* (1983), in which a young Israeli-Jewish poet adopts an Arab from the West Bank as his mentor and in the end finds himself looking on with understanding as the Arab murders the head of the Israeli military administration, himself a Holocaust survivor.

Obviously, such books, whose purpose is to bring Jews to view Israeli policy through the eyes of Arabs in the West Bank, can serve to erode the identification of Israelis with the cause of the Jewish state. But one might say the same of any book that is harshly critical of Israeli government policy in a given area. It goes without saying that even the most dogmatic Zionist might consider the harm done by such works to be a price worth paying if the issue in question is of sufficient importance.

Yet one gains a very different view of Grossman's work by reading those books of his that have nothing at all to do with the West Bank. Of these, the most important is *See Under: Love* (1986), which, like Appelfeld's "Looking Up Close," deals with the Holocaust and with the question of Jewish power in its aftermath. Two story lines dominate its universe of interlocking narratives. The first deals with Momik, the Israeli son of Holocaust survivors, who is growing up in a neighborhood populated by survivors. Momik is an exemplary Jewish child, in terms of both his superior intellectual abilities and his acute moral sensibilities. But at age nine, he becomes aware of the Holocaust and becomes obsessed with defending his family and country from "the Nazi beast" that had committed such horrors against them. As the story unfolds, Momik's need to ready himself for battle against Nazism comes to take precedence over all else. It puts an end to his academic success in school (although his body becomes stronger and he begins to evidence athletic ability). More important, it destroys his moral sense, and his cause begins to supply him with reasons to abuse his elders, to steal, and to torture small animals to death. He also becomes a Nazi-like anti-Semite in his burning hatred for powerless Jews, whom he calls *jude*. Momik's preparations do not, of course, lead to battle with "the Nazi beast," since it is the product of his imagination. But they do transform *him* into a full-fledged

real-life Nazi, who rounds up the aging Holocaust survivors of his neighborhood, marching them into a dark basement for extermination.

The second story line is essentially the same, but in reverse. In it,
Grossman tells the wartime tale of Momik's great-uncle Anshel
Wasserman, a Jewish writer imprisoned in a concentration camp where his
wife and daughter have been murdered. Neither bullets nor the gas chambers can kill Wasserman, and he is brought before Obersturmbannfuehrer
Neigel, the commander of the camp. Neigel is, of course, a real Nazi beast
who killed Wasserman's daughter with his own hands and who urges
Himmler to build more gas chambers so the work can proceed more
quickly. But Neigel has a problem: His wife has left him because she disap-
proves of his extermination camp, and he enlists the Jewish storyteller to
help him win her back. Unlike his Israeli grandnephew, Wasserman has an
unshakable moral sense, and not even the murder of his daughter can move
him to shoot the concentration-camp commander when the opportunity
presents itself. Nevertheless, Wasserman does join battle after his own fashion, using his stories and conversations with Neigel to coax the Nazi into
sympathizing with those he is killing. At first Neigel resists, but eventually
he really does hesitate before murdering an inmate in the camp. Gradually,
the Jew—so Grossman writes—gains the ability to give the Nazi orders.
And with a little help from Neigel's wife, Wasserman in the end succeeds
in morally enlightening him to such a degree that the other Nazis realize
what is happening, and Neigel is left with no choice but to commit suicide.
(A related plot is at the center of Grossman's novel, *The Book of Intimate
Grammar* [1991], in which a brainy Israeli fourteen-year-old, who dreams
of teaching the world Esperanto "so that everyone would speak one
language and understand each other," is gradually driven to commit suicide by the transformation of his childhood friend into a jingoistic Zionist
youth-movement leader, caught up in the fever of immanent war in
1967.)[65]

In these parables, Grossman's message is much the same as that of
Aharon Appelfeld. For Grossman, too, it is not military and political power
that will defeat evil in this world. On the contrary, Jewish children who
grow up desperately wishing to defend their people using worldly power are
on the fast track to becoming Nazis. Genuine resistance cannot, therefore,
be based on the pursuit of power. Instead, the road to victory belongs to
Anshel Wasserman, who will not touch a knife or a gun even to dispose of
his own daughter's murderer—which is to say that victory begins with the
insistence on Jewish powerlessness. Like Appelfeld, David Grossman
earnestly seeks to teach Israelis to recognize that it is *weakness* that gives
birth to virtue. ("Having a body is itself a defect," he writes in *The Book of
Intimate Grammar*.)[66] But again, this is not a lesson that the Jews of our

time can embrace too hastily, for to embrace it is to demolish the foundation on which the entire edifice of the Jewish state rests.

A not dissimilar picture emerges when one considers the leading Israeli poets, Yehuda Amichai, Nathan Zach, and Dalia Rabikovitch. Poetry is traditionally even more complex than fiction in its relationship with the values of the society in which the poet writes, and these particular poets are also very different from one another in temperament and tone. Yet all three share with their counterparts among writers of fiction what appears to be a pronounced difficulty in relating in a constructive fashion to the Jewish state in which they live. Typically aggressive is the poetry of Dalia Rabikovitch, whose "You Don't Kill a Baby Twice" (1987) has words in German emerging from the mouths of Israeli soldiers, so as to ensure that readers understand that the transformation of Jews into genuine Nazis has now been completed. In her poem "New Zealand" (1986), on the other hand, Rabikovitch considers a better country and a better life than she has in Israel:

> As for me,
> He maketh me lie down in green pastures [Ps. 23:2]
> 　　in New Zealand. . . .
> Truehearted people herd sheep there,
> On Sundays they go to church
> In their quiet clothes.
> No point in hiding it any longer:
> We're an experiment that didn't turn out well,
> A plan that went wrong,
> Tied up with too much murderousness.
> What do I care about these people,
> Or those—
> Screaming till their throats are hoarse,
> Splitting fine hairs.
> Anyway, too much murderousness.[67]

Similarly, the recent poetry of Nathan Zach includes "A Small Song of the War Dead" (1996), in which a fallen soldier writes of his homeland:

> In whose throat is the grandeur of the future, . . .
> While she with her steel foot tramples,
> Each whom she finds in her way,
> Each who chances upon her,
> Each who was among her sons.
> How good it is that I have died, am rid of you, my homeland.[68]

Perhaps most disappointing in this regard is Amichai, certainly Israel's foremost poet, who breaks with most of his colleagues in his willingness to defend Jewish nationalist themes, at least when speaking to the press. Yet Amichai is even found using the brilliant irony for which he is famous to cast images that are deeply ambivalent concerning the Jewish political restoration. In his "Biblical Reflections" (1971), for example, Amichai asks whether it would not have been better had the Jews drowned with Pharaoh's army at the Red Sea rather than drowning in the thousands of years of its history; and in "Songs of the Land of Zion, Jerusalem" (1974), he envisions Jerusalem as "a dead city / in which all the people / swarm like worms and maggots."[69] Similarly, in "Jews in the Land of Israel" (1971), Amichai associates the return of the Jews to their land with endless suffering and wonders why the Jews should be in Israel at all:

> The circumcision causes us . . .
> To be in pain all our lives.
> What are we doing here, returning with this pain?
> Our longings were dried out with the swamps . . .
> What are we doing here
> In this dark land . . . ?[70]

Contemporary poets are known for an open style that defies definitive interpretation, and it is therefore likely that no number of such quotations will persuade a devotee of Israeli poetry that something is amiss in the work of such towering cultural figures as Amichai, Zach, and Rabikovitch. But there *is* something amiss. Year after year, Israel's government schools, universities, and media continue to lavish attention on Israel's "national poets," looking the other way whenever they produce some elegantly textured and multilayered metaphor about leaving Israel for Christian New Zealand or ridding oneself of the tyranny that is the Jewish homeland. Yet despite all this adulation, it is hard to escape the conclusion that they rarely see it as their business to produce anything that could be called a serious, positive engagement with the aspirations and achievements of the Jewish state in which they live. Indeed, with remarkable frequency, Israeli poets are found to be saying something in keeping with the spirit of Nathan Zach's recent comment in the daily *Yediot Aharonot* regarding the Jewish state: "Who and what has it not disappointed? . . . Who and what has it not betrayed? . . . What abomination has its soul been spared? What lie and hypocrisy has not issued from its throat? The dream is a monstrosity."[71]

And what of Israel's other writers? Its playwrights, its filmmakers? These fields are, if anything, worse. Israeli theater has for a generation been dominated by the works of Hanoch Levin (d. 1999), whose 1970 *Queen of the Bathtub* depicts the Old City of Jerusalem, captured by Israel in the Six Day War, as a toilet, whose conquest gives Israelis such a power high that they decide not to let their Arab cousin use it—forcing him, for want of a better option, to urinate and defecate on stage. Levin's attitude towards Israel's war dead is not much different. In one famous scene, Levin has a grieving father standing at the fresh grave of his son killed in battle, who is chastised mercilessly by the dead soldier:

> Dear father, when you stand at my grave,
> Old and tired and very alone . . .
> Don't stand so proud . . .
> And don't stand in silence for my honor.
> Something more important than honor
> Is lying now at your feet, father.
> And don't say you made a sacrifice,
> Because I'm the one who made the sacrifice,
> And don't talk in fine-sounding words anymore,
> Because I'm laid lower than low, father.
> Dear father, when you stand at my grave,
> Old and tired and very alone . . .
> Just ask my forgiveness, father.[72]

Hanoch Levin's *The Patriot* (1982) gives his audience a chance to see religious Jews roasting the hand of an Arab over the open flame of a Sabbath candle, and his *Murder* (1997) features a group of Israeli soldiers taking pleasure in stabbing, burning, and cutting the testicles off of an innocent Arab boy.[73] Perhaps second in prominence is the playwright Yehoshua Sobol, whose *Ghetto* (1984) and *Adam* (1989) depicts a Zionist collaborating with the Nazis during World War II. Sobol's *The Jerusalem Syndrome* (1987) portrays the Jews during the Roman siege of Jerusalem (and by analogy, those of today) in a frenzy of politically and, especially, religiously motivated murder, torture, rape, and cannibalism.[74] The kinds of subjects attractive to leading Israeli filmmakers—and that are made into Israel's most important films—are similar. Among these is Judd Ne'eman's *Paratroops* (1977), which depicts IDF training, and by analogy Israeli culture, as a form of total oppression that causes the suicide of a sensitive young inductee. Similarly, Rafi Bokai's *Avanti Popolo* (1986) tells the story of two Egyptian soldiers trying to return home across the Sinai Desert after the Six Day War, encountering various inhumane and vulgar Israeli soldiers en route. The Jews are portrayed as happily wasting precious water on themselves; but they prove uninclined to give the suffering Arabs anything to drink, provoking one of the Egyptians to recite Shylock's "Hath not a Jew eyes?" monologue from *The Merchant of Venice*. Asi Dayan's *Life According to Agfa* (1992) treats a range of Israeli degenerates spending a night in a bar (yet another metaphor for Israel), where a group of IDF officers are getting drunk and trying to rape women. In the morning, the soldiers return and murder everyone in the bar. The list goes on and on like this.[75]

Can the works of these leading Israeli novelists and poets, playwrights and filmmakers be associated with "post-Zionism"? It is unlikely that any of them would choose to be identified in this way. Yet if one were to ask whether they continue to believe in the classic Labor-Zionist dream of the Jewish state, it seems likely that the answers would be more equivocal. Amos Oz, for example, recently wrote with force against the idea of a Jewish state, as though it were self-evident that this idea should be discarded:

> A state cannot be Jewish, just as a chair or a bus cannot be Jewish ... The state is no more than a tool, a tool that is efficient or a tool that is defective, a tool that is suitable or a tool that is undesirable. And this tool must belong to all its citizens—Jews, Moslems, Christians ... The concept of a "Jewish state" is nothing other than a snare.[76]

Moreover, even if they do not come out with explicit and public pronouncements of this sort, almost all of these authors suffer to one degree or another from the syndrome familiar to us from Meir Shalev's *A Russian Romance*. That is, one gets the impression that they feel little obligation to say something positive about the history or ideals or achievements on which the Jewish state ultimately rests, but they *do* feel at liberty to ridicule or disparage these virtually without limit. Oz, who is actually much better on this score than others, nevertheless provided a pointed example when discussing whether he would write fiction about the Six Day War, which had brought the reunification of Jerusalem a year earlier. Oz responded: "I wasn't born ... to liberate lands from foreign yoke. ... If I write something one day about this war, I'll write about sweat and vomit and pus and urine."[77]

One does not have to declare oneself a "post-Zionist" to contribute to the growing contempt for the Jewish state. A consistent attitude such as this one will do just fine.

In the early 1960s, when the rebellion against the idea of the Jewish state among Israel's writers was getting underway in earnest, there were prominent critics such as Baruch Kurzweil and Gideon Katznelson who warned that in severing the connection of the country to the Jewish past, the new literature would soon reduce Israel to a world of "dirty shops, kiosks, and pharmacies."[78] But by now, there are no such voices of genuine resistance to speak of; the leading critics of Israeli literature are professors such as Dan Miron of the Hebrew University and his colleague, Gershon Shaked, who helped to create the present Israeli literary pantheon with their own hands.[79] To find real dissent, one must go to the rare author such as Aharon Meged or Moshe Shamir, who still remain to represent the ideas of the Labor-Zionist founders. Of the writings of these individuals, perhaps the most telling is a

1989 essay by the novelist Moshe Shamir entitled "Is Hebrew Literature Still Zionist?" In it, Shamir breaks with the community of writers to which he devoted his life, confessing, "From the outset, Zionism was [to many Israeli authors] a kind of Molech, which has never ceased to demand sacrifices from our youth and our neighbors." Now, the adulation of powerlessness among Israel's writers has become so severe that Israeli literature as a whole has effectively rejected the Jewish state as the true homeland of the Jews, in its place adopting another, more fitting one. "The Holocaust," he concludes bitterly, "is becoming the common homeland of the Jews, their promised land."[80]

The Arts [81]

As in most Western countries, Israel's artists have been even more radical in rejecting the political ideals of their nation than have other cultural leaders. And yet the radicalism of many of Israel's artists is of special significance because of their direct involvement in mainstream institutions, such as the Israel Museum in Jerusalem and the Tel Aviv Museum of Art, the universities that employ them as instructors, and the mainstream media that readily bring their views to the attention of the public. Indeed, in Israel, the artists are not an esoteric sect but are relatively well integrated into the intellectual establishment. Not only do they provide the artwork that adorns literary and academic endeavors alike, but they also frequently appear at the same social functions and in the same intellectual forums as the rest of Israel's small cultural-political leadership, where they often pioneer themes that are then picked up in academia and literature a few years later.

Of all of the cultural endeavors of the Jewish settlement in Palestine, it may be said that the hope of a Jewish national rebirth in the visual arts was the one most filled with promise. The father of Jewish national art was Boris Schatz, a Bulgarian sculptor who, even before Herzl's Zionist Congresses, sought to capture the national revival through images of Jewish national strength. Among his works were sculptures such as *Mattathias* (1894), in which the Maccabee warrior-priest is depicted standing victorious over a fallen Greek soldier, and *Moses with the Ten Commandments* (1918), in which the prophet is portrayed as a powerful and even muscular leadership figure.[82] Schatz's Betzalel Academy of Art was founded in Jerusalem in 1906, animated by his belief that "nationalist art is the genuine form of art—that which comes from the heart and works in harmony with the heart of the nation."[83] The school featured instructors such as Ephraim Moshe Lilien and Zev Raban, whose drawings, prints, and paintings depicted the degraded condition of the Jew in exile and the burgeoning of Jewish life in the new land. Many of Betzalel's artists gave voice to the Jewish national revival in terms close to Labor Zionism, in sweeping landscapes or in scenes from the new Jewish collective farms. Moshe Matus's *Building Tel Aviv* (1931), for example, shows muscular men dragging a new city out of the earth with their hands, and Abraham Melnikoff's *Roaring Lion* (1934), a massive lion of Judah sculpted in memory of the fallen Jewish soldier and pioneer Joseph Trumpeldor, similarly expresses the majesty and power of the Jewish restoration, even in the midst of tragedy.[84]

Yet Schatz's dream of a Jewish national art effectively came to an end in 1929 when Betzalel was closed due to financial difficulties. The "New Betzalel"—the art academy still in existence in Jerusalem today—was opened in 1935 under the direction of German-Jewish refugees, whose views regarding Jewish nationalism sometimes bordered on overt antagonism. Its students, too, were mostly German Jews, whose inclinations were often in the direction of Franz Rosenzweig's anti-Zionist universalism. Perhaps the central figure in turning the school in this direction was Mordechai Ardon, who headed the New Betzalel from 1940 to 1952 and also taught at the Hebrew University. In his own works, Ardon never fully reconciled himself with the implications of mainstream Jewish nationalism, preferring instead to use kabbalistic-utopian motifs calling for an eternal brotherhood of man. Typical of these ideas are the stained-glass windows he designed for the National Library at Givat Ram (1984), which illustrate a historic process reaching an abstract Jerusalem to which many roads wind, each inscribed in a different language, ending with a field in which spades float over the broken guns of the nations.

The universalistic vision of Judaism advocated by Ardon dovetailed nicely with those instructors at Betzalel and in the Jerusalem art community who sought a new, non-Jewish (and also non-Arab) identity for the residents of Palestine—the "Canaanite" movement, whose foremost student was the sculptor Yigael Tumarkin. Today probably Israel's most influential artist, Tumarkin's work has since the mid-1960s focused on the production of scalding critiques of Jewish national power. Examples include *Bring Me Under Your Wings* (1966), named after a well-known verse from the works of the Jewish-nationalist poet Haim Nahman Bialik, which features a garish array of weapons huddled beneath an iron canopy, suggesting a protective shelter. By representing the speaker of these words as an overstuffed arsenal, Tumarkin accuses the Jewish state of finding salvation in nothing other than the barrel of a gun. More recent works include a series of sculptures of Crusaders and their instruments of war, which—like similar themes in the writings of A. B. Yehoshua and Amos Oz—seem to invite comparisons between the Jewish state and the brutal and racist Crusader state established in Palestine in the Middle Ages.[85]

Perhaps the most famous Israeli sculpture is Tumarkin's *He Walked in the Fields* (1968), whose title is a reference to Moshe Shamir's classic Zionist novel by the same name. Tumarkin's sculpture depicts an Israeli soldier returned from battle, his body bursting with military ordinance, his throat slashed open and his tongue hanging out. Coming as it did on the heels of the decisive victory of the Six Day War, it earned instant notoriety and has long since had its desired effect: By now one cannot make mention of Shamir's novel without immediately conjuring up images of Tumarkin's metal nightmare. "Zionism was a dream," explains Tumarkin, "but reality is a tragedy."[86]

Other leading artists are if anything even harsher in their depictions of Zionism. Yoram Rosov's *The Fall of Goliath* (1969) portrays the Zionist farmer-settler as a repulsively obese giant on the verge of collapse. More so-phisticated are the drawings of Yosl Bergner, such as *Ship of Fools* (1963), showing Jews immigrating to Palestine, and *The Funeral* (1977), which de-picts the result of their efforts. In these works, the Zionist pioneers are por-trayed as emaciated, wide-eyed animals, whose weakness can only inspire pity. Bergner's bottom-line message is perhaps best conveyed in *After the Show* (1972), a sketch of empty chairs ranged around a post with a rag nailed to it. The chairs, hollow stand-ins for human beings, rally around the meaningless, fluttering rag—the national flag of the Jews. The message is frank and unmis-takable: The show of Zionism has ended, and all that is left is the props—hu-man props, unaware that their moment has long since passed.[87]

The empty chair, representing fallen, empty people (and frequently, be-cause of its associations with the Davidic throne, a fallen and empty king-dom), has been so successful as a critique of the traditional aspirations of Judaism and Zionism that by 1991, the Tel Aviv Museum of Art was able to devote an entire exhibition to the subject of the empty chair in Israeli art.[88] In addition to Bergner, the artists promoting this symbol include Uri Lifschitz, one of the leading Israeli artists in any medium, whose depiction of things Jewish is perhaps best represented by his *Ten Commandments* (1993–1995), a series of sculptures depicting the tablets of Moses in various stages of incineration and dissolution, frequently covered by scorpions, ver-min, and human jaws open in screams of agony.[89] Lifschitz's image of Zionism seems to be no less acrid: His *Herzl* (1992) is a larger-than-life metal cast of the founder of the Zionist Organization, on whose chest are spray-painted American comic-book heroes, advancing on an unseen enemy with outstretched fists, swords, and guns. On the reverse of the sculpture, Herzl's face appears riddled through with holes, and a comic-book figure's face is sprayed onto his beard. Herzl, like the creatures crawling all over him, is thus construed as the symbol of aimless power struggles in the ser-vice of imaginary causes.[90]

Of course, not all of Israeli art is so inclined to metaphor, and many of the younger artists devote their energies to more explicit portrayals of the Jewish state as hell. The prominent graphic artist David Reeb, for example, has produced scores of works depicting arrests, beatings, and interrogation of Arabs at the hands of Jewish soldiers. Similarly, Reeb's *Green Line* series (1985–1987) depicts Jews in their mundane apathy, sunbathing or playing backgammon or walking nonchalantly down the street—while all around them are on-duty police officers, assault helicopters, and combat aircraft applying overwhelming force in order to maintain their oppressor regime. Then there is *Bombed Kibbutz* (1982), in which Reeb plays out fantasies of revenge, showing his audience before-and-after portraits of the collective farm, stronghold of Labor Zionism, transformed into a horror of blood, fire, and death as a result of a successful bombing run.[91]

A more intricate yet fundamentally similar picture emerges from the work of Israel's leading photographer, Micha Kirschner, for whom the Jewish state—as expressed by the photo he selected for the title page of his recent collection, *The Israelis* (1997)—seems to be little more than a graveyard. And indeed, Kirschner's works are a tour through a world of insanity, corruption, and death, in which scores of Jewish public figures, representing all parties and points of view, are portrayed as crucified and drowned and hanged, or standing naked with machine guns, or slashing themselves with razor blades, or touched up to look like demons and ghouls and practitioners of the occult. In Kirschner's Israel, it seems that the Jews have built a life of unmitigated decay, an entire nation of ruin and death. The *Arabs*, however, are a different story. Kirschner's Arabs (as portrayed in the same volume) are like creatures from a different universe: Real human beings, crying, resisting, comforting their loved ones in the face of the scourge. A portrait of Arab member of Knesset Hashem Mahmid shows him standing heroically against a gang of white-robed Jewish klansmen, as a large Star of David aflame behind them spells out the Jews' message of hatred and murder.[92]

Once one is living in a hell, the only rational recourse is, of course, emigration—and here, too, Israeli artists have been developing an unequivocal message. In 1991, the Israel Museum in Jerusalem hosted a massive retrospective entitled *Routes of Wandering*—whose theme was not the failings and crimes of the Jewish state but the condition of Jewish alienation and rootlessness that remains once these have been internalized. According to its curator, Betzalel Academy instructor Sarit Shapira, the idea behind the exhibition was the recognition that "the awakening from the Zionist dream has left deep traces upon Israeli art." Says Shapira:

> In the spirit of Jewish thinkers like Martin Buber, Franz Rosenzweig . . . and Jacques Derrida, the present exhibition has chosen works that point to . . . rootlessness and wanderings away from fixation in any defined territory or form: Works that formulate the myth of the exodus from Egypt not as a beginning of the voyage to the promised land, but as a text of the desert genera-

tion. . . . The language and syntax of these works emphasize the aspect of expulsion implicit in the inscription "Get you gone," [Gen. 21:1] rather than the promise "For unto your seed I will give the land." [Gen. 12:7][93]

The fact that Israel's leading museum would host an exhibition devoted to the idea that Israel is *not* home even to the Jews that live there seems to have surprised virtually no one. By 1991, the worldview that had given rise to this exhibition had, after all, become thoroughly accepted. Among the many Israeli artists who have in recent years embraced homelessness as a Jewish principle is Michael Sgan-Cohen, whose *The Wandering Jew* (1983) depicts a birdlike figure standing with a hand pointing to the back of its head, as if it were holding a gun; another hand points down from heaven suggesting the divine origin of the curse.[94] A related image of unending Jewish wandering is found in Michael Druks's *Uganda-Brazil* (1979), which consists of maps chosen at random from around the globe; in each location, Druks uses black ink to blot out the entire map other than a small Israel-shaped enclave along the coast, suggesting that the present-day location of the Israeli place of refuge is in any case arbitrary, exchangeable for any other.[95] The works of Jennifer Bar-Lev likewise imply that the Jews are fundamentally homeless. In *The Gypsy Carnival* (1990), for example, strings of pasteup letters give voice to Bar-Lev's fantasy of being carried off by the paradigmatic nomadic people: "The Gypsies have painted their eyes in black," reads one sequence. "They offer to paint mine too." Another reads: "I'm just passing through on my way to somewhere else."[96]

Nor does the simple assertion of some abstract, existential condition of Jewish homelessness suffice. Many of Israel's artists are preoccupied with advancing the idea that the unnatural transplantation of the Jew in Israel has led to suffocation and death and to urging the actual, physical departure of Jews from the country. Typical of these is Pinchas Cohen-Gan, who in 1973 mounted his *Dead Sea Project,* in which freshwater fish were sent out onto the Dead Sea in semipermeable sleeves filled with fresh water. As the water turned brackish, the fish died; in his published notes on the project, Cohen-Gan compared the fish to the Jews of various lands relocating to Israel.[97] Equally pointed is Cohen-Gan's *Green Card* series of 1978, which reproduces questionnaires and other material related to the test administered to prospective residents of the United States. Similar images are evoked by works such as Benny Efrat's *Quest for Air, Spring 2037* (1989), which features a suitcase open on top of a bed, the entire assembly enclosed in a metal cage; and by Joshua Borkovsky's *Diptychs* (1989–1990), depicting ocean-going ships at full sail, with the land left far behind on the periphery. Moshe Ninio's *Sea States* series (1978–1984) likewise offers an array of views from the rear of a ship that has left shore. In one of them, the caption

"In case of unexpected disaster" appears. In another, the word "Exit" is su-
perimposed on one corner of the image.[98]

In fact, so thick is the post-Zionism of the Israeli art world that one is
hard pressed to name a prominent artistic figure who still identifies with the
ideal of the Jewish state. One can work hard to find an exception here or
there—Naphtali Bezem and Moshe Castel (d. 1991), for example—but
these are lost in a bitter sea of self-hatred and preparations for exile, where
memory of a positive connection with the dream of the Jewish people restored to the land of its fathers has long since vanished.

———————

One hesitates to ascribe too much meaning to the fanaticism of Israel's
artists. After all, they are only artists.

Yet the state of Israel's art is essential as a glimpse into what Israel's culture—and Israel's culture means Israel's *mind*—can easily become only a
few years from now. After all, the arts in Israel began as a vital Jewish national enterprise, arriving at their present terminus through the devotion of
a small group of talented and determined individuals. This same terminus
can be all too easily imagined for Israel's universities and its literature—in
short, for its *entire* public culture, which is already far from being able to
tolerate intellectual works of any kind whose message is too sympathetic to
the Jewish state.

But so what? So what if Aharon Meged is right, and the majority of
Israel's culture makers have been working for decades to prove that the
cause of the Jewish state is misguided or unjust? Cannot an accomplished
fact such as the state of Israel survive the opinions of a few hundred professors, novelists, poets, photographers, and sculptors? The chapter that follows explores the possibility that it cannot.

CHAPTER 2

The Political Struggle
for a Post-Jewish State

WHEN ISRAEL'S LABOR PARTY RETURNED TO POWER in June 1992 after fifteen years in opposition, there were few indications that the country stood on the verge of a cultural upheaval that could jeopardize the very foundations of the Jewish state. If anything, the opposite appeared to be the case: The Labor victory had resulted from the ascendance to party leadership of Yitzhak Rabin—a tough-talking Jewish hawk in the mold of the generation that had founded the state. Rabin had played a key role in the War of Independence, had been chief of staff during the Six Day War, and as prime minister in 1976, had ordered the Entebbe raid. These achievements, plus a stint as defense minister in the "national unity" governments led by Yitzhak Shamir, had given him a reputation as a hard-core continuer of the Labor-Zionist political tradition, as represented by figures such as Ben-Gurion, Moshe Dayan, and Golda Meir.

All this notwithstanding, the fact is that the Labor party that swept into power on Rabin's coattails had long since ceased to be a stronghold of Labor Zionism as an idea.[1] The "Labor" half of the formula had long since become an anachronism, as the children of the laboring families of the 1930s were by now the core of the wealthy oligarchy that dominates every aspect of

Israeli life: The last thing in the world these people wanted was to try to get Israel's proletariat excited about sharing with them the means of production. The result was a party convention in November 1991, at which the Labor party removed the red banner from the rostrum and suppressed the singing of the party anthem, the Socialist "Internationale."[2] The equivalent transformation taking place on the "Zionist" side of the formula had not yet produced such a show-stopping renunciation of symbols, but it was no less real. The renunciation of *these* symbols would begin a few years later.[3] (A similar process has taken place in the right-of-center Likud party, many of whose younger politicians demonstrate little sympathy for the ideological concerns of their fathers.)

Nature abhors a cultural vacuum, and the space that the old Labor Zionism had evacuated was filled by the ideas of Israel's intellectual leaders—the individuals discussed in the previous chapter—whose party connections are largely within the Labor party and its coalition partner, the radical Meretz party.[4] For many of these cultural figures, the Rabin administration was understood as an opportunity to dismantle the policies and institutions of the old, overly "Jewish" state and to create something "normal." And, in fact, the intellectuals quickly demonstrated their ability to influence the course of public policy, making inroads in every area of government activity that has a direct impact on the political culture of Israel: in the educational programs of the public schools, in the constitutional doctrines of the Supreme Court, in the training programs of the Israel Defense Forces, and in the policy aims of the Foreign Ministry. In all these areas and more, 1992 marked the beginning of a cultural revolution—a revolution condemned by few in either of the major political parties and which even the return of the Labor party to the opposition four years later did next to nothing to reverse.

All at once, and in the most dramatic fashion, it became possible to see the contours of the new Israel, pushing up from under the ruins of the old Jewish state.

Education

Over the last few years, as awareness of the work of the "new historians" has increased both in Israel and the Diaspora, there have been occasional flurries of interest in the influence of the new history on the curriculum of the Israeli public schools. In one instance, a single item in the *New York Times* triggered weeks of discussion in the Diaspora and in Israel (the Israeli press followed New York's lead), whose focus was on new Israeli schoolbooks implying that the Jews' struggle during the War of Independence might not have been as heroic as was once thought, since Jewish forces enjoyed battlefield superiority over the Arabs during much of the War of Independence.[5] Yet the argument over the new Israeli schoolbooks has fixated on a handful of such relatively minor issues.[6] What has gone unremarked is the fact that these individual textbooks are but the first fruits of an effort by the Israeli Education Ministry to overhaul the public-school curriculum in virtually everything that touches on the subject of Zionism and the Jewish state—involving the reconstruction of the new curriculum in such areas as Jewish history, general history, civics, and archaeology, and reaching as high as the revision of the legal mandate given to the schools to teach Jewish-national subjects. Also not mentioned is the fact that the labyrinth of committees responsible for these changes is largely staffed by academics from Israel's leading universities, many of whom appear to have been deeply influenced by post-Zionist intellectual trends.

Israel's schools are, of course, one of the principal arenas in which the connection between the state and the Jewish people will be forged or sundered—a fact that was not lost on the founders of the Jewish state. The Israeli school system in its present configuration was created by the State Education Law of 1953, a classic piece of Labor Zionist legislation, which in forty-three words sought to define the purpose of the state education system. First and foremost among its concerns was that the school system inculcate "the values of Jewish culture," "love of the homeland," and "loyalty to the Jewish people." And this mandate was given concrete meaning through a curriculum of required Jewish studies, including Bible, Jewish history, Talmud and Jewish thought, and "motherland" studies such as the geography of Israel, its natural history, and archaeology—a curriculum that, according to the Education Ministry, aimed "to root the children in the land of Israel, the land of our fathers" and to teach them "the basic values of Judaism."[7]

The steep decline in the hours devoted to these subjects was already underway two decades ago, having become pronounced during the years when the Likud's Menachem Begin was prime minister and the Education Ministry was headed by Zevulum Hammer of the hawkish National Religious Party. Nevertheless, the dejudaizing of Israel's schools took on new meaning with the appointment of Shulamit Aloni, head of the Meretz party, as education minister in 1992. Aloni quickly turned her post into a platform for attacking school trips to Auschwitz for stirring up "nationalistic" sentiment among the students ("What's important is that they come back better human beings, not better Jews") and demanding that references to God be eliminated from IDF memorial services.[8] In this Aloni received ample assistance from her deputy, the Labor party's Micha Goldman, who similarly called for changing the text of "Hatikva," the national anthem, "in order to give expression to citizens who are not Jews" and advocated teaching of the poetry of Tewfik Ziyad, the Palestinian nationalist (and anti-Zionist) poet, in the Israeli schools "next to the poetry of Bialik."[9]

In 1994, Aloni was succeeded as education minister by her party colleague Amnon Rubinstein. A former Tel Aviv University law professor, Rubinstein is known in Israel for his trenchant criticism of post-Zionist academic trends. Yet Rubinstein's policies were essentially the same as Aloni's: Both presided over a ministry whose committees—some newly appointed, some left over from the previous Likud government—were engaged in a sweeping re-examination of the mission of Israel's schools. Perhaps the most important proposal to emerge from this work was Rubinstein's 1995 initiative to revise the forty-two-year-old State Education Law, most notably with regard to the Jewish character of Israeli education. The proposed law contained no fewer than ten clauses' worth of values and facts the ministry hoped to teach Israeli students, including "the love of mankind"; "democratic values"; "knowledge of the arts of mankind of all types and periods"; "the language, culture, and unique heritage of the various population groups in the country," as well as recognition of "the equality of fundamental rights of all citizens of Israel." But other than the teaching of the past history of the Jews as a precursor to modern Israeli history (appearing at the bottom of the list, in the ninth clause out of ten), the proposed law was devoid of any references to the Jewish people or Judaism. And the three Jewish-nationalist aims of the school system up until that point—teaching "the values of Jewish culture," "love of the homeland," and "loyalty to the Jewish people"—had been rather pointedly removed. A slightly modified version was endorsed by the government, passed a preliminary vote in the Knesset, and would probably have become law had it not been for the change of government in the general elections of May 1996.[10]

But Rubinstein's failure to overthrow the old Zionist education law did not prevent other committees from working piecemeal to revise the public-school curriculum in the various disciplines as though the new post-Zionist era in education had already arrived. For example, in 1994 an Education Ministry committee issued a new curriculum for the teaching of high-school civics—a mandatory subject in which Israeli students ostensibly learn how to be good citizens of the Jewish state. As the committee explains in its introduction, the new civics curriculum has five normative goals: The course is supposed to teach students:

1. "to work to realize" democratic values;
2. "to understand the fact" that Israel is the state of the Jewish people;
3. "to work to realize" human rights and civil rights;
4. "to be prepared to fulfill" their duties and defend their rights; and
5. "to be involved" in the affairs of the public and of society.[11]

Obviously, this list places disproportional emphasis on purely universal values as opposed to Jewish ones. But this might not be so troubling if the small portion of the course dealing with Jewish subjects were really aimed at encouraging the students' identification with the values of Israel as a Jewish state. Yet the new civics curriculum was apparently not actually written with the aim of encouraging such identification, as one can see immediately from the language of the curriculum's five normative goals, listed above. Of the five goals of the civics class, four are couched in highly active, if not emotional, terms: With regard to democracy, human rights, civic duties, and engagement in public affairs, the students are taught to "work," "realize," "fulfill," "be involved." Only with regard to Israel's character as a Jewish state is the new curriculum aimed at a passive, dispassionate "understanding of the fact"—as though the existence of a Jewish state is not something in which the students have a personal stake. Thus the new Education Ministry civics curriculum actively encourages students to work for the fulfillment of Israel as a democratic state and for the protection of human rights in Israel. But regarding Israel as the state of the Jewish people—as declared in Israel's Declaration of Independence—the curriculum seems not to take a stand.

This same approach characterizes the Education Ministry's long-awaited new civics textbook, *To Be Citizens in Israel* (2000). Written by a team headed by the Education Ministry Coordinator for the Civics Curriculum, Hanna Eden, *To Be Citizens in Israel* is the first government civics text to present the idea of Israel as a Jewish state in essentially neutral terms. Thus the first chapter, "Nations and Nation-States"—which should presumably have made the case for why there should be a Jewish national state—goes no further than to say that many peoples "aspire" to national independence. Nowhere does it consider the possibility that the Jews (or any other people) may have actually *needed* national independence, or that the cause of Jewish independence was desirable or just. Similarly, in a chapter entitled "The State of Israel: Different Approaches," the idea of Israel as a Jewish state is presented not as a matter of settled law and national tradition, but rather as a free-for-all in which no fewer than six different interpretations compete for the students' affections. Among these, the concept of Israel as a non-Jewish "state of its citizens"—whose identity would be "political and not ethnic"—is presented in perfectly neutral language, without any explicit mention of the fact that to adopt such a view would be to undermine the historical and constitutional basis of the state since Ben-Gurion's time. With regard to the Jewish state, it seems as though officials in the Education Ministry would really prefer not to take sides.[12]

This same neutrality toward the Jewish state is even more pronounced in the new elective archaeology curriculum for high schoolers. Obviously, archaeology cannot be a neutral subject in the Jewish state: The entire Zionist movement was built on the premise that the Jews were returning to their historic land, and modern archaeology played a decisive role in demonstrating that this was not only a myth cherished by the pious but a thoroughly "secular" fact that every Jew (and every Christian) could take seriously. In the worldview of leading Zionist figures such as Yigal Yadin and Moshe Dayan, archaeology was transformed into a linchpin attaching the contemporary Jewish identity to the new Jewish state.

Yet in 1995, the Ministry of Education adopted a new archaeology curriculum, designed by a committee headed by Hebrew University archaeologist Yoram Tzafrir. The introduction to the new curriculum offers six full pages of discussion of the new curriculum, including a comprehensive list of the program's aims. Yet not once in all this is there a single reference to Jews, Judaism, the Jewish people, or Jewish history or to the fact that the students are going out to dig in the Jewish state. Instead, there is a profusion of distilled universalism: "To stress to the students the men and the society behind the object," "recommends expanding the discussion to its universal aspects," "the spirit of man," "the culture of mankind," "human culture and its contribution to mankind," and so forth. There is one mention of the land of Israel, but this reference, too, is purely geographic, simply referring to the country in which the students happen to be living ("The student will deepen his knowledge of the country, its landscapes and history, and will increase his connection to the land of Israel and the assets of its past").[13]

Only once in the curriculum overview is there a hint that there might be important differences among the various ancient cultures or that these cultures might have an important meaning to people today. This is in the program's goal number 7, which emphasizes to the teacher that the relationship between peoples should be painted as being "reciprocal," that the various cultures are all to be understood as "the heritage of world civilization," and that, with a little luck, these lessons will disabuse the students of "fundamentalist beliefs":

> The student will learn about the mutual relationships among the societies that lived and created in the East in ancient times, *despite the differences among them* in religion and beliefs, language and ethnic origin.

> The proper reconstruction of cultures of the past will assist the student in understanding the roots of the culture of our age, and in uprooting fundamentalist beliefs.

> The student will learn to appreciate the technologies and artistic creations of the various cultures of the past as part of the heritage of world civilization.[14]

Obviously, some of the archaeology teachers in Israel will add opinions and feelings of their own to these lessons, and in this fashion, some Jewish high-schoolers may benefit from the deep intellectual and emotional resonances of learning about the past of the Jewish people in its homeland. But as far as the new curriculum is concerned, all of this has been obliterated. And the archaeology of the Jewish state retains meaning only to the degree that the "various cultures" of the Middle East's past have contributed to the "world civilization" of the present.

Equally impressive in its radical influences is the new history curriculum being prepared for the public schools. As Hebrew University historian Israel Bartal, chairman of the committee to redesign the curriculum in the high schools, explains, the history books must be revised because they "do not fit in with the historical and political discourse after the smashing of the myths."[15] Although the Bartal committee has yet to present its proposed curriculum, a parallel committee, whose task was to revamp the texts used to teach history to middle schoolers (grades 6–9), completed its work in 1995. The chairman of the latter committee was Bartal's colleague at the Hebrew University, Moshe Zimmermann, mentioned in Chapter 1 as one of the most outspoken of the new historiographers. To the Israeli public, however, Zimmermann is less known for his radical ideas on Jewish history than for his outspoken appearances in the press, in which he has compared "the way that ideology is passed from adults to children" in certain circles in Israel to the education of Hitler Youth.[16]

Having analyzed the problems in the previous curriculum, the Zimmermann committee proposed far-reaching changes, such as the removal of the Bible from the new middle-school history curriculum. Before 1995, all Jewish children in Israel had begun learning history by studying the origins of the Jewish people during the biblical period, with topics such as "From Tribes to a People," "The Kingdom of David," "Prophet versus King," and "Jerusalem as a Capital." In the new curriculum, however, the study of these decisive early centuries of Jewish history has been eliminated entirely, and Israeli children now learn a historical narrative that begins not with Jews but with Greeks: The Greek city-states, the rise of Alexander the Great, and the influence of Hellenism on the various Asian peoples the Greeks conquered. The Jews do not even appear until the fourth unit, which examines the influence of Hellenism on the Jews—so that the Jewish people is first encountered not as an independent people with an important civilization of its own, but rather as a subject people struggling to respond to Greek civilization.[17]

But the new history does not stop at merely removing the biblical basis for Jewish history from the schoolbooks. Many of the "new" Israeli academics find the teaching of the old Jewish historical narrative—in which the Jewish people is the central and unitary actor—to be problematic in itself, claiming, among other objections, that such historiography is a spring for nationalism. Zimmermann's alternative to the old Jewish-national historiography is what he calls "universal history," in which the main actor is not the Jewish people, but a sequence of world civilizations: those of Greece, Rome, America, and so forth. Within the context of *this* narrative, the Jews are essentially a sec-ondary character in a drama in which they are no longer the principle sub-ject. And it is this universalist message that emerges in the new history curriculum. As Zimmermann himself explains, "the emancipation of women has no less important a place than the emancipation of the Jews [in Europe] or of the blacks in the United States." As for the Jews as a people, he says, "Learning about the [Jewish] people and the State [of Israel] appears in pro-gram, *but certainly not as a subject of primary importance.*"[18]

One only needs to go back to Zimmermann's academic writing to see where all this is headed. As he wrote in a recent essay in *Theory and Criticism,* the adoption of "universal" history is for Zimmermann part of a much larger process of reconsidering many of the Jews' most basic beliefs concerning the meaning of their history, including what he calls the Jewish "fixation with sovereignty."[19] As Zimmermann appears to believe, once the Jewish people is no longer "a subject of primary importance" to the student, neither is the existence of a Jewish state likely to remain a subject of primary importance for very long.

The Constitution

The only Israeli institution likely to rival the Education Ministry in its abil-ity to shape the Jewish character of the state of Israel is the country's Supreme Court. Since 1992, the Court has increasingly asserted its claim to be the final arbiter on all constitutional, legal, and even moral issues con-cerning the operation of the Israeli government—a scope of authority ex-ceeding that of even the most "activist" of Supreme Courts in other countries. Moreover, the Court has taken an exceptional interest in the state of Israel's Jewish nature—which Chief Justice Aharon Barak believes stands in tension with Israel's character as a democracy. As a result, there is a strong possibility that the Supreme Court will turn out to be the decisive arena in which the battle over a post-Zionist Israel is decided. And judging by the opinions and rulings issuing from the Court, the chances that it will prove to be a defender of the idea of the Jewish state seem rather dubious.

The shadow of ambiguity that has fallen over Israel's constitutional status as a Jewish state in recent years is, of course, in marked contrast to the self-confidence of government officials on this subject in the early years of the state. Thus, while Israel did not adopt a written constitution when it gained independence in 1948, its constitutional character as a Jewish state was nevertheless understood to derive from the prestate enactments of international bodies such as the League of Nations and the UN; from the right of the Jewish people to its own sovereign state as asserted in Israel's Declaration of Independence; and from fundamental acts of the Knesset such as the Law of Return, which Ben-Gurion considered to be the cornerstone of a Jewish "bill of rights."[20] And this viewpoint was not only the province of politicians but also of the Israeli Supreme Court. As Supreme Court Justice Moshe Landau, later chief justice, wrote in 1961 in responding to the claim that Israel had no standing to prosecute Adolf Eichmann:

> In light of the recognition by the United Nations of the right of the Jewish people to establish their state in Israel, and in light of the recognition of the Jewish state by the law of nations, the connection between the Jewish people and the state of Israel constitutes an integral part of the law of nations. . . . The state of Israel, the sovereign state of the Jewish people, performs through its legislation the task of carrying into effect the right of the Jewish people to punish the criminals who killed their sons with intent to put an end to the survival of this people . . . The state of Israel was established and recognized as the state of the Jews. . . . It would appear that there is hardly need for any further proof of the very obvious connection between the Jewish people and the state of Israel: This is the sovereign state of the Jewish people. . . . These words are not mere rhetoric, but historic facts, which the law of nations does not ignore.[21]

Thus, even the judiciary considered Israel to have been constituted as "the sovereign state of the Jewish people" and held that the legal status of such a state imparted to it a standing unlike that of other nations with regard to its relationship with the Jewish people, past and present, whether in Israel or in the Diaspora.

Yet beginning in the 1970s, prominent Israeli academics such as Tel Aviv University sociologist Yonatan Shapiro began advancing the claim that the state established by the Labor Zionists was a Jewish state *instead* of being a properly constituted democracy.[22] Such arguments, virtually unheard of in the 1950s, at this time began making devastating headway among Israeli intellectuals and political leaders—some of whom, like former education minister Shulamit Aloni, were willing to argue explicitly that the idea of Israel as the state of the Jewish people is "anti-democratic, if not racist."[23] These circles produced a coalition of academics and politicians who believed that Israel would only become a *truly* democratic state once its legal system had been reestablished on the basis of a system of constitutionally guaranteed universal rights, without clear protections for the particularistic Jewish aspects of the state's values and goals.

In March 1992, this coalition succeeded in securing passage in the Knesset of two quasi-constitutional laws ("Basic Laws") dealing with "The Dignity and Liberty of Man" and with "Freedom of Occupation." At the time, both the politicians and the public attached little significance to this legislation, a fact reflected in the small number of legislators who bothered to vote on these bills: There are 120 Knesset members, but the new laws passed by votes of 32–21 and 23–0, respectively. But the politicians and the public were wrong, for these laws were written in such a way as to take precedence over other "regular" Israeli legislation, thereby implicitly putting in place large sections of a new Israeli constitution.

At least one man in Israel understood full well what had happened: Justice Aharon Barak, a former Hebrew University Law professor who is probably Israel's foremost legal theorist and who was shortly thereafter appointed to an eleven-year stint as Chief Justice of Israel's Supreme Court. Immediately upon the passage of the new Basic Laws, Barak issued a lengthy manifesto entitled "The Constitutional Revolution," in which he declared the laws to have conferred upon the Supreme Court the authority to strike down legislation it considered unconstitutional—an authority which he became the first Israeli Chief Justice to exercise a few years later.[24] (This power is far more significant in the hands of the Israeli Supreme Court than it is, for example, in the United States, since the Israeli executive and legislative branches do not have the ability to appoint Supreme Court judges or even to veto candidates who are inappropriate; appointments to the Supreme Court are made by a committee largely controlled by the Court itself.)[25]

The new constitutional legislation challenged Israel's continued existence as a constitutionally Jewish state on two fronts. The first and lesser difficulty is that although both laws declare themselves, in their preambles, to have been legislated "to establish . . . the values of the state of Israel as a Jewish and democratic state,"[26] the fact is that the rights enumerated in them are concerned exclusively with protecting universal values such as freedom of speech, privacy, and so on. That is, neither law addresses the possibility that the Jewish state may have the right or the duty to enact specialized, non-universal provisions in some of these areas. For example, Israeli law limits freedom of speech and religion by restricting efforts to convert Jews to other faiths; and it similarly restricts freedom of occupation by regulating the sale of certain food products during Passover, and by limiting the operation of places of entertainment on Holocaust Memorial Day.[27] By explicitly enumerating only universal rights and saying nothing about Jewish ones, the new Basic Laws would make it difficult for even a balanced Supreme Court to protect Israel's identity and mission as the state of the Jewish people. And given the ideological trends in the country and in the judiciary, these laws are precisely the mandate the Court needed to begin striking down acts of the Knesset and government whose aim is to maintain Israel's character as the Jewish state.

But this is the lesser of the two constitutional difficulties created for the Jewish state by the Basic Laws passed in 1992. Far more important is the fact that these have for the first time created a significant foothold for the claim that Israel cannot *constitutionally* be considered a Jewish state. This crucial change derives from the new laws' reliance on the idea—unprecedented in Israeli constitutional law—that Israel is actually a "Jewish *and* democratic state." Of course, the legislators who coined this phrase did not believe they were at the forefront of a revolution. Israel has been referred to as a Jewish state since its inception, and no organized political party in Israel questions the idea that Israel should be a democracy. Thus, in the minds of most of the legislators involved in drafting these laws and in most public discussion of the new laws, the preamble identifying Israel as a "Jewish and democratic state" has been understood as essentially a truism, a simple statement of fact devoid of any new constitutional content.

This new coinage, however, has proved to be anything other than a simple statement of fact. Quite to the contrary, it has proven to be constitutional dynamite, which has thrown the conceptual foundation of the Jewish state into chaos among the jurists and academics who are at the forefront of interpreting Israeli constitutional law. The reason is as follows. Up until the passage of the new Basic Laws, the idea of "the Jewish state" had been in broad and continual use for nearly a century. It had originated as the title of Theodor Herzl's pamphlet, and from there it had gone on to become a universally understood political ideal in the discourse of Jewish Zionists and anti-Zionists, as well as among leading non-Jewish statesmen from David Lloyd George to Harry Truman. In the end, it was this ideal of a Jewish state that was endorsed by the General Assembly of the United Nations in 1947, and it was this same ideal that all Jewish political parties in Palestine endorsed in Israel's Declaration of Independence the following year. And during all this time, both the friends and the enemies of this state had known exactly what it was, inheriting this knowledge from a well-established political tradition going back to Herzl's *The Jewish State:* "The Jewish state" was a state whose purpose was to serve as the political guardian of the interests of the Jewish people.[28]

But this coherent political tradition sustained heavy damage with the manufacturing of the new constitutional concept of a "Jewish and democratic state" in 1992. On the one hand, the very existence of this new term has cast a pall of illegitimacy on the earlier concept—for if there had been nothing wrong with the idea of the Jewish state, why was it necessary to revise it?[29] (Indeed, one can hardly speak of "the Jewish state" among educated Israelis today without creating the impression that the word "democratic" has been purposefully omitted out of some dark motive.) On the other hand, the new concept of a "Jewish and democratic state" is bereft of any political tradition that can impart specific meaning to it, and the public arena has become a melee of contradictory interpretations, each one as plausible as the next.[30] Asa Kasher of the Tel Aviv University philosophy department, for example, posits that the meaning of the new term is as follows:

> "A Jewish state" in the full sense of the term is a state in whose social coloration there is found the clear expression of . . . the Jewish identities of its citizens. In a "Jewish and democratic" state this social coloration is not created by force, nor in the law, but rather through the aggregation of the free choices of the citizens.[31]

In short, Kasher claims that a "Jewish and democratic" state is one in which the people are Jewish and the state is a universalist democracy. In other words, a "Jewish and democratic state" is a *non-Jewish* state. Yet one would be hard-pressed to demonstrate that Kasher's definition is unreasonable; the term simply has no prior tradition to which one can turn for guidance.

Obviously, if Kasher were the only one who believed this, it would be of little importance. But as the debate has continued, a clear pattern has begun to emerge, according to which the meaning of the term "Jewish and democratic state" is something much closer to what Kasher thinks it means than to the traditional meaning of the term "Jewish state" going back to Herzl. Thus, for example, former Supreme Court justice Haim Cohen recently published a twenty-six-page manifesto entitled "The Jewishness of the State of Israel," in which he argues that the Jewish character of the state of Israel resides principally in the 1992 Basic Laws themselves—since the "true values of Judaism" are really those universalistic rights, such as freedom of speech and privacy, that are enumerated in these laws.[32] Former Supreme Court justice Tzvi Berenzon asserts that the term "Jewish state" is itself really a historical accident anyway, as it was intended solely to distinguish Israel from the neighboring Arab states.[33] And Supreme Court Justice Mishael Heshin, in a 1996 Supreme Court ruling, admitted that the term "Jewish" in "Jewish and democratic" is becoming too confused to have a clear meaning: "What is a 'Jewish state'? A close look teaches us . . . that this combination of terms is overflowing with interpretations and schools of interpretation, and this outpouring is only increasing with time."

Yet while Heshin declined to try to give meaning to the term "Jewish," he did not hesitate to give an explicit response to the question of what "democratic" means—associating this term with the concept of a "state of its citizens," despite the fact that this latter concept was invented and is in common usage to mean a neutral, non-Jewish state: "Is there anyone who maintains that the state of Israel is *not* a 'state of all its citizens'?" he asked. "For it is a basic tenet of democracy that the citizens are equal among themselves."[34]

Most important, of course, have been the views of Chief Justice Aharon Barak. And he too has clearly broken with the traditional meaning of the term "Jewish state," arguing that the Israeli Supreme Court should understand the meaning of the word "Jewish" at such a "high level of abstraction" that it would become precisely identical in meaning to the term "democratic":

> The content of the phrase "Jewish state" will be determined by the level of abstraction which shall be given it. In my opinion . . . the level of abstraction should be so high, that it becomes identical to the democratic nature of the state. . . . The values of the state of Israel as a Jewish state are those universal values common to members of democratic society.[35]

Under this interpretation, the word "Jewish" is no more than a quaint tribal way of saying "democratic." And the meaning of the 1992 constitutional revolution is therefore that the Jewish state—insofar as it is any more "Jewish" than the United States, Canada, or Britain—has ceased to exist.

This interpretation of the term "Jewish and democratic" drew no small amount of criticism, and Barak responded by devoting some twenty pages out of his 2,600-page treatise *Interpretation in Law* (1994) to defending his position.[36] There, Barak vaguely concedes that *both* the "Jewish" and the "democratic" aspects of the state have to be understood at "the highest possible levels of abstraction" before they will reach the desired unity.[37] But he offers no examples as to what this process of dual abstraction might look like and leaves it unclear whether he really believes there are actual cases in which one could thereby end up with something recognizably (which is to say particularistically) Jewish. What is clear is that, this having been said, Barak goes on to offer practical instructions to the jurist who has failed in his efforts at abstraction and still does not know what to do when Jewish interests and aspirations seem to conflict with universal "democratic" values. In such cases, writes Barak, one must make a decision in accordance with what he calls "the views of the enlightened community in Israel." That is, "the judge should act as the enlightened community would."[38] But who is this "enlightened community," whose views concerning the character of the Jewish state are of such significance that the Israeli Supreme Court should in effect serve as its mouthpiece? As Barak explains:

> The metaphor of the "enlightened community" focuses one's attention on a part of the public. One's attention is turned . . . to the educated and progres-

sive part within it. What distinguishes the enlightened community from the rest of the public? . . . The enlightened community represents that community whose values are universalistic, and which is part of the family of enlightened nations.[39]

Thus, the "enlightened community" is that part of the Israeli public that is "educated" and "progressive" and whose values are "universalistic." But there is only one segment of Israeli society that even remotely resembles this description: Israel's *branja* of intellectuals, journalists, and jurists, and those others who are part of their social scene. This is no test based on a hypothetical "reasonable man" such as is known from Anglo-American jurisprudence. These are *actual people,* and the judges of Israel's Supreme Court have their phone numbers.[40]

Aharon Barak's theory that there exists in Israel a certain cultural-political group—*any* group—whose views are automatically the final arbiter of law in the country is problematic in itself. But the people to whom Barak is referring are not just any cultural or political oligarchy. This is the very same community that is now at the epicenter of the struggle to create a post-Zionist Israel—a group whose ideas Barak himself describes (in the passage quoted above) without reference to terms such as "Jewish" or "Zionist." When one understands this, it becomes evident that Israel's "constitutional revolution" is joined at its root to the social and ideological currents that have brought on the Education Ministry's curriculum revolution—currents that have already done much to render the idea of a Jewish state a thing of the past.[41]

The Defense Forces

What is perhaps most remarkable about the advance of the new ideas in Israeli government policy is the way in which even the most sweeping changes in Israel's character as a Jewish state can be effected by a handful of intellectuals, with only the most minimal of opposition from the country's political leaders or the public. This has been true of the issuing of Israel's new public-school curriculum, and it has been true of the "constitutional revolution" as well. Yet even these abrupt changes of policy cannot compete with the breathtaking ease with which the IDF in December 1994 adopted a formal code of ethics that seemed to renounce all Jewish national aims and values as legitimate grounds for Israeli military operations and which has since been distributed to all IDF units and incorporated into the training of all new Israeli officers.[42]

The order to devise and promulgate a general behavioral code for all IDF personnel and operations was given by Ehud Barak, chief of staff under the

Rabin government (and now prime minister of Israel). Under his sanction, a committee chaired by Tel Aviv University's Asa Kasher was formed to develop the code. By the time he was selected to chair the IDF committee, Kasher was well known as one of Israel's most outspoken academic figures, who has called for the effective repeal of the Law of Return, for permitting large numbers of Palestinian Arab refugees to return to Israel, and for the renunciation of Israeli sovereignty over unified Jerusalem.[43] Yet Kasher was asked to take charge of the committee, whose other three members were all career military officers. No other civilian academic or anyone else capable of seriously contending with Kasher's arguments in abstract philosophy was asked to join in the work, so that the final code is essentially a product of his views.

The result of the committee's work was a seven-page code entitled *The Spirit of the IDF*, which Kasher describes in his subsequent book-length commentary published by the Israeli Defense Ministry, as "one of a kind," indeed "the most profound code of ethics in the world of military ethics, in particular, and in the world of professional ethics, in general."[44] The new code may be that, but it is also lacking in any content that the average Israeli soldier could interpret as Jewish or Zionist: Nowhere in its eleven "values" and thirty-four "basic principles" does it refer to the Jewish state, the Jewish people, the land of Israel, or anything else to hint at the Jewish national identity and purpose of the Israeli military. Yet it is these neutral values and basic principles that are now, as the code itself explains, "the moral and normative identity card of the Israel Defense Forces"; the code "according to which every soldier . . . comports himself"; and "the position of the army leadership regarding the spirit of the IDF, as well as the principles and basic guidelines that will serve as its beacon, guiding it in the full spectrum of its activities."[45]

According to *The Spirit of the IDF,* there are eleven essential "values" that must ultimately guide the behavior of every soldier in military operations and in all other contexts: tenacity, responsibility, integrity, personal example, human life, purity of arms, professionalism, discipline, loyalty, representation, and camaraderie. Even a cursory glance, however, reveals that ten of these eleven values are of a purely universalistic nature. That is, values such as "professionalism" and "discipline" could just as easily apply to military personnel in every army in the world. Only one, "loyalty," refers to any kind of purpose specific to a particular army, and it is this value that raises what is really the central question of military ethics, which is: Loyalty to what? The Kasher code answers this question in the following way:

> The soldier will act with utter devotion to the defense of the State of Israel and all its citizens, in accordance with IDF orders, within the framework of

the laws of the state and the principles of democracy. The loyalty of IDF soldiers lies in their . . . continual readiness to fight . . . in defense of the sovereign State of Israel, in accordance with the values of the IDF and its orders,
and while upholding the laws of the state and its democratic principles.

The committee could not have been more clear. With the promulgation
of the code, the acceptable ends of all Israeli military operations are reduced
to the preservation of three objects: the state, its citizens, and the principles
of democracy. What is missing is also abundantly clear: the Jewish people,
the land of Israel, Jewish national values.

Of course, Israeli soldiers must fight to secure the well-being of all Israeli
citizens, whether Jewish or not, as well as all other permanent and temporary residents of the state even if they are not citizens; and they must similarly be prepared to lay down their lives in defense of Israel's free system of
government. Nevertheless, the essential mission of the IDF has never been
the safeguarding of "state, citizens, and democracy." Its purpose was to serve
as the guardian of the Jewish people and to protect Israel's character as the
state of the Jewish people. In recent years, for example, the IDF carried out
extended missions in Ethiopia and the neighboring states, whose purpose
was to protect Ethiopian Jews from bloodshed and famine. IDF operations
in the Soviet Union on behalf of persecuted Russian Jews were of this kind
as well. (The Entebbe raid in 1976 was aimed at rescuing 103 Jewish
hostages, many of whom were Israelis; but it seems likely that the IDF
would have undertaken this operation as well even if all the hostages had
been French Jews.) Such operations on behalf of Diaspora Jews have no basis whatsoever in *The Spirit of the IDF,* since they are not conducted out of
loyalty to "state, citizens, and democracy." The actual moral source for all
such operations is the loyalty of the soldiers to the Jewish people and to
Zionist ideals. And were it not for these, Israeli officers would be fully justified in refusing to send their soldiers out on such "Jewish" missions.

The same can be said concerning the requirement that IDF personnel act
out of loyalty to "democratic principles." This means, of course, that a soldier in the Israeli army must refuse an order to take up arms in support of,
say, a military coup. But is there no such thing as a "Jewish principle" to
which Israeli soldiers must also be loyal? What if Israeli soldiers were ordered
to use force to prevent the entry into Israel of boatloads of Jewish refugees escaping persecution (as British soldiers in Mandatory Palestine were ordered
to do in the not-too-distant past)? Such an order would violate no "principle
of democracy," so long as the government that gave the order were democratically elected. And yet the violation of the constitutive principles of the
Jewish state would be self-evident to anyone still loyal to them. Here, too, a

Jewish soldier attempting to remain loyal to the most rudimentary Zionist principles would find himself without a moral leg to stand on so long as he adhered to the new IDF code. To put the point bluntly, the new code governing the behavior of Israel's soldiers demands that they restrict their concerns to that of good Israeli citizenship; fighting in a Jewish army for the well-being of the Jewish people is simply not part of the mission.

When *The Spirit of the IDF* was first distributed to officers who were expected to teach from it, resistance to the code focused on the fact that the value "love of the land," which had been at the heart of the Zionist movement and of the value system of the IDF since its inception, had been consciously excluded. (The Hebrew *ahavat ha'aretz* has a very specific connotation meaning "love of the land of Israel" or "love of the land of the Jewish people.") Among its other effects, it was "love of the land" that engendered the IDF's "Nahal" units, which to this day combine military service with the establishment of Jewish border settlements. It was this value, too, that motivated IDF educational programs aimed at inculcating in the soldiers a familiarity with the historical and religious significance of the locations it was their job to defend. But members of the committee refused to reconsider its inclusion, explaining that one cannot teach someone to "love" and that the value of "love of the land" in any case amounted to the fetishization of an object.

Other Jewish values and principles proposed fared even worse. The Kasher committee rejected any phrasing that might suggest the soldier was expected to be loyal to Zionism. The committee opposed including the word "Zionism" in the code, arguing that there was no need for this concept and that it was in any case questionable whether Zionism was a doctrine acceptable to the majority of soldiers. Loyalty to Israel as a "Jewish state" or even as a "Jewish and democratic state" was similarly rejected. Because the code had to be suitable in its entirety to every soldier in the IDF, the committee maintained that there was no place in the code for Jewish-national content. The single concession that the committee was in the end willing to make was to include a prefatory statement—almost humorous, given the circumstances under which it was inserted—to the effect that *The Spirit of the IDF* draws its values and principles from, among other sources, "the tradition of the Jewish people throughout the generations."[46]

There is nothing remarkable in the fact that such a thoroughly dejudaized doctrine could be devised by a philosophy professor at Tel Aviv University. But it is something else again when such a code is approved by the highest echelons of the Israeli army. Moreover, the adoption of the Kasher committee's code drew little protest from the media and managed to sail over the heads of the national leadership without even minor scandal—

certainly without damaging anyone's political or military career. More revealing still is the fact that although the years go by and governments of various persuasions come and go, *The Spirit of the IDF* continues to hold fast. Israeli officers continue to be trained by its light and to learn from it the values according to which they will live and perhaps die.[47]

Will the Jewish soldiers of the Israeli Defense Forces resist the new dispensation, insisting that beyond "democracy," there are also Jewish values and principles worth fighting for? Or will they choose not to think about it too much, doing as they are told and internalizing the value system of *The Spirit of the IDF*? For his part, Asa Kasher's preference is clear. As he recently explained in an interview: "The advantage of *The Spirit of the IDF* is that there aren't any dilemmas any more. A soldier has to understand that even when he comes across certain dilemmas, he doesn't need to think or philosophize anymore. Someone else already sat down, did the thinking, and decided. There are no dilemmas."[48]

The Law of Return

Of all the characteristics that make Israel the Jewish state, there is probably none that is as endowed with historical significance as the Law of Return, which guarantees the right of every Jew to immigrate to Israel and claim automatic Israeli citizenship.[49] When it was passed unanimously by the Knesset in 1950, the framers of the law understood themselves to be drawing on the entire range of Jewish and Zionist history—from the biblical promise that the Jews would one day be able to return from the exile, to Theodor Herzl's insistence that the Jewish state must be open to *all* Jews, to the bitter and largely futile struggle of the Zionist Organization to persuade Britain to open the gates of Palestine during the Holocaust. In fact, so essential was this law to the character of the new Jewish sovereignty that had been created in Israel that Ben-Gurion considered the Law of Return to be a "bill of rights . . . guaranteed to all Jews in the diaspora by the state of Israel" and an expression of "the supreme mission of the state." As he explained in bringing the bill before the Knesset: "This is not a Jewish state merely because Jews are the majority of its population. It is a state for Jews everywhere. . . . The Law of Return . . . embodies the central purpose of our state."[50]

For post-Zionist intellectuals, the Law of Return is probably the most tangible demonstration of the fact that Israel is a racist and unjust regime. But as always, what is important is not what the handful of self-described "post-Zionists" are saying but the influence that their arguments are having on the majority of Jewish intellectuals and opinion leaders who do not describe themselves as being part of this trend. And although the Law of

Return still appears to be a consensus issue for Jewish Israelis, recent years have thus seen a dramatic acceleration in attacks on this law by prominent intellectuals, as well as in proposals to "revise" the law so as to reduce its significance, many of them coming from academics and writers who are in the heart of the cultural mainstream.

One cannot understand the change in Israeli attitudes on the Law of Return without considering the position of the country's most prestigious newspaper, *Ha'aretz,* which is not only the "newspaper of record" but also the only Israeli daily whose views are authoritative among the *branja.* As early as 1985, the paper's editor, Gershom Schocken, came out publicly in favor of Jewish-Arab intermarriage as a means of fashioning a new Israeli people distinct from the Jewish people.[51] Under his tutelage, the paper became a hothouse for the development of what today might be called post-Zionist ideas,[52] a trend that has been continued under his successor, Hanoch Marmari.

On November 11, 1994, a few months after Aharon Meged's "The Israeli Urge to Suicide," Marmari published a signed opinion piece arguing that most Diaspora Jews are no longer in danger of persecution and that at this point, the Law of Return is serving no function other than to permit the sick and aged of the Jewish world to be dumped upon the country, fast transforming it into "the old-age home of the Jewish people." Marmari targeted the year 2023—seventy-five years after Israel's founding—as the date on which the Law of Return should expire and called for Israel to adopt a selective immigration policy "as is accepted in enlightened countries." With this, the Zionist mission of the state would come to an end, and it would finally be the case that "a Jew asking for permission to immigrate would not be a preferred candidate for citizenship." More than a year later, Marmari published a follow-up citing the complete lack of public reaction to his proposal as proof that the Israeli public "doesn't care a whit whether the Law of Return exists or is rescinded."[53]

Although *Ha'aretz* has yet to publish a formal editorial supporting repeal of the Law of Return, it has nevertheless been home to an unprecedented series of articles seeking to persuade its readers in favor of repeal.[54] Signed articles by members of the staff in this vein have included pieces by Ran Kislev (the definitions used by the state in granting citizenship are "reminiscent of the Nuremburg laws"), Danny Rubinstein (the Law of Return is "overt discrimination" of the kind that "was the basis for the apartheid regime in South Africa"), and Urit Shohat ("Many [politicians] are convinced that Israel should go over to an immigration policy such as that of other Western countries and should inquire into what its true needs are"), among others.[55] Moreover, the paper's guest opinion columns feature a seemingly endless supply of semi-anonymous "researchers" and "sociologists" who are ready at hand to argue that "the Law of Return is a philosophical anachronism" or that "only changing the Law of Return . . . will liberate us from immigrants' power-mongering . . . and the transformation of Israeli democracy . . . into a wretched variation on the autocratic regimes of the world."[56]

But of all the arguments advanced by Hanoch Marmari and his associates on behalf of repeal of the Law of Return, the most effective seems to be the claim that if the Law of Return is not repealed, Israel may soon be engulfed in hundreds of thousands of unwanted immigrants from Asia and Africa. This line of attack was touched upon by Marmari in 1994, but the definitive statement of this position was contained in an article splashed across several pages of *Ha'aretz* in April 1997 under the headline "A National Home for a Billion Chinese." (The subtitle continued: "And Thais, and Russians, and Filipinos, and Rumanians, and for a handful of mental cases from America.") According to its author, *Ha'aretz* reporter Aryeh Caspi, "Israel must limit immigration, otherwise it will be swamped by immigrants that other countries do not want. The problem is that the Law of Return renders Israel utterly exposed to every would-be immigrant in the world." As Caspi explains, this is because non-Jews can claim to be Jewish by converting with previously unknown streams of Judaism ("Even Woody Allen could set up a rabbinic court for conversions") or by using documents forged by the Russian mafia. Moreover, the Law of Return has *already* permitted Israel to become a "Garden of Eden for criminals and Goldsteins"—the latter referring to Baruch Goldstein, an American-Jewish immigrant who massacred twenty-nine Arabs in the Cave of the Patriarchs in Hebron in February 1994.

But nutty rabbis, Russian hoods, and Jewish murderers are all just a warm-up for the main point, which is this:

> The fact that Israel isn't filled with Thais and Filipinos of the Mosaic persuasion is a result of the fact that they don't yet know about the hole [in Israeli immigration law]. But they will sooner or later. A manpower importer tired of arguing with the Labor Ministry about permits for foreign workers will suddenly discover an obscure Jewish community in the jungles of Vietnam, and will send over a team of top converters to perform a circumcision on anyone looking for construction work in Israel. . . . His emissaries will be Orthodox of the very highest quality . . . For money it will be possible to find the right rabbis. And after the first shipment, the land will be filled with instant Jews, "from India unto Ethiopia."

In other words, the Law of Return must be repealed, because if not, the country will be inundated with refugees from the Third World, who, in cahoots with unscrupulous Orthodox rabbis, will put an end to Israel as we know it. "How long will we keep the door open?" Caspi cries in conclusion.

"Must we allow free immigration even when we are flooded with uninvited guests?"[57]

Like any good piece of demagoguery, the "billion Chinese" argument really does have a basis in fact, and it is this: In the last decade, over three hundred converts to Judaism have actually immigrated to Israel from a remote province in eastern India. Whether there are any more Indians who will in this fashion join the Jewish people is anyone's guess. But in certain circles, this rather unimpressive fact is far less important than the lush layers of rumor and fear that have grown up around the "billion Chinese" argument—to the point that even a prestigious law journal such as Tel Aviv University's *Iyunei Mishpat* is willing to publish an article criticizing the Law of Return, which asserted that "*300 million candidates to become Jews were recently discovered in India.*"[58] This is no slip of the pen. Reports and rumors of this kind have been circulating in *branja* circles for years. And there is no doubt that the fear of losing control of Israel to alien, unseen powers from the Third World has contributed to the sense that the time has in fact come to revoke the Law of Return. And this sense has in recent years made inroads with many of Israel's most prominent intellectual figures.

As in other areas, the pioneer in the field of public demands to revise the Law of Return was Asa Kasher, who as early as 1984 had declared that Jewish immigrants, unless in actual danger, should be allowed to immigrate to Israel only if they are culturally and politically desirable.[59] But the real awakening of public statements on this subject occurred only after *Ha'aretz* began to treat the issue seriously. Since then, Kasher has been joined by Menahem Brinker of the Hebrew University literature department, who has demanded that the Law of Return be repealed, except in cases of clear persecution.[60] The historian Tom Segev has likewise argued that the Law of Return "contradicts the essence of democracy" and that so long as the Law of Return continues in place, Israeli Arabs will never be able to achieve equality.[61] And Haim Ganz of the Tel Aviv University law faculty has published a scholarly article arguing that "in legislating the Law of Return and depriving the Palestinians . . . of rights parallel to those that this law accords to Jews . . . there can be no doubt but that—by dint of the universality of the principles of morality—Israel is doing indisputable damage to the cause of morality and justice."[62]

The historian Amos Elon has similarly explained that Israel has to move beyond the idea that citizenship is related to "history, culture, race, religion, nationality, or language" and that this transition could reveal that "the Law of Return, too, has become redundant."[63] And the author David Grossman has argued that revision of the Law of Return is necessary for achieving "full equality" for the Arabs of Israel:

"Normalization" of life [in Israel] places a difficult and unequivocal question before the millions of Jews of the Diaspora . . . Are you coming here . . . or are you staying there? And if, in spite of everything, you aren't coming—will we, the managers of Hotel Zion continue to keep the empty rooms reserved in your names? Perhaps we'll decide to set a time limit on the problematic Law of Return (without depriving Jews fleeing from danger and privation of the right to return), and thereby begin resolving the problem of full equality for the one-fifth of Israel's citizens who are not Jews?[64]

Most remarkable has been the way in which self-professed opponents of post-Zionism—and even self-professed defenders of the Law of Return—have joined in the rush to explain why the law is really morally problematic or should be substantially modified. Among these is Yael Tamir, of Tel Aviv University's philosophy faculty, who is one of Israel's most prominent defenders of Jewish nationalism, and since 1999 the minister of absorption. According to Tamir, the Law of Return is problematic (and has been for fifty years) because "restrictions on immigration constitute a violation of the right of national minorities to equal treatment." Only when there is a Palestinian Arab state with its own law of return for Palestinian Arabs, she writes, could the Israeli law be considered "justified." (Tamir does not say whether the failure of a new Palestinian state to legislate such a law would mean that Israel must repeal its own.)[65] Hebrew University law professor Ruth Gavison likewise argues that the Law of Return should probably be reconsidered because of the "harm to [Israeli] non-Jews which it entails" and because "there is something repugnant in the fact that a person who has just gotten off the plane can vote and determine the fate of this country."[66]

Similarly, Haifa University historian Yoav Gelber, who is identified with the Israeli political right, has recently argued that "there is room to reconsider the automatic relationship between the right of refuge from persecution, and the right of citizenship. . . . One may have doubts as to the justice of the granting automatic . . . citizenship."[67] And the novelist A. B. Yehoshua, who counts himself among the defenders of the Law of Return, has likewise argued that Jews should be given only a "conditional" right of residency until they are able to demonstrate that they are sufficiently "Israeli":

No longer should citizenship be granted [to diaspora Jews] automatically. Rather it should be suspended for a few years, up until the new Jewish immigrant can prove his belonging to the Israeli identity . . . Of course, the Law of Return will still exist, giving every Jew the right of residence in Israel. *But this will be a right of residence that is conditional.*[68]

Even Israeli environmentalists have not been able to resist getting into the act. Suddenly, Israel has found itself hearing from Yoram Yom-Tov of Tel Aviv University's zoology department that the Law of Return has brought too many Jews to Israel—speaking from a strictly ecological point of view. And Dan Peri, then head of the Israel Nature Reserves Authority, likewise issued a call for Israelis to cut their birth rate, and, if necessary, amend the Law of Return to cut down on Jewish immigration and thereby protect Israel's nature reserves.[69]

All of the individuals cited here (except for the two environmentalists) are prominent in the mainstream of Israeli cultural life, and their need to argue for the abrogation or overhaul of the Law of Return points to a profound change in the way Israeli intellectuals relate to the "bill of rights" Israel once committed itself to guaranteeing for all Jews everywhere. And as we know from the ideological changes that have taken place in the Education Ministry, Supreme Court, and IDF, the radical views of Israel's intellectuals tend to remain divorced from the actual policies of the state for only a limited number of years. Indeed, the first harbingers of a shift in this area, too, can already be felt. In 1994 Welfare Minister Ora Namir (Labor), whose ministry was dealing directly with issues of immigrant absorption, launched a highly publicized attack on the quality of the Jewish immigrants arriving in Israel from Russia, arguing that "one-third of these immigrants are elderly, one-third are crippled and suffering from serious handicaps, and almost one-third are single mothers."[70] Absorption Minister Yair Tzaban (Meretz) was more explicit, demanding changes in the Law of Return in order to prevent the immigration of "millions of people" from "India, Burma, and the Philippines."[71] And in 1995, Uri Gordon, the head of the Immigration and Absorption Department of the Jewish Agency, told the press that the Jewish Agency had begun testing Jews who want to immigrate to Israel to determine whether they would be able to support themselves financially or whether they had psychological problems. Jews who were deemed "unfit" to immigrate would be persuaded to stay in the Diaspora—even though, as Gordon said, "I am aware that these tests contradict the Law of Return."[72]

And it is obvious that the story is just beginning. In 1999, two Arab political parties began an unprecedented campaign to legally redefine Israel as "a democratic and multi-cultural" state, which among other things will have to repeal the Law of Return. As one of the Arab politicians behind the effort, MK Ahmed Tibi, until recently a high-ranking adviser to PLO Chairman Yasser Arafat, explained, this effort is being based on the increasing awareness of the Jews that the country must change:

I could have been bombastic . . . and said that Ahmed Tibi wants to repeal the Law of Return. No, I'm not demanding. I am waiting for the moment the Jews are going to repeal the Law of Return. I want to create a public dialogue, which by the way has already been started, and not at my initiative. Five years ago, Hanoch Marmari, Editor of Ha'aretz, wrote a brilliant article on the need to repeal the Law of Return. It wasn't my suggestion.[73]

Foreign Affairs

Nowhere within the Israeli government was the influence of post-Zionist ideals more in evidence in the years after 1992 than in the Foreign Ministry, which appeared to change course from a foreign policy aimed at securing the interests of the Jewish people and the independent Jewish state, to one aimed at the construction of a "new Middle East" wherein the sovereign character of the present Jewish and Arab states would be attenuated, possibly to the point of erasure. This policy revolution was executed with unparalleled speed and gusto thanks to the leadership of Shimon Peres, one of Ben-Gurion's most devoted disciples, who has over the last decade become the most important advocate of backing away from the idea of an independent Jewish state. His stunning political reversal, at the end a career spanning five decades in which he was one of Labor Zionism's most important figures, has been a decisive factor in gaining legitimacy for the view that even among leading Zionists, the idea of the Jewish state is dying or dead.

Unlike most of the circle with which he is now closely associated, Shimon Peres never attended an Israeli university. It is true that as a youth he was exposed to German-Jewish universalism at length while attending high school at the famous youth village in Ben-Shemen, whose founders were among the opponents of establishing a Jewish state in Palestine. Nevertheless, it is clear that the young Peres resisted the ideological message of the youth village, and his memoirs describe how he publicly denounced Ben-Shemen's instructors—among them Martin Buber—for distorting the Jewish tradition to suit their political ideology.[74] While still in his youth, Peres became a personal protégé of the leading Labor Zionist ideologue, Berl Katznelson, as well as a tireless exponent of Jewish statehood in the Noar Oved ("Working Youth") movement, of which he became a prominent leader. After graduation, Peres turned his back on the Hebrew University, instead choosing a harsh life constructing a collective farm from scratch on a hilltop overlooking the Sea of Galilee. In 1942, at a time when the Nazi invasion of Palestine appeared imminent and the destruction of the Jewish population of the country was a looming possibility, Peres was among forty-seven youth leaders who scaled the dangerous heights of

Masada—the famous desert fortress that was the last remaining stronghold during the great Jewish revolt against Rome. On this fortress, Peres and his friends composed and signed the dramatic nationalist oath that has since entered into legend, swearing that "Masada shall not fall again" and vowing to be "educated by its light."[75] Not long thereafter, he joined forces with the young Moshe Dayan to head the Labor movement's youth wing, which supported Ben-Gurion's insistence that independence be achieved, if need be, by force of arms.

After independence, Peres became one of the central figures in Ben-Gurion's efforts to build Jewish military power, first taking frontline responsibility for arms procurement abroad and subsequently becoming the prime minister's point man in the development of the Jewish state's nuclear capability. Peres was also an articulate spokesman for the imperative of Jewish military force, arguing against many of the intellectuals that the Israeli security situation "would have been desperate had we relied on 'the spirit of conciliation.'" As Peres wrote in 1955,

> Israel's security rests on our treasured strength, on the strength of the IDF, and the security situation has improved because the strength of the IDF has grown. . . . The security of Israel does not depend on . . . conciliation with the Arabs. The degree of our security is the degree to which we are able and ready to defend what has been achieved with so much blood.[76]

Even as defense minister in the last Labor government of the 1970s, Peres continued to be known as a nationalist and a security hawk, insisting that Israel in its pre-1967 boundaries had been so "untenable and indefensible" as to have triggered the Six Day War; and championing the use of force in a government that was prepared to consider capitulation to the demands of the hostage-takers at Entebbe.[77]

It is still unclear what the forces were that drove Peres, during the Labor party's long years in opposition after 1977, to change course after a lifetime of devotion to classic Jewish nationalism. Peres's memoirs faithfully preserve his own earlier attitudes during most of his political career, without any evidence of having given up on the Jewish state. It is only when his narrative reaches the heady days of the reestablishment of Labor government in 1992 that the discussion takes a bizarre turn, as he and his assistants, Yossi Beilin, Uri Savir, and Avi Gil, begin "dreaming"—so Peres writes—"of peace in the Middle East." Suddenly, the sharpness of his thinking evaporates and Peres begins to speak of Israel's diplomatic efforts as having been "based on a misconception," since the entire world "has moved beyond having ideological confrontation." His writing becomes haunted by an eerie refrain to the effect that the very fabric of past reality has dissolved: "The movements of the

Jewish national renaissance and the Arab national renaissance met—and clashed . . . [But] the world in which these two movements were born and grew to fruition no longer exists." And similarly: "We are ending a decades-long history dominated by war, and embarking on an era in which the guns will stay silent while dreams flourish. . . . The world into which I was born no longer exists."[78]

This same giddiness is evident in a speech he delivered at the United Nations in October 1992, less than four months after his appointment as foreign minister, in which he announced that "national conflicts and national rivalries" had come to an end and called for "a new Middle East." Already then, he unhesitatingly told the nations of the world:

> The end of conflict is no longer a utopian fantasy. . . . The forces of change have pushed aside the pillars of conventional wisdom, which proclaimed that military power is the source of national strength and prestige. This is no longer true. . . . The United Nations was established in an era that no longer exists.[79]

But it was only the following year that Peres issued his full programmatic statement in a small book called *The New Middle East* (1993). As Peres explains, the entire idea of the small national state—the Jewish state included—has collapsed. Security, once the central purpose of such states, can no longer be provided on a national basis because of the threat of nuclear-armed terror, which can only be fought with an international armed force. And economic well-being, the second purpose of the national state, can likewise no longer be provided on a national basis because of the overwhelming economic advantages of open-bordered, information-sharing political units such as the European Union. As a result, "national political organizations can no longer fulfill the purpose for which they were established. . . . The social group has expanded, and today our health, welfare, and freedom can be ensured only within a wider framework, on a regional or even a super-regional basis."[80]

But the pressing need to replace national states with vast regional entities has been understood only by certain enlightened segments of mankind. Others, writes Peres, continue to chase after the chimera of nationalism:

> Our era has witnessed the emergence of two contradictory trends: Particularist nationalism and supernational development of regional communities. In every area in which the first has staked a claim, the social order has been subverted and hostility and violence have taken root. The areas of the former country of Yugoslavia are a prime example of this. In contrast, everywhere the supernational trend predominates, there is a sensitivity to human needs, opportunities, and desires, leading to a more lasting international or-

der that strives for prosperity, development, and human rights. Western Europe is a shining example of this.[81]

Arguing from the two examples of Western Europe and Yugoslavia, Peres claims that it is particularist nationalism that induces men to seek domination over others and that inexorably brings injustice and violence. In the case of the Middle East, it was Arab and Jewish nationalism (i.e., his own Labor Zionism) that were responsible for triggering interminable war and spurring an arms race that caused regional economic stagnation, poverty, and religious fundamentalism.[82] The only way to respond to the menace of nuclear-armed fundamentalism, Peres argues, is to transfer political and military power from the Jewish state to "a new political entity," a regional Arab-Jewish government wielding authority and control over the region's military might and economic development. Only such a Middle Eastern federation will be able to offer "regional security" that will truly protect all individuals in the region, as well as a regional common market that would bring wealth to all.

Peres appears to be well aware that his scheme means the end of sovereign Jewish power, but this prospect does not seem to bother him: The independent state, he writes, is in any case a recent invention, and one should not be too concerned with it:

> Moses, Jesus, and Muhammad could not [even] have read the writings of Hugo Grotius, the seventeenth-century thinker who introduced the concept of "sovereignty" to jurisprudence, diplomatic history, and the political lexicon. At the threshold of the twenty-first century, we do not need to reinforce sovereignty, but rather to strengthen the position of humankind.[83]

But if there is to be a new Middle East with a common government, military, and economy, what is to be the identity of the people living in it? The answer is that memories of past national struggles and glories, which only serve to maintain national division, must be jettisoned: "As long as images of the past threaten our present efforts to build a new future, we will get nowhere. We will sentence ourselves to an endless cycle of wars and bloodshed." Instead, Peres demands the creation of a new and non-national "Middle Eastern" identity in the hearts of men, if not something even more universal:

> One day our self-awareness and personal identity will be based on this new reality, and we will find that we have stepped outside the national arena. Western Europe is already showing signs of this new age. . . . In the Middle East, as in Eastern Europe, the process is more complex; people are not yet ready to accept a supernational identity. . . . [Nevertheless] it can be seen that a new type of citizenship is catching on, with a new personal identity, for

Europeans as members of a European society. . . . Particularist nationalism is
fading and the idea of a "citizen of the world" is taking hold.[84]

The effect of Peres's ideal on the policies of his ministry were immediate.
As one of his first acts in office, Peres ordered the closure of the Foreign
Ministry's Information Department, unilaterally suspending the century-
old battle to win the sympathy of the world for the Jewish national cause.
The reason, as Peres was quick to explain, was: "If you have good policy,
you do not need public relations, and if you have bad policy, public relations will not help."[85] Peres's oath as a youth to be "educated in Masada's
light" notwithstanding, sites connoting Jewish nationalism and strength, including both Masada and the Golan Heights, were dropped from the schedules of visiting dignitaries.[86] But Peres's strategy did not stop at merely
downplaying Jewish national symbols and rhetoric. The Israeli Foreign
Ministry diverted its time and energies from traditional diplomacy on behalf of the Jewish state, instead becoming a de facto foreign relations apparatus on behalf of the entire Middle East. Thus, when friends of Israel in the
Congress tried to pass legislation requiring the U.S. government to recognize Jerusalem as Israel's capital, Israel *opposed* the bill because it would upset the Arabs.[87] Indeed, one of the essential responsibilities of Israeli
diplomats became fund-raising for Arab regimes, with the hope that this
would induce them to rally behind Israeli schemes for regional cooperation
and eventual federation. Israel is "a wealthy country," explained then
Deputy Foreign Minister Yossi Beilin (now justice minister), which has no
need of donations from Diaspora Jews; but Jewish philanthropic organizations "have to" provide financial assistance to Jordan and the PLO.[88]
Foreign Ministry Director-General Uri Savir likewise announced that "anyone who objects to American aid to the PLO has no right to be called a
friend of Israel."[89] Assisting in maintaining the American aid package to
Egypt and securing American foreign aid for Syria were also added as important foreign ministry objectives.[90]

And as Peres's new foreign policy aims gained momentum, other ministers also joined in, redirecting their resources as well to the coming fusion of
Jewish and Arab interests. Thus, the Housing Ministry, which is responsible
for Israel's chronically congested highway system, announced it would focus
on the construction of highways that would make Israeli ports accessible to
exporters in Syria and Saudi Arabia. The Religious Affairs Ministry similarly
decided on new funding guidelines that gave preference to groups promoting social encounters between Jewish and Muslim youth and to organizations encouraging pilgrimage to Mecca. And the Tourism Ministry, which
had traditionally focused its efforts on encouraging Jewish and Christian

tourism, embarked on highly publicized efforts to net tourism from places like Muammar Qaddafi's Libya.[91]

Nor was Foreign Minister Peres reticent about revealing where all of this was leading. Once persuaded of the diplomatic and commercial benefits of joining forces with Israel, the Arab states would begin moving toward political union with the Jews. "There can be no doubt," he explained, "that Israel's next goal should be to become a member of the Arab League."[92]

Yet no aspect of Israeli policy more clearly bears the imprint of Peres's campaign for a new Middle East than the Oslo Accords, signed in September 1993 with the PLO. All Israeli governments prior to 1992 had assumed that if Israel were to negotiate with the Arabs over the West Bank, the negotiations would be conducted with the kingdom of Jordan, which was pro-Western and had a long history of under-the-table respect and cooperation with Israel. Such a proposed "Jordanian option," it was believed, would resemble the Camp David Accords signed with Egypt in 1978, in which Israel had conceded territory, a material asset, but had received in return a significant *political* asset sought by the Zionist movement for seventy years: The overt recognition of Jewish sovereignty in Israel by an important Arab-nationalist regime. On this score, both the Camp David Accords and the peace treaty with Egypt had been unequivocal, with Egypt declaring its "respect for the sovereignty, territorial integrity, and political independence" of Israel.[93] And in fact, when a peace agreement was finally signed by Yitzhak Rabin and King Hussein of Jordan in October 1994, the Jordanian government did follow Egypt's lead in explicitly declaring its respect for the Jewish state's "sovereignty, territorial integrity, and political independence."[94]

Prior to 1992, however, virtually no important Israeli leader had ever argued that a "pro-Zionist" diplomatic agreement of the kind reached with Egypt and Jordan could be signed with the fanatically anti-Zionist PLO. Like earlier Jewish anti-Zionist organizations, the PLO had been established to advance the idea, expressed in its charter, that the Zionist claim to Palestine "does not tally with the constituents of statehood in their true sense," because "Judaism, in its character as a religion of revelation, is not a nationality." Thus, Zionism was a historical fraud "organically related to world imperialism," "colonialist in its aims," and "Fascist and Nazi in its means."[95] In keeping with this charter, the PLO eventually became the leading ideological purveyor of anti-Zionism within the Arab world, devoting its propaganda and diplomatic operations to entrenching the idea that a Jewish state in *any* territory is inherently illegitimate (although members of the Jewish faith would be offered a place within the framework of Arab national sovereignty). Moreover, Yasser Arafat's PLO also operated a number of "military" arms that had achieved notoriety for killing Jews around the globe but whose primary mission had been the elimination of Arabs willing to accept the existence of a Jewish state.

Such an organization, it was believed, would not be able to reach a genuine political accord with Israel, because this would require either that Israel give up on its most basic Zionist political demands—that the Arab nationalists recognize "the sovereignty, territorial integrity, and political independence" of a Jewish state in at least part of Palestine, or that the PLO give up on *its* most basic political demand—that the Jews back off from their insistence on these things. For an agreement between the Zionists and the PLO to be reached, it seemed that one side or the other would have to concede the fundamentals of its worldview and the ostensible purpose of its existence.[96]

And sure enough, one side *did* make such a concession. None of the three critical phrases from the peace treaties with Egypt and Jordan—indeed, nothing remotely resembling them—appeared in the agreement Peres negotiated with the PLO through the Oslo back channel.[97]

Why was Shimon Peres willing to make the deal no other Israeli leader had contemplated? The answer seems to be that Peres was not really that interested in questions of "national sovereignty, territorial integrity, and political independence." All three of these diplomatic terms boil down to the same thing—the effort to reinforce the Jewish national claim to military and political supremacy within the borders of the state. But it is precisely the Jewish national claim to military and political supremacy within one set of borders or another that Peres considered to be decreasingly relevant—a position that makes perfect sense if one has given up on the efficacy of anything smaller than "treaties that cover whole regions."[98]

To be sure, it is not easy to believe this—that the Oslo Accords were negotiated within a context of what might be considered near total disregard for issues of Jewish national military and political power. Yet Peres emphasizes time and again that this was the case. Consider, for example, the vexing issue of which of the territories demanded by the PLO are necessary for Israel's defense, or the equally problematic question of permitting Arab military concentrations in the mountains of the West Bank in close proximity to major Jewish population centers. As Peres wrote in his interpretation of the Oslo agreements in *The New Middle East,* all such traditional military issues were to him simply *irrelevant*:

> As far as I can tell, it was not I who had shifted from the traditional concept of national defense, which depends mainly on military and weapons systems. . . . Rather, the world has changed. . . . The physical considerations of the traditional strategy—natural obstacles, man-made structures, troop mobilizations, location of the battlefields—are irrelevant.[99]

Or, as Peres told the IDF's head of intelligence during a cabinet meeting in which the officer argued for greater military preparedness: "There is economics and there is the military, and only a country which goes over to economics will win. Choosing between ten army emplacements and ten hotels, the ten hotels also constitute security. I'm for the European model, which emphasizes economics."[100]

It was such a conception that permitted the team at Oslo to conduct its negotiations and reach an agreement with the PLO without even consulting with the Israeli armed forces. (When news of the Oslo agreement broke, Deputy Chief of Staff Amnon Lipkin-Shahak quickly informed the press that "the army had not been consulted during the secret negotiations leading up to the agreement, and that Chief-of-Staff Ehud Barak saw the document [i.e., the Oslo agreement] for the first time on Monday. No other military man has yet seen the agreement.")[101]

The Oslo agreement reflects a similar disinterest in other types of Jewish national assets that might be damaged by a shift in sovereignty or territorial integrity: air space, water rights, the ability to build basic infrastructure for Tel Aviv and Jerusalem, both of which border the West Bank. All of these could hardly be considered pressing if national borders were soon to be rendered meaningless by the new "world without borders."[102] As Peres explained, his goal was in any case to place much of Israel's basic infrastructure *outside* of Israel's present borders—including new airports, oil terminals, railroad lines, and major highways—since the territory formally remaining under Israeli authority would be too small for such development.[103] In the same manner, the entry of Arab refugees into Israel was for the first time accepted as a subject for negotiation, because the aim was in any case to open Israeli territory to the "free movement of people" from the Arab states.[104] Even Jerusalem, the Israeli capital city, was placed on the negotiating block, since it could hardly matter whether or not the city was united under full Israeli sovereignty in an age when the borders between Israel and the Arab states and their respective sovereignties would effectively cease to exist.[105] In short, the deal with the ideologically anti-Zionist PLO became possible only once every issue related to Jewish "national sovereignty, territorial integrity, and political independence" was recognized as being to a large degree irrelevant—and therefore, of course, negotiable.

In this manner, the Oslo agreement demolished each of the pillars of the traditional Labor Zionist conception of the Jewish state in turn: By turning away from the need for Jewish-national military force, Peres and those who followed him gave up on the essential premises of the search for Jewish national power. By downplaying the need to develop an economic infrastructure within the territory of the Jewish state, they denied the necessity of attracting Jews to live in and create within the boundaries of the Jewish homeland. And by conducting a policy whose highest aim was not the interests of the Jewish people and its state—but rather that of a new, supernational Middle Eastern entity in which the Jews would be a minority—they effectively renounced the concept of the state of Israel as the guardian of the Jews.

This cuts to the heart of why Oslo and the public statements of its chief negotiators at the time created such a sandstorm of opprobrium in Israel: The idea that the Jewish people do not necessarily need political sovereignty is of course a flagrantly post-Zionist proposition—whose meaning is the end of the Jewish people's demand to be, in the words of Israel's Declaration of Independence, masters of their own fate in their own sovereign state.

"A Redeployment in Our Soul"

As befits a country in which public debate rarely focuses on ideas, there was little debate over the theoretical or cultural ramifications of the Oslo Accords. And when, within weeks of the signing of the agreement in 1993, *The New Middle East* appeared to explain the ideological revolution that had taken place in Israeli foreign policy, the book was little read and little discussed. But this does not mean that the transition to effectively post-Zionist foreign policy aims was without effect on the public culture of the state of Israel. On the contrary, it was the downplaying of the concept of the Jewish state in the highest reaches of government—and by one of Ben-Gurion's most trusted heirs—that gave the green light for the sudden eruption into view of post-Zionist ideas that had been simmering in the heart of Israeli political culture for decades. It was the cultural aftershocks of the Oslo Accords that transformed quiet disdain for the Jewish state into the visible political prejudice of many Israeli intellectuals and their swiftly rising political correctness.

Among the few to try and draw attention to what was taking place on the level of political culture was Yoel Marcus, one of Israel's most respected political commentators and an old-time veteran of the Labor-Zionist intellectual establishment. In a blistering column in *Ha'aretz* in the summer of 1995, Marcus made the direct connection between the end of Zionism in the public mind and the foreign policy of the government. "In their worst nightmares," wrote Marcus bitterly, "neither Yitzhak Rabin nor Shimon Peres could have twenty-five years ago imagined themselves as the architects of a government" that had signed an agreement to negotiate over Jerusalem and was seriously considering withdrawing from the Golan Heights—once a potent symbol of the kibbutz movement and Labor Zionism. Asking Israelis to "leave for a moment the preoccupation with the headlines of the hour," Marcus pointed to what he considered "the really dramatic revolution taking place" in post-Oslo Israel: "If these events had taken place in the days of Yitzhak Tabenkin, Israel Galili, Golda Meir, David Ben-Gurion— Rabin and Peres' spiritual fathers— . . . the country would have been in turmoil, the ground would have quaked. But the most all these ideological 'once were's can do now is to turn in their graves."

The reason that such a disavowal of once-sacred Labor Zionist causes could take place without pandemonium, Marcus wrote, was the collapse of the Jewish national ideology that had built the state:

> Our people has long since tired of bearing Zionism on its shoulders generation after generation. . . . While the Arabs have remained faithful to their ideology of the holiness of the land, preferring to forgo peace rather concede anything of their demands . . . Israel is ready lightly to withdraw from the lands that were the cradle of Judaism. . . . in exchange for personal safety and a "normal" life.[106]

But what was for Marcus the painful recognition of the collapse of a life's dream was for others an occasion for rejoicing. Within days, his colleague at *Ha'aretz*, Gidon Samet, responded with an article expressing his pleasure at this same ideological devastation. "Thanks be to God," he cheered, the century-old effort at building a Jewish "national identity" seemed finally to have come to an end. "When did this happen? . . . It was in Oslo."

According to Samet, until the Oslo agreement, Israelis had insisted on living within the fortress of a Jewish national identity that had closed out the world and kept them in perpetual conflict with it. The abandonment of this battle thus represented a profound change not only in Israel's politics but in its very identity. In Oslo,

> one of the ingredients that had acted as the cement in the wall of our old national identity disintegrated. The great majority of us who had always opposed dealing with the PLO finally stopped mumbling that mantra. And even if this majority didn't want to consider the full implications . . . today it is already clear that there is a connection between this change and . . . our new national identity.

The change in Israel's identity, wrote Samet, resulted from the fact that it had for the first time broken with its struggle to create a particularly Jewish state, for the first time demonstrating a "new willingness to engage in a dialogue with our surroundings," and to imbibe the culture of the world: "Madonna and Big Macs are only the most peripheral of examples" of the new identity of "normalness" that Samet saw bursting out around him. "Only those trapped in the old way of thinking will not recognize the benefits."[107]

Not long after this column was published in July 1995, Samet was given a diplomatic posting by the Foreign Ministry and sent abroad to represent the new Israel. But anyone sensitive to the shifting of the tides within Israel's psyche continued to struggle with just this issue—the question of whether Israelis, without fully realizing it, had somehow adopted a "new national identity."

And indeed, for those who looked at events at the level of the ideas that had brought them into being, it was not too hard to understand that Oslo did in fact have a single, overarching meaning, far greater in its importance for the history of Israel than giving up or retaining any particular parcel of land. In some crucial way, the Oslo agreement had signaled the end of *the* mission, a turn of events that the celebrated author David Grossman described—mimicking the language of the accords, which called for an Israel military redeployment—as "a redeployment from entire regions in our soul." And he went on to name them, these "regions of the soul" of the Jewish state that were now being given up:

> The Jews living in Israel are now being asked not only to give up on geographical territories. We must also implement a "redeployment"—or even a complete withdrawal—from entire regions in our soul. . . . Such as "the purity of arms." . . . Such as being a "precious people" [*am segula*] or a "chosen people." . . . Slowly, over long years, we will discover that we are beginning to give them up: . . . Giving up on power as a value. On the army itself as a value. . . . On "It is good to die for one's country," on "The best to the air force" . . . and on "After me." We will discover how we are refining a new existence for ourselves. One which is no longer drenched to the point of suffocation with the myth of our exile from the land, or with the myth of Masada, or with a one-dimensional lesson of the Holocaust.[108]

This is difficult reading for anyone familiar with the "regions in our soul" to which Grossman is referring, all of them building blocks of the Jewish nationalist identity that Labor Zionism had so painstakingly constructed. Giving up on the "purity of arms," for instance, means giving up on the idea that Jewish force was for the great part used justly and for a just cause. Giving up on being a "precious people" or "chosen people" means turning our backs on the idea that the Jewish identity is something especially valuable, that the Jews have a reason to exist distinct from those of other nations. Giving up on the "army as a value" and "power as a value" means the retreat from Ben-Gurion's argument that Jewish powerlessness had been an evil, and that the newly won right of the Jews to bear arms and protect their loved ones is to be cherished. And those slogans, familiar to every Israeli child, that Grossman envisions abandoning: Trumpeldor's dying words after being wounded defending the border settlement of Tel Hai ("It is good to die for one's country"); Ezer Weizman's call for students to volunteer for the crucial, dangerous work of building the newly formed Jewish air force ("The best to the air force"); and the ideal of the first generation of Jewish officers, who were taught that Jews do not send their men ahead to battle but led them with a cry of *aharai* ("After me")—giving up on these means giving up on the idea of Jewish heroism and nobility in the service of the common national effort. And the memory of the Jews sent into eternal exile by Rome; and of Masada, which held out even when all hope was lost; and of the Holocaust, which teaches that even the Jews must be strong. Giving up on these means the abandonment of only one small thing. It means giving up on the ties that bind the Jews to the sacrifices made by other generations on behalf the Jewish people and its ideals.

David Grossman is correct. These are indeed the regions of the Jewish soul that Zionism sought to bring to life, and with such spectacular success, for such a brief time. These are the regions of the soul that burned in men such as Theodor Herzl and David Ben-Gurion, the regions of the soul that had to be brought to a roaring flame for the Jewish state to arise from its tomb after two thousand years, and the regions of the soul that must continue to glow and shimmer and dance if the Jewish state is to live.

The redeployment of which David Grossman speaks is the destruction of the Jewish state in the mind of the Jewish people. It is the return to exile. It is a retreat into the void.

PART

II

CHAPTER 3

An Introduction to the History of the Jewish State

IN THE PREVIOUS TWO CHAPTERS, I have argued that the ideal the state of Israel was intended to fulfill—that of "the Jewish state"—has since the early 1970s come under criticism of the most severe and destructive kind from large sections of the country's intellectual leadership. I do not, of course, mean to say that most Israeli intellectuals are prepared for the immediate rejection of *all* aspects of the idea of the Jewish state. This is not the case. But I do claim that the majority of Israeli cultural leaders have, each in his own way, come to disdain or dissent from central aspects of the traditional idea of the Jewish state. Together with an inability to contribute *positive* substance to it, the rejection of the purpose, values, history, heroes, and symbols that created Israel has brought the ideal of the Jewish state to the verge of dissolution at least among educated Israelis. And it should go without saying that the loss of this ideal will, sooner or later, bring about the end of the Jewish state itself.

The remainder of this book deals with the history of the idea of the Jewish state, from the time of its first great modern advocate, Theodor Herzl, to the present. In researching this story, much of which was unfamiliar to me when I began trying to make sense of it five years ago, I had two principal aims in view. First, I wanted to understand how this condition came into being. I wanted to know how the ideal of the Jewish state, which forty years earlier had been a moral and political axiom for virtually all Jews the world over—and for many millions of others who wished the Jews well—could so quickly have been brought to ruin among the cultural leadership of the Jewish state itself. Second, I hoped to glean clues from the history of the past hundred years that would assist in pointing out the path to restoration, if such a path exists.

These questions have obviously brought to life a story that is very different from the usual histories of the Zionist movement and the state of Israel. This is not so much because what I have written is a "revision" of the known facts. Rather, it is because the questions I have asked turn our attention to ideas, and individuals, and incidents that were rightly thought to have been peripheral before the questions that I am asking became pressing. For example, readers familiar with previous histories of Israel will be surprised to find Martin Buber described as a decisive figure in the history of the Jewish state. Howard Sachar's 1,020-page *A History of Israel*, for example, describes Buber's dramatic impact on the ideas of German Zionism in a single sentence; and it covers Buber's fifty-year-long crusade against the idea of the Jewish state in a single paragraph, which ends as follows: "Yet the Peace Association [i.e., Buber's disciples] were an ideological, not a political, group. Its membership never exceeded two hundred, and in its speeches and publications it made hardly a dent on the leadership of Jewish Palestine. Neither did it evoke even the faintest response from the Arabs."[1]

Nothing that Sachar writes here is false and in need of "revision." He is right in saying that Buber's two hundred ideologues left virtually no mark on "the leadership of Jewish Palestine" in the 1930s and 1940s. But today we know his description was nevertheless missing something important. Writing more than twenty years ago, it could not have occurred to Sachar that these intellectuals—who were not much as politicians, but who *were* the dominant intellectual force at the Hebrew University—had had a tremendous influence on a completely different generation: Students who attended the university in the late 1950s and 1960s, many of whom were only in their thirties when Sachar was writing his book. The evidence of Buber's importance in the history of the Jewish state was then still barely visible.

As soon as one begins to look at the history of Israel from the perspective of today's questions—the most important being whether Israel can continue to fulfill its function as the "Jewish state" envisioned by Herzl—the hard facts of history begin to take on a different weight and value, and a different story emerges. Previously trivial facts seem much more interesting and important. For instance, one's eye is quickly caught by the story of the young Buber's emotional break with his old mentor Herzl or by the role played by Buber's students at the Hebrew University in ending David Ben-Gurion's career. (Of course, the opposite is true as well: The more important the struggle over the question of the Jewish state becomes, the less interesting become the threadbare disputes between Ben-Gurion and Menachem Begin—that is, between the Left and the Right *within* the camp of partisans of the Jewish state—which take on the character of a squabble between the captain and the first mate of a sinking ship.)

I feel constrained to add one last word about the history of the Jewish state before beginning to tell the story as I now understand it. The major works on the history of Israel to this point have quite reasonably been infused by the perspective of mainstream Labor Zionists such as Ben-Gurion, who more than anyone else were the people who actually established the Jewish state. Thus, an old Labor Zionist such as my father can read a history such as Sachar's without feeling that he is seeing things from a new angle. Sachar's is more or less the perspective my father grew up with in Tel Aviv of the 1940s and 1950s.

But as will become clear, there is at least one respect in which my own perspective differs greatly from either that of the mainstream of Labor Zionism or that of the Zionist Right (later the "Likud" party) led by Menachem Begin. And it is this: Labor Zionism tended to see political reality—and therefore political history—as being primarily a function of the physical presence of Jewish workers in the farms and factories of Palestine; the followers of Begin put relatively greater emphasis on the physical effects of Jewish guns and bombs. Neither movement believed much in the power of ideas. And it was this Zionist blindness to the power of ideas that is so evident in the fact that neither Labor Zionism nor its main political opponents had much to do with the founding of the Hebrew University. This institution, in all of its idea-making disciplines, was left to Martin Buber's associates and students, who ultimately believed in nothing if not the ability of ideas to win out over all else in the end. Since Labor Zionists often did not share this belief, they always tended to minimize the effect of the university and other cultural institutions on the political life of their country. And in this the major histories of Israel have, ironically, been faithful chronicles of the way history was viewed by the former farmhands who comprised the Labor-Zionist leadership.

Today, the ideas of Labor Zionism (and even the name "Labor") have all but evaporated from the conscious mind of the Israeli polity, while the ideas of the Hebrew University continue to gather strength, with no end in sight.

And at the same time, the idea of the Jewish state, which was so precious to the leaders of mainstream Labor Zionism and so problematic for many of the fathers of the Hebrew University, has continued its precipitous decline. Only now that this has come to pass is it possible to understand the history of the Jewish state as a story about the power of ideas—a story that most Labor-Zionist leaders would have had difficulty believing but that might have made a great deal of sense to Theodor Herzl.

CHAPTER 4

Theodor Herzl's "Jewish State" Versus Rousseau's Social Contract

IT WAS NIGHT AT THE AKADEMISCHE LESEHALLE, the largest debating and fraternal society at the University of Vienna, where students gathered to pursue their readings, but also to drink and argue, to gamble and hear speeches and pass political resolutions. That night in mid-January 1879, the building was alight, its hundreds of members gathered in anticipation of yet another raucous debate on—what else could cause such heat in the dead of winter?—the Lesehalle's stance toward German nationalism. A young law student stood before the crowd, tall, dark, his dress impeccable, his bearing lofty and condescending. Although only a freshman, his intonation was confident and ironic, in keeping with the style introduced into Vienna by the spread of a pan-German nationalism that threatened to capsize the Austrian empire. No longer would the students sit still for the stolid, bourgeois monotone that had become synonymous with the supporters of the increasingly helpless Austrian emperor. No, this young jurist was of the new type. Caustic, witty, speaking with calculated emotion and a certain cultivated contempt that bore him to heights in praise of the richness of the great German civilization that united the great majority of the assembled students, pan-Germans and loyalists alike.

And why not? As one of the great Liberal leaders at the time of the adoption of the new Constitution two decades before had declared, it was for the Germans to seek cultural hegemony among the backward peoples of Austria—Czechs, Hungarians, Poles, Slovaks, Serbs, Croats—that they should "carry culture to the east, transmit the propaganda of German intellection, German science, German humanism." Among the students of the university, three-fourths were Germans. Among these it was hardly questioned that the empire of Franz Joseph was a creation of the German spirit; its theater, music, philosophy, literature, and science the product of the German genius; its political, military, and business leadership all overwhelmingly German. And how much had taken place in recent years to strengthen this spirit in the empire! The victory of enlightened ideas and tolerant government over the dominance of the Catholic Church in Germany and Austria alike; the humiliation of the papists and their consignment to their cage in the Vatican; the Prussian victory over the decadence of France; the forging of the petty kingdoms of the north into a true German empire—and all this within a decade. Everywhere, Bismarck was triumphant. Everywhere in Germandom one could feel these triumphs through the medium of Richard Wagner's operas, which one could hear in Vienna nearly every night. German civilization was no longer the pale ghost of intellection it had been to Schiller, wandering powerless among the scattered political shards of Central Europe. Now Germany had reached political heights as well and was no longer merely an idea, not merely the greatest of human ideas but an idea with power—world power! And could there be any doubt, then, why so many students at the university were proclaiming their longing to see Austria, creation of the German spirit, joined in political as well as cultural union with Bismarck's empire, which was the representation of this power? Of course the young and impatient German Viennese student longed for such a deed. But what was ultimately at stake was not the great political act itself, but the improvement of mankind. What truly mattered were the deeds of the spirit that followed political deeds like the rain after a clap of thunder that sets the world shuddering. What truly mattered was that German humanism and the idea of freedom might continue their march, bringing civilization to Bohemia, to Hungary, and on to the East, making of Vienna a great capital of the human spirit and of Austria a great German state.[1]

The applause in the packed hall was deafening, the cheers seemingly ready to bring down the rafters of the Lesehalle. The young law student lingered on a few more seconds, grinning with pleasure at the approval of the crowd. Years later, a fellow student wrote to him: "I still recall the first time I saw you—it was in the Akademische Lesehalle. You were making a speech, and you were being 'sharp'—so sharp! . . . You were smiling ironically—and I began to envy you. If only I could speak and smile in that way, I thought to myself."[2] He went to take his seat, obviously pleased, the students around him pounding him on the back in congratulations. It was only the next day that he understood that he had been a bit too sharp. His speech had been understood as favoring annexation to Germany, and he was forced to announce in debate three days later that such had not been his intention. He had meant to express his support for the camp of the Austrian loyalists.[3]

The young Theodor Herzl was not the only student swept up in the defense of German political and cultural hegemony in the face of a rising Hungarian and Slavic separatism that threatened to dismember the German-Austrian state. In the fall semester of the same year that Herzl became a member of the Lesehalle, the society was the scene of a brawl when a Czech student, whose membership had been suspended for organizing a demonstration in favor of Slavic autonomy, assaulted the chairman. The result was a series of motions of no confidence in which the Lesehalle's executive increasingly reflected the rising tide of German nationalism. A year later, the Lesehalle executive sent a letter of support to the rector of the University of Prague, who was embroiled in an attempt to retain the German character of the institution, which was on the verge of crumbling into rival German and Czech faculties. Many of the society's Slavic members left, but the Lesehalle insisted that its gesture of support for the rector was not political but rather aimed at strengthening Austria's "academic principles," which "rested on German traditions, German learning and German culture."[4]

It seems that Herzl supported the Lesehalle in these efforts, since by the fall of his third year, he had been made the Lesehalle's social chairman. (In keeping with the spirit of the period, this officer was charged with organizing festive drink-alongs, in which the free flow of beer rendered more palatable the main course of German nationalist song and doggerel.) At the same time, Herzl was admitted to the German-nationalist fraternity Albia after a saber duel that won him the right to wear the fraternity's sash of black, red, and gold—the colors of the German Reich; he was inducted with the frat name "Tancred," after the warrior prince who conquered Galilee for Christendom in the First Crusade.[5] At the University of Vienna, Herzl studied law, politics, and economics, along with other young men planning a career in the Austrian government bureaucracy. But he spent much of his time writing for the student paper and occasionally publishing in the Viennese press, scribbling novellas and plays and championing Germanness as expressed in the literature "we Germans" had produced, all the while sneering with rage and contempt at the depravity of the French—referring

to Emile Zola's *Nana*, for example, as an "obscene monstrosity of filth.
. . . With the French, their whole literature dances endless circles around the
soiled couch of the whore."[6]

Yet just as "Tancred" was taking fencing lessons to prove himself a vital
link in the tradition of Teutonic knighthood, many of Germany's leading intellectuals, including the historian Heinrich von Treitschke, and the
renowned anti-Marxist Eugen Karl Duehring, were stoking the flames of a
backlash whose aim was to rescind the Jewish emancipation in Germany, then
barely a decade old. Already in 1879, the term "anti-Semitism" had been
coined by Wilhelm Marr, a gutter journalist, reputedly of Jewish origin, who
believed that "the Semitic race" was trying to enslave Germany. But
Duehring's exposition of the Jewish threat, published two years later under
the title *The Jewish Problem as a Problem of Race, Morals, and Culture*, out-
stripped any previous anti-Semitic work in its scale and substance. Seeking to
establish that the perniciousness of the Jews was a function of race rather than
religion, Duehring's book denied the efficacy of the wholesale baptism of
German Jews in recent decades, assailing a vast array of Jewish contributions
to civilization as bearing characteristics intrinsic to the Jews as a racial group.
And since Jewish race was indelible, the only recourse was an immediate ban
on intermarriage with Jews and their expulsion from public office.

Herzl read Duehring in 1882, the year after his initiation into the Albia
dueling fraternity, and he reacted with incredulity. As he noted in his journal, "When so well-schooled and penetrating a mind, enriched by scholarly
and truly encyclopedic knowledge such as Duehring undeniably possesses,
can write this sort of stuff, what, then, can one expect from the illiterate
mob?" But, of course, one could expect nothing. Herzl was well aware of the
massacres of Jews that had been taking place across the border in Russia
over the past year, just as he was aware of the revival of the blood libel at
Tiszaeszlar in his native Hungary that same summer, which triggered anti-
Jewish rioting and murder that did not end until the imposition of a state of
emergency. In fact, Germany had been the one place where educated Jews
such as Herzl had believed that such horrors could not take place. Even in
concluding that Duehring "ought to have his teeth bashed in," Herzl continued to believe that anti-Semitism was alien to the true spirit of Germany.
"I was all the more outraged," he wrote, "because this book is written in so
excellent and pure a German."[7]

Despite Jewish hopes that Germany would be different, it rapidly tran-
spired that the penetration of anti-Semitism deep into the heart of the
German nationalism was no passing tremor. By the following year, the
League of German Students in Vienna, of which Albia had become a mem-
ber organization, conducted a memorial for the arch-anti-Semite Richard
Wagner, in which a North German flag was unfurled and Albia's represen-

tative delivered a pro-German and anti-Semitic tirade so fulsome that the police intervened. Herzl tendered his resignation—the only one of the fraternity's Jewish members to do so—and Albia retaliated by resolving it would accept no more Jews. Yet Herzl still felt compelled to inform the fraternity brother assigned to collect his cap and red-black-gold sash that "the decision to resign has not been an easy one."[8]

Herzl was then twenty-three years old, and for many years thereafter, he attempted to suppress the pain and humiliation of having been drummed out of his position as a student spokesman for the higher mission of German national ideals. On May 16, 1884, he became a doctor of law, and after a year as a law intern, he turned his back entirely on the world of politics. He now submerged himself entirely in a career as a playwright and journalist, through which, it seems, he hoped to redeem his wounded German honor by gaining admission to Vienna's "aristocracy" of German writers. By 1887, Herzl was beginning to gain some acclaim for his essays in the Viennese press and a Leipzig publisher brought out his first book, *News from Venus*, containing eighteen sketches on love. ("True love," he wrote, "pure love free of vanity, selfishness, reservations, free of all petty, narrow-minded and base motives does not exist.") The following year, the Imperial Burgtheater produced the first of Herzl's plays, and in October 1891, he was appointed by the Viennese *Neue Freie Presse,* the leading newspaper in Austria, to be its Paris correspondent. In the French capital, Herzl attended sessions of Parliament at the Palais Bourbon and made the acquaintance of the leading political and creative figures of his age, from Clemenceau to Rodin to that psychologist of civilization, Max Nordau, who achieved instant notoriety across Europe in 1892 with his monster best-seller, *Degeneracy.*[9]

But as surely as Herzl rose in stature, Europe continued undaunted on its course. In Paris, the birthplace of the ideal of a perfect political egalitarianism and of Jewish emancipation, Herzl's attention was drawn time and again to the hatred directed toward the small community of French Jews. In Vienna, too, where he had made his home, the anti-Semitic demagogue Karl Lueger was succeeding in strengthening his political hold on the city from one election to the next. Still, Herzl, like virtually every German Jew he had ever known, clung tenaciously to the promise of Jewish citizenship in an enlightened Europe.

Theodor Herzl was born on May 2, 1860, in a German-speaking home in Budapest, against the backdrop of the titanic struggle between French revolutionary ideals and the old Catholic order of Central Europe, of which the

Austrian emperor, linchpin of the Holy Alliance with Prussia and Russia, had been the protector. During Herzl's youth, however, this struggle appeared to be in its final throes, with the outcome clearly determined in favor of the enlighteners. In 1866, the Prussian chancellor Otto von Bismarck had turned on Austria, pursuing a brief war that ended with the expulsion of Austrian troops from the heavily Catholic German states south of the Main, as well as from northern Italy. The myth of Austria as the political savior of the Roman Church was demolished instantly. The papal secretary of state spoke of "*Casca il mondo*"—the end of the world—and in fact, Catholic influence in Europe never really recovered. The following year, a new constitutional monarchy was installed in Austria under the pro-Liberal prime ministership of Prince Charles Auersperg, which removed the schools from the direct control of the church, placed the appointment and dismissal of priests in the hands of the state, and for the first time granted citizenship to Jews. By 1871, Bismarck had won Prussian control over the Catholic German states, declaring a new German empire under a constitution that extended citizenship to minorities, including Jews, and set the stage for a protracted campaign to subordinate the church to the German state. The Vatican, for its part, responded to these breathtaking losses by declaring Pope Pius IX "infallible," thereby assuring a wide readership for his *Syllabus of Errors,* which condemned "progress, liberalism, and modern civilization," as well as political toleration of other religions.

The German Jews of Central Europe did not have to think too hard in order to recognize which side in this struggle offered them a more tolerable existence. Herzl's father Jakob had left home in Serbia at the age of seventeen without a penny to his name. But thanks to the removal of business restrictions on Jews and the economic liberalizations of the 1860s, he had made a fortune in contracting and finance and had been able to marry into an assimilated German-Jewish family that had made an even larger fortune in textile manufacture. Such Jewish families were of course proud German Liberals, defending the new Austrian order against the reactionary interests of the traditional monopolistic guilds and the church. Like other affluent Jewish mothers in Budapest, Jeanette Herzl naturally identified Germandom with science and art, as well as with political liberty, and it was German nationality and ideals—as opposed to the surrounding Hungarian-Catholic provincialism—which she enthusiastically sought to inculcate in her children. As Herzl himself later wrote of this period,

> The Jews of German culture, whose youth and early manhood came during the reign of liberal ideas, attached themselves to the German nation with all the ardor of their hearts. They dearly loved their Germanness and rendered devoted

and faithful service to the German people as well as to the idea of civil liberty. In times of strife and suffering they clung closely to the German nation.[10]

This is not to say that Herzl's family abandoned Judaism entirely. Herzl's father, at least, retained a strong Jewish attachment, so that his son did receive a Hebrew name, Binyamin Ze'ev, and four years of elementary education in a Jewish school in Pest. Jakob Herzl took young Theodor to synagogue on Friday nights, and later the Herzl family celebrated their son's bar mitzva as well.[11] But by the time Theodor Herzl was introduced to Judaism, most of the Jews of German Central Europe—both liberal and Orthodox—had been drawn into the effort to create a form of Judaism that would be suited to the political environment of the German emancipation. In this, of course, the Judaism that Herzl knew as a child had in critical respects broken with the Jewish-nationalist Orthodoxy familiar to Herzl's grandfather in Serbia.[12] Since the story of Zionism is to a great extent the story of Herzl's revolt against emancipationist German Judaism, it is worth recalling for a moment what this movement entailed.

The story of emancipationist German Judaism begins in France, with the revolution of 1789. Before this time, the Jews of continental Europe had been considered to be a minority people, much like the other national minorities that existed in every land. The Jews for their part had understood themselves in terms that had remained essentially unchanged since the destruction of the classical Jewish state many centuries before. They referred to themselves as *am israel* ("the people of Israel"), a nation living in *galut* ("exile"), and whose only real homeland was *eretz israel* ("the land of Israel"). A thousand times a year, for over a thousand years, this people had repeated the same canonical petition to God to restore the Jewish people, under Jewish rulership, to independence in its homeland: "Sound a great horn—blast for our freedom, raise the banner to ingather our exiles . . . from the four corners of the earth. . . . May you speedily establish there the throne of David. . . . May our eyes behold your merciful return to Zion."[13]

For generations of Jews who remained part of this endless cycle of supplication, there was no question but that the Jews were what they always had been: A people, albeit one deprived of its land and its kingdom, awaiting its return to Zion.

It was Jean-Jacques Rousseau who set in motion the principles of the great revolution that would sunder the ties binding the peoples of Europe to their past. And in this the Jews were no exception. Rousseau's *On the Social Contract* (1762) advanced the claim that there exists only one legitimate political constitution, universally applicable to all countries, which we may call a "social-contract state": A political regime in which all individuals, regardless of the differences of nature and history that divide them, renounce these differences, so that "all become equal through convention," under a state that obliges all equally on behalf of all; the only catch was that individuals unwilling to accept the new convention of equality are to be disposed of through exile or death.[14] During the giddy days following the French Revolution, this conception of the state was transformed from an abstraction into an operative political principle, whose meaning was that even the Jews would now have the right of full and equal citizenship in France, provided only that they were willing to renounce all other political loyalty. For the first time in their history, the Jews were thus asked to give up not their religion—which was suddenly considered to be a "private" matter—but their nationality, which had overnight become a threat to the integrity of France. As the Comte de Clermont-Tonnere famously declared during the debate over the emancipation of the Jews in the French National Assembly in 1789, "To the Jews as individuals we should grant everything. But to the Jews as a nation—nothing."[15]

In the early going of the revolution, the French sometimes seemed to have chosen the latter option, seeking to implement the new ideal through mob actions that more closely resembled pogroms than liberation.[16] Eventually, it was Napoleon who took the issue in hand, and the result was one of the gaudiest pieces of melodrama in a revolution otherwise so amply provisioned. In 1807, having just completed the conquest of the German states, Napoleon convened a "Sanhedrin"[17] consisting of seventy-one rabbis and notables from France and other parts of his empire, who were to legislate a new Jewish law enabling the Jews to cease being a nation and to become Frenchmen "professing the religion of Moses." Of course, the Sanhedrin was not exactly a free agent. In keeping with Rousseau's model, Napoleon threatened that failure to promulgate appropriate laws would result in the expulsion of the Jews from the French empire.[18] The Sanhedrin hastened to find a way of placating him, and in this it succeeded, affirming that the Jewish religion includes two different kinds of law: Religious decrees of eternal validity and political decrees, which were valid only as long as the Jewry was a nation in its own land. Relying on this theory, it determined that the latter were "no longer applicable." Henceforth, all doctrines of Judaism would be subordinated to the civil law of the state, so that Jews might be "in no wise separated from the society of men." As for the Jews' traditional identity, the Sanhedrin solemnly decreed that "Israel no longer forms a nation." The Jews would now "be one with the great family of the [French] state."[19]

When this bargain was struck with Napoleon, the number of Jews in France was in the tens of thousands, and had the revolution stopped at the French frontier, the Sanhedrin's renunciation of the expired Jewish nationality in favor of the perhaps overly vital French one might have had little effect on the rest of Jewry. But by 1806, various of the German states had been reconstituted as puppet regimes closely aligned with France, and much of Prussia was under occupation. The revolution had become a German affair, and many Central European intellectuals seized upon its doctrines as though these were original and fundamental expressions of the German spirit. In this they followed Immanuel Kant, who had rendered Rousseau's often contradictory political principles rigorous and "pure" and had crowned them as the product of "science." It was Kant who had demonstrated that unaided "pure reason" inevitably points to a single correct morality (action devoid of self-interested motives), a single correct religion (reason itself), and a single correct political system (the social-contract state). And it was Kant who proved that since there is only one legitimate constitution, all states must ultimately merge into one in a universal social-contract state "which would continue to grow until it embraced all the peoples of the earth."[20] (Few in Germany seem to have noticed that Kant's "scientific" premises, according to which there exists only one correct answer to every question of politics, morality, and religion, were indistinguishable from the approach of Robespierre, which had made of France a terror state.)

It was in the German-speaking cities of Central Europe that the social-contract state and the Jewish "emancipation" was first dangled before the eyes of hundreds of thousands of Jews, bringing a fleeting French-sponsored removal of all Jewish debilities, which were for the most part reimposed by the German states once these were freed of the French yoke in 1815. But the effects of this abortive emancipation were nonetheless far-reaching. Germany's de-emancipated Jews became ardent advocates of the theory of the social-contract state, which held the key to attaining German citizenship, with the result that nowhere in the West was the repudiation by the Jews of their status as a people so extreme as in German Central Europe. These circumstances were the impetus for the German-Jewish "Reform," which overtly sought to reassemble Jewish belief on an explicitly anti-national—what would by the end of the century be called "anti-Zionist"—basis such as would render it tolerable to the social-contract state they hoped to see arise in Germany. Thus, the leading reformer Abraham Geiger declared that "over and above everything else, I am a human being; it is only second to that, or in constant relation to it, that I am a German, and then a Jew."[21] And the German-Jewish reform leader Leopold Stein likewise pronounced:

> We know but one fatherland, that in which we live. We cannot pray "mayst thou take us back in joy to our land," as though our present home were strange to us and our true home lay a thousand miles distant. . . . We have begun to recognize that our dispersion was a blessing, that God has scattered us over the earth as "the seed of truth."[22]

Nor was the new anti-nationalism restricted only to the German Reform movement. Traditional Judaism, too, was revamped by German Jewry into a new "modern Orthodoxy," whose great exponent, Samson Raphael Hirsch, was able to devise a theory by which Judaism was only a "spiritual vocation," which commands that Jews serve only the state in which they live and "forbids" them from political action on behalf of Jewish restoration in Palestine.[23]

But the principle of "to the Jews as individuals everything," in exchange for which most German Jews abandoned the dream of Jewish national restoration, proved to be a pledge not easily redeemed. In the German states and Austria, as well as further east, political equality for the Jews was implemented only fitfully, suffering repeal and modification time and again; and even full equality, once it was granted, brought a chilling wave of anti-Semitism in its wake, robbing the "liberation" of much of its value. These defeats, none of which had seemed possible when the revolutionary Sanhedrin had made its deal with Napoleon, were accompanied by pogroms and persecutions not only in Russia and Romania, but even within the sphere of influence of the supposedly enlightened West. In 1840, the representative of the French government in Damascus was instrumental in inducing the government of Mohammed Ali to imprison and torture Jewish communal leaders on suspicion they had murdered a Franciscan monk and used his blood for ritual purposes. And in 1858, a six-year-old Jewish child named Edgardo Mortara was seized in Bologna, Italy, by papal officers to be raised a Catholic after a Christian nurse had secretly baptized him during an illness. Both incidents aroused storms of publicity and protest throughout the West. Those Jewish prisoners in Damascus who did not die under torture were ultimately released; but Edgardo Mortara was never returned to his parents.[24]

Among the Jews of France, Germany, and Britain, these outrages led to the belief that emancipation would not come about unless the Jews worked on its behalf. In 1860, in the wake of the Mortara affair, the Alliance Israélite Universelle was founded in Paris as the first Jewish association devoted to the pursuit of equal rights for Jews everywhere; similar missions were adopted by the Anglo-Jewish Association in London in 1871, the Israelitische Allianz in Vienna in 1873, the German Centralverein in Berlin in 1893, and the American Jewish Committee in New York in 1906.[25] Founded by the wealthiest and most powerful Jews in their respective communities, these organizations were composed of individuals who were themselves the great success stories of the emancipation. It is thus no surprise that far from signaling a realistic assessment of the all-too-evident weaknesses of French revolutionary ideals, these groups represented precisely the opposite: the transformation of the theory of the social-contract state and perfect emancipation into a Jewish political dogma, its feasibility and desirability taken to be axiomatic. It was in this manner, too, that the renunciation of

Jewish nationhood and of the idea of a restored Jewish state had by the end of the nineteenth century come to be the "official" point of view of the established Jewish leadership in every Western country.

The more deeply entrenched this political opposition to Jewish nationalism became, the more elaborate and sophisticated were the philosophical arguments mustered in refuting the very idea of a Jewish state. Of these, none better illuminates the meaning of emancipationist German Judaism than the thought of the eminent German-Jewish philosopher Hermann Cohen. Awarded a full professorship at the University of Marburg in 1876, Cohen was the first Jew to hold such a position, so that both by virtue of his appointment and by virtue of his chosen area of expertise—he had by then published a major treatise on Kant, and he was soon to become the principal exponent of what became known as "neo-Kantian" philosophy—he was from the outset of his career a symbol of the German emancipation. And, indeed, his great work *Religion of Reason* stands as the most systematic framework for Jewish anti-Zionist thought ever constructed.

To the unaided eye, Hermann Cohen's teachings seem hardly distinguishable from those of Kant himself: He preached the universality of pure reason and its identity as the one true religion; the existence of a single true morality based on the eradication of self-interest; and, of course, the ultimate triumph of the world social-contract state. But there nonetheless remained a few important challenges to be met at Marburg. One was to redefine the elusive connection between all this "pure reason," which may well have seemed somewhat vapid after Beethoven and Bismarck, and the overriding good of the German state. This he managed to pull off through deft use of the philosophic category of *Deutschtum* ("Germanism"), which he believed consisted of those cultural dispositions that were the heritage of all Germans. This German heritage, as Cohen was always anxious to explain, turned out to be predicated on Kant: "Every German must know his Schiller and his Goethe and carry them in his heart and soul with intimacy and love. Yet this intimacy presupposes that he has won a rudimentary understanding of his Kant as well." For this reason, *Deutschtum* was a national spirit more profoundly related to pure reason than that of any other people. And this, Cohen reasoned, was why the equality of rights granted Jews in Germany was rooted in a moral understanding more profound than anywhere else. It was also the reason that hatred is not a passion characteristic of the German soul.[26]

Having thus established the benevolent essence of Germanism, Cohen turned his attentions to placing Judaism, too, on permanent, universalistic foundations such as would forever close the door on any regression in the direction of Jewish nationalism. The result was his massive *Religion of Reason*, which was fundamentally an effort to reconcile the traditional Jewish sources with Kant's imperatives to pursue "pure" universalism in both personal and national life. Like Kant, Cohen viewed the only "pure" moral act as one of perfect self-renunciation. But whereas Kant was uncertain whether there could ever be a truly moral act, given the complexities of human motivation,[27] Cohen believed he had solved the problem. The hallmark of pure selflessness, Cohen argued, is *suffering*. In suffering on behalf of another—and *only* in suffering on behalf of another—does the individual vanquish his self-interested ego and attain true unity with his neighbor. And only by suffering undertaken on behalf of all men, does the individual attain unity with all mankind—and the ideal of perfect morality:

> The value of human life lies not in happiness, but rather in suffering. . . . The humble man bears the whole of mankind in his heart. Therefore he can become the representative of suffering, because he can fulfill his moral existence only in suffering. . . . The humble man is therefore the true sufferer, he is the representative of suffering. Only he is able to undergo suffering in its moral essence. . . . The ideal man suffers.

Basing himself on the well-known passage in Isaiah, Cohen then associates his "ideal man" with the Messiah, God's "suffering servant," who lives out the ideal on earth by taking the earthly suffering of all men upon his own shoulders.[28]

Thus far, Cohen merely elaborates upon Christian teaching—conceding en passant that Jesus was in fact "the Messiah of mankind." But then his views take a sudden, remarkable turn, in which it is not Jesus alone but the entire Jewish people that is the vicarious sufferer for humanity: "But Jewish history, considered as history, that is, insofar as it exhibits moral ideas, is a continuous chain of human, of national, suffering. These servants of the Lord have always been despised and pierced through, cut off from the land of life. . . . The messianic people suffers vicariously for mankind."[29]

For Cohen, it is therefore the very essence of the Jews that they suffer. Consequently, the very core of Judaism is the rejection of all power such as might ameliorate the worldly condition of the Jews. In this view, the early Jewish state, the kingdom of David, was no ideal but rather "only a short episode," an "anomaly" that "meant little" to the Jews since their "messianic idea" had in any case determined that they would be the first people to exist in the world without a state.[30] Even the word "people" (as in "the people of Israel") is too muscular for Cohen, and he insists that the Jews strive to dissolve even the degree of worldly strength implicit in this term, reaching their ideal form as a *former* people, which he refers to as "the remnant of Israel."[31]

Where does all this lead? To Cohen, it is the beginning of the millennium. Once the Jews have been dispersed, powerless and stateless, as a "divine dew"[32] among the nations, demanding nothing whatsoever for themselves, they are in a position to reach the pinnacle of their "mission" on earth—teaching the other nations to suffer as the Jews do. Eventually, "through this widening of the national limits of suffering, which is demanded by humanitarian ethics,"[33] all the peoples of the earth will have adopted Cohen's Judaism. All of them will have ceased to make demands for themselves, all states will cease to exist just as ancient Israel did, and all conflict will come to an end.

Hermann Cohen was by no means alone in these arguments. His philosophy was only the apex of a century of emancipationist Jewish thought whose conclusions never strayed far from his. And German Jewry of the nineteenth and early twentieth century swallowed these paeans to the Jewish people's self-negation and powerlessness with an enthusiasm that for us, after the Holocaust, is impossible to imagine. Yet within context, it only made sense. For in the face of the social-contract state, whose ideology demanded the Jews' absolute and exclusive political identification, the plain meaning of the words "Next Year in Jerusalem"—the climax of the traditional Passover and Yom Kippur liturgies—simply bordered on subversion. An insatiable hunger was created for an ideology that could reinterpret "Jerusalem," and the Temple Mount at its heart whose name is Zion, into "symbols" of what the Jews might achieve as pure and unblemished devotees of Germany.

It was this desire of much of German Jewry to erase all past memories of the fact that the Jews had once been a people that formed the intellectual soil on which Theodor Herzl became Judaism's greatest counterrevolutionary.

———————

Herzl's college encounter with Eugen Duehring, and his resignation under anti-Semitic duress from Albia the following year, were unassimilable blows. And it hardly seems coincidental that he retreated into a career where the success of his efforts to render faithful service to the German people could henceforth be determined by German Jews such as the publishers of the *Neue Freie Presse*. With their support, Herzl became as celebrated a journalist as German-speaking Europe produced—so celebrated, in fact, that the Conservative government of Austria, which had come to power during Herzl's college years, considered him the leading candidate to edit a new national daily more sympathetic to its policies. But even amid Vienna's spectacularly successful Jewish literati, the cultural undertow was eventually to force itself upon him with an intensity that made the bitterness of his college years appear a child's game.

Herzl's decisive confrontation with Europe's reaction to the emancipation began in 1891, when, at age thirty-one, he accepted the post of correspondent for the *Neue Freie Presse* in Paris. France had been the birthplace of emancipation, and yet here, too, the rise of fanatical anti-Semitism was palpable. In 1886, five years after publication of Eugen Duehring's book, Edouard Drumont published *La France Juive*, a two-volume epic that not only blamed every catastrophe since the revolution on France's minuscule Jewish population but also claimed that there were in France no fewer than half a million crypto-Jews, an invisible Jewish empire within the state, of whom Drumont did not blush to name over 3,000 figures, past and present. *La France Juive* became an instant best-seller, printed in more than two hundred editions. In 1892, Drumont established a weekly called *La Libre Parole,* which succeeded within its first year in accusing Jewish officers in the French military of inclining toward betrayal of military secrets—a libel that led to a saber duel between a young Jewish officer named Armand Mayer and one of Drumont's associates. The thirty-four-year-old Mayer had a crippled right arm and could barely lift his sword but nevertheless chose to accept the challenge rather than be accused of Jewish cowardice. He was cut down within moments.[34]

Herzl must have written his report of the funeral procession with particular grief. It had only been a matter of months since his own closest friend, Oswald Boxer, had died of yellow fever in Rio de Janeiro while on a mission for one of the Berlin Jewish-relief agencies to explore the possibility of resettlement in Brazil of Jewish refugees from Russia. Nor was the connection between the two deaths so difficult to make. Herzl knew from the comportment of educated young men such as Mayer and Boxer that the Jewish people was capable of tremendous acts of courage and loyalty. "Our character . . . had in earlier times been proud and magnificent," he told a fellow journalist. "After all, we were men who knew how to face war and to defend the state."[35] Yet even once freed from the ghetto, these brilliant and courageous Jews continued to dissipate, lost not in great projects of construction but rather in acts of defensive desperation. "There is a Jewish question," he wrote in April 1893, "there can be no doubt about that. Those who deny it are wrong."[36]

The blow that finally brought Herzl to this recognition was another crusade of *La Libre Parole,* which, much to the horror of its opponents, actually succeeded in dredging up a fraud of national proportions initiated by a real conspiracy of Jewish charlatans, who had been milking the public for funds to support the failed project to build a canal across Panama. The fact that the project had capsized had been covered up by means of a vast web of bribes dispensed to journalists and political officials, and by mid-1893 the courts had tried, and in some cases convicted, a number of national figures. Of the original Jewish crooks, one had committed suicide and the other had skipped the country, and there were plenty of non-Jews implicated in the scandal. But the French public had by then been whipped into hysterical fear of Jewish conspiracies, and it was prepared to swallow anything even vaguely matching this description.[37] And this Drumont's paper was happily able to provide.

In the meantime, Herzl's mind continued to pace between the constricting walls of his "Jewish problem," searching every crevice for a way out. In increasing agitation, he pondered the possible salutary effects of seeking a mass conversion of the Jews to Christianity or socialism or of a campaign of pistol duels with the anti-Semites by which the Jews might regain their honor.[38] But these were dead ends, and Herzl knew it. On October 21, 1894, he began furious work on a play, *The Ghetto,* in which he attempted to frame the question in as forthright a manner as he could muster. As he wrote to his college acquaintance, the playwright Arthur Schnitzler: "I have no intention of mounting either a defense or a rescue action on behalf of the Jews. . . . What I do want is to speak out—from the heart, and from the gut."[39]

And indeed he did. The protagonist of *The Ghetto* is an idealistic Viennese lawyer, Dr. Jacob Samuel, who bears a more than incidental resemblance to Herzl himself. Despite years of degrading attempts to adopt gentile mores, Jacob Samuel nevertheless finds himself accused by a German aristocrat of the archetypal "Jewish" crime of having conspired—through inciting the workers and manipulating the stock market—to profit from the ruin of the aristocrat's mining concern. The lawyer is told that he is "Jewish rabble" and accused of cowardice, and in response, he slaps his tormentor in the face. A duel ensues in which Samuel is shot dead, and with his dying breath, he calls upon emancipated Jews to recognize their subservience to gentile prejudice—the invisible ghetto wall behind which they still live. "Jews, my brothers," he cries. "They won't let you live until you know how to die. . . . Out! . . . Out of the ghetto!" Even more remarkable is a speech given by Wasserstein, the coarse, Yiddish-speaking, stock-market Jew, who at first glance seems to embody everything that is contemptible in the Jews of the historical ghetto. Yet it is Wasserstein who reacts to Jacob Samuel's striking the German noble with an admiration that reflected the one unclouded wish in Herzl's heart:

> You do not know how much that thrilled me. A Jew striking back hard, that is great, that is beautiful. He reminded me of the Maccabees. We weren't always such dishrags. Sometimes I think that I too lived to see this . . . but I don't know when it was. It must have been a long time ago. Or when one dreams of something—yes, that's what it was. I dreamed that we too were men who don't allow themselves to be stepped on.[40]

Herzl wrote his first draft of *The Ghetto* in a white heat, completing the entire play in nineteen days.[41] Yet it had not even been completed before it had been rendered obsolete by events. On November 1, eleven days after Herzl had begun work on the play, *La Libre Parole,* under a banner headline screaming "Treason," reported the arrest of a Jewish artillery officer, Alfred Dreyfus, on charges of spying for Germany. The trial opened on December 19, and three days later, after sessions closed to the public and the press, the court reached a unanimous verdict of guilt. But Herzl, like Max Nordau and the Jewish journalist Bernard Lazare, found it difficult to accept that this Jewish officer, a man of means who had chosen military service for no other reason than to be honored by the French state, should voluntarily choose the greatest of dishonors by spying for Germany. It was, he later wrote, "psychologically impossible."[42] Less than a week after the conviction, Herzl's published reports in the *Neue Freie Press* began to reflect his suspicions. On December 27, he reported the rumor that Dreyfus had told a sergeant of the guard, "I am being persecuted because I am a Jew." His January 5 report on the degradation ceremony carried repeated premonitions of Dreyfus's innocence:

> Four soldiers brought him [i.e., Dreyfus] before the general, who declared: "Alfred Dreyfus, you are unworthy to bear arms. I hereby degrade you in the name of the French people. Let the judgment be executed." Thereupon Dreyfus raised his right hand and shouted: "I swear and declare that you are degrading an innocent man. Vive la France." With that, the drums began to roll, and the military bailiff tore the already loosened buttons and straps from the uniform. Dreyfus maintained his proud bearing. . . . Now began the ordeal of filing past the troops. Dreyfus marched like a man convinced of his innocence. As he passed a group of officers who yelled "Judas! Traitor!" he shouted back: "I forbid you to insult me."[43]

His proud bearing? Like a man convinced of his innocence? Herzl was in possession of no shred of concrete evidence to support the contention that the Jewish officer was innocent. But he knew Dreyfus from his own play— *The Ghetto*. Dreyfus was no "dishrag." He was Dr. Jacob Samuel, the "son of the Maccabees" who "would not allow himself to be stepped on." He was the Jew "striking back hard"—with all the strength he had—against those who persecuted him, even though his end was inevitable destruction. In his fictional version, Herzl had made Wasserstein the Jew say that this sight was "thrilling," and "great," and "beautiful." But as Herzl sat there, listening to the throat of the mob, incited by the tide of anti-Semitic reports in the press and bellowing "À mort! À mort les juifs!"[44] his furious little fabrication was beaten to pieces before his eyes. This was no play but the real-life version, in which a lonely Jew stood pitifully before an entire nation seeking his annihilation. This was not beautiful. This was catastrophe.

By the time Herzl had witnessed Dreyfus's degradation, he had already sent out the final version of his play, with Wasserstein's "son of the Maccabees" speech eliminated. It was rejected everywhere, not least because its message—that Europe's Jews could somehow be saved by self-assertion and chutzpa—was still a monstrous piece of self-deception. On April 2, Herzl received the final, and most painful, rejection of all. He was present in Vienna to witness the triumph of the anti-Semite Karl Lueger, who was given a resounding victory in elections for city council by an expanded electorate. Missing an absolute majority by a handful of votes, Lueger was denied the appointment as mayor by the emperor, but this standoff was to prove temporary. Herzl, like other German Jews, began to feel the crushing weight of despair as it became clear that emancipation had been a fraud. "Suddenly they were called parasites," Herzl wrote of this time—and most especially about himself. "All at once they were no longer Germans but Jews. It was a transformation without any transition, abrupt like an awakening from a dream. . . . They walked about in a daze. So everything up to then had been a mistake, the whole pattern of their life had been based on a cardinal error, all their sacrifices had been in vain and all their loyalty futile."[45]

Herzl, who had so recently informed his editor at the *Neue Freie Presse* that "religion is indispensable for the weak,"[46] now stumbled into a synagogue for the first time since his childhood—"solemn and moving," he scratched into his notebook afterward. "Much of it reminded me of my youth." In darkness, Herzl began taking notes for a new novel, unlike any other he had ever contemplated. For in this, the great drama, the Jewish hero no longer strikes back hard at a society that can only defeat him. Instead, he turns his back on Europe, setting sail—so Herzl wrote—"to found the Promised land." And when this new hero learns of the death of a close friend, as Herzl himself had twice in his young life, he no longer searches the event for proof that the Jew had, like Jacob Samuel, succeeded in dying "nobly." "Fool, scoundrel, wretch," he cried out, finally admitting the sense of bitterest loss that had always been there, the loss of a brother. "A life was lost that should have been ours."[47]

Ours—.

———

Herzl was not, of course, the first Jew to set out to found the promised land. The story of Jewish attempts to return to Israel are as old as the exile itself. By the end of the sixteenth century, thousands of Jews expelled from Spain had settled in Safed, Tiberias, Hebron, and Jerusalem, forming the kernel of a Jewish community that, despite periods of great hardship, enjoyed periodic reinforcement from Jews from Europe and the corners of the Ottoman empire eager to contribute to the restoration. Among these were students of Israel Ba'al Shem, founder of the mystical revival movement known as Hasidism, who immigrated to Palestine in 1777. And there were groups led by students of the great Lithuanian leader Elijah of Vilna, called the Gaon, beginning in 1812. Today we would call some of these groups nationalist, and they even corresponded with millenarian groups in England in an effort to arouse interest among the powers in a Jewish restoration in Palestine.[48] After the revelation of French complicity in the Damascus blood libel in 1840, there were also calls from rabbinic figures such as R. Yehuda Bibas of Corfu and R. Judah Alkalai in Serbia—leader of the synagogue in Semlin to which Herzl's grandfather belonged—for the Jews to learn to use arms and prepare to secure their national independence as the Greeks had done a few years earlier.[49]

All these efforts were perhaps doomed to fail in attracting large-scale Jewish activism if only because their efforts were not backed by tangible political and financial abilities. Somewhat more substantive were the efforts at Jewish settlement undertaken in the 1860s in the aftermath of the Mortara outrage, whose immediate result was the publication—this time in enlightened Germany—of Rabbi Tzvi Hirsch Kalisher's *The Demand for Zion* (1862) and of the socialist theorist Moses Hess's *Rome and Jerusalem* (1862) advancing the idea of a Jewish independence in Palestine. These writers came into contact with the alliance and other Jewish emancipationist organizations that had little interest in talk of a Jewish state but were nevertheless willing to support Palestine settlement as a means of providing humanitarian assistance to Jews in distress from the East.[50] This early collaboration between what would later be called Zionist and anti-Zionist Jewish organizations in the effort to create settlements of refuge in Palestine was only marginally successful. Until the beginning of the 1880s, the Jewish population in Palestine increased by 15,000 at most.

It was not until the pogroms in Russia in the wake of the assassination of Czar Alexander II in 1881 that the first stable Zionist organizations in Europe were established. The violence lasted eight months, spreading across the regions of permissible Jewish settlement from Odessa to Warsaw, an area populated by 7 million Jews, most of them living in poverty. Among those who responded to the bloodletting, pillage, and rape as a watershed was Leon Pinsker, a lifelong advocate of Jewish emancipation within a liberalized Russian state. The following year, Pinsker wrote *Auto-Emancipation: An Appeal to His People by a Russian Jew*, a Jewish nationalist pamphlet proposing the reconstruction of an independent Jewish state and explicitly renouncing emancipation as a solution for Jews.[51] Pinsker's words served as a rallying cry for the local Jewish nationalist groups that now sprang up like mushrooms across Russia and beyond, calling themselves Hovevei Zion ("Lovers of Zion") and swearing to work for Jewish restoration in Israel. Pinsker even reached the University of Vienna, where Herzl was studying, establishing a Hovevei Zion club together with the Viennese Hebrew revivalist Peretz Smolenskin. Called Kadimah, a Hebrew word meaning both "forward" and "eastward," and built around a nucleus of Russian expatriates, it eventually grew into a saber-wielding Jewish fraternity that became sufficiently feared to be explicitly disqualified from dueling against members of German fraternities.[52] In a university of only five thousand students, it is hardly plausible that Herzl never heard of the Jewish nationalist organization. It is more likely that he was aware of it but considered it another regrettable echo of the ghetto.

Yet Hovevei Zion, the most substantial Jewish-national movement since the beginning of the emancipation, was nevertheless all but strangled at birth by its Russian oppressors. Unable to organize or raise funds openly because of Czarist surveillance, it was forced to hold its first conference in 1884 in Kattowitz, across the frontier in Germany. There, again for fear of the Okhrana (the Russian secret police), it did not declare itself a national movement but rather masqueraded as a philanthropic organization called the "Society for Supporting Jewish Agriculturists in Syria and Palestine." Leo Pinsker was elected president of the new organization, but not before being briefed not to refer to the Jewish state in his speech, lest the Czar take offense.[53] These conditions meant that even once its Odessa branch succeeded in becoming legal in 1890, Hovevei Zion was dependent on the financial support of the Jewish Colonization Association (ICA) of Baron Maurice de Hirsch in Paris, an organization loosely associated with the alliance and devoted to the philanthropic work of resettling Eastern Jews as a matter of relief—not only in Palestine but in Argentina, and later on in Brazil, Canada, the United States, Turkey, and Cyprus.[54] In the face of rising anti-Semitism, the wealthy Jews of Paris were no longer as willing as they had once been to tolerate agitation for a Jewish state. Thus, the fears of their antinationalist donors combined with the threat of the secret police to ensure that Hovevei Zion became, in practice, much like what it pretended to be—an organization concerned with raising money to support a handful of small agricultural settlements in Palestine.

Was this a political movement or just an illusion? Surely it was both. By 1895, Hovevei Zion in Europe had no more than 10,000 members, and it had lost its leading figure with Pinsker's death four years earlier. In Palestine, Hovevei Zion had contributed to the creation of nine tiny settlements, with a total population of about four thousand, modeled after their own image: outwardly religious, without any real economic foundation or capacity for self-defense, without even having been granted the real protection of the Turkish authorities. It was an achievement, to be sure, but a very small one, whose relationship to the Jewish state was uncertain at best.[55]

Back in Paris two months after the anti-Semitic victory in Vienna, Herzl opened a notebook, in which he inscribed the words: "Of the Jewish Cause." "For some time past," he began, "I have been occupied with a work of infinite grandeur. At the moment I do not know whether I shall carry it through. It looks like a mighty dream. But for days and weeks it has possessed me." Into this notebook he began to pour all that had been pent up within, all that had grieved him and called him to glory. Filling hundreds of pages in a matter of weeks, he wrestled to describe to himself the contents of this mighty dream—a dream far surpassing anything he had ever been able to write as a son of Germany.

Herzl was thirty-five years old, his political hand was completely untried. But he had spent four years in Paris, an observer in the center of one of the world's great politics. "I saw how the world was run," he wrote to himself.[56] And as the weeks progressed, he ceased to think of a novel but contemplated instead the great deed itself, the construction of a Jewish state in reality. Haltingly at first, he began to search for possible allies, writing to the French banking baron Maurice de Hirsch, who had been pouring vast sums into creating agricultural colonies in Argentina for the resettlement of Jewish refugees from the East. "I should like . . . to have a discussion with you about Jewish political matters," he wrote, "a discussion that may have an effect on times that neither you nor I will live to see." On June 2, 1895, he arrived at the baron's mansion with a ream of scribbled notes, almost comically attempting to run through the arguments that rushed forth from his mind: "Throughout two thousand years of our dispersion we have been without unified political leadership"; "there has been no one to train us to become real men"; "new generations will arise whom we must educate for our purposes"; "the principle of philanthropy . . . I consider completely erroneous. You are breeding beggars"; the Jews "must be made strong as for war, eager to work, and virtuous"; to the German kaiser, the Jews must say: "Let our people go. We are strangers here. We are not permitted to assimilate with the people, nor are we able to do so. Let us go."[57]

Hirsch allowed him to speak at length without interrupting, but when Herzl began to propose means for fostering Jewish ambition, creativity, valor, and the desire to work toward greatness—all preliminaries, as he thought, to the great dream of the state itself—Hirsch found himself forced to cut him off: "No, no, no!" he responded.

> "All our misfortune comes from the fact that the Jews want to climb too high. We have too many intellectuals. My intention is to keep the Jews from pushing ahead. They should not make such great strides. All Jew-hatred comes from this. . . . After a few good years [in Argentina] I could show the world that the Jews make good farmers after all. As a result of this, maybe they will be allowed to till the soil in Russia as well."[58]

At this, Herzl came to a dead halt. He was as yet no diplomat, and pride prevented him from proceeding where such a void existed between his premises and those of his interlocutor. Again, for the thousandth time in his life, Herzl heard the accursed theory that the Jews should not gain in strength in this world but that they should rather *withdraw* from it. They should desist from their achievements in the arts, sciences, and professions so as not to inspire "Jew-hatred." Instead, they should become farmers. He stood to leave.

"But you have such fantastic ideas," said Hirsch.

"You don't know what the fantastic is," Herzl retorted.[59]

Back in his room, Herzl poured out page after page of elaboration, continuing his argument with the phantom of the baron in a letter. It is an incredible document, beginning with his recognition that his argument with the baron was that of the Jewish *mind*, struggling to prevail over a conception of life that began and ended with the *material*. "You are the big Jew of money," he wrote impetuously, but with deadly aim. "I am the Jew of the spirit." He argued that his pen and the ideas that it could create represented true power. Even if he were unable to convince the wealthy, it was the ideas themselves—expressed not in farms and funding but in newspapers and books, speech and song—that would ultimately unlock the faith and strength latent in the Jewish people. Had he been able to reach the end of his remarks, he continued,

> I would have had to tell you about the flag. . . . And at that point you would have waxed sarcastic: A flag? A flag is nothing more than a rag on a stick. No sir, a flag is more than that. With a flag you can lead people where you want to, even into the promised land. They will live and die for a flag. It is, in fact, the only thing for which the masses are prepared to die. . . .
>
> Believe me, policy for an entire people—especially one scattered all over the globe—can be made only with lofty imponderables. Do you know what the German empire was made of? Dreams, songs, fantasies, and black-red-gold ribbons. And this in short time. All Bismarck did was to shake the tree planted by the dreamers.
>
> You don't have any use for the imponderables? What, then, is religion? Just think what the Jews have suffered over the past two thousand years for the sake of this fantasy of theirs. Yes, it is a fantasy that holds people in its grip. He who has no use for it may be an excellent, worthy, and sober-minded person, even a philanthropist on a large scale—but he will never be a leader of men, and no trace of him will remain.[60]

Over the course of the summer, Herzl wrote to Albert von Rothschild, head of the Viennese branch of the great Jewish banking family, and also to Bismarck, but neither bothered to respond. He seemed to have better luck with the liberal chief rabbi of Vienna, Moritz Guedemann, who did in fact overcome his aversion for Jewish nationalism long enough to give Herzl a hearing, only to attack Herzl's ideas publicly once they began to make headway.

Only in Paris in November did Herzl succeed in winning his first genuine supporter among the Jews of Western Europe, the celebrated author Max Nordau. It was with Nordau's assistance that Herzl made his way to England, where the idea of Jewish restoration in Palestine had been popularized by George Eliot's novel *Daniel Deronda* (1876) and by the work of the Palestine Exploration Fund, some of whose explorers—all of them Christians—had published proposals for Jewish settlement of the Holy Land. In London, Herzl first made the acquaintance of Jews who were prepared seriously to consider the idea of a Jewish state, among them Israel Zangwill, author of a series of best-selling Jewish novels beginning with his 1892 *Children of the Ghetto,* who was already sympathetic to the idea of Jewish independence; Sir Samuel Montagu, a member of Parliament who told Herzl he felt more a Jew than an Englishman and would settle in Palestine when it became feasible; and Colonel Albert E.M. Goldsmid, a veteran of India and Belfast, who had been raised a Christian but had returned to the Jewish fold and who declared himself prepared to leave his British commission to enter the Jewish armed forces.

Days after his arrival, Herzl made his first public presentation of the idea of the Jewish state at a club of leading English Jews called the Maccabean Society. By this time, he had begun hammering his notes on the Jewish state into a pamphlet for mass distribution, and the stay in London yielded results in this area as well. Asher Myers, editor of the *Jewish Chronicle,* asked him to submit a preview of the pamphlet for publication as an article.

Thus it was that on January 17, 1896, the establishment Jewish newspaper in England published Herzl's "A Solution to the Jewish Question," his first public call for the Jews to recognize that emancipation was a road that led nowhere:

> Everywhere we have sincerely endeavored to merge with the national communities surrounding us and to preserve only the faith of our fathers. . . . In vain are we loyal patriots, in some places even extravagantly so; in vain do we make the same sacrifices of life and property as our fellow-citizens; in vain do we strive to enhance the fame of our native countries in the arts and sciences . . . In our native lands where, after all, we too have lived for centuries, we are decried as aliens, often by people whose ancestors had not yet come to the country when our fathers' sighs were already heard in the country.[61]

In short, emancipation was a pipe dream that offered the Jews of Europe neither physical security nor inner dignity. They had given up their nationhood in exchange for Napoleon's promises, but these had not been delivered upon, and never would be. "We are a people," wrote Herzl, pronouncing the

annulment of the bargain, "One people." And the time had come for this people to recognize its heritage and obligations from its fathers, which had been
so rudely thrust aside: "We shall plant for our children in the same way as our
fathers preserved the tradition for us." The rebuilding that he proposed was
that fantastic idea that had now reached maturity in his mind: "The idea . . . is
an age-old one: The establishment of a Jewish state. . . . Let sovereignty be
granted us over a portion of the earth's surface that is sufficient for our rightful
national requirements. We shall take care of everything else for ourselves."[62]

On February 14, the full-length, German-language edition of Herzl's
manifesto, *The Jewish State,* came off the presses in Vienna. "I was terribly
shaken," he noted in his diary after the bundle was hauled into his room.
"This package of pamphlets constitutes the decision in tangible form."[63] In
the months that followed, Herzl had translations published in English,
French, and other languages, carrying word of his decision to every corner
of Europe. Soon there was hardly a Jew anywhere who did not know of
Herzl's Jewish state—even in Russia, where the police labored to make sure
that nothing made it across the border other than a rumor that salvation
had come to the Jews.

As early as November 1895, Herzl told the chief rabbi of England that he
claimed no novelty for the idea of a Jewish state. It was an idea that dated back
millennia, and Herzl did not claim to be its originator: "I am merely creating
the instrumentality which is to direct the operation."[64] It is perhaps Herzl's
modest claims in this regard that have led to a consistent underestimation of
the theoretical achievement involved in the writing of *The Jewish State**—an
achievement that permitted Herzl to break decisively with those who had writ-

---

*Recent years have seen an increasingly successful effort by Israeli academics to claim that the
name of Herzl's pamphlet is a mistranslation of the German *Der Judenstaat* and that it should
actually be rendered *The State of the Jews.* This semantic change is then used to justify the claim
that Herzl was no supporter of a "Jewish state"—that is, a state that was itself to be in some
fashion intrinsically Jewish. Rather, it is said, he believed only in a "neutral" (i.e., non-Jewish)
state, a majority of whose citizens simply happened to be Jews. This retroactive renaming of
Herzl's work is, however, erroneous. Among the indications that Herzl meant the title of his
pamphlet to refer to a "Jewish state" is the fact that the French and English translations, both
published in 1896, were titled *L'Etat Juif* ("The Jewish State") and *A Jewish State,* respectively;
the Yiddish edition of 1899 was likewise entitled *Die Judische Medineh* ("The Jewish State").
Herzl understood all of these languages well enough to have corrected the titles if he had con-
sidered them to be erroneous. It is true that the Hebrew edition was titled *Medinat Hayehudim*
("The State of the Jews"), but the original Hebrew translation uses the term *Medina Yehudit*
("Jewish State") as interchangeable with the term used in the title. See Yoram Hazony, "Did
Herzl Want a 'Jewish' State?" *Azure* 9 (Spring 2000), pp. 37–73.

ten before him and actually set in motion the events leading to the establishment of an independent Jewish state. It was one thing to declare that the Jews
should be "granted sovereignty over a portion of the earth's surface" and that
they themselves would "take care of everything else." But for this to have been
anything more than hubris, he had to propose a compelling theory as to how a
dispersed people, without a living tradition of national political practice, could
cause the granting of a Jewish sovereignty, or successfully manage the "everything else." What made *The Jewish State* unique in the history of Jewish nationalism, and indeed, in the history of political ideas, was the fact that it
advanced solutions to the various parts of this utterly intractable problem.

Herzl's point of departure, which infused every page of his pamphlet, was
the recognition that the state is not a creation of wood and stone, not a physical thing at all, but an abstraction that exists in the minds of men—a "fantasy"
as he had told Baron de Hirsch, but a fantasy of the kind that was the key to
the way the world works. As Herzl wrote the following year: "The foundation
of a state lies in the will of the people for a state. . . . Territory is only the material basis; the state, even when it possesses territory, is always something abstract."[65] This was something none of his predecessors, and few of his
successors, can be said to have fully grasped. And with this recognition as a
point of departure, Herzl was able to advance a rapid succession of political
theories that permitted him to resolve three apparently insoluble questions
obstructing the creation of a Jewish state: First, what would be the theoretical
justification for constructing a Jewish state in the absence of a population, living on a given territory, which had agreed to the creation of such a state—that
is, in the absence of a "social contract"? Second, how could sufficient political
power be mustered behind the idea of a Jewish state in order to defeat its opponents and cause it to arise in reality? And third, how could the Jews themselves, their ideals and allegiances confused by emancipation, be brought to
believe in the idea of the Jewish state so that they would be prepared to come
to it in body and mind and render it permanent?

In addition to his introductory and concluding remarks, *The Jewish State*
comprised four chapters: The first dealing with the general condition of the
Jews and their need for an independent state, with each of the other three devoted to advancing and elaborating an answer to one of these questions. So far
as I am aware, Herzl's answers constitute the only systematic theory ever advanced to explain how a Jewish state could be made real and permanent. As
such, they continue even in our own time to be critical for understanding
what has been done until now for the sake of this cause, and what has not.

The Guardian State

The first question, that of the right by which Herzl would set out to establish a government that would act on behalf of the Jews, brought him into

direct collision with the theory of the social-contract state popularized by Rousseau's *On the Social Contract,* rendered into German by Kant. According to Rousseau, the state owes its existence and legitimacy to its being the result of a contract among all individuals living in a particular territory. These individuals submit to "the total alienation of each associate, with all his rights, to the whole community," renouncing their peculiar personal advantages and claims and establishing in their place a corporate entity equally responsible for all. It is the perfect formal equality of all residents within the territory of the state that is therefore the cornerstone of the social contract—as Rousseau says, "the basis for the whole system"— while simultaneously constituting the most important "outcome" of the contract: "The fundamental compact . . . substitutes a moral and legitimate equality for whatever physical inequality nature may have placed between men, and though they may be unequal in force or in genius, they all become equal through convention."[66] Thus, the contract takes men with a great variety of natural abilities and cultural differences and transforms them, one and all, into a vast legion of citizens presumed equal before the state.

Remarkably, there is nothing voluntary about the "contract" that brings about this transformation. Indeed, in a passage that Herzl quotes directly in *The Jewish State,* Rousseau argues that "the conditions of this contract are so precisely determined . . . that the slightest alteration would make them null and void. The consequence is that even when they are not expressly stated they are everywhere identical." That is, the social contract is operative universally, determining the legitimacy or illegitimacy of governments everywhere on earth. And it does so without regard for the specific purposes for which a given state has been established, or even for the actual desires of the population in question. Governments that "alter slightly" the prescribed formula are illegitimate and may rightly face popular revolution. Individuals unwilling to accept the premises of the social contract are, in Rousseau's view, to be banished or killed.[67]

Even before turning to Jewish nationalism, Herzl had found this line of argument difficult to swallow, concluding that the state must in reality have a different basis.[68] Certainly in Austria there were few signs that the state drew its legitimacy or granted rights thanks to the agreement, however tacit, of all its subjects. Quite to the contrary, in Herzl's lifetime, it had been obvious that liberalization was the project of the emperor and a portion of the aristocracy, whereas every step toward universal suffrage brought only greater support for the *reversal* of the egalitarian measures promulgated under the new Constitution. It was the constitutional monarchy, based as it was on the premise of the radical *inequality* of men, that in fact defended the ideals of tolerance and freedom in the Austrian empire.

And when Herzl turned to the case of the Jews, he found Rousseau's ideas to be, if anything, even less relevant. It was the theory of the social-contract state that had brought about Napoleon's threat to expel the Jews from the lands in which they lived and that had been responsible for the mirage of emancipation in Germany. In Palestine, of course, the theory of the social contract offered the Jews, who were not even residents there, no rights whatsoever—not even a right to immigrate. Thus, Herzl had every reason to reject the concept of the social-contract state as a fundamentally erroneous theory, which, in addition, doomed the Jews to perpetual helplessness and ruin.

In *The Jewish State,* Herzl therefore offers a radical critique of the social-contract state, based on his recognition that Rousseau had been in error in assuming that the state was formed as the result of a tacit relationship among individuals in a particular, material territory. In fact, Herzl argued, this is never the case.[69] Instead, the state is based in the first instance on the subjective, *conscious* decision of the individual to identify with the cause of the state:

> A state is not formed by an area of land, but by a number of men united under one sovereignty. The people is the subjective, the land is the objective basis of a state, and of these two the subjective basis is the more important. There is, for example, one sovereignty without any objective basis which is, in fact, the most respected on earth: The sovereignty of the Pope.[70]

As opposed to the social contract, which presumes the assent of all men to the government that rules them—an assent that is in fact never given and is nothing but a fiction—Herzl argues that sovereignty actually comes into being within the consciousness of individuals, and ultimately groups, that have subjectively committed themselves to the cause of a nation. As such, sovereignty may be created even without the existence of a population presumed to have accepted a "contract," much less one that is concentrated within a particular physical territory.

For his own description of the source of sovereignty, Herzl sought an alternative to Rousseau's legal metaphor of a "contract," finding it in the Roman legal concept of *negotiorum gestio*—the "conduct of business" on behalf of a proprietor who is unable to conduct it himself: "When the property of an incapacitated person is in danger, anyone may step forward and save it. This man is the *gestor*, the director of someone else's affairs. He has received no warrant—that is, no human warrant. His warrant derives from a higher necessity."[71]

As Herzl emphasizes, business conducted on behalf of an incapacitated person is handled without a contract. Rather, it is conducted unilaterally on the basis of the guardian's recognition of the needs of others who cannot help themselves. Nevertheless, the guardian is presumed to have undertaken the same obligations as if he had signed a contract with those on whose behalf he has acted. And this unilateral action, applied to the political leadership establishing a government over a people, is the sole philosophical basis of the state. The men who take the reins of the state and act on its behalf may have received no human warrant. Instead, it is their subjective recognition of a "higher necessity" that bequeaths sovereignty. And though this "higher necessity" may be formulated differently in different cultures, so that its particulars are anything but invariable and universal, it is the overarching principle that is always the same: "The aim of the guardianship is the welfare of the proprietor, the people."[72]

Considering the political circumstances in Europe, it was clear to Herzl that if there were any people in need of unilateral political action on their behalf, it was the Jews: "The Jewish people," he wrote, "is in a condition of more or less severe distress in a number of places. It needs, above all things, a guardian."[73] But according to Rousseau's theory of the social-contract state, a solution to this obvious case of "higher necessity" was impossible. The Jews of France, as equal citizens, were simply supposed to participate in "the total alienation of each associate with all his rights" to the state, with no room left over for demands or interests such as the well-being of the Jews as a people. The Jews of Russia, on the other hand, who were not equal citizens, lived where the social contract had been violated, and their only recourse was to work to depose an illegitimate regime. Of course, neither side of this dichotomy presented a viable option for the Jews, since neither the "total alienation" of Jewish rights nor revolution would resolve the fundamental problem. Emancipation would not make of France the political guardian that the Jewish people needed, just as revolution would not make such a guardian of Russia.

The concept of the guardian state freed Herzl from the shackles of emancipation theory and permitted him the subjective act of taking it upon himself, along with his colleagues, to become the guardian of the Jews. With this, he began the process of political upbuilding that was the foundation of a new sovereignty—one that did not depend on having already acquired a territory for the Jews. According to Herzl, the guardian of the Jews would initially be what he called "the Society of Jews," and in life, it became known as the Zionist Organization. Eventually, it would be the Jewish state.

The Chartered Company

Once in possession of a theory of state legitimacy that would allow him to go about establishing a state for a people dispersed throughout the world, Herzl was able to turn to the question of power: Even if it were legitimate to do so, how could one amass sufficient military and diplomatic strength to obtain Jewish sovereignty "over a portion of the earth's surface that is sufficient for our rightful national requirements"? As Herzl noted in his diary,

"The transition from Society to state is a complicated problem . . . for it will be some time before we have the power to push through the claims of our citizens or of the state itself."[74] How, in fact, could such massive power be developed?

It was obvious that the existing Jewish philanthropic and settlement organizations could offer nothing. Scarcely able to maintain a handful of ailing agricultural settlements, they were hardly going to establish Jewish authority over Palestine. Sovereignty, a legal claim to a national monopoly on force, would have to be granted by a power possessing sufficient force of its own to bring such a vast Jewish power into being. And in the present political constellation, this meant Turkey, Germany, or Britain. In order to harness any of these world powers to his idea, what Herzl needed was a model, a precedent, according to which a major European power would be willing to invest its strength and prestige in the creation of a sovereignty, or something close to it, for the benefit of a body other than itself.

Herzl found this unlikely possibility in the imperial concept of a "Chartered Company," of which there had been a number of examples, chartered both by Britain and by other imperial powers. Two stood out in Herzl's mind: the British East India Company and the British South Africa Company, both of which are mentioned a number of times in his diaries.[75] The history of both companies is marked by the distasteful qualities of British colonialism at its most audacious, but they are nevertheless important as indicators of what Herzl believed would be feasible in his effort to transform his guardian organization into a real state-building power.

When it was first chartered by Elizabeth I, the British East India Company was created as a shareholder trading company, which was granted a monopoly of all trade from England to the East—a business so lucrative that at the end of the seventeenth century, the company had engendered three major centers of European population in India—Bombay, Madras, and Calcutta.[76] At the height of its power in the 1700s, the company was so successful that its charter had been expanded to grant it almost every characteristic of an independent government: the appointment of governors and legislative councils responsible for both Europeans and native Indians, a court system applying English law, the power of taxation, its own local currency, a conscript military, and the ability to form alliances with native rulers sympathetic to the company's interests.[77] In short, in India, British imperial might had been used to create a protectorate that had been, for all intents and purposes, a sovereign state.

The heyday of the East India Company's effective independence was a mere memory when Herzl wrote *The Jewish State*, direct British rule in India having been proclaimed in 1858. But he also had before him the example of the British South Africa Company, which had been commissioned

in 1887, only nine years earlier. Founded by Cecil Rhodes, a mining mag-
nate and later premier of the Cape Colony, the company was intended to
develop the region north of the Transvaal subsequently known as
Rhodesia—the first step in the construction of a British "Cape-to-Cairo"
route that would dominate the East African coast and the sea approach to
India. The charter, formally promulgated in 1889, granted the company
broad autonomy under which it could build railways and telegraph lines,
develop commerce, encourage British immigration, exploit mineral resources, and regulate liquor and arms; profits from gold and land sales were
expected to cover the costs of administration and maintaining a police force.

And although a British official was supposed to exercise oversight, in
practice the company's administrator, L. Storr Jameson, operated all aspects
of the Rhodesian government: appointing officials who exercised administrative, legislative, tax, and judicial jurisdiction over whites and native
Africans alike; creating a rotating conscription of white settlers in order to
maintain security; and using his armed force to create a favorable political
alignment among neighboring African tribes—extensions of the company's
authority that were often ratified by the British government after the fact.[78]
In fact, it seems likely that the British South Africa Company would have
won virtual independence had it not overreached its foreign policy by
threatening a rival white administration. (In December 1895, Jameson led
an expeditionary force into the Transvaal with the intention of overthrow-
ing the Dutch-Boer government of Paul Kruger in Johannesburg. The infamous "Jameson raid," ended in the capture of the company's war party and
forced the assumption of direct control over the company's lands by the
Colonial Office.)

In the precedent of the British chartered companies, Herzl found the solution to the riddle of how the Zionist Organization would become capable
of mustering the power necessary to erect a Jewish state. Under the protection of an imperial charter, the Jewish organization would be able to settle
Jews in large numbers, building up the right to establish a Jewish government, Jewish courts of law, and a Jewish military—the prerequisites of national independence. In previous cases, the British government had agreed
to the risky business of creating such halfling sovereignties due to its interest
in establishing a crucial imperial outpost without having to invest fabulous
sums out of the state treasury to do it. The company provided a population
willing to brave harsh conditions to establish this outpost, and it covered the
costs as well, at the same time providing Britain with a permanent ally. It
was precisely such a deal that Herzl proposed for the Jewish colony. All that
was needed was for one of the great powers to be persuaded that it could use
such an ally. And such persuasion was feasible, so long as the Society of Jews
that approached the imperial powers itself appeared strong enough—

through the participation of the Rothschilds or other banking magnates—to be taken seriously as a negotiating partner.

Herzl's belief that imperial acceptance of the charter would be tantamount to the creation of the Jewish state was endlessly ridiculed by those who considered it to be the pursuit of a mere piece of paper—as opposed to a "real" state that would be built with sweat and stone. But Herzl was right. Only the mental abstraction of international legality in the form of a charter could give the Jewish mass immigration the right to exist *in the minds of those powerful enough to stop it.* What stood behind Herzl's demand for legality was the belief that an illegal immigration—by 1887 the sultan had formally prohibited Jewish immigration to Palestine—would inevitably be a small one, for as soon as it reached a certain critical size, a backlash would ensue that would destroy the entire enterprise. As he wrote in *The Jewish State:*

> Noteworthy experiments in colonization have been made . . . although they have been based on the mistaken principle of a gradual infiltration of Jews. Infiltration is always bound to end badly. For there invariably comes a moment when the government, under pressure from the native population—which feels itself threatened—bars any further influx of Jews. Consequently, emigration will be pointless unless it is based on our guaranteed sovereignty.[79]

Thus, the charter was the cornerstone of Herzl's Jewish subjective sovereignty in the minds of men. And not only among Jews: It was this slip of paper that demonstrated that the idea of the Jewish state had been fixed in the mind of Europe. This alone would render the use of force by the Jews' opponents illegitimate. And this alone would unlock the possibility that Jewish growth in Palestine would be on a massive scale—a scale such that "there are so many Jews in Palestine, accompanied by Jewish military power, that one need no longer fear that the Turks will attempt to get a stranglehold on them."[80] Along the same lines, Herzl later wrote that he was willing to begin with Palestine as a "vassal state," but only so long as it was granted autonomous authority, guaranteed under international law, in the "constitution, government, and administration of justice" in this state, with law and order "to be managed by the Jews themselves through security forces of their own."[81] Such a vassalage, he wrote to Colonel Goldsmid the following year, would be temporary: "Upon the breakup of Turkey, Palestine would then fall to us or to our sons as an independent country."[82]

The Three Centers

Herzl believed that the abstraction of the Jewish state—and not physical Jewish settlements—would be the basis for winning over the imperial powers to his cause. And he was no less adamant that this same abstraction in the minds of the Jews would be the heart of true national strength once the Jewish state had come into being. This preference for the potentialities of the Jewish mind over those of material construction goes all the way back to his first argument with Baron de Hirsch, in which the banker had informed him that the troubles of the Jewish people stemmed from the fact that it had "too many intellectuals" and that the goal should be to return the Jews to the soil. In the same rejoinder to Hirsch in which Herzl declared himself to be "the Jew of the spirit," he also sprang to the defense of the Jewish intellectual class, which—as opposed to Hirsch's farmers—he insisted held the real key to the future of the Jews:

> All those engineers, architects, scientists, chemists, physicians, lawyers who emerged from the ghetto in the last thirty years. . . . All my love goes out to them. I want to see their breed multiply, unlike you who want to reduce it, because I see in them the inherent future strength of the Jews. They are, in other words, the likes of myself.[83]

In *The Jewish State,* Herzl took this argument a step further, trying to show that through the agency of the company, it would be possible to harness the abilities of the Jewish mind to create a state that would ultimately prove sufficiently attractive to serve as a new and permanent "home" for the Jews.

As an illustration of how the creativity of the mind can be used to defeat the difficulties posed by reality—whereas no amount of material resources will succeed—he proposes a kind of thought-duel between his own methods and those of Baron Hirsch, applied to the problem of how to assemble a crowd of people in a particular field outside Paris on a hot Sunday afternoon.

> By promising them 10 francs each, the Baron will bring out 20,000 perspiring, miserable people who will curse him for having inflicted this drudgery on them. I, on the other hand, will offer 200,000 francs as a prize for the swiftest race horse. . . . The upshot will be that I will get half a million people out there. . . . Most of them will find the exercise in the open air a pleasure in spite of the heat and dust, and . . . I shall have collected a million in admissions and betting taxes. I can get those same people out there any time I want to; but the Baron cannot—not at any price.[84]

Herzl then uses this metaphor as the basis for a discussion of the place of efforts of the mind in constructing a homeland that will attract and hold the loyalty of the dispersed Jews. It is the creativity of the Jewish mind, Herzl argues, that will mold a state whose power will reside in its attractiveness, its magnetism as an idea, for the Jews and for the world. As a consequence, the construction of the Jewish state is primarily a question of mental development, in at least three areas—entrepreneurial, religious, and cultural—and

Herzl argues that the Jewish state will have to become a dynamic "center" for each.[85] If this effort were successful, the Jewish state would become an attractive "home" in the mind of every Jew, and most Jews could be expected eventually to immigrate and make their lives there. If it failed, it would be impossible to win the loyalty of the Jewish people on a permanent basis.

With regard to the first two centers, *The Jewish State* is fairly clear as to what Herzl was proposing. He was outspoken in his belief that the key to creating economic strength lay in constructing an environment that would attract the creative abilities of private enterprise: "In our time, which is made wonderful by technological progress, even the most stupid man . . . sees new commodities appearing all around him. The spirit of enterprise has created them. . . . All our welfare has been brought about by entrepreneurs." In particular, he believed in the existence of a "Jewish spirit of enterprise" that characterized the Jews as a people, and which made them capable of gathering tremendous financial power whenever permitted by law to conduct business freely. Indeed, it was each Jew's desire to unshackle his own abilities that Herzl believed would bring most of the Jews in the world to come to the new Jewish state: "The Jews will soon realize that a new and permanent field has opened up for their spirit of enterprise, which has hitherto been met with hatred and contempt." Far from being a nation like all others, Herzl believed this awesome Jewish economic power would make Israel "a land of experiment and a model country" that would enlighten the world with ideas, discoveries, and achievements. "Ours," he wrote, "must truly be the Promised Land."[86]

The second area of the mind that Herzl believed must be developed if the new state were to flourish was the Jewish religion. He considered Judaism to have been indispensable in nurturing the national idea in the minds of the people in the past ("All through the night of their history the Jews have not ceased to dream this royal dream: 'Next year in Jerusalem'"), and he believed it would continue to be essential in the future ("We recognize our historic identity only by the faith of our fathers"). For this reason, Herzl insisted that the national awakening of the Jews and their ingathering into Israel should be led by rabbis and that the synagogues in the newly built Jewish state "be visible from afar, since the old faith is the only thing that has kept us together."[87] But he considered the most important expression of religion in the Jewish state to be the establishment of "centers of faith"— not synagogues, but historic and holy places such as the Muslims have in Mecca, to which the Jews could come in pilgrimage and which would ignite the imagination of the people, inspiring in them an attachment to their Jewish past and their common destiny.[88] It was concern for this aspect of national religious development that led Herzl to propose the rebuilding of the Temple in Jerusalem and even led him to take interest in proposals to attempt to locate the lost Ark of the Covenant.[89]

With regard to development of the third type of center, which would be devoted to the creation of a Jewish national culture, *The Jewish State* is nearly silent, a failing for which Herzl was to suffer bruising criticism at the hands of his great rival for the heart of the Zionist movement, the essayist Ahad Ha'am. It seems clear from his other writings that Herzl believed in the importance of cultural institutions—not, as Ahad Ha'am instinctively grasped, because these institutions have a direct and decisive effect on politics but because people will no more live without "entertainment" than without food and faith. As Herzl once replied to his friend, the Viennese author Richard Beer-Hofmann, who had insisted that there would be nothing for him in the wastes of Palestine, "We will have a university and an opera, and you will attend the opera in your swallow-tailed coat with a white gardenia in your button-hole."[90]

Once carefully built up, these three centers would together become "home" to every Jew, "for all these centers taken together constitute a long-sought entity, one for which our people has never ceased to yearn . . . a free homeland." But buried amid Herzl's optimistic descriptions of all that might be done to construct the Jewish national state and build the loyalty of the Jews to it, one can also discern a warning, for if the leadership of the new Jewish state were to fail in this formidable task of *mental* construction, there could be little question but that the Jewish state would end up being of only "temporary" interest to the Jews—being just another horse race conducted on a barren field—and would not endure.[91]

Theodor Herzl set out to make a name for himself as a builder of German civilization and a son of German Austria. In this, he found a calling of nobility, excitement, and beauty, to which he probably would have devoted his life, had he not recognized what all the world would know fifty years later: that emancipation had brought not the beginning of life for the Jews of Europe, but its end. As the Dreyfus scandal unfolded in the years that followed, Herzl was confirmed in his early intuition that the Jewish artillery officer had in fact been innocent. Guilt, on the other hand, lay with the bargain struck with Napoleon, which had held out the prospect of a new personal identity for the members of the ancient Jewish nation. The Jews of Europe had striven for close to a hundred years to live up to their end of the deal. Yet for all the changes they had wrought in their own behavior and beliefs, the bargain of emancipation had not been kept. As Herzl wrote:

> Dreyfus is only an abstraction now. He is the Jew in modern society who has tried to adapt to his environment, who speaks its language, thinks its thoughts,

sews its insignia on its tunic—and who has these stripes ripped off by force. Dreyfus represents a position which has been fought for, which is still being fought for, and which—let us not delude ourselves—has been lost.[92]

Herzl's solution was to "return to Judaism" by reclaiming what Napoleon had taken from the Jews at sword point: Their identity as a people, and their dream of the restoration of their state.[93] And this is the meaning of what are probably the most famous words in *The Jewish State,* which we hear so readily today and which were such blasphemy to so many of his Jewish contemporaries: "We are a people—*one* people." Most of the Jews for whom these words were intended adamantly refused to listen, responding to the rising tide of anti-Semitism by becoming ever more supportive of socialist movements promising to bring liberation by stripping the Germans—and all other peoples—of their national loyalties and dreams as the Jews had been stripped of theirs. Herzl, who had himself toyed with such notions, was among the first to warn that the dreams of a withering away of states and nations was based on a counterfeit view of reality. "It might . . . be said that we should not create new distinctions among people, that we ought not to raise fresh barriers but make the old ones disappear instead. I say that those who think along these lines are loveable romantics; but the idea of a fatherland will go on flourishing long after the dust of their bones will have blown away without a trace."[94]

Yet Herzl's call for the Jews of the West to return to their people was not based solely on such cold calculations. On the contrary, the love and admiration he had felt for the cause of a gifted and long-divided people as a German-nationalist student at the University of Vienna remained for him the most honorable and genuine of sentiments even after German nationalism had run black with poison. "The nation is beautiful," he wrote later, after witnessing the festivities marking the thousand-year anniversary of the founding of the Hungarian capital of Budapest. "Not just this or that nation, but any nation. Because the nation consists of what is best in any individual—loyalty, enthusiasm, the joy of sacrifice, and the readiness to die for an idea."[95]

And such, too, were his feelings for the idea of the Jewish nation, which had been—as he wrote to his people in one of his first Zionist essays—the basis for a "great strength, an inner unity which we have lost." To become a whole person once again, the Jew had to return to the struggle on behalf of this idea:

> A generation which has grown apart from Judaism does not have this [inner] unity; it can neither rely upon our past nor look to our future. That is why we shall once more retreat into Judaism and never again permit ourselves to be thrown out of this fortress. . . . We, too, want to work for the improve-

ment of conditions in the world, but we want to do it as Jews, not as persons of undefined identity.

Once we have an ideal, as other nations have an ideal of their own, people will learn to respect us. . . . We shall thereby regain our lost inner wholeness and along with it a little character—our own character, not a Marrano-like, borrowed, untruthful character, but our own. And only then shall we vie with all other righteous people in justice, charity, and high-mindedness, only then shall we be active on all fields of honor and try to advance in the arts and sciences. . . . This is how I understand Judaism.[96]

CHAPTER 5

Herzl As Statesman: The Creation of a Jewish State of Mind

U NTIL PUBLICATION OF HERZL'S *The Jewish State*, the rejection of Jewish nationalism by the Jews of the West had been a highly theoretical position, used as a heuristic to demonstrate how marvelously far Judaism had progressed since biblical times. Not only had there been no actual Jewish state to oppose, but there had been virtually no one seriously proposing one. But with the publication of Herzl's pamphlet in February 1896, and with his trip to Constantinople to discuss Turkish support for the plan a few months later, Herzl succeeded in making hearts stop throughout Western Jewry. It was as though an oft-discussed enemy, long believed dead, had suddenly stepped gamely into the salon—which is of course just what had happened. From Berlin to San Francisco, wherever emancipationist rabbis and Jewish communal leaders began to realize that the move to establish a Jewish state was serious, Herzl's efforts were immediately understood to be a mortal blow to the world they had created for themselves. What difference would it make how much they emphasized that their Judaism was merely a faith, without political implications? The very existence of a Jewish state—even the existence of a political movement for the creation of one—would render all their protestations meaningless. What gentile would be willing to believe that the Jews were not a nation if they commanded armies and navies flying a Jewish flag, protecting Jewish interests, ready to intervene on behalf of Jews in distress? Indeed, if every Jew in the world were also eligible for citizenship in the Jewish state?

In *The Jewish State*, in his diaries, and in conversations throughout 1896, Herzl had expressed the hope that the guardian organization that would take up the political cause of the Jews, and later the Jewish state itself, could be constituted in the form of an aristocratic republic, a form of government he believed would be more stable than democracy for a people with no experience in government. The model to which he looked was the republic of Venice, which for centuries had been governed by the Great Council, composed of noble families that elected the actual government of the state.[1] In England especially, Herzl was at first received respectfully by wealthy Jews and important rabbis, many of whom had long supported the settlement of Russian Jews in Palestine as a form of relief, which encouraged him in his belief that an alliance of Jewish banking families and religious leaders would be best suited to make the case for a resurrected Judea before the powers. His political activities were therefore aimed, first and foremost, at attempting to secure the support of such powerful, established Jews.

But by July 1896, Herzl returned to London to find that his debut as a publicist and diplomat for the cause had transformed him into a lunatic in the eyes of those very Jewish aristocrats whom he had wished to enlist. On the day of his arrival in London, Herzl sat down in conference with businessmen of the Anglo-Jewish Association to discuss the creation of a unified Jewish organization with "the task of acquiring, under international law, a territory for those Jews who are unable to assimilate," only to be told that "the whole plan is unacceptable, and that the Jewish state [is] neither possible nor desirable."[2] He even managed to get into a spat with Colonel Goldsmid's London chapter of Hovevei Zion when he attended a meeting of the group and discovered that their enterprise consisted of providing philanthropic support for the handful of existing Jewish agricultural colonies. As he wrote in his diary:

> They read lengthy reports about a settlement that is to cost I don't know how many hundreds of thousands of pounds: So-and-so many oxen, so-and-so many horses, seeds, timber, etc. The question was asked whether the colonists were protected, and it was answered in the negative. . . . I said I only wanted the kind of colonization that we could protect with our own Jewish army.[3]

In the end, the English Jews referred Herzl to the leader of the Palestine settlement effort, Baron Edmond de Rothschild in Paris, who after Hirsch's death had become the moving force behind the Jewish Colonization Association, and whose purchases of Palestinian wine at above-market prices was single-handedly preventing most of the Jewish settlers from descending into famine. Herzl must have felt a certain sense of déjà vu as he made his second pilgrimage to see Paris's Jewish-settlement moguls. And Rothschild did not in this sense disappoint Hirsch's legacy. He too insisted on a purely materialistic view focused on constructing farming settlements, rejecting out of hand the possibility that Palestine might serve as a refuge for the masses of persecuted Russian Jews.

"He thinks it would be impossible to keep the influx of the masses into Palestine under control," Herzl summed up the meeting in his diary. "The first to arrive would be 150,000 beggars, who would have to be fed. He didn't feel equal to it, but perhaps I would be. He could not undertake such a responsibility. There might be mishaps." The argument went on for two hours before Herzl left in disgust. When he reached his room, he wrote with sorrow, "Edmond is a decent, good-natured, faint-hearted man, who . . . would like to stop it [i.e., the Jewish state], the way a coward tries to stop necessary surgery. I believe he is now aghast to have got himself involved with Palestine. . . . And the fate of many millions is to hang on such men!"[4]

This final refusal by the leading backer of Jewish settlement in Palestine meant the end of Herzl's hopes of a Jewish aristocracy that would assume the guardianship of the Jews. On the other hand, there was no great surprise here; even when Herzl had published *The Jewish State* that spring, he had considered the possibility that the great Jewish bankers would refuse responsibility for the guardian organization. In this case, Herzl had written, it would be necessary to set aside the aristocratic approach in favor of a broad political movement, democratic in character, which would raise the necessary funds through public subscription. A week before the meeting with Rothschild, Herzl had already instructed a supporter in England to begin organizing a propaganda committee in support of a Jewish state among the poor Russian immigrants of London's East End. His diary entry from July 20, two days after the meeting with Rothschild, reads: "I am writing de Haas in London that they should begin to organize the masses. This will be the reply."[5]

A few days later, Herzl was back in Vienna. With the millstone of the Jewish plutocracy loosed from around his neck, he threw himself into the work of organizing a democratic movement. Vienna was home to a number of Hebrew enthusiasts, veterans of the Kadimah dueling society, and other Zionist oddities, who had been meeting every Tuesday night at the Cafe Louvre for years without much of anything to show for it. Herzl had kept the Vienna Kadimah at arm's length since the publication of his pamphlet, but now he called upon them to assist in establishing a head office, which in short order began agitating for a Jewish state among Jews everywhere. His goal was a general Zionist convention—it did not have a name yet—that would assemble supporters of Jewish restoration in Palestine from across

Europe.[6] By mid-October, rumors of Herzl's frantic activities had reached the ICA, which now anxiously began seeking a way to head him off, inviting him to attend a conference of their association in Paris. But Herzl declined. He would henceforth deal with the opponents of the Jewish state only as head of an international movement—one powerful enough to bring them to join him of their own accord.[7]

Within a matter of months, in March 1897, Herzl's office in Vienna began issuing announcements and invitations for the convention, which was now to be the "Jewish National Assembly"—that is, nothing less than a congress. The invitations read:

> Sir:
>   I am desired to announce that preparations are being made for a Zionist Congress at Munich, on August 25th next. . . . Everything will be done to render this Congress, the first to be held by Jews, as imposing, as its discussions will be of importance to Israel.

Exhilaration swept the little office, and Herzl noted in his diary: "Isn't this something so great that every Jewish heart must beat higher at the thought of it? Today still in a foreign land, *leshana haba'a* [Heb., "next year"] perhaps in our ancient home?"[8]

Even more than when Herzl had returned from his Turkish mission, the issuing of announcements for the congress led to an immediate cooling of sympathies among those who had previously received him with favor and an explosion of rage from those who had been inclined to ignore him. A pamphlet, even a mission to see the sultan, were only expressions of one man's idea. But a Jewish congress was a political act by a people, the mustering of power in the service of national interests. Such a brazen attempt at a demonstration of sovereignty—in effect the attempt to create a Jewish parliament in exile—was nothing short of a renunciation, on behalf of all Jews, of their secession from unlimited loyalty to the states in which they lived. The philanthropic organizations again summoned Herzl to Paris, this time holding out the bribe of a "conference of all Zionists" under their own sponsorship, to which he would be invited.

But Herzl could stand no more. His pen dripped with contempt for the weakness and fear that had led these men to refuse consideration of any large-scale plan for the rescue of the Jews of Eastern Europe. "I have waited long enough," he fired back. "In August it will be two years since I took the first practical steps in the Jewish cause. I wanted to act without stirring up the masses, through direction from above . . . I have met with no understanding, no support. I have had to go on alone. At the Munich Congress I shall call upon the masses to resort to self-help, since no one else wants to help them."[9]

This meant war, and the emancipationists threw everything they had into it. Under pressure from Paris, Jewish figures who had intimated support now began distancing themselves from Herzl's congress: Samuel Montagu, the British MP who had told Herzl he felt more Jewish than English, demurred that he rejected mixing Judaism and politics; Colonel Goldsmid objected to speaking the national idea "too loudly"; Zadoc Kahn, chief rabbi of France, found some reason he would not be able to attend; and Hirsch Hildesheimer, publisher of the Berlin Juedische Presse, printed a statement that although he had "held out the prospect of his presence" at a conference to discuss "the manifold tasks of the Palestine project, particularly colonization," he would "emphatically decline to participate in an assembly discussing 'Zionist' theories and future plans, because we are convinced that it threatens to produce grave harm." In Munich, too, the Jewish community threatened a lawsuit to prevent treason from being committed in their city, forcing Herzl to move the congress to Switzerland.[10]

Harshest, however, were the attacks of the rabbis of German Judaism, both liberal and "modern Orthodox," for whom the Jewish national movement was a violation of the social contract and therefore a sacrilege. The first of these came from the liberal chief rabbi of Vienna, Moritz Guedemann, whose mild words of encouragement to Herzl were replaced by a vitreolic pamphlet entitled *National Judaism*, in which he argued that Judaism had no relationship with national aspirations and declared Zion to be not an earthly goal but a "symbol" of future human progress.[11] Similar arguments were advanced as well by the German-Jewish chief rabbi of England, Hermann Adler; and in June, the Association of German Rabbis published a statement in the German press, signed by its executive of three liberal rabbis and two Orthodox rabbis, stating that:

> the endeavors of so-called Zionists to found a Jewish national state in Palestine run counter to the messianic prophesies of Judaism as contained in the Holy Writ and in later religious sources. Judaism obligates its adherents to serve the fatherland to which they belong with full devotion . . . Religion and patriotism thus equally impose upon us the duty . . . to stay away from the aforementioned Zionist endeavors and most particularly from the Congress.[12]

In July, the Central Conference of American Rabbis, representing the overwhelmingly German-Jewish Reform rabbinate in the United States, likewise condemned Zionism as a movement that would "not benefit but infinitely harm our Jewish brethren, where they are still persecuted, by confirming the assertion of their enemies that the Jews are foreigners in the countries in which they are at home and of which they are everywhere the most loyal and patriotic citizens."[13]

Herzl responded to the anti-Zionist din that had broken out on all sides by bringing out a weekly paper of his own, which he seems to have consciously designed to drive his opponents to distraction. The first issue of *Die Welt* ("The World") appeared on June 4, 1897, its masthead bearing a map of Palestine situated in the center of a large Star of David suggesting a globe—an icon that managed to epitomize the myth of international Jewish conspiracy that anti-Semites were so fond of invoking and that Herzl knew would give the congress such potency. The leading article announced: "Our weekly is a *Judenblatt*"—using the pejorative "Jew-rag," which was hurled against Jewish-dominated newspapers such as the *Neue Freie Presse*. "We accept this word . . . and wish to transform it into a badge of honor. . . . What we want is . . . to create a homeland secured by international law for those Jews unable or unwilling to assimilate."[14] The paper carried breathy reports of the international preparations for the congress, and included articles on political, literary, and rabbinic figures, past and present, who were supporters of the idea of a Jewish state. In the summer, when the clamor of anti-Zionist pronouncements by German-Jewish rabbis reached its peak, *Die Welt* joyfully returned fire, broadsiding them for so readily dismissing the most cherished of Jewish aspirations as mere symbolism ("Are we then to believe that when people pray for a return to Zion they mean just the opposite?" Herzl wrote);[15] and for using their doctrine of a Jewish "mission" among the gentiles to justify opposing the establishment of a Jewish state that could provide actual salvation from persecution for millions of Russian Jews ("These are people," he said, quoting Nordau, "who sit in the lifeboat and use their oars to batter the heads of drowning men who try to cling to its sides").[16] Within a year the paper, backed by Herzl's own funds and assistance from his father, had gathered 10,000 paid subscribers.

The scandal over the impending congress assisted in drawing substantial international attention, so that when the congress finally opened in Basel on August 29, 1897, the event was, as Herzl had hoped, attended by delegates and reporters from all over Europe,[17] True, the star-studded extravaganza that Herzl had wanted did not take place. Only the best-selling authors Max Nordau and Israel Zangwill added significantly to whatever prestige Herzl's own name imparted to the event. But the fact that the congress consisted primarily of students, Russians, and a few German businessmen was rendered invisible through the careful manipulation of "imponderables" that Herzl had promised Baron de Hirsch so long before. Herzl attended Orthodox Shabbat services on Saturday morning, even memorizing the Hebrew words of the blessings over the Torah, and with this, the assimilated Viennese journalist was transformed into a true Jewish leader. The Basel municipal casino hall was likewise transformed by a large blue-and-white flag draped over the entrance. And the "delegates" were, through the magic of formal evening attire, turned into a congress. (When Nordau showed up in casual dress, Herzl begged him to return to his room and change: The Jewish congress was "still an absolute nothing; we have to make something of it.")[18]

On Sunday morning, August 29, when Herzl mounted the platform, the crowd burst into a jubilant ovation that lasted for fifteen minutes, complete with cries of *yehi hamelech*—"Long live the king!" To all this Herzl continued to contribute throughout the days of the congress, as he noted in his diary: "Now it became clear why I had had to go to the Palais Bourbon for four years. Subconsciously I was full of all the niceties of parliamentary procedure. I was affable and energetic . . . and at critical moments I endeavored to coin presidential phrases." A state exists first and foremost in the mind, and through a shift in the collective consciousness of the audience, his ragtag band was transformed into a parliament.

> The foundation of a state lies in the will of the people for a state . . . Territory is only the material basis; the state, even when it possesses territory, is always something abstract. . . . At Basel, then, I created this abstraction which, as such, is invisible to the vast majority of people. . . . I gradually worked the people into the mood for a state and made them feel that they were its National Assembly.[19]

He infused in the assembled people, both the delegates and those observing from the galleries, the belief that here indeed was a representation and a power, the guardian of the Jews.

The deliberations at the Basel congress continued for three days, from August 29 to 31, during which the situation of world Jewry was surveyed, an executive was elected, and committees appointed. Most important among its "legislative" achievements was the adoption of what became known as the "Basel program," which was to serve as the platform of the Zionist Organization for the next forty-five years. Bowing to the same kinds of pressures that had prevented the Hovevei Zion conference from speaking publicly of a Jewish state thirteen years earlier—Herzl was particularly concerned not to stir up trouble with the Ottoman sultan, and the Russian Jews pleaded with him to keep the tone restrained so as not to enrage the czar or their financial backers—Herzl agreed to drop the term *staat*, instead electing to use the similar-sounding *heimstaette* (a "homestead," or "home") in the key phrase "the creation of a home for the Jewish people in Palestine secured by public law."[20] But in the privacy of his own diary, all pandering to the sultan and the assimilated grandees of Western Jewry was forgone:

> Were I to sum up the Basel Congress in a word—which I shall guard against pronouncing publicly—it would be this: At Basel I founded the Jewish state.

If I said this out loud today, it would be answered by universal laughter.
Perhaps in five years, certainly in fifty, everyone will know it.[21]

The First Congress was a resounding success. But even in those heady days of
unity and enthusiasm, a nascent opposition faction had already been born in
the figure of Ahad Ha'am ("One of the People"), the leading essayist of
Russian Zionism, who had chosen to attend the congress only as a visitor and
had spent the duration writhing with jealousy in the galleries. Ahad Ha'am,
whose real name was Asher Ginsberg, was in many ways Herzl's opposite: A
prodigious student from an early age, he had spent the first thirty years of his
life in a room in his father's house in Skvira, outside Kiev. In this backyard
ivory tower, he was able to steep himself in book learning (at which Herzl
had never excelled), at the expense of gaining any real understanding of the
workings of the world of politics and diplomacy (in which Herzl did excel).
This protracted incubation also had the effect of implanting in Ahad Ha'am
an abiding faith in his own capacity for criticism—and especially for moral
criticism. Although his essays hardly qualified as being of universal intellectual importance, the leisure of his study nevertheless gave Ahad Ha'am the
opportunity to develop a unique understanding of the needs of the Jewish
national movement—a viewpoint that eventually made him the most important force in the early years of Zionism other than Herzl himself.

Ahad Ha'am's first essay, "The Wrong Way," had appeared in the
Hebrew-language *Hamelitz* in 1889, seven years before Herzl's *The Jewish
State*. Ahad Ha'am had therein mounted a devastating attack on the Russian
settlement committees of Hovevei Zion, blaming the waning enthusiasm in
the movement on the decision to establish physical settlements in Palestine
before the idea that stood behind them had grown strong enough to sustain
protracted action. "What ought we to have done? . . . We ought to have
made it our first object to bring about a revival—to inspire men with a
deeper attachment to the national life. . . . We should have striven gradually
to extend the empire of our ideal in Jewry, until at last it could find genuine,
whole-hearted devotees, with all the qualities needed to enable them to
work for its practical realization." Referring to the new Palestine settlements
as "ruins"—soulless material additions to the ruins with which Palestine was
already covered—he asserted that "it is not on these that we must base our
hope of ultimate success. The heart of the people—that is the foundation
on which the land will be regenerated. . . . Instead of adding yet more ruins,
let us endeavor to give the idea itself strong roots and to strengthen and
deepen its hold on the Jewish people. Then we shall in time have the possibility of doing actual work."[22]

Ahad Ha'am's essay fell like a thunderclap on the struggling movement and gave him the leverage he needed to establish himself as the spiritual leader of a group of younger men, whom he formed into a secret fraternal order—complete with an elaborate system of ethical strictures, ceremonies, and secret code words—that devoted itself to fostering Jewish nationalism through educational and cultural efforts.[23] Calling themselves the Bnei Moshe ("Sons of Moses"), members of the group did succeed in founding a number of "national" Hebrew-language schools in Russia with a modernized curriculum, a similar school in Jaffa, a Hebrew-language publishing house in Warsaw, and a series of newsletters providing accurate information about Jewish Palestine. But their organization was to be short-lived. The group's shroud of secrecy conjured up fierce resistance to its activities, and by 1895, the Bnei Moshe were accused at a meeting of the Odessa Committee—the unofficial leadership of Russian Hovevei Zion—of conspiring to take over the movement. The attack on the Bnei Moshe's unknown aims forced Ahad Ha'am to submit to a humiliating investigation, in which he disclosed many of the order's secret rules, and he subsequently resigned from its leadership. Whether the Bnei Moshe could have survived these events is doubtful, but its demise was in any case assured by external events. Within a matter of months, *The Jewish State* had appeared, and all heads turned to try to understand what was taking place in Vienna. Ahad Ha'am's fraternity of Jewish nationalist educators, which was to have held the keys to a Jewish revolution, dissipated like a whiff of smoke.[24]

It is difficult to underestimate the animosity that Ahad Ha'am harbored for Herzl's Zionism, which to him looked like nothing more than a superinflated version of the same mania for idea-less material construction he had opposed in Russia. In fact, Ahad Ha'am's disgust and resentment was so great that when Herzl personally sent him a handwritten invitation to the congress, Ahad Ha'am replied that he did not know whether he would be able to be in Basel. As it turned out, he was able to attend and proceeded to spend the first Jewish National Assembly peering down from the visitors' gallery, as he himself wrote, "like a mourner at a wedding feast."[25] At the close of the congress, he turned with nerves frayed to writing a letter in which he moaned that there was "no doubt" the Turkish government would now be "much harsher with us . . . Who knows that this was not the last sigh of the dying nation."[26] A few days later, he penned a piece for publication in *Hashiloah*, the Hebrew monthly he had founded the previous year, in which he predicted that Herzl's diplomatic efforts would lead to the destruction of the movement: "The fire suddenly kindled by hope will die down again, perhaps to the very last spark," he wrote. "The salvation of Israel will be achieved by prophets, not by diplomats."[27]

Not until a storm of anger had broken out over these words did Ahad Ha'am go about trying to write a more thoughtful critique of the new Zionist Organization. In his essay "The Jewish State and the Jewish Problem," which appeared in autumn 1897, Ahad Ha'am emphasized that Hovevei Zion, "no less than 'Zionism,' wants a Jewish state and believes in the possibility of the establishment of a Jewish state in the future."[28] However, he was opposed to Herzl's vision as presented in *The Jewish State* and the congress for practical reasons. Following Baron de Rothschild, Ahad Ha'am claimed that the ingathering of large masses of Jews into Palestine and the establishment of a Jewish state within a few decades was "a fantasy bordering on madness." Economic factors alone would permanently preclude the immigration of more than a small number of Jews into Palestine at a time, and the natural increase of Diaspora Jewry would mean that even those who might wish to come to Palestine would have to remain in exile. "We must confess to ourselves that . . . 'to gather our scattered ones from the four corners of the earth' (in the words of the prayer book) is impossible. Only religion, with its belief in a miraculous redemption, can promise that consummation." Moreover, to Herzl's claim that the Jewish state, as a sovereign power, would be capable of alleviating the suffering of Jews in foreign lands through the exertion of political pressure, Ahad Ha'am responded with dismissive contempt:

> We have seen often enough . . . how little diplomacy can do in matters of this kind, if it is not backed up by a large armed force. Nay, it is conceivable that in the days of the Jewish state, . . . [a foreign] government will find it easier . . . to excuse for such [oppressive] action, for it will be able to plead that if the Jews are not happy where they are, they can go to their own state.[29]

In these arguments, Ahad Ha'am proved to be hopelessly wrong. The rapid absorption of millions of Jews into Palestine did prove economically feasible, as did the achievement of Jewish independence in a matter of decades. And even the contemporary Jewish state—more modest in terms of territory than the one being discussed in Ahad Ha'am's day—is large enough for the absorption of further millions. Likewise, the "natural increase" of the Diaspora has proved chimerical, with unprecedented persecution, assimilation, and emigration to Israel reducing the Diaspora by half in the twentieth century. And Israeli diplomatic efforts on behalf of Diaspora Jewry, "backed up by a large armed force" such as Ahad Ha'am could not imagine the Jews would have, has repeatedly proved efficacious in saving Jewish lives. The fact is that respected as his intellect was among nationalist Russian Jews, Ahad Ha'am's ignorance of politics, economics, and diplomacy rendered him worthless as a judge of the practicability of Herzl's Zionism.

Nonetheless, Ahad Ha'am was capable of judging what turned out to be *The Jewish State*'s central weakness—its limited appreciation of the need to strengthen the national Jewish culture and consciousness among the Jews. Without such investment, Ahad Ha'am warned, the Jewish state that might one day come into being would be a construct of "material power" alone— and as such would become a "great danger" to Judaism:

> The secret of our people's persistence is . . . that at a very early period the prophets taught it to respect only spiritual power, and not to worship material power. . . . So long as we are faithful to this principle, our existence has a secure basis: For in spiritual power we are not inferior to other nations, and we have no reason to efface ourselves. But a political ideal which does not rest on the national culture is apt to seduce us from our loyalty to spiritual greatness, and to beget in us a tendency to find the path of glory in the attainment of material power and political dominion, thus breaking the thread that unites us with the past.[30]

Moreover, such a severing of the Jewish people from the thread of its cultural and intellectual heritage was all the more likely when the men taking the helm of the Jewish state were themselves enslaved to foreign cultures— as Ahad Ha'am plainly believed to be true of Herzl. It would be better if the Jewish people were to disappear from the face of history, he wrote, than to find itself trapped in the meaningless power mongering of a small state populated by individuals of Jewish ancestry but which would otherwise not be a Jewish state:

> Almost all our great men, those, that is, whose education and social position fit them to be at the head of a Jewish state, are spiritually far removed from Judaism, and have no true conception of its nature and its value. Such men, however devoted to the state and to its interests, will necessarily regard those interests as bound up with the foreign culture which they themselves have imbibed . . . so that in the end the Jewish state will be a state of Germans or Frenchmen of the Jewish race. . . . Such a Jewish state would spell death and degradation for our people. We should never achieve sufficient political power to deserve respect, while we should miss the living moral force within. The puny state, being tossed about like a ball between its powerful neighbors, and maintaining its existence only by diplomatic shifts . . . would not be able to give us a feeling of national glory; and the national culture, in which we might have sought and found our glory, would not have been implanted in our state and would not be the principle of its life. So we should really be then—much more than we are now—a small and insignificant nation, enslaved in spirit to the favored of fortune. . . . Were it not better for an ancient people which was once a beacon to the world to disappear than to end by reaching such a goal as this?[31]

In contrast to his Malthusianism regarding the practical and political aspects of state building, Ahad Ha'am's warnings concerning the national culture proved deadly accurate. The actual Jewish state, when it finally came, was created through the establishment of a cult of material strength—a fact that did not prevent it from having to shift for its existence in Paris and Washington. And the attachment to Jewish national culture was in fact badly damaged in the all-consuming rush to create Jewish material strength.

Yet astute as was Ahad Ha'am's insight that the basis for the Jewish people's existence would be threatened by an excessively materialist Zionism, there was nevertheless something unfair in his relentless assault on Herzl. For one actually needed to be willfully blind to Herzl's writings and methods to accuse him of abandoning the Jewish people's "spiritual power" in favor of "material power." Such arguments had been perfectly in place when Ahad Ha'am had first leveled them against the Russian Hovevei Zion, but to direct the same accusation against Herzl—whose concerns were almost exclusively in the realm of the nonmaterial and of the mind—required a certain degree of willful prejudice. Herzl, for his part, reacted to Ahad Ha'am's blasts with distance. And when the "cultural issue" eventually began to pick up steam, he dealt with it primarily by trivializing it or delegating it to committees whose deliberations led nowhere—an approach that suggests a rather studied obtuseness on the part of a leader who spent his spare hours writing plays and novels and who had made religion and "entertainment" central pillars of his own theory of how to construct a state.

Here was truly a dialogue of the deaf, a seemingly unnecessary confrontation between positions that, with the perspective of the years, seem to have been quite similar. Both men, after all, believed, in opposition to most Jewish leaders and thinkers at the time, that a Jewish state should be established in Palestine, and both agreed that without a strong national culture there would in the long run be no such state. Two difficulties made a working coalition between them impossible. First, Ahad Ha'am's failed to recognize the abilities Herzl and the Western Jews brought to the table—diplomacy, parliamentarianism, political theory, law, entrepreneurship, mediacraft—for what they are: not materialism at all, but essential components of what Ahad Ha'am referred to as the "spiritual power" of the state. For all his erudition, Ahad Ha'am could not rid himself of the belief, characteristic of the thinking of the East, that only "pure" ideas—those springing from the mind unencumbered by any worldly experience—are worthy of being considered "spiritual" and that these are themselves sufficient to assure a desired end to every endeavor. (Thus, for example, Ahad Ha'am insisted that "Zionists nowadays attach so much importance to questions of organization. But to my mind that is not the essential thing. The idea itself, if it is clearly understood and accepted with thorough conviction, will be the best organizer; it will always produce the necessary ma-chinery in a form suited to its object.")[32]

Herzl, on the other hand, was apparently unable to recognize that diplo-macy and public relations are means of harnessing political power to an idea only in the short term, and that these are capable of creating political con-stellations whose longevity is usually measured in months or years. But in the long term, as measured in generations, national power depends on the vitality of the national culture. As Herzl himself had said, in founding the German state, Bismarck had only to shake the tree that had been planted by the dreamers. Yet if this were the case, then dream weaving—that is, the work of poets and playwrights, academics and artists—is itself ultimately a matter of immense political power. Herzl, it seems, should have been the first to realize this, and his failure in this regard allowed "cultural Zionism," which should have been inseparable from political Zionism, to become its enemy. And once this had happened, it was only a matter of time before the advocates of the national "culture," suppressing the memory of Ahad Ha'am's support for the Jewish state, also declared themselves to be the ene-mies of the idea of the Jewish state itself.

In the year following the First Congress, Herzl moved quickly to consoli-date what had been a smashing political success, building up the Zionist Organization from 117 chapters to 796, so the 350 delegates at the Second Congress in 1898 were the elected representatives of close to 100,000 peo-ple. He worked to organize financial institutions for the movement, includ-ing the Jewish Colonial Bank for the development of Palestine and Syria and the Jewish National Fund to solicit donations from world Jewry for land purchases; and he imposed a poll tax (the "shekel"), through which the burgeoning democratic institution could raise operating funds. And in all these efforts, he carefully cultivated the news organs of the world, which took an ever keener interest in Zionist efforts.

Yet impressive as was Herzl's organizational achievement, it was the ac-companying diplomatic campaign that transformed all these efforts into an event of historic significance—and that still stands as the greatest diplomatic effort mounted by a Jewish statesman on behalf of his people since antiq-uity. Out of the strands of seeming legitimacy and power that he was able to inject into the press, Herzl set to work weaving a network of contacts span-ning the power structure of Europe in his quest to build an international al-liance for a Jewish state. In this effort, Herzl negotiated with Austrian prime ministers Count Kasimir Badeni and Ernst von Koerber over founding a competitor to the *Neue Freie Presse* and established a rapport with Austrian foreign minister Count Goluchowski. He tried to get to the czar but failed, tried to infiltrate a Jewish painter into the czar's court but again failed, and finally succeeded in opening negotiations with Russian interior minister von Plehwe and Russian finance minister Witte. The prince of Bulgaria expressed his sympathy, Romanian prime minister Stourdza was publicly enthusiastic about the Jewish state, and the former president of Romania declared it to be a revolution in the relations between Europe and the Jews. An Indian prince, Aga Khan, was supportive and willing to intercede with the sultan. Herzl enlisted a priest in his permanent service, initiating a series of meetings with Christian clergy, including the Vatican secretary of state Merry del Val and Pope Pius X. Bismarck knew of *The Jewish State* and dismissed it. But Herzl met with the grand duke of Hesse, repeatedly lobbied the grand duke of Baden, and ultimately held a series of negotiations with the kaiser and German foreign minister Bernhard von Buelow. He met with a series of Hungarian notables, enlisting the assistance of the renowned Hungarian diplomat Vambery in negotiations in Constantinople. Herzl wrote to the philosopher Herbert Spencer; British prime minister Gladstone reacted to his approaches with a letter deploring anti-Semitism, but no more. He tried to reach King Edward VII of England, Rudyard Kipling, and Cecil Rhodes; Rhodes agreed to a meeting but died before it could take place. He was able to jump-start substantive negotiations with British colonial secretary Joseph Chamberlain, Foreign Secretary Lord Landsdowne, and Lord Cromer, de facto ruler of Egypt. He held consultations with Oscar Straus, American ambassador to Constantinople, and tried to meet Andrew Carnegie through the American ambassador to Paris, and Theodore Roosevelt with the help of American Zionists. He competed against a group assembled by the French finance minister Rouvier to relieve Turkish debt. He asked Italian foreign minister Tittoni to put pressure on the sultan and found an outspoken enthusiast of the Jewish state in the king of Italy. And then there was the Ottoman court in Constantinople, where Herzl met repeatedly with the sultan, as well as with layer after layer of the advisers and officials who surrounded him.

It is one of the tragedies of Herzl's legacy that this daredevil diplomatic performance—all of it conducted within a span of six and a half years—has been largely dismissed as inherently ill-conceived or else as a failure, since "nothing came of it." Yet Herzl's efforts were on the mark, demonstrating a superb understanding of what his host of armchair critics have since found so difficult to grasp: that the power structure of Europe, which in Herzl's day ruled the entire globe, consisted of a few hundred men, each of them utterly inaccessible unless one could offer him something that would advance his own interests. In bringing into being the Zionist Congresses, backed by hundreds of thousands of members and a not-insubstantial media presence, Herzl was able to create a player on the world stage with access to the leadership of Europe such as no other Jewish leader had ever had. Doors opened before him because Europe understood what he was offering—not a plea to help the oppressed, but tangible benefits: In England's case, protection of Egypt's flank and the route to India, as well as diversion of the deluge of impoverished Jewish refugees arriving in London; in Germany's case, an excuse to become the protector of Palestine and so open a rail route to the East; in Russia's case, the attenuation of the threat from Jewish revolutionary elements and alleviation of the stigma that its pogromist policies had engendered in Western Europe; in Turkey's case, assistance in developing its decrepit economy; and so on.

Herzl has been mercilessly ridiculed for his years of ultimately futile negotiations in the quicksand of the Ottoman court (he himself also suspected that the Turks had only used him as a lever to secure better terms for their loans from the French). But one cannot seriously dispute the creativity and boldness of some of Herzl's other combinations, such as his negotiations to establish a major new Viennese daily under his own editorship—a paper that would support the ruling conservative parties in exchange for their acceptance of an editorial line favoring creation of a Jewish state (the *Neue Freie Presse*, where Herzl worked, was a strictly emancipationist German-Jewish paper, implacably hostile to the idea of a Jewish state). The plan was certainly feasible. Herzl, one of Vienna's most respected journalists, had already been approached with this idea prior to the publication of *The Jewish State* and had turned it down out of strictly professional considerations. And later discussions, which took place after he had realized the significance of such a development for Jewish nationalism, were serious despite the fact that they failed.

The importance of the "near miss" of the Austrian daily can most easily be recognized in Herzl's diplomacy with Germany. Throughout 1897 and 1898, Herzl was making steady progress in winning over members of the kaiser's family and court to the idea of German sponsorship for a Jewish charter company in Palestine. This was conceivable because Germany had in recent years embarked on a global imperial policy—which had also made use of the instrument of imperial charters—and was on excellent terms with Turkey, the ruling power in Palestine. To be sure, Herzl never established anything remotely resembling the stable support of the kaiser. But he did get much farther than any of his critics dreamed, as was later demonstrated by a letter written by the kaiser on September 29, 1898, under the influence of his close friend Count Eulenberg, one of Herzl's most important German sympathizers. The letter, addressed to the grand duke of Baden, the kaiser's uncle and another Herzl confidant, concludes that Germany should indeed consider a Jewish protectorate in Palestine to be in its interest. If such a protectorate were created, he wrote,

[then] the energy, creative power, and productivity of the tribe of Shem . . . addicted to social democracy and busy inciting the opposition will move off to the East, where more rewarding work awaits him . . . Now I realize that nine-tenths of Germans will be horrified and shun me if they find out at some later date that I am in sympathy with the Zionists and might even place them under my protection if they call upon me to do so. On that point, let me say this: That the Jews killed our Savior, the good Lord knows better than we do, and He has punished them accordingly. But neither the anti-Semites nor I nor anyone else has been ordered or authorized by Him to abuse these people. . . . And from the viewpoint of secular realpolitik we cannot ignore the fact that, given the enormous and dangerous power represented by international Jewish capital, it would surely be a tremendous achievement for Germany if the world of the Hebrews would look up to our country with gratitude. . . . All right, then, those who return to the Holy Land shall enjoy protection and security, and I shall intercede for them with the Sultan.[33]

What overturned the kaiser's decision to work out an alliance with the Jews was the opposition of his minister of state and later chancellor, Bernhard von Buelow, who by late 1898 had succeeded in neutralizing the bridgehead that Herzl had built among the kaiser's friends and relations. Buelow's cold assessment was that Herzl was simply not strong enough to hold up his end of a bargain. At Herzl's first meeting with the kaiser, Buelow pointed out that the wealthy Jews were not behind the idea and that "the big papers are not for it, either, particularly your own. You should certainly try to win over one or another of the great papers." Herzl knew that he had no effective response to these remarks, whose point was, as he well understood, "to indicate to the Kaiser that I had no power behind me."[34] But Buelow's comments do make it clear that Herzl's negotiations to establish the conservative Viennese daily, while they would certainly not have been sufficient in and of themselves to fundamentally alter German policy, were nevertheless no exercise at charging windmills. Had he succeeded in establishing a paper powerful enough to make a difference to German politicians in need of favors, this might have been an additional concern capable of thickening the kaiser's passing romance with the Jews into a more useful interest in Zionism in the kaiser's court.

While the German initiative petered out, the sultan himself held open the possibility of granting a charter to a Jewish company in exchange for loans and investment, and Herzl spent much time over the next years in efforts to assemble the financial backing necessary to float a significant loan. But unlike the kaiser, the sultan never had any inclination to give his blessing to concentrated Jewish settlement in Palestine, and neither he nor his lackeys ever suggested otherwise. On the contrary, Herzl's protracted negotiations resulted only in offers of mining concessions and diffuse Jewish settlement in Mesopotamia and the like—perhaps some of them were even sincere—which led Herzl into a labyrinth of lies and subterfuge so dense that it is often impossible to understand what either side hoped to achieve. One example may suffice to give a sense of what he was suffering through. In December 1900, with negotiations over a Zionist loan bogged down, the Turks released a report through a semiofficial news agency that Jews were being turned away from Palestine because of their plans to reestablish the Kingdom of Judea.[35] Understanding that this report amounted to a threat to choke off all Jewish immigration if a deal was not reached on a loan, Herzl responded by issuing a threat of his own: If the Turks did not come to terms, he would conduct a tour of Jewish financiers and instruct them to cut off all ties with Turkey. Incredibly, this threat appeared to work, and Herzl was summoned to Constantinople for an even more involved round of negotiations that continued throughout the next year and on into 1902.[36]

Just as the Russian Zionists' discontent with the Zionist Organization was reaching a boiling point during the summer of 1902, Herzl's diplomacy was rapidly moving toward unprecedented successes that promised to make his disappointment with the Kaiser just so much spilled milk. Herzl had long been toying with the idea of establishing Jewish colonies on the periphery of the lands still firmly under Ottoman control as a prelude to the Jewish entry into Palestine proper. As early as fall 1899, he had considered the possibility of locating such a settlement on Cyprus, which was then under British control ("We would rally on Cyprus, and one day go over to Eretz Israel and take it by force, as it was taken from us long ago").[37] And in the summer of 1900, he had orchestrated a high-profile Zionist Congress in London, followed by an effort to obtain statements of support for Zionism from candidates running for Parliament that year (the new British Parliament included 41 MPs who had gone on record during the elections as favoring Zionism).[38] By March 1901, Herzl was even contemplating relocating to London as the most promising venue for future Zionist activity, and although nothing came of this, the following year he jumped at the chance to testify in Parliament before a Royal Commission considering the question of limiting immigration—the unease being stirred up by the unrestricted flow of Russian Jews into the country being one of the most pressing issues facing the Conservative government of Prime Minister Arthur Balfour. It was against this backdrop that Herzl secured his first meeting with Lord Nathaniel Mayer Rothschild, head of the English branch of the banking family, during which Herzl succeeded in persuading him that a Jewish charter company for settling British-controlled Sinai or Cyprus could divert Jewish immigration from England without recourse to legislation that could be understood as being anti-Jewish.[39] It was Herzl's testimony in Parliament that likewise positioned the option of British sponsorship for Jewish colonization as a real policy option for British leaders.

In late September 1902, Herzl received word from the English Zionist Leopold Greenberg that Colonial Secretary Joseph Chamberlain had agreed to a meeting. The goal was, in Herzl's phrase, "a rallying point for the Jewish people in the vicinity of Palestine"—either at El-Arish in the eastern Sinai or else in Cyprus—and Chamberlain evidently understood that his government had sound electoral reasons for entertaining such possibilities sympathetically. But it was not until the two of them were hunched together over an atlas, staring at El-Arish on a map, that Chamberlain seemed really to take in the possibility that the Russian émigrés could become a substantial colonial force at England's disposal. "The most striking thing about the interview," Herzl wrote later, "was that he didn't have a very detailed knowledge of the British possessions which undoubtedly are at his command now. It was like a big junk shop whose manager isn't quite sure whether some unusual article is in the stock-room. I need a place for the Jewish people to assemble. He's going to take a look and see if England happens to have something like that in stock."[40]

Impressed, Chamberlain ushered Herzl on for discussions with the foreign secretary, Lord Henry Landsdowne. After Greenberg had conducted preliminary meetings in Cairo with both the British and Egyptian administrations, the Foreign Office issued a formal invitation for a Zionist commission to explore possible settlement sites in Sinai—the first recognition by a European power of the Zionist Organization as a partner for negotiations.

The plan for a settlement at El-Arish—which Herzl happily referred to as "the Egyptian province of Judea"[41]—ran aground in the spring, ostensibly because of engineering problems associated with supplying water to the settlement. But the real reason was apparently political opposition from Arab and British officials in Egypt. Herzl met Chamberlain again on April 23, 1903, four days after the Kishinev pogrom. This horror, in which forty-five Jews were killed and six hundred more were badly wounded, marked the resumption of the policy of state-incited terror against the Jews of Russia after an interruption of several years, and it was in this context that Chamberlain made his infamous suggestion that, taking account of the circumstances, the Jews might consider settlement in British East Africa.

Herzl responded negatively at first, insisting that the Jews had to have Palestine.[42] But as the implications of the pogrom unfolded and the Egyptian government cast its final veto against a Jewish settlement in Sinai, he reconsidered. There has been endless argument over whether Herzl actually intended to take up the British offer and establish a Jewish colony in East Africa or whether he was certain nothing would come of the idea and only agreed to explore the possibility as a tactic for drawing Britain deeper into collaboration with the Zionist Organization. A good guess is that his initial impulse, in the wake of the graphic press reports from Kishinev, was closer to the former view and that he ended near the latter.[43] But it is clear that in early summer, Herzl approached Lloyd George, Roberts and Co., the law firm of the Liberal parliamentarian David Lloyd George, to assist in preparing the ZO's proposals for the chartering of a Jewish colony under British protection. Under the draft charter assembled with Lloyd George's assistance, the ZO asked Britain to support Jewish self-government, including legislative, administrative, and judicial authority, the power of taxation, and control over public lands, as well as security services.[44] These negotiations resulted on August 14, 1903, in an official letter from the Foreign Office declaring that Britain was in fact prepared to reach agreement on the establishment of a Jewish colony under Jewish administration:

> Lord Landsdowne will be prepared to entertain favorably proposals for the establishment of a Jewish colony or settlement on conditions which will enable the members to observe their national customs. For this purpose he would be prepared to discuss . . . the details of a scheme comprising as its main features: The grant of a considerable area of land, the appointment of a Jewish official as chief of the local administration, and permission to the colony to have a free hand in regard to municipal legislation and as to the management of religious and purely domestic matters, such local autonomy being conditional upon the right of His Majesty's Government to exercise a general control.[45]

This unprecedented document, buried by subsequent events, constitutes the pinnacle of Zionist diplomatic success, surpassing even the Balfour Declaration in its reflection of Britain's willingness to consider a relationship with the ZO on Herzl's terms—whose essence was that the territory chartered to the Zionists would actually be governed as a Jewish territory by the Jews themselves. As Herzl correctly understood, the fact that the territory in question at that moment was in British East Africa was not, from the British perspective, significant. The territorial basis for the Jewish colony might very well be subject to change with changing circumstances. What *was* significant was that the British government had now accepted the idea that Britain might establish a territory under Jewish charter whose likely consequence would be a Jewish state. As Chamberlain hinted to Herzl regarding the possible future political development of the Jewish settlement, "If your colony is strong enough, I am sure you will assert yourself appropriately."[46]

But Herzl did not rest content with his success in London. Even before the formal publication of the Landsdowne letter, he was already on his way to St. Petersburg to meet the man believed responsible for the massacre at Kishinev, the czar's interior minister, Wjatscheslaw Plehwe. As Herzl had long suspected, the czarist government, ruling 7 million Jews, many of whom were increasingly drawn to socialism, was predisposed to support any scheme that might encourage Jewish emigration, especially if it were granted the legitimacy of Jewish cooperation. Plehwe considered the subject important enough to devote two lengthy meetings to discussions with Herzl, in which he displayed a remarkable familiarity with the Zionist movement, informing Herzl that his government only opposed Zionism of the cultural variety—that is, the movement being fanned by Ahad Ha'am and his followers—whose effect was to sharpen Jewish national feeling without actually resulting in emigration to Palestine.[47] But a Jewish state was a different story, and one that the czar would be prepared to support. "The creation of an independent Jewish state capable of absorbing several million Jews," he told Herzl "would suit us best of all."[48] Plehwe informed Herzl that he should consider this to be the formal position of the czar's government, and he agreed to present this stance to Herzl in writing. The result was a letter, dated August 12, in which a second major power formally expressed its willingness to work toward the fulfillment of Zionism—this one speaking explicitly of an independent Jewish state:

> I had the occasion of explaining to you the point of view of the Russian government regarding the implementation of Zionism. . . . The government of Russia will look upon you with favor so long as Zionism consists of the desire to create an independent state in Palestine, and organizing the emigration from Russia of a certain number of its Jewish subjects. However, the government of Russia will not agree that Zionism be transformed into propaganda for Jewish nationalism in Russia. Zionism of this type will only result in the establishment of a separate national group which will endanger the integrity of the country. Zionism will therefore receive once again the confidence [of Russia] . . . if it returns to its original program. Likewise, it will be able to enjoy both her political support and financial assistance the moment it succeeds in reducing the Jewish population in Russia.[49]

Herzl was now reaping the harvest of six years of ceaseless political initiatives, as England and Russia, two of the four powers capable of exerting themselves in the arena of Ottoman Palestine, had committed in principle to assisting in the restoration of the Jews. Nothing comparable to these events had taken place in the two thousand years of the exile. The dream was becoming policy, and Herzl's fantasy was coming true.

At the moment that these two letters came into his possession, Herzl's heart had already been in a state of continuous deterioration for some time. He had less than eleven months to live.

With a consistency unusual in a political leader, Herzl honored the requests of the various national leaders that he refrain from making use of their conversations with him in public discourse.[50] The result was that even at its most successful, the actual facts concerning his diplomacy in London and Cairo, Constantinople and St. Petersburg, was almost always invisible beneath a dense fog of rumors and speculation. This condition was especially acute in the strongholds of Zionist faith in Russia, where Herzl's every journey was the subject of enthusiastic speculation. And as the legend of the Zionist leader grew, so too did the opposition of Ahad Ha'am, who refused to attend the annual Zionist congresses or to pay membership dues to the ZO and who continued to rail against Herzl's activities as a machine for the manufacture of false hopes.[51]

While overt identification with Ahad Ha'am's rejectionism was at first limited, he did succeed in having a decisive influence on the views of a small circle of disciples, most notably among young Russian Zionist students enrolled in German universities. In 1886, the czar's government imposed matriculation ceilings limiting the number of Jews who could attend Russian universities, with the result that there were soon more Russian Jews studying in Central Europe than in the Russian empire itself. The great majority of these youthful Russian expatriates were attracted to political radicalism, readily assimilating the various "scientific" solutions being offered in Germany to the world's problems—and particularly to the plight of their fellow Jews, groaning under a Russian state that combined all the worst aspects of harsh monarchical government, the Eastern Church, and "capitalist" interests wedded to the ruling order. Usually this radicalism meant adopting the ideas of the Socialist Bund, which argued that a Jewish national identity would only be possible within a new socialist order that would come in place of the old Russia, or else adopting those of Marxism, which proposed that Jewish national identity should be eliminated along with everything else in the old Russia. But there were also some Zionists among them, and these, including Leo Motzkin and Chaim Weizmann, were among the moving spirits of the Russian-Jewish Scientific Society, formed in Berlin in 1887. Under the spell of the "scientific" politics that gave the club its name, these Russian-Jewish students became small-time preachers for socialism—and against capitalism, imperialism, and religion—within the movement for Jewish restoration in Palestine.

Unlike Ahad Ha'am, the Zionist Russian students in Berlin and other German cities attended Herzl's congresses with enthusiasm. Yet their integration into the ZO was not exactly a happy one. In many respects, Herzl was a politician in the traditional European mold, seeking to construct a stable alliance with imperial powers externally, while cementing a coalition of the wealthy aristocracy, middle-class businessmen, and clerical leaders internally. The students were incapable of defending such a strategy, and they found themselves tongue-tied when their non-Zionist competitors argued that Zionism was a reactionary movement.[52] At a very early stage, they began protesting Herzl's inclination toward imperial courts, banking families, and Orthodox rabbis, demanding that the ZO be constructed, as the young Weizmann put it, as "a genuinely modern movement of cultural and scientific responsibility," stripped of all its "unattractive petty bourgeois, conservative, and clerical overtones."[53] As it happened, however, these were precisely the overtones that Herzl had been at such great pains to create.

Particularly galling for the Russian students was the relationship that Herzl and Nordau attempted to develop with the rabbinic leadership of Eastern Europe—that is, with precisely those traditionalists who were the mainstays of the old order in the very communities these students had only recently abandoned. Herzl had only limited interest in the modern Hebrew literature of which Ahad Ha'am was an advocate; the idea that the great European literary and artistic traditions were to be cast aside by the new Jewish state simply held little attraction for him. Religion, however, was a different story. Although he was firmly opposed to the intervention of the religious leadership in the task of governing, Herzl nevertheless felt a certain attraction to traditional Jewish rituals and even ideas,[54] and he assumed religion would have a formal role to play in the Jewish state, just as it did in Austria, Germany, or Britain.* And he conducted the business of the ZO in such a way as to encourage this understanding. Already at the First Congress, Herzl had worked to create a favorable relationship with the local Orthodox synagogue in Basel, announcing the schedule for prayer services from the rostrum.[55] And the possibility of an alliance between Herzl and the traditionalists was given forceful expression at the Second Congress, when he had a group of black-coated Eastern rabbis seated on the dias. (One of them returned the gesture of respect by taking Herzl's

---

* One of the only passages from *The Jewish State* that is well-known in contemporary Israel is Herzl's rejection of theocratic government, in which he says that with respect to rabbis wishing to dictate the terms of governance to the political leadership, "We shall know how to restrict them to their temples." This passage is frequently used to make the case that Herzl supported a constitutional "separation of church and state." In fact, Herzl supported Judaism as an established religion in the Jewish state. The rest of the above sentence makes this clear, with the rabbis having a role in the state analogous to that of the military: "Just as we shall restrict our professional soldiers to their barracks. The army and the clergy shall be honored to the extent that their noble functions require and deserve it. But they will have no privileged voice in the state." The parallel Herzl draws between the established church and the military is clear: Both serve important and legitimate functions in the state, so long as they do not actually usurp the political decisionmaking process. See Herzl, *The Jewish State*, p. 100; Yoram Hazony, "Did Herzl Want a 'Jewish' State," *Azure* 9 (spring 2000), pp. 59–64.

hand and kissing it.) The following year, in 1899, the leadership's courtship of the religious reached its peak, with Herzl arguing that the traditional Jews would yet produce "the very best Zionists," because "they have not yet forgotten the national traditions and have a strong religious sentiment."[56]

By the spring of 1901, the students could no longer stomach Herzl's politics, and Motzkin and Weizmann threw themselves into the creation of a formal opposition party within the Zionist Organization, calling itself the Democratic Faction. As Motzkin emphasized, while all Zionists were united in their pursuit of "the ideal of the Jewish state,"[57] the new party would seek to attain this state through an Ahad Ha'amist program of practical settlement in Palestine, as well as through projects aimed at creating a new Jewish cultural movement based on "modern" tenets. Moreover, Weizmann wrote, the Democrats "will always be . . . in opposition whenever dealings with the clericals and with the bourgeoisie . . . are concerned." In all, thirty-seven delegates arrived at the Fifth Congress committed to advancing this program, with the chief result being an unprecedented display of contempt for diplomacy, capitalism, and traditional Judaism, by the student leaders, Motzkin, Weizmann, and Martin Buber, who even staged a protest walkout during one of the sessions. "Our opponents," wrote Weizmann with satisfaction, "will be wiped out in a few years' time."[58]

At the time at least, Herzl had no reason to fear being "wiped out," and certainly not by the likes of Weizmann and Motzkin. But two factors made the opposition mounted by Ahad Ha'am's followers more than a mere student rebellion. The first was the Russian students' coup in adding to their ranks Berthold Feiwel and Martin Buber, the most talented German student leaders that Herzl had succeeded in recruiting for the ZO during years of strenuous efforts. Feiwel had worked with Herzl in Vienna during the preparations for the First Congress, and both he and Buber had enjoyed Herzl's confidence as editors of the organization's Vienna-based weekly, *Die Welt*. But by 1901, Buber and Feiwel had joined the leadership of the Democrats, promoting Ahad Ha'am's line among German-speaking students as well. This defection of Herzl's closest young sympathizers was no easy turn of events, and it opened a rift that would only grow more bitter.

Herzl's second reason for concern over the Democrats' behavior was his fear of fallout from their shrill attacks on the Eastern rabbinate. Reuben Branin, Herzl's Hebrew-language secretary, wrote that he had not witnessed "such a terrible attitude . . . toward popular Orthodoxy among the most radical parties in all Europe," and Herzl correctly understood that this would reinforce the sense, growing steadily among the traditionalist Jews of the East, that the Zionist movement could not be reconciled with religious piety. As early as 1898, R. Elijah Akiva Rabinowich, one of the rabbinic representatives at the congress, had told Herzl that the attitude toward the ZO among the religious in Russia was deteriorating steadily, emphasizing, "the more the Zionists of our country deal with cultural activities, so will the number of anti-Zionists increase among the Orthodox." And indeed, he pointed to rabbinic figures who were sympathetic to Zionism but found themselves with no choice but to oppose it, since the Russian Zionists continued to "concern themselves only with educating the people in their own freethinking ideology." By the Fifth Congress, Rabinowich had withdrawn from the ZO and begun publishing *Hapeles*, the first trans-European Orthodox publication, which became a leading vehicle for rallying the fragmented camps of traditional Jewry against Zionism.[59]

It is unclear to what degree Herzl understood how much damage had already been done, but certainly by early 1902, it had become evident to him that the threat posed by Ahad Ha'am and his followers could no longer be dismissed. A change in Russian state policy toward Zionism that year had for the first time permitted the Russian Zionists to organize an empire-wide conference to be held in September in Minsk, which they hoped would be the beginning of a legal, officially tolerated movement.[60] Since its inception, Herzl's ZO had been able to operate largely unhindered by the objections of Russian Zionists, since the czar's hostility had in any case foreclosed the possibility of their establishing an effective alternative to the leadership in Vienna. Herzl's encouraging words concerning the convening of the conference of Russian Zionists notwithstanding, the Zionist Organization suddenly found itself faced with a serious threat to its continued viability: Hovevei Zion, virtually wiped out as a political factor five years earlier, had come alive again overnight, conducting what the Russians referred to as a "congress" of their own, which could in practice challenge anything and everything. And this conference came on the heels of a thirty-five-page essay by Ahad Ha'am, which accused Herzl of having contributed nothing to Zionism and dismissed his *The Jewish State* as little more than a shallow plagiarism of the ideas of Hovevei Zion.[61] With Ahad Ha'am and much of the leadership of the Democratic Faction certain to be in attendance at Minsk, the possibility of a takeover of Russian Zionism, the heart of the movement, loomed as an all-too-real possibility.

Even before the plans to convene the Russian conference had been laid, Herzl had determined to fight back, quietly initiating a meeting of both religious and non-Orthodox Zionists in Vilna, where they agreed to establish a united front against the introduction of an Ahad Ha'amist cultural program in the Russian Zionist Organization.[62] The result was the establishment in March 1902 of the movement's second party, the Mizrahi, headed by R. Isaac Jacob Reines, a staunch supporter of Herzl. Under Reines's leadership, Herzl's supporters within Russian Zionism were rapidly organized.

Within months, 130 Zionist chapters in Russia had declared themselves affiliates of the new party, and another thirty were founded, so that by the time the conference opened, one-third of the six hundred delegates were solidly committed to Herzl's line. Weizmann and his circle looked on in helpless horror, with Weizmann commenting, "The rabbinical party is organizing itself in Jesuit fashion, and I think of their machinations with disgust. Everything is vulgar and foul."[63]

Yet Ahad Ha'am's rising authority among Eastern Zionists could not by this point be so easily overwhelmed. When he rose to speak at the Minsk conference on October 7, he stood before a throng of delegates that rivaled those that had attended even the largest congresses. But for once the crowd did not consist of half-assimilated Jews, communicating with one another in German. This was his public, both those who were for him and those who were against. They had followed for five years as he had unleashed his broadsides against the Zionist Organization in Vienna. Now they convened in tense anticipation of the barrage that had been in the making for so long—and they got one.

Ahad Ha'am began by once more affirming that he, no less than Herzl, aimed at "attaining in Palestine, at some distant date, absolute independence in the conduct of the national life." But with that said, he turned his attention to the ravages that the emancipation had visited upon the national culture of the Jews. With the opening of the ghetto, he said, the best Jewish minds had turned their attention to deepening the literature of France and Germany, leaving Jewish literature to become "a barren field for dullards and mediocrities to trample on." Unconcerned for anything other than physical survival, the Jews had reached the brink of a cultural catastrophe: "Our national spirit is perishing, and not a word is said; our national heritage is coming to an end before our eyes, and we are silent."[64]

When Ahad Ha'am said that "we" are silent, he of course did not mean himself. Rather, his target was the Zionist Organization, which wasted those energies available for national revival on the illusion of a fast road to Jewish statehood. With his sights thus locked on the ZO, Ahad Ha'am now threw one bombshell after another. He proposed that the Jews create a second organization in which Zionists and non-Zionists would work together to develop and disseminate Jewish national culture. He demanded that the ZO itself take the lead in establishing the new organization, despite the fact that many of its members would be opposed to Zionism. And he dismissed Herzl's goal of "conquering the communities"—his call to local ZO chapters to wrest control of the synagogues and Jewish communal organizations from the anti-Zionists—insisting instead that the main Zionist effort be devoted to "conquering the schools," so as to prepare the way for successes a generation or two hence:

Conquer the schools! In the synagogue we have to deal with the parents, in the schools with the children. To conquer the parents, to infuse a new spirit into grown men who have already settled down into a certain way of life . . . would be a matter of more labor than profit; the small results would not generally be worth the expenditure of energy. Surely, it were better for our purpose to lay out this energy on the conquest of the children. In them we have a clean sheet on which we may write what we will. If in the course of time we can put into the field a large squadron of younger men to fight their elders, the products of the school against the leaders of the synagogue, where will the victory lie? History bears witness that in a war of parents and children it is always the children who win in the end; the future is theirs.[65]

With the issue of "culture" thus moved to center stage, Ahad Ha'am openly rejected Herzl's compromise version of the Democratic Faction's cultural resolution, adopted the previous year by the Fifth Congress. This resolution had granted that promulgating education "in the national spirit" was incumbent on all Zionists, but it had also sidestepped the question to which the Democrats had demanded an answer with such acrimony: Whether this national education that the congress had endorsed should be traditional or "modernist." Herzl had once again deflected this question for the sake of unity within the movement, but such unity was to Ahad Ha'am nothing more than a ruse. The creation of a "modern" school system was of the essence, and he now demanded that the conference endorse its establishment, alongside the efforts of religious Zionists to infuse national consciousness within the traditional schools.[66]

The effect of Ahad Ha'am's proposals was the dismemberment of the existing Zionist Organization. Instead of continuing as a unified body whose goal was the establishment of a Jewish state, the membership of the ZO would splinter into a confederation of streams, educational and otherwise, some working at cross-purposes with the others and even setting their course in close collaboration with non-Zionists.[67] Subsequent speakers indignantly assailed him as an opponent of Zionism, and the conference verged on explosion. With the dissolution of Russian Zionism—and with it the entire ZO—into two separate organizations now a tangible possibility, the presidium of the conference called upon Ahad Ha'am and Reines to work out a compromise. As the delegates waited in tense anticipation, the two leaders hammered out an agreement that, in the end, mandated the establishment of two separate cultural committees, one modernist and one traditional, that would conduct educational efforts throughout Russia. Reines had capitulated.[68]

Although the Minsk cultural committees quickly ran out of steam for lack of funds, the results of Ahad Ha'am's victory went far beyond what either side realized at the time. The fact was that the Minsk "compromise" was a resounding political defeat for Herzl—his first. Only a year earlier, he had scarcely felt compelled to pass an ambiguous resolution on "culture." Now, having thrown his weight into the fray to prevent the establishment of "modernist" schools from becoming one of the central aims of Russian Zionism, his forces had been routed by a growing coalition of his socialist and anti-religious opponents. Moreover, this defeat sent the clearest possible message to the rabbinic leadership of the East that despite Herzl's own inclinations, Zionists in Russia would become ever more focused on "writing what we will," as Ahad Ha'am had put it, on the tabula rasa of Russia's Jewish children. Indeed, after Minsk there could be no question that the Zionist movement as a whole was lurching away from Herzl's hoped-for coalition of Jewish diplomacy, enterprise, and tradition. Herzl could not know how the looming threat to his leadership would finally express itself, but he was painfully aware, as not many others seem to have been, of how precarious his position had become.

The defeat at the Minsk conference came at the end of a year of humiliations that Herzl had suffered at the hands of the student faction within the ZO—from Martin Buber's resignation after a few months as editor-in-chief of *Die Welt*, to the Democrats' ugly demonstrations at the Fifth Congress, to their active efforts to jump-start a socialist movement within the Zionist Organization over Herzl's protests.[69] The previous eighteen months, too, had seen the dissemination of new German-language publications initiated by the Democrats—Buber and Feiwel's *Juedischer Almanach*, and *Ost und West*, edited by Davis Trietsch and Leo Winz—publications that were translating and circulating Ahad Ha'am's essays in German for the first time.[70] In the Minsk debacle, too, the Russian students had been politically involved on Ahad Ha'am's side, and in Germany the Democrats did what they could to broaden the effects of this defeat as well: The October 1902 issue of *Ost und West* included a translation of Ahad Ha'am's devastating speech, as well as companion essays by Buber and by Feiwel, the former calling Ahad Ha'am "the most profound thinker of the Jewish rebirth," the latter explaining that the participation of Herzl's Orthodox allies in Zionist politics was inherently illegitimate.[71] By this point, Herzl must surely have sensed that the German student leaders were no longer merely expressing dissent from this or that political strategy but that they were now actively assisting in the breakup of the Zionist Organization.

It was against this background that there erupted within the Zionist movement a bizarre little scandal known as the *Altneuland* controversy, which precipitated Herzl's final rupture with the student leaders of the Democratic

Faction. In October 1902, within weeks of Reines's defeat, Herzl published a novel to which he had been devoting spare hours for three years. Entitled *Altneuland* ("Old-New Land"), it was a utopian romance in which a young German-Jewish lawyer who realizes that there is no future for him in Vienna falls asleep and dreams of a time twenty years hence when the Jews have returned to Palestine. The dream is a contemporary reworking of Isaiah's vision, in which the restoration of the Jews to their former glory is achieved as a result of the fact that the lion has come to lie with the lamb: The Jewish society in *Altneuland* has no armies, no borders, no wars; it has no capitalist exploitation, no socialist agitation, and indeed, no work disputes at all; it has no serious crime and no jails; it imposes no citizenship and exists solely by virtue of the voluntary participation of its members, who are free to join and secede as they please; it offers perfect equality among all faiths and nationalities; it wins the respect of all nations, earns endless foreign tourism, and is the center of every international organization for good works and peace on earth; its democracy is populated by pure-hearted Jewish masses, who, although easily incited, are nevertheless immediately brought back to their senses with gentle and sensible words. In short, it is a utopia, and like all utopias, this one also invites the reader to close his eyes and believe. As the famous epigram at the opening of the novel has it: "If you will it, it is no fairy tale."[72]

On its face, *Altneuland* does not seem to pose any great difficulties in interpretation. The central device of the novel—using the seemingly endless technological advances of the beginning of the twentieth century as a stand-in for miracles of the supernatural sort—is a clever means of rendering biblical Messianism palatable to the agnostics and socialists of Herzl's day. But this secularization of the miraculous is hardly sufficient to render the tale plausible, and there is no evidence to suggest that Herzl ever thought it was. In fact, the novel is precisely what it seems to be: An end-of-days vision, not a political program. We know from Herzl's diaries and other sources that, far from trying to actually execute the utopian schemes presented in *Altneuland,* he never wavered from his original goal of seeking an independent and sovereign Jewish state, complete with an army and navy, borders, and power politics. Indeed, during the same period when the novel was being distributed, Herzl was contemplating securing Jewish control of Palestine through armed "influence" across the Sinai frontier, or even by means of a coup d'état in Constantinople.[73] A draft of the charter he hoped to receive from the Turks—from the same period the novel was being written—is similarly hardheaded, granting him the authority to expropriate private land so long as the present owners could be provided with equivalent lands outside of Palestine at the Jewish company's expense.[74]

But if the Messianic utopia presented in *Altneuland* is no reflection of Herzl's actual political aims and activities as the head of the Zionist

Organization, why did he write it? The answer, it seems, appears in *The Palais Bourbon*, a book containing Herzl's insights into politics in France, in which he calls attention to the crucial role played by the utopias presented to the crowds by socialist politicians. Their task, Herzl explains, "is to help the suffering masses through a dark night by duping them with fairy tales, promises, and gory or appealing fantasies."[75] Herzl had said much the same thing in the Zionist context in his meeting with Baron de Hirsch. At that time he had explained that "men are ruled by the simple and the fantastic. . . . To attract Jews to rural areas you have to tell them some fairy tale about how they may strike gold there. In imaginative terms it might be put like this: Whoever plows, sows, and reaps will find gold in every sheaf. After all, it's almost true."[76] A few years later, when Herzl began to realize that his public was growing restless awaiting the results of his diplomacy, he began writing a mass-appeal utopia of his own, which he hoped could buy him some faith, enthusiasm, and patience with a public that could not really understand what their leader was doing. As he wrote to a political confidant: "It is a fable which, as it were, I am telling by the camp-fires to keep up the good spirits of my poor people while they are on the march. To hold out is everything."[77]

Yet from the day *Altneuland* was published, there have been those—and not only among the uneducated Russian-Jewish masses—who insist on reading the novel literally, as though it were intended to be a practical political program. One of them was Ahad Ha'am, whose review of the novel was published in the December 1902 issue of *Hashiloah*—the same issue that carried the Hebrew version of his speech at Minsk. In his review, Ahad Ha'am argued that since the founding of the Zionist Organization, Herzl had never yet explained how the "miracle" of rapid economic development of Palestine could be performed, and claimed that *Altneuland* was the book in which Herzl finally "explains in detail how he himself imagines that his vision is now to be fulfilled." Having set up this straw man, he then goes about tearing it to shreds, ridiculing Herzl for one piece of patent fiction in his novel after another: The completion of the total ingathering of the Jews into Palestine within twenty years; the invisibility of the Jewish settlement's sources of start-up capital; the sudden abundance of superhuman Jewish administrators jumping to the task of building the land; the purchase of much of the country within four months; the organization of the first year's immigration of half a million Jews within a few weeks; the rebuilding of the Temple without a mention as to how this could be done while a mosque is still standing on Mount Zion; and so on.

Once he has demonstrated that Herzl's real-life political efforts to found a Jewish state are nothing more than an impossible fiction, Ahad Ha'am then attacks the book for its blatant efforts to demonstrate that Christian and Muslim interests would be well-treated in a Jewish Palestine, a message repeated in almost every chapter with such enthusiasm and at such length that the suspicion has to arise in the mind of the reader that all the author's labors were "'for them,' so that 'they' will see and be convinced of how beneficial is this 'Zionism.'"[78] And of course, this was exactly the case. Herzl even made one of the central characters in his novel a Prussian military officer who is so impressed with Jewish Palestine that he chooses to live there. Herzl did not really believe that Prussian officers would choose to come live in the Jewish state, any more than he really believed that in the Jewish state there would be no work disputes, no armed forces, and no jails. His utopia was just as carefully aimed at propagandizing against European fears that a Jewish state would harm Christian interests in the Holy Land—upon publication he even sent a copy to his old nemesis Buelow, now chancellor of Germany—as it was fanning Messianic dreams of the coming state among his restless Jewish audience. Here, too, Ahad Ha'am's critique would have been closer to the mark had he dispensed with the foolishness of treating a fantasy as a future political program and instead attempted to grasp the immediate political purpose that the book was intended to serve.

It is a commonplace of Zionist history that the aggressive reaction to Ahad Ha'am's book review on the part of Herzl and Max Nordau was the result of Herzl's vanity. But there is little evidence showing that Herzl cared what a needling Russian reviewer thought of his novel.[79] What Herzl did care about was that Ahad Ha'am, who had for years been fighting a relentless guerrilla war against him, had succeeded, only a few weeks before in Minsk, in blasting a gaping hole in his prestige that threatened to capsize the entire ZO. In this context, the use of *Altneuland* to portray the head of the Zionist Organization and his diplomatic activities as far-fetched fantasies could only do further damage to Herzl's standing and to the viability of his political efforts—especially since the editors of *Ost und West* had announced their intention of publishing Ahad Ha'am's attack in German for circulation in the heartland of Herzl's support.[80]

It was thus not his literary criticism but the political threat that Ahad Ha'am now represented that jolted Herzl into recognizing him as a genuine political enemy. And in the response to the review that Nordau circulated to a number of newspapers in Europe, this is just what he called him—an enemy of Zionism:

> In the last two or three years, some [i.e., the Democrats] have made it their concern to drag [Ahad Ha'am] out of his corner, where he had been . . . unknown and unnoticed, in order to present him to the wider Jewish world. Many of his essays have been translated into German. Studies, meditations and commentaries have been dedicated to him. We smiled, turned our head away and let it happen. It was our Zionism that created the platform and the

audience for all this. The translations from Ahad Ha'am and the "studies"(!) about him were published in our Zionist newspapers. Lectures about this great man were held in Zionist organizations. The interest that was paid to him was an outcome of the involvement in everything Jewish that Zionism had created . . .

We allowed Ahad Ha'am to step out of his darkness, to bask in the light of the wide, Zionist public . . . However, if he abuses our forbearance in order to stir up his naive community against our leader and his difficult, self-sacrificing work; if he expresses his thanks to Zionism, to which he owes so much, by attacking it spitefully and unfaithfully, then forbearance would be an error. The time has come to stop this game, which is no longer harmless. Not for Ahad Ha'am's sake . . . but because of the community that—much through our own fault—believes in him and is being misled by him. Ahad Ha'am is among the worst enemies of Zionism. He fights it differently from those dying to break with Judaism, who would like to see it evaporate without a trace . . . Still, he fights it in no less ferocious and dishonest a way, since he dares to pose as a Zionist and to speak about the real, the only existing Zionism with well-calculated contempt, as . . . "political" Zionism.[81]

From Nordau's response, it is clear that Ahad Ha'am's influence had become a serious problem for the leadership of the Zionist Organization, which not only feared the disintegration or secession of the movement in Russia but had also begun to feel the ground being swept out from under its feet in Germany. Nordau's reference to "some" individuals using the movement's newspapers and local branches to disseminate materials promoting Ahad Ha'am was, after all, the first time that a leader of the ZO had directly condemned the activities of Buber, Feiwel, and their associates, whom Nordau believed to be abetting mutiny.

Nordau's attack on Ahad Ha'am drew an immediate response from the Democrats, with Weizmann, Feiwel, and Buber publishing a defense of their mentor, insinuating that Herzl was a tyrant who opposed free speech within the movement.[82] In a subsequent letter to Buber, Herzl was at pains to emphasize that although he had always supported free speech in the movement—he may have been referring to the Democrats' tirades against the Zionist leadership at the Fifth Congress—Ahad Ha'am's efforts were aimed at undermining the ZO and encouraging its members to leave it.[83] But Buber was by now uninterested in anything Herzl might have said, and his response to Herzl's letter went far beyond the claims of free speech, denouncing the atmosphere Herzl had created by surrounding himself with businessmen and the religious as "intolerable" and accusing him of having prevented the students ("the single great strength of the movement") from taking their rightful place as his natural allies and heirs: "As a friend of the young people you would have rejuvenated the movement and brought into it innumerable modern and capable elements. You have preferred to support a dying generation with dying traditions. . . . All this will probably lead ultimately to reducing the activists to passivity."[84]

Herzl was no fool, and he could not overlook Buber's rejection of his entire politics as the misguided pursuit of "a dying generation with dying traditions." Nor could he miss Buber's none-too-subtle threat that if Herzl's policies remained unchanged, the students would be "reduced to passivity." Written in May 1903, this letter from Buber, the most promising disciple Herzl had ever recruited among German Jewry, spelled the end. If Zionism were to insist on the path that Herzl had originally envisioned for it, Buber was prepared to quit. In a move without precedent for a leader who had gone to such lengths to emphasize that he welcomed all Jews, Herzl wrote back to inform Buber that he could no longer consider him to be within Zionism: "Without going into further detail, I will not conceal from you my view that the so-called Faction, for reasons unknown to me, has gone astray. My advice is: Try to find your way back to the movement." He goes on to say that he "did not know that brothers were going to become enemies."[85]

Two weeks earlier, Herzl had written a similar letter to Weizmann, in which he had told the young Democratic leader that he considered him "temporarily lost" but nevertheless a generally constructive force who would "once more find his way back and proceed along the right road together with all of us." Herzl then concluded: "But I am becoming ever more strongly convinced that not all the gentlemen in your group are in this category, and I am ready for the time when, sooner or later, they will be lost to our movement."[86]

Much as the Democrats believed that they themselves constituted the "the single great strength of the Zionist movement," events proved otherwise. As it turned out, this final rejection of the Democrats' theories by the head of the Zionist Organization was the deathblow that put an end to their grandiose schemes. Within days of this upbraiding from Herzl, Buber wrote to Weizmann and Feiwel in despair that the Democratic Faction "has done almost nothing. . . . No actual organization exists. The Mizrahi shames us in the most painful way." He proposed a "complete reorganization," including dropping the words "Democratic" and "Faction," as well as programmatic and structural changes.[87] But nothing came of any of this. The party failed to operate as a bloc at the stormy congress of 1903, and the party office, which had also served as the campaign headquarters for the great dream of a Jewish university, was closed for good in February 1904. Weizmann left for England, where he devoted himself to chemistry, while Buber made good his threat and withdrew from all activity in the Zionist movement to immerse himself in Hasidic thought somewhere in Italy. Most of the remaining Democrats drifted toward the newly organized Poalei Zion

("Workers of Zion") party, which increasingly carried the standard of so-cialist ideals. Weizmann and Buber seemed to have reached the end of their road as Zionist leaders.

More than ten years were to pass before either of them would reappear as a factor in the public life of the Jews. By that time, Herzl's uncanny prophesy had been proved correct: Weizmann, only "temporarily lost," had assumed the great man's mantle as the only serious statesman of the movement for a Jewish state; whereas Buber, forever "lost to our movement" as Herzl had guessed, was to reemerge as an opponent of the Jewish state.

On Sunday morning, August 23, 1903, Herzl informed the Sixth Congress of aspects of his negotiations in St. Petersburg and of the British offer of a territory in East Africa, the result of the first formal negotiations ever con-ducted between a European power and the Jews as a people. Both achieve-ments were at first greeted by a storm of enthusiastic applause by the nearly six hundred delegates, with Israel Zangwill calling above the din: "Three cheers for England!"[88]

But as the wild details of Herzl's negotiations began to penetrate—a place of refuge in the heart of Africa, two thousand miles from Palestine, and assistance from the blood-soaked Russian tormentor Plehwe—all that many of the Russians could hear were the words that Ahad Ha'am had been preaching for so long: Herzl's insistence on a political salvation for the Jewish masses would bring ruin and despair; there could be no salvation now, only the smallest of steps. And here it was, the single great step that Herzl had been promising for six years—a step into the interior of Africa. Over the hum of the throng, Herzl attempted to speak to the congress of Kishinev, of the condition of the Jews, of the millions endangered: "Jews are being tortured in body and soul"; "considering the plight of Jewry and the need to alleviate that plight as soon as possible"; "I believe the Congress can make use of"; "the offer was made to us in a manner that is bound to im-prove and alleviate." Herzl tried to tell them of the interim goal, that no principle was being abandoned because they would continue to work for Palestine, for Jerusalem.[89] But the spell was broken, and many of the Russians could no longer hear him.

The subsequent debate—technically over the question of whether to es-tablish a committee to study the British offer, but in fact choked with emo-tion over the seeming abandonment of Palestine—began on Tuesday afternoon, continuing late into the night and into the afternoon of the next day. It ended with a vote of 295 in favor, 178 against, although together the opposition votes and abstentions amounted to slightly more than half of the congress. When the results were announced, Yehiel Tschlenov, one of the Russian leaders, left the hall, and most of the opposition followed. Herzl at length succeeded in persuading them to return to the congress, but the wound remained unhealed. In November, Menahem Ussishkin mustered the Russian Zionist leaders in Kharkov and demanded that Herzl withdraw his motion or else they would organize "an independent Zionist Organization without Dr. Herzl." A committee was appointed to handle Zionist affairs in Russia, and financial matters relating to the Russian organization were removed from the hands of Herzl's associates.[90]

Herzl fought back with all the means at his disposal, but by the time a formal British offer of 5,000 square miles near Lake Victoria—a territory about one-half the size of the present state of Israel—was made on January 25, 1904, he was already preparing a face-saving reconciliation. At a conference in April, he told the Russians that even as he had pursued the East Africa option, he had continued to work with all his might for Palestine and that nothing could be achieved if the movement could not trust its leadership to be faithful to its goal. Recalling his views when he had written *The Jewish State* eight years earlier, he pointed out that at the time, he had openly been willing to consider building on Baron de Hirsch's beginning and establishing the Jewish state in Argentina. But those days were long gone:

> It was as a *Judenstaatler* [i.e., proponent of a Jewish state] that I presented myself to you. I gave you my card, and there the words were printed: "Herzl, *Judenstaatler*." In the course of time I learned a great deal. . . . Above all, I learned to understand that we shall find the solution of our problem only in Palestine. . . . I became a Zionist, and have remained one, and all my efforts are directed toward Palestine.[91]

The Russians pronounced that they accepted his statements and agreed to the formality of sending a commission to East Africa. But the possibility of establishing a Jewish settlement there had already evaporated, and everyone knew it. On July 4, 1904, Herzl died, having expended the last strokes of his heart in staving off the destruction of the organization he had founded to be the guardian of the Jews.

Although most of the Zionist Organization seemed prepared to forget the "Uganda" controversy in the wake of Herzl's death, the fact is that it left scars that have never fully healed.[92] Even in our own day, there are those who still point to Herzl's alleged willingness to sacrifice Zion as a precedent for their own efforts to uproot traditional Jewish national concepts, symbols, and values from the public life of the Jewish state. But such efforts only repeat the tragic error of the Sixth Congress, ignoring the lesson that Herzl learned there at such immense cost to himself and to his people.

And the lesson was this: The state is, as Herzl had always claimed, an idea. And as an idea, it is built up in the minds of men through the fashioning of "imponderables" and memories, symbols and dreams. Yet during the period when this political dream weaving was Herzl's central concern, he had never believed that one may make use of just any fantasy or symbol in conjuring up the idea of the state: *Bismarck shook the tree that was planted by the dreamers*—harvesting the mature fruit that had been planted in the heritage of his people generations before. With exacting care, Herzl did the same, choosing a flag that invoked the shield of David and the lion of Judah, ancient symbols of Jewish national power, as well as the azure-blue threads of the prayer shawl. It was with similar care that he courted the rabbinate and attended the Sabbath services at the start of every congress, that he wrote in *Die Welt* of the joy of lighting the traditional candelabra commemorating the holiday of Hanukkah for the first time. Even *The Jewish State*, written before his contact with the Jews of the East, emphasized the immense power that Palestine held as one of the great imponderables: "The very name would be a powerful rallying cry for our people." And his battle against the German rabbis had been waged precisely over this very point— over their grotesque betrayal of their people's deepest longings, when they dismissed Zion, saying, "Never mind all that, it's just a 'symbol.'"[93] So long as Herzl continued to place the most sustained thought and emphasis on the *particular* dreams that the Jewish tradition had implanted in the people, his path was crowned with success.

It was only in the wake of bloodletting in Kishinev that Herzl, shaken to desperation, abandoned the work of harvesting motivating ideals and imponderables from the tree of Jewish tradition, focusing all the energies that remained to him on saving the material existence of the Jews of the East. And who, really, can criticize Herzl for this? For realizing that the sands were running out for the 7 million Jews trapped in the slaughterhouse of Russia, for calling on the Sixth Congress to act to "save those who still can be saved"?[94] Surely it is not for us, knowing what we now know of the fate of Europe's Jews, to disregard the tragic heroism in the opening of the East Africa question. Yet it is also clear that the moment Herzl turned to this cause, the dream that he had built with his own hands was shattered to pieces. And who should have known better that this would happen than Herzl himself? That at the very first utterance of the word "Uganda"—the undreamable, the utterly ponderable, the anti-symbol—the entire state of mind he had created would be run aground on a barren reality with no past and no future, capable of inspiring no one and leading nowhere?

At the congresses, Herzl had succeeded, through signs and wonders, in convincing the delegates that they really were the parliament in exile of Israel, presiding over the future restoration of the Jews, with Mount Zion nearly visible through the windows of the congress hall. But when he told the assembled delegates—not in so many words, but close enough—that the mountain through the window was Kilimanjaro, their fantasy died an instantaneous death. And the "delegates," suddenly awakened from their reverie, found themselves nothing but ordinary Jews again, weak and cold, marooned in the hall of a Swiss casino.

And like a Samson shorn of his braids, they learned that a people shorn of its ideal is incapable of acting to save itself even from persecution and ruin.

———————

Herzl's death at the age of forty-four brought the movement to which he had devoted his last years crashing to the ground. His formal successors had neither his stature nor his depth of vision, and one by one, the movement's accomplishments evaporated. In Russia, Plehwe was assassinated, and the following year brought the fall of the Conservative government in Britain that had for the first time negotiated with the Jews as a nation. Three years later, the coup of the Young Turks in Constantinople ushered in a regime fanatically opposed to any steps implying the erosion of Turkish sovereignty. In the ZO, there was no one with the ability to pick up the trail of Herzl's diplomacy, and in place of any creative counterassault, the hostility of the Turks induced a full-scale retreat. In the years after the advent of Young Turkey in 1908, the entire Zionist leadership, including even Nordau and Herzl's devoted friend David Wolffsohn, threw themselves into fervently denying that the ZO had ever pursued a Jewish state or a charter.[95] That same year, the ZO turned to the consolation of what was called "practical" Zionist work—as opposed to Herzl's "political" work— gradually redirecting its efforts to the establishment of Jewish settlements in Palestine, replicating the nonpolitical work in which the emancipationist philanthropies had been engaged for decades before anyone had ever heard the word "Zionism." The dream of a Jewish state seemed to have dissipated without a trace.

Yet such was the power of the idea Herzl had set in motion that even without substantial assistance from the Zionist Organization, it continued to turn fitfully in the minds of the men whom Herzl had reached in life. Only six years were to pass between the nadir of 1908 and the onset of World War I—when the idea of the Jewish state suddenly enjoyed a complete reversal of political fortune. On November 9, 1914, four days after Britain declared war on Turkey, the man who had been Herzl's lawyer in negotiations with Britain over an imperial charter, the Chancellor of the Exchequer David Lloyd George, raised the issue of the "ultimate destiny" of Palestine during a meeting of the British government, triggering discussions in which he declared himself to favor a Jewish state in Palestine. Another minister, Sir Herbert Samuel, who had read *The Jewish State* under the influence of his uncle, Lord Samuel Montagu, suggested that the war against Turkey might create the opportunity "for the fulfillment of the ancient aspiration of the Jewish people, and the restoration there of a Jewish state." A third, Sir Edward Grey, the foreign secretary, had spoken of creating "a refuge and a home" for the Jewish people somewhere in the empire in Parliament in 1904 during the debate over Herzl's East Africa initiative, and he too now declared himself in favor of a Jewish state in Palestine.[96] Two years later, Lloyd George would become prime minister of Britain. Foreign policy for his new government would be conducted by Foreign Secretary Lord Arthur Balfour, who had been prime minister when Britain had negotiated with Herzl over a Jewish settlement in Sinai in 1902, and by Colonial Secretary Lord Alfred Milner, who had that same year, as high commissioner of South Africa, recognized the ZO's representation in that country as having consular status.[97] Barely a month after coming to power, Lloyd George's government would order British forces to enter Palestine; shortly thereafter, it would formally recognize Jewish aspirations there.

It is to their enduring credit that under the new political circumstances brought about by the war, both Chaim Weizmann and his mentor Ahad Ha'am, now working for the Wissotzky Tea Company in London, jettisoned the antidiplomatic tradition that they had labored to instill in the dying Zionist Organization and personally undertook the renewal of the negotiations with Britain broken off a decade earlier. In these negotiations, Weizmann would pursue a strategy laid down by Theodor Herzl in 1902, seeking to harness the ambitions and sympathies of the British empire to the dream of the Jewish state.

PART

III

CHAPTER 6

The Desperados

ERZL HAD BELIEVED IT POSSIBLE that most of the world's Jews would arrive in Palestine within a few decades of the granting of an imperial charter, and it was this belief that allowed him to imagine that the Zionist Organization, and later on the Jewish state itself, would be launched by educated and prosperous Western European Jews. It would be the mostly Western Jewish directorate of the company that would serve as the government, leading in the development of the new state's political, economic, and cultural institutions and educating the Russian Jews in the operation of a civilized, free, and tolerant Western society such as they had never experienced themselves. He was not blind to the fact that it would be the poorest Jews who would be the first to come over, and in *The Jewish State,* he even estimated that this would be for the best. ("They are the ones we need first. Only desperados make good conquerors.")[1] But these first laborers would construct the physical foundations for the Jewish state. They would not themselves constitute the state, much less become its leadership. On the contrary, they would labor under the aegis of the charter company to earn a small private home and landholding of their own, so as to prepare them to be proprietors in a society that would be defined by the constant immigration of middle- and upper-class Jews from the West.

"Actually," Herzl noted, almost as a throwaway, "our poorest strata alone would suffice to found a state."[2] Yet his disinterest in this possibility was evident throughout his early writings—not least in his diaries, which point to Herzl's concern that a Jewish state would be unable to govern itself in a Western fashion and would turn into a byzantine and fanatical state such as the Boer state in South Africa or the resurrected Greece of his day.[3] For this reason, he was little attracted to the idea—which so charmed many of the Palestine-settlement enthusiasts of his day—of turning the Jews into a people of manual laborers on the soil of Palestine. For Herzl, these efforts at inducing Jews to revert to a more primitive life were worse than useless. They meant artificially attempting to uproot the Jewish intellectual tradition, which for him held the key to the success of the Jewish state. "Will anyone, then, expect Jews, who are intelligent people, to become peasants of the old type?" he wrote. "No effort at artificially lowering the intellectual level of our masses will be able to achieve this."[4]

Yet this was the scenario that had actually begun to unfold even before Herzl's death. As early as 1901, groups of Zionist workers were being organized in Russia, with the assistance of Democratic Faction activists seeking to strengthen their hand against Herzl.[5] These groups soon became hothouses for the inculcation of a Zionism of muscle and agriculture, which disdained the overactive Jewish mind and even held it to be the source of Jewish suffering. Like Tolstoy and the Narodnik movement, which had done so much to promote the cult of the Russian peasant and the Russian soil, these radical Zionists sought salvation in the belief that the Jews were not a real nation because they did not work the land and that the Jewish middle classes were parasites who persisted by the sweat of the Russian workingman. In this they accepted the arguments of the anti-Semites, learning to hate themselves as the Russians hated them and determining that self-respect could only be gained by becoming like the Russian laborers themselves.

No twist in the history of the Jews is as rife with irony as the fact that it was in the hearts of thousands of these revolutionary Russian youths, rather than among Germany's Jewish intellectuals, that Herzl's name and memory continued to resonate even after his death. One of these was David Gruen, a young man from a shtetl called Plonsk, the son of an unaccredited pleader who represented illiterate Polish peasants in the local courts. Gruen himself had not been enrolled in a school since he was thirteen years old, and the summer of 1904 found him in Warsaw, barely feeding himself by working as a teacher and trying to educate himself despite restrictions on the admission of Jews to Russian schools. He was seventeen when the news reached him that the Zionist leader had died. "Only once in a thousand years is a man of miracles such as this born," he wrote to a friend. "Like the expanse of the sea is . . . our loss." But he also believed in the ultimate triumph of Herzl's cause, and in the same letter, he wrote of the poets who would one day arise in Palestine to tell the story of "the great fighter and hero, who . . . awoke a people dwelling in tombs from the slumber of death."[6] A year and a half later, Gruen left for Palestine, where he would become a great fighter and a hero of the Jewish people in his own right—the man who, under the name Ben-Gurion, would bring the Jewish state into being.

In Warsaw, as in the rest of the Russian empire, the air was then seething with theories regarding the millennial peace that was to follow once the workers had overthrown the czar. In January 1905, a railway strike in the city seemingly gave the signal for the revolution to begin but in the end succeeded only in bringing the cavalry down on the heads of the radicals who had supported the strike, many of them Jewish students. Two hundred were killed. In the aftermath, a bespectacled twenty-four-year-old desperado named Ber Borochov arrived from Poltava, seeking to raise the spirits of the defeated by preaching that Jewish political revival in Palestine was preordained and could be adduced from proof texts in Marx and Engels. Following Herzl, Borochov taught that economic factors would force the Jews out of Europe and to an undeveloped land where they could flourish; following Marx, he decreed the process to be historically determined by material conditions and therefore inevitable. "The land of spontaneous concentrated Jewish immigration," he announced firmly, "will be Palestine."[7]

As was often the case with inevitable processes, there was a need for a vanguard to prepare the way, and to this task Borochov now called the Jewish working youth of Warsaw, successfully winning over both David Ben-Gurion and Yitzhak Tabenkin—two of the three young men who would become the giants of Labor Zionism in Palestine. Ben-Gurion may have found it difficult to accept this "scientific" and spiritless determinism, but he had no difficulty in imbibing the rest of Borochov's doctrines, and he quickly became a versatile public speaker in the service of historical materialism, the class war, and the need for Jews to receive weapons training. Upon returning to his village, he began dressing like a peasant, organizing unions and strikes in the tiny tailor shops of Plonsk, and extorting money from well-to-do Jews, sometimes at gunpoint, in order to finance his activities. As the story goes, he once fired two shots from his pistol in the *beit midrash*, the study hall where traditional Jewish books were made available to the community.[8]

In August 1906, not yet twenty, Ben-Gurion immigrated to Palestine, where he immediately set about trying to hire himself out as a farmhand in Petah Tikva. Work was scarce, and Ben-Gurion and his friends were rarely hired for more than a day at a time. Within two weeks of his arrival, he was ill with malaria. Like most of his compatriots, he found himself unable to earn enough money for food, so that his days were wracked not only by the torment of backbreaking physical labor, the sun, and recurring fevers but by chronic hunger as well.[9] The handful of firebrands who survived the battle against their own bodies under these conditions were not the grateful "masses" Herzl had envisioned rescuing but a self-created underclass that had succeeded in doing precisely what Herzl believed Jews would not do: They had reverted to the level of primitive agricultural laborers, under the torch of relentless ideological reeducation that they imbibed in sermons of fire and ice. Fire—in the merciless rages of Yosef Haim Brenner against the Jewish mind: "The Jewish spirit?" he wrote. "Wind and chaff. The great heritage? Sound and fury. . . . We bear no value, we command no respect. Only when we will have learned the secret of labor . . . shall we have deserved the title Man."[10] And ice—in the anaesthetizing astrosophisms of A. D. Gordon, guru and patron saint of the Labor movement's utopians, whose discourses on the relationship between the cosmos and the land ultimately reached conclusions no different from Brenner's: "In as much as we work, the land will be ours. And if not, all the national homes and blood and fire will be of no avail."[11]

The seemingly boundless ability of the Russian immigrants of those years to sustain physical hardship was in no small part a reflection of their age. Few were much older than Ben-Gurion. They had no families, and the majority did not even marry in their first fifteen years in the country. "It should never be forgotten," Gershom Scholem wrote later, "that Zionism was essentially a youth movement."[12] And a youth movement it was, untempered by the wisdom earned in adulthood and untempered by the responsibilities that come with it. And herein lay the secret of its success. The Jewish settlers' willingness to treat physical labor as the single and final value—at the expense of exposure, exhaustion, starvation, and even of life itself—was at its root the revolt of adolescence, colliding with all its furor against the memory of the life they had left behind.

It was this youthful fanaticism, too, that drove Ben-Gurion and the other Jewish farmhands to consume their "spare" hours in organizing themselves into rival political parties—parties whose total possible constituency was at the time no more than a few hundred. Poalei Zion ("Workers of Zion") held its first conference in Palestine on October 4, 1906, before Ben-Gurion had even been in Palestine a month, with seventy members arriving on foot from the various corners of the country. Under the leadership of Israel Shochat—who was twenty years old and had been in Palestine for a whole two years—this gathering hammered out the draft of a party manifesto, which called for the establishment of a Jewish socialist republic in Palestine, as well as for a world classless society without national, political, or other divisions. The completely contradictory nature of the party's two aims evidently did not impress itself upon too many of the participants. Shortly thereafter, Shochat and a number of other party members joined the first collective farm in Sejera, which they used as a base for training Jewish hot-heads in anticipation of an armed revolt against the Ottomans that they believed would bring the establishment of a Jewish state.[13]

Although Ben-Gurion was not invited to join the revolutionary vanguard at Sejera, his politics were at this point no more realistic than those of the other Russian radicals around him. They were, in fact, a nearly perfect example of the materialist naïveté that had divided the Eastern Jews from Herzl. Thus, while Ben-Gurion unabashedly wished for the establishment of an independent Jewish state, he was not embarrassed to refer to the Jewish farming settlements—the largest of which, Petah Tikva, numbered eighty families—as "Hebrew republics."[14] That is, he conceived the coming "Jewish state" as little more than a greatly enlarged version of the Polish shtetl where he was born—an aggregation of houses, farms, and factories peopled by Jews. The necessity of establishing sovereignty by means of amassing the international political support of the great powers was at the time incomprehensible to Ben-Gurion. Likewise, Ben-Gurion had no experience that would allow him to appreciate the role of cultural factors such as religion in forging the state, nor of the importance of capital and enterprise in creating national power. To him, Zionism was simply identical with "transforming the *entire* nation, without exception . . . into workers in Palestine. This is the essence of our movement."[15]

Even after World War I, when Ben-Gurion was already in his thirties, it was these childish views of the state that still permitted him to believe that the Jewish state was something that could be created by an all-encompassing *labor union*—controlling the material means of production and using them toward the end of bringing Jews to Palestine. The full story of this scheme has unfortunately never been told by anyone suitably impressed with its absurdity. Suffice it to say that through the mid-1920s, Ben-Gurion continued to strive to create a union that would in effect be one great Jewish "labor army," all of whose members would take orders concerning "location, nature, and arrangement of the work" they would do and turn over all their income to the union in exchange for food, shelter, and medical treatment. Ultimately, this commune was supposed to absorb every Jew in Palestine.

Failing to sell this plan to his colleagues on the executive of the General Federation of Jewish Labor (usually known only as the Histadrut, "the Federation"), which had been founded in 1920, Ben-Gurion nevertheless continued trying to implement it piecemeal. One noteworthy step was the decision of the Labor Federation in March 1922 to accept Ben-Gurion's plan whereby all Histadrut employees, from the executive down to the janitorial staff, would receive a uniform wage, adjusted only on the basis of family size. This system, which Ben-Gurion judged far superior to the graduated system in place in Leninist Russia, rapidly proved unenforceable. Doctors had to be paid more for fear that they would transfer to the privately operated Hadassah hospital, exceptions for professionals were rapidly followed by a seniority component, and further compromises followed in rapid succession. Ben-Gurion, trying to live on the uniform wage himself, ended up deeply in debt. By 1926, he owed the Histadrut two years' pay. But one of his outstanding traits as a leader, for good and for ill, was that he was not one to allow previous opinions to interfere with his development into a strident opponent of the views he had not long ago espoused. Six years after he had cooked up the plan of a unitary pay scale, Ben-Gurion had become outspoken in his disdain for the idea.[16]

Of course, not all of the Labor movement's materialist experiments were so quickly abandoned. In March 1924, a modified version of Ben-Gurion's all-embracing "Society of Workers" was officially founded by the Histadrut, not as a commune but as a mammoth stock company in which the workers were shareholders. Its principal function was the establishment of monopolistic corporate subsidiaries that would be able to provide for the needs of the workers in all areas of life, including agriculture, contracting, banking, retailing, housing, food processing, insurance, manufacturing, dairy products, and so on. But it was also through these companies (and the private capital that flowed into them through the fund-raising apparatus of the Zionist Organization) that the Histadrut was able to transform itself into the central force in the economy of Jewish Palestine—a role it continued to play into the 1950s, when Ben-Gurion, then prime minister of the state of Israel, began to fear the immense power of the utopian-bureaucratic monstrosity he had done so much to create in his youth.

Yet despite this formidable array of revolutionary ideas, there was one political concept of Herzl's that Ben-Gurion understood immediately and fully, which he carried with him in his earliest steps as a Jewish political leader: the ideal of the guardian of the Jews. It was this that turned out to be Ben-Gurion's essential and immovable political concern, the ideological North Star that permitted him to outgrow one Russian-materialist fixation after another when they had proved useless or dangerous. Thus, physical labor was for Ben-Gurion only a personal ideal until he had had a few years' experience with it ("I have no desire . . . to be and remain a farmer," he wrote to his father. "I hate being possessed by the earth, which binds its owners to itself and enslaves them"),[17] and he quickly abandoned farming for intellectual and political pursuits, founding a party newspaper, attending law school in Istanbul, writing, and even translating into Hebrew Werner Sombart's *Socialism and the Social Movement in the 19th Century*. In the same manner, his opposition to an alliance with Western imperialism at the beginning of World War I was so transformed by political realities that by war's end, he had donned a British imperial uniform so as to participate in forging the British-Jewish political alliance. On socialism, too, his views began to shift, so that by the 1920s, he was arguing that private capital would be necessary for building the Jewish economy in Palestine. And only a few years later, he would make the leap that would position him to become heir to Herzl's policies—leaving behind the Labor Federation that he had long held to be *the* engine of Jewish salvation and seeking instead to revive the Zionist Organization as a body whose purpose was to amass the diplomatic and military might needed to assure Jewish sovereignty in Palestine.

Neither during the first immigrations of Russian-Jewish laborers to Palestine nor thereafter did Zionist leaders seem conscious, as Herzl had been, of the difficulties that might arise if Jewish Palestine were built almost exclusively under the direction of impoverished Russian farmhands; and if the political and intellectual culture of the Jewish state were from the outset guided by the extremism and armchair science of these same desperate men. Or if they were, they kept such concerns to themselves. Under these circumstances, the Jewish cause seems to have had a special need for David Ben-Gurion, a young man respected by his fellow Russian Jews as a sincere, unyielding, and demagogic ideologist—yet whose political principles were constantly subject to dramatic revision in the service of the one goal that mattered to him most, the Jewish state.

More than a decade passed between the spat over *Altneuland* that effectively demolished the Democratic Faction and the reemergence during World War I of the former Democratic leader, Chaim Weizmann, as a critical figure in the struggle to recast the remnants of Herzl's Zionist Organization. In the intervening years, Weizmann had relocated to Britain, where he studied industrial chemistry and pursued a career as a Zionist politico, which, after a decade of machinations, succeeded in catapulting him to the position of one of the English Zionist Federation's two vice presidents. That he would amount to much would have seemed a poor proposition at the time. Yet it is uncertain whether there ever would have been a Jewish state without his decision to turn his back on his youthful tirades against Herzl's diplomacy. As it transpired, it was Weizmann who succeeded in picking up the thread of Herzl's diplomatic missions in Britain and bringing them to a dramatic—although in critical respects, disappointing—conclusion, with the forging of a British-Jewish alliance at the end of World War I and the establishment of the British mandatory regime in Palestine.

It is worth picking up the story of Chaim Weizmann on December 10, 1914, a day that found him engaged in what must surely be one of the strangest conversations in the annals of Zionism. It was a few weeks after Britain's declaration of war on the Ottoman empire, and Weizmann was discussing with Sir Herbert Samuel the needs of the Jews—in what was the first exploration of possible British-Jewish wartime cooperation between a member of the Zionist Organization and a minister of the British government. Samuel, Lloyd George, and others had already been discussing the creation of an independent Jewish state in Palestine, but Weizmann, who had no inkling of this, approached the issue of the Jewish national cause in a more gingerly fashion. After going on at length about the misery of world Jewry, he finally came to his point, explaining to Samuel that what the Jews really needed was "a place where they formed an important part of the population . . . however small this place might be. For example, something like Monaco, with a university instead of a gambling-hall."

The British minister, who was himself at this point pressing for a restored Jewish state in Palestine, must have been dumbfounded to hear a representative of the Zionists speaking of a Jewish "Monaco"—a defenseless principality whose extent was less than one square mile, boasting a total population of perhaps 20,000. Not knowing what else to say, the British minister tried to explain to the Jewish nationalist leader that his demands were simply "too modest." One had to understand, he emphasized, that "big things would have to be done in Palestine."

Now it was Weizmann's turn to be dumbfounded. "In which ways are the plans of Mr. Samuel more ambitious than mine?" he asked.

"I would prefer not to enter into a discussion of my plans," the British minister responded. "But I suggest that the Jews will have to build railways, harbors, a university, a network of schools. . . . I also think that perhaps the Temple may be rebuilt. . . . These ideas are in the mind of my colleagues in the cabinet."

One can only imagine Herzl's reaction to an opening such as this. But Weizmann only mumbled something about desiring "encouragement" from the British government in his efforts to obtain Jewish local government and "freedom for the development of our own culture" in Palestine—and left it at that.[18]

What on earth was going on in this conversation? Why did Weizmann not try, no matter how cautiously, to build up the idea of the Jewish state in the "mind of the cabinet"? The British government, still under the influence of Herzl's dreamweaving, was talking of a Jewish state of its own accord, while at the same time, the Zionist Organization had, since 1911, been under the control of an executive committed to pursuing "practical" Zionism—the support of material Jewish settlements in Palestine and the suppression of talk of a Jewish state, which it was feared would bring them to harm. Even the English Zionist Organization, a decade earlier the most aggressive of Herzl's diplomatic arms, was now represented by a Russian "practical" such as Weizmann. And, in fact, nothing more graphically highlights what had become of the ZO since Herzl's death than Samuel's exchange with Weizmann, who had indeed "found his way back to the movement" as Herzl had predicted—but who continued to have as little grasp of the "imponderables" of which the state is made as in the days when he had prided himself on being at the head of Herzl's detractors.

Weizmann was born in the White Russian village of Motol outside of Pinsk, where two hundred Jewish families lived amid a somewhat larger population of Russian peasants, without paved streets, a rail stop, or regular postal service. And his career as a Zionist might have been much like Ben-Gurion's, had his father not succeeded in sending him away to attend a Russian gymnasium in Pinsk at age eleven.[19] There he became devoted to science, and it was this course of study that brought him to Berlin, where he was trained as a chemist. His head spinning from this newfound world, the young Weizmann quickly lost the ability to identify fully with the terrible condition of the Jews of the East. Returning home to Motol, he wrote to Leo Motzkin that "there is nothing here, and no one: Instead of a town— just an enormous rubbish heap."[20]

This often ugly eagerness to renounce the surroundings of his childhood charted the course of Weizmann's career, both as a scientist and as a Zionist politician. In his pursuit of status, Weizmann became a fanatic in his studies, excelling in them without fail, receiving a doctorate in chemistry in the field of synthetic dyes, and from an early age devoting much energy to patenting and selling his discoveries. And when in 1904 he received an invitation to become a research assistant at the University of Manchester—at the very heart of the world of synthetic dyes—Weizmann jumped at the chance, a decision that eventually won him the social and financial success he so craved. In his Zionist politics, too, Weizmann devoted himself to everything that seemed to represent a negation of his past, becoming the foremost advocate within the ZO of "culture"—the antonym of "rubbish heap"—and of the great enterprise of a Jewish university. To all outward appearances, then, Weizmann seemed to have leaped fully formed out of the shtetl as a confirmed anti-materialist, aristocrat, and capitalist, dedicated to the power of the mind. One could hardly imagine a greater gulf than the one that seemed to separate the lordly and urbane Weizmann, friend to presidents and prime ministers, from the desperate Jewish adherents of labor in Palestine, immersed in their gritty communion with the dirt, the spade, and the rifle.

Yet the fact is that this gulf was an illusion. Although outwardly Weizmann seemed to grow ever more sophisticated, inwardly his mind remained as tied to the earth as it had been in his school days in Motol. It is instructive to consider, for example, Weizmann's assiduously cultivated reputation as a representative of the life of the mind, the champion of Ahad Ha'am's great "spiritual center" in Palestine. Weizmann's standing as a scientist gave him the credibility to speak on such subjects, yet the fact is that his achievements in science were those of an industrial chemist—which is to say that, to put it kindly, he was no great thinker. The achievement that made him famous and wealthy was the discovery, on an ear of corn, of a bacterium (*Clostridium acetobutylicum Weizmann*) that when set loose on corn mash, caused it rapidly to ferment, producing quantities of butanol, acetone, and ethyl alcohol—products that proved to be vital for modern mechanized warfare, being useful in the production of high explosives, plastics, synthetic rubber, petroleum, and aviation fuel. The bacterium of his great rival, the Parisian chemist Auguste Fernbach, used in fermenting potato mash, proved utterly unable to compete, and within a few years, Weizmann's bacterium was breaking down corn, horse chestnuts, and rice all over Britain, Canada, the United States, France, Italy, and India.[21]

But these successes no more qualified him to speak intelligently on the subject of Jewish Palestine as a sovereign power or a "spiritual center" than did the achievements of the farmers who had grown the corn and horse chestnuts in question. For unlike his political allies and opponents—Herzl, Nordau, Ahad Ha'am, Buber, and Jabotinsky, every one of whom was a writer, an artist, and a craftsman of ideas of some ability—the successes Weizmann achieved as an "intellectual" represented quite the opposite. They bespoke nothing better than a more refined materialism, a facility with concrete substances that, while only visible under the microscope, were nonetheless concrete substances, and not cultural "imponderables."

And Weizmann's adeptness in cataloging and manipulating that which was already visible—rather than in conjuring up that which had been invisible—had a dramatic impact on the nature of the leadership he was able to offer the Zionist movement. As one of his biographers has written of Weizmann, "Unlike Herzl, he did not theorize in a systematic manner about the forms the future Jewish state would take: Its constitution, party system, administration, or army. These questions were too abstract for his scientific mind."[22] Indeed, he not only refrained from theorizing but continually drew attention to the special political insights that his "scientific" mind was capable of producing, loosing aphorisms such as: "I am an adherent of the cellular theory [of settlement in Palestine]. It is essential to create the first cell, which should in itself contain the future of the polycellular organism, which may grow out given normal conditions." Or similarly: "In politics, like mechanics, you can only get out of things what you put into them."[23] Such analogies led Weizmann, although absent from Russia since early adulthood, to faithfully reproduce in every instance the materialist politics of the East, seeing the construction of Jewish Palestine not as an activity of the mind but as one of concrete and gravel, the laying of brick upon brick in a linear, physical process, like the fermentation of a corn mash. "If there is another way of building a house," he said famously, "save brick by brick, I do not know it. If there is any other way of building up a country, save dunam by dunam and man by man, and farmstead by farmstead, again I do not know it."[24]

It was Weizmann's bare, incrementalist assumptions about politics—the precise opposite of those Herzl had tried to teach in *The Jewish State*—that likewise guided his contacts with British political leaders. Even once he had developed a taste for diplomacy, Weizmann never entertained the possibility of a policy such as Herzl's, rallying international public opinion, influencing the interests of every great power on the earth, and spinning these against one another in an effort to build a vast coalition of minds supporting the state. On the contrary, Weizmann's natural political method was brick-by-brick sequences of private dinner parties and heart-to-heart chats with English aristocrats behind closed doors—each encounter permitting him to tailor his words for the consumption of the single concrete individual who was his mark. In such intimate circumstances, Weizmann "could charm a bird off a tree"[25]—as one British minister put it—certainly something no one had ever said about Herzl. But this, too, was the result of Weizmann's "scientific" incrementalism. Herzl, despite his extraordinary personal magnetism, could never be truly *charming*, because his goal in conversation was to swing his listener around to sharing the dream of a Jewish state. Weizmann, as far as it is possible to know, never gave up on the dream of the Jewish state either, but he carefully avoided bringing such matters up. In fact, it was his enthusiastic emphasis on unthreatening proximate goals in Palestine that made Weizmann such a thrill to be with at cocktail parties. His fire would rise high into the night, describing the suffering in the East and the need for a Jewish home. But much to the relief of his listeners, the practical conclusions of these perorations were so tame anyone could agree to them. His "practical" Zionism, "cultural" Zionism, "synthetic" Zionism, "non-" Zionism—all the panoply of names he used to avoid seeming to be making any demands that might leave someone feeling uncomfortable—allowed virtually anyone to become his ally, without the cost of ever having really been "converted" to anything.

But then the war came, and Weizmann's world of "scientific" and incremental political growth was turned upside down. On October 27, 1914, Turkey entered the war on the side of Germany, and on November 3, British prime minister Herbert Henry Asquith reported to King George V that "henceforth, Great Britain must finally abandon the formula of 'Ottoman integrity' whether in Europe or in Asia." Days later, in the wake of the formal declaration of war against Turkey, the British prime minister spoke publicly about the "death-knell of Ottoman dominion . . . in Asia."[26] The world as the "practicals" had known it—the world in which the Young Turks would forever rule Palestine's Jewish farmers with an iron fist and the word "charter" would be akin to treason—simply came to an end.

In its place emerged Herzl's world, a world in which Turkey was about to be dismembered, and what was needed above all was the vision of a Jewish state in the minds of Jews and gentiles alike and, conjured up from out of this shared ideal, the political strength to get there. It was in this world that Weizmann's cocktail-party talk landed him in the inner sanctum of British decisionmaking, when C. P. Scott, editor of the *Manchester Guardian*, discovered him at a garden party and volunteered to introduce him to his friends Herbert Samuel and Lloyd George. Only two weeks prior to Weizmann's meeting with Samuel, Sir James Rothschild had specifically warned Weizmann that in imperial diplomacy one had to avoid asking for too little, thereby failing to ignite the imagination of world leaders.[27] Yet Rothschild's warning fell on deaf ears, and the result was Weizmann's proposal that Britain assist in the establishment of a Jewish "Monaco, with a university instead of a gambling-hall."

When, after the war, Ben-Gurion publicly asked Weizmann, "How was it that during all that time the Zionists didn't demand a Jewish state in Palestine?" Weizmann readily responded, "We didn't demand a Jewish state because they wouldn't have given us one. We asked only for the conditions which would allow us to create a Jewish state in the future. It's just a matter of tactics."[28] And it is certainly true that this assessment of what the British "would have given" the Jews guided Weizmann in his contacts with Britain. Yet it is also true that in the absence of a more compelling case for Jewish Palestine being projected by the Zionists, the British had little reason to feel inspired by the dream of a Jewish state themselves. Herbert Samuel's enthusiasm for the state, for example, simply evaporated when, in the six weeks after his meeting with Weizmann, he was subjected to both the anti-Zionist view (as articulated by the establishment Anglo-Jewish organizations) and to further discussions with Weizmann and Russian members of the Zionist executive, who were predisposed to fear talk of a Jewish state as potentially harmful.[29] In the end, Samuel simply gave up on the state, falling back on what he now referred to as "the cultural plan" of "a great spiritual center for Judaism in the Holy Land"—an idea, apparently cribbed from Weizmann, that allowed him to advocate a pro-Jewish policy in Palestine without involving Britain in excessive political complications.[30]

Despite the feeble Zionist diplomatic effort, the political constellation only continued to improve. On December 7, 1916, the Asquith government was replaced by a Conservative government headed by the renegade

Liberal leader David Lloyd George. In politics, one is hardly ever dealt a better hand. Lloyd George seems never to have changed his opinion that the Palestine campaign was one of the only "interesting" aspects of the war,[31] and the new foreign minister, Lord Arthur Balfour, had himself been prime minister when Britain had offered to negotiate a Jewish charter in East Africa. On December 20, British troops captured El-Arish, and less than three weeks later, on January 9, 1917, they were ordered to proceed up the coast to Rafah, in what is today called the Gaza Strip. With the battle for Palestine immanent, the British endorsed the initiative of the Zionist leader Vladimir (Ze'ev) Jabotinsky—quietly supported by Weizmann—to establish a "Jewish Legion" that would fight within the framework of the British armed forces, but representing the Jews as one of peoples supporting the war effort of the Allies. The legion, which in fact saw action in the later stages of the Palestine campaign, quickly won the enthusiasm of most of the future leadership of Labor Zionism; among its recruits were Ben-Gurion, Yitzhak Ben-Tzvi, Berl Katznelson, Moshe Sharett, and Levi Eshkol.

The impending British invasion of Palestine similarly paved the way for a pro-Zionist diplomatic tilt, and on November 2, 1917, Britain, at Weizmann's suggestion, issued a nonbinding, but nonetheless unprecedented, declaration of sympathy with Jewish aspirations in Palestine. Known as the Balfour Declaration, it announced, "His Majesty's government view with favor the establishment in Palestine of a national home for the Jewish people and will use their best endeavors to facilitate the achievement of this object."

Nor did London fail to keep the promise implicit in this declaration, at least so long as Lloyd George and Lord Balfour remained in office. In 1920, the San Remo conference—one of dozens of postwar conferences after Versailles that met to determine the political outcome of the war[32]—formally conferred upon Britain a trusteeship over Palestine, to be called a "Mandate," which included in its terms the British-Zionist concept embodied in the Balfour Declaration:

> An appropriate Jewish agency shall be recognized as a public body for the purpose of advising and co-operating with the administration of Palestine in such economic, social, and other matters as may affect the establishment of the Jewish national home and the interests of the Jewish population in Palestine, and, subject always to the control of the administration, to assist and take part in the development of the country. The Zionist Organization, so long as its organization and constitution are in the opinion of the Mandatory appropriate, shall be recognized as such agency.[33]

Put simply, Britain had, as part of the "new world order," received custody of Palestine, on the strength of international sentiment that part or all of Palestine should be developed by Britain to become a Jewish state.

The Balfour Declaration and the Palestine Mandate were, to be sure, breathtaking achievements. For here, in very real life, Weizmann had succeeded in achieving precisely that which had seemed—to him as well as to many other "practicals"—an impossibility only a few years earlier. The might of the greatest power on earth had been successfully and publicly allied with the cause of constructing a Jewish majority in Palestine and ultimately a Jewish state. For the first time, world leaders of the first rank had rallied behind the idea of constructing what would ultimately be a Jewish state, including Lloyd George, Balfour, Jan Smuts, Winston Churchill, and the American president Woodrow Wilson. Churchill, for example, spoke openly of the establishment of "a Jewish state" protected by England and comprising "three or four millions of Jews."[34] It is no wonder, then, that after the San Remo conference, Weizmann was made president of the Zionist Organization, a title even Herzl had never held, and that Jews the world over were caught up in a wave of gratitude to their newfound ally, Britain.

Yet for all of its importance, the British Mandate was not, as has often been said, the charter that Herzl had sought—an agreement granting the Jews legal authority to govern the territory that was to become the basis for the Jewish state. In fact, the mandatory government in Palestine was in a decisive sense precisely what Herzl had *not* wanted: a *British* regime that would rule the land. From a legal point of view, the Palestine Mandate did not award the ZO control over Jewish immigration, legislation, the courts and police, taxation, the governing bureaucracy, or the allocation of land. Not even the physical protection of the Jewish colonies was in Jewish hands. When one compares the terms of the British Mandate to the draft charters that had been Herzl's basis for negotiations with the powers,[35] or even to the substance of Britain's initial offer in 1903 of a territory in East Africa— which had envisioned the establishment of an autonomous *Jewish* government, with both executive and legislative powers—it becomes apparent that the British Palestine Mandate was, relative to what had been under discussion a decade earlier, a substantial disappointment.

This failure was best expressed by Weizmann himself, when testifying before the Allied council in Paris in 1919. Asked whether the term "national home" in the Balfour Declaration meant that the Jews wished to be granted an "autonomous government," Weizmann responded in the negative:

> No, we do not demand a specifically Jewish government. . . . [but] definite conditions and an administration that will enable us to send immigrants to Palestine. . . . We shall make it our task to create schools where the Hebrew language would be taught and gradually to develop there a Jewish life as Hebraic as the life in England is English. When this nationality forms the majority of the population, then the moment will have come to claim the government of the country.[36]

Thus, the flaw in the mandate was in the first instance a weakness in Weizmann's political conception, which was based on his belief that a favorable British government in Palestine would be able to sustain, as he told the Allied council, a Jewish immigration of "70,000 or 80,000 annually," without any legal authority whatever in the hands of the ZO. The problem with this view was not any lack of goodwill on the part of the British government in London, for there was plenty of this. Rather, the problem was inherent in Weizmann's theory (and Ahad Ha'am's) of a gradual immigration by the Jews until they would "come to form the majority" and "claim the government," a plan that was a political impossibility. It should have been evident that the Arabs would never accept this, and for this reason, no non-Jewish government in Palestine would be able to deliver upon it. Herzl himself had emphasized precisely this point in *The Jewish State*, arguing that "there invariably comes a moment when the government, under pressure from the native population—which feels itself threatened—bars any further influx of Jews." The only remedy, he had understood, was that the Jews must themselves have the right to govern somewhere, or the result would be calamity.[37]

A Zionist diplomacy based on avoiding demands of autonomous Jewish authority proved to be viable only so long as the arena remained that of one-on-one parlor meetings with high-minded Christians in London. But as soon as the "practicals" got to work in Palestine in earnest after the war, an all-too-real reaction appeared claiming that it should be the interests of the Arabs that determined the fate of the country. In April 1920 and May 1921, Arab mobs massacred Jews in Palestine, sometimes with the active involvement of Arab police in the service of the British regime. More than sixty Jews were murdered in these outbursts, and more than 350 were wounded. Herbert Samuel, who arrived in Palestine as high commissioner three months after the first wave of killings, responded just as Herzl had predicted. His past sympathies notwithstanding, he embarked on a series of actions intended to placate the Arabs, including the appointment in March 1921 of Amin al-Husseini, a pan-Arabist fanatic who had been instrumental in instigating the massacres, to the position of mufti of Jerusalem.[38] When Arab violence erupted with even greater force in May, Samuel's support for the Zionists collapsed entirely. He suspended Jewish immigration for a month, permitting it to resume only after 1921, after he had delivered a speech renouncing the right of the Jews to immigrate into Palestine beyond what would be in the "interests of the present population." Moreover, he said, "it must be definitely recognized that the conditions in Palestine are such as not to permit anything in the nature of a mass immigration."[39]

Samuel's tilt away from Zionism in the wake of the Arab massacres was officially ratified in June 1922, when the Colonial Office issued a formal statement of policy, or "white paper," apparently written by Samuel himself, in which the Balfour Declaration was carefully but severely reinterpreted. The territory of Transjordanian Palestine (today, the Kingdom of Jordan), amounting to over three-fourths of the territory of the Palestine Mandate, was closed to Jewish settlement. Regarding the remaining onefourth of Palestine west of the Jordan River, the white paper sought to reassure the Arab population that the status of the ZO in Palestine "does not entitle it to share in any degree in its government." Moreover, it explicitly renounced Weizmann's aim, as presented at the peace conference in Paris, of creating a Jewish majority in the country: "Unauthorized statements have been made to the effect that the purpose in view is . . . that Palestine is to become 'as Jewish as England is English.' His Majesty's Government regard any such expectation as impracticable and have no such aim in view."

Far from being an instrument for the creation of a Jewish state, the British mandatory regime would henceforth be *neutral* toward Zionism, which would essentially be the private business of the Jews. Weizmann, hoping not to harm his relations with Britain, gritted his teeth and pronounced the Zionist Organization's willingness to work within the terms of the white paper.[40] In October, Lloyd George's government fell, and the period of genuine support on the part of the British government in London for the idea of establishing a Jewish state in Palestine passed into history.

Remarkably, the Arabs of Palestine did not follow up their initial political successes with further violence, perhaps because by 1923, the entire Zionist enterprise had begun to appear more pathetic than threatening. Jewish immigration into Palestine remained a trickle for the third year in a row, and Mandatory Palestine, the fruit of the greatest Jewish national diplomatic achievements since antiquity, now verged on becoming a death trap for the idea of a Jewish state: A land where the Jews were a small minority, with nothing but a handful of prematurely discarded paper promises to prevent the imposition of a "democratic"—which is to say an Arab—government.

The Zionist Organization was already operating with a deficit in 1920, and it continued to verge on bankruptcy for the rest of the decade, even as the number of Jewish institutions in Palestine depending on its budget for their survival grew from year to year. The industrial ventures founded by the Labor Federation and its network of collective agricultural settlements were able to subsist only with the help of subsidies from the coffers of the ZO. And when the economy slowed down, the same meager resources were raided for welfare relief handouts as well.[41] The grim fact was that after years of having to smuggle Jews into Ottoman Palestine illegally, it was now possible to openly bring at least *some* Jews into Zion—so long as there were jobs to support them and the British were satisfied that the arrival of more Jews would not unduly irritate the Arabs. Yet for want of economic resources, the Jewish masses of Europe could not be brought into the country, and many who came left. "Only today I received the health statistics from Palestine," Weizmann wrote in January 1924. "The natural increase in Palestine amounts to about 15,000 a year. The Jews brought in last year about 10,000. . . . This will remain always the central axis of my policy, and everything else will be subordinated to this one view and to this one fact, which haunts me like a nightmare."[42]

Weizmann believed that these facts dictated an iron relationship between fund-raising and Jewish national life in Palestine: Increased funding would create jobs, and jobs would bring Jewish immigration. But how to raise funds? The war had destroyed many of the great Jewish fortunes in Europe and, along with them, the prospects of substantial support from European Jewry. If there was to be money for settlement, it seemed there was only one potential source: The wealthy German Jews of the United States—the immediate relations of the same politically anti-Zionist German Jewry that had fought to prevent the Zionist congress and the recognition of the existence of a Jewish people.[43]

But unlike Herzl, whose dream had been to win these people over to the cause of a Jewish state, Weizmann had always treated this goal as irrelevant. One could, he believed, devote tremendous sums to Jewish settlement and cultural institutions in Palestine—understood as philanthropy—without giving up an inch of one's hostility toward the idea of the Jewish state. Thus, all that was needed was to remove the Jewish state itself from the agenda, selling only the "cultural center" in Palestine, and the wealthy Jews would begin constructing the Jewish state with their own hands.[44] As early as the beginning of World War I, Weizmann had therefore begun groping after what he considered to be the great prize: An agreement with the leadership of English Jewry, which consisted largely of self-professed anti-Zionists, to the work of supporting the "nonpolitical" development of Jewish Palestine. And, in fact, when the Conjoint Committee of major British Jewish organizations decided during the war to develop a policy of its own regarding Palestine, it based its proposals on what it called "the 'cultural' policy, including perhaps a Hebrew University, free immigration and facilities for colonization"—a plan virtually identical with the Jewish Monaco program Weizmann had been peddling.[45]

But Weizmann's hoped-for entente with the Anglo-Jewish anti-Zionists never got off the ground. On the contrary, his discussions with their representatives broke down in late 1916 over the question of the character of the regime that was to be established in Palestine, where Arabs still outnumbered

Jews six to one. The English Jewish leaders, like their counterparts in other countries, focused on what they referred to as the Zionists' intention of seeking "special rights" for the Jewish community in Palestine—a concept to which they were vehemently opposed. That is, if the Palestine administration that would emerge from a British-Zionist alliance were to grant any kind of special powers or privileges to the Jews, then the regime would violate the fundamental concept of the social-contract state and thereby serve as a precedent for discrimination *against* Jews in other countries.[46]

So strongly did the leadership of British Jewry oppose any "special rights" for the Jews in Palestine that they eventually launched a full-blown political campaign to prevent the British government from issuing the Balfour Declaration—a struggle that climaxed in May 1917 with the publication of an anti-Zionist manifesto in the London *Times*, signed by Claude Montefiore and David Alexander, the presidents of the Anglo-Jewish Association and the Board of Deputies of British Jews, the two umbrella organizations representing all of English Jewry. Under a headline reading "Palestine and Zionism: Views of Anglo-Jewry," they declared that they supported the idea that the Jews of Palestine should be "secured in the enjoyment of civil and religious liberty" and "equal political rights with the rest of the population." As they explained:

> This policy aim[s] primarily at making Palestine a Jewish spiritual center by securing for the local Jews, and the colonists who might join them, such conditions of life as would best enable them to develop the Jewish genius on lines of their own. . . . [But regarding] the proposal to invest the Jewish settlers in Palestine with certain special rights in excess of those enjoyed by the rest of the population, these rights to be embodied in a Charter . . . any such action would prove a veritable calamity for the whole Jewish people. In all the countries in which they live the principle of equal rights for religious denominations is vital for them.[47]

Although the anti-Zionist effort was ultimately humiliated when the statement in the *Times* was repudiated by one of the organizations whose presidents had signed it, the campaign was not without its effect: In negotiations with the ZO, British ministers appended two clauses to the Balfour Declaration—absent from the original drafts presented both by the ZO and by Lord Balfour himself—which sought to appease anti-Zionist sentiment among British Jews by promising that "nothing would be done" to prejudice the "civil and religious rights" of Arabs in Palestine, nor the "political rights" of Jews in Britain. These two clauses, which constitute the remainder of the text, read: "it being clearly understood that nothing shall be done which may prejudice the civil and religious rights of existing non-Jewish communities in Palestine or the rights and political status enjoyed by Jews in any other country."[48]

The failure of Weizmann's efforts to forge an alliance with London's antinationalist Jews did not serve as much of a warning to him, and when, in the early 1920s, he set about trying to alleviate the chronic financial problems of the subsidized Jewish economy in Palestine, he once again returned to his theory of a grand alliance with emancipationist Jewry. In the United States, too, Jewish anti-Zionists, mostly of German-Jewish extraction, had led a campaign against the American government's support for the Balfour Declaration and the Palestine Mandate—and for the same reasons.[49] As Adolph Ochs, the anti-Zionist German-Jewish publisher of the *New York Times*, told Arthur Ruppin in 1922, the development of Jewish agriculture in Palestine might be interesting, but he could hardly see himself funding Zionist settlements there as "the Jews are not a nation, they share only a religion."[50] Other leading American Jews similarly emphasized that the ZO should stop demanding a Jewish state and render its program in Palestine more attractive by adapting it to "spiritual Judaism."[51] Indeed, so intense was the resistance to Zionism among German-Jewish philanthropists in the United States that at the same time Weizmann was failing to extract commitments from them to fund the resettlement of Russian Jews on agricultural collectives in Palestine, many of them were involved in launching a campaign to raise millions of dollars for a Soviet government plan to resettle urban Russian Jews in agricultural collectives—in the Ukraine.[52]

Weizmann needed little urging on the part of New York Jews to return to his traditional strategy of focusing on proximate, "non-political" goals in Palestine, and at the Thirteenth Zionist Congress in Karlsbad in 1923, he was already calling for a world Jewish "alliance for the land of Israel"— meaning a fund-raising alliance with anti-Zionists, whom he now referred to by the less abrasive term, "non-Zionists."[53] This strategy engendered no small degree of discomfort within the ZO; among its other effects was the establishment by Ze'ev Jabotinsky, a former member of the Zionist executive, of what became known as the Revisionist party, which sought to end the ZO's flirtations with overt opponents of a Jewish state. But Weizmann remained undaunted, targeting particular projects in Palestine that might seem sufficiently harmless to suit the tastes of New York's establishment Jews and dulling their resistance with denials that contributions to Jewish Palestine would lead to a Jewish state. And indeed, Weizmann was eventually so successful at projecting this idea that he had Louis Marshall, the scion of New York Jewry, arguing to his friends that "political Zionism is a thing of the past. There is nobody now in authority in the Zionist Organization who has the slightest idea of doing anything more than to build up the Holy Land and to give those who desire a home there the opportunity they cherish."[54]

In 1924, the flood of impoverished Jews fleeing Russia had brought the proportion of Jews in the United States to almost 4 percent of the population—and here, too, Herzl's warning concerning gradual infiltration came true. In no small part because of this influx, the American government adopted restrictive immigration policies that effectively ended a period of four decades during which the United States had served Jews as their principal place of refuge from an increasingly anti-Semitic Europe. It was against the background of this development that leading American Jews, many of whom had themselves openly supported the new immigration laws, began coming around to Weizmann and Marshall's proposals for supporting "non-Zionist" efforts to build up Jewish Palestine.[55] Within a year, Weizmann was able to chalk up the first major success of his strategy: The establishment in 1925 of a board of governors for the Hebrew University, under the financial leadership of the New York German-Jewish banker and opponent of the Jewish state, Felix Warburg. With this arrangement as a working model, it looked as though it would only be a matter of time before the German-Jewish philanthropists agreed to join the Zionists in a larger "alliance for the land of Israel," which Weizmann believed would solve the financial problems of Jewish Palestine while creating a Jewish state en passant.

It was another four years before Weizmann succeeded in hammering out the deal with the "non-Zionists" for general funding of Jewish settlement activities in Palestine. The basis of the agreement was a loophole in the League of Nations Mandate for Palestine, which did not recognize the Zionist Organization as having any independent standing in Palestine. Instead, it spoke of a "Jewish agency" with which the mandatory government would consult on Jewish matters and whose identity would ultimately be subject to the discretion of the British. Originally, this Jewish agency was the Zionist Organization, but by the summer of 1929, Weizmann had moved to replace the ZO with something more suitable to his needs. Called the "Jewish Agency for Palestine," the new agency was a two-headed organization comprising the democratically governed ZO, on the one hand, and a panel of unelected plutocrats—the non-Zionists—on the other. Under the agreement reached with Louis Marshall, Zionists and "non-Zionists" would have equal representation in all institutions of the Jewish Agency, in return for which the non-Zionists would take the lead in raising the funds for the agency's operations.

The agreement was consummated on August 11, 1929, when the Assembly of the "enlarged" Jewish Agency met for the first time in Zurich. Among the new organization's governors were show-stopping figures such as Herzl had only dreamed of reaching: Albert Einstein; the French socialist leader Leon Blum; the former Palestine high commissioner, Sir Herbert Samuel; the president of the Board of Deputies of British Jews, Osmond d'Avigdor Goldsmid; the prominent English parliamentarian Lord Melchett; the Yiddish writer Sholem Asch; as well as the most prominent figures in American Jewry, Louis Marshall and Felix Warburg. "We never wanted Palestine for the Zionists," Weizmann gushed. "We wanted it for the Jews. The living, evolving Judaism of Palestine is no party matter. The Balfour Declaration is addressed to the whole of Jewry."[56]

Where Herzl had hoped to unite the Jewish people around the idea of a sovereign Jewish state, Weizmann succeeded in bringing about a consensus around practical work for building up the Jewish community of Palestine. Many of those present were at ease with such abstractions and were readily able to draw a clear distinction between the two ideas. For Weizmann, however, the distinction was specious—a view that he shared with the Arabs of Palestine, who, in late August 1929, responded to his new alignment with the wealthy New York Jews with a wave of pogroms that washed all of Palestine with blood.

If Weizmann identified the weakness of Jewish Palestine in its lack of financial resources, David Ben-Gurion identified it with the fact that the authority of the government in Palestine was in the hands of the British—a fact that meant the Jewish community in Palestine could not make decisions regarding immigration or land policy, could not tax itself or set economic policies conducive to creating Jewish places of employment, and could not even defend itself against Arab attack. In 1922, Herzl's diaries began to appear in print for the first time, and Ben-Gurion read them from cover to cover—an activity that must surely have aggravated his already well-rooted inclination to dislike Weizmann. That same year, Weizmann acquiesced in the Colonial Office's rejection of his own pronouncement at Versailles that Palestine was to become a Jewish country, and Ben-Gurion began working in earnest to persuade the Labor movement that the Zionist Organization had simply ceased to seek the "fulfillment" of Zionism. "Until now we thought the Zionist Organization was the means by which Zionism would be fulfilled and we have directed our activity accordingly," he said. "We have been disillusioned in this belief; I am absolutely clear on this. We must find another means. The only one capable of it is the workers' organization in Palestine."[57]

It is impossible to understand the trajectory of the young union leader's career without recognizing how seriously he meant these words, for in Ben-Gurion's eyes, the Jewish labor union in Palestine had ceased to be, if ever it had been, only *part* of the effort of building a Jewish state. Instead, the Histadrut was for him the only suitable candidate to take up the role of the guardian of the Jewish people—an organization whose concern for the interests of the workers of Palestine, or for anything else for that matter, would be secondary to the task of ensuring Jewish immigration and developing the growing Jewish community into a sovereign state. Thus, for example, at the second national convention of the Histadrut in 1923, Ben-Gurion spoke of the uniqueness of the Jewish Labor movement in Palestine, whose "primary motivating force" was not higher wages for the workers, but Jewish immigration. "All traits and characteristics of our movement," he said, "are derived from the process of [Jewish] immigration, its needs, and its strength." At the third national convention of the union four years later, Ben-Gurion was even more emphatic, naming the union, and not the ZO, as the agency that would bring the Jewish state into being: "We don't see ourselves as a government, but in our concept the Histadrut is the beginning of the Jewish socialist state."[58]

The need to create an autonomous Jewish power in Palestine under the rubric of the Labor Federation was far from being self-evident to Ben-Gurion's colleagues. The quasi-sovereignty envisioned in Ben-Gurion's proposal to transform the Histadrut into a "labor army" was rejected by his associates out of hand. And even the institutions affiliated with the Labor movement—the workers' bank and health fund, the collective farms, and the various Histadrut companies—refused to accept central discipline, considering themselves truly bound only by the regulations imposed by the British mandatory government. A change became visible only in June 1923, when Ben-Gurion succeeded in suspending shipments of food and medicine to a northern kibbutz whose members had appropriated the inventory of a neighboring settlement. Ben-Gurion was eventually forced to back down, but the Histadrut had worked for the first time, as he noted in his diary, "as a kind of workers' state." This experience was the first demonstration that the dependence of large segments of the Jewish population on the Labor Federation's health fund could be used to give the Histadrut a measure of coercive authority. And in fact, it was its health insurance that gave the Histadrut a certain ability to "tax" the Jewish population as well; by setting union dues at 150 percent of the value of its health services, the Histadrut was eventually able to secure limited funds for investment in factories and housing for immigrants.[59]

But by 1926, Ben-Gurion had lost patience with the game of trying to govern his nation from the helm of a labor union. Tens of thousands of Jews fleeing the Grabski persecutions in Poland had begun pouring into the country, only to find it in the throes of an economic depression—to which Weizmann's ZO was responding by allocating an increasing proportion of its budget to welfare payments. Ben-Gurion was virtually alone among the leaders of the Labor Federation in demanding that the Zionist Organization cease to focus on relief, concentrating instead on industrial investment. In a spectacular meeting of the Histadrut council on January 31, 1927, he announced that for over two years, the ZO had "hardly done anything except for the dole," demanding the resignation of Labor's representatives in Weizmann's governing coalition.[60] By the end of the year, Ben-Gurion had opened talks with his rivals over the creation, for the first time, of a united Labor party, a political force he believed would be strong enough to seize control of the remnants of Herzl's Zionist Organization. In negotiations over the new party's platform, Ben-Gurion gave away anything that stood in the way of the merger, with the stroke of a pen discarding the references to a "republic of workers," "the class struggle," and "the revolution," which had until now populated his party's platform.

Ben-Gurion was forty-three years old when he bartered all this away. Close associates of twenty years expressed pain over the desocialized platform of the new party, and some threatened to leave it. But he ignored them, signing the agreement that created what would become the Jewish state's Labor party, at this time called Mapai ("The Land of Israel Workers' Party")—the party that would allow him to stand before the Zionist congress and the "enlarged" Jewish Agency as the leader of Jewish Palestine.

CHAPTER 7

Martin Buber and the Rejection of the Jewish State

URING HERZL'S LIFETIME, it was the Russian Jews who had given him instinctive and visceral support, providing him with the popular enthusiasm he needed in order to turn Zionism into a mass movement. But much as Herzl may have learned to respect the Jews of the East, it was the Jews of German Central Europe—that vast storehouse of Jewish intellectual and professional ability concentrated in cities such as Vienna, Berlin, and Prague—on whom he had placed his highest hopes. As he had written to Baron de Hirsch: "All my love goes out to them. I want to see their breed multiply . . . because I see in them the inherent future strength of the Jews. They are, in other words, the likes of myself."[1]

Yet German Zionism during the years of the first Zionist congresses was not composed of men such as Herzl—intellectuals who had rejected the emancipation and who ultimately saw their own place in Palestine constructing a new Jewish state. Indeed, until Herzl's death, German Zionism consisted principally of individuals who, though committed to the idea of the Jewish state, nevertheless conceived of it as a solution to *other* people's problems. Typical of these was the German Zionist leader Franz Oppenheimer, who openly renounced any thought of life in Palestine, writing that "Germany is my fatherland, my homeland, the land of all my yearnings, the land in which my forefathers have been buried, the land of my battles and my ardor, and when I return home from a foreign country, I come home [to Germany]."[2] Even as close an associate of Herzl's as the head of the German Zionist Federation (ZVfD), Max Bodenheimer, bought a house in Cologne upon retirement and admitted that he would have been happy to spend the rest of his life in Germany had it not been for the rise of Hitler.[3] The result was that for the German Zionists, the pursuit of diplomacy and a Jewish state were little more than philanthropy by other means—a fact that all but guaranteed the German Zionist Federation would be a purveyor of institutional boredom and personal irrelevance of precisely the kind that had so stupefied young Jews in their encounters with all other branches of German Judaism.[4]

From an early stage, Herzl sought to remedy this problem by attracting energy and talent from among German-Jewish students. It was his appreciation of the importance of this goal that led him, almost alone among the leaders of the ZO, to sympathize with and support the efforts of Zionist students to make the movement more attractive to their own.[5] Of special importance to him were Berthold Feiwel and Martin Buber, a pair of outspoken Austrian students who were the most outstanding German-speaking students he was able to win over to the cause. Feiwel had been active in assisting Herzl since before the First Congress, and Buber had declared himself loyal to the movement the following year, quickly becoming an impassioned advocate for the cause. ("It is we whom the Maccabees fought for," Buber declaimed before the Third Congress. "As the time has come when once a year the Jewish flag, our flag, flies on the roof of the Basel congress building, so the time will come when, on our own soil, from our own homes, the flag of national freedom will fly in our land.")[6] Herzl appointed first Feiwel and then Buber to the position of editor in chief of his weekly, *Die Welt*, and when the first issue under Buber's editorship came off the presses in September 1901, Herzl wrote to him with pride that "the new generation has arrived."[7] When, shortly thereafter, Buber and Feiwel proposed to found a publishing house for the promotion of Jewish art and literature, Herzl solicited private funds in order to make the venture viable and even agreed, at their request, to contribute his own fiction to their proposed anthologies.[8]

Herzl continued his attempts at a collaboration with the German student leaders despite an ever-growing list of affronts—including their displays of open contempt for the businessmen and rabbis within the Zionist movement, Buber's abrupt departure from *Die Welt* after only a few months as editor, and the establishment of the Democratic Faction as a formal "opposition" to his leadership at the Zionist congress that same year.[9] The author

Stefan Zweig, who was given his start as a Viennese writer by Herzl in the pages of the *Neue Freie Presse*, later wrote bitterly of the behavior of Buber and his circle, whom he knew well, toward Herzl:

> I began to follow the Zionist movement, and sometimes attended, as a spectator, the little meetings that usually were held in the basements of various coffeehouses . . . But I was unable actually to ally myself with the Zionist youth of that day . . . I disliked the evening discussions because of the now hardly imaginable attitude of disrespect which the very foremost of his followers adopted toward the person of Herzl . . . I knew how badly, in that difficult time, Herzl needed the help of perfectly devoted men, and particularly young men . . . and the quarrelsome, contentious spirit of the internal revolt against Herzl made me turn away immediately from the movement to which I was drawn only because of Herzl.[10]

Herzl endured these indignities in silence up until the *Altneuland* controversy in the spring of 1903, when Buber and Feiwel publicly defended Ahad Ha'am in his efforts to dissolve the ZO in Russia. This break more or less marked the end of Herzl's relationship with many of the Democrats. But he reserved his most bitter words for Buber, to whom he referred as a "brother who had become an enemy," and who was apparently the target of his comment to Weizmann that some of the Democrats would sooner or later be "lost to our movement."[11] Why?

A number of factors seem to have been at work, but perhaps the most important one was Herzl's personal disappointment. It was Feiwel who wrote that of the small circle of student leaders, Buber was "the only truly creative person,"[12] and Herzl knew this as well as anyone. Herzl also knew that Buber was the only charismatic leader who had risen among the German students, the only one who had broken through the wall of apathy and socialism that engulfed young German Jews and begun gathering a real following around himself.[13] And yet for all of Buber's talent and dynamism, it is unclear to what degree he was ever fully in or of the movement. Thus, when Herzl had asked him to edit *Die Welt*, Buber responded with seeming enthusiasm, writing of the effect the paper would have on Judaism and all of Europe under his hand. But at the same time he emphasized that he would be able to devote to the project "only a relatively small part of my time," since "aside from completing my dissertation . . . I have literary plans that I cannot evade: Along with various ideas for articles, some larger undertakings, among them some connected with Zionism." And in fact, he proved unable to make anything of his position at the paper, abandoning it after only four months.[14]

But the main difficulty in Buber's relationship with the Zionist Organization was not that it was a low priority for him, competing ineffectively with his interests in Christianity, socialism, mysticism, poetry, drama, and art. Rather, it was ideological. By 1901, the year of his failed involvement with Herzl at *Die Welt*, Buber was deeply immersed in the thought of Christian mystics such as Nicholas of Cusa and Jakob Boehme and was spending his time teaching toward the overhaul of social and spiritual reality at a utopian society in Berlin called "the New Community," of which he had become a member. ("It is not enough that the 'I' unites itself with the world," he wrote in an article on Boehme's teachings. "The 'I' is the world. . . . When I bring a piece of fruit to my mouth, I feel: This is my body. And when I set wine to my lips, I feel: This is my blood.")[15] These interests naturally began to refocus his attention away from the mundane Zion of concern to Jewish nationalists such as Herzl and Ahad Ha'am and toward an amorphous Jewish ideal that Buber began referring to as "the Zion of the soul"—which had to be reborn before "the other, the Palestinian Zion" could come into existence.[16]

It was the search for this "Zion of the soul" that moved his various Jewish cultural projects. And though he insisted that his various publishing efforts seek to inculcate "a radical social and modern cultural standpoint," he did not similarly insist that the writers and artists working with him espouse any particular viewpoint on Zionism. Thus, for example, when Buber decided in early 1903 to convene "a conference for Jewish cultural work," neither Zionism nor Jewish nationalism were mentioned in his letter of announcement.[17]

Within the context of Germany's antinationalist Jewry, the prospects for Buber's "socially radical and culturally modern" movement of Jewish artists to contribute to the eventual establishment of a Jewish state were of course nil, and it was this that led Herzl to the conclusion that Buber would sooner or later be lost to the movement. Buber, for his part, responded by fulfilling Herzl's prediction to the letter. When Herzl died the following year, the animus Buber had stored up against him came spilling forth in all its ugliness: "For him it was the finest time to die," Buber observed; "Herzl laid his hand on it [i.e., Zionism], with a firm, shaping pressure. . . . How many noble possibilities were killed!" And, similarly: "It is fundamentally false to celebrate him as a Jewish personality, as one could celebrate Spinoza, Israel Ba'al-Shem, Heinrich Heine, or Ferdinand Lassalle. In Herzl there lived nothing of an elemental Jewish nature."[18] Even greater was his contempt for David Wolffsohn—who, with Herzl's encouragement, had provided funding for Buber's publications—and the others who now struggled in desperation to keep the movement alive. "With Herzl, the grand seigneur, it was possible to come to an understanding," he wrote. "It is impossible to deal with these pompous nonentities."[19]

At this worst of possible moments, Buber withdrew from Zionism, declaring that he would invest no more in "the organism which is condemned to die." It sufficed that the Zionist Organization had fulfilled its purpose in Buber's personal life. As he told Weizmann, "I needed all that to come to my own real work."[20]

Martin Buber was raised in the German-speaking home of his grandparents in Lvov, capital of the Austrian Polish "crown-land" of Galicia, to which he was consigned at the age of three when his mother abandoned his family. His father was a landowner who devoted his time to farming, greeting herds of horses one by one so as to recognize the unique personality of each animal, tasting kernels from each swaying stalk as he moved about his fields so he could savor the unique character of each plant, but he seems to have been largely absent while the young Buber was having emotional crises over the existence of infinity in space and time, "almost"-suicidal terrors from which he only escaped after reading Kant.[21] Buber's father, however, was sufficiently well off to be able to shelter him financially; and when Buber broke off his activities in the Zionist movement, he was thus able to relocate to Florence and immerse himself in the stories of the Hasidim. There Buber quickly came to regard his earlier nationalist enthusiasms with ambivalence, and after a wave of pogroms swept Bialystok in 1906, he wrote to a friend that his work on Hasidism was now his answer to such questions. "I have a *new answer* to give to everything," he wrote. "I have grown inward into my heaven—my life begins."[22]

That same year, Buber published the first of his volumes of Hasidic stories, mystical-kabbalistic tales translated into German and doctored to express his own views. And although Franz Kafka, for one, pronounced these "meddling adaptations" to be "unbearable," they had a very different reception among other young German Jews.[23] Among these were the members of the Prague Bar-Kochba society, a Zionist student group that had fallen into disarray in the years after Herzl's death, which in 1909 brought Buber to Prague for the first of a series of lectures on Judaism. Thus, Buber's Bar-Kochba speeches were such a sensation that he was invited to deliver them in Berlin and Vienna as well, and he was later able to publish them as a small book—his famous *Three Speeches on Judaism*[24]—which within a handful of years had established him as the philosophical-religious guru of an entire generation of young German Jews, Zionist and anti-Zionist alike. Buber's Bar-Kochba speeches were credited by the novelist and playwright Arnold Zweig with having allowed him to return to Judaism. The poet Franz Werfel wrote Buber that "of all the present Jewish-theoretical literature your writings alone delight my soul and evoke my assent." Hugo Bergmann, later rector of the Hebrew University, wrote that "anyone who

had heard those speeches by Buber has not forgotten them and cannot forget them to his dying day. Judaism was placed before us as a great human issue." Hans Kohn, later a leading historian of nationalism, wrote to Buber
after the talks "You know, sir, what your addresses meant to us. . . . In many
respects they constituted a turning point in all my views." Gershom
Scholem wrote that "we secondary school and university students looked
. . . for an interpreter of the phenomenon of Judaism and its heritage.
. . . Buber's first books on Hasidism and his 'Three Speeches' raised a
tremendous echo in our ears." And the anti-Zionist philosopher Franz
Rosenzweig commented to Buber after the publication of the speeches, "I
am amazed to see to what degree you have become the representative
speaker and the advocate of our generations, mine as well as the one after
me. . . . We see clearly that it was our own words to which you were the first
to give expression."[25]

Even more dramatic was the impact of Buber's writings on the German-
Jewish youth organizations. The German youth "movements" had been
founded in the 1890s by the youth-guru Gustav Wyneken, who initiated
Germany's adolescents into the cult of weeklong outings into the woods to
commune with nature in an environment free from the influence of
adults.[26] In the years before World War I, these movements also began to be
characterized by anti-Semitism, a fact that led to the founding of a number
of Jewish youth movements—the Zionist Blau-Weiss ("Blue-White"), the
anti-Zionist Kameraden, and others—which were established more or less
at the same time Buber's speeches were first in circulation. By the mid-
1920s, perhaps one-third of all young German Jews belonged to one of
these movements, most of which turned to Buber's speeches and his Hasidic
tales for the spiritual guidance they could no longer draw from Wyneken.
Indeed, so great was Buber's impact on these movements that the organ of
Kameraden could speak of the "veneration and gratitude" that the members
of the movement had for Buber's speeches and writings: "We are infinitely
beholden to Buber for the way in which he has activated and enriched
Jewish feeling and perception . . . for his ardent rejuvenation of our spiritual
and intellectual world." And even those few within the youth organizations
who were uneasy with the "indulgence in mystic-maudlin daydreams" induced in the youth by Buber's works could not help admitting that they had
been received with "devastating effect."[27]

What was in those speeches? Buber's Bar-Kochba addresses dealt almost
exclusively with what Buber called "the personal Jewish question, the root
of all Jewish questions, the question we must discover within ourselves."[28]
That is, they were concerned with the subjective feelings of German-Jewish
youth, bewildered by their estrangement both from a German environment
too hostile to absorb them and from a Jewish heritage that, in the forms

they had encountered, had nothing to offer them. (Kafka, for example, wrote of Rosh Hashanah services, "I yawned and dozed through the many hours . . . I don't think I was ever again so bored, except later at dancing lessons.")[29] As Buber explained, the trouble is that the world of the German Jew was divided between his German "environment" and his Jewish "substance." Normally, the national environment corresponds to the individual's inner substance, but for the Jew in Germany, "all the elements that might . . . make this nation a reality for him, are missing; all of them: Land, language, way of life. . . . The world of constant elements [i.e., the environment] and the world of substance are, for him, rent apart. He does not see his substance unfold before him in his environment; it has been banished into deep loneliness."[30]

Buber's answer to this "deep schism" is not, however, for the Jew to exchange the objective German environment for a Jewish land, language, or way of life.[31] Instead, Buber aims for a *subjective* transformation: Amid the pressures of daily life one is aware only of the outer environment; what must be done is to reach in to one's inner substance, to penetrate, to break through into one's own self. As Buber exhorts his audience:

> Let the vision of those stillest hours penetrate even more deeply: Let us behold, let us comprehend, ourselves. Let us get hold of ourselves: Let us draw our life into our hands, as a pail out of a well. . . . When out of our deepest self-knowledge we have thus affirmed ourselves, when we have said "yes" to ourselves and to our whole Jewish existence, then our feelings will no longer be the feelings of individuals; every individual among us will feel that he is the people, for he will feel the people within himself. . . . We shall perceive them, all of them, not merely as our brothers and sisters; rather . . . every one of us will feel: These people are part of myself.[32]

Since Jewish "substance" is what is in the deepest recesses of every Jew's heart, the individual penetrating deep into his own heart achieves a subjective feeling of unity, of becoming one with the entire Jewish people. The same knack for subjectively experiencing himself as becoming one with other things, which had permitted Buber a few years earlier to explain, "When I set wine to my lips, I feel: This is my blood," now allowed him to promise that "Every one of us will feel: These people are part of myself."

But was this not a setback for Buber? Was he not giving up the sublime sensation of oneness with the universe and with God himself envisioned by Jakob Boehme, in favor of a parochial identification with a particular people, the Jews?

Buber leaps past this difficulty by explaining that the identification of the individual Jew with the "substance" of Judaism is no particularism, because the true Judaism—as achieved by the Essenes, Jesus, the early Christians, and the Hasidim—is a Judaism whose essence is nothing other than "unity" itself. Thus, the Jew who affirms his link with the substance of his people does not, in doing so, actually arrive at Jewish particularism but, on the contrary, identifies himself with a people that itself embodies the desire for an interpenetration and unity with all mankind:

> This . . . has always been and will always be Judaism's significance for mankind: That it confronts mankind with the demand for unity . . . Judaism . . . offer[s], ever anew, a unification of mankind's diverse contents, and ever new possibilities for synthesis. At the time of the prophets and early Christianity it offered a religious synthesis; at the time of Spinoza, an intellectual synthesis; at the time of socialism, a social synthesis. And for what synthesis is the spirit of Judaism getting ready today? Perhaps for a synthesis of all those syntheses. But whatever form it will take, this much we know about it: It will, once again, demand unity . . . It will once again say to mankind: All you are looking for . . . is devoid of substance and meaning without unity.[33]

This obsession with the penetration of all barriers and the unity with all things at all times, proclaimed in his Bar-Kochba speeches as the essence of Judaism, was the alpha and the omega of Buber's "new answer to everything," and the point of all his subsequent philosophy. Thus, for example, in a speech a few years later, he asked his audience to imagine that a man is kicking another man: "Let us assume the striker receives in his soul the blow which he strikes: The same blow; that he receives it as the other remains still. For the space of a moment he experiences the situation from the other side. Reality imposes itself on him. What will he do? Either he will overwhelm the voice of the soul [and keep kicking], or his impulse will be reversed." Similarly:

> A man caresses a woman, who lets herself be caressed. Then let us assume that he feels the contact from two sides—with the palm of his hand still, and also with the woman's skin. The two-fold nature of the gesture, as one that takes place between two persons, thrills through the depth of enjoyment in his heart and stirs it. If he does not deafen his heart he will have . . . to love. . . . A transfusion has taken place after which a mere elaboration of [egoistic] subjectivity is never again possible or tolerable to him.[34]

And so on, very far forth—even to the point of achieving "mutuality" with animals, plants, and stones.[35]

Now one might agree with Buber that the key to redemption is for each individual to achieve, within himself, a unity with everyone and everything. Or one might, like the Prague novelist and composer Max Brod, find such narcissism to be indigestible ("But to me it does not seem sufficient for a life of fulfillment that the world be redeemed *in me*").[36] One thing, however, is absolutely clear about the new message that Buber was pushing among the German Zionist student groups: It was *not* Zionism. It was not the Zionism of Herzl, who quested after the Jewish state; nor was it that of Ahad Ha'am, who demanded the upbuilding of Jewish civilization. For while these men may have wrestled bitterly over priorities and means, they had, in the final analysis, shared one common goal: the restoration of a strong and successful Jewish *nation*. In Buber's Bar-Kochba speeches, this final aim simply disappears, and it is the soul of the *individual* Jew that becomes the only arena of consequence. As Buber himself stressed, "Every man whose soul attains unity . . . participates in the great process of Judaism." All else—even the fateful battle between Zionists and anti-Zionists over the question of a Jewish state—is relegated to irrelevance. The search for unity of the soul simply takes no interest in what Buber referred to as the "confrontation between nationalists and non-nationalists, or the like; these concerns are superficial, nonessential."[37]

There can be no appreciating Buber's impact on the subsequent struggle for a Jewish state without recognizing that the revival he was orchestrating among the young Jews of Berlin and Prague during the early 1910s was not a nationalist movement. It was a Jewish outreach organization, whose goal was to achieve an effusive emotional affirmation of one's *being* a Jew. And in pursuit of this end, he consciously sidestepped religious questions of tradition, truth, and the law, as well as national questions of state, land, and language. Buber casually cut away every troublesome particularism known to Judaism and gave the German-Jewish youth what they wanted. He told them that *these concerns are superficial, nonessential.* If only one could truly attain a feeling of "unity" with the other, then one's substance was that of a Jew.

And that—they could do.

In 1904, Martin Buber had dismissed the Zionist Organization as an "organism which is condemned to die," and ten years later, he was still staunchly indifferent toward the movement he had abandoned for dead. Buber's Bar-Kochba speeches do not even contain the word "Zionism." And his other activities evidenced such disinterest that Weizmann in 1913 wrote to Buber that he had not included him in renewed discussions about a university in Jerusalem since Buber had "withdrawn from Zionist affairs."[38] The first volume of Buber's collected essays, published in 1916, was entitled *The Jewish Movement,* without any Zionist connotations, and the essays written in the preceding twelve years likewise do not contain the word "Zionism." And when, in the spring of that year, Buber began publi-

cation of a review of Jewish ideas called *Der Jude,* his first editorial, in which
he laid out his vision of the periodical, still ascribed significance only to the
"personal" problem of the individual Jew. Here, too, the word "Zionism"
did not appear.[39]

But World War I ushered in political changes that breathed life into the
moribund Zionist Organization seemingly overnight, shaking Buber's confidence in its political demise. The entry of Britain into the war against
Turkey in November 1914 had been accompanied by a declaration by
Prime Minister Herbert Asquith to the effect that England sought an end to
the Ottoman empire "not only in Europe but in Asia."[40] And though the
public did not know that ministers in the British government had been discussing a possible Jewish state in Palestine, the formation in March 1915 of
a Jewish military unit, which saw battle under the British flag, caused a rush
of public speculation that an alliance between Britain and the Zionists
might be in the offing.[41] Even Lord Cromer, who had been instrumental in
demolishing Herzl's plans for a Jewish colony in Sinai, now published his
opinion that Zionism was "rapidly becoming a practical issue."[42] In
December 1916, with Britain under a new government headed by David
Lloyd George, Weizmann began circulating a memorandum in government
circles arguing that "a Jewish Palestine" under the auspices of the Crown
would be "a noble ideal, worthy of the British nation."[43]

Buber did not miss these developments, and as the prospects for an alliance between British imperial aspirations in the Middle East and Jewish
nationalist aspirations in Palestine grew, so too did Buber's fear that the de-
tested political strategies of Herzl's Zionist Organization were about to return to haunt the Jewish world. The ZVfD had in 1912 been taken over by
graduates of the Zionist youth movement Blau-Weiss, who had ousted Max
Bodenheimer and the leadership from Herzl's time and adopted an almost
Buberian platform emphasizing the importance of settlement in Palestine
"for the liberation of the personality of the individual."[44] That these young
minds might now be drawn into a corrupt alliance with Britain to create a
Jewish state was an unbearable possibility, which in short order ruined
Buber's pretense that how one stood on Zionism was a "superficial, nonessential" question. "We do not mean to add one more nationality to the
other nationalities that are fighting one another right now," he now wrote.
"The cause of Jewry is not to contribute to the separation of peoples, but to
serve the alliance of peoples." Moreover, the idea of a Jewish state was, as far
as he was concerned, "no longer applicable" when speaking of Palestine. "I
know nothing about a Jewish state with 'cannon, flags, medals,' not even in
the form of a dream," he wrote. What was needed was rather a "building up
of Jewish energy for a *super-national* task."[45]

Of course, none of these ideas falling from Buber's pen were new. They closely resembled the arguments used by Herzl's anti-Zionist detractors, particularly those that had been propounded in Berlin by the anti-Zionist philosopher Hermann Cohen at his popular Monday-night lectures at the Institute for the Science of Judaism.[46] In 1915, at the urging of anti-Zionist Jewish leaders worried by the rapidly mounting excitement over the prospects of Zionism, Cohen had published his *Germanism and Judaism,* in which he again argued for the intrinsic affinity of the Jewish essence for Germany. And in June 1916, he had followed this up with an explicit critique of Zionism, in which he explained that the idea of a Jewish state contravened the most basic teachings of the Jewish religion.[47]

Buber himself, living in Berlin at the time, could easily have applauded most of what Hermann Cohen had to say, offering only minor repairs of his own. But instead he decided that the great interpreter of Kant, now seventy-four years old and at the height of his influence, would serve as a perfect foil for an exposition of his own denationalized views of Judaism, which he began describing around this time as the "true Zionism."[48] Buber attacked Cohen in *Der Jude,* deriding the eminent philosopher for arguing with an "imaginary 'typical' Zionist" (i.e., a supporter of the Jewish state) rather than relating to *Buber's* views, which advocated creating "world-serving" Jewish communities in Palestine, but without political or military power. "We want Palestine not 'for the Jews,'" Buber wrote. "We want it for mankind, because we want it for the realization of Judaism." As for a Jewish state, this was, for the "true Zionism," inconceivable:

> For me, just as the state in general is not the determining goal of mankind, so the "Jewish state" is not the determining goal for the Jews. And the "viable ethnic group's need for power" . . . is completely foreign to me. I have seen and heard too much of the results of empty needs for power. Our argument . . . does not concern the Jewish state, that, yes, were it to be founded today would be built upon the same principles as any other modern state. It does not concern the addition of one more trifling power structure. It does, however, concern the settlement in Palestine, which, independent of "international politics," can affect the inner consolidation of the energies of the Jewish people and thereby the realization of Judaism. . . . This, then, is what I mean by Palestine—not a state, but only the ancient soil which bears the promised security of ultimate and hallowed permanence. . . . Zion restored will become the house of the Lord for all peoples and the center of the new world.[49]

With a wave of his hand, Buber here dismisses, as though it never existed, the essential argument that had divided Zionists and anti-Zionists since the publication of *The Jewish State.* The guardian-state Herzl had believed could save the Jews from the coming catastrophe is to Buber just "one more trifling power structure," just as anti-Zionists had always claimed. In terms of its intellectual substance, the remaining argument dividing Buber from Cohen was basically negligible: A dispute between an "anti-Zionist" who believed that Jewry should remain powerless and dispersed in the Diaspora, and a "true Zionist" who believed that one branch of Jewry should strive to become powerless in Palestine while the rest remained powerless and dispersed in the Diaspora. But if Buber's denunciation of the great anti-Zionist philosopher is understood as a stratagem for assuming Herzl's mantle at the head of an increasingly vibrant Zionist movement in Germany—in a stroke making it seem as though he had never left the ZO but was instead its "true" ideologue—then it was a brilliant success. The Cohen-Buber dispute was circulated in pamphlet form and read throughout German-speaking Europe, with Buber instantly winning accolades as the young Zionist hero defending the honor of the movement.

Having abandoned his disdain for politics, Buber now refashioned himself into a crusader against the Jewish state, calling on German Zionists to denounce Britain's alliance with Jewish nationalism. "Conquest of the land through armies: A bold madness," he sputtered, accusing his old collaborators in the Zionist Organization of having succumbed to the "unholy dogma of the sovereignty of nations" and to a "madness for success, which today presumes to be the real world and is in reality only a power-swollen puppet." As he explained, "Most of the leading . . . Zionists today are rank nationalists . . . imperialists, even unconscious mercantilists and worshippers of success. . . . If we do not manage to set up an authoritative counter-force, the soul of the movement will be corrupted, possibly forever." And as the ZO presented the case for a Jewish Palestine before the Allies in Paris in early 1919, Buber inveighed against any collaboration with the West: "If an agent . . . of English-American capitalism, swollen with power yet soon ready to collapse, is erected on Zion, then all our efforts will be in vain."[50]

The massacres of Jews in Palestine in 1920 and 1921 led Jabotinsky and others to organize a Jewish self-defense organization known as the Hagana ("Defense"), which would become the forerunner of the Israeli armed forces. But for Buber, the violence of the Arab mob only served to reconfirm his view that the Zionists, allied with British force, were creating in Palestine a morally corrupt regime that invited Arab hatred. It was in this frame of mind that Buber appeared at the Twelfth Zionist Congress in Karlsbad in September 1921—the first Zionist congress he had attended in eighteen years—at the head of a faction among the German Zionists demanding a renunciation by the ZO of the idea of the Jewish state. In his speech before the congress, Buber proposed putting an end to Zionist diplomatic efforts in the direction of Britain, calling instead for Zionists to attempt to merge Jewish and Arab political aspirations "in a just union with the Arab people."[51] Three days later, in a caucus of delegates loyal to him, Buber sharpened his attack, excoriating all contemporary nationalism, including that of the Zionist movement since Herzl, deploring it as "power hysteria" and diagnosing it as a "grave and complicated disease." Instead, he announced the arrival of his own "true nationalism"—in which each people would strive to become an "element" in "a more homogenous mankind."[52]

At the Karlsbad congress, Buber advanced what was to become—for anti-Zionists and "true Zionists" alike—the alternative to a Jewish state: a binational Palestinian state or a broader Arab-Jewish federation, into which the Jews living in Palestine would be absorbed as a minority. In presenting this alternate ideal, Buber may have drawn the only possible conclusion from his "new answer to everything," which saw "unity" with all others as *the* inviolable Jewish idea. But in so doing, he also introduced into the Zionist Organization the root concepts of political anti-Zionism, paving the way for a Jewish intellectual leadership in Palestine that would see as its mission the dissolution of the idea of the Jewish state in the minds of the Jews.

CHAPTER 8

The German Intellectuals and the Founding of the Hebrew University

ARTIN BUBER DID NOT CHOOSE to immigrate to Palestine. His various projects, including the Freies Juedisches Lehrhaus for adult education in Frankfurt and the translation of the Bible into German—both projects in collaboration with Franz Rosenzweig—consumed his attention and kept him in Germany until the eve of World War II. But a steady stream of Buber's disciples did make their way to Palestine, forming the country's first small colonies of German Jews. In Jerusalem, there sprang into being a transplanted German-speaking "salon," which soon included Buber's assistant at *Der Jude,* Ernst Simon; Buber's young colleague at the Frankfurt Lehrhaus, Gerhard (Gershom) Scholem; graduates of his Bar-Kochba lectures such as Hugo Bergmann and Hans Kohn; Orientalists such as Fritz (Shlomo) Goitein and David Baneth; Judah Magnes, the former rabbi of New York's German-Jewish aristocracy; and the ZO's point man in making land purchases from the Arabs, Arthur Ruppin.[1] The graphic artist Anna

Ticho hosted regular soirees for German intellectuals and artists in her home, and the parlors of other German immigrants became centers for musical recitals and reading circles in which they struggled to digest the latest works of German-Jewish thought: Hermann Cohen's *Religion of Reason* (1919); Franz Rosenzweig's *The Star of Redemption* (1921); and Buber's *I and Thou* (1923). Thus, even as the desperados of the Labor movement were subjecting themselves to heat, malaria, and hunger in the effort to bring food out of the earth, the German intellectuals in Jerusalem—like their peers in Frankfurt and Berlin with whom they kept up a voluminous correspondence—were wracking their consciences over the question of whether the Arabs in Palestine were being treated as a "thou."

It was this milieu that gave birth to the idea of making a systematic effort to replace the idea of the Jewish state with an alternative political concept that could unite the interest of the Jews with those of Palestine's Arab population. In 1925, this became the formal aim of a group calling itself the Peace Association ("Brit Shalom"),[2] which was established at the initiative of Arthur Ruppin and quickly attracted the support of Buber and a significant number of his associates. Ruppin had briefly visited Europe during World War I after being expelled from Palestine by the Turks, and by the time he returned in 1920, he, like his colleagues in the ZVfD, had concluded that it was not Jewish settlement but an agreement with Arabs that was the most serious difficulty facing Zionism. "Without a friendly arrangement with them," he wrote in his diary, "all our work in Palestine is built on quicksand."[3] It was not long before Ruppin realized the Arabs would never agree to a Jewish state, and by 1923, he had decided that the ZO had to abandon the theoretical foundations laid for it by Herzl:

> I think that I shall not be able to continue working for the Zionist movement if Zionism does not acquire a new theoretical foundation. Herzl's conception of the Jewish state was possible only because he ignored the existence of the Arabs and believed that he could manipulate world history by means of the diplomatic methods of the Quai d'Orsay [i.e., the French foreign ministry]. Zionism has never been able to free itself entirely of this "diplomatic" imperialist conception.

When Ruppin considered what this "new theoretical foundation" for Zionism would be, his point of departure was that "a 'Jewish state' of one or even several million Jews . . . will be nothing more than another Montenegro or Lithuania. There are enough states in the world." Since there was no need for a Jewish state, the Jews of Palestine had to devise a new aim for themselves, and Ruppin had one to suggest: "Their function will have to be to raise the cultural level of the entire Near East . . . and establish a progressive cultural community together with their neighbors"—

a community that would pursue a "new social order," a "new cultural community," and "the teachings of the prophets and Jesus." With such a profound Jewish "mission" available, Ruppin thought, the Jewish settlement movement in Palestine could simply "become a power with a role in the development of the culture of mankind. A few hundred thousand Jews together with thirty million Arabs represent a population large enough to influence the culture of mankind."[4] Unlike Buber, whose views were virtually indistinguishable, Ruppin was honest enough to admit that the new "mission" for the Jews he was devising might be something other than Zionism. As he wrote in his diary, "It seems to me that I am gradually outgrowing Zionism altogether. I have the impression that Zionism has been only a stepping stone for me to a far more important task, the revival of culture in the Near East."[5]

On April 26, 1925, Ruppin organized a lecture in his home by Joseph Horowitz, a prominent Orientalist and a colleague of Buber's at the University of Frankfurt, on the attitude of the Islamic world toward Zionism. Horowitz described his recent visit to Egypt, in which he had discovered that his Muslim colleagues were hostile to the Balfour Declaration. This realization underscored for him the importance of making the Jewish community in Palestine an integral (and therefore tolerable) part of the Orient rather than permitting it to become an alien outpost of the West.[6] The theory that the destiny of the Jews was to somehow fuse with the Orient had been an ideological staple of Buber's circle for over a decade (in stark contrast with Herzl's belief that the Jewish state should be closely aligned with the West),[7] and Horowitz's report only reinforced the sense that a step had to be taken in this direction. The establishment of the Peace Association, dedicated to the study and exposition of the concept of a binational Arab-Jewish state in Palestine, was intended to serve this purpose.

Ruppin's Peace Association quickly gathered around it many of Jewish Palestine's most important intellectuals, including Judah Magnes,[8] the new president of the Hebrew University; Hugo Bergmann, later rector of the university; Ernst Simon, later director of the Hebrew University School of Education; virtually all of the leading Orientalists who later formed the university's School of Oriental Studies, including Shlomo Goitein and Ludwig Mayer; Shmuel Sambursky, later dean of the faculty of sciences; Gershom Scholem; Hans Kohn; the attorney-general Norman Bentwich; Lord Samuel's son Edwin; and the founder of Hadassah, Henrietta Szold. The Peace Association's German and English branches quickly garnered Buber's support, as well as that of the president of the German Zionist Federation, Kurt Blumenfeld; Robert Weltsch, editor of the ZVfD newspaper *Juedische Rundschau* ("Jewish Review"); Werner Senator, later vice president of the Hebrew University; Buber's old alter ego Berthold Feiwel; the Orientalist

Joseph Horowitz; Buber's publisher Zalman Schocken; as well as Lord
Samuel himself, whose stint as high commissioner in Palestine had left him
hostile to his old dream of a Jewish state. Albert Einstein, although never
formally a member, permitted the group to publish his name in association
with its views.[9]

Obviously, a group of thinkers and activists with such credentials can
never be ideologically monolithic. Nevertheless, the general direction of the
Peace Association's ideas—as well as their source in German-Jewish anti-
Zionism—may be appreciated from the following passage by Hugo
Bergmann, published in one of the first issues of the organization's periodi-
cal, *Sheifoteinu* ("Our Aspirations"):

> It is believed in a number of European countries today that the existence of a
> state gives one people, among the many peoples who live in that state, prior-
> ity rights. This people, this nation, is considered "the people of the land," and
> the other peoples are merely residents, guests in that land. In theory, of
> course, each individual, even when he belongs to a minority nation, enjoys
> equal rights, but the state is nonetheless the property of one nation, the ruling
> one . . .
>
> As against this view . . . the Jewish philosopher Hermann Cohen postu-
> lated the philosophy of the prophets. . . . The prophets demanded justice . . .
> And a regime of justice in any country inhabited by two peoples means:
> Abolition of the idea of "the people of the state" which provides priority
> rights to one nation over another . . .
>
> Our entire influence all over the world should be directed towards one
> aim: . . . To set up a new national and political morality in the world, which
> would secure a national minority the same rights enjoyed by the majority and
> eliminate totally the political value of numerical relations between people.
> We thought that our dispersion among the nations had imposed upon us this
> historical mission, of fighting for our existence among the nations—a minor-
> ity existence—while we were struggling for this new interstate and interna-
> tional morality. Palestine, the land on which we hope to have a political
> impact greater than on any other land, will in this respect be an example to all
> nations, because in that land we shall carry out such arrangements in the rela-
> tions between the two peoples inhabiting it, that will serve as a model for our
> brethren who live as minorities in the lands of their dispersion, in their quest
> for equality.[10]

In the search for a political ideal to replace the Jewish state, Bergmann
thus returns to the social-contract doctrine explicitly rejected by Herzl,
while relying on the authority of the anti-Zionist philosopher Hermann
Cohen to establish its moral credentials. In this view, the idea of establishing a sovereign power for the purpose of protecting a particular group—the
Jews—is intrinsically immoral and illegitimate, so that a Jewish state based

on this idea will also be immoral and illegitimate. Although not all of the members of the Peace Association concluded from this that the Jews must immediately renounce the Balfour Declaration and the Palestine Mandate, they did come to believe that the Jews had no moral case for continuing in their efforts to secure unlimited Jewish immigration to Palestine, a Jewish majority, and finally a Jewish state that would be the national home of the entire Jewish people. Sooner or later, they agreed, a different regime would have to be created in Palestine, one in which the Arab character of the land would be able to find its just expression.

In this, the intellectuals of the Peace Association found themselves agreeing on substantial points with the anti-Zionist Arab leadership, as well as with important figures within the British government and Palestine administration who dissented from London's alliance with Zionism and who eventually succeeded in bringing it to an end.

———————

Histories of Zionism have typically maintained that the intellectuals of the Peace Association had virtually no impact on the course of the movement for a Jewish state. But this interpretation of events fails to take into account the tectonic shifts that a small group of intellectuals can induce in the political life of a nation by shaping the understanding of the youth who are the future leaders of the nation. Thus, while Labor Zionism was preoccupied with the physical upbuilding of Palestine, the disciples of Hermann Cohen and Martin Buber were at work shaping the future *cultural* course of the Jewish state.

Even a cursory glance reveals the pivotal position of institutions and organizations led by German-Jewish intellectuals in the cultural landscape of Jewish Palestine. Among the most important of these was the Hashomer Hatzair ("Young Guard") youth movement, founded in Vienna in 1916 and imported into Palestine in the 1920s under the leadership of the Austrian youth leader Meir Wald (later Ya'ari); in Palestine, this movement established a network of collective farms heavily influenced by Buber and the ideal of a binational Palestine, which became a major force in Israeli literature, theater, and art.[11] Of similar significance was the "New Bezalel" Academy for the Arts in Jerusalem, opened in 1935 by German artists with the support of the German Immigrants' Department of the Jewish Agency under Arthur Ruppin,[12] which became a primary force in the inculcation of stridently universalistic views among Israel's artists. Noteworthy as well was the youth village in Ben-Shemen, founded in 1927 by Buber's disciple Siegfried Lehmann, whose prestigious boarding school was the arena for the early development of such figures as Shimon Peres, Shulamit Aloni,

S. Yizhar, and the godfather of low culture in Israel, Dan Ben-Amotz. In this context, mention must also be made of the Hadassah organization, which was founded by young German-Jewish women in the United States to provide humanitarian assistance to Jews and Arabs in Palestine, but which during the 1920s came to view its efforts as "missionary work" in the service of Jewish-Arab social integration (e.g., "playgrounds . . . where Arab and Jewish children can play together")—a line of thinking that rapidly brought many of its outstanding leaders to advocate giving up on the aim of a Jewish state.[13]

But there is no question that the Peace Association's most spectacular institutional coup was its influence over the Hebrew University in Jerusalem, which became the undisputed cultural hegemon in Jewish Palestine.

The idea of establishing a Jewish university in Palestine had long been a fixture in Zionist thought, having been proposed as early as 1882 by the Heidelberg rabbi-turned-mathematician Hermann Schapira, whom Herzl invited to speak on the subject before the First Zionist Congress. Herzl himself also submitted a petition to the Ottoman sultan for the establishment of such a Jewish university in Palestine, and it was the centerpiece of the "cultural" policy advocated by Weizmann and Buber beginning in 1901.[14] In 1913, Weizmann succeeded in securing some private financial support for the idea, as well as the appointment of a university committee by the Eleventh Congress. And toward the close of World War I, with Allenby's forces in control of Jerusalem, he presided over a cornerstone-laying ceremony on Mt. Scopus, in which he spoke of the "integral part" the university would play in the reconstruction of "the Jewish national political existence" by becoming a "center for the development of Jewish consciousness"; "informed by Jewish learning and Jewish energy," it was to be a university in which "our Jewish youth will be reinvigorated from Jewish sources" and "ancient Jewish learning . . . [is] to be brought to light again."[15] Later, he even brought Albert Einstein to Jerusalem to deliver the nonexistent university's first lecture (on the theory of relativity), in a makeshift auditorium studded with Zionist flags, the Union Jack, symbols of the twelve tribes of Israel, and a portrait of Herzl.[16]

Yet all of this amounted to very little. In 1923, Gershom Scholem, recently arrived in Jerusalem, was still able to consider the entire effort something of a farce. As he later wrote:

> I worked for an institution called [the] National and University Library, but except for one building—the Institute of Biochemistry for which Dr. Weizmann, himself a biochemist, had raised the funds, and which was then under construction—the university was not yet in evidence. In Jerusalem there was a committee of a few notables who carried on fruitless discussions

about the coming university and its professorships. For the rest, no one in the country believed that the project which had been decided upon as early as 1913 and for which a symbolic cornerstone had been laid in 1918 . . . would come to fruition in the foreseeable future.[17]

What changed the course of the university's history was the arrival in Jerusalem in 1922 of Judah Leib Magnes, an American Reform rabbi with close ties to New York's wealthy German-Jewish community—which, at Magnes's urging, eventually adopted the struggling Hebrew University project as its own. Magnes grew up in San Francisco, whose Jewish community had been founded by Jewish merchants, many of them German Jews, during the gold rush. At the turn of the century, the city's Jewish community was led by the virulently anti-Zionist Rabbi Jacob Voorsanger of Temple Emanu-El ("Israel's mission," he argued, "is a spiritual one . . . Its political aspirations are dead forever").[18] And it was under his tutelage that the city became a leading center of Jewish anti-Zionist activity, culminating in San Francisco congressman Julius Kahn's 1919 declaration of American Jews against the idea of a Jewish state.[19] Voorsanger's protégé was the young Julius Magnes, son of a local merchant family, who inherited an attachment to German language and culture from his mother. Voorsanger personally tutored Magnes in Judaism and steered him toward the rabbinate, eventually sending him to Hebrew Union College in Cincinnati, where he began a flirtation, which was to last several years, with the idea of establishing a Jewish state in Palestine. Between 1900 and 1902, Magnes traveled to Berlin and Heidelberg to complete his studies.[20]

In 1906, Magnes became associate rabbi at Temple Emanu-El in New York, handily the most prestigious congregation in the United States, boasting as members the leading German-Jewish financiers and businessmen in the city, including the Schiff, Guggenheim, Warburg, Marshall, Lewisohn, Untermyer and Seligman families. Typical among them was the Schiff-Warburg banking family, rulers of a sprawling financial empire with active branches both in Germany and the United States. The Hamburg Warburgs were German patriots and avid readers of Buber, whose scion, Max Warburg, corresponded with Buber about the importance of creating a "new Judaism" in Palestine (at the same time emphatically opposing a Jewish state).[21] Max's younger brother, Felix, had married into the family of the immensely successful New York financier Jacob Schiff, the undisputed lord of Jewish high society in the United States and ruler of its vast array of charitable institutions. Schiff had readily adapted his emancipationist Judaism to the American context, writing that "as an American, I cannot for a moment concede that one can be at the same time a true American and an honest adherent of the Zionist movement."[22] When Felix Warburg was installed at Schiff's firm in New York in 1895, he adopted Schiff's patriotism—and along with it his opposition to the idea of a Jewish state.

By the time Magnes came to Emanu-El, he had become a leader of the struggling American Zionist Federation.[23] But to his new congregants, whose children he tutored for their "confirmations," Magnes explained that Palestine was something like a Jewish California, by which he meant a "romance of the Jewish national frontiersmen" that makes "heroes and heroines of modern Jews."[24] Later, he endorsed a position similar to that which Buber was simultaneously promoting in Germany, arguing that the Jews could succeed in creating what they needed in Palestine as citizens of Turkey: "Zionism must mean . . . the building up of a Jewish cultural center in Palestine through the inner cultural strength of the free Jewish people in Palestine, an Ottoman Province."[25]

These kinds of theories the anti-Zionist New York bankers were at least willing to tolerate, and Magnes quickly succeeded in marrying into the family of Louis Marshall. This kinship with Marshall, as well as his developing friendship with Felix Warburg, permitted Magnes to take an increasingly inside role in determining the course of American Jewish philanthropy. He became one of the founding members of the American Jewish Committee, took a leading role in organizing relief for Russian Jewry, and, in 1914, conducted a meeting at Temple Emanu-El in which Warburg, Schiff, and other leaders agreed to establish the Jewish Joint Distribution Committee (JDC), with the aim of providing charitable relief both in Eastern Europe and in Palestine. So deep was Magnes's commitment to the network of institutions operated by the German-Jewish community that when Louis Brandeis sought to create a representative American Jewish congress—which, like Herzl's congresses, was intended as a springboard for a mass-membership Zionist organization to displace the anti-Zionism of the Jewish philanthropists—Magnes turned his back on his old comrades in the ZO to side with his sponsors. As Magnes explained in a letter to Brandeis, this decision stemmed not only from tactical concerns but was rooted in a deep ideological disagreement between himself and the Zionist Organization over "the attitude to Palestine itself":

> The Congress program of the Zionist Organization is . . . a secure homeland for the Jewish people in Palestine. . . . Have you made it clear to yourselves . . . what you mean by a "secure homeland"? . . . Can the Ottoman government . . . be blamed for viewing us with suspicion if . . . while we want equal rights for the Jews of the world, we want *more* than equal rights in Palestine? I want equal rights for the Jews, no more and no less, in all lands, including Palestine. . . . In this the Jewish people in Palestine would be on the same level as the Moslem, the Christian, the Turkish, the Arabic, the Armenian, and other groups of that empire. All that we have a right to ask is that the Jews be permitted to settle in

and develop their Jewish economic and cultural life in Palestine freely, just as other people of the empire have the same right.[26]

Like his anti-Zionist friends, Magnes insisted that the Jews have a "right" only to equality—never for political strength and sovereignty with which to defend themselves. And it was this belief that later brought him to reject the Balfour Declaration and the British Mandate. "Your Balfour Declaration," he wrote, "decrees a Jewish ruling class from the outset. . . . This gift of political primacy to the Jews in Palestine rather than political equality contains the seed of resentment and future conflict." For this reason he concluded, in a breathtaking foreshadowing of later claims against the Jewish state, that the Jewish settlement in Palestine had therefore been "born in sin": "When I think that Palestine was conquered by force of arms, and that it was made 'Jewish' by the iniquitous [Versailles] Peace Conference, I am reminded of the well-known Jewish description: 'Conceived and born in uncleanliness.'"[27]

Unlike Buber, who won phenomenal success by selling this line to German Jews as the "true Zionism," Magnes paid for his own similar se-mantic agility by being firmly repudiated by both the leadership and the rank and file of American Zionists. But his decision to stand with the phil-anthropists was amply rewarded within the reigning circle of New York Jews. The *New York Times* followed Magnes's lead in launching a furious attack on Brandeis, accusing him of violating judicial norms by participat-ing in the Zionist leadership—an accusation that succeeded in forcing Brandeis to resign all offices in Jewish organizations. And there were other rewards as well. Due in large part to Magnes's unstinting loyalty to emanci-pationist dogma, he was gradually able to win the trust and support of his German-Jewish supporters for agricultural and other "non-political" proj-ects in Palestine. After a relentless lobbying effort by Weizmann and Magnes, Felix and Freida Warburg made the trip to Palestine in February 1924. Accompanying Magnes to Mt. Scopus and hearing a peroration on his vision of the Hebrew University, Warburg was sold, shortly thereafter announcing his intention of giving a $500,000 endowment for the creation of the Institute for Jewish Studies at the university—on condition that Magnes control the funds and that he be assured of a leading position in the new institution.[28]

Warburg's donation had an electrifying effect on the sleepy committees that had for years been ruminating over what a Jewish studies program at the university would look like. By July, Magnes succeeded in imposing his own proposals for the program, and by November, he had been empowered to hire the faculty. In December 1924, Magnes conducted an opening cere-mony at which he delivered the keynote address. This ceremony, which Weizmann learned about from the papers, reflected what had by then become a contest of wills between Weizmann, the promoter of a Jewish university as an "integral part of our national structure," and Magnes, the representative of antinationalist Jews who claimed that ties between the Hebrew University and the Zionist Organization would lead to the politicization of the institution.[29] As Louis Marshall, now the leader of New York's German Jewry, wrote to Weizmann: "It certainly cannot help matters to have the idea go forth that the Hebrew University at Jerusalem is to be a tail to the Zionist kite; in other words, that it is to be controlled by the Zionist Organization. If that were to be the result, it would be far better if the University had never been created."[30]

Thus, even before the Hebrew University opened its doors, the stage was set for what became a protracted battle for control of its ideological underpinnings, pitting the Jewish nationalism of Weizmann, chairman of its Board of Governors, against the political antinationalism of Magnes and Buber and their followers. This was in many respects the same conflict that characterized the disagreements between the leadership of the Zionist Organization and that of the Peace Association, and it naturally translated itself into radically different visions of what the Hebrew University was really all about. Weizmann, the "practical" Zionist, saw the university's significance as being linked to the establishment of strong faculties in the natural sciences, including medicine and agricultural science, whose research would contribute to the physical transformation of the land in preparation for Jewish settlement. For him, ridding the country of malaria—a precondition for large-scale Jewish settlement in otherwise uninhabitable swamplands— was the sort of item that topped the agenda from the very outset.[31]

Magnes, on the other hand, had little interest in the settlement of millions of Jews[32] and therefore only a relatively limited interest in swamps and the scientists who drained them. For him, the mission of the Hebrew University was to be twofold: First, it should take the lead in inculcating a Jewish universalism in the entire Jewish population of Palestine—making it, as one of Magnes's allies wrote later, "a guide for the perplexed for the land of Israel."[33] Second, it would within its walls seek to "bring about the spiritual reconciliation between the two most gifted races of Semitic stock." Warburg similarly planned for it to "play an extraordinarily important part" in bringing Arabs and Jews together.[34] To fulfill this mission, the creation of a "humanistic" humanities faculty, and particularly one that would place great emphasis on Arab culture, was of the essence. The result was that the university in a certain sense consisted of two competing institutions, one teaching physical sciences and animated by traditional practical-Zionist sympathies, the other teaching the humanities and social sciences and largely motivated by the German-Jewish conception of the "true Zion."[35]

Weizmann at first reacted to this challenge to the Jewish university as he had when the Jewish state had become too hard a sell: He responded by massaging his views to make them more palatable to his financial backers ("A university," he now declared, "is nothing if not universal").[36] But he never really had a chance of competing with Magnes on this terrain. On the contrary, the university's German-Jewish donors responded sympathetically to Magnes's pleas that their financial support was crucial if the university were to be a "true university"[37]—that is, one free from the influence of political Zionism. Indeed, until the establishment of the state, it was Magnes's antinationalist associates in New York and elsewhere who contributed the great majority of the Hebrew University's resources.[38] And this fact quickly dictated the nature of the university as well. At Warburg's insistence, the Board of Governors selected Magnes to be chancellor of the university.

Frustrated and humiliated, Weizmann resorted to maneuvering to bring Zionists onto the Board of Governors, a tactic that provoked Warburg into threatening to cut off all donations. At another point, he attempted to have himself foisted onto Magnes as the "academic head" of the institution.[39] "He is constantly playing a game," Magnes wrote of Weizmann in 1928, "very cleverly, and one does not know what he is after."[40] But it is clear what Weizmann was after. He sought, by every means possible, to undermine the influence of Magnes and his friends on the university's appointments and research agenda. And his efforts in this regard must be recognized as a failure.

Magnes remained at the helm of the Hebrew University for twenty-four years—the first ten of them in a position of near-total authority—during which time the core of its staff and the main strokes of its ideology were irrevocably cast. As a direct consequence of Magnes's aims—the propagation of a Jewish universalism and the forging of Arab-Jewish understanding—the Hebrew University's intellectual plan was based on a kind of an academic "binationalism," expressed in the fact that the first two humanities divisions established were the Institute for Jewish Studies and the School of Oriental Studies. One of Magnes's first major decisions was the appointment of Joseph Horowitz of the University of Frankfurt as "visiting director" of the institute, with the authority to design the program of research and studies and to select the faculty.[41] Horowitz, it will be recalled, was the Jewish Orientalist whose lecture at Ruppin's home had been the catalyst for the creation of the Peace Association, and the School of Oriental Studies was similarly inaugurated with a monthlong seminar given by him. With his assistance, virtually the entire faculty of the School for Oriental Studies, including L. A. Meyer, Shlomo Goitein, Levi Billig, Moshe (Max) Schwabe, and David Hartwig (Tzvi) Baneth, came to consist of sympathizers of the Peace Association's binationalist aims. Moreover, the school really did operate as though its mission were the creation of sympathy between Arabs and Jews. Thus, it was decided that the School for Oriental Studies should undertake an "impressive scientific project" that would require much of the institute's attention for a period of years. A member of the institute proposed a critical edition of all of Maimonides' Arabic-language writings for the eight hundredth anniversary of the great rabbi's birth in 1935, but the university administration preferred something that would be "addressed to the Arab world," and Maimonides, one may infer, was too Jewish to qualify. The university therefore chose instead to publish a ten-volume edition, with commentary, of *Ansab al-Ashraf* ("The Genealogies of the Nobility"), a history of the Arabs from the ninth century.[42]

This same trend was visible in other humanities disciplines as well, with the dominant figures frequently drawn from among German Jews opposed to the founding of a Jewish state. No fewer than three of the six founding members of the university's Institute for Jewish Studies—Arthur Ruppin, Gershom Shalom, and David Yellin—were members of the Peace Association.[43] The first courses in Western philosophy, too, were taught by Hugo Bergmann, Buber's faithful disciple and one of the Peace Association's most active members. And when the university formally began offering courses toward a degree in the fall of 1928, more than half of the teaching faculty—seven out of the thirteen instructors in the humanities and social sciences—were openly affiliated with the Peace Association.[44] Similarly, Magnes's deputy chancellor was Max Schloessinger, another Peace Association supporter whom he had known from his school days in Berlin.

Indeed, so confident was Magnes in his pursuit of a "true university" that in the summer of 1929 he approached Buber, still ensconced in Frankfurt, with the offer of a lifetime position as academic head of the university—a step that, as Joseph Horowitz correctly pointed out, would have amounted to appointing Buber permanent minister of education for all of Jewish Palestine.[45] Magnes certainly understood that Buber's views would create tremendous opposition in the ZO, for Buber had only two weeks earlier made a brief appearance at the Zionist Congress in Zurich, in which he had again exhorted the delegates to adopt a "joint national policy" with the Arabs by "imagining the soul of the other . . . through the reality of one's own."[46] Nevertheless, Magnes apparently believed that with Warburg's help, even this, the ultimate act of secession by the university from the movement to build a Jewish state, would be pushed through.[47] There is no way of knowing, however, what the outcome would have been of an all-out struggle over the issue of Buber's appointment. Within three days, there began an outpouring of Arab violence such as Jewish Palestine had never seen, within days obscuring all other questions. Buber's appointment as academic head appears not to have been raised again.[48]

Inevitably, Magnes's insistence on keeping the university aloof from the dream of the Jewish state opened up a chasm between the professors, who saw themselves as the intellectual leadership of Jewish Palestine, and the great majority of the Jewish population—a rift colloquially referred to in those years as the gap between the "mountain" (Mt. Scopus, where the university campus was located) and the "valley" (the Jezreel Valley and the coastal plain), where most Jews lived. Within the Labor movement, many of the leaders came to see themselves has having been betrayed by the intellectuals, while the professors felt, as Hugo Bergmann wrote in his diaries, as if they lived alone on an island, completely misunderstood and surrounded by enemies.[49]

In 1935, after ten years in which Magnes had largely controlled the development of the university in every field of interest to him, Weizmann finally staged a successful assault on the chancellor's position in an effort to bring the university back into ideological alignment with the Zionist Organization. At a meeting of the Board of Governors in Lucerne immediately following his reinstatement as president of the ZO, Weizmann had Magnes stripped of academic control over the university, vesting it instead in the hands of a rector to be elected by members of the faculty.

But this victory proved ephemeral. Hugo Bergmann, one of Buber's most intimate disciples, stepped forward to fill the position, triggering a confrontation in which the Labor leader, Berl Katznelson, recently added to the Board of Governors, pronounced that although professors with Bergmann's views could be tolerated in the name of academic freedom, it was unthinkable that the university's academic head should be a supporter of the "enemies of Zionism."[50] But Hugo Bergmann was nevertheless elected rector, and the crucial humanities faculties continued on their course almost as though nothing had changed—so that two years later, in 1937, Ben-Gurion intimated that the efforts of the professors were not necessarily rooted in "the desires of the Jewish settlement and in its historical aims," a condition that had brought about the "estrangement, if not alienation" of the Hebrew University from the rest of Jewish Palestine.[51]

CHAPTER 9

The Intellectuals' Assault and Ben-Gurion's Response, 1929–1939

THE MEETING OF THE COUNCIL of the newly formed Jewish Agency for Palestine in Zurich on August 11, 1929, represented the high point of Weizmann's diplomatic success, bringing the Zionists into a single organization with the German-Jewish philanthropists Louis Marshall and Felix Warburg, as well as Albert Einstein, Lord Samuel, Lord Melchett, Leon Blum, and others. Here, for the first time, was a gathering of the Jewish aristocracy that at least outwardly resembled the Jewish guardian-organization that Herzl had hoped to create. Yet this new organization, which now inherited the place of the Zionist Organization as Britain's partner in any discussion concerning Jewish Palestine, was not a body even tacitly committed to pursuing a Jewish state. On the contrary, many of its leading figures identified openly with the ideology of the Peace Association, lending the small band of Buber's followers a weight previously unimagined in influencing Zionist policy. The result was that in the ten years that followed, the most important Zionist leaders—Weizmann, Ben-Gurion, and Ze'ev Jabotinsky—spent their best energies in a bitter internecine struggle over when and how to pull away from a politics tailored to suit the "non-Zionist" philanthropists, who did not share in the recognition that only an independent Jewish state held out the prospect of an open gate to Palestine, and therefore of the salvation of millions of Jews trapped in Hitler's Europe.

In the summer of 1929, there were of course few Zionists who recognized that the ZO's new alignment with its erstwhile emancipationist detractors would or could herald catastrophe. Indeed, such was the magnitude of Weizmann's achievement that even a skeptic such as Ben-Gurion found himself looking on in admiration. To his wife Paula, Ben-Gurion wrote that the opening ceremony in Zurich was "astounding and captivating. . . . I myself was profoundly moved . . . All that is sublime and inspiring in the Jewish people was at this gathering." Perhaps the combined Jewish Agency meant the "opening of a new historic chapter in our lives."[1]

But it was not only the Zionists who were struck by this unprecedented show of unity. The Arab leadership was no less impressed by its significance. Already on Friday, August 16, two days after the signing of the formal agreement between the ZO and Louis Marshall's "non-Zionists," Amin al-Husseini—one of the instigators of the anti-Jewish pogroms eight years earlier and now mufti of Jerusalem—used a demonstration by Jewish youths at the Western Wall as a pretext for riots that had left one Jewish youth dead. Crowds of armed Arabs began arriving in Jerusalem from the countryside the following week, but the British police found themselves without sufficient reliable forces (most of the "British" policemen were Arab) to be able to disarm the mob converging on the city. On Friday, August 23, Arab worshippers swept out of the mosques on the Temple Mount and into Jaffa Road, the main Jerusalem thoroughfare, killing the Jews they found in their path. Others attacked Mea Sharim and Yemin Moshe and then continued outward to the other Jewish neighborhoods, where they continued killing for four days. Pleas from Yitzhak Ben-Tzvi on behalf of the Jewish National Assembly—he was one of the only Jewish leaders not in Europe at the time—for the British to arm Jewish defense units were repeatedly rejected. As the slaughter, rape, and looting spread to Hebron, Safed, Haifa, and Tel Aviv, and then to villages in the countryside, it became clear that the British did not believe they had the manpower to interfere. Not until the end of the following week was the blood carnival suppressed with the help of reinforcements from Cairo. By then, 133 Jews lay dead, with more than three hundred wounded. Entire farming settlements had been evacuated. The Jewish community in Hebron, founded four hundred years earlier by refugees from Spain, was decimated. As Husseini explained laconically a few weeks later: "All the troubles started at Zurich, where the Jews held a conference in August and were assured the aid of the rich American Jews for building up Palestine. This made the Palestine Jews so arrogant that they thought they could start driving us out of the country."[2]

In the aftermath of the killings, there were many Jews, including Ben-Tzvi in Palestine and Jabotinsky in Paris, who demanded that Britain permit the establishment of a substantial Jewish military force capable of defending the Jewish settlement.[3] But this view, a distant echo of Herzl's quest for an imperial charter, found no toehold in the bleak political reality that the ZO now faced. The fall of the Conservative Baldwin government in the summer of 1929 had thrown the last of Weizmann's political contacts from the era of Lloyd George and Balfour out of power. When Weizmann arrived in London at the height of the slaughter, he was confronted instead by Britain's first Labor government. Headed by Ramsey MacDonald, the Labor government was without any particular affinity for the dream of a Jewish state. The new colonial secretary, Sydney Webb—shortly to be Lord Passfield—was a renowned socialist, unblemished by any interest in Zionism, and he would not even meet with Weizmann. Weizmann's account of his desperate meeting with Passfield's wife, the socialist author Beatrice Webb, is possibly exaggerated, but nevertheless strongly suggestive of what he now faced in London. According to Weizmann, she told him, "I can't see why the Jews make such a fuss over a few dozen of their people killed in Palestine. As many are killed every week in London in traffic accidents, and no one pays any attention."[4] When Passfield finally agreed to receive Weizmann himself, he insisted on emphasizing that he was simply opposed to large-scale Jewish immigration to Palestine, a none-too-subtle way of saying that he intended to work to suspend the very concept of a British-Jewish mandate in Palestine.[5]

As the Zionist Organization reeled under these blows, the members of the Peace Association realized that the vulnerability of the Jews in Palestine had created an unprecedented opening. Perhaps now the ZO could be brought to recognize the folly in the theory of a British-backed Jewish state. Among the first to sense the opportunity was Buber, who, in a speech before the Berlin chapter of the Peace Association in October 1929, placed blame for the massacres in Palestine with the Jews themselves. After all, it was the Jews in Palestine who had been "excluding" the Arabs from their communal life. "Had we been prepared to live in genuine togetherness with the Arabs," he said, "the latest events would not have been possible." The only recourse was to rebuild life in Palestine on a model of "togetherness"—culturally, by "acquainting ourselves with Islam" and reaching "a cultural accommodation with Arabism," and politically, by establishing "what is called a binational state" in place of the proposed Jewish one. As a first step toward such binationalism, Buber demanded that the Jewish leadership propose amnesty for Arabs who had been convicted of murdering Jews. "We must tell the world," he said, "that we demand that the death sentences pronounced for our sake, for the crimes committed against us, must not be carried out."[6]

Buber's students in Palestine took his words to heart, accepting at least part of the blame for the massacres on themselves. Similar sentiments were expressed by Gershom Scholem, who wrote that a life building Jewish Palestine was proving to be "a dubious undertaking." For him and others in his circle, he said, the face of Zionism was proving to be "that of a Medusa," and the torment of associating with it was "reaching the limits of endurability."⁷ The conclusion that the Jews had been in part to blame for the fact that they had been massacred drove Buber's disciples in Palestine in various directions. Ernst Simon, for one, sought to strengthen his efforts on behalf of the "true Zion" by deepening his association with the anti-Zionist Communists, working under orders from Moscow to undermine British rule in Palestine and establish in its place an Arab state.⁸ Hans Kohn, on the other hand, left for the United States, where he became a supporter of Jewish anti-Zionist efforts there.⁹

But first and foremost, recognition of Jewish complicity prepared the way for a political assault on Weizmann, in an effort to persuade him that there was no choice but to explicitly renounce the Jewish state and accept the binationalist "true Zionism" as the aim of the Zionist Organization.¹⁰ In this, the Peace Association received support from the German Zionist Federation, whose entire leadership now consisted of followers of Buber's binationalism. In a letter signed by Robert Weltsch, Kurt Blumenfeld, and Werner Senator, the ZVfD now called upon the Zionist Executive in London to declare explicitly that "the Jews have no intention of turning the land of Israel into a Jewish State."¹¹ Further efforts emanated from the Peace Association in Jerusalem, which produced a series of papers arguing for a radical shift in the policies of the ZO. Among them was a memorandum prepared by Hugo Bergmann, Gershom Scholem, and Lord Samuel's son Edwin, detailing how Palestine could be reconstituted as a binational state. Even more radical was a proposal from Ernst Simon, which called upon the Jews to "turn to the Arab people with this solemn declaration that the Jewish Agency is striving for nothing but the creation in Palestine of a cultural Jewish minority."¹²

Albert Einstein joined in the peace-plan frenzy as well. Declaring that the conflict between Arabs and Jews was "more psychological than real," he published a plan in the Peace Association's periodical, according to which a "secret council" would be established consisting of Jewish and Arab doctors, lawyers, union leaders, and clergymen—four representatives from each side—who would hold secret deliberations once a week until "slowly but surely, all the difficulties are resolved," and the council would become the de facto governing body of the entire population in Palestine.¹³ (Einstein's position was, like that of the Peace Association, derived from the principles of emancipationist German Judaism. As he explained later, "I would much rather see reasonable agreement with the Arabs on the basis of living together in peace than the creation of a Jewish state. Apart from practical considerations, my awareness of the essential nature of Judaism resists the idea of a Jewish state, with borders, an army, and a measure of temporal power, no matter how modest. . . . We are no longer the Jews of the Maccabee period. A return to a nation in the political sense of the word would be the equivalent to turning away from the spiritualization of our community which we owe to the genius of the prophets.")[14]

Most important were pressures upon the Zionist Organization from Judah Magnes and his associates in the "non-Zionist" half of the Jewish Agency. On September 11, the death of Louis Marshall had left Felix Warburg at the head of the non-Zionist philanthropists, and within two days, Magnes had taken up his pen to ensure that his benefactor recognized the full meaning of the upheaval in Palestine. As Magnes wrote: "We must once and for all give up the idea of a 'Jewish Palestine.' . . . Jews and Arabs . . . have each as much right there, no more and no less, than the other: Equal rights and equal privileges and equal duties. That is . . . the sole ethical basis of our claims there."[15]

Warburg hardly needed to be persuaded. In the wake of the massacres, he was determined that the Zionists must "honestly and officially give up the idea of a Jewish nation,"[16] and he seems to have been considering withdrawing financial support for the Jews in Palestine if they did not. In early October, the existence of such a plan was reported by the Palestine high commissioner John Chancellor, after a meeting with an agent sent to Jerusalem by Warburg and Lewis Strauss. According to the report Chancellor sent to the Colonial Office, Warburg hoped to reach an agreement with the Arabs concerning the establishment of a new order in Palestine—to be negotiated without the Zionists' knowledge. Once negotiated, the deal would be imposed on the Zionists by the philanthropists in New York. "If English Jews [i.e., Weizmann] refuse to accept the policy of moderation," Chancellor wrote, "the Americans [i.e., Warburg] would threaten to cut off supplies and withdraw from the enlarged Agency."[17]

Although no such negotiations are known to have resulted from Warburg's efforts, no more than three weeks went by before Magnes presented his patron with an opportunity to make use of his threat. At the end of October, Magnes was contacted by Joseph Levy, the Palestine correspondent of the *New York Times,* an anti-Zionist who made little effort to hide his desire to see the ZO's influence in Palestine eliminated.[18] Levy brought Magnes together with the rogue adventurer and convert to Islam, Harry St. John Philby, who had the ear of the mufti and his compatriots, and on October 30, in Levy's presence, Magnes and Philby hammered out an agreement similar to the one for which Warburg had been hoping.[19] In effect discarding the Balfour Declaration and any special Jewish status under the mandate, the *Times*-brokered agreement provided for a Palestinian government on a proportional basis—meaning Arab control—with both the Jews and Arabs having a right to free immigration (in accordance with "economic capacity"). Foreign and defense matters would remain in the hands of the British. Philby secured the mufti's agreement in principle and sent the text of the agreement on to Lord Passfield; Magnes informed Warburg, Weizmann, and the British high commissioner.[20] Magnes also attempted to bring Ben-Gurion into the negotiations, sending Irma Lindheim, a former president of Hadassah and a Peace Association sympathizer, to update him on what was taking place. Lindheim told Ben-Gurion that the Jews "have no need for a majority or a state" and that without an agreement with the Arabs, Jewish Palestine would receive "not a cent" from abroad. But Ben-Gurion retorted that the plan would leave the Jews powerless in Palestine, telling Lindheim that "we did not come here to create a new diaspora . . . in addition to all our other ones."[21]

When it became clear that the Magnes-Philby-Levy plan had run into trouble with the Zionists, Warburg personally intervened. Although it seems that Magnes's peace plan was not quite what he himself had envisioned, he nonetheless responded precisely as Chancellor had said he would, twice telephoning Weizmann to demand his support for the initiative and threatening that funding from American Jewry would be jeopardized if he did not. But at this moment, Weizmann was granted a few days' reprieve from an unlikely quarter. The officials at the British Colonial Office, who had plans of their own—a commission of inquiry intended to make proposals similar to those made by Magnes and Philby—sent the Zionists word that Philby was not, as he had claimed, an agent of theirs, and was not to be trusted.[22] With this information in hand, the Zionist Executive rejected Magnes's initiative on November 11, and the National Assembly in Palestine, after an outraged debate, voted to condemn his discussions with Husseini for having granted the Arabs "a premium on violence."[23]

Beaten but not defeated, Magnes took his assault on the ZO to the public. A week after the decision of the Zionist Executive, Magnes opened the academic year at the Hebrew University with a bombshell pronouncement suggesting that the Jewish settlement in Palestine should not exist unless it had the support of the Arab population:

> If we cannot find ways of peace and understanding, if the only way of establishing the Jewish national home is upon the bayonets of some empire, our whole enterprise is not worthwhile, and it is better that the Eternal People, that has outlived many a mighty empire, should possess its soul in patience and . . . wait.[24]

Despite a storm of protest, Magnes went on to press for a binational Palestine in interviews in both the Jewish and foreign press, declaring that "the Balfour declaration was a handicap . . . because it over-emphasized the Jewish relation to Palestine, instead of laying stress on Palestine's position as an international holy land."[25] Weeks later, Magnes published a pamphlet called "Like All the Nations?" in which he cursed the mandate as "an absolutist, colonial regime" and followed Buber's lead in blaming the Jews for the August massacres: "If as a minority we insist on keeping the other man from achieving his just aims, and if we keep him from this with the aid of bayonets, we must not be surprised if we are attacked."[26]

In this public campaign, Magnes received eloquent support from Hugo Bergmann, who in articles and interviews excoriated the Zionist Organization for continuing "to cultivate the ideology of the *Judenstaat*."[27] He received assistance, as well, from the *New York Times*. The American paper, published by the Jewish anti-Zionist Adolph Ochs, was able to provide coverage of Magnes's operations in his home arena in New York, carrying an interview with him, as well as an opinion piece by him, and quoting the Arab newspaper *Falastin*, to the effect that "had the Zionists attempted to work out a plan similar to this . . . Palestine would have been a different country from what it is today."[28] Warburg, too, continued to press, demanding control of the ZO in America, including the closing of the Zionist organ *New Palestine*, and insisting that fund-raising in America would be impossible without "real peace" along the lines that Magnes had advocated.[29]

Weizmann responded to all this with a torrent of telegrams and letters in which he tried in vain to contain the damage. More than one was devoted to begging Warburg to rein in Magnes's attack, which, it was now clear, was toppling the Zionist political position like a house of cards: "Magnes' statements . . . have rendered our position intolerable. . . . We are heading towards the demoralization of the movement, and the inevitable collapse of the Jewish Agency."[30]

But in the face of events, Weizmann was incapable of holding his political line stable. The Jewish population of Palestine now stood at 160,000, a little more than one-fourth that of the Arabs, and as the repercussions of the financial disaster in New York on October 24 spread, hope of financial salvation, for which the enlarged Jewish Agency had been created, evaporated. The Jewish settlement was rife with fear of additional Arab attacks, and Britain was in the process of sending a commission to reevaluate the mandate. On every side—in London, Berlin, New York, and Jerusalem— Weizmann felt the ground disappearing from under his feet. No amount of staring at the hard kernels of this reality could yield a Jewish state, and, just as Buber's circle had hoped, Weizmann's position began to collapse.

On January 3, 1930, Weizmann appeared before the conference of the German Zionist Federation at Jena, and although he practically spat contempt at Magnes's talk of a "cultural home" ("I do not understand this term.

What is it—a museum, a hospital?"), he was nevertheless unable to condemn the binationalists, thereby making himself an extremist in the eyes of the philanthropists and the British government. By the end of the month, he had retreated further, allowing himself to be quoted in a Zionist publication in London as being *opposed* to a Jewish state. "Palestine is not only an Arab country nor is it only a Jewish country," he said. "It is a country belonging to both of us together. The formula 'without a Jewish state there is no existence for the Jewish people' has a lot of assimilation in it. 'The state of the Jews,' 'a national state,' these are terms which do not suit our movement."[31] "The Peace Association has been victorious everywhere," Hugo Bergmann tittered in a letter to one of his colleagues. "Even Weizmann now preaches the gospel of binationalism."[32]

There was much truth in this assessment, but no one familiar with Weizmann methods can take this volte-face at face value. As in everything else, ideological shifts were for Weizmann a matter of being "practical." He understood that the mandate was on the verge of being repudiated; one more push was all that would be needed for MacDonald to award the Arabs a proportional legislature and the complete suspension of Jewish immigration. Fear of such a turn of events was so dense in all camps that even Jabotinsky, who had staked his politics on the tough-minded campaign of public pressure for a Jewish state, at this moment faltered, explaining that when he spoke of a Jewish "state," he meant only a state such as Nebraska.[33] Under these circumstances, Weizmann adopted the rhetoric of a binational state, while at the same time insisting—in a fashion so reminiscent of Buber that one has to wonder whether it was not a conscious parody—that "true binationalism" could not mean majority representation for the overwhelming Arab majority. For the Jews, he wrote, this would be national suicide. What *he* meant by binationalism was a "parity" scheme, in which the gates of Palestine would be held open by a 50-50 deadlock between Jews and Arabs in any Palestinian legislature or government—a scheme he saw as a defeat for Zionism and manifestly dangerous, but that might, if it worked, permit the continued upbuilding of Jewish Palestine. Under the circumstances, it might be the best the Jews would get.[34]

Weizmann's principal concern amid all this maneuvering was to try and soften the conclusions of a commission, headed by an official of the Colonial office, that the MacDonald government had dispatched in the fall to examine the causes of the disturbances in Palestine. In March 1930, the commission issued its report, which, as expected, exonerated the British administration for its performance during the August upheavals and accepted the argument that the Arabs had been driven to perpetrate the massacres by the settlement activities of the Jews. The commission recommended that Jewish immigration and land purchases be curtailed and that it be made clear to the Jewish Agency that the Jews in no way shared responsibility for the government of Palestine. Shortly thereafter, the mandatory government excluded Jabotinsky from the country while he was lecturing abroad, explaining its action as resulting from a "seditious" speech, in which Jabotinsky had held the government responsible for the August massacres and demanded the establishment of a Jewish state.[35] This, effectively the first expulsion of a Zionist leader from Palestine on political grounds, was an unmistakable warning to the other Zionist leaders. When, in August, Weizmann learned that the report of a second British commission was inclining in the direction of the first, he stretched his rhetoric even further, this time actually renouncing the aim of a Jewish state: "Nothing is said about a Jewish state in the Basel program, nor in the Balfour Declaration. . . . The essence of Zionism was not so much the Jewish state as the creation of material conditions for the establishment of an autonomous, productive society. . . . Why should we discuss the academic question of a Jewish state?"[36]

But his efforts had no effect. The second commission amplified the findings of the first, and its results were formally adopted by the government in a white paper published by the Colonial Office on October 20, 1930. This formal pronouncement of British policy, known as the Passfield White Paper, declared that the mandatory government's responsibility to non-Jewish residents of Palestine was "equally important" to commitments made to the Jews and that no further land was available in Palestine for development by Jewish immigrants. Jewish immigration would be shut down completely so long as there was widespread unemployment in Palestine, and the government would establish a legislative council with Arab and Jewish representation in proportion to their respective strengths in the population.[37]

The new policy went well beyond the usual anti-Zionist concerns that the Jews should not have a state in Palestine. It in effect doomed the Jewish community in Palestine to strangulation. Weizmann and Warburg demonstratively resigned their posts at the head of the Jewish Agency, helping trigger a political sandstorm in Britain, which actually threatened to topple the minority MacDonald government. A remarkable constellation of British statesmen—including Lloyd George, former prime minister Stanley Baldwin, Leopold Amery, Winston Churchill, Herbert Samuel, and others—succeeded in averting the impending annulment of the Balfour Declaration and the mandate. But Weizmann proved too weak to press the momentary advantage, and the storm passed without fundamentally altering circumstances. Britain's disinterest in continuing to pursue a Jewish state in Palestine had been amply demonstrated, and the goal of a "democratic" legislature that would, sooner or later, hand power to the Arabs, remained unaltered.

In 1925, Ben-Gurion had appeared at one of the Peace Association's first public meetings, where he had argued that the aim of Zionism was a Jewish majority in the country and that the organization's efforts would only serve to confuse the issue in the minds of both Jews and Arabs. No one would gain from such confusion, he had said. It would end up "damaging us, while giving the Arabs nothing." Only after the Magnes-Philby agreement, however, did Ben-Gurion begin to see the Peace Association as posing an actual threat to Zionism, telling one Peace Association supporter that they were "like lunatics walking around with a knife in one hand, killing children without understanding what you are doing. You are undermining the very essence of our movement."[38]

Berl Katznelson, the Labor movement's leading ideological figure, had similarly considered the Peace Association to be misconceived but benign up until August 1929. As founder and editor of the Labor newspaper *Davar,* he had developed close ties with a number of prominent Peace Association activists, whose contributions to the paper in economics, literature, and other fields he considered crucial in his efforts to "educate" Palestine's Jewish laborers. In the wake of the massacres, however, Katznelson also realized that the calls for a government with an Arab majority were driving Jewish Palestine to hysteria and despair. He quickly shifted gears, damning the intellectuals as *tlushim*—"the uprooted"—in a single, highly celebrated word capturing the feeling among the Russians that the professors' cultural background made it impossible for them to stand up for the vital interests of the Jews as a nation. The writings of Peace Association members were abruptly dropped from *Davar*'s pages, and the paper adopted a stance of unequivocal opposition to the views emanating from Mt. Scopus: "The binationalism they recommend to us," he said, "is a concealed means of creating an absolute government over us. This binationalism is camouflage for an Arab state."[39]

But the angry reactions of Ben-Gurion and Katznelson did little to stem the tide of shock and bewilderment that swept the Labor leadership as first the professors and then Weizmann himself began issuing statements renouncing the traditional aims of the ZO. Until 1929, the Labor leaders had for the most part remained true Russian "practicals," leaving diplomacy to Weizmann in exchange for his support in the financing of their operations on the ground in Palestine. As a consequence, there was hardly a man in the Labor leadership equipped to pass judgment on what Weizmann was or was not doing to fend off the half-perceived forces that now washed over the material contours of the land, threatening to destroy all that they had built. In short order, the collapse of Weizmann's position induced a similar dynamic among the flailing Labor leaders—to the point that, as Moshe Beilinson wrote to Katznelson, the majority of them seemed prepared to capitulate and endorse constitutional proposals not so different from those advocated by the Peace Association, even while most of the Labor Zionist rank and file were determined to hold their ground and fight for Jewish Palestine.[40] That the Labor party did not, in the end, advance any of its own half-baked peace proposals was largely due to Katznelson, who fought for more than a year against the adoption of any of the Labor leaders' constitutional proposals, in the hope that a change in political circumstances would defuse the issue. Only when a Zionist Congress was called for July 1931 did the party, for want of a better alternative, fall in line behind Weizmann's parity scheme.

As Weizmann had planned it, the Seventeenth Zionist Congress in Basel was to be the scene of the Zionist Organization's acceptance of his "true binationalism," which he hoped would prove to the British government and his donors in New York how reasonable Jewish aims in Palestine really were. But the ZO proved itself less than inclined to go along with this even as a tactic. Weizmann's pronouncements on the irrelevance of the goal of a Jewish state, along with pogroms in Poland and the shocking rise of Hitler's power in the Reichstag, had led many to draw precisely the opposite conclusions. A Jewish state to receive European Jews was now needed more than ever, and London's retreat on the Passfield White Paper had provided unprecedented confirmation of Jabotinsky's theory that British policy could be rendered more favorable to the Jewish cause in Palestine through public pressure. Thus, when the Revisionists entered the congress hall on June 30, 1931, they found themselves, together with the hawkish breakaway wing of Weizmann's own General Zionists and the religious Mizrahi, at the head of a working opposition bloc of 146 seats—57 percent of the congress. This was the first time that such a conservative coalition had been close to winning power within the Zionist Organization in two decades.[41]

Weizmann, however, proved himself unwilling to play to the combative mood of the congress. With his eye turned to London and New York, he adamantly continued his efforts to persuade the Zionist Organization's ostensible allies that there was no danger whatsoever of a Jewish state in Palestine. Even Herzl and Max Nordau, he told the congress, had not intended to establish such a state. More radical still was a statement made by Weizmann to the Jewish Telegraphic Agency, published as the congress was in progress, in which he said that he had "no understanding of and no sympathy with the demand for a Jewish majority [in Palestine]. . . . A majority is not required for the development of Jewish civilization and culture."[42] Subsequent "clarifications" only made it obvious that Weizmann was hellbent on leaving the impression that the Jewish state was dead. "Are we not all tired and are we not all nauseated by the constant evasions?" demanded Jabotinsky at one point. "Clearing the atmosphere is a political imperative, and it will be achieved if we tell the truth. Why should we allow the term 'Jewish state' to be described as extremism?"[43]

The congress voted 123-106 to censure Weizmann for his statements, and a resolution by Jabotinsky declaring the "endgoal" of Zionism to be a Jewish majority in Palestine was approved in the political committee of the congress by a vote of 17 to 11. But this initiative was thwarted when a telegram, purportedly from the National Assembly in Palestine, arrived requesting that the discussion be tabled because of unnamed security concerns.[44] The sudden demise of the "endgoal" initiative left the ZO without a real policy—Weizmann's "parity" scheme was not adopted either[45]—and also without a leader, since it was clear that Weizmann would not be reelected if he stood for the presidency. Hesitantly, the congress elected as his successor Nahum Sokolow, an old-time Russian practical with some of Weizmann's views and few of his talents.

In this fog of confusion, the Labor leaders had held fast to their strategy of backing Weizmann through thick and thin, gritting their teeth as he unleashed his devil-may-care public relations stunts on an uncomprehending congress. Yet Ben-Gurion could not stomach this for long. Returning from Europe, he dashed off an article for the party paper in which he declared the congress to have been a "lunatic asylum." No less than Jabotinsky, who had brought the aim of the Jewish majority to a vote, it was the "liquidators" of the Peace Association and Weizmann who "were responsible for the damaging debate about the final aim. . . . If there were not people in the Peace Association . . . working diligently to diminish Zionism and to castrate its national and political [medini] content," the entire debate would never have taken place. Despite the impression left at the congress, Ben-Gurion declared, the Labor movement was utterly faithful to "political Zionism." The Labor party had avoided backing a Jewish majority and a Jewish state "not because . . . of a lack of faith in a majority, and also not because of a lack of faith in the vision of statehood [hazon hamamlachti]," but solely out of tactical considerations. Such considerations, however, could not make up for the damage that Weizmann's declarations had done to the public's faith in the goals of the Zionist movement. It should have been the Labor party and not the Revisionists, he concluded, that had insisted on his removal from the leadership of the ZO. "It was an error of short-sightedness on our part that we supported Weizmann's candidacy at this Congress."[46]

Ben-Gurion's horror over Weizmann's feeble political posture was rendered all the more painful by the situation in Central Europe, which continued to deteriorate from month to month. By July 1932, the ongoing violence against Jews in Poland and Hitler's gathering strength in Germany prompted him to warn that "physical annihilation" was hanging over the Jewish people.[47] But his arguments made little headway with his colleagues, most of whom saw the goal of transforming Labor Zionism into a political force capable of replacing Weizmann in the diplomatic arena as far-fetched, and as a pointless distraction from the pressing concerns of construction in Palestine.

Not until the fall of 1932 did Ben-Gurion hit upon the lever that he could use to push the Labor party into making a bid for control of the ZO—a no-holds-barred battle against Jabotinksy's followers in an effort to secure the Histadrut's monopoly on Jewish labor in Palestine. One of the important political developments in Palestine in the wake of the massacres of August 1929 had been the establishment by Jabotinsky's followers of a military organization and a workers' association operating independently of the Labor-dominated Jewish power structure in the country. These groups, openly calling for a return to Herzl's non-socialist nationalism, certainly posed a challenge to Labor's hegemony in Palestine; Jabotinsky even argued that the days of manual labor were numbered and that the developing Jewish state had to focus on the power of the mind.[48] But Ben-Gurion's decision to throw groups of Labor toughs—who had been training under the cover of Labor's "Hapoel" sporting organizations[49]—into violent confrontation with the Revisionists six months before the elections to the Zionist congress seems to have been motivated by more than just concern for the power of the Histadrut. (Two years later, Ben-Gurion would meet with Jabotinsky and agree to compromise on the Histadrut's exclusive right to represent the workers.) Ben-Gurion's overriding aim was to force the Labor leadership to pull its head out of the Palestinian sand and take cognizance of the arena of real interest—the Zionist Organization, where Jabotinsky's Revisionists represented the only alternative to the impasse created by Weizmann's policies.

In October 1932, Ben-Gurion's athletes went into battle against Revisionist strikebreakers called in to save a factory that had employed a woman who was not a member of the Histadrut. The result, as might have been expected, was a series of street fights between members of the Labor movement and Revisionists, accompanied by flights of gutter rhetoric in which each side managed to compare the other to the Nazis. The campaign reached a crescendo when, on the night of June 16, 1933, with only weeks to go before the balloting, the head of the Jewish Agency's political department Haim Arlosoroff was murdered on the Tel Aviv beachfront, apparently by Arabs.[50] The acrimony of the election campaign spilled directly into the criminal investigation when a Revisionist worker, Avraham Stavsky, was charged with the murder of the young Labor leader. Although Stavsky was later acquitted, the accusation of a politically motivated murder was sufficient to do substantial damage to the Revisionists' public standing. In the elections held on July 23, Labor for the first time became the largest party in the ZO, rising to 43 percent of the congress, while the Revisionists lost ground, dropping to only 16 percent.[51] The way cleared for a Labor-dominated Zionist Organization, in which Ben-Gurion became a member of the executive, and, two years later, its chairman. He was to lead the Zionist movement and the state of Israel for three nearly unbroken decades.

Ben-Gurion's warfare against the Revisionists had forced the Labor movement to conquer the Zionist Organization—something virtually no one in his party had desired other than him. Yet the contest with the Revisionists was far from the top of Ben-Gurion's actual political agenda. When he finally took the helm of the ZO, his policies were principally directed toward reducing the partnership Weizmann had built with New York's German-Jewish philanthropists, which he deplored as a "criminal and shameful mistake." As chairman of the Zionist Executive (which, with the addition of a few "non-Zionists," was also the Jewish Agency Executive), Ben-Gurion went about moving large sections of the Jewish Agency apparatus from London (Weizmann's home base) to Jerusalem, and this was only the beginning of a systematic effort to deprive the non-Zionists of any influence in the policies of the Jewish Agency.[52] His aim was establishing a fully democratized ZO, in which a Jewish mass movement led by Labor would wrestle with the Revisionists and other popular parties for the heart of the Jewish public, while Weizmann and his constituency of non-Zionists would become a trivial force.

That Ben-Gurion was able to pull the Zionist cart out of the binationalist mire, which in 1931 had threatened to capsize the entire movement, was to an important degree testimony to his political acumen. But it also reflected a changed political world. For in January 1933, a matter of months before Ben-Gurion's victory in the Zionist elections, Adolph Hitler ascended to the chancellorship of Germany. That summer, Ben-Gurion bought a copy of *Mein Kampf,* and he quickly concluded that Hitler posed a threat to the entire Jewish people. "Perhaps only four or five years, if not less," he believed, "stand between us and that terrible day."[53] At the same time, however, he recognized that approaching horror in Europe brought with it the possibility of massive Jewish immigration. The number of Jews arriving in Palestine that year was over 30,000—a more than *ninefold* increase since Weizmann's pronouncements that he had no understanding of a Jewish majority at the Seventeenth Congress—and the demand to enter Palestine only continued to grow. Ben-Gurion was soon speaking of the entry of 4 or even 6 million Jews into the country.[54]

These developments also all but destroyed the hope of the Peace Association and its philanthropic supporters for an imminent and final burial of the idea of a Jewish state. In Germany itself, Hitler's grip meant the demise of the German Zionist Federation; its members fled to Palestine, where their influence was to be felt only later. And among Palestine's Jews, even those who had supported Weizmann in his tilt toward Warburg and the Colonial Office could no longer see any point in compromise on immigration, the Jewish majority, and the Jewish state.[55] The escalation of anti-Semitism in Germany, Poland, and Austria had almost overnight made all of these a real possibility—and a dire necessity.

But how could an evacuation of European Jewry to Palestine be achieved in the face of British hostility? Ben-Gurion's answer was similar to Herzl's. The Zionist Organization had to become a mass organization, perhaps divided into various factions but nevertheless united in making the only demand that mattered—the immigration of millions of Jews into what would almost automatically become an independent Jewish state. But the continuing feebleness of the Jewish Agency, now trying to operate without either of its founders, Weizmann and Marshall, made a farce of this aspiration. And Ben-Gurion's Labor Zionists, despite their victory in the ZO, still refused to consider diverting precious resources from the "practical" work in Palestine to pursue fantastic political missions. In fact, the only person ostensibly capable of understanding what Ben-Gurion was talking about was the defeated Weizmann himself. But for all his reputation as a diplomat, Weizmann's "scientific" inability to conceive of a full-scale evacuation, as well as his chronic fear of pressing the British too hard, rendered him virtually useless for such a public relations war. Ben-Gurion could see the window of opportunity passing, but the Zionist leadership remained paralyzed.

In desperation, Ben-Gurion made one of the boldest gambles of his career—he turned to Jabotinsky. Until the summer of 1934, Ben-Gurion had continued to maintain the course that had rocketed the Labor Zionism into the driver's seat in the Zionist Organization, presiding over a war of mutual hooliganism with the Revisionists. This campaign had reached its ugly peak on July 8, 1934, with an attack by Labor activists on Sabbath worshippers in the Great Synagogue in Jerusalem, where Stavsky, having recently been acquitted, was to be honored by being called to read from the Torah. When Stavsky's name was called, the Laborites raised an uproar, triggering a melee in which worshippers were pummeled and benches broken; not until police interfered did Stavsky mount the dais to read. This shameless bit of thuggery provoked no small measure of sympathy for the Revisionists beyond their usual circles in Palestine—a "victory" of sorts that permitted Jabotinsky some breathing space to return to what he regarded as the movement's "main duty,"[56] bringing about a united struggle to open Palestine to Jewish immigration. On July 31, 1934, twenty-three days after the riot at the Great Synagogue, the Revisionist Executive approached the Labor party, proposing to open talks on ending the violence.[57]

What came to be called "the peace letter" touched off a month of acrimonious meetings of the Labor party Central Committee, which tried without success to develop a response to Jabotinsky's overture. This was arguably Ben-Gurion's finest hour, the moment when he turned his back on his party's socialist doctrines and its financial entanglements with Warburg in an effort to reach what only Herzl had achieved—a unified Jewish nationalism in which the struggles between socialists and capitalists, traditionalists and modernists, would be set aside for the sake of securing the movement's foreign policy objectives. Almost the entire veteran leadership of the Labor movement, including Berl Katznelson, Moshe Sharett, David Remez, and Golda Meir, joined with Ben-Gurion in advocating putting an end to the humiliating and fruitless battles with the Revisionists. They were opposed by the party bosses, union leaders, and socialist radicals centered in Tel Aviv, who later became known as "the Bloc"—men such as Zalman ("Ziama") Aharonovitch, who two months earlier had broken into the offices of *Davar* with fifty men, threatening to smash the presses if the paper did not desist from publishing an editorial calling for clemency for Stavsky.[58] The Bloc's interest was straightforward: Any agreement with the Revisionists on labor issues would mean compromise, and compromise would mean the breaking of their monopolistic control of the work schedules in their cities. Less easy to dismiss was the opposition of Yitzhak Tabenkin, leader of the United Kibbutz Movement, whose refusal to compromise with procapitalist forces (i.e., Jabotinsky) in the creation of the Jewish state was a matter of unyielding ideology. Unlike the urban party bosses, Tabenkin was one of the truly leading spirits of the Labor movement, and although he enjoyed only minority support in the party's institutions, his threat to split the party over any deal with antisocialists wrestled the movement into a stalemate. Labor found itself unable to issue any response to Jabotinksy's overture.[59]

But Ben-Gurion would not be stopped. A few weeks later, in London, Pinhas Rutenberg, the mercurial capitalist and founder of the Palestine Electric Corporation, contacted Ben-Gurion with the information that Jabotinksy would be arriving shortly from Paris and asked if he would be willing to meet with the Revisionist leader. Ben-Gurion replied in the affirmative, launching a month of intense negotiations. His first six-hour conversation with Jabotinsky, described by Ben-Gurion in his diary, rambled over the vast field of presumed points of contention between them, from the joint Jewish Agency to Revisionist strikebreaking to the "endgoal" of the Zionist movement. Yet to Ben-Gurion's amazement, their discussion revealed so much common ground that it seemed as though there were almost no important areas of disagreement. Already on that first night, Jabotinsky told Ben-Gurion enthusiastically, "If the two of us make peace it will be a great day for the Jews. The entire Jewish people will rejoice and exult, and such rejoicing should be turned to some great project." Ben-Gurion agreed, suggesting "massive settlement"—the initiation of yet more physical construction in Palestine. Jabotinsky proposed a worldwide petition drive bringing Jews to demand a Jewish state or entrance to Palestine—a scheme consisting of nothing other than altering the subjective views of world Jewry and of the British government.

Both men were taken aback, and Jabotinsky said: "You, who have been a *Judenstaatler* [i.e., a "Jewish-stater"] all your life, how is it that you do not understand and appreciate the value of demonstration and slogan? The word, the statement, the phrase, have tremendous power."

Even through Ben-Gurion's mystified retelling of the story, one can understand the point Jabotinsky was trying to make: He was referring to what Herzl had called the power of "imponderables"—the fact that ideas, as conveyed in words and symbols, are the cornerstone of all political power. The Jewish state was itself ultimately a "word" that people repeated among themselves and eventually came to believe. How could Ben-Gurion, who had taken on the entire leadership of his party to demand a diplomatic offensive at the expense of settlement activity have found this so difficult to understand? Although he had traveled far into the world of abstractions in comparison with his party colleagues, he was still chained too close to the material for a politics such as Herzl's. "I do not see settlement and immigration activities as merely one side of Zionist action, as opposed to political activism," he told Jabotinsky at one point in exasperation. "They are themselves the center of gravity of political action . . . The most effective *argument* is the *deed*."

Ben-Gurion met with Jabotinsky twelve times beginning in mid-October, and they eventually hammered together the first agreements in an intended series of documents reconstructing the Zionist movement: The first forbade party warfare outside the limits of political discussion. The second agreed to a numeric allocation of jobs between the labor federations of the two parties and to binding arbitration in case of disputes, in effect ending the Histadrut's claim to a labor monopoly in Palestine.[60] More important, Ben-Gurion and Jabotinsky drafted a nonbinding trial agreement outlining an alliance between them that would reshape the entire face of Zionist policy: An extraordinary Zionist Congress would be called a few months hence to replace the presidency of the ZO with a cabinet government led by Labor and the Revisionists. The Zionist Organization would seek an independent Jewish state in the entire territory of Palestine, including Transjordan, but this endgoal would not be publicized. Weizmann's fifty-fifty agreement with the non-Zionists, which was in any case not being carried out, would be allowed to die without fanfare. In short, they agreed to the creation of a new and ideologically cohesive Zionist Organization based on two dramatically expanded mass parties, in which Ben-Gurion and Jabotinsky would be the dominant figures.[61] The day the agreements were signed, Ben-Gurion wrote in his diary: "To me it is so important and augurs such great things for the future that I find it difficult to believe it will be consummated. It is too good to be true."[62]

Indeed, it was. Already in London, Ben-Gurion had received telegrams reporting that his negotiations had provoked outrage among Tabenkin's supporters, who viewed the Histadrut's right to strike as sacrosanct, and that the Revisionist workers were simply traitors, with whom there could be no agreement. Grimly, he wired back: "I am sorry to see that our party does not adequately appreciate . . . that in its hands rests the fate of the Jewish people at one of the most grave . . . moments in our generation." Returning to Palestine, he tried to return attention to the fate of the Jews of Europe, asking how the present opportunity could be used if the Zionist parties "are busy making war . . . and all our energies are wasted as we walk forward into destruction?" Katznelson, too, responded in shame to the idea that Labor Zionism could place socialist doctrine before the fate of the Jewish people: "I am not prepared to accept this, that the movement should transform itself and its people into a class." A decisive majority in the party's Central Committee agreed, but Tabenkin refused to recognize the right of the Central Committee to make the decision, threatening to split the party if the decision were not brought to a larger forum. Reluctantly, Ben-Gurion agreed to a referendum of members of the Histadrut, which was held on March 25, 1935. Sixty percent of the rank and file voted against Ben-Gurion; his supporters were able to muster only 40 percent of the vote.[63]

We have no way of knowing what would have happened had Ben-Gurion succeeded in returning the Zionist Organization to what it had been in Herzl's day—an organization geared to a policy of massive evacuation from Europe and the immediate establishment of the state. But we do know the results of the failure, which brought in its wake tragedy and destruction beyond imagination. By the end of 1935, it became clear that although the referendum had temporarily averted the fission of the Labor party,[64] it had also split the ZO. Jabotinsky and his followers withdrew, establishing the New Zionist Organization, which soon attracted a membership greater than that of the ZO, but which failed in the crucial test of being accepted by the West as a partner for negotiations.[65] Ben-Gurion and his party, on the other hand, remained shackled to the non-Zionists in the joint Jewish Agency,[66] incapable of projecting an unequivocal diplomatic stance in favor of a Jewish state for another seven years. For most of Europe's Jews, it would by then be too late.

Looking back on Ben-Gurion's frustrated effort of 1934–1935 to make peace with the Revisionists, one cannot avoid the feeling that this was, to a remarkable extent, a failure of his own making. It is a commonplace of Zionist history that the Labor rank and file rejected the agreement with the Revisionists because they were unable to fathom how one could now simply join forces with an opponent who had been so thoroughly reviled only yesterday. But the fact that Jabotinsky's movement *was* so reviled among Labor Zionists in Palestine was in large part due to decisions made by Ben-Gurion himself. Here, one sees in all its homeliness Ben-Gurion's ability to achieve rhetorical extremes, and even to resort to violence, in defense of sincerely held ideological principles that he himself would not necessarily find compelling a few years later. What he lacked, it seems, was the kind of political balance one finds in a mature political culture—in which, for example, one learns to think twice before casting an opponent as an enemy, hurling the fantastic and the imponderable against him as though these were hand grenades and treating the present contest of wills as though it were the last. Indeed, it was just such ready recourse to absolute vilification as a means of rallying one's forces and winning elections that Herzl had feared when he thought of a Jewish state led by "desperados." One can, of course, win elections this way. But governing a people that has learned to make political decisions on this basis is another story.

At any rate, Ben-Gurion did not have to wait long to beginning reaping the bitter harvest from this mistake. Only a few months later, he was forced to bring Weizmann back as president of the Zionist Organization and as the statesman on whose shoulders rested the fate of European Jewry on the eve of the Holocaust. Weizmann would continue in this capacity even as Britain formally abandoned the idea of a Jewish state in Palestine, as well as the Jews this state had been intended to save.

In September 1935, the Nuremberg laws stripped German Jews of their citizenship, barred Jews from employing German women in their homes, and prohibited marriages or sexual relations between Germans and Jews—a "war of extermination," Ben-Gurion wrote, "liable to drive anyone who is not already insensate mad."[67] Nor was the situation in Austria, Poland, and Romania much better. The only consolation was the onrush of Jewish immigration, which in 1935 alone brought nearly 60,000 Jews to Palestine—an increase of 22 percent in the Jewish population of the country in a single year. In the three years since the establishment of the Nazi government in Germany, the population of Jewish Palestine had nearly doubled to over 350,000, approaching 30 percent of the total population. A Jewish majority was dangled cruelly within reach by the very forces that were rising up to destroy the Jews of Europe.

But as Ben-Gurion had understood, such an opportunity could not possibly hold in the absence of a major Jewish diplomatic initiative. The Arabs could read the map at least as well as the Jews could, and on November 25, 1935, the bickering Palestinian Arab factions united around the leadership of the mufti, Amin al-Husseini, and presented the British administration with three demands: An end to Jewish immigration, a ban on land sales to Jews, and the immediate establishment of a democratic regime, which would effectively hand control of the country to the Arab majority. The British high commissioner, Sir Arthur Wauchope, correctly assessing that he had fulfilled England's pledge to assist the Jews as no other high commissioner had, now felt justified in tilting toward the Arabs by reviving that perennial aim of British policy, the Arab-dominated legislative council.[68] The resulting uproar in Parliament—successfully orchestrated by Weizmann, who accused Wauchope of changing sides at precisely the moment when the Jews of Europe were "drowning in their own blood"[69]— again forced the British administration to back down. But the ZO still hesitated to take a major political initiative in *favor* of Jewish immigration. On March 9, 1936, two days after German forces seized the Rhineland, Ben-Gurion frantically demanded a public campaign in Britain and America for the immigration of 1 million European Jews.[70] Yet his colleagues, pouring every penny and every ounce of their strength into absorbing the present flood of immigrants, met his demands for foreign campaigns and his visions of millions with incomprehension. Weizmann, too, despite musing on the possibility of asking for a Jewish state at this time, could see no reason to begin making rash demands and engaging in pressure tactics. "I cannot repress the bitter and depressing feeling," Ben-Gurion concluded, "that at this time we have no supreme political leadership."[71]

The Arabs of Palestine, on the other hand, *did* have a supreme leadership, and it now landed a stunning blow in the battle to influence British policy. Following the example set in recent months in Egypt and Syria— where strikes and rioting had succeeded in propelling the British and French governments into negotiations over Arab independence— Palestinian Arabs on April 19 began rioting in Jaffa, leaving nine Jews dead. A general strike, called immediately thereafter by Husseini, lasted six months and drew intelligence and financial support from the Nazis, the Italians, and the Soviets.[72] During this period, another eighty Jews lost their lives to attacks on Jewish settlements, and several hundred were wounded. In addition, tens of thousands of fruit trees and thousands of dunams of crops were destroyed, and the cessation of transportation and shipping from the Jaffa port, for which the Jews could at first offer no alternative, crippled the economy of the entire country. By October, the British government once again agreed to send a commission to investigate the "causes" of the disturbances.[73]

Massacres of Jews, Arab demands that immigration be terminated, and then a British commission—all this was the familiar pattern of August 1929, which had come close to destroying Zionism. And the Jewish reactions, as though scripted in advance, were much the same as well. Once more, "non-Zionists" and Peace Association circles sprang into action. In Jerusalem, Judah Magnes again initiated negotiations with the Arabs, in which he suggested restricting Jewish immigration and land purchases and agreed that the Jewish population in Palestine would not exceed 40 percent. In London, Lord Samuel likewise proposed a 40-percent ceiling on the Jewish population, restrictions on land sales, and a binational legislature. In New York, Felix Warburg once more applied pressure on the Zionists to accept Magnes's proposals, and, along with the American Jewish Committee, initiated his own negotiations with the Arabs—negotiations predicated on the principle that the Jewish population in Palestine would remain a minority. It was talk of a Jewish state that had sparked the violence, Warburg declared, and such talk had to come to an end.[74]

Weizmann, once again president of the ZO, resumed his attempts to cement his relations with Warburg and the British government by flaunting his proximity to their own views. He secretly offered to suspend Jewish immigration for a year and preached his parity scheme.[75] And he continued to assure the philanthropists, the British, and anyone else who cared to listen that that no Zionist had asked for a Jewish state and that Palestine could not in any case constitute a "rational" solution for the Jews of Germany, Poland, and Romania.[76] There is no way of knowing, of course, what would have happened had Weizmann instead chosen to endorse Ben-Gurion's demands for an immediate evacuation of European Jewry to Palestine. But if Weizmann expected to win genuine sympathy for Zionism with such pandering, he must have been sorely disappointed. In the Foreign Office, his statements were considered "pure eye-wash."[77]

Although Weizmann's strategy in 1936 was essentially a reprise of his performance after the bloodshed in Palestine seven years earlier, the same could hardly be said for the policy of the Labor Zionists. From his position as chairman of the executive, Ben-Gurion now waged what amounted to a permanent war to contain and control Weizmann's diplomacy. With his sights fixed on massive and immediate immigration ("Vast immigration will bring about Jewish rule in Palestine in not too many years, and when we become a greater power we can shred all the decrees"), Ben-Gurion chaperoned Weizmann in diplomatic meetings and, with Katznelson's support, worked to undermine his political initiatives. And when Weizmann denied that Herzl had intended to establish Jewish independence in Palestine in written materials to be submitted to the Royal Commission, Ben-Gurion literally tore the pages renouncing the Jewish state out of the printed volumes. (Ben-Gurion confronted Magnes as well, telling him: "The difference between you and me is that you are ready to sacrifice immigration for peace, while I am not, though peace is dear to me. And even if I were prepared to make a concession, the Jews of Poland and Germany would not be, because they have no other choice. For them, immigration comes before peace.")[78]

But to no avail. Weizmann continued to manufacture eyewash for public consumption up until the moment that the British Commission of Inquiry, headed by Lord William Robert Peel, arrived in Palestine and began taking testimony in November. Behind closed doors, Weizmann congenially agreed that the "cause" of the Arab disturbances was large-scale immigration and that it would be reasonable to cut Jewish immigration down as a contribution to stability in the country.[79] He did tell the commission that "the hopes of six million Jews are centered on emigration," but when asked whether it was possible to bring 6 million Jews to Palestine, he answered with the confidence of a biochemist decomposing a potato mash: "No. *I am acquainted with the laws of physics and chemistry, and know the force of material factors.* In our generation, I divide the figure by three, and you can see in that the depth of the Jewish tragedy: Two millions of youth, with their lives before them. . . . The old ones will pass . . . They are dust . . . in a cruel world. . . . Only a remnant shall survive. We have to accept it."[80]

Did Weizmann really mean this? That millions of European Jews could not be brought into Palestine because of material factors? That they would not survive? And that the Zionists "had to accept it"? Or was this the most brilliant performance of his career, in which he portrayed the Jewish nation as old and tired, wishing almost nothing for itself and resigned to its unspeakable fate—all in a calculated effort to gain the pity of the Royal Commission, in the hope this would translate into a favorable report to the British government? Perhaps, as is often the case with politicians, both interpretations are correct at the same time. But whatever the case, we know that the Peel Commission reacted unlike any other investigatory body Britain had ever sent to Palestine. Ignoring the proposals of the ZO and virtually everyone else, it cleared the table and made a recommendation of its own: Partition of Palestine into independent Jewish and Arab states. As early as January 8, 1937, Weizmann was asked by the commission what his position might be toward such a partition; his on-the-record answer was noncommittal. But in private conversation with a member of the commission, Weizmann gave the lie to all those who had claimed that he had been "converted" to binationalism. He immediately agreed to what would, by midsummer, be the commission's formal proposal that Britain give its hand to the immediate founding of a Jewish state.

As rumor of the impending report spread, a wave of condemnation of the plans for a Jewish state arose from Martin Buber, Arthur Hays Sulzberger, Lord Samuel, Robert Weltsch's *Juedische Rundschau,* and—perhaps before anyone else—Felix Warburg.[81] It is unclear how news of developments in Palestine reached Warburg and his friends in New York, but it is clear that, by mid-February, Warburg had grasped that the Jewish Agency, running amok without his consent, was hurtling toward consummation of the Zionists' long-suppressed goal, the Jewish state. In Warburg's papers, there is a draft of what was apparently to have been his response and that of his associates to this realization. The letter accuses "one or two members of the Executive" of undertaking to speak for the entire Jewish Agency, "in terms which the non-Zionists cannot accept," reflecting "a conception of Jewish life which is abhorrent." It was the "lust for power" of the Zionist leadership that was in large part responsible for the Arab violence in Palestine and that now threatened to destroy "the achievements which have been accomplished at the expenditure of so much effort and money. . . . Success can only follow a change of heart on the part of the Zionists and a realization that the dream of a Jewish state in Palestine must be abandoned."[82] Such was the beginning of Felix Warburg's last battle against the Jewish state, which shortly took the form of a full-blown struggle to restore the original fifty-fifty partnership between his camp and the Zionists in the Jewish Agency.

The Peel commission published its recommendation that Palestine be partitioned between Jews and Arabs in July 7, 1937, and a month later, the Council of the Jewish Agency was convened in Zurich to consider the question of Jewish independence. The Jewish state proposed by the Royal Commission was minuscule—consisting of a mere 4 percent of the territory of the original Palestine Mandate (about 20 percent of the size of Israel in 1949)—but it was a sovereign state nonetheless. The rest of the territory, including Transjordan, would become an independent Arab state. The sacrifice involved in accepting such a plan was considerable, but Weizmann and Ben-Gurion nevertheless swung into line behind independence at any cost, with Ben-Gurion arguing, as was surely true, that "Herzl would have accepted as a godsend a charter for any part of Palestine and put his stake in a Jewish state, without any commitment that this and only this will always be the Jewish state." Even the state proposed by the commission would mean the establishment of a Jewish guardian-state, a Jewish armed force holding open the gates to Palestine, "without an alien, unconcerned . . . hostile administration, but with a Zionist government making its own laws . . . and holding the key to immigration in its hand."[83] Weizmann similarly declared that the Jews "would be fools not to accept it, even if it were the size of a table-cloth."[84]

Ranged against this position were old-time practicals, for whom partition was essentially a repetition of the East Africa chimera, with Ben-Gurion and Weizmann taking Herzl's side, proposing to trade the soil of Zion in exchange for a mere political abstraction. For them, it was not the land that should be compromised to gain the Jewish state, but the state that should be deferred in order to retain Jewish access to the breadth of the physical land. "Nothing outweighs the importance of building another settlement and another," thundered Tabenkin. "The state we will leave to future generations."[85] But at Zurich, the ZO was also confronted by a faction that Herzl would hardly have permitted into the chamber—non-Zionists and "true Zionists" such as Warburg and Magnes, who rejected partition because they opposed a Jewish state, in any territory, on ideological grounds. On August 18, Warburg took the rostrum, calling upon the Zionist leaders "not to give up on our ideals," painting for them a picture of the Arab-Jewish "second Switzerland" that could be created if they would only give up the dream of a Jewish state and threatening to cut off their funds if they did not.[86] Magnes appeared as well, presenting a resolution in support of a binational state on behalf of the non-Zionists, comparing Ben-Gurion's calls for a Jewish state and massive Jewish immigration to the "false Messianism" of Shabtai Tzvi, and assuring his listeners that a Jewish state, too, would have to close the gates of Palestine lest it be "overrun" by Jews.[87]

As was his way, Weizmann played for a compromise, seeking to avoid the impending schism with his patrons. But Ben-Gurion held his ground, referring to Warburg and his allies as "enemies of the Jewish state" and insisting that no amount of philanthropy could be weighed against the prospect of Jewish sovereignty, the only thing that could save the Jews alive out of Europe: "We must divert attention from all other considerations. . . . We must not consider endangering in the least the possibility of establishing a Jewish state in exchange for the donations of Warburg and his associates."[88] In the end, the Jewish Agency Executive was reconstituted with seven Zionist and five non-Zionist members—a "compromise" formula that guaranteed that the Zionist Executive continued to make the decisions for the Jewish Agency, ensuring that any negotiations with Britain would be conducted on the basis of partition and the establishment of a Jewish state. A few months later, Felix Warburg died of a heart attack, and the threat that the guardian-organization of the Jews might be transformed into a "non-Zionist" institution committed to a binational Palestine passed from the world.

But as it transpired, it would be years before the ZO would see the fruits of this victory. Husseini's Higher Arab Committee rejected the Royal Commission's recommendation of partition, returning with even greater

force to its campaign of violence. On September 26, 1937 the British acting district commissioner of the Galilee was shot to death in Nazareth, and
further acts of terror against British and Jews followed in rapid succession.
By the following year, armed Arab organizations had gone into action in
Jaffa, Jerusalem, Nablus, Ramallah, and the Galilee, attacking and destroying police stations, government offices, post offices, train stations, and
banks. Over the two-year period of the Arab terror, attacks on Jews alone
left 415 dead.[89]

With much of the Arab population in rebellion against the mandatory
government, Britain for the first time responded with tenacious military and
political action, arming and training Jewish military units that participated
in British operations, disbanding the Higher Arab Committee, and exiling
numerous Arab leaders. But the new British collaboration with Jewish
armed forces in Palestine—a collaboration that permitted an unprecedented
growth in the Palestinian Jewish military—reflected no change in London's
views on Zionism. On the contrary, within weeks after the publication of
Lord Peel's recommendations, the British cabinet, at Prime Minister Neville
Chamberlain's insistence, determined to send yet another commission. This
new commission was publicly charged with exploring ways of implementing
partition, but it had been quietly instructed that it might also conclude the
partition plan was not "workable." By the time it completed its research in
August 1938, Hitler had assumed control of Austria and had begun his
great political offensive against the Sudetenland, the mountain ridge sepa-
rating the Nazi German state from Prague. On September 29, Chamberlain
and French prime minister Edouard Daladier flew to Munich to strike a
bargain with Hitler, where they infamously sold out the Czechs in exchange
for "peace in our time." The independent British state was itself quickly
ceasing to be "workable," and if it would not honor a written alliance with a
pivotal ally such as Czechoslovakia, it was evident that it would not lift a
finger to honor a promise made to the Jews. "The world's leaders are deaf,"
wrote Ben-Gurion, "unable to hear anything other than the sound of cannon. And the Jews of the diaspora have none."[90]

On November 9, 1938, forty days after the betrayal of the Czechs, the
Chamberlain government announced the results of its new study of conditions in Palestine, which concluded that "the political, administrative, and
financial difficulties involved in the proposal to create independent Arab
and Jewish states inside Palestine are so great that this solution of the problem is impracticable." Hours later, as night fell upon Central Europe, the
Nazis launched their first nationwide pogrom against the Jews of Germany,
burning hundreds of synagogues and demolishing Jewish places of business.
Scores were murdered and tens of thousands dragged off to concentration
camps. What later came to be known as Kristallnacht, the night of broken

glass, was the exact moment when it became clear that being a Jew had become a punishable offense in the German state. It was also the night that the only real hope of escape—the guardian-state of the Jews—was snuffed out of existence.

A conference was subsequently convened by the British in London, whose purpose was to resolve the problem of Palestine once and for all and whose farcical proceedings included a statement by the moderator, Colonial Secretary Malcolm MacDonald, to the effect that Hitler was not as wrong as many thought and that there were already too many Jews in Palestine.[91] The outcome was not even a deadlock. The Arab states refused to be seated with the Jewish delegates, so that each side held separate discussions with the British. In the end, MacDonald read the British "proposals": An additional 75,000 Jews would be allowed into Palestine during the next five years. Thereafter, a Jew would be allowed to enter Palestine only with the approval of the Arab majority. Within ten years, Palestine was to be reconstituted as an independent Arab state.

On May 17, 1939, these terms became British policy with the publication of the Chamberlain White Paper. The British-Jewish alliance for Jewish Palestine was dead. Herzl's dream of creating a Jewish state that would rescue European Jewry had ended in failure.

CHAPTER 10

The Professors' Struggle Against the Jewish State, 1939–1948

THE CHAMBERLAIN WHITE PAPER OF MAY 1939 marked the formal end of Britain's support for Jewish restoration in Palestine. Henceforth, British policy would be unequivocally aimed at reconstituting Palestine as an Arab state. For David Ben-Gurion, the implications of the new British policy were clear: Only the rapid growth of Jewish power—military power in Palestine, and diplomatic strength abroad, especially in Washington—could now induce Britain to either reconsider or get out of the way. Others were not so certain, and many of the Zionist leaders continued to fear public action in support of a Jewish state that might only further alienate Britain. The course of the next eleven years was thus the story of how Ben-Gurion and his allies, facing stiff resistance from Jews opposed to a Jewish state both in Palestine and in America, nevertheless succeeded in moving most of the Jewish world to support a policy of diplomatic and military activism, whose ultimate result was Jewish political independence in Palestine.

Even before returning to Palestine from the London conference, where the Jewish delegation was informed of Britain's new policy, Ben-Gurion was already firing off defiant messages to Jerusalem, pronouncing that "we must . . . concentrate all our efforts on increasing our strength in Palestine— quickly, with all the means available to us."[1] In this he received the support of Berl Katznelson, who called upon the Zionist leadership to recognize that times had changed and that no amount of practical settlement work would suffice to secure the Jewish presence in Palestine if political circumstances continued to deteriorate.[2] On May 18, the day after publication of the white paper, a wave of strikes and rioting organized by the Jewish Agency's under-ground armed force, the Hagana, swept Palestine, claiming the life of a British policeman. At the same time, Ben-Gurion circulated an open letter to the British administration in which he branded the white paper as "a breach of faith and a surrender to Arab terrorism" and declared that the Jews would not accept it, "even if their blood will be shed." He now threw himself into the work of strengthening the Jewish settlement's armed force, seeking ways of acquiring aviation and naval training, siphoning off Histadrut funds for purchasing arms, and imposing a war tax on the Jewish settlement. New kib-butzim were established along the coast in order to provide cover for the clandestine importation of illegal immigrants and material.[3]

But Ben-Gurion could not rest satisfied with stockpiling illegal arms, and he wracked his mind for a means of erecting a de facto Jewish sovereignty that could hold open the gates of the country to Jewish refugees despite British policy. In discussions with Katznelson and Hagana commander Eliahu Golomb, Ben-Gurion seems to have contemplated radical expansion of the clandestine Jewish military and its use in combating British restric-tions on immigration.[4] What precisely he intended is not known, but we do know that he approached the Labor party with a proposal to form a small body—a kind of war cabinet—empowered to take secret decisions on issues of military and foreign policy. In effect, Ben-Gurion was asking that the Zionist Organization simply ignore the fact that it had no charter in Palestine, attempting to unilaterally establish an executive branch of govern-ment like that which sets foreign and military policy for independent states. Such an executive authority had existed in Herzl's time, when he had, by virtue of his position as chairman of the Executive,[5] conducted all foreign policy initiatives in secret.

But the ZO no longer functioned in this way. The interlocking commit-tees and councils of the Labor party, the Zionist Organization, and the Jewish Agency constituted a constellation of dozens of individuals who were consulted on important issues, most of whom were unwilling to give up their say in foreign policy, rejecting Ben-Gurion's initiative out of hand. Among the loudest of his detractors were Palestinian-Jewish leaders of

German origin, whose aversion to an independent Jewish state was readily transformed into opposition to an independent Jewish executive authority. Thus, Arthur Ruppin denounced Ben-Gurion as "a zealot liable to drag us into the abyss"; Meir Ya'ari, head of Hashomer Hatzair, accused Ben-Gurion of seeking to make himself "dictator"; and Werner Senator, a "non-Zionist" member of the Jewish Agency Executive and later the Hebrew University's chief administrator, declared that Ben-Gurion was promoting "national fascism."[6]

Nor did Ben-Gurion and Katznelson do much better in persuading their colleagues to place pressure on Britain by means of diplomatic and public relations initiatives in the United States. The mass rallies organized by American Jews in late 1938 to protest Britain's Palestine policy had powerfully demonstrated the potential for such a campaign,[7] and Ben-Gurion now found himself demanding precisely the kind of politics of "demonstration and slogan" that had so mystified him in discussions with Jabotinsky a few years earlier. But here, too, the Labor Zionist majority evidenced little sympathy for his initiatives, throwing back at him the same materialist arguments he himself had been making not so long ago. As Tabenkin put it: "The true political phenomenon is only that which creates facts, not that which is formal and juridical. . . . Our political fact is not the Balfour declaration. . . . Our political fact is the 400,000 Jews who are here. That is a political fact. Beyond this there are no political facts."[8]

On September 1, 1938, Hitler invaded Poland and Britain went to war. Overnight, whatever hope there may have been of pushing the ZO into a confrontation with the British evaporated, and the concern to avoid any action that might harm London's war effort became paramount. The Chamberlain government was unimpressed by the favor, and in February 1940, it took time out from its faltering war with Nazism to issue land regulations restricting free Jewish land purchase in Palestine to a tiny ghetto composing roughly 5 percent of the area west of the Jordan River (about 1 percent of the original Palestine Mandate). With this, Ben-Gurion reached the end of his tether, announcing that he was resigning from the leadership of the Zionist Organization and moving to a kibbutz.[9] In a statement quivering with emotion, he accused his colleagues on the Zionist Executive of acquiescing—out of fear, petty self-interest, and insensitivity to the fate of European Jewry—in the transformation of what was to have been the Jewish guardian-state in Palestine into yet another powerless Jewish community in a British-Arab Diaspora:

> I believe that Zionists still exist. How many I cannot say. . . . For Palestinian Jewry can be just like German Jewry or American Jewry. . . . A Palestinian Jew, too, might think: Might I not be damaged through this [i.e., political ac-

tion against the Chamberlain White Paper]. . . . But this is not a Zionist assessment. . . .

The interests of the Jews of Palestine are not important to me—not more so than the interests of the Jews of Germany or of any other country. The fate of Poland's 3 million Jews is much closer to my heart than the fate of 500,000 Jews in Palestine. . . . For the Zionist perspective says: . . . We act as a people, not as individual Jews, not as a collation of individuals, not as any Jewish community. Rather, we act *as the Jewish people*. . . .

I say that a Zionist politics is unwilling to turn Palestine into a diaspora community under Chamberlain's command. . . . A Zionist program that seeks to preserve . . . the possibility of immigration and settlement of masses of Jews cannot allow these land regulations. . . . The Jewish people must not be silent: Neither in Palestine, nor in America.[10]

But Ben-Gurion never reached the kibbutz. Within days he had left for London, continuing from there to the United States, where he would spend much of his time for the next two years. He no longer traveled in his capacity as leader of the Zionist Executive but rather as a freelance recruiter for a Jewish national army that—if the Allies consented—would join in the fight against Hitler; and as a freelance diplomat for a Jewish state, to be named Judea or Eretz Israel.[11] Like Herzl before him, he now traveled carrying Jewish independence with him in his suitcase, a subjective sovereignty of one, but the guardian of the Jewish people nonetheless.

In the United States in the fall of 1940, Ben-Gurion discovered a Zionist movement that had retreated into almost complete inaction for fear of troubling Britain. Its leading figure, Rabbi Stephen Wise, preached tirelessly that "to add the weight of a feather to the crushing burdens now borne by England is to sin against the Holy Spirit,"[12] and after only a day of meetings, Ben-Gurion already noted that the Zionist leaders he met were "wallowing in personal problems, afraid of what the non-Jews will say."[13] But he nonetheless set about systematic efforts to persuade the constituent parts of American Zionism to come out publicly for a Jewish national army and Jewish sovereignty in Palestine.

Perhaps most important were his appearances before Hadassah, the largest and best organized of the American Zionist groups, which had close personal ties to Judah Magnes (the Hebrew University president was also chairman of the committee overseeing Hadassah's activities in Palestine) and which in October decided to devote funds to developing the idea of a binational Arab-Jewish state in Palestine.[14] These prejudices notwithstanding, Hadassah proved willing to consider Ben-Gurion's views, at one point extending an evening session at its national convention to 5:00 A.M. so that its leadership could give Ben-Gurion a full hearing.[15] Finally, on November 14, after six weeks of reconnaissance, he moved to the main stage of his offensive, submitting his plan for a Jewish army and a new "regime" in Palestine to the "Emergency Committee for Zionist Affairs," the coordinating body of the various Zionist groups in the United States. Twelve days later, he attended a meeting of the national board of Hadassah, where he pressed for the adoption of the Jewish state as the explicit aim of American Zionism.[16]

It is not difficult to imagine Ben-Gurion's proposals being dismissed by American Jewish leaders, just as they had been dismissed by Zionist leaders in Palestine. But events now conspired to give weight to Ben-Gurion's demands. In the days immediately prior to his meeting with the Hadassah national leadership, Hungary and Romania joined the war on the side of Germany, bringing huge new Jewish populations under Nazi influence. That same week, Britain announced the deportation to Mauritius, an island five hundred miles off the coast of Madagascar, of nearly 2,000 Jewish refugees who had arrived in Haifa from Europe. The Hagana attempted to disable the deportation ship by detonating an explosive charge against its hull, but the plan misfired. The ship sank, and 240 refugees were killed. Nevertheless, the tragedy left the British unmoved, and the deportation of Jewish refugees to the Indian Ocean was resumed two weeks later.

The trauma of watching Britain use force to turn away ships overloaded with refugees from Nazi Europe made a profound impression on American Jews, and the gathering shame and anger gave Ben-Gurion the opening he needed to begin building an opposition to Wise's policy of silence. In this he found an ally in Abba Hillel Silver, a Reform rabbi from Cleveland who had headed the United Palestine Appeal since 1938.[17] In early December, Silver broke ranks with the entire American Jewish leadership to pronounce that he could no longer be still while Britain was escalating its struggle against Jews fleeing to Palestine:

> Our desire to help Great Britain in this war is maneuvering us into a policy distinctly harmful to Zionism. We are asked not only to withhold criticism of outrageous acts on the part of the Palestine government, but actually . . . to become apologists for the Palestine government and to make its position "understood by the Jews of America." In the meantime, England intends to pursue her policy of appeasing the Arabs even more aggressively than she did before the war . . . In this way we practically acknowledge . . . that the United States government will do nothing to help us . . . This is an intolerable situation . . . Every people speaks up for its own rights in these desperate times, and for its own needs. The Jews alone, the most hard-pressed of all, must speak up only on behalf of—Great Britain.[18]

Three days later, at a meeting of American Zionist leaders with Ben-Gurion in New York, Silver pointedly told Wise that it was only the exercise

of Jewish power that would induce Britain to make room for Jewish interests in its war calculations. "If the British think that the Jews are powerless,
from their point of view they are no doubt right—having the greater objective before them—to sacrifice us," he said. "But they must be made to realize that we are a factor, and only thus can we save the honor and the future
of the Jewish people."[19]

Ben-Gurion's alliance with Silver resulted in a joint conference of the ex-
ecutives of the four largest Zionist organizations, which for the first time issued a statement publicly condemning Britain's policies in Palestine. The
days that followed brought additional successes: The small American Labor
Zionist organization backed Ben-Gurion's demand for a Jewish state, as did
New Palestine, the publication of the Zionist Organization of America
(ZOA).[20] And in late January 1941, Silver presided over a "National
Conference for Palestine" in Washington to inaugurate a newly independent United Palestine Appeal cut loose from collaboration with non-Zionist
fund-raising efforts. There Silver issued his first public call for the establishment of the Jewish state after the war, and the conference followed his lead
in resolving that "only by large-scale colonization of . . . Jews in Palestine,
with the aim of its reconstitution as a Jewish commonwealth, can the Jewish
problem be permanently solved."[21]

These developments constituted a breach in the wall. Certainly not victory, as the majority of American Zionists continued to fear a public struggle for a Jewish state. But it was a breach nonetheless—and one that
surpassed anything Ben-Gurion had been able to achieve in Palestine.
Indeed, returning home for several months that spring, Ben-Gurion joined
Katznelson on a heartbreaking tour of Labor strongholds in an attempt to
rally his party around the declaration of the state as the immediate aim of
the ZO for war's end. If the Zionists did not set clear and undisputed goals
now, he argued, the end of the war would bring only disunity and chaos.[22]
But to no avail. The Labor party was loath to take any step that might ag-
gravate Tabenkin's group, now on the verge of secession, and all external
concerns were held to be irrelevant when compared to the need for cooperation with Britain in preparing defenses against a possible Nazi invasion of
Palestine.[23] Remarkably, a successful political battle for the birth of the
Jewish state seemed more plausible in New York than it did in Tel Aviv.

Returning to the United States in November 1941, Ben-Gurion set up
shop in Washington, the city he believed held the key to a postwar political
constellation that would bring the Jewish state into being. In his absence,
the willingness of American Jews to accept his arguments had grown significantly. Hitler had by now penetrated deep into Russia, bringing most of the
Jews in Europe under his control, and harrowing rumors of their destruction were in circulation. Within a few months, the rumors were supple-

mented by eyewitness accounts released by the Soviets attesting to the killing of tens of thousands, perhaps even hundreds of thousands of Jews in the Ukraine and Belarus. From then on, the toll of the murdered only increased, even as Britain continued its interception of Jewish refugee ships and the deportation and internment of the Jews captured in these operations. Never in their worst nightmares had Zionists imagined so grisly a confirmation of Herzl's warnings regarding the futility of Jewish settlement in Palestine in the absence of political control of the country. In a stinging position paper, Ben-Gurion gave voice to what Jews the world over were finally coming to understand all too well: that there would be no guardian of the Jews until the establishment in Palestine of "a Jewish administration— an administration completely identified with the needs and aims of the Jewish settlers . . . *To secure the homeland for homeless Jews, Jews themselves must be entrusted with its reconstitution.*"[24]

The developments in Europe had an electric effect on Jewish politics in America. In September 1941, Silver's forces had achieved an impressive victory at the annual conference of the ZOA, which called for "the reconstitution of Palestine in its historic boundaries as a Jewish commonwealth."[25] A month later, they had produced a stunning upset at Hadassah's national convention, which revolted against its most venerated leaders to adopt a resolution in favor of a Jewish commonwealth.[26] This breakthrough, led by Judith Epstein—who later reported that Ben-Gurion's all-night appearance at the Hadassah convention the previous year had constituted a political turning point for her[27]—meant the first defeat for the leadership sympathetic to the aims of Magnes and Buber, presaging Epstein's ascendancy to the presidency of Hadassah in 1943. With all of the American Zionist parties lined up behind the Jewish state, the way was paved for the master stroke, a great Zionist assembly that would at long last speak the name of the Jewish state as the goal of the movement. Even Weizmann joined in the campaign in January 1942 with an article in *Foreign Affairs,* arguing that "a Jewish state in Palestine . . . is a moral need and postulate . . . I believe that after the war Jews everywhere can gain in status and security only through the rise of a Jewish state."[28]

The Extraordinary Zionist Conference convened at the Biltmore Hotel in New York on May 9, 1942, and continued for three days with the participation of Weizmann, Ben-Gurion, and other Zionist representatives from seventeen countries. The American Zionist movements were represented by 586 delegates. It was the closest thing to a Zionist congress that would be possible during the war, and Ben-Gurion used it to deliver the speech he had been unable to give during the debate over the Zionist end goal eleven years earlier at the Seventeenth Congress. Now he demanded "a clear and unequivocal reaffirmation of the original intention of the Balfour declaration and the Mandate to re-establish Palestine as a Jewish commonwealth."[29] And this he received. Significant opposition came only from former Hadassah president Rose Jacobs, who spoke for the binational-ist line pioneered by the Peace Association, arguing that the conference should make no political statements until a formula could be found that was acceptable to the Arabs.[30] In the decisive resolution, which came to be known as the Biltmore Platform, the conference swept aside Jacobs's objec-tion and that of the Palestinian Hashomer Hatzair representative and openly called for the establishment of a Jewish commonwealth in Palestine.[31] The resolution, which was adopted by a consensus of all four streams of American Zionism, read:

> The Conference declares that the new world order that will follow victory, cannot be established on foundations of peace, justice and equality, unless the problem of Jewish homelessness is finally solved. The Conference demands that the gates of Palestine be opened; that the Jewish Agency be vested with control of immigration into Palestine and with the necessary authority for upbuilding the country . . . and that Palestine be established as a Jewish Commonwealth integrated into the structure of the new democratic world. Then and only then will the age-old wrong to the Jewish people be righted.[32]

This was indeed a great moment, one for which the Zionist Organization had waited four decades: The moment in which the Zionist Left, following Weizmann and Stephen Wise, turned its back on its partnership with "non-Zionism," uniting with the more hard-line Zionism of Ben-Gurion, Silver, and the Mizrahi in a virtually wall-to-wall coalition for a Jewish state. Not since the early days of Herzl's ZO had there been such a singleness of spirit. This spirit was captured well in the speech of Emanuel Neumann, an ally of Silver's, who called for the American Zionists to become the diplomatic arm of the Zionist Organization, declaring, "If we can effectively mobilize our forces and talent throughout the country, if we go in now for an all-out ef-fort for winning the battle of America, there is a good prospect that we will win the battle of Palestine."[33]

This assessment soon proved itself completely on the mark. With the die already cast by the American Zionists, Ben-Gurion returned to Palestine, where his resignation from the leadership of the Zionist Organization seemed to have been forgotten. In October, he and Katznelson easily se-cured the support of the Labor Zionists and of the other major Zionist par-ties in Palestine for the Biltmore Platform. And on November 8 and 10, days after the British defeated the Germans at El-Alamain, once and for all ending the threat of a Nazi invasion of Palestine, Ben-Gurion appeared be-fore the Jewish Agency Executive and the Zionist Executive to collect their endorsements of his Jewish-state policy.[34] In the United States, too, the idea of the Jewish state continued to gain momentum, with its supporters capturing an overwhelming majority of the seats at a representative assembly of American Jewry organized at the initiative of B'nai B'rith. The American Jewish Committee, the stronghold of New York's German Jews led by the anti-Zionist Joseph Proskauer, won only token representation.[35] Ignoring State Department and Jewish anti-Zionist pleas for a "restrained" conference, Silver read to the assembly from a "Declaration on Palestine," which included the call for a Jewish commonwealth. A wave of emotion swept the chamber, and the delegates rose to sing "Hatikva," the Jewish nationalist anthem. Silver's declaration passed by a vote of 478 to 4. Zionism and the Jewish state had become the policy of organized American Jewry.[36]

Perhaps no words capture the feelings of world Jewry during this period as well as those with which David Ben-Gurion addressed the Jewish National Assembly in Palestine, at a special session called on November 30, 1942—three weeks after the adoption of the Biltmore Platform by the Zionist Executive—when incontrovertible evidence reached Palestine that all of Europe's Jews were being systematically exterminated:

> We do not know exactly what goes on in the Nazi valley of death, or how many Jews have already been slaughtered . . . We do not know, whether the victory of democracy and freedom and justice will not find Europe a vast Jewish cemetery in which the bones of our people are scattered . . . We are the only people in the world whose blood, as a nation, is allowed to be shed. . . . Only our children, our women . . . and our aged are set apart for special treatment, to be buried alive in graves dug by them, to be cremated in crematoriums, to be strangled and to be murdered by machine guns . . . for but one sin: . . . Because the Jews have no political standing, no Jewish army, no Jewish independence, and no homeland . . .
>
> As long as the gates to our land are closed, your hands, too, [Britain,] will be steeped in Jewish blood . . . Give us the right to fight and die as Jews. . . . We demand the right . . . to a homeland and independence. What has happened to us in Poland, what God forbid, will happen to us in the future, all our innocent victims, all the tens of thousands, hundreds of thousands, and perhaps millions . . . are the sacrifices of a people without a homeland . . . We demand . . . a homeland and independence.[37]

From the moment the Nazis took control of the state in Germany, the professors of the Peace Association and their associates had found themselves on the defensive in a Jewish community that had become ever more inclined to view the political environment as implacably hostile to its interests and that was ready to seek a response in terms of Jewish force. Yet almost until the eve of World War II, Martin Buber, the one man who could have lent public stature to the professors' arguments against this trend, remained immured in Frankfurt, working on his translation of the Bible into German. Letters from key members of the university faculty and administration, especially Hugo Bergmann and Gershom Scholem, continued to flow to Buber, pleading with him to come to Palestine and assist in refurbishing the true Zionism, which they feared was foundering. "You do not know . . . how much some persons here wait for your coming," wrote Werner Senator, Hebrew University's chief administrator. "For there are those here who believe that you . . . could bring together and make effective forces that today are unrecognized, ineffective. . . . Come quickly!"[38]

Buber finally arrived in Palestine in March 1938, where he became the head of the Hebrew University's fledgling program in sociology. Nor were the hopes of his disciples disappointed. Within a year of his arrival, he had succeeded in contributing his substantial prestige to the establishment of a new binationalist organization, this one named the "League for Jewish-Arab Rapprochement and Cooperation."[39] The league was established in April 1939, in the immediate aftermath of the London conference, where the Chamberlain government had announced its intention of ending Jewish immigration to Palestine after the entry of a final 75,000 Jews into the country—a policy that was not received as entirely invidious by those who in any case considered large-scale Jewish immigration to be the main obstacle to peace with the Arabs. Within this new political context, the prospects for a binational state in Palestine became substantially more plausible. And to this end, the league drew together an alliance of veteran Peace Association activists, new immigrants from Germany and Austria,[40] and representatives of the Hashomer Hatzair collective farms—in short, a grand reunion of all the movements in Palestine whose opposition to the Jewish state had been cut from the cloth of Buber's "true Zionism."[41]

With this coalition behind him, Buber quickly adapted himself to his new role as Jewish Palestine's arbiter of moral truth. In one of his earliest public statements after arriving in the country, he excoriated unnamed Zionists who were working "to establish our own national egoism," declaring that even in a time of crisis, those who did so "are performing the acts of Hitler in the land of Israel, for they want us to serve Hitler's god after he has been given a Hebrew name."[42] The League's first pamphlet, carrying articles by Buber and a number of his followers, argued against the Jewish state and called for the limitation of Jewish immigration to 45 percent of the population of Palestine. A second pamphlet, appearing in August 1939, again attacked the ZO for trying to settle Jews in Palestine without the consent of the Arabs, asserting that "it will not be the theory of Hitler and the worshippers of force which will win, but the teachings of the prophets of Israel." In October, weeks after the German invasion of Poland, Buber headed a delegation of members from the league in a meeting with Ben-Gurion aimed at persuading him that only the adoption of a binational Arab-Jewish state as the ZO's ultimate aim stood a chance of inducing Britain to reopen the question of Jewish immigration. Ben-Gurion, at this moment devoting every fiber in his mind to steering the Jews toward a confrontation with the British over the white paper, must have cut a grim figure as he listened to Buber, almost fresh off the boat, preaching to him the benefits of seeking immigration on the Arabs' terms. "We all want to bring Jews today to Palestine," Ben-Gurion told Buber. "I ask you, and I asked Magnes years ago . . . Did you come to Palestine with the consent of the Arabs or against their wishes? He came against their wishes, and with the force of British bayonets. . . . I say, there is no example in history of a nation opening the gates of its country . . . because the nation that wants to enter has explained its desire to it."[43]

The league, like Magnes a few years earlier, took its failure to change the aims of the ZO as a signal to begin conducting a foreign policy of its own, initiating discussions with Arabs inside and outside of Palestine. These meetings generated various schemes for promoting Arab-Jewish coopera-tion, which, it was hoped, would be funded by the Peace Association's tradi-tional sympathizers in New York.[44] As a result, the league directed a stream of material promoting a binational Palestine at Magnes and Henrietta Szold's contacts in the United States—including a two-hundred-page pro-posal for a federal Arab-Jewish Palestine, whose president would be alter-nately an Arab and then a Jew.[45]

Of particular importance was the distribution of these materials to Hadassah president Tamar de Sola Pool and her colleagues, who a few months later announced the formal establishment of a Hadassah committee whose objective was to devise a "compromise solution" in Palestine. The committee was chaired by Hadassah binationalist Rose Jacobs[46] and staffed by Dr. Moshe Perlmann, a Hebrew University graduate living in New York, who claimed he had been expelled from the Labor party in the early 1930s because of his opposition to a Jewish state.[47] The conclusions of the com-mittee's work seemed foregone, but the committee did not have time to draw them. Within a few months, the first hard news of the extermination of European Jewry reached the United States, and this, combined with the ongoing reports of the British blockade of Palestine, soon ended Hadassah's flirtation with binationalism. The largest Zionist organization in the United States ended up endorsing the Biltmore Platform along with all other American Zionist organizations.

Only in Jerusalem was the commitment to the "true Zionism" so strong that it was possible to contemplate a renewed campaign against the Jewish state at precisely the moment when reports from Europe had begun to suggest a slaughter of unimaginable proportions. By the end of June 1942, the entire movement of Hashomer Hatzair collective farms had reacted to Biltmore by associating itself with the league's demand for a binational Arab-Jewish state—albeit with the critical caveat that this state would have to permit massive Jewish immigration. In effect, this decision meant that the league could not be relied upon to negotiate with the Arabs and the British on the basis of severely restricted immigration, which many of the professors in the league viewed as a precondition for any agreement.

The result was the establishment of a new organization that *would* be willing to accept limitations on Jewish immigration. Calling itself Ihud (or the "Union Association" in English),[48] the new group was essentially a revived Peace Association under the formal leadership of Buber and Magnes, with the active participation of Peace Association activists and sympathizers such as Henrietta Szold, Moshe Smilansky, Ernst Simon, Hugo Bergmann, Benjamin Radler-Feldman, Robert Weltsch, Werner Senator, and Norman Bentwich.[49] At the organization's first public gathering, on August 11 in the lecture hall of the German Immigrants' Association in Jerusalem, Magnes once again spelled out the familiar principles of emancipationist German Judaism, calling for the abandonment of the idea of a Jewish state, which would inevitably mean war in Palestine: "Is the Jewish state of such importance as to justify this war? For myself, I answer: No! Because the warfare may destroy the Jewish settlement here . . . Because it will breed a hatred difficult to assuage for generations . . . Because the resultant state will not be a Jewish State but a pagan state."[50]

Less than a month later, Ihud issued a platform, which was circulated among members of the Hebrew University staff. The program called for a "union between the Jewish and Arab peoples" that would span "all branches of life—social, economic, cultural, political." On the question of Jewish immigration, the platform was silent.

The founding of Ihud was greeted with horror in the ZO, which had almost been capsized by the professors' independent foreign policy in 1929, and which now faced the possibility of a separate peace between Britain and a more "reasonable" Jewish leadership in Palestine and America than the one the Zionists represented. Implausible as this may seem in retrospect, such a scenario was not considered impossible by Zionist leaders, considering the Peace Association's earlier success in transforming the crucial German Zionist Federation into a swamp of "non-politicals," "cultural Zionists," and binationalists, due to the professors' close ties with Jewish organizations and publications in Germany. The leadership of Ihud was similarly endowed with connections among *American* Jews—Henrietta Szold was still the revered honorary president of Hadassah; Werner Senator was the official representative of the wealthy American "non-Zionists" in the

Jewish Agency; and Magnes was the official representative in Palestine of two of the most important American Jewish organizations, the Joint Distribution Committee and B'nai B'rith. Moreover, sympathy for Magnes ran strong in the still-influential American Jewish Committee, which, in the wake of Biltmore, had elected Judge Joseph Proskauer, an outspoken anti-Zionist, as President.[51] And the publisher of the *New York Times,* Arthur Hays Sulzberger, had a few years earlier instructed his paper that its editorial policy on Palestine "should be predicated on the Magnes point of view."[52]

For anyone who knew how to read the map, the possibility that American Jewry would be lost, or at least politically neutralized with regard to the Jewish state, was a very real possibility—and one that would snuff out hope of winning support for the Jewish state from the American government. And in fact, in the months that followed Ihud's appearance, the Jewish press in Palestine was spattered with nervous reports of the favorable reactions to the new organization from senior British officials, the American press, and the anti-Zionist Orthodox organization, Agudat Israel.[53] Moreover, news of Ihud's appearance gave opponents of the Jewish state in Hadassah an excuse to sidestep Biltmore and launch a new offensive to have Buber and Magnes's proposals considered by American Zionist groups. (Hadassah continued to waver until the meeting of its national board, during which Ben-Gurion's supporters crushed the effort by Hadassah president Tamar de Sola Pool to withdraw the organization's support for the Biltmore program.)[54]

Ben-Gurion, still in America, was beside himself, sputtering that the goal of Ihud was "to destroy organized Zionism, and to influence the American government to believe that there is a cheaper solution to the Palestine problem than the Jewish commonwealth."[55] And other Zionist leaders followed suit. Yitzhak Ben-Tzvi, chairman of the Jewish National Assembly in Palestine, spoke of the appearance of an "anti-Zionist constellation" capable of endangering everything that the movement had achieved. Yehoshua Suprasky of the hard-line General Zionists and Joshua Heschel Farbstein of the Mizrahi attacked Ihud, calling its independent political line "a knife stabbed in the back of the Jewish settlement . . . and treason against the Zionist movement as a whole." Benzion Mosinson of the dovish pro-Weizmann faction of the General Zionists called the Ihud program "the suicide of the Jewish people, the loss of our last hope; that is why we oppose it with all the might of an organism that wants to live and not to die." Moshe Sharett, head of the Jewish Agency's political department, described Ihud as "a pack of anti-Zionists" and accused Buber of having abandoned his own students in Germany: "If I were a Jew in Germany right now, and this were to reach me, and I saw the signatures of former German Zionists, and of the man who was teacher and guide to the Zionist movement in Central

Europe . . . I would want to know . . . what they are telling me? After the war, will I be able to join Martin Buber [in Palestine] or not? . . . Does Martin Buber support my right to immigrate or not?"[56]

The Jewish papers in Palestine responded similarly, with the Labor paper *Davar* deploring the group's positions, writing of Magnes: "Go out and look among the democratic nations to see if one can find presidents of universities who in the very midst of wartime conduct their own independent foreign policy, hold[ing] discussions with foreign agents in opposition to their government."[57]

When Ben-Gurion returned to Palestine in October 1942, he immediately pronounced Buber and his followers to be "national apostates."[58] In early November 10, when the Biltmore Platform was brought before the Zionist Executive, Ben-Gurion castigated Hashomer Hatzair and Ihud for their circulation of binationalist propaganda among the leadership of Hadassah in New York: "All this talk of a binational state, and of these [federal] districts—they are the sick phantasmagoria of Jewish boys sitting and addling their brains. . . . You stand before a situation which you do not dare see as it is. The Arabs are unwilling to allow Jewish immigration."[59]

The ZO in Palestine adopted Ben-Gurion's position by an overwhelming majority, but this did nothing to soften Ihud's sense that it had a moral mandate to pursue an opposing policy. As Magnes noted in his diary, "The slogan 'Jewish state' (or commonwealth) is equivalent, in effect, to a declaration of war by the Jews on the Arabs." It was a slogan that Ben-Gurion was using to prime "the Jewish storm troops" for the dirty deeds ahead, and no stone might be left unturned to ensure that these deeds were prevented.[60] Thus did Herzl's observation that "brothers had become enemies" come to its full fruition in December 1942, when Ihud launched an international campaign aimed at winning converts both among "Zionists and non-Zionists" to its platform.[61] In January 1943, *Foreign Affairs* published Magnes's rejoinder to Weizmann's Jewish-state article, in which he denounced what he termed "official Zionist policy" and called upon the United States and Britain to impose a binational solution on Palestine against the will of the Jewish leadership.[62] Similar articles by Magnes appeared in the *Nation,* the London *Economist* and the London *Times.* Once again, this position received support from the *New York Times,* which publicized Ihud's views in its news stories, opinion pieces, and letters. In all this, Ihud and its supporters continued to follow Buber's expositions of the true morality, according to which even the goal of a Jewish majority in Palestine was illegitimate, because the only reason to want such a majority was so that the Jews might have the power, "at decisive moments," to "determine the fate of the minority."[63] As Magnes explained in the *New York Times,* the

Zionists' declarations that they intended to establish a democratic state in Palestine was simply misleading: "It is a profound distortion of the truth. . . . What they want is a Jewish state, dominated by Jews."[64]

In its diplomacy in the United States, Ihud's goal was a coalition of Jewish and non-Jewish opponents of the Jewish state, which would be capable of pushing the American government into imposing a settlement in Palestine over the objections of the Zionist Organization.[65] In search of this coalition, Magnes reached out to such figures as Hans Kohn, the former Peace Association activist, who now went public with his view that "Zionist ideology . . . is dramatically opposed to the liberal concepts of the West, especially [the] United States."[66] His efforts were also supported by Hannah Arendt, another German-Jewish intellectual who argued that Herzl had been a "crackpot" and a proto-fascist, and that Ben-Gurion's continuation of his policies reflected nothing less than suicidal insanity, coming "terribly close" to being a repetition of the false Messianism of Shabtai Tzvi.[67] Magnes was also in touch with Joseph Proskauer, under whose guidance the American Jewish Committee maintained an anti-Zionist line, demanding the reintegration of Holocaust survivors into their countries of origin and ruling out Palestine as the destination for Jewish refugees.[68] Along the same lines, Magnes later sought the support of Christian anti-Zionist groups such as the Committee for Justice and Peace in the Holy Land, whose executive director, Kermit Roosevelt, was one of the architects of the anti-Zionist policies of the State Department and the Central Intelligence Agency.[69]

Perhaps most remarkable, however, was Magnes's effort to recruit for Ihud such leading Jewish anti-Zionist figures as Morris Lazaron, a Reform rabbi and a family friend of the Warburgs, whom Magnes knew from his days as a student at Hebrew Union College. Under the influence of Zionist rabbis such as Stephen Wise and Abba Hillel Silver, the central institutions of the Reform movement had in 1937 tempered their opposition to Zionism, for the first time accepting the idea that the land of Israel was, in fact, the "Jewish homeland."[70] It was at this time that Lazaron had emerged as one of the leading voices demanding that Reform hold fast to its opposition to the creation of Jewish national power, which he held to be akin to fascism. As he explained:

> I believe in the rebuilding of the ancient homeland, both from the philanthropic and the cultural points of view. My life has been made richer because I have been privileged to serve humbly in that cause. . . . But . . . nationalism . . . is a *hukat hagoyim* [i.e., an illicit custom of the gentiles]. Behind the mask of Jewish sentiment, one can see the specter of the foul thing which moves Germany and Italy. Behind the camouflage of its unquestioned appeal to Jewish feeling, one can hear a chorus of "Heil!" This is not for Jews. . . . Shall

we condemn it as Italian or German, but accept it as Jewish? . . . We must cry out the universal message of Israel. Not the blood cult, state cult, hate cult, war cult of nationalism, but one humanity on earth. . . . That is the meaning of the great *Aleinu* [prayer] and the high challenge of the holiest Yom Kippur.[71]

As the Jewish state became a real possibility with the recommendations of the Peel Commission that year, Lazaron threw himself into a personal diplomatic offensive against it, informing Felix Warburg—on the eve of Warburg's departure for the Jewish Agency assembly in Zurich in 1937— that to accept the idea of the Jewish state would mean that "we turn our backs on everything we've stood for."[72] In the years that followed, he became one of the Jewish state's most effective opponents, lobbying a web of contacts that included Max Warburg, Arthur Hays Sulzberger and his wife Iphigene, as well as other leaders of the American Jewish Committee and the Joint Distribution Committee, upper-crust British Jews, high-ranking officials in the State Department, British foreign minister Anthony Eden, and First Lady Eleanor Roosevelt.[73]

On June 1, 1942, three weeks after the adoption of the Biltmore Platform by American Zionists, an assembly of Lazaron's allies in the Reform rabbinate was called in Atlantic City to discuss options for combating Zionism—both the Jewish state and the campaign to create a Jewish army to fight with the Allies on a national basis. Among those attending were six former presidents of the Reform Rabbinic Assembly and the president of the Reform seminary, Hebrew Union College. The result was a "Statement of Principles by Non-Zionist Rabbis," endorsed by nearly a hundred members of the Reform rabbinate, which, while expressing support for the cultural development of the Jewish community in Palestine, categorically rejected the ZO's efforts to create a Jewish state.[74] This manifesto soon led to the establishment of an outspokenly anti-Zionist organization called the American Council for Judaism, which was to stand "against the claims of Zionists for rights of *all* Jews, as Jews, in their 'Jewish national state.'"[75] The group soon gathered around itself a small but devoted laity, which included such names as Lessing Rosenwald, former chairman of Sears Roebuck (son of Julius Rosenwald, the moving spirit behind the "Agro-Joint" project for settling Jews in the Ukraine); the chief executives of Levi Strauss and Company, Daniel Koshland and Walter Haas; former president of B'nai B'rith Alfred Cohen; Admiral Lewis Strauss, former president of Temple Emanu-El in New York; former congresswoman Florence Kahn; and the prominent jurist and legal theorist, Judge Jerome Frank. Close associates of Felix Warburg such as Paul Baerwald and Maurice Hexter, the latter formerly of the Jewish Agency Executive, also threw their weight behind the effort. So did Arthur Hays Sulzberger, publisher of the *New York Times*, who helped draft its first statement of principles.[76] The group was also successful in attracting the public support of a number of prominent Protestant religious leaders, including Henry Sloane Coffin and H. Richard Niebuhr (Reinhold Niebuhr's brother), and Lazaron's ties to undersecretary of state Sumner Welles soon yielded a close collaboration between the new organizations and the State Department.[77]

As early as September 1942, Lazaron wrote to Magnes in Palestine about the possibility of organizing "non-Zionist sentiment" in the United States, enclosing a copy of the "Statement of Principles by Non-Zionist Rabbis." Magnes immediately responded with a letter praising Lazaron and his associates, pronouncing himself willing to endorse the council's statement of principles (albeit with certain "questions" requiring clarification), agreeing that the Jewish nationalism of the Zionists was "unhappily chauvinistic and narrow and terroristic," and inviting Lazaron to participate in the establishment of an organization similar to Ihud in the United States "so that we may all be working together."[78] And although Ihud in the end shied away from publicly acknowledged ties with the council—Lazaron's impolitic publication of a brazenly anti-Zionist letter by Magnes put a chill on their romance—the two groups maintained a comfortable underground relationship for years. The staff of the council received Ihud's publications from Magnes, and it reprinted and distributed Magnes's speeches in the United States, endorsing them in the most laudatory terms. When necessary, the council also requested Ihud's assistance in researching events in Palestine. Similarly, Magnes remained on affable terms with the council's president, Lessing Rosenwald, soliciting funds from him for the Hebrew University and sending him copies of Ihud's materials. He also engaged in behind-the-scenes diplomatic efforts in the United States with the financial assistance of Rosenwald and other council members. Moreover, Ihud's fund-raising efforts in the United States were conducted with the active assistance of anti-Zionists such as Arthur Hays Sulzberger and Admiral Lewis Strauss.[79]

Beginning in 1943, under the leadership of Abba Hillel Silver, the Emergency Committee for Zionist Affairs was transformed into a political fighting machine on behalf of the Jewish state. With its stunning array of public relations and lobbying organs—including Committees for Labor Relations, Mobilization of Intellectuals, Community Contacts, Jewish Religious Forces, Christian Clergy, Press and Radio, Publications, Research, Contact with Postwar Planning Groups, and Postwar Political Planning—the Emergency Committee constituted the first standing, nationally organized effort by American Jewry to influence the American government on the issue of Palestine.[80]

Pressure created by Silver's organization soon succeeded in introducing pro-Zionist planks into the platforms of both major political parties and even induced the president himself to utter an uncharacteristic comment in favor of the Jewish state. And although Franklin Roosevelt remained more or less unmoved by Zionist aspirations until his death on April 12, 1945, four weeks before the end of the war in Europe, Zionist political fortunes took an unexpected turn with the accession to the presidency of Harry Truman. Lacking Roosevelt's Olympian demeanor, Truman proved sur-prisingly sensitive to press reports from the liberated concentration camps, in which the remains of human beings were to be found in piles ten feet high and skeletons in harlequin uniforms lingered near death. In the sum-mer, Truman sent a personal envoy to the Displaced Persons Camps in which the Jewish remnant had been collected. "We appear to be treating the Jews as the Nazis treated them," the president was told, "except that we do not exterminate them." Truman was genuinely moved, and he now went public with a request, which he had earlier communicated privately, that Britain permit as many of the Jews remaining in Europe as possible to go to Palestine.

The new British Labor government, which had committed itself to al-lowing Jewish immigration into Palestine on the campaign trail, now bowed to the same Arabist concerns that had kept the gates to Palestine sealed throughout the Holocaust. And when, in August 1945, the Colonial Office informed Weizmann that there would be no change in Britain's Palestine policy, Ben-Gurion approved preparations for the establishment of a joint military resistance with the two Jabotinskyite underground organizations, the Irgun, under the command of Menachem Begin, and Yitzhak Shamir's Lehi. This marked a breathtaking change of course. Only a year earlier, hoping that diplomatic efforts might bring Churchill to reverse the white paper policy, Ben-Gurion had outdone even his earlier use of violence against his Palestinian Jewish opponents by ordering the Hagana to collabo-rate with the British in their struggle against the Revisionist underground groups. This decision had led to an eight-month manhunt conducted by the Hagana, that has gone down in history as the *saison,* the "hunting season," and which had resulted in hundreds of members of these organizations be-ing handed over to the British. Only Menachem Begin's adamant insistence that his followers refrain from resistance had averted civil war.

Now, with hope of political deliverance from the white paper dashed and the *saison* discredited among broad sections of Palestinian Jewry, Ben-Gurion decided on another of his full-throttle policy reversals: He ordered the Hagana to join in a united resistance against the British alongside the same groups he had only months before branded as enemies. That fall, a matter of months after the end of the war in Europe, Hagana forces joined the Irgun and Lehi in operations against British targets throughout Palestine, including railways, telephone installations, oil refineries, and police naval craft. In early 1946, attacks were carried out on British police and radar stations, a coast-guard base, the Lydda and Kfar Syrkin airstrips and the military base at Sarafand.

In the meantime, the British determined that they could hardly ignore Truman's request to allow Jewish refugees in Europe to emigrate to Palestine. Buying time, Britain agreed to the dispatch of yet another study commission—what became known as the Anglo-American Commission of Inquiry—which held hearings in Washington, New York, London, the Displaced Persons Camps in Europe, Cairo, Jerusalem, Beirut, Amman, Damascus, Baghdad, and Riyadh, before retiring to Lausanne, Switzerland at the end of March 1946 to ruminate on its experiences. Among those who testified was Albert Einstein, who once again rejected the idea of a Jewish state, insisting that Palestine should be ruled by the United Nations.[81] Lessing Rosenwald appeared as well, reasoning that a Jewish state would of necessity be one based on racial or religious foundations, in which the Jews would dominate others, and so would lead to war.[82] The Protestant theologian Reinhold Niebuhr, on the other hand, demanded a Jewish majority and a Jewish state, as did Leo Baeck, the former leader of German Jewry, who had survived the Theresienstadt concentration camp.[83] In Jerusalem, Buber and Magnes, speaking for Ihud, advocated a federal Arab-Jewish government in Palestine under UN authority, as a step toward binational independence, and perhaps a Near Eastern federation in which the Arabs would have such an overwhelming majority that they would no longer feel a need to oppose Jewish immigration.[84]

Amid this cacophony, Ben-Gurion and the representatives of the ZO strained to explain just why one might believe—less than a year after the liberation of Auschwitz—that there should be a Jewish state. "When we say 'Jewish independence' or a 'Jewish state,'" he told the commission, "we mean Jewish safety, security. . . . If there is one thing a Jew lacks everywhere, it is security. Even in countries where he seems secure, he lacks the feeling of security. Why? Because even if he is safe, he has not provided his safety for himself. Somebody else provides for his security. . . . We came here to take care of ourselves."[85] Most of the commission was unimpressed, and when its report became public on May 1, 1946, its recommendations were similar to those presented by Ihud and the other opponents of the Jewish state. While calling for an end to discriminatory land laws and the facilitation of Jewish immigration into the country, the committee utterly rejected Jewish independence, since the establishment of any independent state, Jewish or otherwise, would bring certain war. Instead, the British Mandate was to continue, eventually giving way to a UN trusteeship, whose mission would be to bring about a "self-governing state, guarding the rights of Muslim, Jew, and Christian alike." The mandatory or trustee administration should effectively renounce the Balfour Declaration, "proclaiming the principle that Arab economic, educational, and political advancement in Palestine is of equal importance with that of the Jews."[86]

The report of the Anglo-American commission was the first clear statement of British and American postwar intentions concerning Zionism—and a bitter defeat for the Zionist Organization. Not even the death of most of the Jews in Europe seemed to have affected Anglo-American officialdom, and for a moment, it appeared that the labors invested over six long years by Ben-Gurion, Weizmann, and Silver had been for nothing. Both Ihud and the American Council for Judaism, on the other hand, were quick to claim victory. The director of the council, Elmer Berger, described the committee's report as a "Magna Carta," which had done for the cause of "integration" in Palestine—that is, the political integration of Arabs and Jews in a single polity—what the Balfour Declaration had done for Jewish nationalism; he and Rosenwald prepared for an all-out political offensive supporting implementation of the plan.[87] Magnes left Palestine immediately in order to campaign for implementation of the committee's recommendations, stopping in Cairo to lobby the secretary-general of the Arab League, Azam Pasha, later known for his threats of genocide against the Jews of Israel.[88] From there he proceeded to the United States, where he stayed for six months, working to deepen support for the report in the American government and among "non-Zionist" members of the Jewish Agency. He continued to devote articles, pamphlets, and radio appearances to explaining the virtues of binationalism in both America and England. Perhaps the demand of the Jews for a state could be brought to naught after all.

Ben-Gurion understood the meaning of the commission's report as well as Magnes and his friends did, and after publication of the Anglo-American commission's recommendations in May, the underground organizations went into action as well, blowing up trains, destroying bridges connecting Palestine to the neighboring Arab states, and kidnapping a number of British officers. The British retaliated on Saturday, June 29—"Black Sabbath"—occupying the Jewish Agency's offices in Jerusalem and Tel Aviv and arresting nearly three thousand Jewish leaders throughout the country. The Zionist Organization was effectively outlawed, with only a few of its Palestinian leaders escaping arrest. One was Ben-Gurion, who had been out of the country in Paris; another was Weizmann, who took advantage of the chaos to order an end to Hagana violence against the British.[89] But the Jabotinskyite organizations resolved to carry on their campaign, on July 22, 1946, bombing the headquarters of the British administration's Criminal Investigations Division in the King David Hotel, demolishing the hotel's entire south wing, and killing ninety-one people. Thereafter, they maintained a constant pressure of shootings and bombings aimed at British military personnel. This campaign was so successful that by mid-1947, British civilians and dependents had been evacuated from the country and nearly 100,000 British military personnel had withdrawn into a life of imprisonment in security areas enclosed by barbed wire.

Late summer 1946 was the nadir of Ben-Gurion's campaign to bring the state into being, with both Jewish diplomacy in America and the Hagana's military options in Palestine apparently at a dead end. Fearful that the Zionist Executive was about to be replaced as Britain's negotiating partner in Palestine by Jews who would be more pliable—perhaps Weizmann, perhaps Ihud—Ben-Gurion decided on another gamble, pronouncing at a rump meeting of the Jewish Agency Executive in Paris that he would be willing to "moderate" the Zionist diplomatic line. Four years earlier, the Biltmore Platform had been passed with the tacit assumption that there would be millions of Jewish refugees in Europe at war's end, making an immediate Jewish majority feasible in all of western Palestine. Now these millions were no longer among the living, and a Jewish majority could probably be created only in a part of the country. The ZO, of course, had not rushed to scale down its claims. No one wanted to grant Hitler yet another success. But now, Ben-Gurion had the chance to make a diplomatic virtue of what was otherwise only ugly necessity. He offered a "compromise," according to which he would be ready to discuss any plan granting the Jews autonomy—including control over immigration—in an "adequate" part of Palestine.[90]

The Zionist Organization's proposal came at precisely the moment that American officials not previously sympathetic to the aim of a Jewish state, and even some Jewish anti-Zionists, were reaching the end of their ability to stomach Britain's position on the refugees. It had now become clear that Britain would go to war against the Jews of Palestine rather than allow Holocaust survivors to enter the country. As against this policy, which was becoming more tyrannical with every passing week, Ben-Gurion's "compromise" seemed to offer a way out, perhaps the only way out. As American secretary of war Robert Patterson told Joseph Proskauer: "It makes sense . . . I don't know what to do with these poor people anymore. MacDonald's White Paper keeps them out of Israel. I can't get them into America because of our terrible immigration laws. I'm for it."[91]

Proskauer himself was an outspoken anti-Zionist and heir to Felix Warburg as head of New York's German-Jewish community, but he too began to feel his opposition to the Jewish state slipping before the reality of hundreds of thousands of Jews languishing in Displaced Persons Camps and detention camps. Two weeks after news of Ben-Gurion's initiative,

Proskauer issued an unprecedented statement, supporting the Jewish Agency's effort to create a "governmental unit" capable of accepting Jewish immigration into Palestine. The reason for this historic shift in a community that had for so long greeted the Jewish state with unbending hostility was the pressure of reality. Even hard-core emancipationists could now see that a national home for homeless Jews was a dire necessity, and that Herzl might have been correct in his belief that such a home could not exist in the absence of sovereign Jewish power. Proskauer masterfully hinted as much in a speech in which he signaled the change that had taken place in the American Jewish Committee: "If we can get it with partition, let's get it that way. If we can get it without partition, let's get it that way. If we can get it without a state, let's get it; *and if we can get it with a state, let's get it.* But let's get immigration into Palestine."[92] Proskauer would soon become one of the ZO's most important allies in the political struggle to secure American and United Nations support for the establishment of the Jewish state.

Ben-Gurion's partition proposal had a similar effect on Harry Truman. On Yom Kippur eve, October 4, 1946, Truman reiterated his demand for large-scale Jewish immigration into Palestine and for the first time signaled that a Jewish state might well be the only means of achieving such immigration. "The Jewish Agency," he said, has "proposed a solution to the Palestine problem by means of the creation of a viable Jewish state in control of its own immigration and economic policies in an adequate area of Palestine. . . . It is my belief that a solution along these lines would command the support of public opinion in the United States."[93]

Truman's Yom Kippur address caused pandemonium among opponents of the Jewish state, with State Department officials warning that the president's policy would lead to "bloodshed and chaos."[94] In London, too, the president's words were greeted with anger. But it was also becoming evident that Britain would not be able maintain its course. Seeking to regain lost ground, the British veered sharply toward a more conciliatory policy, releasing imprisoned Zionist leaders and issuing an amnesty for Ben-Gurion and Hagana commander Moshe Sneh. But these steps were far too little, far too late. The first postwar Zionist Congress, held in Basel in December 1946, was dominated by a hard-line coalition led by Ben-Gurion and Abba Hillel Silver, which again endorsed the Jewish state as the immediate Jewish aim. Weizmann, who had denounced the use of force against Britain, was removed from the presidency of the ZO, and Ben-Gurion, now the undisputed head of the Zionist movement, was given the defense portfolio.

Only overwhelming British force, it seemed, would now achieve the goal of an Arab-dominated Palestine, and without at least tacit American support, such a policy would be doomed from the outset. Two months later, on

February 14, 1947, British foreign secretary Ernest Bevin, speaking for a government exhausted by its inability to mold American opinion and tormented by its inability to end Jewish underground operations in Palestine, pronounced that "the whole problem" was to be referred to the United Nations.[95] British rule in Palestine was dying, and the future of the country had now been thrown wide open.

The last phase of the political battle over Palestine began on April 28, 1947, with the opening of deliberations on the subject in the General Assembly of the United Nations. Abba Hillel Silver presented the case of the Jews on behalf of the Zionist Organization, ascribing the violence in Palestine to Britain's determination to abort the mission of the mandate. Silver demanded that the UN inquire into "why shiploads of helpless refugees . . . who have been through all the hells of Nazi Europe, are being driven away from the Jewish national home by a Mandatory government which assumed as its prime obligation the facilitation of Jewish immigration into that country." The goal of establishing a Jewish national home, he told the assembled delegates, "must now be fully restored."[96]

The Zionist Organization now had the ear of the world, and its opponents worked frantically to make sure that its message would be rejected. Ihud began distribution in the United States of a heavy English-language publication entitled "Towards Union in Palestine," in which professors and administrators at the Hebrew University—including Martin Buber, Judah Magnes, Ernst Simon, and the university's leading historian, Richard Koebner—expressed their opposition to the establishment of a Jewish state in Palestine.[97] The American Council for Judaism, too, initiated a broad series of contacts with the American government. And the State Department began work on a series of plans for a UN trusteeship in Palestine, which would lead to an in independent Palestine with a stable Arab majority but which would "continue to provide a Jewish national home in its spiritual and cultural aspects"—a plan that quickly won the support of Secretary of State George Marshall.[98]

After two weeks of deliberations, the United Nations determined that it, too, would have to send a commission to investigate the situation in Palestine. Consisting of representatives from Australia, Canada, Czechoslovakia, Guatemala, Holland, India, Iran, Peru, Sweden, Uruguay, and Yugoslavia, the United Nations Special Committee on Palestine was given "the widest powers" to investigate "all issues and problems relevant to the problem of Palestine," holding hearings in Palestine during June and July with the country quaking beneath its feet. The commission's hearings were rocked by another round of strikes in the Arab sector and by the British government's decision to resume hanging Jews associated with the underground—a policy that provoked the Irgun to hang two British servicemen in retaliation, in turn triggering the murder of five Jewish civilians by rampaging British troops in Tel Aviv. At the same time, the Hagana ship *Exodus* left the French port of Sète for Palestine with 4,550 Jewish refugees on board. After being tracked for a week by British warships, the *Exodus* was boarded off the coast of Haifa, touching off a melee in which British troops fought Holocaust survivors for possession of the ship. Three Jews were killed and scores wounded, with the entire event being broadcast by live radio to Hagana headquarters, which released it to the world press. Outraged, British foreign secretary Ernest Bevin ordered the survivors returned to Europe, removing them from shipboard by force and depositing them in internment camps in Germany. There, they refused to speak to their captors when addressed, other than to utter the words *eretz israel*—"the land of Israel."

It was against this backdrop that Magnes rose to give testimony before the UN commission on behalf of Ihud. Claiming that he would like to create a Jewish state if he could, Magnes emphasized that this was impossible. "We are here in this country with two peoples," he said, "[and] so long as it is inhabited by two peoples, the Jewish people will have to do without the state, as it has done for many hundreds of years."[99]

Ben-Gurion, too, testified. But this time it was a different Ben-Gurion who took the podium: For the first time, he appeared as the undisputed leader of the Zionist Organization and the de facto leader of the Jewish people—in Palestine, in America, and in the Displaced Persons Camps in Europe—which had overwhelmingly given its blessing to the cause for which he had struggled for five decades. This people, he told the committee, had suffered enough for its statelessness, and it would bear its suffering no more. As for the claims of men such as Buber and Magnes and their allies, he rejected them outright:

> By depriving the Jews in Palestine of a national home, by preventing them from becoming a majority and attaining statehood, you are depriving not only the 600,000 Jews who are here, but also the millions of Jews who are still left in the world, of independence and statehood . . . A Jewish minority in an Arab state [of Palestine], even with the most ideal paper guarantee, would mean the final extinction of Jewish hope, not in Palestine alone, but for the entire Jewish people.[100]

The committee finished its report on August 31, and for once, the moral and political confusion that had reigned in so many other reports on Palestine dissipated. With Britain now practically one of the combatants, the commission was able to decide unanimously to end the mandate.

Palestine was to be granted independence. Seven of the participating nations voted for partition and the creation of an independent Jewish state in keeping with the aims of the ZO; three others, India, Iran, and Yugoslavia supported a binational federal state in which foreign policy, defense, and immigration would be determined by a legislature in which an Arab majority would be assured.[101] With most of the commission supporting partition and Jewish independence, a supportive majority in the General Assembly appeared likely. But how large a majority? The procedures of the United Nations called for "important questions" to be settled by a two-thirds majority,[102] and Ben-Gurion, Sharett, and Silver now poured all the strength the Zionist Organization possessed into the effort to forge the implausible coalition of Western, Communist, and Latin American states on which the Zionist dream now depended. Weizmann, too, was brought in to speak about the international commitments made to him as the representative of the Jewish people, declaring that "full, sovereign independence for the Jewish national home was clearly envisaged by the authors of the Mandate," and that nothing could be done to make viable the idea of a "binational" and Arab-dominated state such as that proposed by the minority of the UN committee. The Jewish community in Palestine "would burst out of such an unnatural framework."[103]

In the battle to secure the two-thirds majority, the Zionists received vital assistance from Joseph Proskauer's American Jewish Committee, which made use of its banking connections to place pressure on Latin American governments and used its ties to the Alliance Israélite to influence the French. Another formerly hostile organization, the Jewish Labor Alliance headed by David Dubinsky, similarly mounted round-the-clock operations aimed at activating its connections to American labor leaders and European socialists, who in turn used their influence to swing votes in Europe, Mexico, Liberia, and Ethiopia.[104] Ihud, of course, responded to these defections from its cause with anger, with Magnes pronouncing, at a speech before the assembled faculty and students of the university, that the Jews in Palestine and America who were now fighting on the side of the Zionist Organization had "left the Jewish tradition of purity and holiness" in favor of an official ideology of "Zionist totalitarianism, which seeks to extend its rule over the entire people . . . if necessary by means of power and violence." Only at the Hebrew University, concluded Magnes, could there be found an institution that, "in spite of all the votes of the majority," continued to hold out against "the totalitarian idea."[105]

On November 29, the United Nations voted, by a margin of 33 to 13, to accept the partition of Palestine.[106] Jews throughout the world greeted the decision with jubilation, but the rejoicing was short-lived. Already on the day after the vote, Arabs opened fire on a Jewish bus, killing five. The next day

Arabs rioted in Jerusalem, leaving seven Jews dead. In the weeks that followed, Jewish casualties in Palestine rose into the hundreds, even as Arab mobs attacked Jews in Egypt, Syria, Iraq, Yemen, and other Arab states. In the meantime, the United States announced an arms embargo on Palestine, and Britain declared that its troops would unilaterally evacuate the country by May 15, 1948—leaving the country without a government. The Arabs recognized that London's strategy was to create a chaos that would result in an Arab state in Palestine, and they set about realizing this policy. In January, three months before the planned British withdrawal, Syrian paramilitary units began operations in northern Palestine with the aim of bringing the Galilee under Arab control, while at the same time forces loyal to Amin al-Husseini escalated attacks on Jewish positions in and around Jerusalem.

The Jews were now fighting in the hills of the Galilee and Judea in a wall-to-wall coalition the likes of which the early Zionists had only dreamed possible: The Labor Zionist followers of Ben-Gurion and Tabenkin fought side by side with members of Hashomer Hatzair, who had only recently supported a binational state in Palestine; with contingents from the Jabotinskyite underground groups; and with black-coated haredi youths whose rabbis had been critical of a secular Jewish state.[107] In America as well, the war against Jewish Palestine brought together virtually all Jews— including New York's German Jewry—in support of the effort to bring the state into being, a phenomenon vividly described by Hannah Arendt, herself one of the Jewish state's only remaining Jewish opponents:

> There is now no organization and almost no individual Jew that doesn't privately or publicly support partition and the establishment of a Jewish state. Jewish left-wing intellectuals who a relatively short time ago still looked down upon Zionism as an ideology for the feeble-minded . . . Jewish businessmen whose interest in Jewish politics had always been determined by the all-important question of how to keep the Jews out of the newspaper headlines; Jewish philanthropists who had resented Palestine as a terribly expensive charity, draining off funds from other "more worthy" purposes; the readers of the Yiddish press, who for decades had been sincerely, if naively, convinced that America was the promised land—all these, from the Bronx to Park Avenue down to Greenwich Village and over to Brooklyn are united today in the firm conviction that a Jewish state is needed . . . that the reign of terror by the Irgun and the Stern groups is more or less justified, and that Rabbi Silver, David Ben-Gurion, and Moshe Sharett are the real, if somewhat too moderate, statesmen of the Jewish people.[108]

Yet as Palestine descended into anarchy, the opposition to the Jewish state rapidly began to reclaim ground. Only ten weeks after the UN vote, Arab forces were doing so well that the State Department began preparing the ground for an American offensive to rescind partition, in late February informing Truman that since the partition resolution could clearly not be implemented, the only recourse would be the State Department's plan for a UN trusteeship. The anti-Zionist counteroffensive involved pressures on the secretary of state and the president, as well as a redoubled public relations offensive, including the creation of a new Christian organization called the "Committee for Justice and Peace in the Holy Land," assembled with the assistance of American officials and Jewish anti-Zionists with the express aim of lobbying for a reversal of the UN vote in favor of partition.[109]

By the beginning of March, the tilt against partition within the American administration had become evident to all. Only Truman himself remained ominously silent. On March 18, the ZO succeeded in spiriting Weizmann into the White House for an unpublicized, off-the-record meeting, in which Truman assured the aging Jewish leader that American policy would be determined by his personal commitment to the partition plan,[110] but even this assurance failed to dispel the sense of looming disaster. Only a day later, Warren Austin announced at the United Nations that the American government had decided "that a temporary trusteeship for Palestine should be established under the Trusteeship Council of the United Nations."[111] Release of the speech was apparently a maneuver designed to force Truman's hand by prematurely pronouncing what was in effect a backup plan as though it were settled policy. On his office calendar, the president scribbled, "This morning I find that the State Department has reversed my Palestine policy. The first I know about it is what I see in the papers. Isn't that hell? I am now in the position of a liar and a double-crosser. I've never felt so in my life."[112]

Although Truman sent his reassurances to the Zionists,[113] his words could not now alter the fact, understood clearly by all, that a UN trusteeship in Palestine was a live option in the American administration—and one that could yet snuff out the plan for a Jewish state, perhaps forever. At the United Nations, Silver declared that the partition plan was the minimum that the Jewish people would be willing to accept and that proposals calling for further sacrifice "will have to be imposed on the Jewish community in Palestine by force."[114] Under Silver's guidance, the anguished reactions of American Jews to the administration's about-face were poured into the open, with protest rallies staged by the Jewish War Veterans, B'nai Brith, Jewish labor, Orthodox and Conservative rabbis, and Agudat Israel, culminating in a demonstration on April 4 by 100,000 people in Madison Square Park and a tidal wave of letters asking the president to save the Jewish state.[115] Non-Jews reacted with great emotion as well, with the author Thomas Mann, for example, decrying the American reversal under threat of Arab violence as "the most humiliating and revolting political event since the treachery against Czechoslovakia in 1938."[116]

None of this moved Buber and his circle, however, who were so pleased by the revival of the State Department's UN trusteeship plan that they plastered Palestine with placards declaring, "Long live the Jewish-Arab Union of Peace."[117] Lessing Rosenwald reacted similarly, calling for an immediate truce in Palestine, reconsideration of the partition decision, and a UN trusteeship for an indefinite period.[118] In April, with the deadline for the British withdrawal only weeks away, Hannah Arendt prepared an article for publication in *Commentary,* in which she denounced the "fanaticism and hysteria" that had brought almost all of Jewry to demand a Jewish state, calling for the Zionist Organization to be "denied authority" in Palestine. Instead, Arendt called upon the United Nations to "summon up the courage to take an unprecedented step" of opening negotiations with Ihud and non-Zionist Jews, whom she believed would be willing to reach an agreement "at once"—along with unnamed moderate Arabs—to hand Palestine over to foreign troops.[119]

Magnes went even farther, calling upon the United Nations "in its wisdom and strength" to *force* a cease-fire on the Jewish and Arab combatants, because "we need the authority and might of the Security Council to make us lay down our arms."[120] This was, of course, music to the anti-Zionists' ears, and on April 21, Lessing Rosenwald and other leading anti-Zionists brought the Hebrew University president to the United States to attempt to sell this idea in meetings with Secretary of State Marshall, UN ambassador Warren Austin, British colonial secretary Arthur Creech-Jones, representatives of the French government, and leaders of major Jewish American bodies.[121] Marshall, at least, was so dumbfounded to hear Magnes speak of "imposing" foreign trusteeship on Palestine that he had to stop and check whether he had heard him correctly. "When you say 'impose,'" he asked Magnes, "that means, does it not, the use of military force?" When Magnes affirmed that he had heard correctly, the secretary of state said that such a plan did not seem advisable to him, but he was sufficiently impressed that he promised to consider the idea, even arranging for an unscheduled meeting with Truman so that he could hear Magnes out.[122]

By the time Magnes's operations were in full swing in Washington, however, the military constellation in Palestine, which in February had led to the revival of the idea of UN trusteeship, had for the first time turned in favor of the Jews. In late April, Jewish forces succeeded in breaking Arab resistance in Haifa and Tiberias, and further victories in Safed, Jaffa, and in the mountain passes leading up to Jerusalem followed shortly. But in early May, with only days left before the British pullout, opponents of the Jewish state in Washington nevertheless made their last, desperate bid to avert a declaration of Jewish independence. The State Department offered the Zionists a diplomatic package that was to include a cease-fire, non-declaration of either an Arab or a Jewish state, an embargo on arms and manpower entering Palestine, and the establishment of a UN committee as the highest authority in the country. To sweeten the offer, Marshall, who had been American chief of staff during World War II, warned Moshe Sharett that the assessments of the Jewish military in Palestine could not be relied upon and that the Jewish state would not be able to expect help from the United States if things went badly.[123]

On Wednesday, May 12, the invasion of Palestine by the armies of the neighboring Arab states began with an assault by Jordanian forces on the Jewish settlements in Gush Etzion, south of Jerusalem, that ended in the massacre of 240 inhabitants. That same day, Ben-Gurion faced grim deliberations before the Jewish emergency government[124] and the Labor Central Committee over the American plan to postpone the declaration of the state. Although Ben-Gurion had ordered the clandestine importation of heavy weaponry and factories for the production of arms as early as the summer of 1945, the results of three years of efforts were mixed. Of all the weapons needed to stave off a mechanized invasion with aerial support, only one piece of equipment had thus far gone into production: "Piat" antitank charges, which were being manufactured in secret factories around the country. Only a handful of artillery pieces had as yet arrived; no aircraft had made it into Palestine at all. Most of the weapons that had been purchased by emissaries of the ZO were still abroad or on shipboard. Moreover, rumors that Britain would lift the sea blockade allowing Jewish immigrants to arrive freely were as yet unsubstantiated, and the threat loomed that British gunboats would continue to prevent Jewish immigration even after the declaration of a Jewish state. On Monday, May 10, Ben-Gurion had reported to the Histadrut Executive, "It would be correct, it seems to me, if I say that overall we are not ready. We don't have the power necessary to withstand the possible invasion."[125]

But if the danger of invasion was great, the danger of relying on the foreign powers was if anything worse. UN rule in Palestine would mean the reversal of the international support that had been proffered for Jewish independence a few months earlier. And having reversed its decision to partition Palestine once, the chances that such a decision would be made a second time were nonexistent.[126] There remained only one path to the Jewish state: The vacuum left by the withdrawal of British authority on May 14 had to be filled immediately by a new and sovereign Jewish power. Not all of Ben-Gurion's colleagues in the ZO saw this as clearly as he did. Fearful at the prospect of taking so great a responsibility on themselves, two Labor leaders flew to Paris to ask the advice of Leon Blum, the Jewish socialist and former president of France. The old non-Zionist told them that Ben-Gurion was right: "It's now, or never."[127]

On Wednesday, Ben-Gurion brought the American proposal to a vote in the Jewish emergency government, where he succeeded in mustering six out of the ten votes for rejection of trusteeship—thus securing the decision to declare independence by a single vote. That night, the Labor Central Committee brushed aside feeble opposition to independence at a meeting that lasted past midnight. On Friday, May 14, 1948, fifty-two years after the publication of Herzl's pamphlet, and with war impending on all sides, the Jewish state was declared.

PART

IV

CHAPTER 11

Ben-Gurion's Jewish State and Buber's Dissent, 1948–1961

Ｏｎ Friday, May 14, 1948, minutes before 3:00 P.M., the National Assembly[1] endorsed the text of the Jewish declaration of independence. With this, it assumed the role of a sovereign legislative assembly in Palestine, immediately thereafter suspending the white paper that had excluded the Jews from Palestine for nine years and appointing a temporary government with Ben-Gurion at its head, including representatives of all Jewish political parties in the country—from the Communists to Agudat Israel.[2] A public ceremony followed in which those members of the new legislature who were not trapped in besieged Jerusalem signed the declaration of independence, and a band played the Jewish nationalist anthem, "Hatikva" ("The Hope"). Ben-Gurion closed the meeting with this pronouncement: "The state of Israel is established." In his diary, he wrote: "Jewish independence has been declared."[3]

And, indeed, the document that was adopted was a declaration of *Jewish* independence: It designated no specific territorial base, reflecting only the subjective decision of the Jewish people to establish its own sovereign state. The declaration emphasized that Jewish people in exile had "never ceased to pray and hope . . . for the restoration of its political freedom," and that the European cataclysm was "a clear demonstration of the urgency of solving the problem of their homelessness by reestablishing in the land of Israel a Jewish state which would open the gates of the homeland wide to every Jew." And while the United Nations resolution of November 1947 was cited, it was only the Jewish people in Palestine and in the Diaspora that was recognized as having the authority to establish a Jewish state:

> This recognition by the United Nations of the right of the Jewish people to establish its state is irrevocable. This right is the natural right of the Jewish people to be masters of their own fate, like all other nations, in their own sovereign state. Accordingly we, members of the People's Council, representatives of the Jewish community of the land of Israel and of the Zionist movement . . . hereby declare the establishment of a Jewish state in the land of Israel, to be known as the state of Israel.

In all, the Jewish declaration of independence uses the term *medina yehudit*, "the Jewish state," or otherwise refers to the restored political independence of "the sovereign Jewish people" no fewer than nine times, and its meaning can be disputed by no honest interpreter. The state that was declared was no social-contract state such as Rousseau or Kant had demanded. It was not a neutral or universal or binational or multinational state such as Hermann Cohen and Martin Buber, Judah Magnes, Lessing Rosenwald, and the American State Department wished to see established. For better or worse, the state of Israel founded in 1948 was in the most explicit way possible the guardian-state of which Herzl had written in *The Jewish State*—a state in which non-Jewish residents were invited "to participate in the upbuilding of the state on the basis of full and equal citizenship," but one whose meaning, mission, and purpose would nevertheless be derived from "the right of the Jewish people to be masters of their own fate . . . in their own sovereign state."[4]

Ben-Gurion's reading of the declaration of independence was broadcast live on Friday afternoon at 4:00 P.M. But even before word had reached Washington of its contents, Harry Truman had already prepared—without so much as bothering to inform the State Department—a statement of recognition of Ben-Gurion's government. Since he did not yet know the name of the state that was declared, Truman's communiqué read: "This Government has been informed that a Jewish state has been proclaimed in Palestine, and recognition has been requested by the Government thereof. The United States recognizes the provisional government as the de facto authority of the new Jewish state." Only later was the name "Israel" added.[5]

The next day, Egyptian aircraft began bombing missions against Tel Aviv, and on Saturday night, after the conclusion of the sabbath, Ben-Gurion again took the microphone to speak to the newborn state, now under invasion on four fronts. He announced that the United States had become the first nation to recognize the new state, and that an Egyptian warplane had been downed, the pilot taken prisoner, and the craft itself added to the "Jewish air force."[6] By this time, opposition to the Jewish state had virtually disappeared from the Jewish world. After the gas chambers and all that had transpired since, few Jews remained who could not feel tears of pride with the announcement of the existence of a "Jewish air force." The state declared by Ben-Gurion—Israel—had really become the state of the Jewish people.

For weeks, the success of the Jewish military effort hung in the balance. The Egyptian army had seized the Negev and thrust up the coast toward Tel Aviv from the south; Jordanian and Iraqi forces had secured the highlands east of Tel Aviv and threatened to sever the narrow corridor leading up to Jerusalem. The Jordanian siege of the Old City of Jerusalem ended with the collapse of the Jewish defenders. Only after a cease-fire was declared on June 11 did weapons and ammunition, combat aircraft and artillery pieces, begin to arrive in quantities from Czechoslovakia and France, with substantial assistance from Jewish communities in the Diaspora. It was this successful supply operation that tilted the balance of forces, despite Arab efforts to build up their formations. When the fighting resumed, the IDF was able to drive Arab forces out of the coastal plain and then the Galilee; toward the end of the year, the Egyptians were routed in the Negev and in Sinai. But Ben-Gurion's efforts to defeat Jordanian forces under British command in the Samarian hills ended in dismal failure, and the Old City of Jerusalem remained in Arab hands. By the time the war had ended on January 8, 1949, over 6,000 Jews—one percent of the Jewish population—had been killed in the fighting.

The Jewish state, for so many years no more than an idea, had established itself politically by holding its own on the field of battle. On January 25, general elections were held in which Ben-Gurion's Labor party won 46 seats out of 120 in the new legislative assembly. His first government followed Herzl's model, rejecting a coalition with the parties of the Left in favor of an alliance with the United Religious party. The small Progressive and Sephardi lists were also represented. But the work of forging the Jewish state did not end with the achievement of victory on the battlefield and the establishment of an elected government. It was only just beginning.

The Jewish settlement in Palestine had always viewed itself as the guardian of the interests of the Jews as a whole, and now it had to be transformed into a Jewish sovereign power. This effort of construction was evidenced in a host of specialized laws, administrative measures, legal rulings, and accepted norms of political behavior that began filling out the conception of the Jewish state as a tool, as Ben-Gurion liked to say, "for the redemption of Israel." Among these was the Law of Return, passed unanimously by the Knesset in 1950, which granted the automatic right of immigration to any Jew in the world who wished to take up residence in Israel. Ben-Gurion considered this law "to contain in itself the aim of the 'ingathering of the exiles,'"[7] a concept drawn from the prophesies of the Bible and the traditional Jewish prayer service, as well as from Herzl's writings.[8] And this vision was immediately given practical meaning by Ben-Gurion's activist policy of seeking out communities in the Jewish dispersion that could be brought to Israel. As a result of hard and dangerous work done by the emissaries of the state and its security services, nearly all of the survivors in the Displaced Persons Camps in Europe and the great majority of the Jews of the Arab world were soon "ingathered" into Zion. The fledgling state's Jewish population, which had stood at 650,000 in 1948 had more than doubled—rising to 1.4 million—four years later.

Moreover, under the Nationality Law (1952), Jews arriving in Israel were formally recognized in state records as being of Jewish nationality—perhaps the most important step in fusing the diverse diasporas into a single Jewish people, not only in theory but in practice. (A later effort by a Jewish individual to be registered as being of "Israeli" nationality was rejected by the courts, on the grounds that the creation of an "Israeli nation" in place of the Jewish one was inconsistent with Israel's character as the Jewish state.)[9] Other critical steps were taken in the realm of what Herzl had called "imponderables," symbols whose power resides in their ability to mold a public, Jewish identity for the state. Thus, the Flag and Emblem Law (1949) formalized the earlier decision of the provisional government, which had selected the banner of the Zionist Organization as the flag of the new state, whose design includes representations of the star of David and the traditional Jewish prayer shawl, its azure-and-white coloration being a reference to the hue in the Jewish fringed garments of antiquity.[10] The state seal, too, was the emotionally laden image of the *menora*, the ceremonial candelabrum in the Temple in Jerusalem, which had been infamously portrayed being born into captivity on the Arch of Titus in Rome. It was this ancient symbol of Jewish grief that was now adopted as the emblem of Jewish national restoration. No national anthem was formally adopted, but in practice the hymn of the Jewish state was "Hatikva" ("The Hope"), the anthem of the Zionist movement.

Under the Law and Government Ordinance (1948), the official days of rest of the state were declared to be the Jewish Sabbath and the traditional festivals of the Jewish calendar. Protection for the Sabbath as a personal day of rest for Jews was similarly afforded by the Hours of Rest and Work Law (1951).[11] And although Arabic remained an "official" language from the time of the mandate, Israeli laws and court decisions are written in Hebrew, and knowledge of Hebrew was required by the Nationality Law as a condition for acquiring citizenship through naturalization.[12] Among the most important symbols is the declaration of independence itself, which, beginning in 1948, was held by the Israeli courts to be a constitutional document embodying "the aspirations of the people and its fundamental credo."[13] But perhaps the most important symbol of all was the name of the state: "Israel"—the traditional Hebrew name for the Jewish people itself.

In addition to such laws protecting the Jewish "character" of the state, Ben-Gurion's government sought to inculcate Jewish pride and loyalty on the part of the population through the medium of the government schools. This "spiritual ingathering" was mandated in the State Education Law (1953), which provided a mission for the entire educational system consonant with the purposes of the Jewish state as a whole. It opened by listing the aims of the state educational system, first and foremost among them being the inculcation of "the values of Jewish culture," "love of the homeland," and "loyalty to the state and to the Jewish people."[14] As Ben-Gurion later said, this law was intended to express "our aspiration to be a 'precious people' [am segula, "God's treasured people"] and a model state, and to maintain our continual connection with the Jewish people around the world." The State Education Law, together with the Law of Return, were for Ben-Gurion, "the highest laws of the State of Israel . . . which point the direction in which our state wishes to and must go if it is to exist and fulfill its historic purpose."[15]

Indeed, a few years later, the Ministry of Education, at Ben-Gurion's urging, issued a syllabus aimed at teaching nonreligious students "the light which is hidden in some of the customs that constitute the religious way of life." To this end, it sought to disseminate knowledge of "sabbath and holiday customs . . . the literature which describes the Jewish national and religious way of life; the structure of the prayer book and the high-holiday prayer book; prayers and festival hymns; the framework of the religious way of life (such as the scroll of the Law, procedures in reading of the Tora, prayer shawl and tefillin, mezuza, bar mitzva, and so forth)." And these instructions were in the toned-down version issued after the parties of the Left had insisted that the original was too religious.[16]

But the Jewish aims of the state school system were only a part in Ben-Gurion's campaign to foster a *public* Judaism around which the young Jewish country could unite. He himself kept a Bible on his desk in the prime minister's office, held a biweekly Bible study session in his home, and at one point even called a press conference to announce a new interpretation he had hit upon.[17] Similarly, the state stepped in to fund the Maccabia, a quadrennial olympics for Jews from around the world, and government radio carried live broadcasts of the annual Bible contest for Jewish youth from around the world. The Hebrew language was supported by the Institute for the Science of the Hebrew Language Law (1953), which created a state-funded academy to research, develop, and advance the national language. Similarly, the national library was not merely the library of the state but the "Jewish National and University Library," which was also to be the library of the Jewish people, with a mandate to collect books, periodicals, documents, and manuscripts reflecting the life and culture of the Jews throughout history. The Broadcasting Authority Law (1965) likewise stated that the mission of state-operated radio and television was to be, among others, "strengthening the connection with the Jewish heritage."[18]

One of the most striking aspects of Israel's character as the Jewish state was its relationship to Germany and the crimes committed against the Jewish people in the years before the founding of Israel. If the new democratic German state of Konrad Adenauer had to take steps on behalf of the German people to compensate, if at all possible, for the crimes committed against the Jews, it was the Jewish state that similarly assumed responsibility for the response of the Jewish people to what had taken place. As Ben-Gurion emphasized, "the Jewish state, which is called Israel, is heir to the six million . . . For these millions . . . regarded themselves as the sons of the Jewish people, and *only* as the sons of the Jewish people [i.e., not as Poles or Lithuanians]. If they had lived, the great majority of them would have come to Israel."[19]

This approach of kinship to the murdered millions—a great many of whom were of course direct relations of Palestinian Jewry—expressed itself in a series of laws and policies, all of which asserted a legal and moral relationship between the Jewish state and the European Jews who had been murdered outside its borders, and before it had even been created. The first of these, the Nazi and Nazi Collaborators Punishment Law (1950), asserted the legal right of the Jewish state to punish German war criminals for "a crime against the Jewish people."[20] The most famous of the operations conducted under the rubric of this law was, of course, the capture of Adolf Eichmann in Argentina by the Israeli security services, which brought him to trial in Jerusalem for his leading role in the German extermination program. But there were other less-publicized anti-Nazi operations of the Jewish state's security service, including the elimination of Nazi leaders who had escaped formal justice and had found safe haven outside of Germany.[21] Similarly, when in 1952 Ben-Gurion's government concluded negotiations with the West German government over reparations for the war crimes committed by Hitler's Germany, it did so on behalf of the Jewish people as a whole.[22] Other steps taken by the Labor Zionist government with regard to the fate of European Jewry included the Holocaust Memorial Law (1953), which created a state authority, called Yad Vashem, whose task was to study the Holocaust and conduct activities in memory of its victims; and the Martyrs' and Heroes' Remembrance Day Law (1959), which established a national day of mourning in "commemoration of the disaster which the Nazis and their collaborators brought upon the Jewish people, and the acts of heroism and revolt performed in those days."[23]

The Labor Zionist government also laid the foundations for a special constitutional relationship that would permit the Jewish people outside of Israel to participate in shaping the policies of the Jewish state. The 1952 Zionist Organization–Jewish Agency Status Law recognized the ZO as the agent empowered to continue immigration and absorption activities in Israel and implied a far broader international role as well, embracing the entire Jewish people:

> The State of Israel regards itself as the creation of the entire Jewish people . . . The mission of ingathering the exiles, which is the central task of the state of Israel and the Zionist movement in our days, requires constant efforts by the Jewish people in the diaspora; the state of Israel, therefore, looks to the cooperation of all Jews, as individuals and groups, in building up the state and assisting the immigration . . . [Israel] regards the unity of . . . Jewry as necessary for this purpose. The State of Israel looks to efforts on the part of the World Zionist Organization for achieving this unity.[24]

Subsequent Israeli government application of this law interpreted the Jewish Diaspora to be a legally recognized partner not only in securing the well-being of the Jewish state itself. It was also seen as a partner in fostering Hebrew-language study abroad, bringing Diaspora Jews for educational programs in Israel, deepening "Jewish consciousness and unity" among the Jews of the world, and combating "all signs of assimilation and denial of Jewish peoplehood."[25] Moreover, numerous specific laws of the Knesset grant the Jewish Agency and the ZO representation in Israeli government agencies, particularly where development of the country is concerned, in this way providing Diaspora Jewry with indirect responsibility within the structure of the Israeli government.[26]

On the question of land ownership, too, the government of Israel saw itself as an agent for the Jewish people, claiming and developing properties abandoned by Arab landowners during the War of Independence in order to settle Jewish refugees from Europe and from the Arab states. Under the Absentee Property Law (1950) and the Land Acquisition and Compensation Law (1953), the state of Israel in effect created a population and property exchange between the Arab and Jewish states, setting compensation for land acquired from Arabs during the military engagements and in effect compensating Jewish refugees from Arab countries, who had frequently been stripped of their possessions in those countries. Moreover, the Jewish National Fund Law (1953) paved the way for transferring portions of these lands to the Jewish National Fund (JNF), an affiliate of the ZO founded by Herzl, whose function was to purchase lands that could become "the perpetual property of the Jewish people." In the early years of the state, the JNF's central function became land reclamation work to make these lands hospitable for resettling the Jewish communities flooding into the state from the various diasporas.

In the same fashion, Ben-Gurion built the Israel Defense Forces as a Jewish national army. Although Israeli law theoretically required all residents to serve in the IDF, in practice the armed forces were recruited almost exclusively from the Jewish population. Indeed, during the War of Independence, the Jewish armed forces were substantially augmented, and in many cases commanded, by Diaspora Jews, including Paul Shulman, commander of the Israeli navy, and Mickey Marcus, commander of the Israeli army on the Jerusalem front. Most of the Israeli air force's fighter and bomber pilots were Diaspora Jews as well.[27] Only later, in the late 1950s, did the IDF systematically begin induction of non-Jewish populations such as the Druze community, which was willing to join in a full political and military alliance with the Jewish state. But the sincere desire to create such positive and permanent relations with minority communities did not change the fact that the IDF was principally a Jewish armed force. Its Star of David–studded insignias; its induction ceremonies in which soldiers received their rifle together with a Bible; its educational programs aimed at familiarizing the troops with Jewish history; its special units for creating Jewish settlements in border areas; its special mode of operations on the Jewish Sabbath—all these sought to foster a sense of connection to the Jewish people and its past and to bolster what was explicitly referred to as the army's "Zionist motivation."[28]

In its aims, too, the IDF operated as a Jewish force, assisting in enabling Jewish immigration from oppressed diasporas, conducting educational programs for the absorption of Jewish immigrants and carrying out operations against Nazi war criminals. In fact, it was in the IDF's ability to project Jewish force around the globe that Ben-Gurion saw the fundamental change in the Jewish condition that had taken place with the birth of Israel. And it was for this reason that he did not blush to express publicly his love for the Israel Defense Forces: "I confess that I love the Israel Defense Forces with a fierce and profound love . . . I see in the military not only the fortress that secures us, although this would be sufficient, but also an educational force for raising up the Jewish man, a cement for bringing together the nation, and a faithful mechanism for the absorption of immigrants."[29]

No, this was not a neutral technocratic state but rather a polity suffused with direction and purpose. It was a Jewish state not merely in name but in essence, pursuing the interests of the Jews as a people at home and abroad. To the complaints of Buber and his associates, who argued that the state, as an instrument of violence, could not merit love and that a particularistic Jewish state must be considered a corruption, Ben-Gurion responded firmly:

> Professor Buber says the state is only an instrument—but it is a precious instrument without which there can be no freedom and independence, no possibility of free, creative activity, suitable to our needs, our aspirations, and our values. . . . For that reason, give honor to the State of Israel. It is not merely an instrument. . . . it is the beginning of the redemption, a small part of the redemption.[30]

Even as the War of Independence raged on every border—in the Galilee and in the kibbutzim in the Negev, on the road to Jerusalem and in the Old City, and in Gush Etzion—Buber and his circle worked frantically to undermine the Jewish sovereignty that had just been established. On May 27, a day before the collapse of Jewish forces under siege in the Jewish quarter of Jerusalem's Old City, Ihud published a new issue of its periodical *Ba'ayot Hazman* ("Issues of the Day"), which included an article by Buber excoriating the Jewish state as a "desecration" of Jewish ideals:

> Never in the past have spirit and life been so distant from each other as now, in the period of "rebirth." Or perhaps you are willing to give the name "spirit" to a collective selfishness which acknowledges no higher standard? . . . This "Zionism" desecrates the name Zion. It is nothing more than one of the crassest nationalisms of our time . . . We are not obliged to conquer the land, for no danger is in store for our spiritual essence or our way of life from the population of the land. . . . Yet the inclination to power *[megamat hahisun]* makes only one demand: Sovereignty.[31]

In November, Buber felt compelled to speak out again, this time against the idea that the Jews were fighting a defensive—and therefore just—war. "It is characteristic for modern warfare," he wrote, "that each of the two fighting sides is convinced his is a war of defense. . . . Let us make an end to these ambiguities. The truth of the matter is that when we started our infiltration into the country, we began an attack 'by peaceful means.' . . . Let all who know the meaning of responsibility seek their own hearts as to what we have done."[32]

But Buber's feelings were perhaps best captured in an unpublished poem from this time, in which the famous thinker explored the relationship between the Jews of Israel and the dark forces that had swept over Europe a few years earlier:

> The destroyers are now long since disposed of
> A vile band of hangmen and thieves . . .
> But we, are we speakers of the Word? . . .
> I see us struggling—for the sake of what hoard?
> Powerful the arm—and the heart withered?
> O homeless voice
> In which the Word remained.[33]

Nor was Buber alone. His views were shared by other supporters of Ihud and anti-Zionists, who like him could not stand to be silent at this moment. Magnes, for example, suffered a stroke four weeks after Israeli independence and was hospitalized in New York; but even this could not stop him. From his hospital bed, he wrote to contacts in the State Department, proposing that the newborn Jewish state be replaced by an Arab-Jewish confederation that would strip the Jews of control over Jerusalem, foreign policy, defense, supreme judicial authority, and religious sites.[34] For him, the struggle against the Jewish state only ended with his death in October. Hannah Arendt, who had taken upon herself the organization of a new grouping of anti-Zionists and Ihud supporters in the United States,[35] in August 1948 appeared in *Ba'ayot Hazman*, reiterating her view that Jewish military victory in Palestine would lead to the spiritual ruin of Palestinian Jewry.[36]

Buber and his associates continued taking potshots at the embattled Jewish state so long as the outcome of the struggle for Jewish independence in Palestine remained uncertain. Yet by the beginning of the following year, it was clear that circumstances had changed beyond recognition. With the end of the fighting and the election of the first Jewish parliament in January 1949, the great majority of Jews who had previously given Ihud's views a sympathetic hearing had become supporters of Ben-Gurion and the new Jewish state. Even a pillar of Buber's movement for a binational Palestine such as the German immigrants' party, Aliya Hadasha, had decided shortly before the war that it would support a Jewish state. (When outraged members attacked this deviation from emancipationist German-Jewish principle, the head of the party, Felix Rosenbluth, responded that "we must get used to the fact that we cannot say publicly everything we think.")[37] Moreover, with Magnes's death, Ihud had to face not only the loss of one of its leading spirits but also its lifeline to sympathizers and sources of funding in New York and Washington.

In the spring of 1949, Buber gathered together what remained of his forces to discuss the disaster that had befallen them. "The cry of victory does not have the power of preventing the clear-eyed from seeing that the soul of the Zionist enterprise has evaporated," he told his colleagues. Yet he urged them not to give up their struggle, promising that "the day will yet come when the victorious march of which our people is so proud today, will seem to us like a cruel detour."[38] In recognition of the task that lay ahead, Ihud's newsletter was renamed *Ner*—meaning "lantern," or "candle," the implication being that only herein did the faithful light endure. The lead article in the first issue was penned by Martin Plessner, a student of Joseph Horowitz who became an instructor of Arabic literature at the Hebrew University. Plessner emphasized the continued loyalty of his circle to the ideas of the Peace Association, arguing that those who had been ideologically committed to binationalism in Palestine could not give up now "just because another 'solution' has supposedly proven itself feasible *for the time being.*" Despite the apparent success of Ben-Gurion's policy, the fact that Jews had chosen "the path of power" was nonetheless "a terrible blow," as Ihud had always claimed, and the existence of a Jewish government still "does not offer any means of distinguishing between our state and the state of Mussolini and Hitler." Invoking the ideas of "our teacher, Martin Buber," Plessner declared that "there is no problem that it is too late to treat," pronouncing Ihud's new mission to be "the penetration of the spirit of the true Zionism into the public life of the state of Israel."[39]

And what exactly was the message of the "true Zionism" that Ihud now sought to penetrate into the state of Israel? Not surprisingly, it was quite similar to the message of the binational state, albeit updated to suit the new circumstances. Thus, while Buber did say he had "accepted" the existence of the new Jewish state (according to his disciple Ernst Simon, "he accepted it with a heavy heart"),[40] this "acceptance" was deprived of much of its meaning by Buber's relentless efforts to promote the idea that the arrival of Jews in Palestine in large numbers had amounted to a "sin." As Buber explained time and again, the Jewish settlement in Palestine had retained its moral quality only during the period when Jewish immigration consisted mostly of radical socialist youths. These Jewish radicals, he believed, had been well on their way to achieving a "true humanity," while at the same time generating very little "sin" against the Arabs because there were too few of them to pose a tangible threat. Only in the mid-1920s, when Palestine began to flood with refugees from Poland and Germany, were the Arabs driven to violence, and only then was there "an enormous increase in our objective guilt."[41]

It was this revision of the history of Zionism, in which the absorption of Jewish refugees fleeing Hitler was not a virtue but rather the subject of "enormous" and "objective" Jewish guilt, that became the prism through which Buber interpreted all subsequent policies of the Jewish state. Thus, even after the establishment of the state, he and his associates continued to argue for the curtailment of further Jewish immigration into Israel (in the name of maintaining what was sometimes referred to as the "quality" level of the immigrants).[42] And they did this even as they agitated *in favor* of the absorption of large numbers of Arabs into Israel[43]—since the Arab refugees, unlike the Jewish refugees, were to be considered an essential part of the land. As Buber said, "There is nothing sillier than to be overjoyed because the Arab population has left. One day we will realize that the *fellah* [i.e., Arab farmer] is the column that holds up the edifice of the land of Israel."[44]

By advocating that the state of Israel accept fewer Jewish immigrants while seeking to increase the size of its Arab population, Buber in effect continued his earlier advocacy of a binational state. The word "binational" was retired from use, but its substance remained. And this was in evidence not only on the question of immigration policy but also in other areas. Buber continued to insist, for instance, that peace would never be possible unless Israel agreed to be absorbed into a political federation with the Arab states, effectively bringing Jewish sovereignty to an end.[45] He likewise continued to call for the Jewish state to hand Jerusalem over to an international regime ("I have always wanted the internationalization of Jerusalem").[46]

Moreover, although Buber and his colleagues had, in the years prior to independence, argued against sovereign Jewish power on the grounds that such power would be morally corrupting *in theory*, after the declaration of the state, they simply made the transition to arguing that virtually every pursuit of Jewish interest by this power, now that it existed, was corrupt *in practice*. Thus, Ihud criticized Ben-Gurion's government and defense forces in the harshest terms: for anti-terror operations involving civilian casualties; for the military administration of the Arabs of the Galilee; for the expropriation of Arab property in building new cities and towns; for Israel's nuclear program; for abandoning neutrality in world politics and aligning the Jewish state with the West; and so on. "The tormented of yesterday," *Ner* summed up, "have become the tormentors of today."[47] Or, similarly: "Israel has only just returned to its land and to its state, and it immediately acts like the most corrupt among peoples."[48]

Now that there was an actual Jewish state to accuse of moral corruption, Ihud naturally focused its ire on Ben-Gurion, the individual who, more than anyone else, had made the state and its policies. Certainly, the first prime minister was not exactly a genial figure. His rhetoric was still overcharged and his demeanor self-righteous on a remarkably broad range of subjects—traits that were hardly endearing in a prime minister whose party controlled much of the state bureaucracy and the economy, and, to an extent, the media as well through the office of the military censor.[49] On the other hand, Ben-Gurion *was* the founder of one of the only stable democracies beyond the frontiers of the West—and he was also responsible for leading a country that was still at war. Most Jews at the time were capable of factoring such central considerations into the equation. But they largely escaped the calculations of Ihud's intellectuals, whose publications denounced Ben-Gurion and his government with terms such as "totalitarianism," "fascism," and "pseudo-democracy."[50] Similarly, when Ben-Gurion dismissed the more compromsing Moshe Sharett from the foreign ministry, he was greeted by an Ihud poster campaign in the streets of Jerusalem crying, "The General has driven out the Diplomat."[51] As far as Buber's circle was concerned, the issue crying for attention was not the threat posed to Israel by the Arab regimes. As one headline in *Ner* put it, "The Danger Is—David Ben-Gurion."[52]

But it was not until the Sinai campaign of October 1956 that the professors of Ihud finally reached a climax in their hostility toward Ben-Gurion's leadership. The political background to the war was the Soviet decision, thirteen months earlier, to supply Egypt and Syria with unprecedented quantities of modern tanks, combat aircraft, and other heavy weapons. This was at a moment when officials of the Eisenhower administration were courting Arab affections by pressing for Israel to give up the Negev Desert (the southern half of the state of Israel) in exchange for peace, and even pushing for a limit to Jewish immigration into Israel. In the wake of the new Arab-Soviet axis, the young Egyptian dictator Gamal Abdel Nasser pronounced that the Arabs finally had the power to destroy Israel and proceeded to enforce a blockade on the Israeli port of Eilat, while escalating cross-border terror raids against the Jewish state from the Gaza Strip.

With both the Soviets and the Americans spoken for, Ben-Gurion forged an alliance with France—itself under pressure from Nasser in Algeria—seeking to land a blow that would loose Nasser's grip on Israeli shipping before Egypt could fully assimilate its new weapons. Moreover, Nasser's nationalization of the Suez Canal in late July 1956, enabled Israel to bid for an alignment with its former enemy, Britain, whose security interests were now also in jeopardy. On October 29, Israeli forces entered Sinai with the backing of the French, crushing Egyptian opposition and prying open the waterway to Eilat; a combined British-French force then joined battle against Egyptian positions along the Suez Canal.

In the end, the entire operation was brought to a halt by threats first from Moscow and then from Washington, resulting in the withdrawal of Israeli forces from Sinai a few months later.[53] Yet despite this humiliation, Ben-Gurion's first experiment in gun-barrel diplomacy was a breathtaking success, not only demolishing the Egyptian menace and putting an end to demands that Israel cede the Negev but also solidifying a strategic alliance with France that permitted Israel to purchase advanced Western armaments. In addition, it was the French alliance that gave Ben-Gurion the assistance he needed to bring Israel's nuclear program to maturity—arguably Israel's most important political achievement in its first fifteen years after independence.

If Buber and his associates had refused to accept as justifiable Israel's War of Independence—when the Jews were fighting against Arab invasion on four fronts—one can easily imagine their reaction to the decision to enter Sinai with the support of the imperial powers. Even more galling for them, however, was the fact that Ben-Gurion insisted on interpreting the Sinai campaign as a *Jewish* cause. Not only were the Jewish forces struggling to free the present Jewish state from the tightening Nasserist-Soviet noose, but they were simultaneously breaking a path into Jewish history by returning the Jewish people to their origins in the wilderness of Sinai. In this context, Ben-Gurion did not hesitate to compare the Jewish fighters of the IDF to those who had participated in the wars of Joshua, David, and Judah Maccabee, as well as the Warsaw ghetto uprising. As he emotionally told his troops once the victory was in hand, "You have done something immense. You have brought us closer to the ancient history of our people, to the place where the Law was given, and where our people was chosen as God's precious people." And in fact, much of the country responded to the brush with Mt. Sinai just as Ben-Gurion had. Jewish soldiers and civilians descended into the wilderness in search of evidence of the biblical exodus, while songs lush with Herzlean "imponderables" circulated in the army, the youth movements, and the schools. One went:

> It is no fable, my friend, it is no fable,
> And it is no passing dream.
> For you can see it, facing Sinai, you can see it,
> There the bush, the bush, still burns.[54]

Such an admixture of Jewish ideas and images from the past with the present political aims of the state was perhaps not unusual for a people at war. But for many of the professors, it represented precisely the kind of corruption of Judaism against which Hermann Cohen had warned. Within two weeks of the outbreak of hostilities, professors and students at the Hebrew University were organizing protests against the war, and on November 15, Ihud publicly called upon Ben-Gurion to "obey world opinion" and to renounce the hope of political gain through warfare by ending the Sinai operation "without victors and vanquished."[55]

Encouraged by the withdrawal of Israeli troops from Sinai in the months that followed, the professors began groping for a means of discrediting not only this particular war but Ben-Gurion's entire strategy of amassing political power in the service of Jewish interest. One of the first indications of what was coming took place in August 1957 at a Jewish Agency conference of Jewish thinkers and political figures in Jerusalem. Ben-Gurion was in attendance, and this time, when he referred to the Jewish state as a miracle, Buber attacked him sharply and personally, comparing him to the false prophets of antiquity who had urged the Jews to follow the path of evil:

> Behind everything that Ben-Gurion has said . . . there lies . . . the will to make the political factor [i.e., worldly power] supreme. He is one of the proponents of that kind of secularization which cultivates its "thoughts" and "visions" so diligently that it keeps men from hearing the voice of the living God. . . . This "politicization" of life here strikes at the very spirit itself.[56]

The following spring, Buber went even further in a speech before the American Friends of Ihud, in a program he shared with the noted psychologist and anti-Zionist Erich Fromm.[57] Buber subsequently published a written version of the speech under his name in the *Jewish Newsletter,* an anti-Zionist bulletin appearing in New York. (Its editor, William Zuckerman, had once said that the Jews had returned to Palestine "not because of any idealism . . . [but] because that is the only country where they can have a fascism of their own.")[58] In it, Buber argued that significant numbers of Jews—and here too he may have been thinking of Ben-Gurion and other Zionist leaders—had turned to the "way of power" after having been witness to Hitler's successes. According to the article, he and Magnes had advocated a binational Palestine as a way of permitting the Jews to pursue the "way of the spirit" in their relations with the Arabs. "But the majority of the Jewish people preferred to learn from Hitler rather than from us. Hitler showed them that history does not go the way of the spirit but the way of power, and if a people is powerful enough, it can kill with impunity as many millions of another people as it wants to kill." (In the wake of criticism in the Israeli press, Buber claimed that in his original speech he had referred to only "a certain part" rather than the majority of the Jewish people.)[59]

When Buber wrote these words in 1958, there were still few in Israel willing to take this message seriously. And they would not be prepared to heed them for another two and a half years—not until the Lavon Affair had finally cracked Ben-Gurion's hold on the imagination of his country, and of his people. By that time, Ben-Gurion and Buber would be locked in a public struggle so complex that even today it is no simple matter to understand exactly what was at stake. Yet in the midst of the Lavon Affair and its aftermath, history inserted a small postscript, an allegory seemingly aimed at making it perfectly obvious what Ben-Gurion and Buber each stood for, so that no one should misunderstand. The postscript went as follows.

On May 22, 1960, the Mossad reported to Ben-Gurion that it had captured Adolf Eichmann, head of the Jewish Section of Nazi Germany's Main Security Office and the man who had masterminded the destruction of

European Jewry.[60] Kidnapped in Argentina and smuggled to Israel, he was to stand trial under the provisions of the Nazi and Nazi Collaborators Punishment Law, which Ben-Gurion's government had promulgated ten years earlier. No one at the time could miss the fact that such a trial was possible only because there now existed a sovereign Jewish power with security services capable of operating around the globe, an executive authority able to guard Jewish interests wherever they might be, and a system of laws and a judiciary capable of meting out justice in the defense of innocent Jews. As Ben-Gurion said himself: "Here, for the first time in Jewish history, historical justice is being done by the sovereign Jewish people. . . . For the first time Israel is judging the murderers of the Jewish people. . . . And let us bear in mind that only the independence of Israel could create the necessary conditions for this."[61]

In other words, the Eichmann trial in many ways encapsulated the meaning of the Jewish state, which had been Ben-Gurion's lifework.

For Buber, precisely the opposite was the case. The Eichmann trial encapsulated everything that he had devoted his life to trying to *prevent*. And this was true not only with regard to the Jewish state. On the subject of the Holocaust, too, Buber had invested a decade in attempting to achieve a feeling of mutual disempowerment with the "pro-human" circles in Germany, traveling there to accept various prizes and to call out to the Germans, "Let us not let the Satanic element in men hinder us from realizing man! . . . Let us dare, despite all, to trust!"[62] For Buber, the Eichmann trial, a kind of retroactive pitting of the power of the Jewish state against that Nazi Germany, was the apotheosis of all that Judaism must not be. "I am disgusted," he wrote at the time. And he could not stop finding reasons why: He was disgusted because it was a Jewish court rather than an "impartial" international tribunal that was to conduct the trial; disgusted because the state has no right to take the life of any man; disgusted because "for such crimes there is no penalty"; disgusted because "killing him was too facile and commonplace a way out of this unique dilemma." And when, after eight months of reliving hell's scenes of annihilation, incineration, and extermination, the court in Jerusalem finally handed down a sentence of death, Buber was disconsolate, running from meeting to meeting with other professors from the university—including Gershom Scholem, Hugo Bergmann, Ernst Simon, Natan Rotenstreich, and Leah Goldberg—writing letters and hoping against hope that Adolf Eichmann might be granted clemency and given a life sentence of agricultural work on a kibbutz instead.[63]

Buber's pleas went unanswered. In the margin of one of the documents submitted to him pleading for clemency, President Yitzhak Ben-Tzvi penciled in the biblical verse, "As your sword has made women childless, so shall your mother be childless among women."[64] Eichmann was executed at midnight on May 31, 1962. Only afterward did Buber publicly confess the thought that had been motivating him throughout his struggle to free Eichmann: "Is it for us, Israel, again to fasten the chains of death?"[65]

It seems that for Buber, no horror was greater than the reality of Jewish power.

CHAPTER 12

The Incubator:
The Hebrew University,
1948–1961

I N THE FIRST HEADY YEARS AFTER INDEPENDENCE, hardly anyone in
Israel was much interested in the attacks of Buber and his circle on the
government of the newborn Jewish state. Indeed, when someone did
take notice of the professors' doings, these were greeted with almost universal disdain—to the point that a sympathetic disciple could report to Buber
after five months of traveling around the country that nowhere was he able
to find the slightest sympathy for Ihud's views: "Whether on the street or in
a cafe, among intellectuals of Jerusalem or Tel Aviv, in Tiberias or Safed, in
a kibbutz of Mapai, Mapam, or Hapoel Hamizrahi—nowhere did I hear a
kind word about Martin Buber."[1]

Yet in this sea of hostility, the Hebrew University in Jerusalem was an oasis
in which Buber nevertheless continued to be venerated. The sharp contrast
between the assessment of the public and that of the university is evidenced,
for example, by the fact that in March 1953, at the lowest point of Ihud's influence, the professorate of the Hebrew University chose to honor Buber with
its highest accolade, the honorary doctorate, which in the preceding thirty
years had gone only to Einstein, Magnes, and Weizmann.[2] A few years later,
the newly founded Israel Academy of Sciences and Humanities, led by profes-

sors of the Hebrew University, followed suit by electing Buber its first president. And this reverence for the Ihud leader likewise infected the students, hundreds of whom, on the occasion of Buber's eighty-fifth birthday in 1963, marched in a torchlit procession to his home in Jerusalem for a midnight ceremony, in which they adorned Buber with flowers, kissed him, and inducted him into the student union as an honorary member.[3] This is not to say that the academic community necessarily *liked* Buber.[4] But this did not alter the fact that he had been and remained the intellectual godfather of the current of ideas being developed and taught at the university. As Gershom Scholem said, Buber's writings on Hasidism had left "a deep impression on our age. In one sense or another we are all his disciples."[5]

Indeed, despite Weizmann's efforts to reduce the anti-nationalist tendencies of the Hebrew University, the fact is that its humanities and social sciences faculties had never been subjected to the kind of serious reshaping that would have moved it to a new intellectual course. Magnes remained president of the university until his death in 1948, and the position of rector, or academic head, was likewise filled, until after World War II, by professors who were generally committed to views similar to those that Magnes had stood for: Hugo Bergmann, Abraham Adolf Fraenkel, Leon Roth, and L. A. Mayer. Indeed, so powerful was this intellectual stream that in the first years after independence—twenty-five years after the founding of the Hebrew University—the humanities and social sciences faculties were still dominated by the same figures who had worked to advance the binationalist agenda of the Peace Association in its various permutations: Richard Koebner in history, Martin Buber in sociology, Hugo Bergmann and Leon Roth in philosophy, Norman Bentwich in international relations, Moshe Schwabe in classics, Ernst Simon in education, Alfred Bonne in economics, Dov Sadan in literature, Gershom Scholem in Jewish philosophy, Isaac Fritz Baer in Jewish history, and David Baneth, Shlomo Goitein, and L. A. Mayer in Islamic studies.[6]

Surveying the ideological landscape at the university shortly before his death, Magnes confessed his pride in the fact that he had succeeded in establishing the Hebrew University as *the* intellectual epicenter in Palestine of views such as his. As he wrote to Leon Simon:

> I have come to believe that it is providential that a man with my views is president of the Hebrew University . . . The charge is made against the university, that it is the stronghold of those who are against chauvinism and terror and who are for peace . . . I think that this is so, and it is this which gives me more genuine cause for thankfulness than anything in life. If it is, in however small part, because of me . . . what a great thing it is to have been president of the Hebrew University.[7]

But the War of Independence brought changes even to the Hebrew University. Magnes's death and the evacuation of the Mt. Scopus campus during the war left the university administration devastated, both financially and spiritually. Moreover, with the university's Labor-Zionist opponents and their ideology in power in Israel and the attenuation of the connection with Magnes's American friends, the situation appeared so bleak that the Hebrew University administration actively considered closing the institution for good and letting Ben-Gurion and his friends found a new university of their own.[8] This possibility receded only when the presidency of the university was taken over by Benjamin Mazar, a mainline Labor Zionist and the brother-in-law of Yitzhak Ben-Tzvi, one of the founders of the Jewish Labor movement in Palestine.

In 1951, Mazar was a mere lecturer in archaeology, when suddenly he was promoted to full professor, and then, a few months later, to the position of rector. In March 1953, only eighteen months after becoming a full professor, he became president of the university, while at the same time, it was announced that his brother-in-law Ben-Tzvi—who in December 1952 succeeded Weizmann as the president of the state of Israel—would concurrently serve as the "honorary president" of the Hebrew University. Ben-Tzvi introduced Mazar to Ben-Gurion,[9] and, one has to assume not coincidentally, he quickly succeeded in turning the university's finances around, for the first time gaining large-scale funding from both the state and the ZO, as well as being granted a new campus in the heart of Jerusalem.[10] Nor did Mazar disappoint his newfound friends. In the face of relentless opposition from the clique of mostly-German humanities professors and their students, Mazar carried out a sweeping program of university-building along classic practical-Zionist lines, introducing programs in law, business administration, social work, criminology, psychology, medicine, Asian and African studies, physiology, genetics, dentistry, and pharmacology. In fact, by the time Mazar resigned as head of the university in March 1961, at the age of fifty-five—a matter of weeks after the Lavon Affair had brought down Ben-Gurion's government[11]—he had successfully transformed the university into an integral part of the effort to construct the new Jewish state, much as Weizmann had conceived of it.

But successful as Mazar may have been in his battles to bring the Hebrew University in line with the "practical" needs of the Zionist enterprise, his tenure left the idea-making core of the Hebrew University—its humanities and social science faculties—nearly untouched. And it was here that the transformation of the political ideals of emancipationist anti-Zionism into a worldview suitable for consumption by Israelis proceeded apace. Of course, the professors did not speak openly against the idea of the Jewish state once it came into being. But, on the other hand, neither did they necessarily change the way that they taught and researched. The result was that history, philosophy, and other basic disciplines, as presented at the Hebrew University, for the most part continued to militate toward a "pure" universalist ethics, the social-contract state, an anti-nationalist politics, and, of course, variations on Hermann Cohen's ideal of Jewish disempowerment.

Thus, although the explicit term "binationalism" may have been driven underground in the years after the birth of Israel, all the vast arsenal of ideas that had led to this political conclusion remained intact. In fact, by examining some of the major themes emphasized by professors in the humanities and social sciences at the Hebrew University, it is possible to see the ideological substructure upon which the subsequent trend toward "post-Zionism"—and the delegitimization of the idea of the Jewish state—among the students of the professors was based.

Shabtai Tzvi and Hasidism

A striking example of the filtering of academic subjects through the lens of emancipationist political ideas is the study of Hasidic mysticism, which originated with Buber's numerous writings on Hasidism and was transformed into a respectable academic discipline by Gershom Scholem's lifelong research on the subject at the Hebrew University. And though Scholem worked to distance himself from Buber's ideas, in the end this effort highlighted relatively small areas of disagreement. In the larger scheme of things, Scholem's superior scholarship ultimately served to give maximum academic credibility to an overall scheme on whose broad strokes he and Buber were in fact largely in agreement.[12]

Both Buber and Scholem sought to bring out the importance of the eighteenth-century Hasidic movement by placing it at the center of a broader historiographic revision embracing all of Jewish thought and history. According to this view, the Judaism of the Hasidim was understood to have developed in opposition to the mystic Messianism of Shabtai Tzvi, which had shaken Eastern Jewry to its foundations after his promises of redemption and of the immanent return of the Jews to Palestine had ended in his apostasy in 1667. Before the establishment of the Buber-Scholem school of thought on the subject, it had been common to view apocalyptic movements such Sabbateanism (i.e., the Shabtai Tzvi movement) as a menace, because their claims that the very fabric of reality—including the laws of nature and morality—was on the verge of revolutionary revision were seen as leading to fanaticism, apostasy, and nihilism. What was new in Buber and Scholem's interpretation was the idea that the Hasidic movement of the mid-1700s was in its essence an effort to "neutralize" the destructive Messianic potential latent in Judaism by transferring hope of redemption from the historical-political world to the arena of the heart.[13] As Scholem explained, this neutralization took place through the Hasidic suppression of the real, physical meaning of terms such as "Egypt," "the land of Israel," "exile," and "redemption," which "were turned into allegorical catchwords ... standing for a personal state of mind, for a moral condition, or ... for existential situations of man." The result was a Judaism in which "every individual is the Redeemer, the Messiah of his own little world," and the historical-political aspect of Judaism—which had anticipated an actual return to Israel as part of a historic Jewish redemption—is consequently "shelved" or "liquidated." Indeed, the very greatness of Hasidism is inseparable from the fact that in order to achieve this neutralization of the Messianic, "the movement as a whole had made its peace with the Exile."[14]

Without entering into the question of whether this interpretation of Hasidism is correct—recent research suggests that it is not[15]—one can readily appreciate why such an interpretation of Hasidism would be attractive to German-Jewish thinkers. After all, it in effect attributes to the Jewish mystical tradition, which is hundreds (if not thousands) of years old, the very same ideas that were the cornerstone of nineteenth-century emancipationist Judaism: that "Zion" is essentially a metaphor; that redemption can be brought about equally by every man, wherever he may be; and that there is consequently no longer any need to hope for a particular leader or movement ("the Messiah") to bring about historical-political Jewish restoration in Palestine, since this aim within Judaism has been "liquidated." Moreover, by opposing Hasidism to Sabbateanism, Buber and Scholem created a deceptively simple analytic tool for evaluating the entire course of Jewish history. One had only to ask whether a given leader or movement within Judaism was characterized by a belief in the efficacy of human efforts to achieve historical-political redemption within the world, or whether it had succeeded in neutralizing such a dangerous, "Messianic" view of history and politics.[16] With this litmus test in mind, a student could quickly consider what he knew about the Hasmonean kings, Masada, Bar-Kochba, Shabtai Tzvi, or even Herzl, and without too much effort reach the conclusion that some, if not all of them, were standing on the dark side of Jewish history.

Nor did the students have to look very hard to understand how this theory applied to contemporary politics, for Ben-Gurion was *constantly* speaking of the Jewish state as playing a decisive role in the redemption of the Jews, not only physically but spiritually. For him, this "redemption" was the purpose of the existence of a Jewish state. Yet as anyone who studied Hasidism at the Hebrew University knew—or believed he knew—one could not make such claims for historical-political actors and instruments without approaching the threshold of heresy.[17] It was this belief that informed Buber's warnings that Ben-Gurion's ideas "strike at the very spirit" of Judaism and that "only" by drawing closer to Hasidism could Zionism avoid "destroying . . . its right to exist."[18] Scholem's views were more complicated, but their implications were the same. He too feared that Labor Zionism was gravitating toward "Sabbateanism," and he too demanded that Zionists "neutralize" the Messianic element in their movement by systematically stripping its Jewish basis of political pretensions.[19] Among its other effects, this line of reasoning fed directly into Buber and Scholem's opposition to the Jewish state.

Many of those who knew Scholem in his later years believe that he went a long distance toward embracing the Jewish state. Yet even if this is so, it is striking that this change of heart effected no change at all in his doctrine of the neutralization of the Messianic, with its sweeping implications regarding the antipolitical nature of Judaism and the personal, non-national nature of the Jewish conception of redemption. In the final analysis, the theory of Jewish history taught at the Hebrew University under the rubric of courses in Jewish mysticism was in fact a grand recapitulation—albeit in mystical, rather than rationalistic, garb—of the understanding of Jewish history that Scholem had imbibed as a youth in what he described as Hermann Cohen's "awe-inspiring" lectures in Berlin in the 1910s.[20]

The Pharisees, Franz Rosenzweig, and Irish Independence

Although no other original theory minted by the Hebrew University's "first-generation" professors can compete with Buber and Scholem's revision of Jewish history for the depth of its anti-political influence, this message was powerfully reinforced by the teachings of other leading professors, whose presentation of historical and philosophical material was heavily colored by the premises of emancipationist German Judaism. Thus, Richard Koebner, who headed the university's department of general history, was a binationalist who created a department that—in the words of one of his students, the historian Joshua Prawer—had "a far more universal outlook than any university that I know of, anywhere. Anywhere."[21] Koebner, who had been active with Buber and Magnes in the campaign against the establishment of the Jewish state, liked to explain that if one would only learn enough world history, one would recognize that a successful national politics had "never" been built on the defeats and tragedies of others.[22] National independence in particular, he argued, was not a pressing goal, as it is "neither directly nor indirectly the most important means of creating sound economic and cultural conditions." Eamon De Valera's successful drive to create an independent Irish state, for example, had brought nothing but disaster, alienating segments of the Irish people and foreign public opinion and harming the country economically. "Does this fact," Koebner asked, "not convey a warning to us?"[23]

Similarly, Hugo Bergmann, who was the founder of the department of philosophy and was a fervent disciple of Buber, based his opposition to the Jewish state on Kantian universalism, as interpreted by Hermann Cohen.[24] Even in the 1960s, Bergmann was still advocating the idea that Zionist thought had been "completely mistaken" in claiming Jewish sovereignty would alter the prospects for Jewish well-being in some fundamental sense. Instead, Bergmann continued to support what he called Franz Rosenzweig's "un-Zionistic attitude" that the Jewish people "could ensure its survival only step by step . . . generation by generation, by means of a specific solution for each period"[25]—a worldview that leaves open the possibility that the Jewish state could yet be abandoned by future generations. Similarly, Buber's follower Ernst Simon taught the education department's courses on Jewish values and history, which naturally lent themselves to the exposition of his claim that the Pharisaic rabbis had wisely recognized that there was in fact no need for a Jewish state, even before this state was destroyed by the Romans:

> The world has not yet outgrown the stage in which power and the state are viewed as a necessity, but we outgrew it in the year 70 C.E. [i.e., with the destruction of Jerusalem] at the latest. . . . We must accept the assessment of the Pharisees regarding the last Jewish state . . . The inner power [of the mind] that turned this national catastrophe into a source of life . . . is our power even today . . . We have no legitimate power other than this.[26]

And Yeshayahu Leibowitz, although a biochemist, became an important influence on many students in the humanities and social sciences, whom he taught philosophy of science. Leibowitz's erratic philosophizing generally defended the idea of a Jewish state, and he was often critical of Buber and his followers.[27] But Leibowitz also left a lasting mark on his students with his strident assertions that the state "is nothing but an apparatus of coercion and violence that exists for its own sake" or that heroism and courage on the battlefield cannot be considered a virtue:

> In the Jewish sources one cannot find admiration for the fighting man . . . If it is biblical sources we are talking about, the Bible includes the prophet Isaiah, not David Ben-Gurion . . . Weren't the scum of humanity, the Crusaders, whom we know from their deeds in the Jewish communities of Speyer, Mayence, Worms and Jerusalem, weren't they courageous? . . . The men of the S.S., under whose jurisdiction were Auschwitz and Maidanek and Treblinka, weren't they heroic in battle? . . . Since when is it praise to say of a man that he is heroic in battle?[28]

The dramatic impact of such views on students at the Hebrew University was compounded by the paucity of competing viewpoints, which resulted from the university's hesitation to hire instructors who might undermine the prevailing views on sensitive topics. A case in point was the decision not to offer a position to the historian Joseph Klausner. On the surface of it, Klausner would seem to have fit in perfectly with the Hebrew University's profile. A member of Weizmann and Buber's Democratic Faction in his youth, Klausner had been an outspoken advocate of the Hebrew cultural revival, taking over publication of Ahad Ha'am's monthly *Hashiloah* after his mentor's retirement. Klausner had given up a position at the University of Odessa to immigrate to Palestine in 1919, where he was one of the initiators of the Jerusalem committee on behalf of the establishment of a university. At the time of the university's founding, Klausner had written four volumes on the history of the Second Temple period (i.e., the classical Jewish kingdom). And yet when the Hebrew University was founded in 1925, Klausner was not offered a position—despite the fact that there was no other candidate qualified to fill the post. It is difficult to avoid the conclusion that this was because of Klausner's outspoken political views, which were close to Jabotinsky's, and included overt support for a Jewish state. Apparently, it was feared that such beliefs might influence his presentation of ancient Jewish history and lead students to draw the wrong conclusions about Jewish independence in antiquity. (Klausner's reading of history, for example, was sympathetic to the Hasmoneans and the Saducees in their struggle against the Pharisees.)[29]

In the end, Magnes offered Klausner a professorship in Hebrew literature, where he would presumably do less harm. And in fact, Klausner taught Hebrew literature at the Hebrew University for twenty-five years, for most of this period under a ban that prohibited him from teaching about the ancient Jewish state. Only in 1943—when Klausner was sixty-nine years old—did the university lift the decree, permitting Klausner to teach about the history of the Second Temple period until he was forced to retire a few years later.[30]

Kant and Hermann Cohen

Such, then, was the climate of political correctness created by the "first generation" of professors at the Hebrew University. But at least as important to the future course of the Jewish state were the academic theories propounded by the university's "second generation"—professors who had arrived as students from Central Europe during the 1930s and who had received much of their academic training under the tutelage of Buber, Bergmann, Koebner, and Scholem. Typical of these next-generation academics were the philosopher Natan Rotenstreich and the historians Joshua Prawer and Jacob Talmon. All three had been raised in Galicia, where German was spoken as "almost" a mother tongue;[31] all three were active as youths in movements of the utopian Left under the influence of Buber and German Zionism: Prawer and Talmon in Hashomer Hatzair, which had begun tilting toward binationalism in

1927;[32] and Rotenstreich in Gordonia, whose leader, Pinhas Lubianker (later Lavon) declared himself a binationalist around that time as well.[33] These students entered a university in which Hebrew was stammered out as the official language of instruction but where many of the students and most of their professors spoke German among themselves.[34] Their studies, leading directly to a master's degree, involved a course of study lasting five to seven years,[35] during which time they were subjected to countless hours of listening to the professors in frontal lectures—Prawer described the students at the Hebrew University as "probably the most lectured-at academic audience in the world"—a system apparently intended to make up for the fact that most of the readings were not available in Hebrew.[36] The resultant intimacy with the interpretations of the professors was further amplified by the fact that the faculty did not have offices on the campus due to lack of space, so that discussion sessions were commonly conducted in the professors' homes.[37]

Unlike their mentors, most of the students who came of age in this environment did not like to refer to themselves as "true Zionists." They were willing to accept the Jewish state as a necessary lesson in the wake of the Nazi cataclysm, and they were careful not to associate themselves with Ihud. Moreover, some of them—Nathan Rotenstreich comes immediately to mind—were ardent patriots whose devotion to the Jewish state cannot seriously be questioned.

Nevertheless, these young professors continued to conduct research and teach on the basis of ideas derived from German-Jewish anti-Zionist thought, no less than did their mentors. Thus, for example, Nathan Rotenstreich, later the leading force in the university's philosophy department, grew up under the tutelage of Hugo Bergmann—with whom he worked to translate Kant into Hebrew—and Gershom Scholem.[38] It is therefore no surprise that, like Bergmann, Rotenstreich found in Kant (and to a lesser degree in Hermann Cohen) the foundation for his worldview, characterized by a general distaste for the ways of worldly power ("Damage must not be done to the humanity in man. Violence must be avoided at all costs; rational persuasion must govern human relations").[39] From Scholem, he adopted the view of Ben-Gurion's "Messianism" as fundamentally misguided—a view that in 1957, in the wake of the Sinai campaign, led him to publish a celebrated, although relatively tame, critique of Ben-Gurion's political ideals in the national press.[40]

The forceful application of Rotenstreich's academic theories to the arena of the Jewish state would come only a few years later, during the Lavon Affair. By then, Rotenstreich would take the lead in organizing the faculty and students of the Hebrew University in the effort to remove Ben-Gurion from power. It was then that the arresting similarity between his views and those of his mentors would be on full display, as he called for an end to the "Messianic

period" in Israel's history—at the same time arguing that unless Jewish politicians began to treat one another with "care" and "mutual respect," the "historical warrant" for the existence of the Jewish state would be "eliminated."[41]

The Crusaders

Among the younger professors in the general history department, by far the
most influential were two of Richard Koebner's students, Joshua Prawer and
Jacob Talmon, the former specializing in the medieval period and the latter
writing about the history of the modern period. Of all the possible topics of
study during the Middle Ages, Prawer devoted his life to examining the brutal
and racist Crusaders who took Palestine from the Muslims in 1099, and then
struggled for nearly two hundred years to construct a Christian state in the
country until finally being driven out in 1187. Professors at the university
had, since their earliest meetings with Arab leaders, been told in no uncertain
terms that the Jewish settlement in Palestine was nothing more than a resurrected Crusade, and that Jewish Palestine would in the end be obliterated just
as the Crusader state had been.[42] And Prawer, who began studying this subject
at Koebner's suggestion,[43] became preoccupied with the analogy, struggling to
resolve for himself whether the Zionists were indeed like the Crusaders. In attempting to resolve this problem, Prawer pioneered the academic discipline of
trying to understand the history of Palestine from the point of view of the
Arabs. "I tried to see the Crusades not from the European point of view," explained Prawer, "but from the other way around."[44] And, indeed, his scholarly
writing did not shrink from referring to the Christian settlers as "the destroyers"—even as he described their attempts to create a Christian farming community rooted in the soil and border outposts to defend themselves from the
incessant threat of Arab attack.[45]

This affinity for the Arab historical perspective—which, it will be re-
called, had been one of Magnes's central ideological goals in establishing the
Hebrew University—had a direct impact on the manner in which Prawer's
students viewed Zionism. A good example is the historian Meron
Benvenisti, today a well-known journalist. Benvenisti was raised in a classic
Labor-Zionist household but also became sympathetic to the Arab side of
the conflict while studying the Crusades as a graduate student of Prawer's.
"The knowledge of Moslem reaction to the Crusaders made me aware of the
similarity of Arab reaction to the . . . loss of Jerusalem" in 1967, says
Benvenisti, "and, in a curious way, also sensitized me to their emotional suffering." In fact, so sensitive did Benvenisti become to Arab emotional suffering that when he learned that a medieval artifact symbolizing the Muslim
military victory over the Crusaders had been destroyed in a fire, he found
himself "overwhelmed with grief." Indeed, he began crying.[46]

Not surprisingly, Meron Benvenisti's ability to see contemporary politics from the Arab perspective has left its mark on his own politics, and today he is one of the leading exponents of reconstituting Israel as a binational Arab-Jewish state.[47] In this way Prawer, who was no opponent of the Jewish state, nevertheless devoted his academic career to evoking emotional sympathy for an anti-Zionist historical narrative adopted from Arab political propaganda—in so doing transmitting the binationalism of his own mentor, Koebner, to a new generation of students.

Robespierre, Political Messianism, and Totalitarian Democracy

But by far the most breathtaking example of the anti-Zionist premises underlying the scholarship of the young professors at the Hebrew University is found in the work of Israel's most influential historian, Jacob Talmon. When Talmon's *The Origins of Totalitarian Democracy* was published in 1951, the only professor at the Hebrew University acknowledged as having reviewed the manuscript before publication was Martin Buber, and there is reason to think the book was based on ideas first advanced by Buber in a course at the university in 1938.[48] In fact, despite the ostensible political differences between the two—Talmon had been supportive of the establishment of a Jewish state—the book was unmistakably the product of the philosophical and historical ideas of Buber and his followers. "The most vital issue of our time," Talmon asserts on the first page, is the "headlong collision between empirical and liberal democracy on the one hand, and totalitarian Messianic democracy on the other"[49]—and one does not have to read too far to realize that this dichotomy simply imitates the Buber-Scholem opposition between Hasidic "neutralism" toward redemption within history, on the one hand, and Messianic-Sabbatean pursuit of such historical and political redemption, on the other.

Talmon achieves the transposition of these concepts as follows. According to his retelling of history, the philosophers of the Enlightenment were unable to conceive of a contradiction between the demands of a free society and those of a just society, believing that if men were freed from bad government, justice would follow as a matter of course. It was only during the French Revolution, when the old regime was destroyed, that it become clear that freedom would not, in fact, produce what the revolutionaries conceived to be a just society. At this moment, Talmon argues, there appeared what he calls "the great schism," the split between those who believed that democratic rule was essentially a matter of securing individual liberties, and those for whom the revolution had not attained its aims unless it achieved human salvation by establishing the reign of reason and equality on earth. It was the choice of the second path—the pursuit of an overriding collective *purpose* by the state—that in Talmon's view led to the orgy of terror and bloodshed that ensued. "Both schools," he writes, "affirm the supreme value of liberty. But whereas one finds the essence of freedom in spontaneity and the absence of coercion, the other believes it to be attained only in the pursuit and attainment of an absolute collective purpose."[50]

Thus, on Talmon's reading, it was neither the hopelessly utopian and extremist aims of Robespierre and Saint-Just nor their willingness to resort to the most bloodthirsty methods in pursuit of these aims that was the cause of the catastrophe. Rather, the essence of the Jacobin error was the belief that the state could have any "collective purpose" or "final aims" other than the rights of its citizens, for which it is justified in "directing the physical and moral forces of the nation."[51] For the moment one is willing to compromise the rights of the individual for the sake of an alternative overarching purpose—what Talmon calls a "salvationist creed"—the state invariably uses this creed as the excuse to muster force for the coercion of recalcitrant individuals, and the inexorable slide toward totalitarianism begins,[52] hence Talmon's term "totalitarian democracy," or "Messianic democracy" (he uses the two interchangeably). Thus, the essential point of his book, as well as of Talmon's subsequent volumes, is that a salvationist creed of any kind cannot be reconciled with liberty. As he explains,

> The two ideals correspond to the two instincts most deeply imbedded in human nature, the yearning for salvation and the love of freedom. To attempt to satisfy both . . . is bound to result, if not in unmitigated tyranny and serfdom, at least in the monumental hypocrisy and self-deception which are the concomitants of totalitarian democracy. This is the curse on salvationist creeds: To be born out of the noblest impulses of man, and to degenerate into weapons of tyranny.[53]

Again, one has to consider the impact that such a theory had on students at the Hebrew University in the years when these lines were penned. One can hardly imagine anything that more closely resembles a higher "collective purpose" of the state, or even a "salvationist creed," than the Zionism of Herzl or Ben-Gurion.[54] The idea of the Jewish state was from its inception no less than to redeem an oppressed people from debasement and suffering. Moreover, when Talmon's book first appeared in 1951, it was at the height of Ben-Gurion's mobilization of Israel's resources, with a regime of painful austerity imposed to enable the government to absorb hundreds of thousands of refugees from Europe and the Arab states. Massive government works were underway with the aim of creating Jewish population centers on the new state's periphery, and large sections of the country were still under martial law. Indeed, the postponement of the drafting of a written constitution—as opposed to the urgent passage of the Law of Return, for example—

rendered it obvious to anyone paying attention that Israel was at this moment preoccupied with "collective purposes" of life and death, and not with
absolute guarantees of individual rights.

But if it were true, as Talmon emphasized, that "the most vital issue of
our time is the headlong collision between . . . liberal democracy on the one
hand, and totalitarian Messianic democracy on the other," what was one to
think of Labor-Zionist Israel? If one were to adopt Talmon's taxonomy, the
Jewish state was certainly no "liberal democracy"—and there was only one
other thing it could be.[55]

As suggested earlier, Talmon's division of all modern history into a struggle between "Messianic" movements and their opponents is nothing more
than an application to general history of a theory that the first generation of
Hebrew University scholars had already applied to Jewish history. In
Talmon's world, "liberal democracy" plays the role that Hasidism played for
Buber and Scholem: It is "liberal democracy" that seeks to "neutralize" the
"Messianic element" in politics, delegitimizing any "collective purpose" or
"final aim" greater than the achievement of political rights for the individual—just as in Jewish history it is Buber and Scholem's "Hasidism" that
seeks to neutralize the Messianic element in religion by rejecting any collective purpose of final aim greater than the achievement of redemption in the
heart of the individual. In Talmon's thought, as in Buber's, this dichotomy
between the totalitarian-Messianic approach to public life and the personal-
humanistic one is presented in such a radical form that every leader arousing
the hopes of a people for collective historic improvement can immediately
be suspected of being a reincarnation of either Shabtai Tzvi or Robespierre—or, as in the case of Labor Zionism, both.

Ben-Gurion correctly understood that the extreme stance of the professors on this subject ruled out not only fanatical and violent collective purposes but even such benign collective efforts as the construction of Jewish
settlements in the Negev Desert—which, of course, had nothing to do
with anyone's personal rights, being derived from the greater aim of constructing a Jewish state capable of absorbing millions of immigrants. For
this reason, Ben-Gurion argued, the denial of the legitimacy of higher collective purposes was in effect a denial of the legitimacy of the entire Zionist
enterprise. "The fears of Professor Talmon and his students or friends," he
wrote, "that a Messianic faith leads to despotism and dictatorship, are the
result of a mistaken and misleading reading of history. . . . Without the
Messianic faith, the last three generations of our people would not have
done what they did."[56]

Put simply, if one accepts the idea that placing the nation's physical and
moral forces in the service of some greater purpose is the root of totalitarianism, then any political movement or political state that sets as its pur-

pose saving the Jews of Europe from destruction, for example, or protecting and rebuilding Jewish civilization is of necessity an incipient totalitarianism. And from here, it is no great distance to the conclusion that if Israel
were to pay more than lip service to its purpose as a *Jewish* state, it would
risk becoming—just as the emancipationists had insisted in the time of
Herzl—intrinsically illegitimate.

Buber, Bergmann, Leibowitz, Scholem, Simon, Koebner, Rotenstreich,
Prawer, Talmon—and so on. It was these scholars who taught the children
of the Zionist movement when they came to college in the first years of the
state. In virtually every field of the humanities and social sciences, the students at the Hebrew University encountered towering academic figures who
had presumably made peace with the idea of a Jewish state, but whose intellectual output was not necessarily compatible with this claim. In fact, one
can say that from behind his desk at the Hebrew University, seated beneath
a picture of a church with the cross proudly visible,[57] Buber sat at the hub of
the great intellectual contrivance that he and his associates had succeeded in
creating in the course of over forty years, and that continued to broadcast
his ideas and variations on his ideas in virtually every idea-making discipline
in the university.

Among the professors, too, there were always some who would go out of
their way to make sure that the students were able to draw the appropriate
political conclusions from the theories they learned in class. In Magnes's
day, the professors of the Peace Association and the League for Arab-Jewish
Rapprochment had sponsored lectures and "clubs" that sought to influence
the political views of the students.[58] And in the early years of the state, a
concerned professor such as Yeshayahu Leibowitz would summon promising students to off-campus encounters in which they were fed the professors' political line.[59] Moreover, there were always those professors who gave
voice to their political opinions in their lectures or articles, as a colleague in
the history department recalls concerning Jacob Talmon's work:

> When discussing critically policies advocated by the government or the pub-
> lic, Talmon frequently inserted remarks such as "history teaches." It was of-
> ten difficult to distinguish when he really thought that his views were formed
> by what one could consider "historical lessons," from when he used historical
> arguments rhetorically in order to strengthen his arguments. . . . His political
> pronouncements and opinions were fused with [his] historical insights.[60]

And yet there is something strange, even eerie, about the vast generational divide that opened up between the Zionist immigrants of the 1920s

and 1930s and their university-educated children, a scandalous proportion of whom ended up with views much closer to those of the professors than to the ideas they had heard in their homes. Even if a few were simply mesmerized by what they learned in college, surely there must be a deeper explanation if—as journalists and academics had already begun emphasizing by the early 1970s—the "generation of the sons" was drifting ever farther from the beliefs that had animated the work of the Zionist founders.[61]

The key to understanding the remarkable openness with which students from staunchly Zionist homes received the views of the teachers lies, it seems, with Berl Katznelson's description of Labor Israel in the 1930s, as a country characterized by what can only be called intellectual famine: "Our sole occupation is piling up gravel and cement and putting up the frames for buildings."[62] Certainly, some of the members of the Labor movement, Katznelson and Ben-Gurion among them, were keen on their own intellectual development and that of others. But the vast majority of Labor Zionists in the 1930s had neither the means nor the time, even if they had the inclination, to collect books of philosophy in Greek as Ben-Gurion did. Instead, the opposite was the case. In becoming laborers rebuilding their land, they reversed whatever intellectual gains their fathers had made in Europe, giving up most of their nonphysical abilities and sinking into a world devoid of abstract thought. "Work filled every cranny of our souls," wrote Shmuel Dayan, one of the founders of the kibbutz movement and Moshe Dayan's father, "for there was nothing else all day long, from two hours before dawn until after dark. . . . It was clear that we could not triumph over ourselves in any other way."[63]

But if the collective farms, the pride of the Labor movement, were not centers of intellectual or ideological activity, neither did Labor Zionism provide itself with any alternative venues for intellectual development. As Yitzhak Ben-Aharon, one of the leaders of the kibbutz movement, charged in a speech before the Labor Central Committee in 1937: "If we examine the situation, we can say that in our movement today there is no intellectual center, no place for exchanging ideas, for reflection, no place for studying our ideals, for developing and expounding them. Practical life is not accompanied by any ideological activity. Today there are hardly any such centers among the workers." At this point, when Ben-Aharon repeated that "today" there were no intellectual centers in the Labor movement, Yosef Sprinzak interrupted him, shouting: "When did they exist? Can you give us any examples?"[64]

To those few intellectuals who were familiar with what was happening in Jewish Palestine, the mental privation entailed in the construction of the country was obvious. Even Buber, a lifelong enthusiast of kibbutz socialism, was sober about the meaning of kibbutz life when his son-in-law, the poet Ludwig Strauss, was in 1936 considering joining a kibbutz founded by disciples of Buber's from Germany. As Buber wrote to Strauss:

When you wish to take root in a kibbutz, you must forget to some extent who you are. . . . That will be more onerous than you imagine. . . . You will no longer be able to hold fast to the rhythm of activities and the leisure that you as a poet need. If you join a kibbutz, you must let yourself be swallowed hide-and-hair by the equal and common, by the command of the earth that needs to be plowed, and only accord yourself the poet's breath when and if the situation of the kibbutz frees you for it.[65]

And even this none-too-subtle message was perhaps an overly euphemistic description. This, at least, is the impression one gets from the description of the young Shimon Peres, who, after years of Labor movement indoctrination during high school, decided to join a collective farm rather than attend university. What Peres found was that

smiles were few and far between. Mistakes were seldom glossed over. . . . Here each person was under constant collective scrutiny, and was required to measure up to rigidly demanding criteria. Woe betide anyone leaving for work in the fields after the sun had risen, and woe betide him if he returned before it had set. . . . Our labor, as A. D. Gordon had taught us, was the essence of our life. Anyone wielding his scythe without the requisite energy, anyone betraying a careless slip during milking, could be certain of being censured by the entire kibbutz.[66]

Peres himself escaped subjugation to this socialist utopia by wrangling a job tending the sheep, spending long days and nights out with his flock, far from the prying eyes of other members of the collective. "I loved my job," he later wrote, "for the freedom it gave me to roam around for hours on end, not answerable to a soul, at liberty to dream."[67] But Peres seems not to have drawn any conclusions as to what this meant for those who were not assigned to tend the sheep.

What Katznelson and Buber already understood in the 1930s had become a blight by the time Israel reached independence. Not only the collective farms but the cities as well had by now produced an entire generation whose central concern was works of "gravel and cement," and that had come to value *bitzuism*—a Hebrew word that can be roughly translated as "executionism," meaning doing much while thinking little—above all else. In 1950, Natan Rotenstreich, himself a graduate of the kibbutz-oriented Gordonia movement, was forced to admit that there existed an inverse relationship between the realization of Zionism and intellectual activity of any kind. "This explains what might otherwise seem paradoxical," wrote Rotenstreich, "namely that the awakening of Jewish life [in Israel] and the faith in its potential did not lead to a renewal of Judaic thought and its invigoration."[68] By this time, Buber, too, was aware that a wrong turn had been taken and began to speak of Jewish Palestine as "a reality devoid of ideas": "The members of this generation, whether openly or secretly in their hearts, suspect ideas as ideas and put their trust only in tangible reality as such." Indeed, such emphasis had been placed on material achievements in Jewish Palestine that by now the material world had become a kind of adversary to thought, which "threatens to swallow up the ideas that are still alive."[69]

In an essay from 1934, Berl Katznelson had prophesied that the creation of such a reality in Palestine, stripped of ideas and meaning by the very labor that had brought it into being, would be the cause of immense hardship among future generations. "Many Jews will yet live in this land, and they will have no rest on account of our cultural suffering,"[70] he had said. And indeed, the youth who tried to survive amid this intellectual suffocation paid the price that he had understood they would. Thus, the novelist Amos Oz recalled his alienation from the stark reality he encountered upon joining a kibbutz as a teenager in 1954: "They had contempt for everything I was. Contempt for emotions other than patriotism. Contempt for literature other than [nationalist poet Nathan] Alterman. Contempt for values other than courage and stout-heartedness. Contempt for law other than the law of 'might makes right.'"[71] The historian Meron Benvenisti went straight to kibbutz after finishing high school in 1952, as he had been encouraged to do in his youth movement, but he too collided headlong with the stultification he found there:

> The reality of kibbutz life was totally at odds with my expectations. I remember those back-breaking early dawns harvesting clover with a sickle. I earnestly tried to perceive the cosmic meaning of my work, but could perceive only deadly boredom, and at the same time shame and disappointment at my weakness. I longed for intellectual challenges, but my physical exhaustion left me unable to read a page in the evening. I dreaded the sound of the gong waking us for another day in the fields.

Too uncreative or too honest to find himself a safe haven from the collective as Shimon Peres had done ten years earlier, Benvenisti, like many others of his generation, simply quit. "One day I . . . simply notified the kibbutz office I was leaving. I did not take anything with me, just a terrible feeling of shame. I have a vivid recollection of walking slowly down that unpaved road, hoping not to meet any of my comrades, of boarding a bus and going directly to the registrar's office of the Hebrew University in Jerusalem."[72]

It was no secret that Labor Zionists often spoke with contempt of the "materialism" and lack of ideals that seemed to pervade the lives of their children. And when S. Yizhar famously labeled them "the espresso generation," the name stuck, seemingly encapsulating in a word the selfishness and irresponsibility that had brought a generation to turn its back on its parents' ideals.[73] But "espresso" is not precisely a materialistic word, and the life of the cafes, galleries, and libraries that it sought to capture was not necessarily a life of selfishness and irresponsibility, either. Far from being a sign of advancing materialism, the turn against practical Zionist values reflected much the opposite: The search for something *higher* on the part of many intelligent, even spiritual young Jews, for whom trying to persist on Labor Israel's mediocre physicality—incongruously called "redemption" by Ben-Gurion and the generation that had lived through the Holocaust—meant little more than asphyxiation. And it was this intellectual asphyxiation, and the students' resentment of their parents who had created it, that the professors seized upon to such great effect. It was the professors who sympathized with the students' predicament, and it was they who provided the children of the Zionist movement with what they wanted and needed most—a worldview that gave moral sanction to their disillusionment with the suffocating ideals on which they had been raised.

Thus, while the attacks by the professors on the moral foundations of Ben-Gurion's Zionism may have missed their mark with most of the public, they succeeded in finding an enthusiastic audience at the university—especially after the 1956 Sinai campaign, in the wake of which many leading professors, authors, and artists for the first time joined in open criticism of the presumptions of mainstream Labor Zionism. "The turning point for some," Amos Oz recalled later, "was the Sinai campaign. It became clear that the founding father, or the group of the founding fathers, in fact errs, in both senses of the word: They make mistakes, and they do evil."[74]

By 1959, the hostility toward Ben-Gurion's government had reached such proportions among the students that the Labor party was for the first time defeated in student-union elections at the Hebrew University—by a group that called itself the "Independents" and was openly opposed to the governing ethos. That year, too, recent graduates from the Hebrew University and its new daughter institution in Tel Aviv began publishing a literary journal called *Achshav* ("Now"), which launched a bitter assault on the prevailing themes of Labor Zionism. Writing in 1960, one of the journal's editors, Gavriel Moked, took careful aim at what he called the "pseudo-Messianism" that was the driving cultural force in Labor Zionist Israel:

> If we look as objectively as possible at cultural life in our Israel . . . there stands out the official worldview of most of our educators and our public figures. This worldview is common to the Education Ministry and our veteran authors . . . and to the editors of the newspapers. . . . According to this worldview, there is no room in the literature and culture of Israel for being "uprooted" . . . What there is room for is topics like "Holocaust," "redemption," "the triumph of Israel," "the forging of far-flung communities into a people." . . .

Our audience . . . is buckling under the weight of these visions routinely heaped upon its shoulders . . . which endlessly fall from the mouths of our senior officials . . . And really, what do people living in Tel-Aviv . . . have to do with the covenant of Abraham? Is the General Staff of the IDF really some kind of local chapter of the general staff of the Lord of Hosts, as claimed in a poem by an anonymous poet from the diaspora, published in one of the papers last Independence Day? . . . I do not believe officials from the Defense Ministry when they speak of the Jews standing at Mt. Sinai a second time, or when they speak of the Third Kingdom of Israel . . .

Perhaps our literary environment will finally be able to shake itself free from them, from their primitive chatter and their anachronistic spiritual and cultural associations, and we will be able to go back a bit to an atmosphere . . . in which problems are experienced by us without first being filtered through the ideological-metaphysical prism of "the redemption of Israel," or through the national-societal prism of "the enterprise of reconstruction," or of "the revival of the land."[75]

The editors of *Achshav* went on to become pivotal figures in Israel's cultural establishment, with Moked and Dan Miron becoming leading professors of Israeli literature, while their coeditors Yehuda Amichai and Nathan Zach were eventually recognized as Israel's most important poets. But the worldview that their publication promulgated was not unique to them. On the contrary, it spoke for a generation of students in the humanities and social sciences who chose the path of the professors over that of Ben-Gurion.

In fact, one may speak to individuals of this generation who went on to become prominent in Israel's cultural establishment almost at random and in nearly every case find that they trace their own views back to what they learned at the university in the 1950s and 1960s. Thus, Israel Segal, producer of Channel 2's *Mishal Ham*, probably Israel's most influential political interview program, says: "I can't imagine intellectual life without the German Jews that came. They plowed the ground of the thinking here. They brought . . . Hermann Cohen and Franz Rosenzweig and Franz Kafka. They opened a rich world for us."[76] It was Scholem and Leibowitz, he says, who taught him the value of truth and intellectual integrity. "Then there was Talmon. I happen to have things that he said about the Messianism in Israel that cause shivers when read even today." Yael Dayan, parliamentarian, leading spokesman for the Israeli Left, and daughter of Moshe Dayan, reports that she was not influenced by her studies with Buber and Bergmann. What had a real impact on her was reading "Talmon, his big book on totalitarianism." Ze'ev Sternhell, a prominent professor of political science at the Hebrew University, names the instructors who most influenced him as Talmon, Rotenstreich, Prawer, and Yehoshua Arieli, explaining that "they contributed to the formation of my comprehensive outlook . . . They opened a humanistic outlook for me."

Ilan Pappe of Haifa University, perhaps the most outspoken advocate of a "post-Zionist" historiography, reports that he was "very influenced" by the writings of the members of the Peace Association, and especially by Buber: "I read Martin Buber, and I was very impressed by what I read . . . For me, Buber is the man who succeeded in bridging between abstract philosophy . . . and the concrete reality of Palestine." Tom Segev, the noted journalist and revisionist historian, likewise refers to Talmon first among his intellectual influences ("He was outspoken, very outspoken"). A. B. Yehoshua, one of Israel's most important authors, studied philosophy and literature, emphasizing that it was the philosophy department that was "the major for the good people, for the serious people" and that was critical "to forming a person and his way of thinking." He had had a personal relationship with Bergmann, but he names Rotenstreich as foremost among those who influenced him during his studies. Hanoch Marmari, editor in chief of the leading Israeli daily, *Ha'aretz*, says that "the impressive personalities were Talmon and Prawer. Talmon in particular was influential . . . He taught the French revolution and dealt with the revolution itself. Anyone who wanted could make the connections. Of course it was influential. These were things that you internalize."[77]

Asa Kasher, professor of philosophy at Tel Aviv University, columnist, and author of the IDF code of ethics, mentions Bergmann, Leibowitz, and their student Shlomo Bar-Hillel as the professors who most interested him in the classroom. But he stresses that the greatest impact on him was the "work" of the philosophers outside the classroom, especially Rotenstreich's crusade against Ben-Gurion during the Lavon Affair. Says Kasher, "I wouldn't be doing what I am, if they hadn't done what they did." The revisionist historian Benny Morris studied history and philosophy and says he was most influenced by Prawer ("who always talked about his great mentor Koebner") and Talmon.[78] Amos Oz studied philosophy and literature at the Hebrew University, joining Rotenstreich in the public battle to bring down Ben-Gurion.[79] Shulamit Aloni, founder of the Citizens' Rights Movement ("Meretz"), says she "had a wonderful relationship with both Bergmann and Buber, as well as with Gershom Scholem . . . It was my private conversations with the philosophy professors that had impact on me."[80] Meron Benvenisti, historian and leading columnist, learned Buber's essays "almost by heart" as a youth but developed much of his worldview while studying the Crusades under Prawer.[81] The historian and educator Mordechai Bar-On lists as his greatest influences Koebner, Talmon, Prawer, and the economist Don Patinkin.[82]

And then there is Aharon Appelfeld, the respected novelist and inter-preter of the Holocaust, ascribes his ability to understand life to his mentors at Hebrew University: "I studied under Buber and Scholem at Hebrew University . . . Buber and Scholem opened new gates for me. It was a new life."[83]

CHAPTER 13

The Triumph of
the Intellectuals

THE MAINSTREAM OF LABOR ZIONISM that Ben-Gurion represented accepted the premise that Zionism was in its essence about the empowerment of the Jewish people—and the self-confidence, respect, and even honor that Jews might gain once they were again able to pursue Jewish interests and aspirations as "masters of their own fate" in a sovereign Jewish state. As discussed in the previous chapter, this aim was difficult to reconcile with the heritage of emancipationist German Judaism, and was therefore problematic for leading figures at the Hebrew University. Thus, even after they had announced their acceptance of the Jewish state in which they now lived, many of them nevertheless continued to devise and defend historical and philosophical systems in which the use of Jewish political power in the service of collective Jewish purposes—the conceptual cornerstone of the Jewish state—was of questionable legitimacy. And inevitably, such systems tended to lead to the conclusion that the use of Jewish power in the service of Jewish collective purposes (or "final aims" or "salvationist creeds") had to be "neutralized" somehow: if not by means of a binational state or a Near Eastern federation, then through "Hasidism" or "liberal democracy." Those who did not see the merits of such a neutralization could without difficulty be suspected of treading the path of Shabtai Tzvi or Robespierre, if not worse.

For more than a decade, these ideas were rarely encountered outside of Israel's universities. And even when the professors permitted themselves a public confrontation with Ben-Gurion over his conception of the Jewish state—as at the 1957 Jewish Agency conference in which Buber compared the prime minister's ideas to those of the false prophets of the Bible who used God's name to sanction evil[1]—it was noticeably without political effect.

Yet intellectuals cannot develop, publish, and teach theories according to which their government is being operated as a nascent totalitarian state without eventually bringing about some kind of a reaction among the public for whom these theories are being produced. Sooner or later, scholars and writers who believe such things are either marginalized by the educated public as cranks—as the professors who openly identified with Ihud were in the 1950s—or else an event comes along whose effect is to render their ideas plausible and brings them crashing into the mainstream of public thought. Reality may appear ambiguous. But it is in the nature of powerful ideas that they force reality to speak clearly, responding to such theories with a resounding "no" or "yes."

During the first decade after independence, educated Israeli Jews, their cultural leaders, and other public figures who were exposed to the theories of the professors had heard reality say only "no." There were, of course, exceptions, including those students at the Hebrew University who, even before the Lavon Affair, had understood exactly what their professors were talking about. But for the majority, the theory of "totalitarian democracy" in its various forms remained irrelevant to the mainstream public ideas of the Jewish state until the eruption of "the affair" in October 1960, when suddenly broad and influential circles found themselves believing that reality might just be shouting "yes."

The Lavon Affair was a who-authorized-the-spy scandal that pitted Ben-Gurion—along with a group of his defense-establishment protégés such as Moshe Dayan and Shimon Peres—against a Labor party official named Pinhas Lavon, who had served a brief term as defense minister five years earlier. Now, Lavon came before the Knesset Defense and Foreign Affairs Committee, where he presented testimony whose gist was that despite the facade of Israeli democracy, the IDF had in fact achieved operational independence from civilian government, and the country was in danger of being transformed into a military dictatorship under Ben-Gurion's rule.[2]

On the face of it, the allegation had little going for it. Israel was by this point a vital parliamentary democracy, heir to over sixty years of Zionist experience in democratic rule, which had seen the downfall of revered leaders and witnessed peaceful transitions of power. Indeed, within a matter of months—by March 1961—Ben-Gurion had been stripped of his ability to form a government by a democratically elected Knesset using routine democratic means. If ever there was a moment for the putative "dictator" to take things in hand, this was it. But nothing of the sort happened, of course. Instead, Ben-Gurion's standing as a leader rapidly plummeted, and his career wound to a close.

Yet despite these seemingly obvious facts, at the time Lavon's allegations did strike a receptive chord with Ben-Gurion's political opponents and some of the press, which had for years been chafing against his high-handed style of governing and against various of his policies they believed to be inappropriate for a democratic state (such as the ongoing military administration of the Galilee and the military censor, to pick two obvious examples). And this time the politicians were joined in their denunciations of the government by the leading professors of the Hebrew University and their students, who made the Lavon Affair the occasion for their first collective sally into politics since the establishment of the state. Fusing Lavon's conspiracy theories and allegations of crypto-dictatorship with their own theories as to how illegitimate government is born, they threw the full weight of their prestige into a campaign to convince the public that Israeli democracy was really on the brink of disaster.

The results of this incursion into politics were of the first order. There is even evidence that the activism of the professors during the Lavon Affair had the direct *political* effect of bringing on new elections and triggering the downward spiral that ended Ben-Gurion's career. But more important for the history of the Jewish state is the *cultural* victory that the triumph over Ben-Gurion represented.[3] For in the minds of the student demonstrators, Lavon and his wild accusations were only the tip of an iceberg, a convenient pretext to fight a much deeper battle: the struggle to "smash the monstrosity" of Ben-Gurion's leadership—as Amos Oz later described it[4]—and put an end to the collective historical missions that had meant everything to the generation of the founders.

And though very few of the professors and students who fought Ben-Gurion would have said at the time that they opposed a Jewish state, this does not change the fact that the state they demanded left little room for a Jewish state such as Herzl had advocated.[5] Thus, the Lavon Affair marked the precise moment when the idea of the Jewish state began to falter in the mainstream of Israeli political life—the moment when most Israelis were first reminded of that other, alternative conception of the state that had been waiting on the fringes of public consciousness for so long.

Although it is difficult to remember today, the Lavon Affair revolved around the political rise and fall of Pinhas Lavon, a Labor party leader who had for many years been the leading light of Gordonia, a kibbutz-oriented youth movement originally centered in Galicia and styled after the utopian labor-guru A. D. Gordon. It was this choice of a role model that led the young Lavon to describe the Jewish nation using such terms as "a spiritual-cultural-cosmic entity." He also declared himself a binationalist when this became the fashion in Austria in the late 1920s, but he gave up on this idea a few years later.[6] In his position as secretary-general of the Histadrut and Ben-Gurion's stalking horse within the Left wing of the Labor party, Lavon set himself up as a flamboyant advocate of views that at times approached those of the professors. Like many of the academics, he was an opponent of Ben-Gurion's policy of political alignment with the orthodox parties, and he also objected to the militarily "activist" line that Ben-Gurion had adopted as the means of pressuring the Arab states to cease terror operations against Israel. Lavon likewise joined Buber and other professors in dissenting from the mass immigration of hundreds of thousands of Jews from the Arab lands into Israel, claiming that the "poor quality" of the immigrants would lead to "counter-revolution" and the ruin of the Labor party. "The question is simple," he said on this subject. "Will there arise here a Levantine people, or a people bearing the divine image of the Hebrew Labor movement—that which was dreamed of, written of, and for which two generations at least sacrificed their lives? Are we to be reduced to a Jewish version of the Lebanon, Syria, and Egypt?"[7]

The Lavon Affair had its roots in Ben-Gurion's abrupt—and to this day not fully explained—elevation of Lavon to the post of defense minister in 1954. Ben-Gurion himself had held this position, along with the prime ministership, since independence, and had seen it as being at the very heart of his state-building. After six years in office, he announced his intention to take a break from holding formal positions, leaving Moshe Sharett and Lavon at the helm. The appointment of the fifty-year-old Lavon to this post was no small shock to the Labor leadership, which received his promotion as a bid by Ben-Gurion to anoint the younger and perhaps more pliable man his successor. In accepting the appointment, Lavon took charge of a ministry operated almost entirely by individuals in their thirties—among them Chief of Staff Moshe Dayan and Ministry Director-General Shimon Peres—the "young men" who had been handpicked and tutored by Ben-Gurion and whose loyalty was not to the party establishment but rather to the old man's vision of a continued and aggressive upbuilding of Jewish national strength.

Much to the amazement of the onlookers, Lavon did not let his new-found benefactor down. Without giving up a stitch of his ideological affinity for the radical Left, Lavon immediately set upon a course of "heating up" relations with the neighboring Arab states in an effort to outdo even Ben-Gurion in the war against Arab terrorism. Sharett, now prime minister, found himself bypassed time and again as his defense minister took matters into his own hands, initiating cross-border operations, reprisals, and even the hijacking of a Syrian airliner. The dumbfounded Sharett scribbled in his diary that since assuming control of the IDF, Lavon had "incessantly advocated acts of lunacy, inculcating the army command with the diabolical notion of igniting the Middle East, fomenting disputes, bloody assassinations, attacks on objectives and assets of the powers, desperate and suicidal acts."[7]

Although many of Lavon's proposals for operations against the Arab states were blocked by the army, at least one of them did manage to go through: In the spring of 1954, after only four months in office, Lavon began considering options for containing the rapidly increasing power of Gamal Abdel Nasser, the Egyptian strongman. What he came up with was a scheme for disrupting the expected departure from Egypt of the British forces garrisoned there—considered a serious obstacle to Nasser's ambitions—by means of a series of terrorist acts against British targets in Egypt, to be carried out by Egyptian Jews posing as Muslim extremists. By midsummer, the entire operation had been penetrated by Egyptian counterintelligence, which activated the unit on its own initiative and then followed up by imprisoning the entire Israeli network. When news of the arrests and the impending trials of the Israeli spies reached Jerusalem, it touched off frantic cover-up efforts by Lavon and his erstwhile collaborator on the Egyptian project, IDF Director of Military Intelligence Binyamin Givly, with each attempting to pin blame for the debacle on the other. Both sides manufactured evidence and accusations—with Lavon even threatening suicide[8]—for the benefit of the government and ultimately for the Israeli public, which would clear one of them at most. An unofficial commission of inquiry was unable to clear either of them of responsibility, and Lavon's term as a senior minister, prime-ministerial contender, and superhawk, came to an end with his resignation in February 1955, just over a year after it had begun. With Ben-Gurion's assistance, Lavon returned to his earlier post as secretary-general of the Labor Federation, and Ben-Gurion himself returned to office as defense minister.

But this was only the beginning. Lavon continued to nurse the conviction that his career had been sabotaged by a conspiracy of top army officers orchestrated by Dayan and Peres,[9] and this belief only grew more malignant during the years after his departure from the government. For their part, Ben-Gurion's clique of military-establishment protégés seemed more than willing to go out of their way to act the part Lavon designed for them. Even before the destruction of the Israeli spy network in Egypt, the chief of staff,

Dayan, had demonstrated a marked tendency to meddle in civilian public life, founding his own political movement at a national convention with Ben-Gurion in attendance. In June 1955, he called for the youth of the country "to storm the Knesset and other key redoubts" in order to "replace the aging, defeatist leadership in the party, the Histadrut and the government." Dayan's tactless attacks on the Labor leadership, Ben-Gurion's well-known plans for constitutional reform (he favored a district-based electoral system that was expected to increase the power of the prime minister in the Knesset), and the relentless rumormongering of their political opponents, all worked to raise the fear—treated by certain Israeli leaders as fact—that Dayan and Peres were planning a military putsch to make Ben-Gurion dictator. Lavon assisted in fanning this fear, and Ben-Gurion's 1959 election victory, winning Labor an unprecedented 47 Knesset seats with its egregious campaign slogan "Say 'Yes' to the Old Man," brought the dread of dictatorship, among those who were disposed to take this seriously, to a crescendo. After the elections, Ben-Gurion's new coalition government made Dayan a junior minister and Peres a deputy minister, redoubling the fear among the party old guard that the prime minister wished to drive them out.[10]

Finally, in September 1960, five years after he had left the government, Lavon reemerged from exile with new information provided to him by opponents of Peres and Dayan. According to a story leaked to *Ma'ariv*, then the largest daily paper, Lavon had been framed with documents fabricated by the army, and he demanded that the government clear him of all responsibility for the Egyptian spy disaster. Primed with years of dictatorship innuendo—in the form of the professors' "totalitarian democracy" fetish, as well as in Uri Avneri's sensationalist weekly, *Ha'olam Hazeh*[11]—several of the leading newspapers bought the conspiracy story and proceeded to abet a smear campaign that in short order brought Lavon and his accusations before the Knesset Defense and Foreign Affairs Committee. In a series of Knesset appearances in October, Lavon loosed a savage campaign of accusations—Sharett referred to them as "a weave of atrocities"[12]—against Dayan and Peres, depicting the defense establishment during his year in office as operating without ministerial control, and insinuating that senior officers and officials had been participants in criminal activities that had resulted in his elimination from his post.[13]

Although the sessions of the Knesset committee were supposedly closed, virtually everything that Lavon said was leaked directly to the press, and within a matter of days, the country was awash with rumors that the army had spun out of control. Both genuine fear and rank rumormongering by Ben-Gurion's political opponents seem to have contributed to magnifying the importance of what was reported in the press. Moreover, what actually appeared in the papers was perhaps even more frightening than straightfor-

ward reporting of Lavon's accusations would have been: Due to the con-
straints imposed by the military censor, the entire story was reported in a
bizarre code with no names attached, using shadowy expressions such as
"the senior officer," "the reserve officer," and "the third man" as stand-ins
for the actual human beings involved.[14] At any rate, Lavon rapidly managed
to do so much damage that Moshe Sharett, who had been prime minister
during the original spy debacle, felt constrained to issue a statement in an
attempt to stem the tide. On October 25, five days after Lavon's final appearance in the Knesset, Sharett issued a statement to the effect that Lavon
had been innocent of wrongdoing. But the effort backfired. By this point,
an exoneration of Lavon by the Labor leadership could only be understood
as a clear indication that his accusations of a frame-up had been substantially correct. Suddenly, Ben-Gurion found himself, his young protégés, and
the Israel Defense Forces itself publicly convicted of a shopping list of
crimes against which they were powerless to defend themselves.[15]

With an anguished compulsion that few seem to have been able to
fathom, Ben-Gurion threw himself into the maelstrom. Insisting that neither the press nor the Knesset had the right to determine innocence and
guilt, he demanded a commission of inquiry with full judicial powers to get
to the bottom of the affair once and for all. This call for justice to be rendered by means of a judicial proceeding may today seem like a reasonable
enough demand, but by the time Lavon and his allies had finished their
handiwork at the end of October, the prime minister's standing had been
damaged so badly that he could not even muster a majority to push it
through his own government. The party old guard flailed in a swamp of rumors that Ben-Gurion, if not actually plotting a literal coup d'état, was at
least bent on democratically replacing the government with one composed
of his young friends. Faced with the possibility of such a politically legitimate "putsch," they were by now too panicked to initiate a judicial commission of inquiry that might clear Dayan and Peres completely.

Instead, the ministers of the government resolved to investigate the affair
themselves—appointing no fewer than seven sitting ministers to a committee
that conducted its own inquiry, despite the fact that some of the ministers
had already pronounced themselves disposed to clear Lavon.[16] After nineteen sessions, the ministerial committee unanimously concluded that
"Lavon did not give the instructions" to initiate operations in Egypt, and
the government approved these findings on December 25. Ben-Gurion resigned, dissolving the government and vowing to appoint a new one that
would agree to refer the issue to a judicial commission of inquiry. The entire
country held its breath as the Labor party skidded to the brink of a split—
gasping for air as Finance Minister Levi Eshkol, who had orchestrated the
ministerial committee in order to reach a bogus "exoneration" of Lavon in

the first place, now moved, for the sake of party unity, to have Lavon dismissed as head of the Histadrut.

Looking back on these events, it is somewhat difficult to see what Ben-Gurion might have done differently, at least as far as the substance of the issue is concerned. Lavon *did* in fact do serious damage to the image of the armed forces, not to mention to the prime minister; and the ministerial committee *was* in fact a travesty of justice. It is difficult to imagine an American president or a British prime minister being expected to sustain an assault of this kind from a member of his own party and not responding by eliminating the threat to his government.

But Israeli Jews had never had a prime minister before, and many were, it seems, genuinely afraid of the power entailed in this post. Certainly Ben-Gurion, whose outbursts of spleen had always been insufferable and only grew worse with age (he called Menachem Begin an "outstanding example of the Hitlerian type" and Pinhas Lavon "human scum"),[17] was hardly the man to reassure them. For these, Eshkol's decision to switch sides and seek Lavon's dismissal was the final straw. Ben-Gurion, it was said, was prepared to dismiss the entire government for the crime of having ruled that Lavon was an innocent man; indeed, he was willing to have Lavon dismissed from his post *after* he had been found innocent by the government itself. And the government was so intimidated by the threat of Ben-Gurion's resignation that it was willing to do his bidding, despite the fact that it had found Lavon innocent. Was it not a sure sign of dictatorship when the state punishes an innocent man for fear of the prime minister's whim?

Of course, this was what Buber and his associates had been claiming with regard to Ben-Gurion since the founding of the state. Even the simple dismissal of a foreign minister over policy disagreements had been treated by Ihud as a totalitarian step ("the General has driven out the Diplomat").[18] No wonder, then, that the parties closest to Buber's circle, Mapam and the Progressives (which had been the binationalist Hashomer Hatzair and German immigrants' parties, respectively, prior to independence) suddenly went public with the recognition that the professors just may have been right. Perhaps Lavon really *had* uncovered a "totalitarian" current within Israeli democracy. "We are all in danger—all of us," Meir Ya'ari, head of Mapam, told the press, pointing to "the danger of dictatorship" posed by "the group surrounding Ben-Gurion."[19] Israel, he said, was showing "all the signs of the consolidation of a totalitarian regime. . . . The fate of the democratic regime in the country . . . is now in the balance and dangling by a thread."[20] Similarly, Yizhar Harari of the Progressives compared the campaign against Lavon to the French reign of terror, the original "totalitarian democracy" that Talmon had described in his book: "This reminds me too much of the days of the French constituent assembly. . . . Robespierre went to the guillotine, and Danton went to the guillotine, and everyone went to the guillotine. . . . It's simply frightening from a democratic perspective."[21]

The same sentiment quickly spread to other parties as well. Thus, Israel Bar-Yehuda, secretary-general of Tabenkin's Ahdut Ha'avoda party, similarly warned that a leader could come to power by democratic means and yet, "by force of a personality cult, determine every aspect of life in the country." It was possible, he said, that Israel might give up on democracy, "find some old man to say 'yes' too, and be done with it."[22]

Ben-Gurion's conservative opponents were only too happy to join the bandwagon as well, with Yosef Sapir, leader of the General Zionists speaking of the "gradual but rather rapid advancement of a ruling clique within the ruling party, which has dictatorial aspirations."[23] And Menachem Begin's Herut got in its revenge, too, with one of the party's leaders, Yohanan Bader, comparing David Ben-Gurion to a Molech, lusting after human blood—that of Pinhas Lavon. As he said in a speech before the Knesset: "When flesh and blood turns into a god . . . according to the ancient tradition one must bring this god a sacrifice of flesh and blood, from a man. A living man. I call upon every man who has not yet gotten down on his knees . . . to lend a hand against this menace."[24]

In the early stages of Lavon's assault on the Israeli military, the universities were already seething with hostility toward Ben-Gurion and the "young men" around him. The professors of Buber's generation were not alone in this. The dean of the Hebrew University humanities faculty, Natan Rotenstreich, had publicly challenged Ben-Gurion's "Messianism" in a series of open letters in the wake of the Sinai campaign; and when the Lavon Affair became public in the fall of 1960, he had already been agitating on Lavon's behalf in Labor party circles for over two years.[25] There is no reason to think that other young professors close to Rotenstreich differed significantly from him on these issues, and when the ministerial committee reported its findings and Ben-Gurion rejected them, he and his colleagues found themselves prepared for a much more significant mobilization.

The result was an unprecedented public campaign against Ben-Gurion by much of the intellectual leadership of the Hebrew University, which commanded the overt support of more than sixty of its professors and instructors—including over half the faculty in the fields of history, sociology, education, and religion, and a significant proportion of the instructors in the departments of literature, philosophy, law, and Jewish studies. Professors from Tel Aviv, as well as other prominent intellectuals, writers, and artists quickly joined in as well. After lengthy deliberations, on December 29 the professors issued a statement drafted by Talmon, Rotenstreich, Prawer, and Efraim Urbach—a scholar of Judaic studies from Breslau who had fled from Germany in 1938—and signed by scores of others, including Buber, Bergmann, and Scholem. This first statement asserted that it was "not intended to place blame or offer support to one side or the other," but its message was nevertheless obvious. Execrating the events of the preceding months, in which certain leaders had placed their desire for power above all concern for principle—Ben-Gurion was not yet mentioned by name—the professors argued that "there could be no graver danger to the democratic system."[26] Buber followed up with a letter to Ben-Gurion in which he directly accused the prime minister of threatening Israeli democracy,[27] while Rotenstreich gave an interview to *Ma'ariv* in which, in response to the question of whether there was actually danger of the collapse of Israeli democracy, he affirmed that present trends were indeed "truly dangerous."[28]

A subsequent rally of professors in mid-January, 1961, led by Rotenstreich and Jacob Katz—the dean of the faculty of social sciences, who had been Buber's student at the Frankfurt Lehrhaus[29]—gathered support for a second letter composed by the professors, this one explicitly calling on the political system to reject Ben-Gurion's demands and asserting that "a worldview that subordinates the fate of the country to any particular individual contravenes the very basis of democracy, and could bring the country, sooner or later, to one-man rule."[30] Elaborating on the new declaration, Shmuel Noah Eisenstadt—a sociologist trained by Buber, who was now head of the Hebrew University's sociology department—explained that the affair constituted an attempt to gather all the authority of the government "into the hands of one man," and that there was "a genuine danger to Israeli democracy."[31]

Others who signed onto the second declaration included Buber, Bergmann, Ernst Simon, Prawer, and Talmon.[32] Buber even granted a rare interview to the press, in which he declared that he had signed the statement against Ben-Gurion because "I felt—and when I say that I felt, I mean that my whole mind was enveloped by this feeling—and I felt that this was . . . an hour of danger."[33] Similarly, Yeshayahu Leibowitz declared that "this 'affair' of ours demonstrates that the state of Israel is not a democracy . . . Napoleon was much more honest than Ben-Gurion. He didn't claim that he was fulfilling a prophetic vision."[34]

Talmon, too, seemed constantly available in the media to explain that though the present threat of an actual military coup in Israel was "small," history nevertheless taught of a "tendency" for groups of individuals with "monopolistic responsibility for national security . . . to regard parliamentary paralysis or severe internal crisis as a challenge or an opportunity to take emergency measures to save the nation."[35] And Rotenstreich, appearing in the press again, issued a demand that the country's "Messianic period," which, he said, had now lasted fifteen years, be brought to an end.[36]

But the idea that Labor Zionist "political messianism" had transformed Israel into an embryonic "totalitarian democracy" was not alone in the matrix of theories now being lobbed like mortar shells at Ben-Gurion's leadership by professors at the Hebrew University. Among their central claims was that Ben-Gurion's battle was intrinsically immoral because it was, at bottom, a struggle over power. Thus, the original manifesto issued by the professors accused Ben-Gurion of engaging in "a battle over positions of power," declaring this to be "a grave danger to the state of Israel." And it implied that a homely battle for political power was somehow a violation of the Jewish ethical tradition: "The best among the nations of the world expect that the state of Israel will live up to the spiritual heritage of our people. We may not . . . disappoint these hopes."[37] Of course, this was the view of some of the older professors, who had opposed the very existence of a Jewish state as morally problematic since it involved the pursuit of Jewish political power. It was therefore little surprise to hear Ernst Simon, for example, sighing that "we are burying a dream . . . the dream of the land of Israel, the state of the pure and the moral."[38] But this line of argument, which sought for the state of Israel the same virtue that Hermann Cohen had claimed for the Jewish Diaspora—the *renunciation* of worldly power—was also strongly in evidence among the professors trained at the Hebrew University. Natan Rotenstreich, for instance, repeatedly argued that Ben-Gurion was turning Israel into a place wherein "man is a wolf to man" and that this trend toward power politics in public life was rendering the historical basis for the Jewish state potentially *illegitimate*:

> If we do not act with care, each one towards his neighbor, and out of mutual respect, while refraining from polishing swords against one another, and if this is not going to be the content of our life here, how will we be able to turn to the Jews of the world and say to them that we are the center? Without all this, the historical warrant for our work will be eliminated.[39]

Indeed, at the height of the drama, while standing before the Labor Central Committee, Rotenstreich accused the party of the worst crime that the German-Jewish intellectual heritage permitted him to imagine: The party had turned "a man and a friend" into "an object and a means." In other words, Lavon was no longer being treated as a citizen in a Kantian "kingdom of ends"; he was no longer involved in a Buberian "dialogue" with the Labor party. Urging the grown men seated before him to return to the path of good-neighborliness they had shared with him and with Lavon in the youth movement in Galicia, Rotenstreich cried out in anguish, "Do not destroy the dream of our youth!"[40]

Such arguments may not have been perfectly tailored for winning over the Labor party Central Committee, but they worked wonders on the students at the Hebrew University—to the point that when Dayan came to speak on campus in the early stages of the affair, he found himself facing hysterical students accusing him of involvement in a possible military coup, in what the press reported to be "a lynch atmosphere."[41] As matters progressed, the professors grew bolder in their incitement of the students, with some issuing public calls for the students to involve themselves in the efforts against Ben-Gurion. "Before the student body is one task," Yeshayahu Leibowitz told the student newspaper. "To speak its mind without fear! The students should say what lies behind the Messianic vision." Ernst Simon, too, spoke publicly in favor of student participation in the struggle of the professors, and others, including Rotenstreich, held discussions with their students over what actions should be taken.[42]

The students, not surprisingly, responded with enthusiasm, with the chairman of the Hebrew University Student Union appearing at the head of a rally warning that Israeli democracy was in danger. The editors of the campus newspaper, *Pi Ha'aton* ("The Mouth of the Ass") likewise expressed themselves in opposition to Ben-Gurion, and the paper issued a ringing endorsement of student action in the affair:

> The professors, our spiritual leaders [*anshei haruah shelanu*], have spoken their minds . . . They have spoken explicitly . . . and there are clear signs that our professors are ready to take vigorous, practical action with regard to the "affair." And what will the students do? Has not the time come for them to break their silence?[43]

The result of these efforts was the organization of a "National Movement of Students for the Defense of Democracy," which mounted demonstrations, rallies, and teach-ins against "dictatorship," including a mass "funeral" for democracy, complete with coffin. Their chants and banners carried messages such as "All hands to the defense of democracy," and "We won't give the government to Dayan and Shimon."[44] And at the decisive meeting of the Labor Central Committee in which Lavon's dismissal was being debated, crowds of students gathered outside, chanting "Democracy! Democracy!" Some even shouted "Heil Ben-Gurion!"[45]

One may glimpse the depth of the convulsion that seized much of the student population from the description of Amos Oz, who entered the Hebrew University the following year. It was during the Lavon Affair that Oz came to see that the real meaning of Ben-Gurion's ideas was the "tyranny" of dreams that had belonged to people long dead, over the present state of Israel:

I saw that the root [of Ben-Gurion's Messianism] was in a distortion of the soul ... in the tyranny of the dead over the living. Because this very idea means that through it the dead send messages and commandments to the living, and these messages may very well be murderous ones ... There, in Ben-Gurion, I saw the black demon-fire. ... He embodied in himself the entire Jewish mystique, the kabbala, Shabtai Tzvi, and the suicides to sanctify God's name. All of this converged in him as though at a sort of crossroads.[46]

For Oz, Ben-Gurion thus represented the call of the great historical drama, the "commandment" of generations of Jewish dead to fulfill *their* dreams by restoring a Jewish state in Israel—as opposed to the more mundane needs of the present, living citizens of the state. It was during this elemental confrontation with "the great drama" of Ben-Gurion's Zionism that Oz recognized, with perfect clarity, "that the cost of the great drama is death, and that one must choose life." But how? How was a twenty-one-year-old student to "choose life," while living in a Jewish state that had been conceived and created for the very purpose of playing a decisive role in "the great drama"? For Amos Oz, as for his peers, the answer was Pinhas Lavon:

When I met Lavon, and he referred to some of the heroes of the paratroops, the idols of Israel, calling them "those hot-headed thugs," the very hearing of those sentences was a kind of redemptive experience for me. A liberating experience. Suddenly I realized—here was the force that could smash this monstrosity.[47]

Others, though less articulate, described their feelings in much the same way. Yossi Sarid, today minister of education and head of the Left-wing Meretz party, studied philosophy and literature at the Hebrew University at the same time and recalls the anguished arguments in his home over the subject of Ben-Gurion. "Although my father never raised his voice at me, we had arguments, almost fights, over Ben-Gurion. ... For my father, everything Ben-Gurion said was holy. And I said: What do you mean, 'Ben-Gurion said'?" Like many other students, Sarid found a focus for his resentment of Ben-Gurion in the Lavon Affair. And like many others, his resentment was inextricably entangled with the image of Ben-Gurion as "the father" of the country—a father figure, Sarid says, whom he felt "an urge and a need to undermine." Asked recently whether it hurt him to lend a hand in destroying the founder of the Jewish state, Sarid's answer was nonchalant: "On the contrary. I loved smashing myths."[48]

———

While the students were demonstrating in the streets, Finance Minister Eshkol coordinated the efforts to have Lavon removed from his position as head of the Histadrut and one of the leaders of the Labor party. Eshkol's initiative culminated in a meeting of the Labor party Central Committee on February 4, 1961, where the issue was to be decided. Minister of Labor Giora Yoseftal rose to deliver a summary of what had befallen Labor Zionism in the four months since Lavon had begun his crusade.

> Lavon has created a psychosis in this country . . . to the effect that the subordination of the army to the civilian authorities is not guaranteed. This is one of the fears that has led to the hysteria that democracy is supposedly in danger. Lavon has conjured up fears that there are those in the army and in the military establishment who wish . . . to act without the oversight of the Knesset and of the government. As though there are organized "cells" among us that would actually support a "putsch." . . . In this atmosphere that has been created, the parties of the Left have . . . jumped onto a bandwagon whose driver is Lavon. . . . Never before has there been . . . such a tide of lack of confidence [in the government], and of hysteria over the danger to democracy.[49]

Lavon, Yoseftal said, had gone too far. And if Labor was to take responsibility "for what will happen in this country tomorrow," it had to decide to put an end to his campaign against the government.[50] By a vote of 159 to 96, the Central Committee voted to relieve Lavon of his post.

For those who feared that Israel was becoming a "totalitarian democracy," Lavon's demise was the final proof—if any were needed—that the worst had come to pass. Declared innocent of the charges against him, Lavon had nevertheless paid with his political life. Outraged, the professors made public their demand that Lavon be reinstated, informing the press that "our battle has not ended."[51] And in the days that followed, they threw all their weight into preventing Ben-Gurion from establishing a new government by persuading Labor's coalition partners that Ben-Gurion had ceased to be a legitimate democratic leader. Yet another professors' statement was composed, this one declaring that "a great injustice has been done in Israel, and we believe that it is forbidden to reestablish the national leadership on the basis of this injustice. We call upon the parties and their leaders . . . not to render assistance to Mr. Ben-Gurion in his efforts to build a new government coalition."[52]

The professors pressed their views on the leaders of Mapam and the Progressives, while their students assisted by staging rowdy demonstrations in the streets. And the results were as hoped. When Ben-Gurion tried to assemble his new government, he found his coalition partners unwilling to enter into the government so long as he continued at its head. In March, he was forced to inform the president that he had been unable to form a government.

We cannot know for certain that the activism of the professors and their students gave the Lavon Affair the additional push it needed to make it impossible for Ben-Gurion to form a coalition in March 1961. But there are indications that this was in fact the case. Moshe Dayan, for example, believed that it was the signed declarations of the professors that had really "created a movement of hysteria against Ben-Gurion."[53] Labor party secretary-general Yosef Almogi likewise reported that consternation at party forums was particularly focused on the campaign of demonstrations by the professors and their students, whose unprecedented attacks on the government were perceived as "the ground quaking beneath the party's feet."[54]

Moreover, it appears that the National Religious Party (NRP)—the one party in the coalition that was unsympathetic to the "prohibition" slapped on Ben-Gurion's leadership by the professors and the parties of the Left,[55] and that was also large enough to give the prime minister a ruling majority in the Knesset—changed course and decided against salvaging Ben-Gurion's government because of pressure emanating from the university. As reported by the head of the NRP, Interior Minister Haim Moshe Shapira, and emphasized by contemporary press accounts, the party's leaders had originally intended to support Ben-Gurion. But they were dramatically affected by the demonstrations of religious university students and of the party's youth wing, which had adopted the position of the professors and the Hebrew University student government.[56] It was the young protesters' meetings with party leaders, as well as the demonstration outside of party headquarters on the day of the decision, that apparently tipped the balance in the party executive, which finally decided against Ben-Gurion by a vote of 8 to 7.[57]

With nowhere else to turn, Ben-Gurion conceded defeat and the country went to elections. Ben-Gurion would never again be able to muster the confidence of a majority of the Knesset.

In retrospect, we know that the rest of the story, although it was to go on for a few years, was nothing more than a postscript. The humiliation of being placed "off limits" continued after the elections of August 1961, when Ben-Gurion's former coalition partners, led by Mapam,[58] again refused to join a government formed by him unless a new "civilian" body were erected with the power of inquiry into all doings in the military and unless they were collectively given a majority in the government capable of forcing Ben-Gurion to bow to its will.[59] These unprecedented demands returned him to the days of the British Mandate, when Meir Ya'ari had opposed his efforts to create a national executive with the authority to wage war. They were, after all, aimed at depriving an elected prime minister of the authority to govern the armed forces and to preside over the development of the power of the Jewish state.

Ben-Gurion broke off negotiations, issuing a public statement in which he declared his faith with the Jewish military that had been at the center of his life's work:

For the entire period of the state's existence apart from fifteen months . . . I have been responsible, as minister of defense, for the organization, training, education, equipment, and operations of the Israel Defense Forces. . . . The IDF has become the fortress of the security of our state, a workshop for the creation of a pioneering youth fighting and building our homeland, the blast furnace for the forging together of the various exiles, a mighty vehicle for the uplifting of the Jewish man [*adam beisrael*], and a faithful executive arm of the elected leadership of the sovereign nation—no less than the most experienced and properly trained armies in the most outstanding democracies in the world. . . . Our entire people has a right to be proud of the IDF.[60]

His message was unmistakable. Errors there may have been, but the foundation on which the Jewish state had been built—a Jewish military ready and able to protect the interests of the Jewish people—was no source of fear. It was no "totalitarianism," no "monstrosity," no creeping dictatorship, but only a source of pride for any Jew who was able to keep events in perspective.

But the back of Ben-Gurion's political strength had been broken, and his perspective was no longer shared by the majority of the Knesset. Levi Eshkol, the genial apparatchik who had served as Ben-Gurion's finance minister, was charged with the task of forming a new government. On November 2, 1961, after ten months of agony, Ben-Gurion was again presented to the Knesset as prime minister—this time as the head of a government he himself had been unable to assemble. Eighteen months later, Ben-Gurion resigned as prime minister, leaving the Labor party and the country under Eshkol's stewardship, only to return to his efforts to have the army's reputation cleared. In January 1965, Ben-Gurion staged a final showdown, in an attempt to bring about a judicial commission of inquiry into the Lavon Affair. Eshkol, insisting that the issue be buried at all cost, announced that "it is either Ben-Gurion or me," forcing a choice between the party machine and the man whose spirit had given it life. With the help of a speech by a terminally ill Sharett, who spoke from a wheelchair, and not without the obligatory telegram from professors at the Hebrew University,[61] the Labor Central Committee tilted against Ben-Gurion, forcing him out of the party. The old man's new party, founded with Dayan and Peres, contested the 1965 elections. But it returned only 10 seats in the Knesset, as opposed to Labor's 45.

With this, his final humiliation, the era of David Ben-Gurion's "totalitarian democracy," such as it had been, came to an end.

Epilogue:
The Specter of
David Ben-Gurion

EN-GURION'S RESIGNATION AS PRIME MINISTER in 1963 created a bizarre twilight period in the history of the Jewish state—one in which the old man's visionary leadership had evaporated, even though prominent intellectuals continued to live in perpetual fear of his return. "A specter is haunting Israel," wrote a young professor of political science at the Hebrew University named Shlomo Avineri, two years after Ben-Gurion's resignation. "The specter of David Ben-Gurion, erstwhile national leader and secular Messiah . . . now wandering in the political wilderness with a small band of followers . . . Is he doomed to old-age failure . . . or is it a cold-blooded maneuver, calculated to bring about major changes in Israeli society?"[1]

Defending the proposition that the Jewish state was better off without Ben-Gurion, Avineri was at pains to explain to his readers what seems to have been entirely lost upon the Labor party apparatus: that the destruction of Ben-Gurion was not primarily a political event, achieved through political means. Rather, it was a *cultural* event, achieved principally through cultural means. In attempting to explain what had happened, Avineri referred to the arrival of a "post–Ben-Gurion" era in Israel's history—an era that was "a spiritual as well as a narrowly political phenomenon." One of the main characteristics of this period was "that the state is here, and the military ma-

chinery for its security is well geared to its function" and with these fundamental achievements spoken for, there would no longer be any need for the
kind of leadership Ben-Gurion had provided. True, the resignation of
Israel's first prime minister had been traumatic. But the country would
quickly find a way to do without him: "However one evaluates Ben-
Gurion's contribution in 1948 . . . no man is indispensable in the long run.
Government [is] running smoothly."[2]

Yossi Sarid, now Israel's minister of education, would later describe this
period in similar terms, arguing that the main task of the Israeli government
in the years after Ben-Gurion was "to initiate the era of normality . . . to extricate us from the syndrome of the Holocaust, from the syndrome of the
founding of the state, from the syndrome of the battle for survival—and to
bring us into a space where one could breath normally."[3]

To breath normally. There could be no better metaphor than this one for
what Ben-Gurion's opponents had wanted: A state whose heart and lungs
no longer strained with the effort of battle; and therefore a state of mind no
longer preoccupied night and day with grand and pressing purposes, with
"the fantastic," as Herzl had called it.

And such, in fact, was the government of Levi Eshkol, which operated
for four years after 1963 as a deal-cutting technocracy, taking care of business in the absence of any grand vision or burning need to achieve anything
in particular. And even as the old Labor-Zionist way of looking at the world
declined, so too did the ideas of the professors, which had once been so peripheral, expand to fill the void. As the historian Anita Shapira explains:

> In everything related to the shaping of the national ethos, the status of the
> university changed . . . There was a correspondence between the decline in
> the standing of the Labor movement and the rise of the university's moral
> standing . . . The university entered the vacuum that was created, and began
> playing a critical role in the consolidation of a [new] national ethos.[4]

A sense of the new "post-Ben-Gurion" ethos ushered in by the professors
and their students—in all its idealism and hubris—may be gleaned from a
small but celebrated incident that took place on May 15, 1967, during the
celebration of Israel's nineteenth Independence Day. The officials responsible for the ceremonies had chosen to include in them the reading of a famous poem by Nathan Alterman, a leading Labor-Zionist poet and
confidant of Ben-Gurion, which had been written eleven years earlier.[5] The
poem spoke of the "thin line" dividing peace from war—a message that
could be appreciated by almost everyone in the 1950s but had now become
an unforgivable breach of the newly fashioned era of "non-Messianism."
When word reached the university of the planned inclusion of Alterman's
poem in the official ceremonies, one of the professors protested and was in

fact successful—or so it was reported in the press—in stifling the original version of the poem, which was in the end read in an altered form, the offending line having been neutered to suit the dictates of the new culture.[6]

At least in this case, however, Alterman's decade-old intuitions proved to be more accurate than the professor's contemporary ones. The real reason for the change in the poem was apparently the government's desire not to provoke a war already on the threshold: The day before the ceremony, Nasser began pouring tens of thousands of troops into the previously demilitarized Sinai, sweeping away the irrelevant UN "peacekeepers" who had been stationed there and positioning them on the Israeli border. Eight days later, Nasser announced the blockade of the southern Israeli port of Eilat—an action accompanied by calls for all of the Arab regimes to join hands in the eradication of the Jewish state, which they obligingly answered in the affirmative.[7] As the days went by, armed forces from Syria, Jordan, Iraq, and Kuwait piled upon one another along Israel's eastern and northern borders. Abandoned by both France and the United States, Israel was left to face the threat alone.

Eshkol, that master of political novocaine, whom the professors and their students had so admired for his ability to induce a sense that all was running "smoothly" and that everyone was "breathing normally," responded with hesitation and confusion, with endless meetings that went nowhere, and finally with an infamous radio address intended to inspire public confidence but which was stammered so badly that it left the country submerged in panic. Terrified of the impending catastrophe, representatives of various parties scurried to Ben-Gurion's home in Sde Boker to explore the possibility of returning him to the prime ministership. But once there, they found that the fire had deserted the old man, now eighty, and that he would be able to do little more than to watch the war run its course from the sidelines.[8] The specter of Ben-Gurion's leadership—at least in the form of his own personal direction of Israel's path—was no more.

Of course, the story did not end this way. The shadow of Ben-Gurion's policies was to have a life of its own that lasted a few more years, as various of his supporters attempted to step into his shoes. On June 1, 1967, two weeks after the crisis had begun, Eshkol buckled in the face of pressure to bring in a stronger personality, retrieving Ben-Gurion's protégé Moshe Dayan from the political wilderness to become defense minister. Five days later there was war; six days thereafter peace reigned—with Israel suddenly in command of territories extending from the Suez Canal to the outlooks over Damascus. Moreover, the Jews had suddenly returned to Hebron, Mt. Efraim, Jericho, and, most dazzling of all, the Old City of Jerusalem with its Temple Mount—the literal Zion for which Herzl had named his movement. Four years after Ben-Gurion's fall from power, the Six Day War brought the Jewish state to most of the places to which the biblical prophets had foretold the Jews would one day return.

At first at least, the new territories, so heavy with historical Jewish associations, seemed a godsend for the flagging spirit of practical Zionism. A startling array of the prominent Labor Zionist figures immediately organized themselves into an ideological lobby whose aim was to infuse Zionist life and settlement ideals into Eshkol's policies—including poets such as Alterman and Haim Guri; the novelists S. Y. Agnon, Moshe Shamir, Yehuda Burla, and Haim Hazaz; and Labor elder statesmen such as Rachel Yanait-Ben-Tzvi, Eliezer Livneh, and Tzvi Shiloah, as well as two of Yitzhak Tabenkin's sons. (Outstanding figures in the Jabotinskyite tradition also joined, including the poet Uri Tzvi Greenberg and the former Lehi leader Israel Eldad.) It was this revivalist current, too, that moved the editorial writers at *Ha'aretz* to exult that "the majesty of the past is no longer a distant image. It is now part of the new state . . . Cry out and shout, you inhabitant of Zion!"[9] And it was this current, too, that inspired a number of the Jewish state's most beloved popular songs, such as Naomi Shemer's "Jerusalem of Gold" (1967), whose final stanza is about the return to Old Jerusalem and Jericho.

There was also a political expression of this revival, with some of the most important Labor party figures, including Ben-Gurion's protégés Moshe Dayan and Shimon Peres, as well as their rival Yigal Allon—heir of the tradition of the kibbutz movement—sponsoring the establishment of dozens of small agricultural settlements in the Jordan Valley, Mt. Hebron, the Golan, and northern Sinai. Their rhetoric, too, hearkened back to Ben-Gurion's "great drama," with Dayan, in a famous eulogy two months after the Six Day War, promising the fallen Jewish soldiers of the War of Independence that

> we have not abandoned your dream . . . We have returned to the [Temple] Mount, to the cradle of our nation's history, to the land of our forefathers, to the land of the Judges, to the fortress of David's dynasty. . . . Our brothers, we bear your lesson with us . . . We know that to give life to Jerusalem, we must station the soldiers and armor of the IDF in the mountains of Samaria and on the bridges over the Jordan.[10]

Allon likewise called for settlement so that the Cave of the Patriarchs in Hebron and Rachel's Tomb in Bethlehem, "precious to us from a national and traditional point of view, would remain within the boundaries of the state of Israel."[11] Similar sentiments were expressed by Shimon Peres, and sometimes by Ben-Gurion, as well as by the Jabotinskyite Right led by Menachem Begin. They were also characteristic of the group of young rabbis, students of R. Tzvi Yehuda Kook, who would soon lead a practical-

Zionist revival among religious youth that would later spearhead the neosettlement movement in these territories.

In intellectual circles, all of this was of course greeted with dismay. The
specter of David Ben-Gurion's "totalitarian democracy" was resurrected
once more, and the campuses again resounded with the professors' condem-
nations—with Jacob Talmon, the country's leading historian, comparing
the ideas of leading public figures to those of Heinrich von Treitschke and
Shabtai Tzvi, and Yeshayahu Leibowitz, the country's leading philosopher,
accusing the government of colonialism and terrorism, predicting that it
would soon lead to putting the Arabs in "concentration camps" (his infamous description of Israel as falling into "Judeo-Nazism" came a few years
later).[12] But they need not have exercised themselves quite so much. By the
time of Ben-Gurion's death on December 1, 1973, the revivalism being
urged by his aging Labor-Zionist allies had failed miserably. It had run
aground on the complete disinterest of the generation of their university-educated children, who had long since come to see matters much the way that
the professors did.

With hindsight, it is obvious that the collapse of Labor Zionism was already
well underway in the years before Ben-Gurion's departure from government
in 1963. And yet no less than thirty years were to pass—until after the Oslo
Accords in 1993—before this fact was openly recognized in public discourse
in Israel. In Chapters 1 and 2, I described these years from the perspective of
Israel's cultural leadership. There, I traced the ascent to prominence—in
academia, literature, journalism, and the arts—of the generation of the sons,
which had rebelled against central aspects of the Labor Zionist understanding of history and of the role of the Jewish state. And I tried to show how
their prominence in the intellectual life of Israel has contributed to very real
changes in Israeli policy, all of which militate toward dismantling the idea
of Israel as the Jewish state.

But this description inevitably raises the question of what Israel's political
leaders were doing during all this time—for the thirty years during which
the generation of their own children was growing ever more open and aggressive in its rejection of the world they had devoted their lives to creating.
What was going on? Was the political leadership not involved in issues of
culture, or at least in those issues that were relevant to the Jewish national
character of the state of Israel?

The answer is that for the most part they did not. This is not to say that
they were any less "Zionist" than Ben-Gurion was. On the contrary, for an
entire generation, the state of Israel, whether governed by the Labor party or

by the Likud (a generally more conservative party headed by the former commanders of the Jabotinskyite underground organizations), was blessed with leaders whose understanding of the meaning of the Jewish state never wavered. Indeed, leaders such as Golda Meir, Moshe Dayan, Shimon Peres, Yitzhak Rabin, Menachem Begin, and Yitzhak Shamir were—each in their own way—notorious for their insistence on the basics of the Ben-Gurionist tradition of Jewish statecraft: the emphasis on the upbuilding of the IDF and the value of Jewish military self-reliance; the constant efforts at securing Jewish immigration and settlement; the cultivation of ever-deepening relations on every level with the Jewish Diaspora, the strong diplomatic tilt toward the West; and, above all, the belief in Israel as the guardian-state of the Jewish people. In short, every one of them saw themselves as playing a part in "the great drama" from which many Israeli intellectuals were so alienated. In this sense, these political leaders were faithful heirs to the Labor Zionism of Ben-Gurion.

But all of these Israeli leaders differed from Ben-Gurion in one crucial regard. None of them were idea-makers of any significance. That is, they were not people who could be considered, along with Herzl, Ahad Ha'am, Ben-Gurion, or Buber, to have shaped the public mind of the Jewish state to any significant degree. Thus, while Golda Meir, who headed the Labor government from 1970 to 1974, unhesitatingly invoked the Jewish missions of the state of Israel, inspiring the same kind of contempt among many of the professors and their students that Ben-Gurion had inspired, her influence on the ideas of the Jewish state was negligible. Meir made no effort to ignite a great national romance with the Hebrew Bible; did not hold meetings with leading cultural figures to berate them for their failure to address the pressing issues of Jewish restoration; did not engage in public disputations with professors from the Hebrew University on the nature of Jewish history. Not that Ben-Gurion himself had won these battles. He had lost them all. But he *did* fight them, where Golda Meir did not. Meir made sure that Israel would continue to be shaped by the political course set by Ben-Gurion, yet she all but withdrew from the struggle over the culture of the Jewish state—which was the struggle over whether there would be further generations of Zionists.

Much the same can be said regarding the Likud's Menachem Begin, who became the first non-Labor prime minister of Israel in 1977. Begin's emotional Jewish-nationalist speeches have often led to him being referred to as an "ideologue." But there is little to be said for this claim. Begin had indeed changed the name of the Israeli currency from the pound to the Hebrew *shekel*, and images of Irgun and Lehi fighters began to appear on postage stamps during his years in power. And there was more cosmetic cultural tinkering of this kind. But Begin, unlike his mentor Jabotinsky, actually had little interest in the power of ideas. His government was characterized by an almost complete preoccupation with the classic Labor-Zionist concerns of material armament, land, and settlement and by the use of these as a lever to secure diplomatic recognition from the Arab states—an old Ben-Gurionist strategy that finally bore fruit in 1978 when Begin signed the Camp David Accords with Egypt.[13] It is no coincidence, either, that Begin was at ease appointing Moshe Dayan as his foreign minister. His years in office were simply far more of a continuation of traditional Labor-Zionist rule than politicians from either party care to admit.

Indeed, if there was a noticeable shift in Israeli public culture during the fifteen years of Likud governments, it had little to do with the ideas of Menachem Begin or his party and everything to do with the peculiar fate of Labor Zionism in the years after the Yom Kippur War in October 1973. The Yom Kippur War was a unique catastrophe in Israeli military history, whose most important aspect was the failure of the IDF to respond in time to intelligence reports warning of an impending Egyptian and Syrian attack. The result was the loss of 2,550 Israeli lives (nearly four times the number that had been lost in the 1967 war), and the battlefield situation on both fronts was transformed only by virtue of exceptional actions by commanders in the field. The war might just as easily have been lost. And when the awareness of this fact began to harden, the result was widespread disaffection whose most obvious result was the end of the Labor party's four decades at the helm of the Zionist movement. (The elections of December 1973 were held too early to reflect the public reaction to the war, which was registered only in the general elections four years later.)

On the cultural level, the effects of the war were if anything more significant. For many educated Israelis, the Yom Kippur War fiasco provided unequivocal confirmation of a premise raised forcefully for the first time during the Lavon Affair in 1961: the idea that Israeli power, especially military power, was in a profound sense a fallacy, which could not be relied upon to protect even the Jews of Israel, much less anyone else. Whatever prospects there may have been for a genuine revival of Labor Zionism in the mainstream of Israeli culture died with those thousands of young Israelis in October 1973. The Labor Zionist idea—which many Labor leaders felt could be resuscitated after the Six Day War—had now become all but irrelevant to the search of young, educated Israelis looking for a way to make sense of their lives and their world.[14]

It is important to emphasize that this tidal shift away from the intellectual presuppositions of the Jewish state was not restricted to the supporters of the Labor party. Rather, it was a general change in Israeli culture that touched virtually *everyone*—the children of Labor-Zionist families and those of families affiliated with General Zionism or with Jabotinsky's movement—who had sought intellectual leadership and training from Israel's universities. This included the vast majority of educated Israeli Jews, although there were some who were not in this category. Among the more traditional Jews, especially, there had always been some who continued to spurn Western-German scholarship, instead preferring to study in traditional Jewry's alternate system of higher education, the yeshivas. And though Israel's yeshivas varied in their willingness to accommodate Zionism, almost all of them had in common an exceptional level of intellectual and political independence from the Hebrew University (and, later, from the academic cartel controlled by the main universities). For better and for worse, this made the Orthodox system of yeshivas the only substantial organized intellectual counterforce in the state of Israel.

And indeed, by the time the yawning void left in the heart of Israel's political culture by the demise of Labor Zionism began to be felt in the mid-1970s, the only publicly discernible source of ideas preventing the intellectual monopoly of the Hebrew University and its progeny was a single yeshiva—Yeshivat Mercaz Harav Kook ("The Yeshiva of the R. Kook Center") in Jerusalem, founded in 1924 by Palestine's first chief rabbi, Avraham Yitzhak Kook. Like Buber and the professors, R. Kook was sharply aware that the Jewish state being built in Palestine was shot through with an all-corroding materialism that was creating a reality devoid of ideas.[15] And like the professors, he sought to respond to this menace with an institution that would create in Palestine a rejuvenated Jewish scholarship that would be "universal" in its breadth and appeal. When he died in 1935, he left his students with a vast collection of his essays and aphorisms on the philosophy of Judaism, the Jewish nation, and its history—the first original philosophic system Jewish Palestine had produced. In time, the close-knit circle of his students—the most influential of whom was his son R. Tzvi Yehuda Kook—edited and published these works, placing them at the center of a new yeshiva curriculum that was to have a dramatic impact on the movement of "religious Zionists."

The philosophy of the elder R. Kook was based on the fusion of Jewish kabbalistic concepts with a historical dialectic strikingly similar to that of Hegel. The Jews had been a people of ideas alone for generations, R. Kook argued, and there could be no possibility of a return of the Jews to their land without a descent into the basest form of materialism. Only once the material basis for the Jewish state had been built would it be possible for the Jews to concern themselves again with ideas and with God. It was this theory—that materialism was a necessary way station on the road to redemption—that served as the basis for what eventually became the sanctification of Labor-Zionist materialism on the part of the "national-religious" stream within Zionism. In this way, R. Kook succeeded in creating an entire educational and spiritual movement among traditional Jews in Israel, whose devotion to learning was able to rival that of the students of the universities, but which, in terms of substance, reached the opposite conclusions. The students educated in Mercaz and its satellite institutions were inculcated with a deep love of all that students at the Hebrew University were moving away from: the old Labor-Zionist religion of physical labor, the power of gunpowder, and the importance of physical settlement of Jews on the land, preferably in agricultural communities. And they also held tightly to that most critical tenet of mainstream Labor Zionism—the belief that through the material and the practical, the Jews would somehow find salvation.[16]

It was during the mid-1960s, at almost exactly the time that Buber's intellectual grandchildren were finishing their studies in history, literature, and philosophy at the Hebrew University, that R. Kook's intellectual grandchildren began to emerge from Mercaz—young rabbis who were, somewhat incongruously, to become the principal guardians of the flame of Zionist materialism. Three months after the Six Day War, a young Mercaz rabbi led a group of religious families onto a hill south of Jerusalem called Kfar Etzion. The following spring, other graduates of Mercaz led a group of sixty settlers who rented an Arab building in the heart of Hebron.[17] Only a handful of years earlier, the religious-Zionist students, who had joined the university's revolt against "the great drama," had been the straw that broke the back of Ben-Gurion's government during the Lavon Affair. But by the time young religious-Zionists had made their way for the first time to Old Jerusalem, Hebron, Shiloh, and Rachel's Tomb, their identification with the cause of the professors had disappeared virtually without a trace. With the ideas of Mercaz Harav Kook to serve as an intellectual rejoinder, they now did precisely what the youth of all other Zionist streams had so pointedly refused to do: They embraced the ideals of their parents' generation.

The Yom Kippur War of 1973, which crushed whatever life had remained in the old Labor Zionist ideal among the young of Tel Aviv, had precisely the opposite effect in religious-Zionist circles. In direct response to the debacle, young religious-Zionists founded a movement called Gush Emunim ("Alliance of the Faithful"), whose purpose was to keep the faith not only with Jewish tradition but with Labor-Zionist historical missions that the rest of their generation was giving up for dead. The result was a neosettlement movement that established Jewish settlements in the heart of the West Bank with the support of the Labor government of Yitzhak Rabin. (It was Shimon Peres, then defense minister, who was the settlement movement's patron in the government.) True, Menachem Begin, when he came to power in 1977, offered the settlers his support. But it was not Begin who had—on the level of political ideas—created the phenomenon of ideological Jewish settlement in the West Bank. Just the opposite is true. It was principally through the alliance with the Mercaz-inspired settlement movement that Likud leaders were able to catch some of the adrenaline of the Ben-Gurionist revival taking place among religious Israelis and feel they stood at the helm of something grand, perhaps even at the head of a great Jewish nationalist reawakening.

But in the end, there was no such reawakening—at least not outside of limited circles—and the attempt of R. Kook's yeshiva to forge ideas capable of sustaining the Jewish state ended in failure. Nor is it difficult to understand why. For in 1973, the idea of the Jewish state was already in state of steep decline. What Israel needed more than anything else was conceptual and ideological refinement of the kind that could return meaning and purpose to the enterprise of Jewish restoration. In short, the state of Israel was in need of *ideas*—just as the elder R. Kook had believed it would be, the moment the Jews discovered that they could no longer bear to live for physical construction alone. And at precisely this moment, when the Jewish people in Israel began to ask hard questions regarding the ideas that were supposedly at stake in all this construction, the Mercaz-trained rabbis turned their backs on idea-making, instead pouring all they had into a renaissance of practical-Zionist "gravel and cement" in which they believed they would find salvation. This, of course, was the very same act of cultural suicide that had caused the death of Labor Zionism in the previous generation.

And it had the same results. Jewish communities arose where none had been before in the Samarian and Judean mountains, the Golan Heights, the Jordan Valley, the Sinai, and in the eastern reaches of Jerusalem. But even as they grew in material dimension, the motivating idea that had summoned these communities into existence continued to decay, becoming ever more shallow and vague, ever more unreasoned and inexplicable, until it ceased to be compelling to anyone who was not himself perched atop some crucial mountaintop somewhere.

There were, of course, those who had suspected this might be the result. Immediately after the Six Day War, R. Adin Steinsaltz, the celebrated translator of the Talmud, had warned the settlement movement leaders that although the Jews had a moral right to the West Bank, it would be a grave mistake to invest such great energies in the upbuilding of a piece of territory when the Jewish people itself, both in Israel and in the Diaspora, was drifting further away from the ideas of the settlers with each passing day.[18]

By 1982, it seems that even R. Tzvi Yehuda Kook, the last great prophet of practical Zionism, may have come to suspect the flaw in the course he and his students had chosen. The signing of peace accords in Egypt by Prime Minister Menachem Begin had included an agreement to uproot thousands of Jewish settlers from their homes in northern Sinai, wiping out Jewish farms and factories and school buildings as though they had never existed. As the date of the final evacuation approached, so the story goes, R. Tzvi Yehuda for the first time told his students that "the people aren't with us"[19]—in a phrase conceding the bitter truth that it is not physical settlements but rather ideas with which all political battles are ultimately fought and won.

The old rabbi was spared having to find out how right he was. He died on March 9, 1982, six weeks before the first razing of a Jewish community by the government of the Jewish state.

———

From the time David Ben-Gurion came to Palestine at the age of twenty, he regarded himself as personally responsible for the fate of the Jewish people. Even the act of immigrating to Palestine came in the wake of Herzl's death, and Ben-Gurion's decision to come and build the Jewish state with his own hands expressed his effort to ameliorate his people's loss in the only way he knew. And it was this relationship of guardianship that was in evidence at every moment of Ben-Gurion's nearly fifteen years at the head of the Jewish state itself. As he described it in a letter to Shmuel Sambursky of the Hebrew University:

> To some extent, [security] is the most important problem, but—this is at any rate what I feel—it does not conceal from my eyes and blur in my consciousness the importance of other problems and needs, because I experience every day, not just all the problems of the state, but the main problems of the whole of the Jewish people.[20]

It was this principle of governing the Jewish state by means of a daily confrontation with "the problems of the whole Jewish people" that was the motive force behind all of Ben-Gurion's actions and policies—as expressed in the Law of Return, the State Education Law, the efforts at bringing mass Jewish immigration, the trial of Adolf Eichmann, and Ben-Gurion's numerous other legal, political, symbolic, and cultural efforts. All of these were aimed at ensuring that Israel would not simply be a neutral, social-contract state but that the new country would in fact understand itself as Herzl had believed it would: As a *Jewish* state, committed to the ideal of Jewish strength in the service of Jewish interests and aspirations.

Ben-Gurion himself could not have continued governing the Jewish state forever, but this does not mean that the "Ben-Gurion era" had to end as it did. It is not difficult to imagine the aims and purposes of Ben-Gurion's Jewish state being inherited by a successor generation such as he himself always believed would arise—a generation of Israeli Jews that would bring the idea of the Jewish restoration to the various aspects of the national culture and the concept of Jewish national sovereignty to the political efforts of the state. But Ben-Gurion and his colleagues did not raise such a next generation, and even those young Israelis who wanted to be loyal to the traditional ideals of the Labor movement found they had inherited nothing they were capable of holding on to. Having despaired of the mindless materialism of kibbutz life, they found that they had exhausted Labor Zion's store of ideas. No reworking or recasting of the old ideas, such as might have rendered them of value to this new generation, was ever achieved.

It was this, the collapse of the Labor Zionist ideology, that transformed the denouement of Ben-Gurion's political career into the end of a cultural era and the most important fact of Israel's history up until our own time—more important than any of Israel's subsequent wars, including the Six Day War, and more important, too, than the peace agreements with Egypt and other Arab regimes. For in the disappearance of David Ben-Gurion, the Jewish state lost not only its first prime minister but also its only commanding advocate and theorist. And this loss was sustained during the period of the country's infancy, before the establishment of any firm tradition or culture of the state that could infuse it with form and direction over any length of time. No, the idea of the Jewish state did not have to end in this way—but it did.

"No man is strong or wealthy enough to move a people," Herzl had written. "Only an idea can do that." In *The Jewish State*, he had tried to provide his people with such a motivating idea as best he was able. But when Herzl died, it was as though the *vision* of the Jewish state died with him—much as was the case with Ben-Gurion. How could it be that both Herzl and Ben-Gurion produced such exhilaration over the idea of the Jewish state during their lifetimes, only for this idea to begin a precipitous decline the moment they had left the arena?

In this context it is worth recalling again Herzl's letter to Hirsch, in which he described the relationship between the motivating idea and the creation of the unified German state: "Believe me, policy for an entire people . . . can only be made with lofty imponderables. Do you know what the German empire was made of? Dreams, songs, fantasies and black-red-gold ribbons. . . . All Bismarck did was to shake the tree planted by the dreamers."[21] Herzl recognized that the "tree planted by the dreamers"—a living tradition of ideas that have taken root in the mind of a people—is potentially the source of immense political power. And in this he was proved correct. It was in fact the age-old Jewish dreams and songs and fantasies of a restored kingdom in the land of Israel that made it possible to establish the political Zionist Organization and, fifty years later, to erect the Jewish state itself. All Herzl did was to shake the tree planted by the dreamers, speaking to Jews and Christians alike on the basis of ideals that they had already held dear before he ever entered the room.

Yet Herzl seems never to have established in his mind the direct connection between "the tree planted by the dreamers" and the instruments of cultural transmission that ensure that a tradition of ideas is preserved and strengthened from one generation to the next. Certainly, Herzl cherished such institutions as the Imperial Burgtheater in Vienna, where his own plays appeared, and he expected the reborn Jewish state to have its own opera houses and universities and so forth. But nowhere in Herzl's writings do we find such institutions being associated with the problem of political strength, as we do, for example, in Ahad Ha'am's demand that Zionism focus on "the conquest of the schools," because "history bears witness that in a war of parents and children it is always the children who win in the end."[22] Indeed, all of the tools in Herzl's political arsenal—congresses, newspapers, diplomatic conversations, rallies, membership drives—were of the kind capable of unleashing great waves of popular sentiment, affecting the course of events in a matter of months or even days. But these are not tools for the inculcation of *stable* ideas, for their effects recede as quickly as they are introduced; nor are they appropriate for the development of *profound* ideas, those that can withstand the results of application across many times and places. It is only in books, journals, and other serious intellectual creations, which take years to circulate and decades to digest, and in universities, seminaries, and schools, wherein the views of the individual are refined over long years of effort, that stable and profound ideas can be worked into the fabric of the mind.

But Herzl seems to have cared little whether professors at this university or that preferred Rousseau's theory of the state to his own. His short-term political calculus was far more concerned with whether Zionism was being treated credibly in the *Neue Freie Presse* than in some classroom at the University of Vienna. And the case can certainly be made that Herzl was right in making the choice he did. In dealing with the fate of European Jewry, time was of the essence. But even so, it is evident that it was the Zionists' abandonment of the deep end of the pool of cultural and political idea-work that rendered the Zionist Organization so defenseless before the "new answer to everything" that the young Martin Buber had discovered in his readings in Hasidism. In the deep end of the pool, Martin Buber's "true Zionism"—a Jewish-flavored reconstitution of Kant inimical to the very notion of a Jewish state—won by default.

Buber always postured against the idea that political power should or could be used to advance Judaism. Yet there was something misleading in this claim. Although Buber himself did not actually pursue elected office, he was nevertheless a decisive political figure in the broader sense of the matter: for Buber was an indefatigable and lifelong conqueror of schools. Operating through a torrent of books and speeches, through the publishing house that he helped establish and through his journal *Der Jude*, he worked relentlessly to promote his ideas, especially among university and high-school students. None of this had much to do with Zionism, as all of Buber's intellectual projects embraced anti-Zionists warmly. But by the time Buber showed up at a Zionist congress again in 1921, declaring himself a "true nationalist" and spouting his opposition to the alliance with Britain and the Jewish state, he was—again, by default—the most important theoretician of nationalism that the congress had. Even if the "practicals" had been able to understand the threat posed by Buber's theories, it is unclear whether anyone could have challenged the participation of the most prominent German intellectual willing to associate himself with their movement.

The opening of the Hebrew University in Jerusalem in 1925, with an administration and faculty closely aligned with Buber's ideas, was a reprise of the same story. Even a leading Labor Zionist intellectual such as Berl Katznelson allowed this to pass without serious objections. For who else, if not Buber's German disciples, was supposed to open a Jewish university in Palestine? When in the mid-1930s Ben-Gurion and Katznelson began to understand the implications of what was happening on Mt. Scopus, the resources simply did not exist to alter the character of the university and Jewish Palestine's other cultural institutions. Ben-Gurion was, like Herzl in his own day, immersed in the short-term political battle for the state, and he had no time to take stock of the intellectual circumstances in the country for another fifteen years—not until after independence.

Ben-Gurion was sixty-one years old when he became prime minister of Israel, and by this point, he had become deeply aware of the critical role that the culture of the country would play—or fail to play—in determining the fate of the nation. This recognition led him, from his very first days as prime minister, to initiate repeated meetings with the professors and other intellectual figures, who were, after all, the most obvious candidates to lead in the flowering of a civilization that would be capable of sustaining the state. At one of these meetings, Ben-Gurion opened with such questions as: "Can we become a chosen people? Can we become a light unto nations? Is the redemption possible?"

There is no reason to doubt the prime minister's sincerity in posing such questions, but it is also the case that he could not have chosen topics better suited to irritating the professors, for whom such talk was what they would soon be calling "totalitarian democracy"—issues of collective purpose that were morally questionable because they diverted the attention of the state from the real issue of personal welfare for the citizens. Instead of answers to his questions, what Ben-Gurion received was an assault on his policy of attempting to build up Jewish settlements in the Negev, which he believed had to be established in preparation for the future immigration of additional millions of Jews. Leading the criticism was Don Patinkin, a Hebrew University professor who was the founding father of the study of economics in Israeli academia. Had anyone considered, Patinkin demanded to know, how many schools could be constructed with the money spent on building Jewish settlements in the South? Ben-Gurion responded angrily that none of his most important goals had a solid basis in economics or security. Like the rest of the Zionist enterprise, they were based on a vision of things not yet extant but which might be brought into being. "Man," he asserted in exasperation, "is capable of vision."[23]

As the years went on, Ben-Gurion's disappointment with the intellectuals grew, and he became ever more concerned with trying directly to engage the high-school and university students and inspire them with an attachment to the Jewish people and a belief in its cause. This he did through his appointment of the Labor Zionist historian Benzion Dinur as minister of education; support for the new Hebrew University president Benjamin Mazar; the initiation of Jewish identity programs in the public schools; the manufacturing of new memorial days on the calendar; and by means of his own personal efforts to raise public interest in the Bible, and to cajole prominent writers into using their abilities in a less destructive fashion ("I want to tell you," he wrote to S. Yizhar after reading about the War of Independence in *Days of Ziklag*, "that your young men were better than the ones you describe in your book").[24] In 1954, Ben-Gurion even attempted an end run around the entire educational system, assembling 8,000 high-school juniors and seniors in a field in Tel Aviv for an open-air lecture from him on Zionism.[25] Thus, there was more than a grain of truth to Shlomo Avineri's accusation, so indicative of the professors' views regarding Ben-Gurion's activities, that "security affairs were increasingly left in the hands of . . . Shimon Peres . . . Ben-Gurion himself cared more for biblical quizzes."[26]

But with hindsight we know that all these efforts were hopeless, for the simple reason that the most important centers of idea-making in the new Jewish state were unsympathetic and even hostile to the entire effort. By virtue of their position as the schoolmasters of the public mind, the professors and their students were already far advanced in the process of creating a new infrastructure of imponderables and dreams and myths that would replace those that Herzl and his Labor Zionist heirs had created. For this, after all, is what Buber and his associates and successors have done, not only smashing old Zionist myths but repopulating the Jewish mental universe with hoards of new myths of their own: The myth of the "suffering servant" and the Jewish "remnant," and its "mission" to live a life of eternal political powerlessness; the myth of the apolitical and anti-Messianic Hasidic saint; the myth of a purity and selflessness that has the power to bring an end to political strife among peoples; the myth of a "dialogue" and a "union" among all individuals and peoples and things; the myth of the social-contract state in which such dialogue can bring salvation to the Jews through emotional identification with the interests of the "other"; the myth of the "Oriental" or "Semitic" heritage or essence of the Jews, who will one day reunite with the Arab world; the myths of Bar-Kochba and Shabtai Tzvi, whose perverse rejection of the Jewish "mission" brought inevitable destruction upon the Jews; the myth of the "original sin" committed against the "other" by virtue of the establishment of a Jewish state; and the myth of the "totalitarian democracy" that the Jewish state eternally threatens to become. And then there is the myth of Martin Buber, believed by many to have been a great thinker and even a great Zionist; and the myth of Herzl, a dissolute madman whose works all ended in failure; and, of course, the hideous anti-myth of Ben-Gurion and "the black demon-fire" that issued forth from the innermost recesses of his being, seeking to consume the world.

It is these myths, and others like them, that now haunt the public mind of Israeli Jewry, casting long conceptual shadows even where they are not seen clearly, compelling the uprooting of any idea that is felt to contradict them. In this way, they progressively reshape the culture of the state, and the state itself, to conform to their lessons—the most important being the conclusion that there is no theoretical justification for the claim that a state can be "Jewish," and that anything specifically "Jewish" about the state of Israel is, in principle, morally wrong. As the outstanding spokesman for contemporary Israeli culture Amos Oz wrote not long ago: "A state cannot be Jewish, just as a chair or a bus cannot be Jewish. . . . The concept of a 'Jewish state' is nothing other than a snare."[27]

Of course, the argument that a state cannot be Jewish any more than a chair is specious. A chair is an inanimate object; it cannot truly be "Jewish" because it has no subjective aims or interests. But any organization that is composed of human beings can have subjective aims and interests, just as an individual can. Just as there can be Jewish organizations, there *can* be such a thing as a Jewish state. The only question is whether one wants to have one, or not.[28]

For all its faults, Ben-Gurion's Israel was without question such a Jewish state. Like any political state, it was one that needed much improvement. But the revolt against Ben-Gurion's Zionism in which Oz and his young compatriots took part was, as they themselves said, about "smashing."[29] And the results of this revolt are clear. The hole that opened up in the heart of the Jewish state in 1963 has long since been filled by these students—so that today, in virtually every realm of the mind, it is they who are Israel's cultural establishment. And it is they who have, to one degree or another, turned the Jewish state's cultural institutions to continuing this task, "critiquing" or discrediting virtually everything that was precious to Israel's founders: from historians obsessed with exposing the invidious character and crimes of the Labor Zionist settlers; to artists with their ghastly assault on traditional Jews and the defense forces; to novelists fixated on the Arab claim to the land and images of Israel's future annihilation; to a court system bent on replicating Canadian legal institutions; to screenwriters and dramatists issuing one savage attack after another against the country's heroes, from Hannah Senesh to Yoni Netanyahu; to "philosophers," whose ruminations inevitably seem to hit upon the fact that Zionism is a medusa, or that Judaism is inimical to the state, or that the defense forces are engaged in Nazism. Israeli culture has become a carnival of self-loathing, offering little from which one could construct the renewed Jewish civilization that was to have arisen in Israel, or the restored state of the Jewish people that was the dream of its founders.

Whenever I have the opportunity to speak on the subject of Israeli culture before Jewish communities in the Diaspora, I make a point of emphasizing, as often as my audience permits me, that a state is not a material object. The state is an idea, bereft of existence outside of the human mind. Consequently, it is first and foremost a matter of culture. Whether people believe in the state or not, whether they are willing to make efforts and sacrifices on its behalf or not—all this is a matter of the culture within which a people lives. And when people stop believing in the cultural artifact that is a particular state—as happened in the Soviet state, East Germany, Czechoslovakia, and Yugoslavia, and as threatens to happen in Canada as well—it is only a matter of time before the entire construct proves as shallow as is the belief in it, crumbling into the dust of memory at the first unfavorable wind. As a consequence, the state need not be defeated militarily to be defeated utterly. The entire job may be done on the battleground of ideas.

These simple facts are generally not challenged. On the contrary, these statements garner surprisingly easy assent, perhaps because the Soviet example is so compelling and tangible, having happened before our eyes only yesterday. Yet when the subject turns to the Jewish state, the hall is in every instance filled with a dense silence, and the hum of the ventilation system suddenly becomes clear and pronounced. The Jewish state, too, I say as carefully as I am able, is undergoing such a cultural disintegration, the result of decades of neglect and hostility at the hands of its own intellectual and cultural leadership. If we wish for the Jewish state to end otherwise than did the Soviet Union, then we must turn our attention back to the motivating idea that has grown faint and unintelligible.

Only an idea can move a people. But an idea *can* move a people—and this means that the present, difficult circumstances of the Jewish state may be altered by the same kind of effort that originally brought them about.

The story of Martin Buber's lifelong struggle against the idea of the Jewish state is indeed a tragedy: the tragedy of the People of the Book, which chose to abandon its life in the realm of ideas in order to pursue heroic, virtuous, and saving deeds in the realm of the material—only to discover that it is ideas that *make* material facts into heroic, virtuous, and saving deeds; and that just as easily smash them again, calling them myths and villainy. It is the tragedy of a people that, having given up on ideas to pursue deeds, was soon enough without ideas, and without deeds as well.

Yet the story of Martin Buber's victory over Theodor Herzl and his Jewish state is not only tragedy, a cautionary tale with a lesson for those who would put their faith in things material. It affords optimism, in my opinion, because it also offers a different lesson: the lesson of how a small fellowship of intellectuals, without the benefit of exceptionally sensible ideas or especially cogent means of expressing them, nonetheless succeeded in changing the life of a nation, against all odds, and despite the deepest longings of an entire people. With this lesson in mind, one cannot help considering what a few individuals might yet be able to do, if their ideas were just a bit more sensible, and if these ideas *did* correspond in some way to the dreams and desires of our people. I have in mind writers and thinkers and "men of the spirit" who look upon the specter that continues to haunt Israel, the specter of David Ben-Gurion and of the Jewish state, and see in it not a totalitarian repression or a Sabbatean heresy but rather a promise—the most noble promise ever made.

It seems to me that such individuals could even now return to the work that was left undone, reestablishing the idea of the Jewish state on solid foundations, that it might actually become the guardian of the Jews and a source of strength to them. And in this way, too, they might assist the Jewish people to again become a nation of grandeur and a blessing to all who befriend them, perhaps even to all the families of the earth. And it seems to me that the Jewish people and its friends among the nations await just such an effort.

Appendix

Declaration of the Establishment of the State of Israel

The land of Israel was the birthplace of the Jewish people. Here their spiritual, religious and political identity was shaped. Here they first attained statehood, creating cultural values of national and universal significance, and giving the world the eternal Book of Books.

After being forcibly exiled from their land, the Jewish people kept faith with it throughout their dispersion, never ceasing to pray and hope for their return to it, and for the restoration of their political freedom there.

Moved by this historic and traditional attachment, Jews strove in every generation to re-establish themselves in their ancient homeland, and in recent decades they returned in numbers. Pioneers, "illegal" immigrants, and defenders, they made deserts bloom, revived the Hebrew language, built villages and towns, and created a thriving community, controlling its own economy and culture, loving peace but knowing how to defend itself, bringing the blessings of progress to all the country's inhabitants, and aspiring towards independent nationhood.

In the year 5657 (1897), at the summons of the spiritual father of the Jewish state, Theodore Herzl, the First Zionist Congress convened and proclaimed the right of the Jewish people to national rebirth in its own country.

This right was recognized in the Balfour Declaration of November 2, 1917, and re-affirmed in the Mandate of the League of Nations which, in particular, gave international sanction to the historic connection between the Jewish people and the land of Israel, and to the right of the Jewish people to rebuild its national home.

The catastrophe which befell the Jewish people—the massacre of millions of Jews in Europe—was another clear demonstration of the urgency of solving the problem of its homelessness by re-establishing in the land of Israel the Jewish state, which would open the gates of the homeland wide to every Jew and confer upon the Jewish people the status of a full-fledged member of the family of nations.

Survivors of the Nazi holocaust in Europe, as well as Jews from other parts of the world, continued to immigrate to the land of Israel, undaunted by difficulties, restrictions and dangers, and never ceased to assert their right to a life of dignity, freedom and honest toil in their national homeland.

During World War II, the Jewish community of this country contributed its share to the struggle of the freedom- and peace-loving nations against the forces of Nazi evil, and, by the sacrifices of its soldiers and its war effort, gained the right to be reckoned among the peoples that founded the United Nations.

On November 29, 1947, the General Assembly of the United Nations passed a resolution calling for the establishment of a Jewish state in the land of Israel. The General Assembly required the inhabitants of the land of Israel to take such steps as were necessary on their part for the implementation of that resolution. This recognition by the United Nations of the right of the Jewish people to establish their state is irrevocable.

This right is the natural right of the Jewish people to be masters of their own fate, like all other nations, in their own sovereign state.

Accordingly we, members of the People's Council, representatives of the Jewish community of the land of Israel and of the Zionist movement, are here assembled on the day of the termination of the British Mandate over the land of Israel, and, by virtue of our natural and historic right, and on the strength of the resolution of the United Nations General Assembly, hereby declare the establishment of a Jewish state in the land of Israel, to be known as the State of Israel.

We declare that, with effect from the moment of the termination of the Mandate, being tonight, the eve of the Sabbath, the 6th of Iyar, 5708 (May 15, 1948), until the establishment of the elected, regular authorities of the state in accordance with the constitution which shall be adopted by the elected Constituent Assembly not later than October 1, 1948, the People's Council shall act as a Provisional Council of State, and its executive organ, the People's Administration, shall be the Provisional Government of the Jewish state, to be called Israel.

The State of Israel will be open to Jewish immigration and to the ingathering of the exiles. It will foster the development of the country for the benefit of all its inhabitants. It will be based on freedom, justice and peace as envisioned by the prophets of Israel. It will ensure complete equality of social and political rights to all its inhabitants irrespective of religion, race or sex. It will guarantee freedom of religion, conscience, language, education and culture. It will safeguard the Holy Places of all religions. And it will be faithful to the principles of the Charter of the United Nations.

The State of Israel is prepared to cooperate with the agencies and representatives of the United Nations in implementing the resolution of the General Assembly of November 29, 1947, and will take steps to bring about the economic union of the whole of the land of Israel.

We appeal to the United Nations to assist the Jewish people in the upbuilding of its state, and to receive the State of Israel into the family of nations.

We appeal—in the very midst of the onslaught that has been waged against us for months—to the Arab inhabitants of the State of Israel to preserve peace and to participate in the upbuilding of the state, on the basis of full and equal citizenship and due representation in all its provisional and permanent institutions.

We extend our hand to all neighboring states and their peoples in an offer of peace and friendship, and appeal to them to establish bonds of cooperation and mutual assistance with the sovereign Jewish people settled in its land. The State of Israel is prepared to do its share in the common effort for the advancement of the entire Middle East.

We appeal to the Jewish people throughout the diaspora to join the Jews of the land of Israel in the tasks of immigration and upbuilding, and to stand by them in the great struggle for the realization of the age-old dream, the redemption of Israel.

Placing our trust in the Almighty, we affix our signatures to this proclamation at this session of the Provisional Council of State, on the soil of the homeland, in the city of Tel Aviv, on this Sabbath eve, the 5th day of Iyar, 5708 (May 14, 1948).

David Ben-Gurion	*Meir David Loevenstein*
Daniel Auster	*Tzvi Luria*
Mordechai Bentov	*Golda Myerson [Meir]*
Yitzhak Ben-Zvi	*Nachum Nir*
Eliyahu Berligne	*David Tzvi Pinkas*
Fritz Bernstein	*Berl Rapter*
Rachel Cohen	*David Remez*
Eliyahu Dobkin	*Felix Rosenbluth [Pinhas Rosen]*
R' Yehuda Leib Hacohen Fishman	*Tzvi Segal*
Rabbi Wolf Gold	*Moshe Shapira*
Meir Grabovsky	*Mordechai Shattner*
Dr. Abraham Granovsky	*Moshe Shertok [Sharett]*
Yitzhak Gruenbaum	*Bechor Shitreet*
R. Kalman Kahana	*Ben-Zion Sternberg*
Eliezer Kaplan	*Herzl Vardi*
Abraham Katznelson	*Zerach Warhaftig*
Sa'adia Kobashi	*Meir Wilner-Kovner*
Moshe Kolodny	*Aharon Zisling*
R. Yitzhak Meir Levin	

Archives Consulted

Secondary works are fully cited in the notes. Below are the most important archival collections consulted. Where the name of a given archival collection has been abbreviated in the notes, the relevant abbreviation appears below in parentheses.

American Jewish Joint Distribution Committee Archive, New York City, New York.

Amos Oz Archives, Beersheva.

Archives and Museum of the Jewish Labor Movement, Institute for Labor Research in Memory of Pinhas Lavon, Tel Aviv.

Archives of the Israel Defense Forces, Ministry of Defense Archives, Tel Aviv.

Archives of the Labor Party, Beit Berl, Kfar Saba. (Beit Berl Archives)

Archives of the Prime Minister of the State of Israel, Jerusalem. (Prime Minister's Archive)

Ben-Gurion Archives, Sde Boker. (Ben-Gurion Archives)

Bergmann Archives, Department of Manuscripts and Archives, Jewish National and University Library, Jerusalem.

Buber Archives, Department of Manuscripts and Archives, Jewish National and University Library, Jerusalem. (Buber Archives)

Central Archive of the Hebrew University, Hebrew University, Mount Scopus, Jerusalem.

Central Archives for the History of the Jewish People, Papers of Judah L. Magnes, Hebrew University, Givat Ram Campus, Jerusalem. (Magnes Papers)

Central Zionist Archives, Jerusalem. (Central Zionist Archives)

Colonial Office Archives, London. (Colonial Office Archives)

Degania Archives, Degania Aleph.

Department of Newspapers and Periodicals, Sha'arei Zion Library, Tel Aviv University, Ramat Aviv.

Genazim Archives, Tel Aviv.

Ha'aretz Archive and Database, Tel Aviv.

Hareali School, Haifa.

International Herald Tribune Library, Neuilly Cedex.

Israel Documentation Center for the Performing Arts, Tel Aviv University, Ramat Aviv.

Israel State Archives, Jerusalem.

Jacob Rader Marcus Center of the American Jewish Archives, Felix M. Warburg Papers, Cincinnati, Ohio. (Warburg Papers)

Knesset Archives, Knesset, Jerusalem.

New York Public Library, Jewish Division, New York City, New York.

New York Times Archive, Adolph Ochs Collection, New York City, New York.

Oral History Division Collection of the Avraham Harman Institute of Contemporary Jewry, Hebrew University, Mount Scopus, Jerusalem. (Oral History Division Archives)

Records of the American Council for Judaism, State Historical Society of Wisconsin, Madison, Wisconsin.

Weizmann Archives, Weizmann Institute of Science, Rehovot.

YIVO Institute for Jewish Research, New York City, New York.

Notes

Introduction

1. See Chapters 1 and 2.
2. Yoram Hazony, "The End of Zionism and the Last Israeli," *Weekly Standard*, October 9, 1995. A version of this essay appeared in Hebrew as well.
3. Theodor Herzl, *The Complete Diaries of Theodor Herzl*, Raphael Patai, ed., Harry Zohn, trans. (New York: Herzl Press, 1960), p. 10.
4. Theodor Herzl, *The Jewish State*, Harry Zohn, trans. (New York: Herzl Press, 1970), p. 34.
5. Herzl, *Diaries*, pp. 131–132.
6. *Yediot Aharonot*, April 8, 1992.
7. Theodor Herzl, "Judaism," *Oesterreichische Wochenschrift*, November 13, 1896 [German]. Compare Theodor Herzl, *Zionist Writings: Essays and Addresses*, Harry Zohn, trans. (New York: Herzl Press, 1973), vol. 1, pp. 57–58.
8. Declaration of the Establishment of the State of Israel, May 14, 1948.
9. See Chapters 4 and 7–11.
10. See discussion in Chapter 1.
11. According to Rubinstein, the state of Israel "is creating a criminal legal system that isolates Israel in the world. And one day, I have a dream that Israel will join the European Union. I want this for other reasons anyway. And all these [Israeli] verdicts and all these laws will come before the Court in Strasbourg, which throw them in the appropriate place." *Kol Israel*, May 27, 1998. The "Court in Strasbourg" is the European Court of Human Rights.
12. See discussion in Chapter 1.
13. See Chapters 7–11.
14. Even prior to 1925, there had been Jewish opponents of the Jewish state in Palestine, usually members of the Communist party beholden to Moscow. But this organization had been placed outside the law by the British administration, and its long-term effect, as opposed to that of the German-Jewish intellectuals, was marginal.
15. See Chapters 11–13.
16. Ibid.

Chapter One

1. Aharon Meged, "The Israeli Urge to Suicide," *Ha'aretz*, June 10, 1994.

2. Dan Michman, ed., *Post-Zionism and the Holocaust, 1993–1996* (Tel Aviv: Bar-Ilan University, 1997) [Hebrew].

3. For an exposition of the idea that the opposition to Zionism was fundamentally an opposition to Jewish empowerment, see "The Problem of Jewish Power," in Benjamin Netanyahu, *A Place Among the Nations: Israel and the World* (New York: Bantam, 1993), pp. 358–401.

4. Martin Buber, "Old Zionism and Modern Israel," *Jewish Newsletter*, June 2, 1958. See Chapter 10.

5. Yeshayahu Leibowitz, "On the Territories, Peace and Security," *Ha'aretz*, November 3, 1972. Compare Yeshayahu Leibowitz, *Judaism, Jewish People and the Jewish State* (Jerusalem: Schocken, 1979), p. 427 [Hebrew]; for "Judeo-Nazis," see *Yediot Aharonot*, June 21, 1982; Yeshayahu Leibowitz, "Forty Years After," in Yeshayahu Leibowitz, *Judaism, Human Values, and the Jewish State*, Eliezer Goldman, ed. (Cambridge: Harvard University Press, 1992), pp. 243–245; *Jerusalem Post*, January 19, 1993.

6. Jacob Talmon, "Is Force Indeed an Answer to Everything?" *Dispersion and Unity* 17/18 (1973), pp. 12, 18.

7. On November 10, 1975, the General Assembly of the UN ruled "that Zionism is a form of racism and of racist discrimination." UN General Assembly Resolution 3379, "Elimination of All Forms of Racial Discrimination."

8. Avi Shlaim, *The Iron Wall*, pp. 28, 49, 104, 137, 149, 238, 283–284.

9. Benny Morris, *Righteous Victims*, pp. 652, 654.

10. Ibid., pp. 253, 659; Benny Morris, "Arab-Israeli War," in Roy Gutman and David Rieff, eds., *Crimes of War: What the Public Should Know* (New York: W. W. Norton, 1999), pp. 31–32. See also *The Birth of the Palestinian Refugee Problem, 1947–1949* (Cambridge: Cambridge University Press, 1987); Benny Morris, *1948 and After: Israel and the Palestinians* (Oxford: Clarendon Press, 1994). The fact that many of the Arabs who left Israel during the War of Independence did not do so of their own accord was well known before Morris's books. Thus, a thoroughly mainstream history such as Sachar's *A History of Israel*, which appeared in 1979, said that "in many cases . . . Jews captured Arab villages, expelled the inhabitants, and blew up houses to prevent them from being used as strongholds against them." He even quotes Ben-Gurion in April 1948 as having said, "The Arabs are wrong if they think they have nothing to lose in entering the war," specifically predicting "a great change in the composition of the population of the country." Howard Sachar, *A History of Israel: From the Rise of Zionism to Our Time* (New York: Knopf, 1979), pp. 333, 335. The previous generation of historians did not, however, believe that these actions were necessarily morally "tainted" or "atrocities."

11. See, for example, Ilan Pappe, *The Making of the Arab-Israeli Conflict, 1947–1951* (London: I. B. Tauris, 1994), pp. 45–46, 111, 138; Avi Shlaim, *Collusion Across the Jordan: King Abdullah, the Zionist Movement, and the Partition of Palestine* (Oxford: Clarendon Press, 1988).

12. Yonatan Shapiro, *The Formative Years of the Israeli Labor Party: The Organization of Power 1918–1930* (Tel Aviv: Am Oved, 1975), p. 257–261 [Hebrew]; Yonatan Shapiro, *Democracy in Israel* (Ramat Gan: Masada, 1977), pp. 191–194 [Hebrew]; Yagil Levy, "A Policy of Warfare, Inter-Ethnic Relations, and the Internal Spread of the State: Israel, 1948–1956," *Theory and Criticism* 8 (Summer 1996), pp. 203–223 [Hebrew].

13. Ze'ev Sternhell, *Nation-Building or a New Society? The Zionist Labor Movement, 1904–1940, and the Origins of Israel* (Tel Aviv: Am Oved, 1986) [Hebrew]. Published in English under the title *The Founding Myths of Israel: Nationalism, Socialism, and the Making of the Jewish State* (Princeton: Princeton University Press, 1997). For Sternhell's argument against the Jewish national state, see pp. xii, 320, 402–403 of the English. See also Sternhell, "The Zionism of Tomorrow," *Ha'aretz*, September 15, 1995.

14. Yehuda Shenhav, "The Conspiracy of Silence," *Ha'aretz*, December 27, 1996; Yehuda Shenhav, "Iraqi Jewry and the National Interest," *Theory and Criticism* 12–13 (Spring-Summer 1999), pp. 67–77 [Hebrew]. See also Shlomo Swirski, *Israel: The Oriental Majority* (London: Zed Books, 1989).

15. Tom Segev, *The Seventh Million: The Israelis and the Holocaust*, Haim Watzman, trans. (New York: Hill and Wang, 1993), pp. 95–96, 109. It is worth noting, however, that Segev is chronically self-contradictory, asserting that the Zionist leaders cared little about the fate of European Jewry and did next to nothing to save them even when they had the opportunity to do so, while at the same time conceding that they "could not have done more to save them; the yishuv was helpless" (p. 514).

16. Idith Zertal, *The Gold of the Jews: Underground Jewish Immigration to the Land of Israel, 1945–1948* (Tel-Aviv: Am Oved, 1996) [Hebrew]. Published in English under the title *From Catastrophe to Power: Holocaust Survivors and the Emergence of Israel* (Berkeley: University of California, 1998), especially pp. 263–269. See also Yosef Grodzinsky, *Good Human Material: Jews Against Zionists, 1945–1951* (Or Yehuda: Hed Artzi, 1998) [Hebrew].

17. Baruch Kimmerling, "Academic History Caught in the Crossfire: The Case of Israeli-Jewish Historiography," *History and Memory* (Spring-Summer 1995), pp. 42–43. See also Moshe Zimmerman, "The Historians' Debate: The German Experiment and the Israeli Experience," *Theory and Criticism* 8 (Summer 1996), p. 91 [Hebrew].

18. Baruch Kimmerling, "Militarism in Israeli Society," *Theory and Criticism* 4 (Spring 1993), pp. 125–129 [Hebrew]. See also Gershon Shafir, *Land, Labor, and the Origins of the Israeli-Palestinian Conflict, 1882–1914* (Cambridge: Cambridge University Press, 1989); and Gershon Shafir, "Introduction to the New Edition of Land, Labor, and the Israeli-Palestinian Conflict, 1882–1914," *Theory and Criticism* 8 (Summer 1996), pp. 247–254 [Hebrew].

19. See Ilan Pappe, interviewed in *Yediot Aharonot*, August 27, 1993; Ilan Pappe, "The New History of the War of 1948," *Theory and Criticism* 3 (Winter 1993), pp. 102–103 [Hebrew]; Ilan Pappe, "A Lesson in New History," *Ha'aretz*, June 24, 1994; Uri Ram, "Zionist Historiography and the Invention of Modern Jewish Nationhood: The Case of Ben Zion Dinur," *History and Memory*, Spring-Summer 1995, pp. 93, 100; Uri Ram, "Post-Zionist Ideology," *Ha'aretz*, April 8, 1994; Amnon Raz-Krakotzkin, "Exile Within Sovereignty: Towards a Critique of Negation of the Exile in Israeli Culture," *Theory and Criticism* 4 (Spring 1993), pp. 29, 35 [Hebrew]; Amnon Raz-Krakotzkin, "Did Religion Protect the Jewish People?" *Ha'ir*, April 1, 1994. Compare *Davar*, February 18, 1994.

20. For example, Gabi Peterberg of Ben-Gurion University argues against the belief that medieval Europe was characterized by a coherent pattern of anti-Semitism. Instead, he argues that every Jewish community had its own unique experience, and the Spanish Expulsion, for example, was merely part of the unique story of the Spanish reconquista, in which the Muslims suffered as well as the Jews. Dan Michman, "The Scourges of Zionism: Essentials of the Worldview of the Post-Zionist Current in Contemporary Israeli Society," in Michman, *Post-Zionism and the Holocaust*, p. 14.

21. On this point, Zimmermann cites a study by Hebrew University historian Israel Ya'akov Yovel, who suggests that the medieval blood libel was based partly on the fact that the Jews of the Middle Ages really *were* murderers—arousing Christian hatred by killing their own children in times of persecution. Israel Ya'akov Yovel, "The Vengeance and the Curse, the Blood and the Libel," in *Zion* (Spring 1993), pp. 33–90 [Hebrew].

22. Zimmermann, "The Historians' Debate," pp. 91–93, 102.

23. *Jerusalem Post*, September 29, 1995.

24. Amos Elon, *The Israelis: Founders and Sons* (New York: Penguin Books, 1983), p. 230; Amos Elon, "Israel and the End of Zionism," *New York Review of Books*, December 19, 1996.

25. Yosef Agasy, Yehudit Buber-Agasy, and Moshe Brandt, *Who Is an Israeli?* (Rehovot: Kivunim, 1991), pp. 14–16 [Hebrew]. Agasy has also written against the Law of Return. See Yosef Gorny, *The State of Israel in Jewish Public Thought: The Quest for Collective Identity* (New York: New York University Press, 1994), p. 200. Compare Ben-Gurion University historian Hagai Ram, who argues that Ben-Gurion's Zionism can be profitably compared to Iran under the Ayatollah Khomeini. Hagai Ram, "The Hobgoblin Is Not So Bad," *Ha'aretz*, March 15, 1996.

26. See, for example, Adi Ophir, foreword to *Theory and Criticism* 8 (summer 1996), pp. 3–6 [Hebrew].

27. Ariella Azoulay and Adi Ophir, "100 Years of Zionism, 50 Years of a Jewish state," *Tikkun*, March-April 1998, pp. 68–71.

28. Emphasis added. Eliezer Schweid, "The Jewish Qualities of the Israeli Democracy," *Et Hada'at* 1 (1997), p. 103 [Hebrew].

29. Avishai Margalit and Moshe Halbertal, "Liberalism and the Right to Culture," in Menahem Mautner et al., eds., *Multiculturalism in a Democratic and Jewish State: The Ariel Rosen-Tzvi Memorial Volume* (Tel Aviv: Ramot, 1998), pp. 94, 104 [Hebrew].

30. Danny Rabinovitch, "The Original Sin," *Ha'aretz*, April 10, 1994.

31. Yehuda Elkana, "In Favor of Forgetting," *Ha'aretz*, March 2, 1988. The head of the history program of the School of Education at Tel Aviv University, Avner Ben-Amos, has scored Holocaust Memorial Day in the Israeli schools as unduly focused on Jews, demanding that they be imparted a "universal meaning" by including discussion of "other holocausts." According to Ben-Amos, the commemoration ceremonies in the schools have created an atmosphere that is "Messianic." In principle, he says, such ceremonies should really not take place in schools at all. *Ha'aretz*, April 23, 1998.

32. Yaron Ezrahi, *Rubber Bullets: Power and Conscience in Modern Israel* (Berkeley: University of California, 1997), p. 117f., 271–272.

33. Yael Tamir, *Liberal Nationalism* (Princeton: Princeton University Press, 1993), pp. 151, 170 n. 7. In 1999, Tamir was appointed absorption minister in the new Barak government; upon assuming her post, she gave a broad-ranging interview in which she seemed to reverse herself, advocating nation-states in the Middle East. Her book never appeared in Hebrew. *Ha'aretz*, August 13, 1999.

34. See, for example, Shlomo Avineri, "Hatikva Will Not Die," *Ha'aretz*, October 20, 1997; Anita Shapira, *The Sword of the Dove: Zionism and Power, 1881–1948* (Tel Aviv: Am Oved, 1992) [Hebrew]; Anita Shapira, "Politics and Collective Memory: The Debate over the 'New Historians' in Israel," *History and Memory*, Spring-Summer 1995, pp. 9–40; Shabtai Teveth, *Ben-Gurion and the Holocaust* (New York: Harcourt Brace, 1996); Moshe Lissak, "The Zionist Dream and Its Demise," *Ha'aretz*, October 25, 1995; Amnon Rubinstein, *From Herzl to Rabin and Beyond: One Hundred Years of Zionism* (Tel Aviv: Schocken, 1997), pp. 228–282 [Hebrew].

35. See *Theory and Criticism* 12–13 (1999) [Hebrew]; Assaf Sagiv, "Fifty Faces of Post-Zionism," *Azure* 8 (Autumn 1999), pp. 23–31.

36. *Jerusalem Post*, September 6, 1991. *A Russian Romance* (published in English under the title *The Blue Mountain*) spent sixteen weeks on the "Bookreport-Bestsellerlist" in Germany beginning on April 8, 1991, appearing between the twenty-fifth and forty-ninth places.

37. Meir Shalev, *The Blue Mountain*, Hillel Halkin, trans. (New York: HarperCollins, 1991), pp. 171–172, 293, 322.

38. Ibid., pp. 118, 172.

39. Ibid., p. 123.

40. Ibid., pp. 124–127, 136.

41. Ibid., pp. 242, 247, 275.

42. Moshe Shamir, *He Walked in the Fields* (Merhavia: Hakibbutz Ha'artzi, 1947) [Hebrew].

43. For an early view critical of the accepted Zionist approach to war and statehood, see, for example, Pinhas Sadeh's 1958 cult classic, *Life as a Parable*, Richard Flantz, trans. (Jerusalem: Carta, 1989), p. 108.

44. Gershon Shaked, ed., *Hebrew Writers: A General Directory* (Tel Aviv: Institute for the Translation of Hebrew Literature, 1993), p. 136; see also Nurit Gertz, "Israeli Novelists," *Jerusalem Quarterly* 17 (Fall 1980). A. B. Yehoshua similarly says of Yizhar's work that since it first appeared, "I haven't stopped reading it." A. B. Yehoshua, "The Injustice of Death," *Modern Hebrew Literature*, Fall 1989, p. 9. See also Nurit Gertz, *Hirbet Hiza and the Morning After* (Tel Aviv: Hakibbutz Hameuhad, 1984), pp. 15, 36–37, 40–41, 60, 77 [Hebrew].

45. S. Yizhar, "The Prisoner" and "Hirbet Hiza," in *Four Stories* (Tel Aviv: Hakibbutz Hameuhad, 1971) [Hebrew]. The quote appears on pp. 110–111.

46. "Before Zero Hour," in *Four Stories* (Tel Aviv: Hakibbutz Hameuhad, 1971), pp. 30–31 [Hebrew]; S. Yizhar, *Days of Ziklag* (Tel Aviv: Zmora-Bitan, 1996), vol. 3, p. 1096 [Hebrew].

47. Baruch Kurzweil, "The Chain Has Not Yet Been Broken," in Kurzweil, *Beyond the Pale: Disputations and Satire on Issues of the Day*, Ya'akov Avramson, ed. (Jerusalem: Carmel, 1998), p. 123f. [Hebrew]; Gertz, *Hirbet Hiza*, pp. 60–61; Ezra Spicehandler, "The Fiction of the 'Generation of the Land,'" in S. Ilan Troen and Noah Lucas, eds., *Israel: The First Decade of Independence* (Albany: State University of New York Press, 1995), p. 326.

48. Nathan Zach, "Reflections on the Poetry of Alterman," *Achshav* 3–4 (Spring 1959), pp. 111–112, 120–121 [Hebrew]; Gavriel Moked, "Notes from a Possible Discussion," *Achshav* 3–4 (Spring 1959), p. 27 [Hebrew]; Dan Miron, "Comments on 'Efraim Returns to the Clover,'" *Achshav* 5–6 (1960) [Hebrew]. See also Dan Miron, "From Creators and Builders to the Homeless," *Igra* 2, 1985–1986, pp. 104–106 [Hebrew]. A second new journal, *Keshet* ("Bow"), edited by Aharon Amir, was more inclusive and less inclined to total war, but it too served as a venue for writers whose stance was openly critical of the Zionism of their parents. The difference between the two groups was, however, more one of style than substance. A. B. Yehoshua emphasizes in choosing to write in *Keshet* that he was declining to be openly identified with *Achshav*'s vocal rejection of the previous generation's writings: "We did not see it as our job to undermine someone else's literature [i.e., that of the literary establishment]. We simply felt that what they were writing was not the best." Quoted in Gertz, *Hirbet Hiza*, p. 40. See also Gershon Shaked, interviewed in Yona Hadari-Ramage, *Stopping to Think: Conversations on Public Thought in Israel* (Ramat Efal: Yad Tabenkin, 1994), pp. 647, 649, 661 [Hebrew].

49. Since the early 1980s, nearly all of the authors awarded the Israel Prize in literature by the Ministry of Culture have been selected from among their ranks. Recent recipients of the Israel Prize in literature include Yehuda Amichai (1982), Aharon Appelfeld (1983), Nathan Zach and A. B. Yehoshua (1995), Nissim Aloni (1996), Amos Oz and Dalia Rabikovitch (1998). Only two prizes—to Haim Guri and Moshe Shamir (1988)—stand out as representatives of the older Labor Zionist literary tradition.

50. Nurit Gertz, *Amos Oz: A Monograph* (Tel Aviv: Sifriyat Poalim, 1980), pp. 25, 27 [Hebrew].

51. Amos Oz, *My Michael*, Nicholas de Lange, trans. (London: Chatto and Windus, 1972), p. 242.

52. Amos Oz, *Black Box*, Nicholas de Lange, trans. (New York: Vintage International, 1989), pp. 141–142.

53. Amos Oz, *Fima*, Nicholas de Lange, trans. (London: Vintage, 1994), pp. 5–6, 43, 67, 85–86, 163.

54. Gertz, *Hirbet Hiza*, p. 43.

55. Amos Oz, *In the Land of Israel*, Maurie Goldberg-Bartura, trans. (San Diego: Harcourt Brace and Company, 1993), pp. 130–131. Oz compares the dream of the early Zionist leaders that the Jews should be allowed to join in the "family of nations" to wanting to join a "family" in the Mafia (p. 141).

56. A. B. Yehoshua, "Facing the Forests," in A. B. Yehoshua, *All the Stories* (Tel Aviv: Hakibbutz Hameuhad, 1993), pp. 102, 106, 108, 110, 112–116, 118 [Hebrew].

57. Dan Polisar, unpublished study of the high-school literature curriculum by the Shalem Center.

58. Ellipses in the original. A. B. Yehoshua, *The Lover* (Tel Aviv: Schocken, 1981), pp. 311–312 [Hebrew]. Compare A. B. Yehoshua, *The Lover*, Philip Simpson, trans. (San Diego: Harcourt Brace, 1993), p. 250.

59. Address of A. B. Yehoshua at the World Jewish Congress in Jerusalem, January 23, 1996. The Associated Press paraphrased Yehoshua as having said, "Neither does most of Israel's population want more Jewish immigration." *Jerusalem Post*, January 24, 1996. The WJC's transcript of the speech reads as I have it. From the transcript, however, it is clear that Yehoshua is not saying that he himself is opposed to additional Jewish immigration; rather, it is only what he believes most Israelis want.

60. Kol Israel, March 31, 1987; A. B. Yehoshua, interviewed in Hadari-Ramage, *Stopping to Think*, p. 267; A. B. Yehoshua, *For the Sake of Normalcy* (Jerusalem: Schocken, 1980), p. 163 [Hebrew]. Compare A. B. Yehoshua, *Between Right and Right*, Arnold Schwartz, trans. (Garden City, N.Y.: Doubleday, 1980), p. 173; *Ha'aretz*, December 29, 1995.

61. Hadari-Ramage, *Stopping to Think*, pp. 285–287. Although others are not so extreme, this view is not much further afield than that of other cultural figures. Amos Oz, for example, believes that for Jews there is "nothing wrong with . . . conversion" to other religions. Amos Oz, "The Meaning of Homeland," in *Under This Blazing Light*, Nicholas de Lange, trans. (Cambridge: Cambridge University Press, 1995), p. 84.

62. Aharon Appelfeld, *The Searing Light* (Tel Aviv: Hakibbutz Hameuhad, 1980) [Hebrew]. Compare Lilly Rattok, *A Precarious House* (Tel Aviv: Heker, 1989), pp. 141–145 [Hebrew]; Gershon Shaked, *Wave After Wave in Hebrew Literature* (Jerusalem: Keter, 1985), pp. 27–32 [Hebrew]; Gila Ramras-Rauch, *Aharon Appelfeld: The Holocaust and Beyond* (Bloomington: Indiana University Press, 1994), pp. 112–113.

63. Emphasis added. Aharon Appelfeld, "Looking Up Close," *Ma'ariv*, August 8, 1997; Aharon Applefeld, *Life Story* (Jerusalem: Keter, 1999), pp. 121–128 [Hebrew]. Similar,

albeit less extreme, criticism of the "ingathering of the exiles" is directed on behalf of Sephardi Jews by the immensely successful writer Sami Michael in books such as *Some Men Are Equal But Some Are More* (Tel Aviv: Bustan, 1974), p. 54 [Hebrew]. Although this book is relentless in its anger, the ending is ambiguous, with the possibility left open that the future will offer improvement. Michael's later works, such as *Victoria* (Tel Aviv: Am Oved, 1993) [Hebrew], also open the possibility that Israel in some ways bettered the life of the Iraqi immigrants.

64. David Grossman, *The Yellow Wind*, Haim Watzman, trans. (New York: Farrar, Straus and Giroux, 1988), pp. 7–8.

65. David Grossman, *See Under: Love*, Betsy Rosenberg, trans. (London: Picador, 1991); David Grossman, *The Book of Intimate Grammar*, Betsy Rosenberg, trans. (New York: Riverhead, 1994), p. 357.

66. Grossman, *Grammar*, p. 395.

67. Dalia Rabikovitch, "You Don't Kill a Baby Twice," in Dalia Rabikovitch, *True Love* (Tel Aviv: Hakibbutz Hameuchad, 1987), pp. 63–64 [Hebrew]; Dalia Rabikovitch, "New Zealand," in *The Window: New and Selected Poems*, Chana Bloch and Ariel Bloch, eds. and trans. (New York: Sheep Meadow Press, 1989), pp. 105–106.

68. Nathan Zach, *Because I'm Around* (Tel-Aviv: Hakibbutz Hameuhad, 1996), p. 258 [Hebrew].

69. Yehuda Amichai, "Biblical Reflections," in Yehuda Amichai, *Not in Order to Remember* (Tel Aviv: Schocken, 1971), p. 132 [Hebrew]; Yehuda Amichai, *Behind All This There Hides a Great Happiness* (Tel Aviv: Schocken, 1974), p. 27 [Hebrew]. Compare Yehuda Amichai, *A Life of Poetry, 1948–1994*, Benjamin and Barbara Harshav, eds. and trans. (New York: HarperPerennial, 1994), pp. 228, 242.

70. Amichai's answer is that only the continuing bloodshed—here he refers to circumcision as *dam shafuch* ("spilled blood"), a term associated with war or murder—continues to keep the Jews in the land: "Spilled blood . . . /Is the closest thing to roots/That human beings have." Yehuda Amichai, "Jews in the Land of Israel," Amichai, *Not in Order*, pp. 13–14. See also Amichai, *A Life of Poetry*, p. 193.

71. Nathan Zach, "No Time for Celebrations," in *Yediot Aharonot*, February 8, 1998.

72. Hanoch Levin, *The Queen of the Bathtub*, in Hanoch Levin, *What Does the Bird Care* (Tel Aviv: Hakibbutz Hameuhad, 1987) [Hebrew].

73. Hanoch Levin, *The Patriot*, in Levin, *Bird*; Hanoch Levin, *Murder*, in Hanoch Levin, *Plays VII* (Tel Aviv: Hakibbutz Hameuhad, 1999) [Hebrew].

74. Yehoshua Sobol, Ghetto (Tel Aviv: Or Am, 1984) [Hebrew]; Yehoshua Sobol, Adam (Tel Aviv: Or Am, 1989) [Hebrew]; Yehoshua Sobol, Jerusalem Syndrome (Tel Aviv: Or Am, 1987) [Hebrew].

75. Judd Ne'eman, "The Death Mask of the Moderns: A Genealogy of *New Sensibility* Cinema in Israel," *Israel Studies*, Spring 1999, pp. 100–128; Nurit Gertz, "Historical Memory: Israeli Cinema and Literature in the 1980s and 1990s," in *Critical Essays on Israeli Society, Religion, and Government*, Kevin Avruch and Walter P. Zenner, eds. (Albany: State University of New York Press, 1997), pp. 209–226; Ilan Avisar, "Israeli Cinema and the Ending of Zionist Ideology," in *Israel in the Nineties: Development and Conflict*, Frederick A. Lazin and Gregory S. Mahler, eds. (Gainesville: University of Florida Press, 1996), pp. 153–168; Glenda Abramson, *Drama and Ideology in Modern Israel* (Cambridge: Cambridge University Press, 1998); Linda Ben-Zvi, ed., *Theater in Israel* (Ann Arbor: University of Michigan Press, 1996).

76. Amos Oz, "A Laden Wagon and an Empty Wagon? Reflections on the Culture of Israel," *Free Judaism*, October 1997, p. 5 [Hebrew].

77. Gertz, *Amos Oz*, p. 27.

78. Gideon Katznelson, "Where Are They Going?" *Moznaim* 19 (August–September 1964), p. 263 [Hebrew]. See also Baruch Kurzweil, *In Search of Israeli Literature* (Ramat Gan: Bar Ilan University Press, 1982) [Hebrew].

79. See Gertz, *Hirbet Hiza*, p. 60. Shaked and Miron, however, seem not to be without at least some qualms, with Shaked admitting that Israeli literature has become obsessed with "morbid characters who are declining towards death without a heroic justification." Gershon Shaked, "Through Many Small Windows by the Back Door: An Introduction to Postrealistic Hebrew Literature, 1950–80," *Prooftexts*, September 1996, p. 290. Miron, too, has warned that the most important Israeli authors were leading away from the arena of national awareness and responsibility and instead being carried "into a fantasy land to be found in the depths of a brave new world of Israeli hedonism." Dan Miron, "An Unholy Trinity," *Yediot Aharonot*, June 3, 1994.

80. Moshe Shamir, "Is Hebrew Literature Still Zionist?" *Nativ* 1 (1989), pp. 41, 44 [Hebrew]. See also Assaf Inbari, "Towards a Hebrew Literature," *Azure* 9 (Spring 2000), pp. 99–154.

81. This section is based in large part on Avraham Levitt, "Israeli Art on Its Way to Somewhere Else," *Azure* 3 (Winter 1998), pp. 120–145. My thanks to the author for allowing me to make use of this material and for his assistance throughout the project.

82. Boris Schatz, *Betzalel: History, Essence, and Future* (Jerusalem: Snunit, 1910), p. 8 [Hebrew].

83. Attributed to Schatz in Binyamin Tammuz, *History of Israeli Art* (Givatayim: Masada, 1980), p. 14 [Hebrew].

84. Avraham Melnikoff, *The Awakening Judah* (Haifa: The University of Haifa, 1982), p. 20 [Hebrew].

85. See Tumarkin's *Kingdom of Jerusalem* (1970), *Horns of Hittin* (1970), in *Tumarkin: Sculptures, 1957–1992* (Tel Aviv: Tel Aviv Museum of Art, 1992), nos. 55 and 57; *The Order* (1972), *Goliath* (1972), *Crac des Chevaliers* (1972), and *Horns of Hittin VIII* (1972) in *Tumarkin: Yodfat Gallery* (Tel Aviv: Yodfat Gallery, 1972), n.p.

86. Yigael Tumarkin, *Tumarkin: Etchings, Texts, Photos and Drawings*, Yael Lotain, trans. (Givatayim: Massada, 1980), n.p.

87. Yosl Bergner, *Paintings: 1938–1980* (Jerusalem: Keter, 1981), pp. 61, 98; Yosl Bergner, *Between Seas* (Tel Aviv: Rubin Museum, Autumn 1996), p. 34.

88. Exhibition catalogue, *The Presence of the Absent: The Empty Chair in Israeli Art*, The Genia Schreiber University Gallery, May–August 1991 (Tel Aviv: Tel Aviv University, 1991).

89. Uri Lifschitz, *Index* (Tel Aviv: Ministry of Defense, 1995), pp. 11, 28, 41–46, 48, 49, 51 [Hebrew].

90. Lifschitz's sculpture was on display at the Diaspora Museum in Tel Aviv during its Zionist centennial retrospective, "Blue and White in Color" (1997). The sculpture, however, is inexplicably missing from the museum's official catalogue of the exhibit. See Rachel Arbel, ed., *Blue and White in Color: Visual Images of Zionism, 1897–1947* (Tel Aviv: Bet Hatefutsoth, 1997).

91. See, for example, David Reeb, "Painting with Green Line No. 1" (1985), in *Routes of Wandering*, p. 173.

92. Micha Kirshner, *The Israelis: Photographs, 1979–1997* (Or Yehuda: Hed Artzi, 1997).

93. Sarit Shapira, "Waymarks: Local Moves," in *Routes of Wandering: Nomadism, Voyages and Transitions in Contemporary Israeli Art* (Jerusalem: The Israel Museum, 1991), pp. 235, 244.

94. *Routes of Wandering: Nomadism, Voyages and Transitions in Contemporary Israeli Art* (Jerusalem: The Israel Museum, 1991), p. 79.
95. "Borders" exhibition catalogue (Jerusalem: The Israel Museum, 1980), p. 48.
96. *Routes of Wandering*, pp. 28–29.
97. Pinchas Cohen-Gan, *Figure, Form, Formula* (Greensboro, N.C.: Weatherspoon Art Gallery, 1996), p. 57; *Routes of Wandering*, p. 25.
98. *Routes of Wandering*, pp. 46–47, 107, 137, 147, 168.

Chapter Two

1. The death of David Ben-Gurion in 1973 had more or less signaled the passing of the generation of the fathers who had devoted their lives to establishing a Jewish state, and these were soon replaced by the "generation of the sons"—a group whose disinterest in continuing in their fathers' ideological footsteps was already something of a scandal even then. See, for example, Aharon Meged's novel, *Living on the Dead* (Tel Aviv: Am Oved, 1965) [Hebrew]; and a journalistic account by Amos Elon, *The Israelis: Founders and Sons* (New York: Penguin Books, 1983), originally published in 1971. See also Yonatan Shapiro, *An Elite Without Successors* (Tel Aviv: Sifriyat Poalim, 1984) [Hebrew].
2. *Ha'aretz*, November 20, 1991; *Jerusalem Post*, November 20, 1991.
3. The renunciation of Zionist symbols by the new generation of Labor politicians was particularly obvious, for example, when the young Laborite Haim Ramon challenged and defeated the aging Haim Haberfeld for the secretary-generalship of one of the Labor party's most powerful and central institutions, the Histadrut Labor Federation. On January 30, 1995, Ramon had the traditional name of the union, the "General Federation of Labor in the Land of Israel" changed to the "New General Federation of Labor." The term "land of Israel," which for the Labor Zionist founders of the union had been paramount, was now simply erased.
4. Typical of this process was the growing friendship between Shimon Peres, once one of Ben-Gurion's devoted ideological protégés, and Amos Oz. See Amnon Lord, "Oslo, the Bomb, and Other Home Remedies," *Azure* 4 (Summer 1998), pp. 117–136.
5. See *New York Times*, August 14, 1999; Jim Hoagland, "Fresh Breezes in Israel," *Washington Post*, August 29, 1999; Norman Podhoretz, "Has Israel Lost Its Nerve?" *Wall Street Journal*, September 10, 1999. In Israel, see *Jerusalem Post*, September 3, 1999. The claim of Jewish battlefield superiority can plausibly be demonstrated regarding the later engagements of the war, but not its early ones. See Amitzur Eilan, "The War of Independence," in Benny Micholson et al., eds., *The Struggle for the Security of Israel* (Tel Aviv: The Israel Association for Military History at Tel Aviv University, 1999), pp. 40–73 [Hebrew]; Shabtai Teveth, "Charging Israel with Original Sin," *Commentary* 1989, pp. 24–33.
6. Daniel Polisar, "Making History," *Azure* 9 (Spring 2000), pp. 14–22.
7. Ministry of Education and Culture, *Curriculum for the Elementary School: State and State-Religious Schools* (Jerusalem, 1954), pp. 1, 3 [Hebrew]; David Zisenwine, "Jewish Education in the Jewish State," *Israel Affairs*, Spring-Summer 1998, p. 148f.
8. *Jerusalem Post*, September 15 and 25, 1992; May 10, 1993; and July 2, 1993; *Yediot Aharonot*, March 22, 1999.
9. *Yediot Aharonot*, April 13, 1995. Amendment of the national anthem to accord with Arab sensibilities was included by Shimon Peres's staff in its postelection planning during the 1996 election campaign and was revived again two years later by the recently retired state controller Miriam Ben-Porat. *Ha'aretz*, May 29, 1998.

10. The original text of the law appeared in *Ha'aretz*, December 10, 1995. I first published a reference to this in Yoram Hazony, "The Zionist Idea and Its Enemies," *Commentary*, May 1996, p. 34. For Rubinstein's reaction and my own detailed discussion of Rubinstein's initiative, see *Commentary*, October 1996, pp. 14–16.

11. Ministry of Education, *Civics Curriculum for General and Religious High Schools* (Jerusalem, 1994), p. 8 [Hebrew].

12. Hanna Eden, et al., *To Be Citzens in Israel: A Jewish and Democratic State* (Jerusalem: Ministry of Education, 2000), pp. 22, 29–40 [Hebrew].

13. Similarly, the curriculum does refer to the "biblical period" and the "Second Temple period," but these are temporal designations used side by side with the "Roman period" and the "Byzantine period."

14. Emphasis added; I have also inserted space breaks between the sentences. Ministry of Education, *Archaeology Curriculum for High Schools* (Jerusalem, 1995), pp. 5–7 [Hebrew].

15. *Ha'aretz*, March 29, 1998.

16. *Yediot Aharonot,* May 1, 1995.

17. The first four units of the curriculum are as follows:
    1. The polis: Athens, Sparta, and Greek culture.
    2. The conquest of the East by Alexander.
    3. The meeting between Greek culture and the cultures of the East.
    4. The meeting between Hellenism and Judaism during the Ptolemaic period.
    Ministry of Education, *History Curriculum for Grades 6–9 in the Public Schools* (Jerusalem 1995) [Hebrew].

18. *Ha'aretz*, February 15, 1994.

19. Moshe Zimmermann, "The Historians' Debate: The German Experiment and the Israeli Experience," *Theory and Criticism* 8 (Summer 1996), p. 92 [Hebrew].

20. Speech before the Knesset, July 3, 1950.

21. *Verdicts of the District Courts in Israel,* 1965, vol. 45, pp. 7–8, 55–56 [Hebrew]. Indeed, as late as 1985, the Knesset reconfirmed the constitutional standing of Israel's character as a Jewish state by enacting legislation prohibiting the participation in national elections of parties explicitly opposed to Israel's standing as the state of the Jewish people. See Basic Law: The Knesset, Amendment 12, April 17, 1985.

22. See, for example, Yonatan Shapiro, *A Society Held Prisoner by Its Politicians* (Tel Aviv: Sifriyat Poalim, 1996), p. 46f. [Hebrew].

23. Shulamit Aloni, "The State of Gutnick and Moskowitz," *Ma'ariv*, November 30, 1998. See also Shulamit Aloni, "Basic Law: The Dignity and Liberty of Man," *Theory and Criticism* 12–13 (Spring–Summer 1999), pp. 367–375 [Hebrew].

24. Aharon Barak, "The Constitutional Revolution: Protected Fundamental Rights," *Mishpat Umimshal* 1 (1992), pp. 16–17 [Hebrew]. For further discussion of Israel's constitutional revolution, see Ruth Gavison, *The Constitutional Revolution: A Reality or a Self-Fulfilling Prophecy?* (Jerusalem: The Israel Institute for Democracy, 1998) [Hebrew]; Hillel Neuer, "Aharon Barak's Revolution," *Azure* 3 (Winter 1998), pp. 13–49; Evelyn Gordon, "Is It Legitimate to Criticize the Supreme Court," *Azure* 3 (Winter 1998), pp. 50–89; Evelyn Gordon, "How the Government's Attorney Became Its General," *Azure* 4 (Summer 1998), pp. 75–116.

25. See Mordechai Haller, "The Court That Packed Itself," *Azure* 8 (Summer 1999), pp. 64–92.

26. Basic Law: Human Dignity and Liberty, section 1a. A parallel clause appears in Basic Law: Freedom of Occupation, section 4. For an analysis of the purpose of this clause,

see Aharon Barak, *Interpretation in Law* (Tel Aviv: Nevo Publishing, 1994), vol. 3, p. 347 [Hebrew].

27. Amendment to the Criminal Justice Law (Inducement to Convert from One's Faith), 1977; Martyrs' and Heroes' Remembrance Day Law, 1959. For food products, see Passover Law, 1986.

28. For Herzl's view, see Chapter 4; for Ben-Gurion's view see Chapter 11. See also Yoram Hazony, "Did Herzl Want a 'Jewish' State?" *Azure* 9 (spring 2000), pp. 37–73. I am unaware of any Zionist thinker who ever argued that this definition of the Jewish state made it in any way incompatible with a democratic system of government.

29. The new term seems to have been the result of two decades of efforts by Israeli academics to dissociate the term "Jewish state" from Herzl and the early Zionist movement.

30. As former president of the Supreme Court Meir Shamgar said recently, the terms "Jewish" and "democratic" have become "a pretext . . . for disagreement and interpretation." Former vice president of the Supreme Court Menahem Elon goes even further, saying that Israel had been a model democracy before 1992 but that "since the legislation of these Basic Laws, the tension has mounted, as well as the divide, misunderstandings, and friction between segments of the public." Chief Justice Aharon Barak, on the other hand, sees this new tension as a positive development: "All of Israeli society will [now] have to contend with this duality. Thinkers and researchers, rabbis and professors, yeshiva students and university students. All strands of Israeli society will have to ask themselves: What are the values of the state of Israel as a Jewish and democratic state?" See the proceedings of the Twelfth World Congress of Jewish Studies, August 1, 1997, published as Ron Margolin, ed., *The State of Israel as a Jewish and Democratic State* (Jerusalem: World Union of Jewish Studies, 1999), pp. 6, 10, 34 [Hebrew].

31. Asa Kasher, "The Individual, When He Is for Himself," *Ma'ariv*, December 11, 1998.

32. Haim Cohen, "The Jewishness of the State of Israel," *Alpayim* 16 (1998), pp. 9–35 [Hebrew].

33. According to Berenzon, the source for the term is in the United Nations partition decision of 1947. Tzvi Berenzon, "The Declaration of Independence: Vision and Reality," booklet published by the Education Ministry, 1988, p. 12 [Hebrew].

34. Opinion by Mishael Heshin, *Verdicts*, 1996, vol. 50, pt. 2, pp. 548–549 [Hebrew].

35. Barak, "The Constitutional Revolution," p. 30.

36. In this, his definitive position on the subject, Barak appeared to backtrack by conceding that Israel was indeed mandated to be a "Jewish state" according to the declaration of independence and that such a state can in fact be one that is informed by values drawn from Jewish nationalism and Jewish tradition. Barak, *Interpretation*, vol. 3, p. 332. But as subsequent pages make clear, Barak's recognition of what a Jewish state would be like has little to do with what the State of Israel, as a "Jewish and democratic state," should be.

37. Barak, *Interpretation*, vol. 3, p. 343. This passage contradicts a much more interesting position presented earlier, in which Barak argues that one should seek the "universal" streams within the Jewish tradition, while at the same time bringing democratic theory closer to Judaism by selecting those democratic models that are closest to the particularistic Jewish tradition. Barak, *Interpretation*, vol. 3, pp. 340–341. This position does, in fact, offer a way to bridge the problem of "Jewish democracy"—and without requiring any "abstraction" of either Judaism or democracy. But Barak mentions it only in passing, and it is lost entirely in his subsequent discussion of the importance of high levels of abstraction and of the ultimate authority of the "enlightened public."

38. Barak, *Interpretation*, vol. 3, p. 230; Neuer, "Aharon Barak's Revolution," pp. 31–35.

39. In Barak's original, there are quotation marks around the phrases "enlightened community," "to the educated and progressive part within it," and "the family of enlightened
nations." These expressions are drawn from the writings of Justice Alfred Vitkon, upon
whom Barak relies repeatedly in dealing with this subject. Barak, *Interpretation*, vol. 3,
pp. 234–235.

40. In recent restatements of his judicial philosophy, Barak has retained the concept of "the
highest level of abstraction" as a means of reaching the "universal" values of Judaism,
while omitting the references to the "enlightened community." See, for example,
Margolin, *Israel as a Jewish and Democratic State,* pp. 14–15. But Barak has not explicitly renounced this idea, and there is no reason to believe that his views on the subject
have changed.

41. Thus far, the Supreme Court has largely refrained from putting these theories into practice. Two minor cases stand out as exceptions: In 1994, the Court ruled unconstitutional
a statute prohibiting the importation into Israel of certain nonkosher food products; and
in 1996, it for the first time permitted Knesset representation—previously understood to
be illegal—to an Arab political party advocating that Israel be reconstituted as a non-
Jewish "state of its citizens." Both of these decisions were unimportant in terms of their
substance; Israel can, of course, be a perfectly good Jewish state while importing
nonkosher food products and allowing Knesset representation to Arab parties calling to
sever its ties to the Jewish people. But what these cases *do* demonstrate is that the Israeli
Supreme Court is now ready and able to begin clearing away Jewish-national legislation
that offends its sense of democracy and its interpretation of the 1992 Basic Laws.

42. The material in this section is based on Tzvi Hauser's "The Spirit of the IDF," *Azure* 2
(Spring 1997), pp. 47–72, which includes the complete text of the code.

43. *Koteret Rashit,* October 31, 1984; *Al Hamishmar,* December 20, 1991; Asa Kasher,
"There Are Limits," in Yishai and Dina Menuhin, eds., *The Limits of Obedience* (Tel
Aviv: Yesh Gvul, 1985) [Hebrew].

44. Asa Kasher, *Military Ethics* (Tel Aviv: Israel Defense Ministry, 1997), p. 244 [Hebrew].

45. The first two of these quotes are from the code itself; the third is from the cover letter
accompanying the code that was distributed to all IDF units. See Hauser, "Spirit of the
IDF," p. 48.

46. See Hauser, "Spirit of the IDF," pp. 57–59.

47. IDF Spokesman, September 8, 1999.

48. *Yediot Aharonot,* October 31, 1997.

49. What is colloquially referred to as "the Law of Return" is in fact two laws: The Law of
Return (1950) and the Citizenship Law (1952); the first recognizes the right of immigration and the second grants the right of automatic citizenship for Diaspora Jews
choosing to immigrate. For the sake of simplicity, I have here retained the colloquial
Israeli usage, which speaks of these two laws as a single concept.

50. Speech before the Knesset introducing the Law of Return, July 3, 1950; *Jerusalem Post,*
July 19, 1957.

51. Gershom Schocken, "Ezra's Curse," *Ha'aretz,* August 28, 1995.

52. An editor close to him assesses that he was moving toward calling for repeal of the Law
of Return and would have done so had he lived longer. Dan Margalit, *I've Seen Them
All* (Tel Aviv: Zmora Bitan, 1997), p. 222 [Hebrew]. Margalit reports that Schocken
never allowed him to join the editorial board that set the paper's ideological line because
he was "a Zionist square." Margalit, *I've Seen Them All,* p. 221.

53. Hanoch Marmari, "The Law of Return," *Ha'aretz,* November 11, 1994; Hanoch
Marmari, "Life After Zionism," *Jerusalem Report,* February 8, 1996.

54. The other major media, including the national dailies *Ma'ariv* and *Yediot Aharonot,* have likewise made themselves available to those advancing this line of argument, although far less frequently. See, for example, Yaron London, "Abolish the Law of Return," *Yediot Aharonot,* November 13, 1988; Yael Paz-Melamed, "The Media Is to Blame for Everything," *Ma'ariv,* June 7, 1998; Haim Baram, untitled column, *Kol-Ha'ir,* August 22, 1997.

55. Ran Kislev, "The Gentiles Are Coming," *Ha'aretz,* July 31, 1990; Danny Rubinstein, "Part of the Family or Tenants?" *Ha'aretz,* July 29, 1991; Urit Shohat, "The Unexpected Immigrants," *Ha'aretz,* September 15, 1993. See also Aryeh Gelbloom, "The Right of Citizenship," *Ha'aretz,* February 17, 1992.

56. Yosef Barnea, "An Anachronistic Anthem," *Ha'aretz,* January 27, 1993; Shlomit Avdor, "Pop-Politics," *Ha'aretz,* December 17, 1998. See also Uzi Ornan, "The Art of Camouflage in the Wording," *Ha'aretz,* May 17, 1991; "Conversion and Extraneous Rights," *Ha'aretz,* February 12, 1998.

57. Aryeh Caspi, "A National Home for a Billion Chinese," *Ha'aretz,* April 18, 1997.

58. Haim Ganz, "The Law of Return and Ameliorative Discrimination," *Studies in Law,* July 1995, p. 696 [Hebrew]. Such references to India are allusions to the "ten lost tribes" deported from ancient Israel after the Assyrian conquest of the biblical northern kingdom. In recent years, the "lost tribes" have become the object of small-scale but systematic work on the part of a few Israeli devotees. Although most of these efforts have led to little, much attention has been paid to one particular ethnic group, the so-called "Bnei Menasheh," of whom there may be (according to different reports) between 1 and 4 million. Of these, several hundred have converted to Judaism and immigrated to Israel. No one has yet produced evidence that substantial numbers of people in India really wish to return to or join the Jewish people or to immigrate to Israel. See Yair Sheleg, "Descendents of the Tribe of Menasheh Are Living in Eastern India," *Ha'aretz,* August 16, 1999.

59. *Koteret Rashit,* October 31, 1984.

60. *Jerusalem Post,* September 29, 1995.

61. *Ha'aretz,* October 15, 1995; June 12, 1998.

62. Ganz, "The Law of Return," p. 684 n. 3.

63. Amos Elon, "Israel and the End of Zionism," *New York Review of Books,* December 19, 1996.

64. David Grossman, "Imagine the Peace," *Yediot Aharonot,* September 29, 1993.

65. Tamir clearly states that the Arab law would render the Jewish one justified, but she then backtracks and considers that this might not be sufficient, since a state has a broader obligation to "assure equality among *all* nations." Emphasis mine. Yael Tamir, *Liberal Nationalism* (Princeton: Princeton University Press, 1993), pp. 160–161. For a more favorable view of the Law of Return, see Tamir's interview after being appointed absorption minister in 1999. *Ha'aretz,* August 13, 1999.

66. Margolin, *Israel as a Jewish and Democratic State,* p. 47; Gavison, "A Jewish and Democratic State," pp. 243, 276–277.

67. Yoav Gelber, "The Law of Return and the Right of Return," *Davar Rishon,* November 26, 1995.

68. Emphasis added. *Ha'aretz,* December 29, 1995.

69. Yoram Yom-Tov, "The Necessary Balance," *Ha'aretz,* December 23, 1996; *Yediot Aharonot,* January 12, 1995.

70. *Ha'aretz,* October 2, 1994. Although Namir told the press a few days later that she had not meant to call for changes in the Law of Return, she nevertheless emphasized, as the *Jerusalem Post* summarized her view, that "she had been overwhelmed by the number of

people, both immigrants and veteran Israelis, who had called in support of her opinion" regarding the quality of the immigrants. *Jerusalem Post*, October 5, 1994.

71. *Jerusalem Post*, August 8, 1993.

72. *Ha'aretz*, July 7, 1995; *Ma'ariv*, January 2, 1995. Gordon's emissaries, however, were more zealous in the creation of categories of Jews who should not be encouraged to immigrate than he himself was willing to tolerate. When the head of the Jewish Agency's immigration emissaries in North America, Judy Amit, called for a "redefined" Zionism that would be of a cultural character and would not necessarily seek Jewish immigration to Israel, Gordon angrily had her recalled. *Davar*, April 16, 1995; *Jerusalem Post*, April 17, 1995.

73. Kol Israel, November 2, 1999.

74. Shimon Peres, *Battling for Peace: Memoirs* (London: Weidenfeld and Nicolson, 1995), p. 26.

75. Muli Brog, "Young Peres Atop Masada," *Ha'aretz*, February 2, 1996.

76. Shimon Peres, "Conciliation Is Not Security," in *Niv Hakvutza*, September 29, 1955. Reprinted in Shimon Peres, *The Next Stage* (Tel Aviv: Am Hasefer, 1966), pp. 22, 24 [Hebrew].

77. Peres's memoirs vividly describe his views in 1974 on the indefensibility of Israel without the territories and on the determination of the PLO to destroy Israel. Peres, *Battling*, pp. 301–302.

78. Peres, *Battling*, pp. 316–318, 320, 355–356.

79. Address before the General Assembly, October 1, 1992.

80. Peres, *The New Middle East* (New York: Henry Holt, 1993), pp. 80–81. I have replaced "ultraregional," which is a mistranslation, with "superregional."

81. Ibid., p. 73. I have replaced "ultranational," which is a mistranslation, with "supernational."

82. Ibid., pp. 37–38.

83. Ibid., pp. 62–83, 171–172. Peres conceives of the continued existence of borders, but he conceives of them as being "soft" and permeable: "By definition, a 'soft' border is open to movement. . . . the free movement of people, ideas, and goods." Ibid., p. 172.

84. Ibid., pp. 76, 81, 98. I have replaced "ultranational," which is a mistranslation, with "supernational." Peres's 1998 book, *A New Genesis*, which declares that a "second Genesis" is now taking place in which "human nature will change" and that the world will be "freed from the barbed wire of territories and from the demarcation lines of sovereignty," is likewise insistent on this point—the Jewish "faith and people are one." Shimon Peres, *A New Genesis* (Tel Aviv: Zmora-Bitan, 1998), pp. 135, 191, 197–198 [Hebrew].

85. *Jerusalem Post*, May 3, 1993.

86. *Davar*, January 12, 1995; *Al Hamishmar*, January 12, 1995.

87. *Jerusalem Post*, May 19, 1995.

88. *Ma'ariv*, January 16, 1994; *Ma'ariv*, March 2, 1995.

89. "The Orwellian Corner," *Nativ*, May 1995, p. 9.

90. *Jerusalem Post*, May 31 and June 16, 1995; *Decision Brief*, Center for Security Policy, June 19, 1995.

91. *Ha'aretz*, June 4, 1993, and July 2, 1995; *Jerusalem Post*, May 31, June 4, and October 15, 1993.

92. *Ha'aretz*, December 21, 1994.

93. "A Framework for Peace in the Middle East Agreed at Camp David," preamble, clause 6; "Peace Treaty Between Israel and Egypt," March 26, 1979, article 3, clause 1a.

94. "Peace Between the State of Israel and the Hashemite Kingdom of Jordan," article 2, clause 1, October 26, 1994.

95. "The PLO Charter," as amended in 1968, Articles 20, 1, 22, 20. Unlike Jewish anti-Zionists, however, it also held that "the establishment of Israel is fundamentally null and void, whatever time has elapsed." "The PLO Charter," Article 19.

96. This position was held not only by the Israeli Labor party, but also by key American policymakers such as Secretary of State Henry Kissinger. Thus, when despite his formally anti-Zionist stance, Arafat offered in 1973 to "recognize" Israel in exchange for sovereign control over a territorial base on Israel's borders, the Americans concluded that what the PLO was asking for "could only be an interim step towards their final aims." Henry Kissinger, *Years of Upheaval* (Boston: Little, Brown, 1982), p. 626. This suspicion was backed up over the years by Arafat's record of declarations that if such a territorial base were secured, then, "After its establishment, the Palestinian [Arab] government will fight . . . to complete the liberation of all of the Palestinian land." These are the words of a resolution of what is known in the West as the "Plan of Phases," which was approved by the PLO Council on June 8, 1974. Article 8; see also Article 2, which for the first time sanctions establishing a government on only a part of Palestine. Reproduced in Benjamin Netanyahu, *A Place Among the Nations: Israel and the World* (New York: Bantam, 1993), p. 433.

97. There does exist a side letter from Arafat to Yitzhak Rabin, in which he declares that the PLO recognizes Israel's right to "exist in peace and security." But it too declines to mention the key terms "sovereignty, territorial integrity, and political independence." Thus, even Arafat's letter declines to recognize the essential Zionist component of the Jewish state's existence: The fact that it is not merely a "state" that "exists"—so is Nebraska—but that it has the right to be an *independent* state that is *sovereign* in at least a part of Palestine. Arafat to Rabin, September 9, 1993. On the unprecedented character of the Oslo Accords, see also Ze'ev Sternhell, *The Founding Myths of Israel: Nationalism, Socialism, and the Making of the Jewish State*, David Maisel, trans. (Princeton: Princeton University Press, 1998), pp. 339–340, 343.

98. Peres, *New Middle East,* p. 34

99. Ibid., pp. 33–34.

100. *Ha'aretz,* January 29, 1996.

101. *Jerusalem Post,* September 1, 1993.

102. Peres, *A New Genesis,* p. 100. Compare Peres, *New Middle East,* p. 171.

103. *Jerusalem Post International Edition,* October 28, 1995.

104. Peres, *New Middle East,* p. 172.

105. In the context of the Oslo negotiations, Peres provided the PLO with a promise in writing that it would be able to operate Palestinian national institutions in Jerusalem. See Shimon Peres to Norwegian Foreign Minister Johan Jorgen Holst, October 11, 1993. David Makovsky, *Making Peace with the PLO: The Rabin Government's Road to the Oslo Accord* (Boulder: Westview Press, 1996), p. 231. Members of Peres's team such as Beilin were similarly outspoken in their conviction that East Jerusalem should be given over to PLO "self-administration." *Davar,* March 12, 1995.

106. Yoel Marcus, "Ideology Is Taking Off for Anatolia," *Ha'aretz,* July 4, 1995.

107. Gidon Samet, "Our People Has Moved Up a Class," *Ha'aretz,* July 28, 1995.

108. Grossman, "Imagine the Peace."

Chapter Three

1. Howard Sachar, *A History of Israel: From the Rise of Zionism to Our Time* (New York: Knopf, 1979, and revised edition 1996), pp. 66, 180. I have replaced the Hebrew terms

"Brit Shalom" and "Yishuv" with the English equivalents "Peace Association" and "Jewish Palestine," respectively. Similarly, Conor Cruise O'Brien's excellent history of Zionism, *The Siege: The Saga of Israel and Zionism* (New York: Simon and Schuster, 1986), does not mention Buber once. The Peace Association in its various incarnations receives less than three paragraphs (pp. 174, 186). Martin Gilbert's *Israel: A History* (New York: Doubleday, 1998) also devotes three paragraphs to the Peace Association's activities (pp. 62, 256), and Buber's opposition to the Jewish state is not mentioned at all.

Chapter Four

1. I am unaware of any actual record as to the content of Herzl's speech of January 15, 1879, in which Herzl was apparently mistaken for a radical pan-German. What I have constructed here is a conjecture, based upon what we know of Herzl's inclinations at the time and of the reactions the speech elicited. See Jacques Kornberg, *Theodor Herzl: From Assimilation to Zionism* (Bloomington: Indiana University Press, 1993), p. 39. The Liberal leader quoted is J. N. Berger, cited in Carl E. Schorske, "Politics in a New Key: An Austrian Triptych," *Journal of Modern History*, December 1967, p. 343.
2. Arthur Schnitzler to Herzl, August 5, 1892. Quoted in Joel Carmichael, trans., "Excerpts from the Correspondence Between Theodor Herzl and Arthur Schnitzler, 1892–1895," *Midstream*, Winter 1960, p. 48. As Schnitzler was younger than Herzl, it seems that the speech to which he was referring must have been later than the one reconstructed above.
3. Kornberg, *From Assimilation*, p. 39; Herzl to Academische Lesehalle, first half of 1897. Theodor Herzl, *Briefe und Tagebuecher* (Vienna: Propylaeen, 1983–1996), vol. 1, pp. 73–74 [German].
4. Quoted from the Lesehalle's 1879–1880 annual report. Kornberg, *From Assimilation*, p. 44.
5. Robert Wistrich and David Ohana, eds., *The Shaping of Israeli Identity: Myth, Memory, and Trauma* (London: Frank Cass, 1995), p. 8. Other Jewish students who joined the German nationalist student organizations in Vienna at the time included Sigmund Freud, Gustav Mahler, and the historian Heinrich Friedjung. Kornberg, *From Assimilation*, p. 46.
6. Herzl diary, January 19 and 30, 1882. Herzl, *Briefe und Tagebuecher*, vol. 1, pp. 588, 596. Compare Ernst Pawel, *The Labyrinth of Exile: A Life of Theodor Herzl* (London: Collins Harvill, 1989), pp. 73–74.
7. Herzl diary, February 9, 1882. Herzl, *Briefe und Tagebuecher*, vol. 1, pp. 611, 615–616. Compare Pawel, *Labyrinth*, p. 76.
8. Pawel, *Labyrinth*, pp. 70–71. Twelve years later, he noted in his diary that the Jewish state would have saber duels as well: "I must have the duel in order to have good officers." Herzl diary, June 9, 1895. Herzl, *Briefe und Tagebuecher*, vol. 2, p. 92. Compare Theodor Herzl, *The Complete Diaries of Theodor Herzl*, Raphael Patai, ed., Harry Zohn, trans. (New York: Herzl Press, 1960), p. 58.
9. Pawel, *Labyrinth*, pp. 117, 176–178.
10. Theodor Herzl, "The Hunt in Bohemia," *Die Welt*, November 5, 1897. Theodor Herzl, *Zionist Writings: Essays and Addresses*, Harry Zohn, trans. (New York: Herzl Press, 1973), vol. 1, pp. 170–171.
11. Pawel, *Labyrinth*, pp. 13, 18–19.
12. Herzl's grandfather, Simon Loeb Herzl, belonged to the congregation of the famous Jewish nationalist rabbinic leader Yehuda Alkalai. Alex Bein, *Theodor Herzl*, Maurice Samuel, trans. (Philadelphia: Jewish Publication Society, 1940), pp. 5, 15.

13. "Shemoneh Esrei," traditional daily prayer service.

14. Jean-Jacques Rousseau, *On the Social Contract: With Geneva Manuscript and Political Economy*, Roger D. Masters, ed., Judith R. Masters, trans. (New York: St. Martin's Press, 1978), pp. 58, 130–131.

15. Elie Barnavie, ed., *Universal History of the Jews* (Paris: Hachette, 1992), p. 158 [French]. Compare Paul R. Mendes-Flohr and Jehuda Reinharz, eds., *The Jew in the Modern World: A Documentary History* (New York: Oxford University Press, 1980), pp. 103–105.

16. Simon Schwartzfuchs, *Napoleon, the Jews, and the Sanhedrin* (London: Routledge, 1979), pp. 13–21.

17. The Sanhedrin was the great rabbinic court that had served as a kind of Jewish national parliament in antiquity.

18. Schwartzfuchs, *Sanhedrin*, p. 85.

19. See decisions of the Paris Sanhedrin, in Mendes-Flohr and Reinharz, *The Jew in the Modern World*, pp. 123–124; Schwartzfuchs, *Sanhedrin*, pp. 69, 93.

20. Immanuel Kant, "Perpetual Peace: A Philosophical Sketch," in Hans Reiss, ed. and trans., *Kant's Political Writings* (New York: Cambridge, 1970), pp. 94, 99–100, 105–106, 114–115; Immanuel Kant, "On the Common Saying 'This May Be True in Theory But It Does Not Apply in Practice,'" in *Kant's Political Writings*, pp. 73–80; Immanuel Kant, *Fundamental Principles of the Metaphysic of Morals*, T. K. Abbott, trans. (Buffalo: Prometheus, 1987), p. 35.

21. Max Wiener, ed., *Abraham Geiger and Liberal Judaism: The Challenge of the 19th Century* (Philadelphia: Jewish Publication Society, 1962), p. 71.

22. David Philipson, *The Reform Movement in Judaism* (New York: Ktav, 1967), p. 179.

23. Samson Raphael Hirsch, *Horeb: A Philosophy of Jewish Laws and Observances*, Isidor Grunfeld, trans. (New York: Soncino Press, 1981), p. 461. For his belief in the Jewish "mission" among the nations, see Samson Raphael Hirsch, "Studies on Isaiah and Essays on the Psalms," in Samson Raphael Hirsch, *The Collected Writings*, Karin Paritzky, trans. (New York: Feldheim, 1986), vol. 4, p. 380.

24. Ben Halpern, *The Idea of the Jewish State* (Cambridge: Harvard University Press, 1961), pp. 13–14.

25. Even in Russia, a similar group, The Society for the Spread of Culture Among the Jews of Russia, was established in 1863. Leo Pinsker was an active member, calling upon Jews to adopt Russian as their first language. Arthur Hertzberg, ed., *The Zionist Idea: A Historical Analysis and Reader* (New York: Atheneum, 1969), p. 179.

26. Hermann Cohen, "Germanism and Judaism," in Hermann Cohen, *Jewish Writings* (Berlin: Schwetschke, 1924), vol. 2, pp. 279, 283 [German]. Compare Nathan Rotenstreich, "Hermann Cohen: Judaism in the Context of German Philosophy," in Jehuda Reinharz and Walter Schatzberg, eds., *The Jewish Response to German Culture* (Hanover: University Press of New England, 1985), pp. 55–56.

27. Kant, *Metaphysic of Morals*, p. 35.

28. Hermann Cohen, *Religion of Reason: Out of the Sources of Judaism*, Simon Kaplan, trans. (Atlanta: Scholars Press, 1995), pp. 263–264, 265–266, 282–284.

29. Ibid., pp. 239–240, 267–268.

30. "But how little the [ancient Jewish] state meant to this people [i.e., Israel] is manifested in the continuation and the blossoming of the people even after the destruction of the state. . . . With this people . . . the great event occurred: Without the state, even after the destruction of the state, the people flourished and grew into an inner unity." Moreover: "David's realm is not the proper soil for the world of monotheism. Neither in this short and bygone past nor in any political present does Israel's historical calling

lie. . . . Only a spiritual world can fulfill this national existence. . . . The endurance of the Jewish state . . . would have been an anomaly, as it already was in its origin, with regard to 'the Lord over all the earth.'" Cohen, *Religion of Reason*, pp. 251–253. Note that this reverence for statelessness was first a German idea before Cohen attempted to make it into a Jewish one. Thus, Schiller, viewing a Germany consisting of a kaleidoscope of disunited and bickering ministates, was able to write of the unique German spirit detached from political success: "Sundered from politics, the German has founded . . . ethical greatness; it is inherent to the culture and character of the nation, which is independent of its political destiny. . . . Each people has its day in history, but the day of the German is the harvest of time as a whole." Friedrich Schiller, "German Greatness," in Norbert Oellers, ed., *Schiller's Works* (Weimar: Hermann Boehlaus Nachfolger, 1983), vol. 2, pt. 1, pp. 431, 433 [German].

31. Cohen, *Religion of Reason*, pp. 259–260.

32. "The downfall of the Jewish state is, in our view, the best example of historical theodicy. . . . It is our proud conviction that we are to continue to live as divine dew in the midst of the peoples . . . All of the prophets place us in the midst of the peoples and their common perspective is the world mission of the remnant of Israel." Cohen, in Mendes-Flohr and Reinharz, *The Jew in the Modern World*, p. 450.

33. Cohen, *Religion of Reason,* pp. 267–268.

34. Pawel, *Labyrinth*, p. 165.

35. Herzl diary, Pentacost 1895. Herzl, *Briefe und Tagebuecher*, vol. 2, p. 49. Compare Herzl, *Diaries*, pp. 9–10.

36. Bein, *Theodor Herzl*, pp. 93–94.

37. Pawel, *Labyrinth*, pp. 170–173.

38. Kornberg, *From Assimilation*, pp. 115–126.

39. Herzl to Schnitzler, December 17, 1894. Pawel, *Labyrinth*, p. 204.

40. Theodor Herzl, *The Ghetto: A Play in Four Acts*, (unpublished, 1894), pp. 141–142, 163 [German], Central Zionist Archives, H–525. Compare Kornberg, *From Assimilation*, pp. 146–147. Herzl subsequently reworked his play and toned down its message. The revised, published version was called: *The New Ghetto*. See Theodor Herzl, *Collected Zionist Works* (Berlin: Juedischer Verlag, 1935), vol. 5, pp. 111, 124 [German].

41. Herzl's November 8 letter to Schnitzler, written the day Herzl finished the play, says that he began work on October 21 and then calculates: "Seventeen days, in other words." Pawel, *Labyrinth*, p. 202. But this period comprises nineteen days.

42. Herzl wrote later: "The whole thing seemed improbable to me. . . . A Jew who was an officer on the General Staff and as such was assured of a distinguished career could not commit such a crime. . . . [It] was psychologically impossible. A man of means, who had chosen this career only out of a desire for honors, could not possibly have committed this most dishonorable of crimes. Because they were deprived of the honors of citizenship for such a long time, the Jews have a desire for honor that frequently borders on the pathological, and in this respect a Jewish army officer is a Jew with a high potential to desire honor." Theodor Herzl, "Zionism," unpublished essay from 1899. Leon Kellner, ed., *Theodor Herzl's Zionist Writings* (Berlin: Juedischer Verlag, 1920), pp. 257–258 [German]. Compare Herzl, "Zionism," in *Zionist Writings*, vol. 2, pp. 112–113.

43. Pawel, *Labyrinth*, pp. 206–207.

44. "Death! Death to the Jews!" Herzl, "Zionism," p. 112.

45. Herzl, "The Hunt in Bohemia," pp. 170–171.

46. Herzl to Moriz Benedikt, December 27, 1892. Herzl, *Briefe und Tagebuecher*, vol. 1, p. 507.

47. Herzl diary, Pentecost, June 2, 1895. Herzl, *Briefe und Tagebuecher*, vol. 2., pp. 50–52. Compare Herzl, *Diaries*, pp. 11–13.

48. See Arie Morgenstern, *Redemption Through Nature: Students of the Vilna Gaon in the Land of Israel, 1800–1840* (Jerusalem: Maor, 1997), pp. 135–157 [Hebrew].

49. Halpern, *The Idea of the Jewish State*, p. 115; Yosef Klausner, "R. Yehuda Bibas: One of the Forerunner's of Zionism," *Ha'olam*, December 2, 1943 [Hebrew]; Yehuda Alkalai, "The Third Redemption" (1843), in Hertzberg, *The Zionist Idea*, pp. 105–107.

50. See Hertzberg, *The Zionist Idea*, pp. 111–114, 119–139; Halpern, *The Idea of the Jewish State*, pp. 117–118; Yosef Salmon, "The Beginnings of Jewish Nationalism as Understood Through Research," in *Studies in the Restoration of Israel* (Sde Boker: Ben-Gurion University, 1998), p. 578 [Hebrew].

51. See Hertzberg, *The Zionist Idea*, pp. 183, 198. Ahad Ha'am, too, considered emancipation in the West to have been a disaster, offering the Jews status, but at the cost of a spiritual enslavement to the emancipating regime. See Halpern, *The Idea of the Jewish State*, pp. 74–75.

52. Pawel, *Labyrinth*, p. 271.

53. Jehuda Reinharz, "Jewish Nationalism and Jewish Identity in Central Europe," in Wolfgang Beck, ed., *The Jews in European History: Seven Lectures* (Cincinnati: Hebrew Union College Press, 1994), p. 95.

54. Theodor Norman, *An Outstretched Arm* (London: Routledge, 1985), p. 6.

55. Yossi Ben-Artzi, *Early Jewish Settlement Patterns in Palestine, 1882–1914* (Jerusalem: Magnes Press, 1997), pp. 60–64 [Hebrew]; David Vital, *The Origins of Zionism* (Oxford: Clarendon Press, 1980), p. 183.

56. Herzl diary, June 2, 1895. Herzl, *Diaries*, pp. 3, 5.

57. Herzl to Hirsch, late May 1895. Herzl, *Diaries*, p. 14.

58. Herzl diary, June 2, 1895. Herzl, *Diaries*, pp. 19–23.

59. Ibid.

60. Herzl to Hirsch, June 3, 1895. Herzl, *Diaries*, pp. 26–28.

61. Theodor Herzl, "A 'Solution of the Jewish Question,'" *Jewish Chronicle*, January 17, 1896.

62. Ibid. I have used the English text of these passages from Herzl, *The Jewish State*, Harry Zohn, trans. (New York: Herzl Press, 1970), pp. 27, 33–34, 49. The meaning is identical, but the latter dispenses with a few grammatical problems in the original.

63. Herzl diary, February 14, 1896. Herzl, *Briefe und Tagebuecher*, vol. 2, p. 301. Compare Herzl, *Diaries*, p. 299.

64. Herzl to Adler, November 23, 1895. Herzl, *Diaries*, November 23, 1895, p. 279.

65. Herzl diary, September 3, 1897. Herzl, *Diaries*, p. 581.

66. Rousseau, *Social Contract*, pp. 53, 58. For Kant's version of the social contract, see Kant, "On the Common Saying," pp. 73–80.

67. Rousseau, *Social Contract*, pp. 53, 130–131.

68. "Since the state did not by any means arise historically from the social contract, another legal principle must be operative. This is the *negotiorum gestio*. The people are and will always be incapable of directing their own affairs, whose scope and magnitude are beyond their comprehension." Theodor Herzl, *The Palais Bourbon* (Leipzig: Dunker and Humbolt, 1895), p. 243 [German]. Ccompare Kornberg, *From Assimilation*, p. 168.

69. "Rousseau believed that there was such a thing as a social contract. This is wrong. In the state there is only a *negotiorum gestio*." Herzl diary, June 7, 1895. Herzl, *Briefe und Tagebuecher*, vol. 2, p. 76. Compare Herzl, *Diaries*, p. 41.

70. Herzl, *The Jewish State*, p. 92.

71. Theodor Herzl, *Der Judenstaat* (Vienna: M. Breitenstein, 1896), p. 69 [German]. Compare Herzl, *The Jewish State*, pp. 92–93.

72. Ibid.

73. Herzl, *Der Judenstaat*, p. 69 [German]. Compare Herzl, *The Jewish State*, p. 94.

74. Herzl diary, June 12, 1895. Herzl, *Diaries*, pp. 87–88.

75. Herzl, *The Jewish State*, p. 55; Herzl diary, November 18, 1898. Herzl, *Diaries*, p. 765. When Herzl sought in 1899 to have the first draft charter written, he also considered German charters in East Africa and New Guinea to be of relevance. Max Bodenheimer, *Prelude to Israel: The Memoirs of M. I. Bodenheimer*, Israel Cohen, trans. (New York: Thomas Yoseloff, 1963), p. 145.

76. Philip Lawson, *The East India Company: A History* (London: Longman, 1993), pp. 17–20, 45–46.

77. Ibid., pp. 46–48, 90–117.

78. John S. Galbraith, *Crown and Charter* (London: University of California Press, 1974), pp. 263, 288–293, 312–323, 326–336; Anthony Sillery, *Founding a Protectorate* (The Hague: Mouton, 1965), pp. 128, 153–156.

79. Herzl, *The Jewish State*, p. 51. See also Herzl diary, April 25, 1896. Herzl, *Diaries*, p. 338.

80. Herzl diary, July 8, 1896. Herzl, *Diaries*, p. 412.

81. Herzl diary, August 25, 1896. Herzl, *Diaries*, p. 458. Compare letter to Goldsmid of May 20, 1897, in which "self-protection is again emphasized as a condition of becoming Turkish subjects." Herzl, *Diaries*, p. 551.

82. Herzl diary, March 29, 1897. Herzl, *Diaries*, p. 533.

83. Herzl to Hirsch, June 3, 1895. Herzl, *Briefe und Tagebuecher*, vol. 1, p. 65. Compare Herzl, *Diaries*, p. 28. Compare with his diary a few days later, where he writes, "We shall be a nation of thinkers and artists." Herzl diary, June 10, 1895. Herzl, *Diaries*, p. 66.

84. Herzl, *Jewish State*, pp. 85–86. In the pamphlet, Herzl refers to Hirsch only as "the Baron."

85. I have used the term "centers" where Herzl referred to religious, entrepreneurial, and entertainment *Zielpunkte* ("goal-points") or *Anziehungspunkte* ("attraction-points") in the new land, which would serve both as personal objectives and attractions to the Jews. Herzl, *Der Judenstaat*, pp. 62–63.

86. Herzl, *The Jewish State*, pp. 31, 48–50, 61, 105. Herzl's understanding of the importance of private enterprise seems to have come not only from the experiences of his father but also from studying political economy with Carl Menger at the University of Vienna, whose influence can also be felt in the work of another student who was later at the university, Ludwig von Mises. Herzl's loyalty to the market principle was, however, far from absolute. As is clear from his diary entries, Herzl was strongly attracted to the idea that those aspects of the economy that no longer needed entrepreneurial risk in order to operate could reasonably be transferred to the state for the good of the population. That this kind of argument did not make it into *The Jewish State* may have been the result of Herzl's interest in attracting the great Jewish bankers to his cause.

87. Herzl, *The Jewish State*, pp. 38–39, 59, 71, 81.

88. Ibid., p. 88. Herzl's close friend Max Bodenheimer similarly recorded in his memoirs his disappointment upon visiting such sites in Palestine in 1926: "The grave of Rachel left me with nothing but a sorrowful recollection. It is regrettable that the Jews so neglect their holy places, while in the vicinity of monasteries and of Christian and Moslem places of pilgrimage one finds well-kept gardens. Why does Rachel's tomb lie bare, somber and neglected in a stony desert? As there can be no lack of money about, it can

be assumed that the Jews, during the long exile of the Ghetto, lost all sense of beauty and of the significance of impressive monuments . . . The poor, indeed even wretched condition in Palestine of many buildings and institutions connected with the Jewish religion permits of hardly any other conclusion." Bodenheimer, *Prelude to Israel*, p. 327.

89. Herzl, "A 'Solution of the Jewish Question,'" *Jewish Chronicle*, January 17, 1896; Pawel, *Labyrinth*, p. 361.

90. Olga Schnitzler, *Reflection of Friendship* (Salzburg: Residenz, 1962), p. 96 [German]. Quoted in Kornberg, *From Assimilation*, p. 178.

91. The reference to the temporary nature of such attractions appears where Herzl raises it as an objection to his plans "that the masses can be attracted to such centers of faith, of business, or of amusement only temporarily." His response to this objection is that "One of these objects can only attract the masses, but all of the centers combined are designed to hold them and give them permanent satisfaction." Herzl, *The Jewish State*, p. 88. The possibility that there will be no such development of the three centers, or only limited development, and that this, indeed, would render the state "temporary" is obvious enough that it must have been evident to Herzl as well.

92. Herzl, "Five to Two," *Die Welt*, September 15, 1899. Herzl, *Zionist Writings*, vol. 2, p. 128.

93. "We have returned home as it were. Zionism is a return to Judaism even before there is a return to the Jewish land." Speech before the First Zionist Congress, *Minutes of the First Zionist Congress in Basel (August 29–31)* (Prague: Barissa, 1911), p. 16 [German]. Compare *Zionist Writings*, vol. 1, p. 133.

94. Herzl, *The Jewish State*, pp. 33, 107.

95. *Neue Freie Presse*, May 14, 1896, quoted in Alex Bein, *Theodor Herzl: A Biography* (Vienna: Fiba, 1934), pp. 301–302 [German]. The quote does not appear in the English edition of Bein's biography, but it is quoted in Pawel, *Labyrinth*, p. 287.

96. Theodor Herzl, "Judaism," in *Oesterreichische Wochenschrift*, November 13, 1896 [German]. Compare Herzl, *Zionist Writings*, vol. 1, pp. 57–58.

Chapter Five

1. Theodor Herzl, *The Jewish State*, Harry Zohn, trans. (New York: Herzl Press, 1970), p. 99. See also Theodor Herzl, *The Complete Diaries of Theodor Herzl*, Raphael Patai, ed., Harry Zohn, trans. (New York: Herzl Press, 1960), May 19, 1896, pp. 353–354; Frederic Chapin Lane, *Venice: A Maritime Republic* (Baltimore: Johns Hopkins University Press, 1973), p. 429.

2. Frederic Mocatta, quoted in Herzl diary, July 6, 1896. Herzl, *Diaries*, p. 408.

3. Herzl diary, July 14, 1896. Herzl, *Diaries*, pp. 419–420.

4. Herzl diary, July 19, 1896. Herzl, *Diaries*, pp. 427, 429.

5. Herzl, *The Jewish State*, pp. 75–77; Herzl diary, July 20, 1896. Herzl, *Diaries*, p. 430.

6. The term "Zionism" was apparently coined in 1890 by the Jewish nationalist circle in Vienna around Nathan Birnbaum, who considered it to be synonymous with Jewish nationalism. Like Herzl, Birnbaum viewed the "ultimate aim" of Zionism to be political "restoration of the Jewish commonwealth in Palestine." Nathan Birnbaum, *The National Renaissance of the Jewish People in Its Country as a Means Toward a Solution to the Jewish Question* (1893), quoted in Alex Bein, "The Origin of the Term and Concept Zionism," in *Herzl Year Book* 2 (New York: Herzl Press, 1959), pp. 20–21; see also pp. 10, 14–15. Max Bodenheimer explains that the early German Zionists who opposed Herzl were united in their support of the Jewish state as he was but wished to keep this

goal secret for tactical reasons. Max Bodenheimer, *Prelude to Israel: The Memoirs of M. I. Bodenheimer,* Israel Cohen, trans. (New York: Thomas Yoseloff, 1963), pp. 74, 93, 140. See also Bambus to Herzl, April 8, 1897, quoted in Bein, "Origin," p. 25 n. 69.

7. Herzl diary, October 11, 1896. Herzl, *Diaries,* p. 480.

8. De Haas's original English translation of the invitation, in Pawel, *Labyrinth,* p. 320; Herzl diary, March 29, 1897. Herzl, *Diaries,* p. 534.

9. Herzl diary, March 29, 1897. Herzl, *Diaries,* p. 532. However, see Herzl, *Briefe und Tagebuecher* (Vienna: Propylaeen, 1983–1996), April 4, 1897, vol. 2, pp. 497–498 [German].

10. Pawel, *Labyrinth,* pp. 321–322; Paul Goodman, *Zionism in England* (London: English Zionist Federation, 1929), p. 13; Herzl diary, May 9, 1897. Herzl, *Diaries,* pp. 543–544. For Montagu's earlier profession of sympathy, see Herzl diary, November 24, 1895. Herzl, *Diaries,* p. 280.

11. Moritz M. Guedemann, *National Judaism,* Miriam Dinur, trans. (Jerusalem: The Dinur Center, 1995), pp. 33–34 [German and Hebrew]. Compare Theodor Herzl, "Dr. Guedemann's National-Judentum," *Oesterreichische Wochenschrift,* April 23, 1897 [German]. Reprinted in Theodor Herzl, *Zionist Writings: Essays and Addresses,* Harry Zohn, trans. (New York: Herzl Press, 1973), vol. 1, pp. 62–70, especially p. 69.

12. The statement also distinguished between Zionism and the "practical" efforts of the philanthropic organizations in settling Palestine, which it held to be legitimate. Theodor Herzl, "Protest Rabbis," *Die Welt,* July 16, 1897. Herzl, *Zionist Writings,* vol. 1, pp. 119–120.

13. *Yearbook of the Central Conference of American Rabbis, 1897–1898* (Cincinnati: May and Kreidler, 1898), p. xli.

14. *Die Welt,* June 4, 1897.

15. Herzl, "Dr. Guedemann," p. 69.

16. Herzl, "Protest Rabbis," p. 119.

17. The Congress was also attended by agents of the powers. The German ambassador's report made it all the way up to the Kaiser, who scribbled in the margin: "Let the kikes go to Palestine, the sooner the better. I am not about to put obstacles in their way." Pawel, *Labyrinth,* p. 342.

18. Herzl diary, September 3 and 6, 1897. Herzl, *Diaries,* pp. 581, 584, 588–589.

19. Ibid.

20. Alex Bein, *Theodor Herzl,* Maurice Samuel, trans. (Philadelphia: Jewish Publication Society, 1940), p. 227.

21. Herzl diary, September 3, 1897. Herzl, *Diaries,* p. 581.

22. Ahad Ha'am, "The Wrong Way," in Ahad Ha'am, *Ten Essays on Zionism and Judaism,* Leon Simon, ed. (London: Routledge, 1922), pp. 12, 14.

23. Steven J. Zipperstein, *Elusive Prophet: Ahad Ha'am and the Origins of Zionism* (Berkeley: University of California, 1993), p. 29f.

24. In the wake of his publication of the "The Wrong Way," Ahad Ha'am had been elected to this body in 1890 after its activities had been legalized. By 1895, three of the committee's members were Bnei Moshe, under whose influence its allocations for educational programs had been increased from year to year. In 1896, the committee at long last adopted the line Ahad Ha'am advocated and determined to take responsibility for supervising the schools and designing curricula for them. See Ehud Luz, *Parallels Meet: Religion and Nationalism in the Early Zionist Movement, 1882–1904,* Lenn J. Schramm, trans. (Philadelphia: Jewish Publication Society, 1988), p. 101. For the breakup of Bnei Moshe, see Zipperstein, *Elusive Prophet,* pp. 100–104.

25. Ahad Ha'am, "The First Zionist Congress," in *Ten Essays*, p. 30.

26. Ahad Ha'am to Ravnitsky, September 1, 1897. Aryeh Simon, ed., *The Letters of Ahad Ha'am* (Tel Aviv: Dvir, 1956), vol. 1, pp. 251–252 [Hebrew].

27. Ahad Ha'am, "The First Zionist Congress," pp. 30–31. For a discussion of Ahad Ha'am's motives, see Zipperstein, *Elusive Prophet,* pp. 128–132.

28. Ahad Ha'am, "The Jewish State and the Jewish Problem," in *Ten Essays*, p. 48.

29. Emphasis added. Ahad Ha'am, "The Jewish State and the Jewish Problem," pp. 36–39.

30. Ahad Ha'am, "The Jewish State and the Jewish Problem," pp. 45–47, 51.

31. Emphasis in the original. Ahad Ha'am, "The Jewish State and the Jewish Problem," pp. 45–47, 51. Quotation marks inserted by the author to indicate phrases quoted from his earlier essay, "The First Zionist Congress," have been removed from this passage for clarity.

32. Ahad Ha'am, "The Spiritual Revival," in Ahad Ha'am, *Selected Essays*, Leon Simon, trans. (Philadelphia: Jewish Publication Society, 1912), p. 305.

33. Pawel, *Labyrinth*, pp. 368–369. After a preparatory meeting with Herzl in October 1898, the Kaiser did in fact broach the subject of a German protectorate for the Jews in Palestine with the Ottoman Sultan on his state visit in Constantinople, and Abdul Hamid apparently responded with a carefully worded rebuff. For the various versions of this meeting, see Pawel, *Labyrinth*, p. 378.

34. Herzl diary, October 19, 1898. Herzl, *Diaries*, p. 729. Pawel quotes Buelow as having said: "I had a very good impression of Dr. Herzl, but I don't believe in his cause. Those people don't have any money. The rich Jews won't go along, and with the Polish riffraff you can't do a thing." Pawel, *Labyrinth*, pp. 393–394.

35. *Politische Correspondenz*, Vienna, December 27, 1900. See Herzl, *Briefe und Tagebuecher*, vol. 6, pp. 131–132.

36. Herzl diary, December 28–31, 1900. Herzl, *Diaries*, pp. 1015–1018.

37. Herzl diary, January 4, 1901. Herzl, *Diaries*, p. 1023. A year later, his determination to find a site for Jewish concentration near Palestine that could be used as a base for extension into Palestine had only increased. "This must be my . . . task now," he wrote. "Then I would be a serious but friendly neighbor to the sanjak of Jerusalem, which I shall somehow acquire at the first opportunity, as the Bulgarians did with Eastern Rumelia." Herzl diary, August 4, 1902. Herzl, *Diaries*, p. 1344. The disputed territory of Eastern Rumelia became an autonomous province within the Turkish Empire according to treaty in 1878, only to proclaim itself a part of Bulgaria seven years later in 1885.

38. Oskar K. Rabinowicz, "Herzl, Architect of the Balfour Declaration," in *Herzl Year Book* 1 (New York: Herzl Press, 1958), pp. 5–8.

39. Herzl diary, July 12, 1902. Herzl, *Diaries*, p. 1302.

40. Herzl diary, October 23, 1902. Herzl, *Diaries*, pp. 1362–1363.

41. Herzl diary, December 22, 1902. Herzl, *Diaries*, p. 1382.

42. Herzl diary, April 24, 1903. Herzl, *Diaries*, p. 1473.

43. Herzl decided to explore the East Africa proposal in the wake of the pogrom, writing to Nordau: "We must give an answer to Kishinev, and this is the only one . . . We must, in a word, play the politics of the hour." Herzl to Nordau, July 6, 1903. Bein, *Theodor Herzl*, p. 444. The belief that the ZO must negotiate over East Africa as a bargaining tactic was also the position of Leopold Greenberg, who was Herzl's chief representative in the negotiations with Britain. On June 7, 1903, he wrote to Herzl: "It seems to me that intrinsically there is not great value in East Africa. It will not form a great attraction to our people for it has no moral or historical claim. But the value of the proposal of Chamberlain is politically immense . . . It will for the first time since the diaspora al-

most be a recognition of the necessity of aiding our people as a whole . . . and hence will be the first recognition of our people as a nation. . . . It matters not if East Africa is afterwards refused by us—we shall have obtained from the British government a recognition that it cannot ever go back of[:] . . . the recognition of us as a nation. It also follows naturally that as we got the British government on with the Sinai scheme and that going off they suggested a substitute, so if it is found that East Africa is no good they will have to make a further suggestion, and this it is possible will gradually and surely lead us to Palestine." Greenberg to Herzl, June 7, 1903, in Rabinowicz, "Herzl," pp. 50–51.After the Sixth Congress, too, when Bodenheimer showed Herzl a news report depicting the violent opposition of English settlers in East Africa to the Jewish colonization scheme, Herzl is said to have responded: "So the report of the [ZO's] expedition will prove negative, and we shall have what we want. You will see. . . . The time is coming when England will do everything in her power to have Palestine ceded for us as a Jewish state." Bodenheimer, *Prelude to Israel*, p. 161.

44. Such were the terms of the draft sketched by Herzl on June 8, 1903. *Briefe und Tagebuecher*, vol. 7, pp. 680–681. The proposed charter submitted by Lloyd George on Herzl's behalf on July 13 preserved all of these authorities, as well as requesting a Jewish name, a Jewish flag, a form of government that would be "Jewish in character," and explicit recognition that the purpose of the colony would be to secure "the wellbeing of the Jewish people." It also envisioned the possibility of extension of the colony, with Britain's permission, to other territories "whether . . . contiguous to the said territory or not." Text of the proposed charter reprinted in Oskar K. Rabinowicz, "New Light on the East Africa Scheme," in Israel Cohen, ed., *The Rebirth of Israel: A Memorial Tribute to Paul Goodman* (London: Goldstein and Sons, 1952), pp. 81–91.

45. Sir Clement Hill to Leopold Greenberg, August 14, 1903. Reprinted in *Die Welt*, August 29, 1903.

46. Herzl diary, April 24, 1903. Herzl, *Diaries*, p. 1474.

47. As Plehwe explained to Herzl, "We used to be sympathetic to your Zionist movement, as long as it worked toward emigration. You don't have to justify your movement to me. You are preaching to a convert. But ever since the Minsk conference we have noticed a change [among the Russian Zionist leaders] . . . There is less talk now of Palestinian Zionism than there is about culture, organization, and Jewish nationalism. This doesn't suit us. We have noticed in particular that your leaders in Russia—who are highly respected persons in their own circles—do not really obey your Vienna committee. Actually, Ussishkin is the only man in Russia who is with you." Herzl diary, August 10, 1903. Herzl, *Diaries*, p. 1525.

48. Herzl diary, August 14, 1903. Herzl, *Diaries*, p. 1535.

49. Plehwe to Herzl, July 30/August 12, 1903. Central Zionist Archives H-877.

50. Even the Zionist leaders were generally informed only of what they needed to know to execute the tasks Herzl assigned them. See Bodenheimer, *Prelude to Israel*, pp. 153–154.

51. Ahad Ha'am himself had by this point stopped paying dues and so was not officially a member of the ZO. As he wrote to the Zionist Executive, "I am not a regular shekel-payer, by which I mean that in principle I am neither for the shekel nor against it. I do not regard payment of the shekel as a sign of adherence to Zionism, because on the one hand I sacrificed much more than the shekel for Zionism before the shekel became an institution, and on the other hand I know many shekel-payers whom I cannot regard as Zionists. Hence I pay the shekel only when a collector asks me to do so; and though I used to be asked in the early years, I have not been asked recently." Ahad Ha'am to the Zionist Executive, February 4, 1902. Ahad Ha'am, *Essays, Letters, Memoirs*, p. 280.

52. Luz, *Parallels Meet*, pp. 175–177.

53. Weizmann to Herzl, May 6, 1903. Chaim Weizmann, *The Letters and Papers of Chaim Weizmann*, Meyer Weisgal and Barnet Litvinoff, eds. (London: Oxford University Press, 1968–1972, and Jerusalem: Israel Universities Press, 1973–1980), ser. A, vol. 2, p. 319.

54. Herzl, "The Menorah," *Die Welt*, December 31, 1897. *Zionist Writings*, vol. 1, pp. 203–206. He even conducts discussions in his diaries on the nature of God. Herzl diary, June 12 and August 16, 1895. Herzl, *Diaries*, pp. 96, 231. For Herzl's interest in the Hebrew language, see Michael Berkowicz, "Herzl and Hebrew," in Meyer W. Weisgal, ed., *Theodor Herzl: A Memorial* (New York, 1929), p. 74.

55. Michael Berkowitz, *Zionist Culture and West European Jewry Before the First World War* (Chapel Hill: University of North Carolina Press, 1996), p. 15.

56. With characteristic hyperbole, Nordau likewise told the rabbis at the Third Congress that "in one day, with a single gesture, you can turn nine-tenths of the Jewish people from Zionists in their hearts, as they are today, to Zionists in word and deed." Luz, *Parallels Meet*, pp. 141–142.

57. Ibid., p. 187. His partner Weizmann described his group as believing that "the free development of the nation find[s] its highest expression in the idea of statehood." Weizmann to Menahem Ussishkin and others, October 26, 1903. Weizmann, *Letters*, vol. 3, p. 81.

58. Weizmann to Motzkin, November 23, 1901, in Weizmann, *Letters*, vol. 1, p. 206; Weizmann to Vera Khatzman, September 8, 1901, in Weizmann, *Letters*, vol. 1, p. 178. A party program from 1902 explained what the Democratic leaders meant by the group's "modernism": "By the Jewish cultural heritage, Zionism designates past and present creations of the Hebrew spirit, to the extent that they can be associated with general human culture." Luz, *Parallels Meet*, p. 186.

59. Luz, *Parallels Meet*, pp. 188, 209, 219–220.

60. Yitzhak Ma'or, *The Zionist Movement in Russia* (Jerusalem: Hasifria Hatziyonit, 1986), p. 198 [Hebrew]. One previous conclave of Russian Zionists had taken place, without government approval, on the eve of the Second Congress in 1898. See Ma'or, *The Zionist Movement in Russia*, p. 152f.

61. Ibid., p. 198; "Pinsker and Political Zionism," in Ahad Ha'am, *Ten Essays*, pp. 56–90.

62. Herzl apparently covered the costs of the convention that created the organization out of his own pocket. Joseph Adler, "Religion and Herzl: Fact and Fable," *Herzl Year Book* 4 (New York: Herzl Press, 1961–1962), pp. 298–300; Pawel, *Labyrinth*, p. 453.

63. Weizmann to Vera Khatzman, August 23, 1902. Weizmann, *Letters*, vol. 1, p. 379.

64. Ahad Ha'am, "The Revival of the Spirit," in *Selected Essays*.

65. Ibid.

66. Ibid., pp. 254, 273, 286–287, 295–296, 300–301. My description relies on sections of the Hebrew original which do not appear in Simon's translation. See Ahad Ha'am, "The Spiritual Revival," in *Hashiloah*, December 1902, pp. 484, 489–491 [Hebrew]. In addition, Simon misleadingly translates the slogan *kavshu et beit hasefer!* as "Win over the educational organization!" In my version here I have replaced this with "Conquer the schools!" which may be more embarrassing, but is nevertheless correct. See the Hebrew original, p. 487.

67. Ahad Ha'am's interest in collaboration with "non-Zionists" stemmed from a common interest in encouraging Jewish national culture, which he shared with supporters of the Socialist Bund. The historian Simon Dubnow, who was known as an anti-Zionist but supported the dissemination of Jewish nationalist culture in the Diaspora, was one of

Ahad Ha'am's collaborators. Steven J. Zipperstein, *Elusive Prophet: Ahad Ha'am and the Origins of Zionism* (Berkeley: University of California Press, 1993), pp. 224–226.

68. However, Ahad Ha'am's proposal for the establishment of a new organization outside of the ZO to include non-Zionists was rejected by the conference. Ma'or, *The Zionist Movement in Russia*, p. 202.

69. See Luz, *Parallels Meet*, p. 190.

70. The *Juedischer Almanach*, which appeared in 1902, included a translation of Ahad Ha'am's "Priest and Prophet"; *Ost und West* published essays by Ahad Ha'am under the titles "Autonomous Realms" (May 1901), "Nietzscheanism and Judaism" (March–April 1902), "On Culture" (October–November 1902), and "Altneuland" (April 1903). After the Democrats' rupture with Herzl in 1903, *Ost und West* distanced itself from the Zionist Organization, eventually becoming a successful publication affiliated with the non-Zionist Alliance Israélite Universelle and catering to a principally non-Zionist audience. David A. Brenner, *Marketing Identities: The Invention of Jewish Ethnicity in Ost und West* (Detroit: Wayne State University Press, 1998), pp. 38, 45–47.

71. Buber's article, in particular, made sure to take direct aim at Herzl's Orthodox allies, demanding that "the rule of an old sick culture be broken and a young one be placed on the throne." See Martin Buber, "A Spiritual Center"; Ahad Ha'am, "On Culture"; Berthold Feiwel, "Currents in Zionism"; and Davis Trietsch, "A Russian-Jewish Congress," all in *Ost und West*, October 1902.

72. Theodor Herzl, *Altneuland* (Berlin: Benjamin Harz, 1902), p. 1 [German].

73. The plans for the coup d'état are mentioned explicitly in Herzl diary, February 14, March 22, and April 10, 1904. Herzl, *Diaries*, pp. 1614–1615, 1619. The assumption that the existence of a Jewish settlement and armed force in Sinai, whether under British rule or not, would bring about the eventual incorporation of Palestine into the Sinai Jewish state was politely but explicitly present in all of Herzl's discussions with Chamberlain about a "rallying point for the Jewish people in the vicinity of Palestine." Herzl diary October 23–24, 1902, and April 24, 1903. Herzl, *Diaries*, pp. 1362, 1368–1369, 1474. None of these conversations with the imperialist Chamberlain would have been possible if Herzl had accepted the premises of disarmament and powerlessness in *Altneuland*. In the area of social and economic innovation, however, the novel does contain ideas that Herzl actually toyed with, such as the establishment of newspapers on a cooperative basis, in which subscribers are the paper's shareholders. See Herzl diary, May 27, 1899, and January 25, 1902. Herzl, *Diaries*, pp. 838, 1203.

74. Undated draft charter reproduced in Adolf Bohm, *The Zionist Movement* (Berlin, 1935), vol. 1, pp. 705–709 [German].

75. Theodor Herzl, *The Palais Bourbon* (Leipzig: Dunker and Humblot, 1895), p. 28 [German].

76. Herzl diary, June 2, 1895. Herzl, *Diaries*, pp. 19, 21.

77. Herzl to the Grand Duke of Baden, October 5, 1902. Herzl, *Diaries*, pp. 1356–1357. Another important factor that led Herzl to write *Altneuland* as he did was his need to avoid any suggestions that he wished to establish an independent state of a kind that might be offensive to the sultan. In a letter from this time, he explains that his explicit plans in *The Jewish State* were written when he was "inexperienced and irresponsible"; in *Altneuland*, on the other hand, Herzl says, "I was forced to be discreet." Herzl to Ernst Mezei, March 10, 1903. *Briefe und Tagebuecher*, vol. 7, pp. 76–77 [German]. Most important is the fact that Herzl simply did not consider *Altneuland* to be very important when compared to his other works, writing: "Of my works, my book *The Palais Bourbon* is—apart from *The Jewish State*—my most important book from a political

point of view." Herzl to Highly Respected Doctor, October 23, 1903. Herzl, *Briefe und Tagebuecher*, vol. 7, pp. 428–429 [German].

78. Ahad Ha'am, review in *Hashiloah*, December 1902, pp. 567, 572–574.

79. The theory of Herzl's wounded vanity does not conform to the fact that Ahad Ha'am had been broadsiding Herzl in public over and over since the first Zionist Congress five years earlier, including criticizing him for the 1899 reissue of his play, *The New Ghetto*, without meriting so much as a rebuttal. Kornberg, *Theodor Herzl: From Assimilation to Zionism* (Bloomington: Indiana University Press, 1993), p. 158. Nor does it explain why Nordau, himself an art critic of international standing who certainly could not have thought *Altneuland* to be much of a masterpiece, would have bothered to brutalize a small-time literary reviewer in papers all over Europe for having attacked a mediocre fantasy.

80. For a description of the course of events, see Leo Winz to Adolf Friedemann, August 15, 1903. Michael Heymann, *The Uganda Controversy*, vol. 1, pp. 68–71 [German].

81. Emphasis added. Max Nordau, "Ahad Ha'am on Altneuland," *Die Welt*, March 13, 1903 [German].

82. *Hatzefira*, March 23–April 5, 1903. Not all the Democrats, however, were united in taking this step; Shemaryahu Levin, for one, wrote an open letter to Ahad Ha'am arguing that "Herzl builds and you destroy" and demanding that he "stop destroying and begin to build." Shmaryahu Levin, *In the Days of the Transition* (New York: Asaf, 1919), pp. 207–212 [Hebrew].

83. Herzl to Buber, May 23, 1903. Martin Buber, *The Letters of Martin Buber: A Life of Dialogue*, Nahum Glatzer and Paul Mendes-Flohr, eds., Richard Winston et al. trans. (New York: Syracuse University Press, 1996), pp. 94–95.

84. Buber to Herzl, May 26, 1903. Buber, *Letters*, pp. 96–97.

85. Herzl to Buber, May 28, 1903. Buber, *Letters*, p. 97.

86. Herzl to Weizmann, May 14, 1903. Weizmann, *Letters*, vol. 2, p. 339 n. 3.

87. Buber to Weizmann and Feiwel, June 12, 1903. Buber, *Letters*, p. 98.

88. The Plehwe letter published in *Die Welt*, August 25, 1903; *Minutes of the Sixth Zionist Congress* in Basel, August 23–28, 1903 (Vienna: Industrie, 1903), pp. 8–10, 120–124 [German].

89. *Minutes of the Sixth Zionist Congress*, pp. 4, 8.

90. Pawel, *Labyrinth*, p. 516; Luz, *Parallels Meet*, p. 259.

91. Minutes of the meeting of the Greater Actions Committee of the ZO, April 11–15, 1904. Bein, *Theodor Herzl*, p. 496. I have replaced the English translation's awkward term, "Jewish statist" with the term used in the German original, "Judenstaatler." Compare Herzl, *Zionist Writings*, vol. 2, pp. 248–249.

92. There were in fact, those few who were not prepared to forget Uganda. Israel Zangwill and a handful of others angrily rejected the Zionist insistence that a Jewish state be established only in Palestine, breaking from the movement after the Seventh Congress in 1905 and establishing the Jewish Territorial Organization (ITO), which continued the quest for a territory on which to found a Jewish state outside of Palestine.

93. The design of the flag chosen by Herzl for the First Congress combined elements proposed by Wolfssohn (the prayer shawl) and Bodenheimer (the lion) and was a departure from the colorless flag of seven gold stars (representing his proposed seven-hour workday) on a white field proposed in Herzl, *The Jewish State*, p. 101. But the claim that Herzl did not propose the Star of David on the flag himself is incorrect. He decided that his seven stars should themselves be formed into a Star of David at least as early as June 1896, more than a year before the congress. See Herzl to Jacob de Haas on July 20 and 27, 1896. Herzl, *Briefe und Tagebuecher*, vol. 4, pp. 121, 127. Also Amos Elon, *Herzl* (New York: Holt, Rinehart, and Winston, 1975), p. 213. See also Herzl, "The

Menorah," pp. 203–206; Herzl, *The Jewish State*, p. 52; Herzl, "Dr. Guedemann," p. 69.

94. *Minutes of the Sixth Zionist Congress in Basel*, p. 4.

95. Leonard Stein, *The Balfour Declaration* (London: Valentine, Mitchell, and Co., 1961), pp. 64–65.

96. Stein, *The Balfour Declaration*, pp. 103–104, 114; Rabinowicz, "Herzl," pp. 100–101. For the influence of Lord Montagu on Herbert Samuel, see Bernard Wasserstein, *Herbert Samuel: A Political Life* (Oxford: Clarendon Press, 1992), pp. 201–202.

97. For an analysis of Lord Milner's contacts with the Zionist Organization in South Africa, see Rabinowicz, "Herzl," pp. 80–89. In their pro-Zionist policy, the government had the important support of the London *Times*, whose editor, Wickham Steed, had also been drawn to Zionism after meeting Herzl in 1896 and 1902. Rabinowicz, "Herzl," pp. 103–104.

Chapter Six

1. Theodor Herzl, *Der Judenstaat* (Vienna: M. Breitenstein, 1896), p. 84 [German]. "Desperados" appears in the original German. Compare Theodor Herzl, *The Jewish State*, Harry Zohn, trans. (New York: Herzl Press, 1970), p. 109.

2. Herzl, *The Jewish State*, p. 85.

3. Theodor Herzl, *The Complete Diaries of Theodor Herzl*, Raphael Patai, ed., Harry Zohn, trans. (New York: Herzl Press, 1960), July 24, 1895, and February 23, 1896, pp. 213, 306. See also Jacques Kornberg, *Theodor Herzl: From Assimilation to Zionism* (Bloomington: Indiana University Press, 1993), pp. 164–169.

4. Herzl, *Der Judenstaat*, p. 24. Compare Herzl, *The Jewish State*, pp. 46, 85.

5. In this they had been greatly assisted the following year by the resolution of the Bund to seek Jewish national autonomy within the boundaries of Russia—a decision that drove from their ranks anyone who sympathized with Lovers of Zion. Ehud Luz, *Parallels Meet: Religion and Nationalism in the Early Zionist Movement (1882–1904)*, Lenn J. Schramm, trans. (Philadelphia: Jewish Publication Society, 1988), p. 190.

6. Michael Bar-Zohar, *Ben-Gurion: A Biography* (Jerusalem: Keter, 1980), p. 18 [Hebrew].

7. See Borochov's "Our Platform," published in 1906, in Arthur Hertzberg, ed., *The Zionist Idea: A Historical Analysis and Reader* (New York: Atheneum, 1984), pp. 360–366.

8. Shabtai Teveth, *Ben-Gurion: The Burning Ground, 1886–1948* (Boston: Houghton Mifflin, 1987), pp. 30–34.

9. David Ben-Gurion, *Memoirs* (Ramat Gan: Am Oved, 1971), vol. 1, pp. 26–30 [Hebrew].

10. Yosef Haim Brenner, *Writings, Stories, Novels, Plays* (Jerusalem: Hakibbutz Hameuhad, 1978), vol. 2, pp. 1293–1294 [Hebrew].

11. Quoted in Gideon Shimoni, *The Zionist Ideology* (Hanover: Brandeis University Press, 1995), p. 351.

12. Gershom Scholem, *From Berlin to Jerusalem: Memories of My Youth*, Harry Zohn, trans. (New York: Schocken, 1980), p. 166.

13. See Yehuda Slutsky, ed., *Poalei Zion in the Land of Israel, 1905–1919: Documents, Ideas and Programs* (Tel-Aviv University, 1978), pp. 19–20 [Hebrew]; Teveth, *Burning Ground*, pp. 54, 56–57.

14. Teveth, *Burning Ground*, pp. 40–41, 50.

15. Ben-Gurion to Isaac Nahman Steinberg, September 7, 1928. Ben-Gurion diary manuscript, p. 326. Ben-Gurion Archives.

16. Teveth, *Burning Ground*, pp. 183, 242–248, 329.

17. Ben-Gurion to his father, June 30, 1909. David Ben-Gurion, *The Letters of David Ben-Gurion*, Yehuda Erez, ed. (Tel Aviv: Am Oved, 1971), vol. 1, p. 136 [Hebrew].

18. I have reconstructed Samuel's response from Weizmann's report of it, which reads: "Mr. Samuel preferred not to enter into a discussion of his plans, as he would like to keep them *'liquid,'* but he suggested that the Jews would have to build railways, harbors, a university, a network of schools, etc. The university seems to make a special appeal to him. He hopes great things may be forthcoming from a seat of learning, where the Jews can work freely on a free soil of their own. He also thinks that perhaps the Temple may be rebuilt, as a symbol of Jewish unity, of course, in a modernized form. . . . He added that these ideas are in the mind of his colleagues in the Cabinet. He advised me to work quietly, continue the investigation step by step and prepare for the hour to come." Report to the Zionist Executive, January 7, 1915. Meyer Weisgal and Barnet Litvinoff, eds., *The Letters and Papers of Chaim Weizmann* (London: Oxford University Press, 1968–1972; and Jerusalem: Israel Universities Press, 1973–1980), ser. B, vol. 1, pp. 123–124.

19. Norman Rose, *Chaim Weizmann: A Biography* (New York: Viking, 1986), p. 19.

20. Weizmann to Leo Motzkin, June 20, 1895. Weizmann, *Letters*, vol. 1, p. 48.

21. Rose, *Chaim Weizmann*, pp. 153–154.

22. Ibid., p. 265.

23. Weizmann to Israel Zangwill (?), November 20, 1914. Weizmann, *Letters*, vol. 7, p. 48; Rose, *Chaim Weizmann*, p. 265.

24. Address before the Seventeenth Zionist Congress, July 1, 1931. Weizmann, *Papers*, vol. 1, p. 634. Even "spiritual" and "cultural" growth was, for Weizmann, the result of "the intimate contact between man and soil" in agricultural communities, whereas "the towns do no more than 'process' the fruits of the villages." Chaim Weizmann, *Trial and Error: The Autobiography of Chaim Weizmann* (New York: Harper and Brothers, 1949), p. 278.

25. Blanche Dugdale, *Baffy: The Diaries of Blanche Dugdale, 1936–1947*, N. A. Rose, ed. (London: Valentine, Mitchell, 1973), p. 216.

26. Bernard Wasserstein, *Herbert Samuel: A Political Life* (Oxford: Clarendon Press, 1992), p. 206.

27. "He [i.e., Rothschild] . . . thought that the demands, which only amount to asking for an encouragement of colonization of Jews in Palestine, are too modest and would not appeal sufficiently to statesmen. One should ask for something which is more than that and which tends towards the formation of a Jewish state." Note of the conversation with Baron James de Rothschild of November 25, 1914. Weizmann, *Letters*, vol. 7, p. 56.

28. Minutes of the Eighth Assembly of the Temporary Committee of Palestine Jewry, Jaffa, October 22, 1919, pp. 15, 24. Central Zionist Archives, J1/8783.

29. Wasserstein, *Herbert Samuel*, p. 207. These included Nahum Sokolow, one of the greatest partisans of the line denying the ZO had ever had any interest in a state. See Leonard Stein, *The Balfour Declaration* (London: Valentine, Mitchell, and Co., 1961), pp. 407, 466.

30. Samuel by then believed that the cultural plan "would suffice" in allowing the Jews to demonstrate to the world that they were not "insensible to their great traditions." Moreover, such a plan "would be safe from the political point of view, and as an effort to create a great spiritual center for Judaism in the Holy Land would probably satisfy the imagination even of Christian well-wishers." Lucien Wolf's record of a conversation with Samuel on February 28, 1915. Stein, *The Balfour Declaration*, pp. 107–108. Samuel's in-

voking the "spiritual center" suggests the possibility that it was Ahad Ha'am himself who was guiding the negotiations with Britain from behind the scenes. "Practically nothing," claimed Weizmann "was undertaken without his [i.e., Ahad Ha'am's] knowledge and consent." Report to the Zionist Executive, January 7, 1915. Weizmann, *Letters*, vol. 7, p. 119.

31. David Lloyd George, *War Memoirs* (London: Ivor Nicholson and Watson, 1934), p. 1536.

32. See David Fromkin, *A Peace to End All Peace: The Fall of the Ottoman Empire and the Creation of the Modern Middle East* (New York: Avon, 1989), p. 403f.

33. The League of Nations Mandate, Article 4.

34. Churchill, February 8, 1920. *Illustrated Sunday Herald*, February 8, 1920, quoted in Stein, *The Balfour Declaration*, p. 662.

35. See, for example, Herzl's draft charter, submitted to the British government, July 13, 1903. Reprinted in Oskar Rabinowicz, "New Light on the East Africa Scheme." Israel Cohen, ed., *The Rebirth of Israel: A Memorial Tribute to Paul Goodman* (London: Goldstein and Sons, 1952), pp. 81–91.

36. Weizmann, *Papers*, vol. 1, p. 231.

37. Herzl, *The Jewish State*, p. 51. When the Zionist Organization was finally revived in the spring of 1920, Herzl's trusted partner, Max Nordau, now in his seventies, vehemently attacked Weizmann's capitulation on Jewish participation in the government of Palestine. But his arguments were ignored because of the expectation that the mandate would be "favorably interpreted" by Britain. "This was an error," Bodenheimer later conceded. Max Bodenheimer, *Prelude to Israel: The Memoirs of M. I. Bodenheimer*, Israel Cohen, trans. (New York: Thomas Yoseloff, 1963), pp. 280–281; Nordau's speech before the Actions Committee, February 24, 1920, in *Minutes of the Zionist Action Committee, 1919–1929* (Jerusalem: Hasifria Hatziyonit, 1985), pp. 164–165 [Hebrew].

38. From conversations with Samuel only a few weeks after the massacres, it was clear to Arthur Ruppin that the High Commissioner had "lost his confidence and, I fear, his belief in [the possibility of] realizing the Zionist idea." Ruppin noted that Samuel believed only concessions would bring calm, a policy that even Ruppin suspected might be misguided. Ruppin diary, June 4, 1921. Arthur Ruppin, *Arthur Ruppin: Memoirs, Diaries, Letters*, Alex Bein, ed., Karen Gershon, trans. (New York: Herzl Press, 1971), p. 191.

39. *Palestine Weekly*, June 3, 1921.

40. J. E. Shuckburgh to the Zionist Organization, June 3, 1922; Weizmann to the Colonial Office, June 18, 1922. Reprinted in *Palestine: Correspondence with the Palestine Arab Delegation and the Zionist Organization* (London: His Majesty's Stationery Office, 1922), pp. 18, 20, 31.

41. See Hagit Lavsky, *The Financial Bases of the Zionist Enterprise* (Jerusalem: Yad Yitzhak Ben-Tzvi, 1981), pp. 149–202. See also Scholem, *From Berlin to Jerusalem*, pp. 162–163; Teveth, *Burning Ground*, pp. 308–309.

42. Weizmann to Robert Weltsch, January 15, 1924. Weizmann, *Letters*, vol. 12, p. 94.

43. See Ruppin diary, January 3, 1922. Ruppin, *Memoirs, Diaries, Letters*, p. 195.

44. Weizmann had personal experience to suggest that this was true. On January 3, 1914, he had succeeded in persuading Edmond de Rothschild—who in 1896 had rejected Herzl's idea of a Jewish state as "harmful to the welfare of the Jews all over the world"— to promise 650,000 francs for a bacteriology laboratory that was to be the beginning of a university-level research institute in Jerusalem.

45. This quote is from Lucien Wolf's notes on his discussion with Samuel, February 15, 1915. See Stein, *The Balfour Declaration*, pp. 177–179.

46. Stein, *The Balfour Declaration*, pp. 180, 443. The "special rights" in question were not specified.

47. London *Times,* May 24, 1917.

48. See Stein, *The Balfour Declaration,* p. 664, for the various drafts of the declaration. The possibility of "special rights" for the Jewish people, however, was not ruled out and was, in theory, the most important achievement of the declaration.

49. Thomas A. Kolsky, *Jews Against Zionism: The American Council for Judaism, 1942–1948* (Philadelphia: Temple University, 1990), pp. 30–32.

50. Ruppin diary, November 14, 1922. Ruppin, *Memoirs, Diaries, Letters,* p. 201. Under Ochs, the *New York Times* had itself backed this anti-Zionist line, objecting to the Jewish state on the grounds that Judaism was a religion. See Monty Noam Penkower, "The Genesis of the American Council for Judaism: A Quest for Identity in World War II," *American Jewish History,* June 1998, p. 170; Adolph Ochs, "The Truth About Palestine," *American Israelite,* April 27, 1922.

51. Ruppin diary, February 20, 1923. Ruppin, *Memoirs, Diaries, Letters,* p. 203.

52. Magnes, who was a member of the JDC, was ideologically committed to the project, which he saw as a way of exposing a large community of Jews to the "special experiment" of the Soviet Union. Magnes to Weizmann, October 5, 1926, in Arthur A. Goren, *Dissenter in Zion: From the Writings of Judah L. Magnes* (Cambridge: Harvard University Press, 1982), p. 259; Ron Chernow, *The Warburgs: The Twentieth-Century Odyssey of a Remarkable Jewish Family* (New York: Vintage Books, 1994), pp. 292–296; Ben Halpern, *The Idea of the Jewish State* (Cambridge: Harvard University Press, 1961), p. 181.

53. The American Jewish Committee had been anti-Zionist until April 1918, when it accepted the goal of creating a cultural center in Palestine—without giving up its opposition to Jewish nationalism and the idea of a Jewish state. Kolsky, *Jews Against Zionism,* p. 31. But the term "non-Zionists" to describe such an outlook was misleading, since none of the anti-Zionist groups had ever opposed the cultural center concept. Moreover, even groups that called themselves anti-Zionist referred to themselves as "non-Zionist," and there was no clear boundary between the two groups. See Kolsky, *Jews Against Zionism,* pp. 51, 54.

54. Marshall had long been concerned that Britain and America would close their borders to Jewish immigration from the East, and by 1924, these fears had become a fact. The upshot was that anti-Zionists concerned for an alternate target for Eastern Jewish immigration had to look to Palestine. Halpern, *The Idea of the Jewish State,* pp. 199–200.

55. Ruppin diary, December 31, 1924. Ruppin, *Memoirs, Diaries, Letters,* p. 215.

56. Rose, *Chaim Weizmann,* p. 243. Even a skeptic such as Ben-Gurion found the scene at Zurich breathtaking: "I myself was moved down to the core by this profound and shocking experience. The exalted and the sublime in the Jewish people was gathered together in this scene, expressing the elevated and the profound in the thoughts of the Jewish people and its feelings." Anita Shapira, *Berl Katznelson: A Biography* (Tel Aviv: Am Oved, 1980), p. 302 [Hebrew].

57. Teveth, *Burning Ground,* p. 388.

58. Ibid., pp. 274, 345.

59. Ibid., pp. 219, 363.

60. Ibid., pp. 309–311, 347.

Chapter Seven

1. Herzl to Maurice de Hirsch, June 3, 1895. Theodor Herzl, *The Complete Diaries of Theodor Herzl,* Raphael Patai, ed., Harry Zohn, trans. (New York: Herzl Press, 1960), p. 28.

2. See Jehuda Reinharz, "Three Generations of German Zionism," *Jerusalem Quarterly* 9 (Fall 1978), pp. 98–99.

3. Max Bodenheimer, *Prelude to Israel: The Memoirs of M. I. Bodenheimer*, Israel Cohen, trans. (New York: Thomas Yoseloff, 1963), p. 334.

4. See, for example, Buber's rejection of German Zionism as "vulgar and just as self-satisfied as the usual philanthropy." Jehuda Reinharz, "Ahad Ha'am, Martin Buber and German Zionism," in Jacques Kornberg, ed., *At the Crossroads* (Albany: State University of New York Press, 1983), p. 150. The failure of Zionist ideas among the German students was evident, among other places, in the bottom-line immigration figures to Palestine: Despite the fact that the East produced thousands of youthful immigrants, by World War I, the number of German Jews who had come to Palestine was no more than thirty. Jehuda Reinharz, "Ideology and Structure in German Zionism, 1882–1933," *Jewish Social Studies,* Spring 1980, p. 137.

5. For example, of the Western leaders of the ZO, only Herzl supported the effort to establish a university. Chaim Weizmann, *Trial and Error: The Autobiography of Chaim Weizmann* (New York: Harper and Brothers, 1949), p. 68.

6. Minutes of the Third Zionist Congress in Basel, August 15–18, 1899 (Vienna: Industrie, 1899), p. 193 [German]. Compare Gilya Gerda Schmidt, *Martin Buber's Formative Years: From German Culture to Jewish Renewal, 1897–1909* (Tuscaloosa: University of Alabama Press, 1995), pp. 55–56.

7. Michael Berkowitz, *Zionist Culture and West European Jewry Before the First World War* (Chapel Hill: University of North Carolina Press, 1996), p. 127. Also Herzl to Buber, August 7, 1901; Buber to Herzl, August 11, 1901; Herzl to Buber, September 28, 1901. All in Martin Buber, *The Letters of Martin Buber: A Life of Dialogue*, Nahum Glatzer and Paul Mendes-Flohr, eds., Richard Winston et al., trans. (New York: Syracuse University Press, 1996), pp. 73–74, 77.

8. Although Herzl opposed official ZO funding for the publishing venture, the Juedische Verlag, he encouraged private donations from members of the Congress; the most important source of funding was David Wolffsohn, a Cologne businessman who was one of Herzl's closest associates and his successor as head of the ZO. Berkowitz, *Zionist Culture*, p. 66.

9. Ibid., pp. 91, 127–130.

10. Stefan Zweig, "Koenig der Juden," in Meyer W. Weisgal, ed., *Theodor Herzl: A Memorial* (New York, 1929), pp. 56–57.

11. Herzl to Weizmann, May 14, 1903. Chaim Weizmann, *The Letters and Papers of Chaim Weizmann*, Meyer Weisgal and Barnet Litvinoff, eds. (London: Oxford University Press, 1968–1972, and Jerusalem: Israel Universities Press, 1973–1980), ser. A, vol. 2, p. 339 n. 3.

12. Feiwel to Buber, July 28, 1902. Buber, *Letters*, p. 84.

13. See Magnes's description of Buber's youthful magnetism in Magnes to Buber, February 1948, n.d. Buber, *Letters*, pp. 529–530.

14. Buber to Herzl, August 11, 1901. Buber, *Letters*, pp. 74–75; Jehuda Reinharz, "Martin Buber's Impact on German Zionism Before World War I," *Studies in Zionism* 6 (Autumn 1982), p. 173.

15. Martin Buber, "On Jakob Boehme," *Wiener Rundschau*, June 15, 1901 [German]. Compare Buber's speech on the "New Society," in which he in his own name advocates a "life that is liberated from all boundaries and concepts," attaining "a feeling of co-essentiality, of blissful, blessed fusion with all things in time and space." Buber, "Old and New Society," quoted in Paul R. Flohr and Bernard Susser, "*Alte unde neue*

Gemeinschaft: An Unpublished Buber Manuscript," *Association of Jewish Studies Review,* 1976, p. 47.

16. Martin Buber, "The Zion of the Jewish Woman: From a Speech," *Die Welt,* April 26, 1901 [German]. Reprinted in Martin Buber, *The Jewish Movement: Collected Essays and Speeches, 1900–1914* (Berlin: Juedischer Verlag, 1920), pp. 28–29 [German].

17. Maurice Friedman, *Martin Buber's Life and Work* (Detroit: Wayne State University Press, 1988), vol. 1, p. 60; Berkowitz, *Zionist Culture,* p. 134. Also Buber to the Zionist Actions Committee, March 21, 1903, and Herzl to Buber, April 14, 1903. Buber, *Letters,* pp. 90–91.

18. Buber to Paula Winkler Buber, July 6, 1904. Buber, *Letters,* p. 106; Martin Buber, "Herzl and History," *Ost und West,* August 1904, reprinted in Buber, *The Jewish Movement,* pp. 152–173. According to Buber's close friend and disciple, Ernst Simon, these feelings against Herzl were to continue to affect Buber's behavior for years to come. Friedman, *Martin Buber's Life and Work,* vol. 1, p. 65.

19. Buber to Ehrenpreis, September 13, 1904, in Reinharz, "Martin Buber's Impact," p. 175.

20. Buber to Weizmann, August 18, 1906. Buber, *Letters,* p. 113.

21. Friedman, *Martin Buber's Life and Work,* vol. 1, pp. 11–12, 29, 96.

22. Emphasis in the original. Buber to Hans Kohn, December 1906. Hans Kohn, *Martin Buber: His Work and His Times* (Koeln: Joseph Melzer Verlag, 1961), pp. 309–310 [German].

23. *Tales of Rabbi Nahman* was published in 1906, *The Legend of the Ba'al Shem* in 1907. In 1909, Buber followed these with a book entitled *Ecstatic Confessions,* containing first-person accounts of mystic ecstasy from various cultures. Kafka's response to them may be found in Kafka to Felice Bauer, January 20–21, 1913. Franz Kafka, *Letters to Felice,* Erich Heller and Juergen Born, eds. (New York: Schocken, 1967), p. 260 [German]. Compare Kafka to Max Brod, January 1918, referring to a different round of Buber books: "Buber's last books are terrible, loathsome books, all three of them together.... They make you despair ... If these books were the only ones in the world, even the healthiest lung would almost run out of breath ... Their loathsomeness is growing beneath my hands." Franz Kafka, *Letters 1902–1924,* Max Brod, ed. (New York: Schocken, 1958), pp. 224–225 [German].

24. Martin Buber's *Drei Reden ueber das Judentum* (Frankfurt: Ruetten and Loening, 1911) [German] was the published version of his three Bar-Kochba speeches. They have been reprinted in English as "Judaism and the Jews," "Judaism and Mankind," and "Renewal of Judaism," in Martin Buber, *On Judaism,* Nahum N. Glatzer, ed. (New York: Schocken, 1967).

25. For Zweig, see Friedman, *Martin Buber's Life and Work,* vol. 1, p. 140. For Werfel, see ibid., p. 212. For Bergmann, see Aharon Kedar, "Brit Shalom," *Jerusalem Quarterly* 18 (Winter 1987), p. 58; compare Bergmann to Buber, January 31, 1928, in Buber, *Letters,* p. 357. For Hans Kohn, see Kohn to Buber, September 22, 1911, in Buber, *Letters,* p. 130; compare Kohn to Buber, October 20, 1912, in Buber, *Letters,* p. 138. For Scholem and Rosenzweig, see Friedman, *Martin Buber's Life and Work,* vol. 1, p. 145; compare Rosenzweig, writing later: "I would be unable to mention any other book about Judaism of those years, which even came close to having such an effect." Quoted in Roger Kamenetz, Foreword to Martin Buber, *On Judaism,* Nahum Glatzer, ed. (New York: Schocken, 1995), p. ix. Additional similar reactions include: Ludwig Strauss to Buber, August 6, 1913, in Buber, *Letters,* p. 149; Salman Schocken to Buber, February 4, 1914, in Buber, *Letters,* p. 153; Ernst Rappeport to Buber, October 22, 1915, in

Buber, *Letters*, p. 180; Hermann Gerson to Buber, November 25, 1926, in Buber, *Letters*, p. 346.

26. See Walter Z. Lacqueur, *The German Youth Movement: A Historical Study* (Koeln: Verlag Wissenschaft und Politik, 1962), pp. 7, 13 [German]; Michael Brenner, *The Renaissance of Jewish Culture in Weimar Germany* (New Haven: Yale University Press, 1996), p. 47.

27. Review of "The Jewish Movement" in the Kameraden newsletter, April 1921; VJJD newsletter, June 1922. Both quoted in Chaim Schatzker, "Martin Buber's Influence on the Jewish Youth Movement in Germany," *Leo Baeck Institute Yearbook*, 1978, pp. 164, 170.

28. Martin Buber, "Judaism and the Jews," in Buber, *On Judaism* (1995), p. 19.

29. Franz Kafka, *Letter to His Father*, Ernst Kaiser and Eithne Wilkins, trans. (New York: Schocken, 1966), p. 77.

30. Buber, "Judaism and the Jews," pp. 16–17.

31. Buber's refusal to be pulled into any of these concrete expressions of Jewishness is notorious: Over twenty years, he steadfastly evaded the calls of his disciples in Palestine to make a break with Germany and rebuild his life on Jewish land. See, for example, his correspondence in Buber, *Letters:* Bergmann to Buber, December 30, 1918, p. 237; Scholem to Buber, November 15, 1928, p. 362; Scholem to Buber, February 2, 1934, p. 414; Buber to Hirsch, March 1, 1934, p. 416; Buber to Gerson, August 14, 1934, p. 423; Buber to Gerson, September 7, 1934, p. 424; Buber to Bergmann, April 16, 1936, p. 441. Buber's approach to Hebrew was similar, and he continued throughout most of his adult life to insist that "I am and shall remain a German-Jewish author," unable to write in Hebrew, and "content . . . with living and dying as a border guard." See Bergmann to Buber, September 19, 1919, p. 249; Buber to Bergmann, October 21, 1919, p. 251; Buber to Kohn, January 31, 1926, p. 336; Buber to Salman Schocken, May 19, 1934, p. 419; Buber to Gerson, September 7, 1934, p. 424. With regard to a Jewish way of life, Buber was famously a "religious anarchist" without recognizing any given Jewish tradition as being applicable to him except at times when he personally felt he was being "addressed" by God. See, for example, Buber to Maurice Friedman, March 27, 1954. Buber, *Letters*, p. 576.

32. Buber, "Judaism and the Jews," pp. 18–20.

33. Buber, "Judaism and Mankind," p. 32.

34. From his August 1925 lecture to the conference of the International Work Circle for the Renewal of Education, Heidelberg. Friedman, *Martin Buber's Life and Work*, vol. 2, p. 27. It was this same argument that Buber applied with such conviction to the relationship that the Jews must have to the Arab population in Palestine. See Friedman, *Martin Buber's Life and Work*, vol. 2, p. 18. One should note here the influence of Hermann Cohen's view that morality is in its essence the identification with suffering. See, for example, Buber's claim that true spiritual leaders "recognize in their own pain the formation of a new way of life for humanity"; "They suffer as the prophets once did . . . We have to trust their prophesy which is born from suffering." From "Die Juedische Renaissance," quoted in Schmidt, *Martin Buber*, p. 56.

35. See Bergmann to Buber, December 1, 1947, and Buber to Bergmann, December 14, 1947. Both in Buber, *Letters*, p. 525.

36. Friedman, *Martin Buber's Life and Work*, vol. 1, p. 140.

37. Buber, "Judaism and Mankind," p. 31.

38. Weizmann to Buber, May 16, 1913. Buber, *Letters*, p. 147. Buber's response to Weizmann's invitation to attend the Eleventh Zionist Congress in Vienna, where the issue was to be debated, was to ignore it.

39. Buber did mention creating "an organic center" in Palestine, but this concern appears only as an appendage to his demand for a strengthening of the Diaspora. Martin Buber, "The Watchword," *Der Jude* 1 (April 1916), p. 3 [German].

40. London *Times*, November 10, 1914, cited in Leonard Stein, *The Balfour Declaration* (London: Valentine, Mitchell, and Co., 1961), p. 103.

41. Already in July 1915, for example, the *Jewish Chronicle* referred to a "gathering of favorable omens," declaring that the war "has brought the fate of Palestine and of Jewish hopes into the region of practical politics." *Jewish Chronicle*, July 2, 1915. Compare Magnes to Weizmann, January 28, 1916, which speaks of the newspapers being "full of reports" on the developing British-Jewish alliance. Arthur A. Goren, *Dissenter in Zion: From the Writings of Judah L. Magnes* (Cambridge: Harvard University Press, 1982), p. 154.

42. *Spectator*, August 12, 1916. Stein, *The Balfour Declaration*, p. 301.

43. Stein, *The Balfour Declaration*, p. 301.

44. The resolution also referred to emigration to Palestine "as a means to achieve our final goal" as an almost contentless allusion to the former ideal of a Jewish state that had animated Max Bodenheimer and his colleagues. Quoted in Jehuda Reinharz, *Fatherland or Promised Land: The Dilemma of the German Jew, 1893–1914* (Ann Arbor: University of Michigan Press, 1975), p. 161. See also Reinharz, "Ahad Ha'am, Martin Buber and German Zionism," pp. 152–153; Hagit Lavsky, *Before Catastrophe: The Distinctive Path of German Zionism* (Detroit: Wayne State University Press, 1996), pp. 29–30.

45. Martin Buber, "The Watchword," *Der Jude* 1 (April 1916) [German]; Buber to Gustav Landauer, December 24, 1915, in Buber, *Letters*, p. 182; Buber to Stefan Zweig, February 4, 1918, in Buber, *Letters*, p. 229; Buber to Julius Bab, August 7, 1916, in Martin Buber, *Correspondence from Seven Decades* (Heidelberg, Lambert Schneider, 1972), vol. 1, p. 451 [German]. Emphasis added.

46. Scholem, *From Berlin to Jerusalem: Memories of My Youth*, Harry Zohn, trans. (New York: Schocken, 1980), p. 68; David N. Myers, *Re-Inventing the Jewish Past: European Jewish Intellectuals and the Zionist Return to History* (New York: Oxford University Press, 1995), pp. 24, 69–70.

47. Hermann Cohen, "Zionism and Religion," *K.C.-Blaetter* 11 (May–June 1916) [German]. A second article, which responded directly to Buber, was Hermann Cohen, "Response to the Open Letter of Dr. Martin Buber," *K.C.-Blaetter* 12 (July–August 1916) [German]. The second article was translated in part in "A Debate on Zionism and Messianism," in Paul Mendes-Flohr and Jehuda Reinharz, eds., *The Jew in the Modern World: A Documentary History* (New York: Oxford University Press, 1980), pp. 449–451. See also David Engel, "Relations Between Liberals and Zionists in Germany During World War I," *Zion*, November 1982, p. 447f. [Hebrew].

48. "A true Zionist is not interested in 'nationalism,' but in building up Jewish energy for a super-national task." Buber to Julius Bab, August 7, 1916. Martin Buber, *Correspondence*, vol. 1, pp. 450–451. Compare Buber's speech in *Minutes of the Sixteenth Zionist Congress in 1929*, p. 205. For the "true nationalism," see Martin Buber, "Nationalism," in Martin Buber, *Israel and the World: Essays in a Time of Crisis* (New York: Schocken, 1963), p. 221.

49. See Martin Buber, "Concepts and Reality," in *Der Jude* 5 (August 1916); Martin Buber, "Zion, State and Humanity," *Der Jude* 7 (October 1916) [German]. Translated in part in Mendes-Flohr and Reinharz, "A Debate on Zionism and Messianism," pp. 449, 451–452.

50. Buber, "The Holy Way: A Word to the Jews and to the Nations" in Buber, *On Judaism* (1995), p. 135; Buber to Hugo Bergmann, February 3–4, 1918, in Buber, *Letters*, p.

229; Friedman, *Martin Buber's Life and Work*, vol. 1, pp. 226, 230, 259–260. Friedman's paraphrases.

51. Buber called for "the removal of external obstacles that do not lie in people and land, but in things that are independent of people and land. That is politics in the narrow sense or, let us be more accurate, diplomacy." Speech at the Twelfth Congress on September 2, 1921. *Minutes of the Twelfth Zionist Congress in Karlsbad, September 1–14, 1921* (Berlin: Juedischer Verlag, 1922), pp. 124, 129 [German].

52. Buber, "Nationalism," pp. 216, 219, 220–221.

Chapter Eight

1. David N. Myers, *Re-Inventing the Jewish Past: European Jewish Intellectuals and the Zionist Return to History* (New York: Oxford University Press, 1995), p. 158.

2. Many writers have translated Brit Shalom as "Covenant of Peace," after the traditional English translation of the term in Numbers 25:12. But the actual English-language name chosen by the organization itself was as I have rendered it.

3. Ruppin diary, March 11, 1920, in Arthur Ruppin, *Arthur Ruppin: Memoirs, Diaries, Letters*, Alex Bein, ed., Karen Gershon, trans. (New York: Herzl Press, 1971), pp. 185–186. Like Buber, Ruppin came to believe that it was nationalism and the idea of the national state that had brought about the conflagration in which millions had perished. "We want to extricate ourselves," he wrote later, "from the error which was prevalent in Europe for one hundred years, and which caused the catastrophe of the World War—namely that only one nation can rule in the state." Speech before the Sixteenth Zionist Congress, July 29, 1929. Minutes of the Sixteenth Zionist Congress in Zurich, July 28–August 14, 1929 (London: Central Bureau of the Zionist Organization, 1929), p. 46 [German].

4. Ruppin diary, March 29, 1922, April 13 and 29, 1923, October 30, 1923. Ruppin, *Memoirs, Diaries, Letters*, pp. 197, 205–206, 208, 211.

5. Ruppin diary, April 29, 1923. Ruppin, *Memoirs, Diaries, Letters*, p. 207.

6. Aharon Kedar, "On the History of the Peace Association, 1925–1928," in Yehuda Bauer et al., eds., *Research Chapters in Zionist History* (Jerusalem: Hasifriya Hatziyonit, 1976), p. 230 [Hebrew].

7. See Buber's 1912 essay, "The Spirit of the Orient and Judaism." Martin Buber, *On Judaism*, Nahum Glatzer, ed. (New York: Schocken, 1995), pp. 56–78.

8. Various writers have claimed that Magnes was not a member of the Peace Association, in part due to a diary entry in which he wrote that he could not join the Peace Association because it was not sufficiently universalistic. Magnes diary, September 14, 1928. Arthur A. Goren, *Dissenter in Zion: From the Writings of Judah L. Magnes* (Cambridge: Harvard University Press, 1982), pp. 272–273. But Magnes was in fact closely involved with the Peace Association and its activities, appearing in both its public and its internal lists of supporters and providing it with advice and assistance. See Aharon Kedar, "Brit Shalom," in *Jerusalem Quarterly* 18 (Winter 1987), p. 67; membership list from Magnes Papers, file P3/2662. When the group was revived in 1942 under the name Ihud, Magnes formally served on its directorate.

9. Kedar, "Peace Association," pp. 281–285. Weltsch was the major conduit for Peace Association materials and influence reaching Germany. See Hagit Lavsky, "German Zionists and the Founding of the Peace Association," *Contemporary Judaism*, 1988, p. 99 [Hebrew]. For Buber's argument supporting the Peace Association, see Martin Buber, "Soul-Searching," *Juedische Rundschau*, April 16, 1926 [German]. Part of this

article is translated in Martin Buber, *A Land of Two Peoples: Martin Buber on Jews and Arabs*, Paul R. Mendes-Flohr, ed. (Oxford: Oxford University Press, 1983), p. 77.

10. Hugo Bergmann, "On the Majority Problem," *Sheifoteinu* 3 (1929), pp. 24–29 [Hebrew].

11. Yitzhak Ben-Aharon, one of the leading figures of Hashomer Hatzair in Palestine, reports that in the movement in Austria in the 1920s: "I came in contact with the [Hasidic] stories of the Ba'al Shem Tov and with Buber—this was the basic material that the youth leaders in Hashomer Hatzair carried around with them. . . . We read Hasidic stories and we studied Buber." Yitzhak Ben-Aharon, interviewed by Dan Shavit in *Conversations with Ben-Aharon* (Tel Aviv: Hakibbutz Hameuhad, 1974), p. 24 [Hebrew]. Similarly, see Meir Ya'ari, interviewed by Avraham Yisor in "Interview with Meir Ya'ari on Anarchism, Socialism, and the Kibbutz," *Sources for Research into the History of Hashomer Hatzair* (Givat Haviva: Hashomer Hatzair, 1986), vol. 4, p. 29 [Hebrew].

12. Gidon Shachtel, "The German Immigration from Germany to Palestine During the Years 1933–1939," Ph.D diss., Hebrew University, 1995, p. 157 [Hebrew].

13. Rafael Medoff, *Zionism and the Arabs: An American Jewish Dilemma* (Westport: Praeger, 1997), pp. 36–37, 56–57.

14. Herzl to Sultan, May 3, 1902; Herzl to Izzet Bey, May 3 and June 20, 1902. In Theodor Herzl, *Briefe und Tagebuecher* (Vienna: Propylaeen, 1983–1996), vol. 3, pp. 392–394, 403–404 [German].

15. Speech delivered on Mt. Scopus, July 24, 1918. Chaim Weizmann, *The Letters and Papers of Chaim Weizmann*, Meyer Weisgal and Barnet Litvinoff, eds. (London: Oxford University Press, 1968–1972, and Jerusalem: Israel Universities Press, 1973–1980), ser. B, vol. 1, pp. 191–195.

16. Arthur A. Goren, "The View from Scopus: Judah L. Magnes and the Early Years of the Hebrew University," *Judaism*, Spring 1996, p. 208.

17. Gershom Scholem, *From Berlin to Jerusalem: Memories of My Youth*, Harry Zohn, trans. (New York: Schocken, 1980), pp. 170–171.

18. Marc Lee Raphael, "Rabbi Jacob Voorsanger of San Francisco on Jews and Judaism: The Implications of the Pittsburgh Platform," *American Jewish Historical Quarterly*, December 1973, pp. 200–201. See also Fred Rosenbaum, "San-Francisco-Oakland: The Native Son," in William M. Brinner and Moses Rischin, eds., *Like All the Nations? The Life and Legacy of Judah L. Magnes* (Albany: State University of New York Press, 1987), p. 24.

19. The petition declared that a Jewish state would necessarily be racialist or theocratic; that the Jews had ceased to be a nation in antiquity; and that "we do not wish to see Palestine, either now or at any time in the future, organized as a Jewish state." It was signed by Kahn, Ambassador Henry Morgenthau, and Adolph Ochs, among others. *New York Times*, March 5, 1919. See also Morris Jastrow, *Zionism and the Future of Palestine: The Fallacies and Dangers of Political Zionism* (New York, 1919), pp. 151–159.

20. Fred Rosenbaum, "San-Francisco-Oakland," pp. 22, 24; Marc Lee Raphael, "Cincinnati: The Earlier and Later Years," in Brinner and Rischin, *Like All the Nations?* p. 31; Magnes diary, December 17, 1941, in Goren, *Dissenter*, pp. 381–382. Like the Democrats and Ahad Ha'am, Magnes was, while in Berlin, still sympathetic to the aim of a Jewish state. See, for example, Magnes to his parents, December 26, 1901, in Goren, *Dissenter*, pp. 67–70.

21. Ron Chernow, *The Warburgs: The Twentieth-Century Odyssey of a Remarkable Jewish Family* (New York: Vintage, 1994), pp. 106, 248, 399, 426.

22. Like Warburg, Schiff supported Jewish Palestine financially, referring to himself sometimes as a "cultural Zionist," and even, after the Russian revolution, coming to see Palestine as a possible home for Jewish refugees. Chernow, *Warburgs*, p. 248.

23. Magnes apparently returned from Berlin a "practical" under the influence of Ahad Ha'am. In 1905, the year after Herzl's death, Magnes became secretary of the American Zionist movement, a position he used to tilt it away from its previous Herzlean course. See Evyatar Friesel, "Magnes: Zionism in Judaism," in Brinner and Rischin, *Like All the Nations?* pp. 71ff.

24. Deborah Dash Moore, "A New American Judaism," in Brinner and Rischin, *Like All the Nations?*, p. 50.

25. Magnes to Brandeis, September 2, 1915. Goren, *Dissenter*, p. 150.

26. Emphasis added. Magnes to Brandeis, September 2, 1915. Goren, *Dissenter*, pp. 149–150. See also Goren, *Dissenter*, pp. 21–23. Like the new leadership of the ZVfD in Germany, Magnes insisted that "this does not mean . . . that I cease to be a Zionist." Magnes to Brandeis, September 2, 1915, in Goren, *Dissenter*, p. 152.

27. Magnes to "Dear Friend," May 1920. Parts of this letter were published in the *Jewish Chronicle* in London on August 26, 1921. Goren, *Dissenter*, pp. 183–189.

28. At Magnes's urging, Warburg dropped these conditions, but their effect was nonetheless overwhelming, delivering the clear message that Magnes's influence at the university would determine Warburg's involvement. Indeed, when Weizmann learned of the donation, he implored Magnes to have the funds earmarked for the Jewish studies institute transferred to the general university fund, but to no avail. Goren, "View from Scopus," pp. 211–212. Compare David N. Myers, "A New Scholarly Colony in Jerusalem: The Early History of Jewish Studies at the Hebrew University," *Judaism*, Spring 1996, p. 148.

29. Goren, "View from Scopus," pp. 209, 212; Weizmann to Magnes, December 25, 1924. Magnes had in fact sent Weizmann an invitation to the ceremony—which arrived five days after the ceremony had taken place. Myers, "New Scholarly Colony," pp. 149–150, 157.

30. Marshall to Weizmann, May 28, 1926. Goren, "View from Scopus," p. 215. Compare Magnes to Warburg, July 25, 1929: "I regard it as fatal to the spirit of the university and its scientific spirit for one man to be running a political movement and at the same time to be president of a university. We must try as far as possible to keep the university as far as possible out of the muck of politics." Goren, "View from Scopus," p. 215.

31. See, for example, his speech at the cornerstone-laying ceremony of the Hebrew University, July 24, 1918, in Weizmann, *Papers*, vol. 1, pp. 194–195.

32. Unlike Ahad Ha'am, who believed the Diaspora would continue because a wholesale Jewish resettlement in Palestine was impossible, Magnes followed Hermann Cohen in believing that the Jews were a *Weltvolk* ("world-people") and had to stay in the Diaspora in order to fulfill their "mission." Magnes diary, December 24, 1922, in Goren, *Dissenter*, p. 12. See also "The Land of Israel and Exile," address delivered in Jerusalem, May 22, 1923, in which this idea is elaborated at length. Goren, *Dissenter*, pp. 208–214. Similarly, Magnes was prepared to accept settlement of "many hundreds of thousands of Jews" in Arab countries as a substitute for settlement in Palestine. *New York Times*, July 18, 1937, in Goren, *Dissenter*, p. 327.

33. Leon Roth, rector of the Hebrew University in 1943, quoted in Anita Shapira, "The Labor Movement and the Hebrew University," in Katz and Heyd, *History of the Hebrew*

University, p. 683 [Hebrew]. Magnes also conceived Arab studies at the Hebrew University as having the purpose of bringing Arab opinion to accept the Jewish university as a positive presence in Palestine. Magnes diary, March 22, 1925. Goren, *Dissenter*, p. 231. Moreover, in Magnes's mind, the university also had a distinctly political mission of its own: "The University is *the* place where Arab-Jewish relations can and must be worked out. That is . . . I am to bring the University into politics in *my* sense and on behalf of my views." Emphasis in the original. Magnes to Warburg, September 13, 1929. Goren, *Dissenter*, p. 281.

34. Magnes to Ahad Ha'am, April 1925. Goren, *Dissenter*, p. 235. Warburg, *Jewish Daily Bulletin*, December 30, 1926; Selig Brodetsky, of the university's Board of Governors, similarly trumpeted the idea that the university would embody "to the Jews of Palestine and the world at large, the international idea." *Jewish Daily Bulletin*, December 22, 1926. Both in Medoff, *Zionism and the Arabs*, pp. 37–38. Similarly, Magnes told Warburg a few years after the founding of the university, "the University is *the* place where Arab-Jewish relations can and must be worked out. That is . . . I am to bring the University into politics in *my* sense and on behalf of my views." Emphasis in the original. Magnes to Warburg, September 13, 1929, in Goren, *Dissenter*, p. 281.

35. Hagit Lavsky, "Between the Laying of the Cornerstone and the Opening: The Founding of the Hebrew University, 1918–1925," in Katz and Heyd, *History of the Hebrew University*, p. 156 [Hebrew]; Ze'ev Rosenkrantz, "Albert Einstein's Involvement in the Affairs of the Hebrew University, 1919–1935," in Katz and Heyd, *History of the Hebrew University*, pp. 389–390 [Hebrew]; David Biale, "The Idea of a Jewish University," in Brinner and Rischin, *Like All the Nations?* pp. 133–134; Paul R. Mendes-Flohr, "The Appeal of the Incorrigible Idealist," in Brinner and Rischin, *Like All the Nations?* p. 144. Remarkably, the political rift between nationalistic physical scientists and universalistic humanities professors is still in evidence today. See, for example, Yossi Melman, "We Are Analytical, They Are Disconnected from Reality," *Ha'aretz*, July 5, 1995.

36. Chaim Weizmann, speech at the "opening" ceremony of the Hebrew University, April 1, 1925, in Katz and Heyd, *History of the Hebrew University*, p. 321.

37. As Magnes wrote to Warburg: "One of the evils of the educational system [in Palestine] is its absolute dependence, financially and spiritually, upon the Zionist political machinery. The fact that the University is, fortunately, independent of this is helping us to create a true University." Magnes to Warburg, April 28, 1929. Goren, *Dissenter*, p. 274.

38. Norman Bentwich, *For Zion's Sake: A Biography of Judah L. Magnes* (Philadelphia: Jewish Publication Society, 1954), pp. 129–137.

39. Chernow, *Warburgs*, p. 253; Rosenkrantz, "Einstein," pp. 390–392.

40. Magnes diary, February 13, 1928. Goren, *Dissenter*, p. 265. In later years, Magnes himself admitted that "one of the reasons why the Zionists in England [i.e., Weizmann] opposed me from the very beginning was because I kept the university from becoming a part of the Zionist political organization" and instead placed it in the service of an alternative allegiance to "a larger, freer humanity." Magnes to Eugene Untermeyer, March 1945. Goren, *Dissenter*, p. 429. See also Biale, "The Idea of a Jewish University," pp. 134–135.

41. Menahem Milson, "The Beginnings of Arabic and Islamic Studies at the Hebrew University of Jerusalem," *Judaism*, Spring 1996, pp. 172–174, 177.

42. S. D. Goitein, "The School of Oriental Studies: A Memoir," in Brinner and Rischin, *Like All the Nations?* pp. 170–172; Milson, "The Beginnings of Arabic and Islamic Studies," pp. 170–171. When the first volume appeared, it was reprinted in Baghdad with all references to the Hebrew University omitted. Buber, too, argued that Oriental

studies would bring with it a "sympathetic knowledge of our neighbors," which would be the basis for bringing about a unity of interests between Jews and Arabs. Martin Buber, "Soul-Searching," *Juedische Rundschau*, April 1926. Buber, *Two Peoples*, p. 77.

43. Myers, *Re-Inventing the Jewish Past*, p. 59. See also George L. Mosse, "Central European Intellectuals in Palestine," *Judaism*, Spring 1996, p. 135.

44. For course listings, see *The Hebrew University, Jerusalem: Yearbook 1927–28 and 1928–1929* (Jerusalem: April 1929), pp. 78–94. For supporters of the Peace Association, see Kedar, "Peace Association," pp. 281–285.

45. Buber to Rosenzweig, August 15, 1929; Buber to Paula Buber, n.d. Martin Buber, *The Letters of Martin Buber: A Life of Dialogue*, Nahum Glatzer and Paul Mendes-Flohr, eds., Richard Winston et al., trans. (New York: Syracuse University Press, 1996), pp. 365–366.

46. Speech before the Sixteenth Zionist Congress, August 1, 1929, in Minutes of the Sixteenth Zionist Congress, p. 207. Compare Buber, *Two Peoples*, pp. 79–80.

47. Buber himself believed that Magnes would have the power to ratify this appointment with the university council because "he has the Americans on his side." Buber to Paula Buber, n.d., in Buber, *Letters*, p. 366; Buber to Paula Buber, August 20, 1929. Buber, *Letters*, p. 369.

48. The August massacres led to Magnes's decision to reenter the political arena on behalf of binationalism. It seems likely that this change in Magnes's public behavior turned the effort to bring Buber into such a sensitive position into a nonissue.

49. Michael Keren, *The Pen and the Sword: Israeli Intellectuals and the Making of the Nation-State* (Boulder: Westview, 1989), p. 28; George L. Mosse, "Central European Intellectuals in Palestine," *Judaism*, Spring 1996, p. 135.

50. Katznelson to Hugo Bergmann, November 1935 (no exact date), in Berl Katznelson, *Berl Katznelson's Letters, 1930–1937*, Anita Shapira and Esther Raizen, eds. (Tel Aviv: Am Oved, 1984), pp. 207–208 [Hebrew]. It is unclear whether this letter was ever sent.

51. Speech of Ben-Gurion before friends of the university, December 2, 1937, quoted in Anita Shapira, "The Labor Movement and the Hebrew University," p. 685.

Chapter Nine

1. David Ben-Gurion, *The Letters of David Ben-Gurion*, Yehuda Erez, ed. (Tel Aviv: Am Oved, 1971), vol. 3, p. 66 [Hebrew].

2. Jewish Telegraphic Agency Bulletin, August 21, 1929; *Jewish Chronicle*, September 27, 1929. Compare Weizmann, who writes of the massacres: "This, then, was the answer of the Arab leadership to the Congress and the Agency meeting. They had realized that our fortunes had taken an upward turn, that the speed of our development in Palestine would soon follow the same curve." Chaim Weizmann, *Trial and Error: The Autobiography of Chaim Weizmann* (New York: Harper and Brothers, 1949), p. 331. For a more complete account of events, see Conor Cruise O'Brien, *The Siege: The Saga of Israel and Zionism* (New York: Simon and Schuster, 1986), pp. 178–188; Shmuel Katz, *Lone Wolf: A Biography of Vladimir (Ze'ev) Jabotinsky* (New York: Barricade Books, 1996), pp. 1119–1128.

3. Katz, *Lone Wolf*, pp. 1131–1135.

4. Weizmann, *Trial and Error*, p. 331.

5. In October, Britain made good on its intentions by sending yet another in what was to become a long series of investigatory commissions to Palestine—there had already been

two in the wake of the riots of 1920–1921—with the goal of submitting recommendations for a new policy that was to take the August bloodshed into account.

6. Martin Buber, "The Wailing Wall," October 1929. Reprinted in Martin Buber, *A Land of Two Peoples: Martin Buber on Jews and Arabs,* Paul R. Mendes-Flohr, ed. (Oxford: Oxford University Press, 1983), pp. 93–95; Martin Buber, "The National Home and National Policy in Palestine," October 31, 1929. Reprinted in Buber, *A Land of Two Peoples,* pp. 82–91. Buber returned repeatedly to the demand for clemency for the Arab murderers, including in letters to Weizmann pleading for his participation: "It would not be a sign of weakness but of power and of consciousness of power if I save the life of my enemy." Maurice Friedman, *Martin Buber's Life and Work* (Detroit: Wayne State University Press, 1988), vol. 2, p. 13. Compare Buber to Weizmann, November 11, 1929, in which he continues to press to have the murderers reprieved. Martin Buber, *The Letters of Martin Buber: A Life of Dialogue,* Nahum Glatzer and Paul Mendes-Flohr, eds., Richard Winston et al., trans. (New York: Syracuse University Press, 1996), p. 372.

7. Scholem to Buber, May 22, 1930. Buber, *Letters,* p. 377. Only a year earlier, Bergmann had written to Buber to confess, on behalf of himself and his circle in Jerusalem, that they felt "more than ever" how unclear was their relationship to Palestine and to Zionism. Bergmann to Buber, January 31, 1928. Buber, *Letters,* p. 357.

8. Shmuel Dotan, *Reds: The Communist Party in Palestine* (Kfar Saba: Shabna Hasofer, 1991), pp. 298, 388–390 [Hebrew].

9. See Hans Kohn to Buber, August 26, 1929, in which he writes: "The events in Palestine are very bad. All of us share in the blame. . . . Now, because of our cowardice and inaction . . . great misfortune will flow . . . Years of hatred, military suppression, the moral defeat of Zionism." Buber, *Letters,* p. 370. Seven years earlier, Kohn had written in *Der Jude* that Buber had liberated the Jewish nation from "the vain delusion of political independence." Hans Kohn, "Nationalism," *Der Jude* 6, August 1922, translated in Arthur A. Cohen, *The Jew: Essays from Martin Buber's Journal* Der Jude, *1916–1928,* Joachim Neugroschel, trans. (Tuscaloosa: University of Alabama Press, 1980), p. 28. But in the wake of the massacres, he informed Buber that the "Zion" that they had sought in Palestine was now leading him elsewhere—to America. See Hans Kohn to Buber, December 10, 1929. Buber, *Letters,* pp. 372–373. Compare Hans Kohn to Berthold Feiwel, November 21, 1929, in Aharon Kedar, "Brit Shalom," *Jerusalem Quarterly* 18 (Winter 1987), pp. 78–82. A few weeks later, Kohn left Palestine for the United States.

10. See, for example, Ernst Simon to Buber, October 10, 1929. Buber, *Letters,* p. 371.

11. Memorandum submitted to the Zionist Executive in London on September 16, 1929. Aharon Kedar, "On the History of the Peace Association, 1925–1928," in Yehuda Bauer et al., eds., *Research Chapters in Zionist History* (Jerusalem: Hasifria Hatzionit, 1976), p. 261 n. 87 [Hebrew].

12. Bergmann's initiative dated February 27, 1930; Simon's dated March 12, 1930. Susan Lee Hattis, *The Binational Idea in Palestine During Mandatory Times* (Haifa: Shikmona Publishing, 1970), pp. 51–55.

13. For the peace plan, see Einstein to the editor of *Falastin,* February 25, 1930; for the abandonment of the Jewish state, see Einstein to Dear Friend, June 19, 1930. Reprinted in *Sheifoteinu* 4 (1930), pp. 33–34.

14. Albert Einstein, *Ideas and Opinions* (New York: Crown Publishers, 1954), p. 190.

15. Magnes to Warburg, September 13, 1929, in Arthur A. Goren, *Dissenter in Zion: From the Writings of Judah L. Magnes* (Cambridge: Harvard University Press, 1982), p. 279. Already at the end of August, Max Warburg had written Felix from Berlin, urging upon him the recognition that development of Palestine would be impossible without a peace

agreement between Jews and Arabs. Max Warburg to Felix Warburg, August 29, 1929. Ron Chernow, *The Warburgs: The Twentieth-Century Odyssey of a Remarkable Jewish Family* (New York: Vintage Books, 1993), p. 302. The "non-Zionist" members of the Jewish Agency quickly reached similar conclusions, arguing that the rights of the Jewish people in Palestine did "not accord with the conscience of people bred in America" and that the rights of the Arabs in Palestine were "perhaps even more basic than those of the Jewish people." Julian Morgenstern to Judah Magnes, December 23, 1929; James Marshall, "Home Rule in Palestine," *New Palestine*, January 10, 1930. Both quoted in Raphael Medoff, *Zionism and the Arabs: An American Jewish Dilemma* (Westport: Praeger, 1997), p. 54.

16. Felix Warburg to Aby Warburg, October 30, 1929. Chernow, *Warburgs*, pp. 302–303.

17. Sir John Chancellor to Sir John Shuckburgh, October 4, 1929. Colonial Office Archives, 733/175. On October 30, Chancellor personally asked Magnes whether it was not the case that "the rich American Jews control the situation now" and pressed him to bring Warburg to speak publicly against the views of the Zionists. Judah L. Magnes, "The Magnes-Philby Negotiations: A Personal Record," in Menahem Kaufman, ed., *The Magnes-Philby Negotiations, 1929: The Historical Record* (Jerusalem: Magnes Press, 1998), p. 94. The American consul in Jerusalem, Paul Knabenshue, also spent the fall lobbying the State Department to take a publicly anti-Zionist line. See his dispatches of October 19, November 2, November 16, and December 9, as quoted in Lawrence Davidson, "Competing Responses to the 1929 Arab Uprising in Palestine: The Zionist Press Versus the State Department," *Middle East Policy*, May 1997, pp. 102–103, 110. He was eventually reprimanded by the State Department for trying to drag the United States into a confrontation with the ZO. See Davidson, p. 106.

18. Naomi W. Cohen, *The Year After the Riots: American Responses to the Palestine Crisis of 1929–1930* (Detroit: Wayne State University Press, 1988), pp. 99–100.

19. The text of the agreement can be found in Magnes, "A Personal Record," pp. 108–109. Levy also told Magnes that Knabenshue was involved and that Levy wanted to use the American consulate as a place for meetings between Arabs and Jews. The following week, Levy and Knabenshue attempted to arrange a meeting between Magnes and the Mufti, but Magnes declined. Magnes, "A Personal Record," pp. 136–137.

20. Warburg's cabled response to Magnes reflected anger that Magnes had concluded an agreement with Philby without bringing Warburg into the negotiation: "Much distressed and disturbed at receipt of your cable and lone hand proceedings. Had hoped that you would offer to cooperate with other sound minds . . . so that I could be put in a position of conferring with my colleagues on a joint suggestion." Warburg to Magnes, November 2, 1929, included in Magnes, "A Personal Record," p. 127. From this it is evident that Warburg was *not* angered by Magnes's negotiations with Philby but only that he had expected to be included.

21. Shabtai Teveth, *Ben-Gurion and the Arabs: From Peace to War* (Jerusalem: Schocken, 1985), pp. 152–153 [Hebrew]. Irma Lindheim was a founder of Hadassah and its president from 1926–1928.

22. Hattis, *Binational Idea*, pp. 68–69; Cohen, *The Year After the Riots*, pp. 77, 163; Warburg to Magnes, November 13, 1929, included in Magnes, "A Personal Record," p. 151. See also Weizmann's telegram to Warburg, arguing that Magnes's diplomacy threatened "complete destruction" and demanding that Magnes be restrained. Weizmann to Warburg, November 6, 1929. Meyer Weisgal and Barnet Litvinoff, eds., *The Letters and Papers of Chaim Weizmann* (London: Oxford University Press, 1968–1972, and Jerusalem: Israel Universities Press, 1973–1980), ser. A, vol. 14, p. 62.

23. *Jewish Daily Bulletin*, November 21, 1929.

24. Opening speech of the academic year, November 18, 1929. Reprinted in Judah Magnes, *Addresses by the Chancellor of the Hebrew University* (Jerusalem: Hebrew University, 1936), p. 102.

25. As for the Jews, he stated that enough of a basis had been laid for "an Ahad Ha'amist intellectual center" within a binational state, calling on the Jews to "prepare for the negotiations that are bound to come." All quotes as paraphrased by Jewish Telegraphic Agency, *Jewish Daily Bulletin*, November 20, 1929; compare *New York Times*, November 21, 1929.

26. Judah Magnes, *Like All Nations?* (Jerusalem: Herod's Gate, 1930), pp. 13, 28.

27. "We have continued to cultivate the ideology of the Judenstaat in our own circles and have considered the White Paper [of 1922, which implied a British policy of evenhandedness between Arabs and Jews] as a concession which was forced from us and which we were not obligated to fulfill. . . . If we wish to express the contents of the White Paper in a short formula, it means: Palestine is a binational state." *Jewish Daily Bulletin*, November 21, 1929.

28. *New York Times*, November 21 and 24, 1929.

29. See Warburg to Weizmann, November 15, 1929; Warburg to Melchett, November 15, 1929; Weizmann to Warburg, November 25, 1929. Warburg Papers, boxes 266 and 289.

30. I have filled in missing words in Weizmann's cable. The original text reads: "Magnes statements utterances rendered our position intolerable . . . we heading demoralization movement inevitable collapse agency." Weizmann to Warburg, November 25, 1929. Warburg Papers, box 289. Compare Weizmann's letter to Albert Einstein, in which he savages Magnes—and, by implication, Einstein himself—for his binationalist efforts: "Little Palestine was the one place on earth where we stood upright," he wrote. "Now come the Magneses, the Bergmanns, and break our united front. . . . That hypocrite, that Tartuffe, Magnes, lightly abandons the Balfour declaration. He did not bleed for it, he only gained by it. . . . Bergmann and Magnes, and even you . . . are now quoted against us, and from the mouths of the murderers we are told: 'Yes, if all Zionists were like Bergmann.'" Weizmann to Einstein, November 30, 1929. Weizmann, *Letters*, vol. 14, pp. 123–124. The reference to "the mouths of the murderers" apparently refers to an article in the Arabic newspaper *Falastin*. Its English-language edition carried an article entitled "Jabotinsky and Weizmann or Magnes and Bergman," comparing the position of the Peace Covenant group to that of the ZO, which was prepared to rely on British force to bring about the establishment of a Jewish majority. Palestine, September 30, 1929, cited in Weizmann, *Letters*, vol. 14, p. 124 n. 7.

31. *Juedische Rundschau*, January 3, 1930; *Ha'olam*, January 24, 1930. Both quoted in Hattis, *Binational Idea*, pp. 87–88.

32. The quotation is Bergmann's phrasing of an evaluation he attributes to Leon Simon. Bergmann to Robert Weltsch, January 10, 1930. Bergmann, *Tagebuecher und Briefe*, vol. 1, p. 300 [German]. Compare Stephen Wise's comment: "The August disaster . . . has given the nons [i.e., non-Zionists] the excuse for reverting to anti-Zionism, and . . . they are dragging the Zionists with them and coverting them into non-Zionists." Quoted in Cohen, *The Year After the Riots*, pp. 145–146.

33. Appearing before the Shaw commission in London in 1930, Jabotinsky asserted that a Jewish state "does not necessarily mean the right to declare war on anybody . . . [but] that measure of self-government which, for instance, the state of Nebraska possesses. That would satisfy me completely." Ben Halpern, *The Idea of the Jewish State* (Cambridge: Harvard University Press, 1961), p. 206.

34. Weizmann to James Marshall, January 17, 1930. Weizmann, *Letters*, vol. 14, pp. 206–211.

35. Jabotinsky's exclusion from Palestine was apparently endorsed by the attorney general of Palestine, Norman Bentwich, a Jew and an adherent of the Peace Association, who was later member of the faculty at the Hebrew University. Katz, *Lone Wolf*, pp. 1174–1182.

36. Katz, *Lone Wolf*, pp. 1210, 1212.

37. Under this version, the council's 22 members would consist of 10 Britons, 9–10 Arabs, and 2–3 Jews.

38. Teveth, *Ben-Gurion and the Arabs*, p. 155, 158.

39. Anita Shapira, *Berl Katznelson: A Biography* (Tel Aviv: Am Oved, 1980), pp. 244, 252, 256, 263, 305, 309–311 [Hebrew]; Berl Katznelson, "The Political Future of Palestine," 1931, in Enzo Sereni and R. E. Ashery, eds., *Jews and Arabs in Palestine: Studies in a National and Colonial Problem* (New York: Hechalutz, 1936), p. 211.

40. Beilinson to Katznelson, n.d. Shapira, *Berl*, p. 329. Ben-Gurion said that he was willing to consider going to war against Britain if Jewish immigration were suspended. Teveth, *Burning Ground*, p. 396. He did, however, react to the Magnes-Philby plan with a proposal of his own for a federal constitution with binational elements, although his plan also placed control over Jewish immigration in Jewish hands. Teveth, *Ben-Gurion and the Arabs*, p. 154.

41. In elections to the Seventeenth Congress, Jabotinsky's party won an unprecedented 52 seats out of 254, or 20 percent of the representatives, while Labor had 75 seats, or 30 percent of the representatives. In Palestine as well, the 1931 elections for the Jewish National Assembly steeply strengthened the Revisionist representation, bringing it to nearly one-fourth of the seats.

42. Address before the Seventeenth Zionist Congress, Basel, July 1, 1931, in Weizmann, *Papers*, vol. 1, pp. 621–623; interview with Jewish Telegraph Agency, July 3, 1931, in Weizmann, *Papers*, pp. 641–642.

43. Katz, *Lone Wolf*, p. 1254. So universal was the consternation that even Haim Arlozoroff, one of the Labor leaders most outspoken in favor of tactical compromise, was forced to declare Weizmann's statement "factually as well as politically wrong and harmful." Minutes of the Seventeenth Congress, p. 304 [German].

44. The telegram was subsequently shown to be a fraud. Nevertheless, the telegram was sufficient to induce members of the political committee to reverse their decision. See Katz, *Lone Wolf*, pp. 1262–1264.

45. This point was to result in much subsequent confusion, because the Jewish Agency Council, meeting in the wake of the Congress, did pass a resolution that was at times interpreted as an endorsement of parity. It stated that the agency would "carry on working on an establishment of harmonious relations between Jews and Arabs under the Mandate, relations that are founded on the acceptance by both parties of the principle that no party should rule or be ruled by the other." Protocol of the Seventeenth Zionist Congress and the Second Conference of the Council of the Jewish Agency for Palestine, pt. C, p. 593.

46. David Ben-Gurion, "The Seventeenth Congress and Our Future Course," *Hapoel Hatzair*, August 14 and 21, 1931.

47. Teveth, *Burning Ground*, p. 399. Teveth has "physical and spiritual annihilation."

48. Ze'ev Jabotinsky, "The Crisis of the Proletariat," in Ze'ev Jabotinsky, *Writings: Articles* (Tel Aviv: Eri Jabotinsky, 1958), pp. 313–114 [Hebrew]. The original article was published in *Posledniye Novosti*, April 9, 1932 [Russian].

49. Teveth, *Burning Ground*, pp. 412–413, 461.

50. To this day, no consensus has emerged concerning the identity of the actual murderers; a state commission of inquiry into the subject, launched in 1982, cleared Stavsky and two other Revisionists. It was unable to reach any conclusions regarding the actual identity of the murderers. See Shabtai Teveth, *The Murder of Arlosoroff* (Jerusalem: Schocken, 1982) [Hebrew]. Shmuel Katz summarizes the Revisionist view in *Lone Wolf*, pp. 1353–1398. But see also Dan Margalit's account of his grandfather's futile efforts to submit evidence to Labor party officials supporting the case that the killers were Arabs. Dan Margalit, *I Saw Them All* (Tel Aviv: Zmora-Bitan, 1997), pp. 204–205 [Hebrew].

51. Labor won 138 seats out of 318, while the Revisionists, split into two factions, won only 52. The Mizrahi and General Zionists B roughly retained their strength, and together with the Revisionists, they composed 52 percent of the Congress. But Jabotinsky's clear defeat at the polls eliminated the possibility of Revisionist leadership.

52. By 1933, it was clear that the participation of non-Zionists had not had the expected dramatic impact on fund-raising, and non-Zionist participation in the institutions of the Jewish Agency had commensurately dwindled. The Jewish Agency executive elected that year was composed of ten members of the ZO and only three non-Zionists. By 1939, participation of non-Zionists in decisionmaking of the Jewish Agency was practically nil, and the joint organization with the Zionists existed on paper only. Menaham Kaufman, *An Ambiguous Partnership: Non-Zionists and Zionists in America, 1939–1948* (Jerusalem: Magnes Press, 1991), pp. 31–32, 43, 93, 173; Teveth, *Burning Ground*, p. 439.

53. Speech before the Fourth Convention of the Histadrut, January 9–13, 1934. Reprinted in David Ben-Gurion, *From Class to People* (Tel Aviv: Ayenot, 1955), p. 475 [Hebrew].

54. Ben-Gurion took the lead in meeting with Magnes's Arab friends; and when he met with them, he informed them that the Jews did indeed seek peace—on the basis of "a Jewish homeland and a Jewish state" on both banks of the Jordan, comprising 6 million Jews. Teveth, *Burning Ground*, p. 465, 475.

55. Outside of the immediate circle of the professors of the Hebrew University, sympathy for the Peace Association's arguments simply evaporated—to the point that when Magnes prepared a new pamphlet entitled "Palestine, an Arab-Jewish State," even Arthur Ruppin was moved to ask what he hoped to achieve with it. Ruppin diary, February 4, 1932. Arthur Ruppin, *Arthur Ruppin: Memoirs, Diaries, Letters*, Alex Bein, ed., Karen Gershon, trans. (New York: Herzl Press, 1971), p. 259.

56. Katz, *Lone Wolf*, p. 1422.

57. Yehoshua Ofir, *The History of the National Labor Movement in the Land of Israel* (Tel Aviv, 1987), pt. 1, pp. 162–163 [Hebrew].

58. The paper backed down, and the editorial did not appear. Shapira, *Berl*, p. 414.

59. Tabenkin himself once summed up his movement's ideology as: "The entire Jewish people, settled in the entire land of Israel, all of them in communes, within an association of the world's communist peoples." Minutes of the assembly of the United Kibbutz Movement, December 17–19, 1953. Quoted in Ze'ev Tzahor, *Awakening: The Dream of the State and Its Outcome* (Tel Aviv: Modan), p. 235 [Hebrew].

60. A third agreement set old accounts straight by reinstating the Revisionists' right to immigration certificates from the Jewish Agency and the end of Jabotinsky's boycott of Zionist fund-raising.

61. Fears of such an alliance were rife among supporters of Weizmann and the Zionist left. See comments by Kurt Blumenfeld, Abraham Katznelson, and Tabenkin, in Teveth, *Burning Ground*, pp. 483–484, 491.

62. David Ben-Gurion, *Memoirs* (Tel Aviv: Am Oved, 1972), entries for October 9–November 11, 1934, vol. 2, pp. 185–233 [Hebrew]; Katz, *Lone Wolf*, p. 1431.

63. Shapira, *Berl*, p. 417, 422–423; Teveth, *Burning Ground*, pp. 485, 490–491; Katz, *Lone Wolf*, p. 1431.

64. The final split with Tabenkin took place nine years later, in 1944. Tabenkin's breakaway movement, which accused Ben-Gurion of having sold out on Labor Zionist ideals, was called Ahdut Ha'avoda. It merged with the main Labor party, Mapai, in 1968.

65. The NZO was, however, successful in forging diplomatic ties with Poland and other Eastern European countries. It was Jabotinsky's ties with the Polish government that permitted the military training of the Irgun ("Jewish Military Organization"), the underground group in Palestine that, under the command of Menachem Begin, would become the main military opponent of the British presence in Palestine. Katz, *Lone Wolf*, pp. 1629–1631.

66. The new Jewish Agency executive consisted of the seven members of the ZO executive (Weizmann, Ben-Gurion, two Labor Zionists, two General Zionists, and one representative of Mizrahi) and three other members representing non-Zionists: Maurice Hexter, Julius Simon, and Maurice Karpf.

67. Teveth, *Burning Ground*, p. 514.

68. The proposal developed in London was for a Legislative Council in which the Arabs would have 14 members, the Jews 7, and the British 8. The British chairman would also have veto power.

69. Meeting with Wauchope, January 26, 1936. Rose, *Chaim Weizmann*, p. 312.

70. Minutes of the meeting of the Mapai political committee, March 9, 1936. Beit Berl Archives.

71. Teveth, *Burning Ground*, pp. 517, 521–522.

72. John Marlowe, *Rebellion in Palestine* (London: Cresset Press, 1946), pp. 194, 202; Yehoshua Porath, *The Palestinian Arab National Movement, 1929–1939: From Riots to Rebellion* (London: Frank Cass, 1977), p. 188; Dotan, *Reds*, pp. 233–237.

73. Porath, *Palestinian Arab National Movement*, pp. 163–178.

74. Magnes to Reginald Coupland, January 7, 1937, in Goren, *Dissenter*, p. 316; Hattis, *Binational Idea*, pp. 146, 159–160; Bernard Wasserstein, *Herbert Samuel: A Political Life* (Oxford: Clarendon Press, 1992), pp. 383–384; Chernow, *Warburgs*, pp. 449–452.

75. Teveth, *Burning Ground*, pp. 525–533, 564f.; Hattis, *Binational Idea*, pp. 162–163.

76. Hattis, *Binational Idea*, p. 162; Weizmann to Warburg, June 18, 1936. Warburg Archives, 332/11. Compare Weizmann in 1935: "I am afraid that we replace today the concept of rescue of Jews with that of redemption. When I consider if these German refugees can fit in the style of life that we are creating here . . . I should sincerely say: no . . . Zionism is eternal life, whereas the rescue of thousands of Jews is not for me but temporary lives." Speech before the Zionist Executive in Jerusalem, April 1935. Reprinted in Chaim Weizmann, *Works* (Tel Aviv: Mitzpeh, 1937), vol. 4, pp. 788–794 [Hebrew].

77. Foreign Office memorandum dated September 21, 1936, quoted in Hattis, *Binational Idea*, p. 163.

78. Teveth, *Burning Ground*, pp. 525, 533, 539, 564–570.

79. Ibid., p. 580.

80. Emphasis added. Weizmann's speech before the Twentieth Zionist Congress, August 4, 1937. Weizmann, *Papers*, vol. 2, p. 286.

81. Shmuel Dotan, *The Debate over Partition During the Period of the Mandate* (Jerusalem: Yad Yitzhak Ben-Tzvi, 1980), pp. 144–145, 147–148, 206–207, 209–211 [Hebrew].

82. American Non-Zionist Members of the Jewish Agency Administrative Committee to Weizmann, February 17, 1937. Unsigned draft, Warburg Archives, 346/9.

83. Teveth, *Burning Ground*, pp. 611–612. Teveth's quotation has "the key to immigration" in italics. Both he and Weizmann agreed with Herzl on another point as well: Once sovereignty was attained, even on 5 percent of Palestine's soil, there always existed the possibility that the boundaries would be redrawn somewhere along the line. Weizmann: "The kingdom of David was smaller; under Solomon it became an empire. Who knows?" Weizmann to Mrs. A. Paterson, July 7, 1937. Weizmann, *Letters*, vol. 18, p. 146. Ben-Gurion: "A Jewish state in part of Palestine is not the end but the beginning.... The establishment of such a Jewish state ... will serve as a powerful means in our historical efforts to redeem the country in its entirety. We shall bring into the country all the Jews that it can contain ... We shall build a Jewish economy ... We shall organize a sophisticated defense force—an elite army. I have no doubt that our army will be one of the best in the world. And then I am sure that we shall not be prevented from settling in all the other parts of the country, either through mutual understanding and agreement with our Arab neighbors or by other means." Ben-Gurion to his son Amos, October 5, 1937. In David Ben-Gurion, *Letters to Paula and the Children* (Tel Aviv: Am Oved, 1968), p. 211 [Hebrew].

84. Blanche Dugdale diary, February 1, 1937, quoted in Rose, *Chaim Weizmann*, p. 320.

85. Teveth, *Burning Ground*, p. 614.

86. "If this Council's efforts will be directed merely towards the establishment of a Jewish state and not the simultaneous fulfillment of responsibilities towards its neighbors, we won't be able to go along with you." Warburg's speech before the Jewish Agency Council, August 18, 1937. Minutes of the Twentieth Zionist Congress and the Fifth Session of the Jewish Agency, p. 31 [Hebrew].

87. Address before the Council of the Jewish Agency, August 18, 1937. Goren, *Dissenter*, pp. 329, 333–334. See also Henrietta Szold's undelivered speech, quoted in Joan Dash, "Doing Good in Palestine: Magnes and Henriette Szold," in William M. Brinner and Moses Rischin, eds., *Like All the Nations? The Life and Legacy of Judah L. Magnes* (Albany: State University of New York Press, 1987), p. 108.

88. Teveth, *Burning Ground*, p. 619.

89. Yitzhak Ben-Tzvi, ed., *The History of the Hagana* (Jerusalem: Hasifria Hatziyonit, 1964), vol. 2, pt. 2, p. 801 [Hebrew].

90. Teveth, *Burning Ground*, pp. 635, 669.

91. Hattis, *Binational Idea*, p. 201.

Chapter Ten

1. Shabtai Teveth, *Ben-Gurion: The Burning Ground: 1886–1948* (Boston: Houghton Mifflin Company, 1987), p. 707. Second half of the quoted passage is in italics in the original.

2. "You may think it strange that I and my kind ... are forced now to disagree with those who say: We'll go on as always.... [building] new settlements, erecting industries.... It was to this that we were educated.... But now we see before our very eyes the [German] Tyrolean farmer, rooted in his soil [in northern Italy] since ancient times ... and how a quarter of a million farmers is torn up from their soil and expelled from their homeland, and no one says a word.... We must recognize the nature of the times we are living in, and what awaits us under the coming Anglo-Arab regime." Berl

Katznelson, speech at the Twenty-First Zionist Congress, August 16–25, 1939. Berl Katznelson, *Writings* (Tel Aviv: Mifleget Poalei Eretz Yisrael, 1948), pp. 61–82 [Hebrew]. In 1939, Germany and Italy signed an agreement under which most of the German-speaking South Tyrolese were to be transferred to Germany.

3. Teveth, *Burning Ground*, pp. 713–715, 720, 722.

4. For a discussion of small-scale clandestine operations conducted against the British at this time, see Yehuda Bauer, *From Diplomacy to Resistance: A History of Jewish Palestine, 1939–1945* (Philadelphia: Jewish Publication Society, 1970), pp. 57–60.

5. In Herzl's time, the Executive of the ZO was called the Small Actions Committee.

6. Teveth, *Burning Ground*, pp. 730, 739.

7. See *New Palestine*, October 14, 21, 28, and November 4, 1938.

8. Proceedings of the Mapai Council, April 14–16, 1939, quoted in Allon Gal, *David Ben-Gurion and the American Alignment for a Jewish State* (Jerusalem: Magnes Press, 1991), pp. 61–62; see also p. 39. Compare Ussishkin: "Upon whom can we depend in our struggle for the future of Palestine? . . . Can we depend upon England? . . . Can we depend upon America, on Roosevelt's elegant smile, on his handshake with Weizmann? . . . On the Jewish people in America, afraid to open its mouth? . . . The only force [we have] is the half million Jews in Palestine and the 1.5 million dunams beneath our feet." Minutes of the Select Zionist Executive, March 14, 1940, in Gal, *David Ben-Gurion*, pp. 95–96.

9. Teveth, *Burning Ground*, pp. 740–741.

10. Emphasis in the original. Speech before the Select Zionist Executive, March 14, 1940. Central Zionist Archives, S 25/1829.

11. Teveth, *Burning Ground*, p. 791.

12. Wise to Goldman, December 5, 1940, in Gal, *David Ben-Gurion*, p. 148.

13. Gal, *David Ben-Gurion*, p. 119.

14. Susan Lee Hattis, *The Binational Idea in Palestine During Mandatory Times* (Haifa: Shikmona Publishing, 1970), pp. 171–172, 225; Gal, *David Ben-Gurion*, p. 127; David H. Shpiro, *From Philanthropy to Activism: The Political Transformation of American Zionism in the Holocaust Years, 1933–1945* (Oxford: Pergamon Press, 1993), pp. 91–92. Magnes and Hadassah's founder, Henrietta Szold, had collaborated both ideologically and practically since 1903. See Joan Dash, "Doing Good in Palestine: Magnes and Henrietta Szold," in William M. Brinner and Moses Rischin, eds., *Like All the Nations? The Life and Legacy of Judah L. Magnes* (Albany: State University of New York Press, 1987), especially pp. 100–102, 105. For funding of binationalist efforts, see note 78 below.

15. Ben-Gurion's report before the Jewish Agency Executive, February 16, 1941. Gal, *David Ben-Gurion*, p. 129.

16. Proceedings of Ben-Gurion's Meeting with the National Board of Hadassah, November 26, 1940. Gal, *David Ben-Gurion*, p. 156.

17. Shpiro, *From Philanthropy to Activism*, p. 38; Gal, *David Ben-Gurion*, pp. 110–112, 123–124.

18. Silver to Emanuel Neumann, December 2, 1940. Gal, *David Ben-Gurion*, p. 146.

19. "Report of a Meeting with Mr. Ben-Gurion at the Winthrop Hotel, New York City, on December 5, 1940, at 2 p.m." Gal, *David Ben-Gurion*, p. 151.

20. Gal, *David Ben-Gurion*, pp. 153, 168–170. Ben-Gurion began to use the term "Jewish commonwealth" after he determined that by using this phraseology he could bring the authority of Woodrow Wilson into the discussion of the Jewish state. Thus, on January 5, 1941, he told the leadership of the ZOA that creating a Jewish commonwealth in Palestine "is not a new thing; it is not a new invention. This is what America said in the last war; this is what Wilson wanted; and I know that the present America, which certainly is not worse

than the America of Wilson . . . will understand us." Proceedings of the ZOA National
Administrative Council Meeting, January 5, 1941. Gal, *David Ben-Gurion*, p. 169.

21. See Gal, *David Ben-Gurion*, pp. 182–185; Shpiro, *From Philanthropy to Activism*, p. 78.

22. "There is a danger that after the war there will be confusion among the Jewish people,"
Ben-Gurion told the Labor Central Committee, "all sorts of witch-doctor solutions will
come forth, and there will be a great catastrophe. If a carefully considered effort is not
made now by all of us, we will have to suffer the consequences." Teveth, *Burning
Ground*, p. 783.

23. During 1940 and 1941, German troops invaded Egypt and entered Vichy Syria, and the
pro-Nazi coup of Rashid Ali overthrew the Iraqi government; Italy began bombing operations against Haifa and Tel Aviv from its bases in Libya, which left over a hundred dead.

24. "Jewish Immigration and Palestine After the War," Memorandum to Judge Rosenman,
February 10, 1942, pp. 7–8. Ben-Gurion Archives.

25. American Mizrahi had adopted such a platform in May 1941. *New Palestine*,
September 19, 1941.

26. *Hadassah Newsletter*, December 1941–January 1942.

27. Gal, *David Ben-Gurion*, p. 129.

28. Chaim Weizmann, "Palestine's Role in the Solution of the Jewish Problem," *Foreign
Affairs*, January 1942, pp. 337–338.

29. Proceedings of the Extraordinary Zionist Conference, May 9–11, 1942. Gal, *David
Ben-Gurion*, p. 200.

30. The majority position was also opposed by one of the Palestinian delegates, Moshe
Furmansky, who spoke on behalf of Hashomer Hatzair in opposition to a Jewish state.

31. Both Weizmann and Ben-Gurion responded that there had never been any progress in
finding an Arab leader who would agree in writing to the immigration of millions of
Jews to Palestine. That being the case, Ben-Gurion continued, "Any attempt on our
part to achieve an Arab-Jewish accord is doomed to failure unless we give up on immigration—and there is no point in trying to achieve such an accord . . . without giving
up on immigration." Shpiro, *From Philanthropy to Activism*, pp. 93–94.

32. *New Palestine*, May 15, 1942.

33. Proceedings of the Extraordinary Zionist Conference, May 9–11, 1942. Gal, *David
Ben-Gurion*, pp. 198–199.

34. Proceedings of the Jewish Agency Executive, November 8, 1942, pp. 8840–8851 and
Proceedings of the Zionist Executive, November 10, 1942, pp. 3478–3487. Central
Zionist Archives, S100/36b and S25/294.

35. Thomas A. Kolsky, *Jews Against Zionism: The American Council for Judaism, 1942–1948*
(Philadelphia: Temple University, 1990), pp. 41, 75. Proskauer became an ally of the ZO
in the years after the Holocaust. Kolsky, *Jews Against Zionism*, pp. 146–147.

36. Of course, this high point could not last. Proskauer's American Jewish Committee resigned in protest and was subjected to a boycott by pro-Zionist organizations in response. Nevertheless, with periodic swings in political fortune, the alliance of American
Jewry behind the Jewish state was a presumption up until, and including, the struggle
for the establishment of the state in 1947.

37. Speech by Ben-Gurion before a special session of the National Assembly, November
30, 1942. Central Zionist Archives, J/1366.

38. Senator to Buber, January 29, 1938. Martin Buber, *The Letters of Martin Buber: A Life
of Dialogue*, Nahum N. Glatzer and Paul Mendes-Flohr, eds., Richard Winston et al.,
trans. (New York: Syracuse University Press, 1996), p. 463.

39. Even before the establishment of the league, Buber had joined forces with the "League for
Human Rights"—yet another avatar of the Peace Association, this one featuring Magnes,

Ernst Simon, and the writer Arnold Zweig—in demanding clemency for Arab terrorists and denouncing the ZO for seeking security in the Balfour Declaration instead of through "common interests" with the Arabs. See Maurice Friedman, *Martin Buber's Life and Work* (Detroit: Wayne State University Press, 1988), vol. 2, pp. 288, 294. Compare Zweig to Freud, July 16, 1938, in Ernst L. Freud, ed., *The Letters of Sigmund Freud and Arnold Zweig* (New York: Harcourt, Brace, and World, 1970), p. 165.

40. The German immigrants' party Aliyah Chadasha, one of the constituent groups of the league, had favored binationalism "in principle" from its founding in 1938, although it had also evidenced a willingness to support partition under certain conditions. Hattis, *Binational Idea*, p. 215.

41. The league also maintained active involvement with Communists, through the assistance and encouragement of Magnes, Ernst Simon, and others among the professors, whose contacts with the Communists were through their students. Shmuel Dotan, *Reds: The Communist Party in Palestine* (Kfar Saba, Israel: Shabna Hasofer, 1991), pp. 297–300, 388–390 [Hebrew].

42. Martin Buber, "They and We," *Ha'aretz,* November 16, 1939.

43. This, of course, did not mean that there would not eventually be an agreement with the Arabs. On the contrary, he told Buber: "My prognosis is that agreement will be reached, because I believe in our power, in our power which will grow." Hattis, *Binational Idea*, pp. 216–219, 221, 223–224.

44. Hattis, *Binational Idea*, pp. 224–225.

45. Report of the League's Committee on Constitutional Development in Palestine (Jerusalem, June 1941), pp. 104, 112 [Hebrew].

46. Gal, *David Ben-Gurion,* p. 173.

47. See Rafael Medoff, *Zionism and the Arabs: An American Jewish Dilemma, 1898–1948* (Westport: Praeger, 1997), pp. 96–98; Shpiro, *From Philanthropy to Activism*, pp. 91–92. On Perlmann's expulsion from Mapai, see Hattis, *Binational Idea*, pp. 102–104. As a member of the Hadassah study group in New York in 1941 and 1942, Perlmann advocated a "spiritual or cultural Zionism," which aimed only at the establishment of a "spiritual center or nucleus" that would not need "a state, an army, or political status recognized internationally." Hattis, *Binational Idea*, p. 261. Hadassah funds were also used to pay a special "informant" on Jewish-Arab affairs in Palestine: Lotta Levensohn, a former secretary of Magnes's who was the head of the English-language publicity department of the Hebrew University.

48. This was the organization's formal name in English and was reported in this manner in the foreign press. See, for example, the *New York Times,* September 5, 1942.

49. Hans Kohn, now a professor in the United States, also joined. Meir Margalit, "The Establishment of 'Ihud' and the Response of the Yishuv to the Reorganization of the Peace Association," *Zionism,* vol. 20, 1996, p. 152 [Hebrew].

50. Speech before Ihud public rally, August 11, 1942. Magnes Papers, file P3/2541. I have replaced "yishuv" with "Jewish settlement."

51. Despite the fact that Ben-Gurion had had some success with Proskauer's predecessor in attempting to swing the American Jewish Committee toward a less ascerbic line on Zionism, he nevertheless reckoned the AJC to be "a strong, anti-Zionist organization," particularly after Proskauer became its president in February 1943. Kolsky, *Jews Against Zionism*, p. 66; Margalit, "Establishment of Ihud," p. 165.

52. Arthur A. Goren, *Dissenter in Zion: From the Writings of Judah L. Magnes* (Cambridge: Harvard University Press, 1982), p. 44. On July 8, 1937, Sulzberger sent Magnes a copy of a *Times* editorial with a note saying, "I felt it was important to put across your

point of view which is now quite my own." Magnes Papers, P3/200. The *Times* correspondent in Palestine, Julius Meltzer, was similarly oriented. Margalit, "The Establishment of Ihud," p. 171.

53. The Palestinian press also reported rumors of contacts being conducted by Ihud and the British authorities. Margalit, "The Establishment of Ihud," pp. 156–157, 164, 172. Agudat Israel announced that Ihud's binationalist program was "perhaps not perfected in its specifics, but in the right direction." Margalit, "The Establishment of Ihud," p. 169. Ihud actually conducted negotiations for bringing Agudat Israel into Ihud as a constituent group. These discussions foundered not because of any difference in political outlook between the two groups but rather because Ihud insisted that its members should pay the "shekel" (a poll tax instituted by Herzl) to the ZO in order to emphasize their continuing association with the organization. Hattis, *Binational Idea*, p. 260.

54. Shpiro, *From Philanthropy to Activism*, p. 105.

55. Minutes of the Meeting of the Executive (the so-called Office Committee) of the American Emergency Committee for Zionist Affairs, September 9, 1942. Central Zionist Archives, F39/444.

56. Margalit, "The Establishment of Ihud," pp. 152, 157–160.

57. Davar, December 29, 1942. Compare Margalit, "The Establishment of Ihud," pp. 153–155.

58. Margalit, "The Establishment of Ihud," p. 152.

59. Hattis, *Binational Idea*, pp. 254–255.

60. Magnes diary, August 30, 1942. Goren, *Dissenter*, p. 382.

61. Magnes to Alexander Dushkin, January 7, 1943. Goren, *Dissenter*, p. 388.

62. "In view of the intransigence of many responsible leaders on both sides, the adjustment may have to be imposed over their opposition." Judah Magnes, "Toward Peace in Palestine," *Foreign Affairs*, January 1943, p. 241.

63. Martin Buber, "A Majority or Many? A Postscript to a Speech," *Bayot*, May 1944. Reprinted in Martin Buber, *A Land of Two Peoples: Martin Buber on Jews and Arabs*, Paul R. Mendes-Flohr, ed. (Oxford: Oxford University Press, 1983), pp. 166–168.

64. *New York Times*, December 3, 1946.

65. Magnes diary, August 30, 1942. Goren, *Dissenter*, p. 383.

66. Kohn to Sidney Wallach, September 16, 1944. This letter was read by Wallach at the first conference of the American Council for Judaism, held in Philadelphia on January 13–14, 1945. Kolsky, *Jews Against Zionism*, pp. 110–111. Magnes's approaches to Kohn are mentioned in many of his letters, including his hope that Kohn will publicly support Ihud's views. See, for example, Magnes to Setty Kuhn, May 30, 1944. Goren, *Dissenter*, pp. 403–404.

67. Hannah Arendt, "The Jewish State, Fifty Years After: Where Have Herzl's Politics Led?" *Commentary*, May 1946, pp. 1–2, 8.

68. Proskauer pointed to Ihud's program as an alternative to that of the Zionist Organization. Menahem Kaufman, *An Ambiguous Partnership: Non-Zionists and Zionists in America, 1939–1948* (Jerusalem: Magnes Press, 1991), pp. 159–166, 178–179; Kolsky, *Jews Against Zionism*, p. 66.

69. Magnes to Leon Simon, March 16, 1948. Goren, *Dissenter*, p. 468. The only Jew on the league's executive seems to have been Morris Lazaron.

70. The Pittsburgh Platform, adopted in 1885 under the leadership of Isaac Mayer Wise, declared: "We consider ourselves no longer a nation, but a religious community, and therefore expect neither a return to Palestine, nor a sacrificial worship under the sons of Aaron, nor the restoration of any of the laws concerning a Jewish state." It was officially

adopted by the Central Conference of American Rabbis (Reform) in 1889. See Monty Noam Penkower, "The Genesis of the American Council for Judaism: A Quest for Identity in World War II," *American Jewish History*, June 1998, pp. 171–172.

71. Sermon delivered by Rabbi Morris S. Lazaron before the Council of the Union of American Hebrew Congregations (Reform), January 16, 1937. Remarkably, Lazaron had been active in the Zionist Organization of America, maintaining a "cultural-Zionist" and politically anti-Zionist line that was virtually indistinguishable from that of Warburg and Magnes. Penkower, "Genesis," pp. 167–168.

72. Morris Lazaron to Paul Baerwald, July 22, 1937. A copy of this letter, proposing a clear, politically anti-Zionist policy—which would, however, support the upbuilding of Palestine as "a place of refuge"—was also sent to Felix Warburg. In it, Lazaron intimates that he had discussed such an anti-Zionist platform with Warburg a month earlier. Warburg Papers, file 343/8.

73. Sulzberger himself, in addition to carrying anti-Zionist material in the *New York Times*, also approached Eden and British Colonial Secretary Lord Cranborne with the proposal that Iraq, Syria, and Palestine be reconstituted as a single Arab state with room enough to absorb Jewish immigrants and forestall demands for Jewish sovereignty. Penkower, "Genesis," pp. 173–188.

74. Kolsky, *Jews Against Zionism*, p. 54.

75. Circular of the council issued November 20, 1947, quoted in Kolsky, *Jews Against Zionism*, p. 173.

76. Kolsky, *Jews Against Zionism*, pp. 69–70, 88.

77. Ibid., pp. 43–44, 140. H. Richard Niebuhr was open about Buber's influence on his thinking, writing, "More than any other person in the modern world, more even than Kierkegaard, Martin Buber has been for me, and for many of my companions, the prophet of the soul." Friedman, *Martin Buber's Life and Work*, vol. 3, p. 330.

78. See Lazaron to Magnes, September 7, 1942; Magnes to Lazaron, October 6, 1942. Magnes Papers, file P3/2548. Subsequent reactions when Magnes's words found their way into print did not succeed in dislodging him from these views. When colleagues proposed that he must have meant that a "few extremists" were, as he had said, "chauvinistic and narrow and terroristic," he denied this interpretation explicitly. Magnes to Alexander Dushkin, January 7, 1943. Goren, *Dissenter*, p. 387.

79. For solicitation of funds from Rosenwald, see Magnes to Rosenwald, January 22, 1947, in which Magnes points to the affinity of their views on upbuilding Palestine and Jewish religion. Magnes Papers, file P3/221(b). For Magnes's distribution of materials to Rosenwald, see Rosenwald to Magnes, April 8, 1947. For Rosenwald's reprinting of Magnes's speech, see Elmer Berger to Magnes, December 10, 1947. Magnes Papers, P3/1983. For Rosenwald's request of research assistance, see Rosenwald to Magnes, June 28, 1947. Magnes Papers, P3/221(b). For Rosenwald's assistance to Magnes's diplomacy, see below, note 120. For Sulzberger and Strauss's fund-raising efforts on behalf of Ihud, see Sulzberger to Magnes, June 6, 1946. Magnes Papers, P3/1958; a list of donors is to be found in Magnes to Leon Crystal, August 27, 1946. Magnes Papers, P3/2552.

80. At this point, the group was renamed the American Zionist Emergency Council (AZEC). Silver was technically cochairman of the council with Stephen Wise, but as the head of that body's "Office Committee" (later its Executive Committee), Silver was in practice responsible for Zionist political activity directed at the American government.

81. *New York Times*, January 12, 1946; Einstein-Buber, January 29, 1946. Einstein reiterated his belief in a binational regime under UN auspices in early 1947. Albert Einstein, "Partition or Binationalism?" *Ba'ayot*, January–February 1947, p. 20 [Hebrew].

82. Kolsky, *Jews Against Zionism*, pp. 124, 130–132.

83. Kaufman, *Ambiguous Partnership*, pp. 207, 211–212.

84. Hattis, *Binational Idea*, p. 288.

85. David Ben-Gurion, testimony before the Anglo-American Committee of Inquiry, March 11, 1946.

86. Report of the Anglo-American Commission of Inquiry, May 1, 1946.

87. Kolsky, *Jews Against Zionism*, p. 140.

88. Harry Sachar, *Israel: The Establishment of a State* (London: George Weidenfeld, 1952), p. 198.

89. Norman Rose, *Chaim Weizmann: A Biography* (New York: Viking, 1986), pp. 413–414.

90. Nahum Goldmann, *Memories: The Autobiography of Nahum Goldmann*, Helen Sebba, trans. (London: Wiedenfeld and Nicolson, 1969), p. 232; Michael Bar-Zohar, *Ben-Gurion: A Biography*, Peretz Kidron, trans. (New York: Adama Books, 1977), pp. 134–135.

91. Menahem Kaufman, *Ambiguous Partnership*, p. 227.

92. Emphasis added. Menahem Kaufman, *Ambiguous Partnership*, p. 231.

93. Truman's statement also referred to the Morrison plan, backed by Britain, which advocated a scheme of provincial autonomy that might lead ultimately to a binational state or to partition. Truman pointed out that his plan—which deferred indefinitely any Jewish state—had been strongly opposed by leading Democrats and Republicans in the United States. Truman's observation that Ben-Gurion's plan, in contrast, "would command the support of public opinion in the United States," amounted to an implicit but rather clear endorsement of the Jewish Agency's position. However, the two sentences that follow purposely blur this endorsement: "I cannot believe that the gap between the proposals [i.e., British and Jewish] which have been put forward is too great to be bridged by men of reason and goodwill. To such a solution Government could give its support." Thus, the literal meaning of Truman's words was that he would be prepared to back a compromise between Britain's position and the ZO's. But it was clear that the statement indicated a tilt in favor of the Jewish proposal, backed by American public opinion, rather than the British one, which was not. *New York Times*, October 5, 1946.

94. State Department memorandum by Gordon Merriam, Director of the division for Near Eastern Affairs. Kolsky, *Jews Against Zionism*, p. 150.

95. The claim that the Jewish underground was in large part responsible for having driven Britain out of Palestine is an old argument between the Labor movement and the Jabotinksyite groups. It is interesting to note that Magnes agreed with Menachem Begin on this point: "It is largely the Jewish terror groups which have made the people of Britain weary of their task in Palestine." Judah Magnes, "Report on Palestine: UNSCOP partition plan is opposed, binationalism urged," *New York Times*, September 28, 1947. Goren, *Dissenter*, p. 453.

96. Address before the General Assembly of the United Nations, May 8, 1947. Abba Hillel Silver, *Vision and Victory: A Collection of Addresses by Dr. Abba Hillel Silver, 1942–1948* (New York, Zionist Organization of America, 1949), pp. 124–133.

97. Martin Buber et al., eds., *Towards Union in Palestine* (Jerusalem: Union Association, 1947).

98. Kaufman, *Ambiguous Partnership*, pp. 254–255.

99. Bentwich, *For Zion's Sake: A Biography of Judah L. Magnes* (Philadelphia: Jewish Publication Society, 1954), p. 267. I have replaced the word "Jews" with "Jewish people" in order to avoid the grammatical error in Bentwich's text.

100. *The Jewish Plan for Palestine: Memoranda and Statements Presented by the Jewish Agency for Palestine to the United Nations Special Committee on Palestine* (Jerusalem: The Jewish Agency for Palestine, 1947), p. 325.

101. Australia abstained.

102. Report of the Preparatory Commission of the United Nations, 1945, Rule 69.

103. Address before the UN Ad Hoc Committee on Palestine, October 18, 1947.

104. Kaufman, *Ambiguous Partnership*, pp. 259–273.

105. Address opening the Hebrew University academic year, October 29, 1947. Magnes Papers, file P3/2114.

106. There were ten abstentions.

107. See, for example, the Agudat Israel youth publication *Digleinu*, March 1948 [Hebrew]. The articles in this issue deal in various ways with Haredi recruits in the Jewish armed forces. See also Menachem Friedman, "The Structural Foundation for Religio-Political Accommodation in Israel: Fallacy and Reality," in *Israel: The First Decade of Independence*, S. Ilan Troen and Noah Lucas, eds. (Albany: State University of New York Press, 1995), pp. 67–69.

108. Hannah Arendt, "To Save the Jewish Homeland: There Is Still Time," *Commentary*, May 1948, pp. 398–406. I have replaced "Shertok" with "Sharett."

109. Magnes tendered his assistance in gaining prestige for the group by writing a letter in support of it, which was dutifully published by the *New York Times*. Goren, *Dissenter*, p. 473 n. 5.

110. See Zvi Ganin, *Truman, American Jewry and Israel, 1945–1948* (New York: Holmes and Meier Pub., 1979), pp. 167–168. For a less complimentary portrayal of Truman, see Michael J. Cohen, *Truman and Israel* (Berkeley: University of California Press, 1990), pp. 173–198.

111. *Foreign Relations of the United States, 1948* (Washington: Government Printing Office, 1976), vol. 5, p. 743.

112. Ganin, *Truman*, p. 161. Compare notes taken by Truman's press secretary, Charles G. Ross, in a meeting ten days later, which clearly depict the president's humiliation over the policy reversal and his political sense that truth could not be made public. Ganin, *Truman*, pp. 162–163.

113. Kaufman, *Ambiguous Partnership*, p. 305.

114. Silver, *Vision and Victory*, p. 180.

115. *New York Times*, April 5, 1948; Kaufman, *Ambiguous Partnership*, pp. 323–326, 353.

116. See Magnes to Thomas Mann, April 12, 1948. Goren, *Dissenter*, p. 480.

117. Bentwich, *For Zion's Sake*, p. 270.

118. Kolsky, *Jews Against Zionism*, p. 185.

119. Hannah Arendt, "To Save the Jewish Homeland," pp. 398–406.

120. Bentwich, *For Zion's Sake*, p. 271. Magnes conceived of the UN Trusteeship that would be imposed as being of "indefinite duration," ending only when "the Arab and Jewish communities of Palestine agree on the future government of their country." Magnes to Thomas Wasson, April 6, 1948. Goren, *Dissenter*, p. 475.

121. In addition to Lessing Rosenwald, the group of Magnes's friends who brought him to the United States in 1948 included anti-Zionist figures such as Admiral Lewis Strauss and Judge Jerome Frank, both of whom had been prominent members of Rosenwald's organization. As the American Council for Judaism's director, Rabbi Elmer Berger, later recalled Magnes's assistance to the anti-Zionist effort during this period: "We were on common ground . . . in our total and complete abhorrence of Zionism as it had come to be in Palestine. . . . Magnes . . . could, with greater authority than we American anti-Zionists, name the Palestinian Zionist leadership for what it was: Brutal, power-mad,

militaristic." Elmer Berger, *Memoirs of an Anti-Zionist Jew* (Beirut: Institute for Palestine Studies, 1978), p. 25. The feeling was, it seems, mutual. To Werner Senator, Magnes wrote bitterly of the weakness and ineffectualness of opponents of the Jewish state in America: "The one person who seems to have any courage at all is Lessing Rosenwald." Magnes to Senator, February 18, 1947. Goren, *Dissenter*, p. 450.

122. Magnes diary, May 5, 1948. Goren, *Dissenter*, p. 493. According to the minutes of the meeting approved by Marshall, Magnes demanded that the United States cut off donations of the UJA, which were going to help Jewish forces. Kaufman, *Ambiguous Partnership*, p. 351.

123. Meir Avizohar and Avi Bareli, eds., *Now or Never: Proceedings of Mapai (The Labour Party of Eretz-Israel) in the Closing Year of the British Mandate, Introductions and Documents* (Kfar Saba: Bet Berl, 1989), pp. 481, 508 [Hebrew].

124. On March 1, 1948, a new National Assembly—which bore the name *moetzet ha'am*, the "People's Council"—was appointed by the Jewish Agency Executive and the Executive of the old National Assembly. This body consisted of 37 members, representing all Jewish political parties in Palestine. An executive committee, consisting of 13 members, was called *minhelet ha'am*, the "People's Executive." After the declaration of independence on May 14, the former body assumed the authority of a provisional legislature and the latter that of a provisional government.

125. Avizohar, *Now or Never*, p. 480.

126. As Shertok, famed for his moderate political approach and temperate personality, told the Mapai Central Committee, "The risk involved in delaying the declaration of the state . . . is worse than the risk in taking this step. . . . It seems that we have no choice, and we must go forward." Avizohar, *Now or Never*, p. 484.

127. Ibid., p. 483.

Chapter Eleven

1. On March 1, 1948, a new National Assembly—which bore the name *moetzet ha'am*, the "People's Council"—was appointed by the Jewish Agency Executive and the Executive of the old National Assembly. This body consisted of 37 members, representing all Jewish political parties in Palestine. An executive committee, consisting of 13 members, was called *minhelet ha'am*, the "People's Executive." After the declaration of independence on May 14, the former body assumed the authority of a provisional legislature and the latter that of a provisional government.

2. Particularly striking was the speech of Meir Wilner, representative of the Communist party, who said, "All of us are united in our appreciation of this great day for the Jewish settlement and for the Jewish people—the day of the termination of the Mandate and the declaration of the independent Jewish state." Minutes of the National Assembly and the Temporary State Assembly (Jerusalem: The State of Israel, 1948), vol. 1, p. 13 [Hebrew].

3. Eli Shaltiel, ed., *Ben-Gurion, The First Prime Minister: Selected Documents (1847–1963)* (Jerusalem: Israel State Archives, 1996), pp. 27–28 [Hebrew].

4. Declaration of the Establishment of the State of Israel, May 14, 1948. See Appendix.

5. This was the original text signed by Truman before the arrival of the official announcement from Israel. The revised text read: "The Government has been informed that a Jewish state has been proclaimed in Palestine, and recognition has been requested by the provisional Government thereof. The United States recognizes the provisional government as the de facto authority of the State of Israel." Shaltiel, *Ben-Gurion: Selected Documents*, p. 31.

6. Ben-Gurion's address aimed directly at connecting the struggle of the Jews in Palestine for national independence with the struggle of their ancestors in the lands of the dispersion: "We have achieved what has been achieved because we have received and kept guard over a precious heritage, the heritage of a small nation, which has suffered and been tried much, but which is great and eternal in its spirit, its vision, its faith, and the unique traits of its soul." Shaltiel, *Ben-Gurion: Selected Documents*, p. 30.

7. Ben-Gurion's "Farewell Address" to the Knesset, October 25, 1971. Compare English translation in *Azure* 6 (Winter 1999), p. 250.

8. The right of citizenship for all Jewish immigrants returning under the Law of Return is recognized in the Nationality Law (1952). Herzl's intention to take all Jews without exception appears repeatedly in his diaries. See, for example, June 7, 8, and 13, 1895, in Theodor Herzl, *The Complete Diaries of Theodor Herzl*, Raphael Patai, ed., Harry Zohn, trans. (New York: Herzl Press, 1960), pp. 38, 44, 135.

9. Justice Simon Agranat in *George Rafael Tamarin v. State of Israel*, January 20, 1972, in *Decisions of the Supreme Court of Israel* (Jerusalem: Supreme Court, 1972), vol. 26, pt. 1, p. 197 [Hebrew].

10. Numbers 15:38.

11. Non-Jews, however, may have their own days of rest in accordance with Christian or Muslim practice. David Kretzmer, *The Legal Status of the Arabs in Israel* (Boulder: Westview Press, 1990), p. 21 n. 32.

12. The Interpretation Law (1981) explicitly states that the binding version of any law is the language in which it is written—that is, Hebrew. Kretzmer, *Legal Status*, p. 165.

13. *Tzvi Ziv v. Yehoshua Gubernik*, November 23–24, December 2, 1948, in *Decisions of the Supreme Court of Israel* (Jerusalem: Justice Ministry, 1948), vol. 1, p. 85 [Hebrew].

14. In addition to these primary Jewish-national values, the law also mentions other Labor Zionist concerns such as education in agriculture and industrial craft and "pioneering education," before it finally lists more universal values such as freedom, equality, and tolerance.

15. Ben-Gurion's "Farewell Address" to the Knesset, October 25, 1971. Compare English translation in *Azure* 6 (Winter 1999), pp. 250–251.

16. *Jerusalem Post*, February 24, 1958; *Ha'aretz*, February 16–18, 1958. Interestingly, familiarity with the basics of Jewish national history was also a requirement in Arab schools, where it was presumed to be part of the cultural literacy needed to take part in the life of the Jewish state. Baruch and Joel Migdal, *Palestinians: The Making of a People* (Cambridge: Harvard University Press, 1933), p. 169.

17. Michael Keren, *Ben-Gurion and the Intellectuals: Power, Knowledge, and Charisma* (Dekalb: Northern Illinois University Press, 1983), pp. 100–108.

18. Kretzmer, *Legal Status*, p. 19.

19. Emphasis mine. Ben-Gurion to Joseph Proskauer, July 18, 1960. Quoted in Tom Segev, *The Seventh Million: The Israelis and the Holocaust*, Haim Watzman, trans. (New York: Hill and Wang, 1993), p. 330.

20. *Laws of the State of Israel* (Jerusalem: Government Printer, 1950), vol. 4, p. 154 [Hebrew].

21. See Michael Bar-Zohar, *The Day of Vengeance: The Story of Jewish Vengeance Against the Nazis* (Tel Aviv: Tefer, 1991), pp. 163–164, 279–280 [Hebrew].

22. Neimah Barzel, "Israel-German Relations," in Tzvi Tzameret and Hannah Yablonka, eds., *The First Decade, 1948–1958* (Jerusalem: Yad Yitzhak Ben-Tzvi, 1997), p. 202 [Hebrew].

23. *Laws of the State of Israel* (Jerusalem: Government Printing Office, 1958), vol. 13, p. 120 [Hebrew].

24. Ibid., vol. 7, p. 3.

25. As described in the Israeli government's 1953–1954 yearbook, "the new law established the bond between the State of Israel and the entire Jewish people." *Israel Government Book, 1953–1954* (Government Printing Office, November 1953), p. 57 [Hebrew].

26. Kretzmer, *Legal Status*, p. 94. A "covenant" was later signed between the State of Israel and the Zionist Organization on July 26, 1954. See Meron Madzini, *Collection of Documents on the History of the State* (Jerusalem: Ministry of Defense, 1981), pp. 135–137 [Hebrew].

27. Jeffrey Weiss and Craig Weiss, *I Am My Brother's Keeper: American Volunteers in Israel's War of Independence, 1947–1949* (Atglen, Pa.: Schiffer Military History, 1998).

28. IDF educational programs aimed at fostering Jewish identity were shaped by explicit guidelines from Ben-Gurion himself. See Anita Shapira, "Ben-Gurion and the Bible: The Forging of an Historical Narrative?" *Middle Eastern Studies*, October 1997, pp. 653–654. See also Tzvi Hauser, "The Spirit of the IDF," *Azure* 2 (Spring 1997), p. 55.

29. David Ben-Gurion, *The Sinai Campaign* (Tel Aviv: Am Oved, 1960), p. 44 [Hebrew].

30. David Ben-Gurion, "Zionism and Pseudo-Zionism," in Proceedings of the Jerusalem Ideological Conference, published in *Forum* 4 (Spring 1959), pp. 148–154.

31. Buber, "Zionism and 'Zionism,'" *Ba'ayot Hazman*, May 27, 1948 [Hebrew].

32. Buber, "Let Us Make an End to Falsities!" *Ba'ayot Hazman*, November 1, 1948, in Martin Buber, *A Land of Two Peoples: Martin Buber on Jews and Arabs*, Paul R. Mendes-Flohr, ed. (Oxford: Oxford University Press, 1983), pp. 226–228.

33. Maurice Friedman, *Martin Buber's Life and Work* (Detroit: Wayne State University Press, 1988), vol. 3, p. 32.

34. The most detailed exposition of this proposal is found in Judah Magnes, "For a Jewish-Arab Confederation," *Commentary*, October 1948, pp. 379–383.

35. See minutes of the first meeting in New York, April 26, 1948, in Arthur A. Goren, *Dissenter in Zion: From the Writings of Judah L. Magnes* (Cambridge: Harvard University Press, 1982), p. 482f.; Magnes to Robert McClintock, June 14, 1948, in Goren, *Dissenter*, p. 501. Magnes defended the inclusion of anti-Zionists such as Lessing Rosenwald in the group, arguing that "Lessing has been the one man in the country who has had the courage to buck the terror of the Zionist political machine." Magnes to James Marshall, September 11, 1948. Goren, *Dissenter*, p. 510.

36. Hannah Arendt, "Warning from America," *Ba'ayot Hazman*, August 13, 1948 [Hebrew]. This article reproduced parts of Arendt's May 1948 article in *Commentary*.

37. Minutes of the Aliya Hadasha executive, January 1, 1948, in Segev, *Seventh Million*, p. 62.

38. Unpublished speech before Ihud, Spring 1949, in Buber, *Two Peoples*, pp. 245, 249–251.

39. Martin Plessner, "The Periodical and Its Circle" in *Ner*, February 1950, pp. 1–3 [Hebrew].

40. Reading Buber's article in the inaugural issue of *Ner*, one cannot help being astonished at his apparent about-face regarding Jewish national "independence and self-determination," for which, he says, the Jewish people longed for two thousand years. See Martin Buber, "The Children of Amos," in February 1950, translated to English in Buber, *Two Peoples*, pp. 255–257. But as Buber makes clear in subsequent articles, the "independence" that he now touts is not sovereignty but rather autonomy within a Near Eastern Federation modeled on Switzerland. See note 45 below. On Buber's "heavy heart," see Akiva Ernst Simon, "Buber's Legacy for Peace," *New Outlook*, October–November 1966, p. 21.

41. Martin Buber, "We Need the Arabs, They Need Us!," January 21, 1954, in Buber, *Two Peoples,* p. 267; Buber, "Instead of Polemics," *Ner*, September–November, 1956. Translated into English in Buber, *Two Peoples*, p. 271.

42. Anita Shapira, "The Labor Movement and the Hebrew University," in Shaul Katz and Michael Heyd, eds., *The History of the Hebrew University in Jerusalem: Origins and Beginnings* (Jerusalem: Magnes Press), p. 688 [Hebrew]; Tzvi Tzameret, "Ben-Gurion and Lavon: Two Standpoints on Absorption During the Great Wave of Immigration," in Dalia Ofer, ed., *Israel in the Great Wave of Immigration, 1948–1953* (Jerusalem: Yad Yizhak Ben-Tzvi, 1996), pp. 78–80 [Hebrew].

43. Buber, *Two Peoples*, pp. 279, 287, 295.

44. Speech before the members of Ihud, Spring 1949, in Buber, *Two Peoples*, p. 251. I have replaced the word "caryatid" in Mendes-Flohr's translation with the word "column."

45. On federation with the Arabs, see Martin Buber, "Old Zionism and Modern Israel," *Jewish Newsletter*, June 2, 1958; see also Martin Buber, "The Time to Try," *New Outlook*, January–February 1965, reproduced in Buber, *Two Peoples*, p. 305. On Jerusalem, see Friedman, *Martin Buber's Life and Work*, vol. 3, p. 334.

46. Friedman, *Martin Buber's Life and Work,* vol. 2, p. 334.

47. "The Kfar 'Ara Affair," *Ner*, October 1952, p. 8 [Hebrew].

48. Yehoshua Hatalmi (Benjamin Radler-Feldman), "Mr. Ben-Gurion: Will You Really Not Respond?" *Ner*, May 1955, pp. 5–6 [Hebrew].

49. Moshe Negbi, *Freedom of the Press in Israel* (Jerusalem: Jerusalem Foundation for Research on Israel, 1995), pp. 40–47 [Hebrew]. During the 1950s, there were examples of decisions to censor that were made by Ben-Gurion and Moshe Sharett themselves.

50. Yehoshua Hatalmi (Benjamin Radler-Feldman), "I Saw a Small Country and the Corruption There Was Great," *Ner*, June 1951, p. 10 [Hebrew]; Yehoshua Hatalmi (Benjamin Radler-Feldman), "The Danger Is—David Ben-Gurion," *Ner*, June 1955, pp. 3–5 [Hebrew].

51. *Ner*, June–July, 1956, p. 31 [Hebrew].

52. Hatalmi, "Danger," pp. 3–5.

53. Michael B. Oren, *The Origins of the Second Arab-Israeli War: Egypt, Israel and the Great Powers, 1952–1956* (London: Frank Cass, 1992), p. 145.

54. Nurit Gertz, *Amos Oz: A Monograph* (Tel Aviv: Sifriyat Poalim, 1980), p. 22 [Hebrew]; Michael Bar-Zohar, *Ben-Gurion* (Tel Aviv: Am Oved, 1977), p. 1276 [Hebrew]; Ben-Gurion, *The Sinai Campaign*, p. 241.

55. Gertz, *Amos Oz*, pp. 11–12; resolution of the Ihud council, quoted in *Ner*, November–December 1956, p. 38 [Hebrew].

56. Martin Buber, "Israel's Mission and Zion," in Martin Buber, *Israel and the World: Essays in a Time of Crisis* (New York: Schocken Books, 1963), p. 261.

57. Friedman, *Martin Buber's Life and Work*, vol. 3, pp. 236, 446.

58. William Zukerman, "The Menace of Jewish Fascism," *Nation*, April 25, 1934.

59. Martin Buber, "Old Zionism and Modern Israel," *Jewish Newsletter*, June 2, 1958. The *Jewish Newsletter* carried on its masthead the names of such well-known anti-Zionist Jews as Fromm and the leader of the American Council for Judaism, Rabbi Morris Lazaron. After protest both in Israel and the United States, Buber reread the article in the *Newsletter* and concluded that the text was "somewhat misleading"—although he also conceded that this was "my own fault," apparently because he had personally approved it. Buber's notes, prepared before the talk, are worded in a less noxious fashion, but their meaning is not much different: "In the days of Hitler the majority of the Jewish people saw that millions of Jews had been killed with impunity, and a certain part made their own doctrine that history does not go the way of the spirit but the way

of power." Friedman, *Martin Buber's Life and Work*, vol. 3, p. 237. The key passages from Buber's article in *The Jewish Newsletter* were reprinted in Israel two weeks after they appeared in the United States, but it was not until July 20 that Buber issued a clarifying statement in *Ha'aretz*. In this statement, Buber did not retract his article in *The Jewish Newsletter*, and in fact did not even admit that he had published it. Instead he claimed to have been misquoted in the Israeli papers. His version in the Israeli press was identical to the version to be found in his notes from before the lecture. See H. Yustus, "The Professor from Jerusalem Encourages Haters of Israel," *Ma'ariv*, June 17, 1958; Y. Eisenberg, "The Jews Learned from Hitler," *Haboker*, June 4, 1958; Martin Buber, "Things as They Were," *Ha'aretz*, July 20, 1958. A revised version of the article appears in Buber, *Two Peoples*, pp. 289–293; Buber, *Israel and the World*, pp. 253–257.

60. Isser Harel, *The House on Garibaldi Street* (New York: Viking Press, 1975), pp. 156–157.

61. Howard M. Sachar, *A History of Israel: From the Rise of Zionism to Our Time* (New York: Knopf, 1996), p. 558.

62. Friedman, *Martin Buber's Life and Work*, vol. 3, pp. 110, 307.

63. Buber et al., to Yitzhak Ben-Tzvi, May 30, 1962. Buber Archive, ms. var. 350/88d/3h; Friedman, *Martin Buber's Life and Work*, vol. 3, pp. 356, 358–359.

64. I Samuel 15:33; Segev, *Seventh Million*, p. 365.

65. Friedman, *Martin Buber's Life and Work*, vol. 3, p. 363.

Chapter Twelve

1. Baruch Litvin to Buber, May 2, 1951, in Martin Buber, *The Letters of Martin Buber: A Life of Dialogue*, Nahum Glatzer and Paul Mendes-Flohr, eds., Richard Winston et al., trans. (New York: Syracuse University Press, 1996), p. 560. Compare Buber's disciple Hermann Gerson, who wrote to Buber in 1934 that the Labor Zionist public in general harbored "an enormous, constantly noticeable prejudice against you in particular." Gerson to Buber, July 24, 1934. Buber, *Letters*, pp. 419–420.

2. The decision to award Buber the honorary doctorate was made by the Senate and confirmed by the Board of Governors. *Ha'aretz*, March 26, 1953.

3. Maurice Friedman, *Martin Buber's Life and Work* (Detroit: Wayne State University Press, 1988), vol. 3, pp. 397–398.

4. See the memoirs of Nahum Glatzer, who was Buber's student and colleague at the Freies Juedisches Lehrhaus. Glatzer says he "never forgot" the moral callousness that "the man of *I and Thou*" displayed toward him when his father was murdered in Jerusalem. He also goes out of his way to describe the manner in which Buber tried to cheat Rosenzweig, after the latter's death, of credit for the work he did with Buber on their joint translation of the Bible. Nahum Glatzer, *The Memoirs of Nahum N. Glatzer*, Michael Fishbane and Judith Glatzer Wechsler, eds. (Cincinnati: Hebrew Union College Press, 1997), pp. 86, 91.

5. Gershom Scholem, "Martin Buber's Interpretation of Hasidism," in Gershom Scholem, *The Messianic Idea in Judaism and Other Essays on Jewish Spirituality* (New York: Schocken, 1971), p. 229.

6. All of these professors were teaching in 1948. See *The Hebrew University, Jerusalem: Its History and Development*, foreword by Leon Simon (Jerusalem: Azriel Printing Works, 1948).

7. Magnes to Leon Simon, March 16, 1948. Goren, *Dissenter*, p. 472. Compare Magnes's claim to have become "for professors and assistants, academic staff and workers, the

ruhende Pol [i.e., axis] spiritually both in large problems and in small." Magnes diary, March 23, 1932. Goren, *Dissenter*, p. 291.

8. This was proposed by Magnes's administrator, Werner Senator. Interview of Benjamin Mazar, October 23, 1983, Oral History Division Archives, (117) 24. After the founding of the state, it seems that Ben-Gurion did what he could to marginalize the professors and the Hebrew University. See Anita Shapira, "The Labor Movement and the Hebrew University," p. 687.

9. According to Bernard Cherrick, at the time director of the Hebrew University's Department of Organization and Information, Ben-Tzvi broke the ice with the government by inviting Mazar to join him for some of his regular, weekly luncheons with Ben-Gurion. Interview of Bernard Cherrick, August 21, 1983, Oral History Division Archives (117) 14. See also Ben-Gurion's requests after independence for Selig Brodetsky to come to Israel and "take on" the Hebrew University. Selig Brodetsky, *Memoirs: From Ghetto to Israel* (London: Weidenfeld and Nicolson, 1960), pp. 286, 295.

10. *Ha'aretz*, March 24, 25, 27, 1953; Y. Shochman, "The Hebrew University's Other Front," *Davar*, March 29, 1953. No direct evidence of the Labor party's direct involvement in Mazar's appointment and the subsequent drastic changes at the university has yet come to light. But a suggestive letter from Minister of Education Ben-Zion Dinur to Prime Minister Ben-Gurion asks the prime minister to consider "what I told you in person concerning the urgent need to make order in matters of the University at the earliest possible opportunity." First among the matters Dinur lists is "the presidency of the University." Other subjects include funding and land for a new campus. Dinur to Ben-Gurion, July 20, 1952. Prime Minister's Archives, File 17/16/1/0-460.

11. Interview of Benjamin Mazar, October 23, 1983, Oral History Division Archives (117) 24; interview of Benjamin Mazar, July 13, 1990, Oral History Division Archives (174) 1. See Eli Ayal, "Professor Mazar's Nine Years," *Ha'aretz*, March 23, 1961.

12. See Gershom Scholem, "Martin Buber's Interpretation of Hasidism," in Scholem, *Messianic Idea*, pp. 227–250; David Biale, *Gershom Scholem: Kabbalah and Counter-History* (Cambridge: Harvard, 1982), p. 91.

13. Gershom Scholem, *Major Trends in Jewish Mysticism* (New York: Schocken, 1946), p. 329.

14. Gershom Scholem, "The Neutralization of the Messianic Element in Early Hasidism," in Scholem, *Messianic Idea*, pp. 180, 200–202; Scholem, *Major Trends*, p. 336. See also Scholem, *Major Trends*, pp. 341, 346.

15. Arie Morgenstern, *Mysticism and Messianism* (Jerusalem: Maor Press, 1999), pp. 180–208 [Hebrew]; Mor Altshuler, *The Messianic Root of Hasidism* (Haifa: Haifa University, forthcoming) [Hebrew].

16. For if Hasidism recognized that—as Buber wrote—"all mankind is accorded co-working power, all time is directly redemptive, all action for the sake of God may be called Messianic action," then Shabtai Tzvi's heresy was none other than his "differentiation of one man from other men, of one time from other times, of one act from other actions." One only had to ask whether a given leader or his movement was engaging in "differentiating" a particular man, or a particular set of actions, as uniquely capable of bringing redemption to the Jews. Martin Buber, *The Origin and Meaning of Hasidism*, Maurice Friedman, ed. and trans. (Atlantic Highlands, N.J.: Humanities Press, 1988), p. 111.

17. It is important to note that while Buber was clear in his view of what constituted "true" Judaism and "false" Judaism, Scholem's evaluations were hardly ever couched in such terms. In fact, it is unclear whether Scholem believed that anything could be a funda-

mental deviation from Judaism at all. Nevertheless, Scholem did not refrain from using adjectives, and from his descriptions of apocalyptic Messianic movements, it is evident that he found them destructive, as Buber did.

18. Martin Buber, *Israel and the World: Essays in a Time of Crisis* (New York: Schocken, 1963), p. 261; Buber, *The Origin and Meaning of Hasidism*, p. 218.

19. Gershom Scholem, "On the Three Crimes of the Peace Association," *Davar*, December 12, 1929, in Gershom Scholem, *Od Davar: Writings on Heritage and Restoration* (Tel Aviv: Am Oved, 1992), vol. 2, pp. 88–89. Similarly, see Gershom Scholem, "The Theology of Sabbateanism in the Light of Abraham Cardosos," *Judaica* 1 (Frankfurt am Main: Suhrkamp Verlag, 1963), p. 146 [German]. Quoted in Biale, *Gershom Scholem*, pp. 96–97. On Scholem's refusal to bring Jewish religious attachment to the Western Wall into political discourse, see Biale, *Gershom Scholem*, p. 102.

20. Scholem, *From Berlin to Jerusalem: Memories of My Youth*, Harry Zohn, trans. (New York: Schocken, 1980), p. 68.

21. Interview of Joshua Prawer, January 25, 1984. Oral History Division Archives (117) 34, tape 26a, p. 10.

22. Richard Koebner, "Apolitical Reflections on Our Political Problems," *Ba'ayot*, December 1944, pp. 8–13 [Hebrew]. Koebner had been active in radical politics almost since arriving in Palestine in 1934, taking part in activities sponsored (apparently without his knowledge) by student members of the Communist party, along with Hebrew University professors such as Ernst Simon, Hugo Bergmann, and David Yellin. See Shmuel Dotan, "The Beginnings of Jewish Nationalist Communism in Palestine," in Daniel Karpi, ed., *Zionism: An Anthology on the History of the Zionist Movement and the Jewish Settlement in Palestine*, vol. 2, pp. 217–218, esp. n. 20 [Hebrew].

23. Richard Koebner, "Ireland: The False Analogy," in M. Buber, J. L. Magnes, E. Simon, eds., *Towards Union in Palestine: Essays on Zionism and Jewish-Arab Cooperation* (Jerusalem: Ihud, 1947), pp. 48–49. The Hebrew version was originally published in December 1945.

24. See, for example, Hugo Bergmann, "On the Majority Problem," *Sheifoteinu* 3 (1929), pp. 24–29 [Hebrew].

25. Bergmann interviewed by Ehud Ben-Ezer, May 1966, in Ehud Ben-Ezer, *Unease in Zion* (Jerusalem: Jerusalem Academic Press, 1974), p. 93.

26. Ernst Simon, "Against the Sadducees," *Sheifoteinu* 6 (July 1932), pp. 160–162 [Hebrew]. Simon's views remained essentially unchanged through the 1960s. See, for example, Ernst Simon, "Buber or Ben-Gurion," *New Outlook*, February 1966, pp. 9–17.

27. Yeshayahu Leibowitz, "After Kibya," in Yishayahn Leibowitz, *Tora and Commandments in Our Day* (Tel Aviv: Masada, 1954), p. 169 [Hebrew].

28. Leibowitz interviewed by Ehud Ben-Ezer, April 1970, in Ben-Ezer, *Unease*, p. 198; Yeshayahu Leibowitz, "War and Heroism in Israel, Past and Present," in Yeshayahu Leibowitz, *Belief, History, and Values* (Jerusalem: Hebrew University Student Union, 1982), pp. 176–178.

29. Joseph Klausner, *The History of the Second Temple* (Jerusalem: Ahiasaf Publishing House, 1968), vol. 3, pp. 122–123, 126, 132, 136 [Hebrew]; Magnes once told Klausner that if he had lived in the days of the Pharisees, he would have joined them in assisting to destroy the Hasmonean kingdom. Yosef Klausner, *My Journey Towards Restoration and Redemption* (Tel-Aviv: Masada, 1955), vol. 2, p. 167 [Hebrew].

30. Klausner, *My Journey*, vol. 2, pp. 85–92, 199–200, 263.

31. Interview of Joshua Prawer, November 13, 1983. Oral History Division Archives (117) 34, tape 26, p. 6.

32. Hashomer Hatzair began debating binationalism in 1927. This position was embraced by the head of the movement, Meir Ya'ari, in 1930, and was formally adopted by the movement as a whole in 1933. Levi Dror and Israel Rosenzweig, eds., *The Book of Hashomer Hatzair* (Merhavia: Sifriat Poalim, 1956), vol. 1, p. 186 [Hebrew].

33. On Lavon's early binationalism, see Eyal Kafkafi, *Lavon: Anti-Messiah* (Tel-Aviv: Am Oved, 1998), p. 18, 26 [Hebrew].

34. All of Prawer's professors spoke German among themselves. Prawer, interviewed on November 13, 1983. Oral History Division Archives (117) 34, tape 26, p. 9.

35. Prawer, tape 26, p. 20.

36. Prawer, tape 26, p. 22; tape 26a, pp. 21–22.

37. Nathan Rotenstreich, interviewed on November 2, 1983. Oral History Division Archives (117) 30, tape 22, p. 19; Prawer, tape 26a, p. 15.

38. Rotenstreich, tape 22, pp. 19, 23, 28.

39. Natan Rotenstreich, *Spirit and Man: An Essay on Being and Value* (The Hague: Martinus Nijhoff, 1963), pp. 235–252. The quote is on p. 242.

40. Natan Rotenstreich, "An Awareness of a Need for a Homeland," and the subsequent correspondence between Ben-Gurion and Rotenstreich on the subject, reprinted in *Hazut* 3, July 1957, pp. 12–29 [Hebrew]. In general, Rotenstreich's philosophy demanded that politics be understood as within its proper sphere only when it is engaged in the "establishing circumstances in which man will be able to cultivate values and create them." Politics "oversteps its boundaries" when it becomes involved in the creation of values or their cultivation. See Natan Rotenstreich, *On the Human Subject: Studies in the Phenomenoloy of Ethics and Politics* (Springfield, Ill.: Charles C. Thomas, 1966), pp. 161–166. This view is similar to that of Talmon and is a secularized recapitulation of Scholem's theory of the "neutralization" of the Messianic by Hasidism. See discussion of Talmon's *Origins of Totalitarian Democracy* below in Chapter 12.

41. *Ma'ariv*, January 12, 1961; *Lamerhav*, February 20, 1961. See discussion in Chapter 13.

42. For example, Jamal Husseini in conversation with Joseph Klausner. Quoted in Susan Lee Hattis, *The Binational Idea in Palestine During Mandatory Times* (Haifa: Shikmona Publishing, 1970), p. 240.

43. Ironically, Prawer reports that he was actually more interested in studying the Second Temple Period, but that as the university would not permit Klausner to instruct him, he ended up searching for a different topic. Transcribed interview with Nana Sagi, October 1989, pp. 11–12. Oral History Division Archives (214) 3.

44. Interview with Joshua Prawer in *Scopus*, Summer 1989, p. 20.

45. Joshua Prawer, "Colonization Activities in the Latin Kingdom of Jerusalem," *Revue Belge de Philologie et d'Histoire*, Winter 1951, pp. 1064–1065.

46. The famed lectern was destroyed in 1969. Meron Benvenisti, *Conflicts and Contradictions* (New York: Villard Books, 1986), pp. 98–99.

47. For Benvenisti's binationalism, see "Who's Afraid of a Binational State?" *Ha'aretz*, August 16, 1996.

48. J. L. Talmon, *The Origins of Totalitarian Democracy* (New York: Norton, 1970), p. vii. For Buber's ideas on the "secular messianism" of Hegel and Marx, see Martin Buber, *The Problem of Man* (Tel Aviv: Mahbarot Lesafrut, 1943), pp. 37–38 [Hebrew]. For the likely influence of this on Talmon's similar concept of "political messianism" in European thought, see Avraham Shapira, "Political Messianism and Its Place in Martin Buber's Conception of the Redemption," in *Lectures in Memory of Martin Buber* (Jerusalem: National Academy of Science, 1985), p. 60 [Hebrew]. Compare Talmon's Hebrew edition, in which it is Koebner, and not Buber, who is credited with being the

inspiration for the book. Talmon, *The Origins of Totalitarian Democracy* (Tel Aviv: Dvir, 1954), n.p. [Hebrew].

49. Talmon, *Totalitarian Democracy*, p. 1.

50. Ibid., pp. 1–2.

51. Talmon declines to hazard an opinion on whether liberal democracy has any clear "final aims," but he does concede that if there are any such aims, they are not of a "concrete character." Talmon, *Totalitarian Democracy*, pp. 2, 118.

52. "Liberal democracy flinched from the specter of force. . . . Totalitarian Messianism hardened into an exclusive doctrine represented by a vanguard of the enlightened, who justified themselves in the use of coercion against those who refused to be free and virtuous." Talmon, *Totalitarian Democracy*, p. 5.

53. Ibid., p. 253.

54. For an explicit application of Talmon's concept of political messianism to the case of Zionism, see Israel Kolatt, "Zionism and Political Messianism," in *Totalitarian Democracy and After: International Colloquium in Memory of Jacob L. Talmon* (Jerusalem: The Israel Academy of Sciences and Humanities, 1984), pp. 342–353.

55. The power of Talmon's work lay not only in its political philosophy but in its ability to transform the terror of the French Revolution, a century and a half past, into "the most vital issue of our time"—through its shocking portrayal of Robespierre and his cronies in terms that Israeli readers could easily recognize from experience. The totalitarian-Messianic leadership, wrote Talmon, was possessed of "a most intense and mystical sense of mission"; "not satisfied with acquiescence . . . it wanted to exact living, active communion with the absolute purpose"; "it is the psychology of the neurotic egotist, who must impose his will—rationalized into divine truth—or wallow in an ecstasy of self-pity"; "this is a self-righteous mentality which is quite incapable of criticism, divides reality into watertight compartments and adopts contradictory attitudes to the same thing, making judgment wholly dependent on whether it is 'me,' by definition representing truth and right, or the opponent who is associated with it"; "with the personal misery and the passionate dedication to an ideal there went a passion for self-dramatization, a deliberate acting for history, that cannot fail to evoke a feeling of revulsion"; and so on. Talmon, *Totalitarian Democracy*, pp. 81, 83, 172. All of these descriptions refer to Robespierre, except for the last, which describes the later revolutionary leader, François-Noel (Gracchus) Babeuf.

56. David Ben-Gurion, "In Defense of Messianism," *Midstream* 12 (March 1966), p. 68. Ben-Gurion's frequent defense of the "Messianic faith" at this time was a consequence of his search for a more ecumenical term he could use in place of the European-sounding expression "Zionist faith," which he feared would have little meaning for Jewish immigrants arriving from the Arab countries. Thus, he wrote that "the Jews of Eastern Europe and their way of thinking . . . no longer exist . . . The Jews of Yemen, Morocco, and Iraq—immigrated to Israel as a result of their consciousness of history and their Messianic vision, and not as a result of 'Zionist' ideology." Ben-Gurion to Natan Rotenstreich, January 9, 1957, reprinted in *Hazut* 3, July 1957, p. 17 [Hebrew]. Buber, Scholem, and others insisted that the term "Messianic" should only refer to a religious ideal, which could not properly refer to Zionism as a movement within the political world. Ben-Gurion flatly rejected this view, arguing that Messianism meant the desire to perfect the world, to whatever degree this was possible, within the natural course of history. See Rotenstreich to Ben-Gurion, April 3, 1957; Ben-Gurion to Rotenstreich, April 29, 1957, reprinted in *Hazut* 3, July 1957, pp. 27, 29 [Hebrew]. Ben-Gurion's view that Zionism and Messianism were historically intertwined later received important support in Jacob Katz, "Israel and the Messiah," *Commentary,* January 1982, esp. p. 41. The pro-

fessors' opposition to Ben-Gurion's use of the term "Messianic" was part of a more general theory of the illegitimacy of using Jewish religious terms within the framework of Zionism. For the positions of Buber, Scholem, and others on this subject, see Shapira, "Political Messianism," p. 57; Mendes-Flohr, "The Appeal of the Incorrigible Idealist," p. 149; Scholem to Rosenzweig, December 26, 1926, quoted in Shapira, "Political Messianism," pp. 69–71.

57. See Baruch Litvin to Martin Buber, May 2, 1951; Martin Buber to Baruch Litvin, May 3, 1951. Buber, *Letters*, pp. 560–561.

58. Magnes Papers, P3/2399; Hattis, *Binational Idea*, p. 224.

59. See, for example, Dan Margalit's experience at such a session with Leibowitz during his first year at the Hebrew University in 1960. Dan Margalit, *I Saw Them All* (Tel Aviv: Zmora-Bitan, 1997), p. 54 [Hebrew].

60. Yehoshua Arieli, "Jacob Talmon: An Intellectual Portrait," in *Totalitarian Democracy and After*, pp. 3–4.

61. See Amos Elon, *Founders and Sons* (New York: Penguin Books, 1983), first published in 1971; and Yonatan Shapiro, *An Elite Without Successors* (Tel Aviv: Sifriyat Poalim, 1984) [Hebrew].

62. Berl Katznelson, *Writings* (Tel Aviv: Mifleget Poalei Erez Israel, 1947), vol. 6, p. 337 [Hebrew].

63. Shmuel Dayan, *The Promised Land: Memoirs of Shmuel Dayan*, Sidney Lightman, trans. (London: Routledge and Kegan Paul, 1961), p. 30.

64. Minutes of the Mapai central committee, September 29, 1937. Ze'ev Sternhell, *The Founding Myths of Israel: Nationalism, Socialism, and the Making of the Jewish State*, David Maisel, trans. (Princeton: Princeton University Press, 1998), p. 267.

65. Buber to Ludwig Strauss, 1936. Friedman, *Martin Buber's Life and Work*, vol. 2, p. 249. See March 9, 1936, in Buber, *Letters*, p. 440.

66. Shimon Peres, *Battling for Peace: Memoirs* (London: Weidenfeld and Nicolson, 1995), pp. 37, 45.

67. Ibid.

68. Nathan Rotenstreich, "New National Thought," in Tzvi Adar, et al., eds., *Values of Judaism* (Tel Aviv: Mahbarot Lisafrut, 1953), p. 115 [Hebrew].

69. *Ba'ayot Hazman*, May 27, 1948, in Buber, *Two Peoples*, p. 221; speech before the Jerusalem Ideological Conference of the Jewish Agency, August 1957, reprinted as "Israel's Mission and Zion," in Buber, *Israel and the World*, pp. 262–263.

70. Katznelson, *Writings*, vol. 6, p. 338.

71. Nurit Gertz, *Amos Oz: A Monograph* (Tel Aviv: Sifriyat Poalim, 1981), p. 28 [Hebrew].

72. Benvenisti, *Conflicts*, pp. 56–57.

73. Speech before the Mapai central committee, June 30, 1960. Beit Berl Archives.

74. Interview with Nurit Gertz, quoted in Nurit Gertz, *Hirbet Hiza and the Morning After* (Tel Aviv: Hakibbutz Hameuhad, 1984), p. 58 [Hebrew].

75. Gabriel Moked, "Notes in Possible Debate," *Achshav* 3–4 (1959), pp. 30–33 [Hebrew].

76. All interviews from unpublished study by Dina Blank. Interviews were conducted with Segal, January 4 and 8, 1996; Dayan, July 7, 1996; Sternhell, August 16, 1996; Pappe, January 2, 1996; Segev, December 28, 1995; A. B. Yehoshua, January 1, 1996; Marmari, August 27, 1996; Kasher, January 19, 1996; Morris, December 27, 1995.

77. Ibid.

78. Ibid.

79. Gertz, *Amos Oz*, p. 24.

80. Interview conducted by Dina Blank, July 16, 1996.

81. Benvenisti, *Conflicts*, pp. 31–32, 54.

82. Interview conducted by Dina Blank, January 7, 1996.

83. Joseph Cohen, *Voices of Israel* (Albany: State University of New York Press, 1990), p. 132.

Chapter Thirteen

1. Martin Buber, "Israel's Mission and Zion," in Martin Buber, *Israel and the World: Essays in a Time of Crisis* (New York: Schocken, 1963), p. 261.

2. Lavon's charges in the Knesset committee were not public, but information about his testimony was leaked to the newspapers, which commented on the basis of these leaks as well as further embellishments and insinuations made off the record. Shabtai Teveth, *Ben-Gurion's Spy* (New York: Columbia, 1996), pp. 202–206.

3. Some of my conclusions in this regard are supported by a recent article published on the subject of the intellectuals and the Lavon Affair, which came to my attention as this book was going to press. See Yehiam Weitz, "The Involvement of the Intellectuals in the Lavon Affair," *Zion*, Fall 1999, pp. 370–377.

4. Nurit Gertz, Amos Oz: A Monograph (Tel Aviv: Sifriyat Poalim, 1981), pp. 28–29 [Hebrew].

5. Gideon Shimoni, *The Zionist Ideology* (Hanover: Brandeis and University Press of New England, 1995), p. 215; Eyal Kafkafi, *Lavon: Anti-Messiah* (Tel-Aviv: Am Oved, 1998), pp. 18, 26 [Hebrew].

6. See Tzvi Tzameret, "Ben-Gurion and Lavon: Two Approaches to the Appropriate Absorption of Immigrants in the Great Wave of Immigration," in Dalia Ofer, ed., *Between Immigrants and "Oldtimers": Israel in the Great Wave of Immigration, 1948–1953* (Jerusalem: Yad Yitzhak Ben-Tzvi, 1996), pp. 74 n. 4, 78–80, 88–90 [Hebrew]. See also Meir Avizohar and Avi Bareli, eds., *Now or Never: Proceedings of Mapai (The Labor Party of Eretz-Israel) in the Closing Year of the British Mandate, Introductions and Documents* (Kfar Saba: Beit Berl, 1989), pp. 483, 508 [Hebrew].

7. Teveth, *Spy*, pp. 134, 136–137.

8. Teveth, *Spy*, pp. 135–136.

9. Ibid., p. 136. The belief that Peres and Dayan had conspired to "publicly annihilate him" actually dated at least as far back as January 5, 1955, when he was still defense minister and under investigation by the Olshan-Dori commission. Ibid., p. 135.

10. Ibid., pp. 171, 174–180.

11. Uri Avneri was the son of German immigrants and a veteran of the Jabotinskyite underground organization Lehi, who in the 1950s briefly flirted with joining Ihud before striking out on his own in search of a "Semitic" fusion between Jews and Arabs. This activism, along with books such as *Israel Without Zionists* (New York: MacMillan, 1968), made Avneri one of the only successful popularizers of such ideas, with which he ran for Knesset and for which in 1960 he sought funding from the anti-Zionist American Council for Judaism. It was his weekly, *Ha'olam Hazeh,* that pioneered the revolt against Labor Zionism and the "smashing" of its myths, training "an entire generation" of investigative journalists who later became integrated into the mainstream media. See Dan Margalit, *I Saw Them All* (Tel Aviv: Zmora-Bitan, 1997), p. 213f. [Hebrew]; Shaika Ben-Porat, *Conversations with Motti Kirschenbaum* (Tel-Aviv: Sifriyat Poalim, 1998), pp. 58–59 [Hebrew].

12. Teveth, *Spy*, p. 204.

13. Kafkafi, *Lavon*, p. 367. Kafkafi, whose biography defends Lavon, claims that Lavon only said he feared that Dayan and Peres were involved.

14. Teveth, *Spy*, p. 198.

15. Dayan in particular bore the brunt of what *Davar* called "numerous accusations of totalitarian and anti-democratic tendencies" and found himself having to appear at party forums to explain his views on parliamentary democracy, peaceful transitions of power, and readiness to submit his actions to the judgment of the voter. *Davar*, January 25, 1961.

16. Teveth, *Spy*, pp. 219–220, 231.

17. Michael Bar-Zohar, *Ben-Gurion* (Tel Aviv: Am Oved, 1977), p. 1547 [Hebrew]; Kafkafi, *Lavon*, p. 380.

18. *Ner*, June–July 1956, p. 31.

19. *Ma'ariv*, October 14, 1960.

20. Ibid., January 6, 1961.

21. Ibid., January 31, 1961.

22. *Davar*, November 2, 1960; *Ha'aretz*, November 3, 1960.

23. *Ma'ariv*, October 9, 1960.

24. Ibid., January 17, 1961.

25. Ibid., January 12, 1961.

26. *Ha'aretz*, December 30, 1960.

27. Buber to Ben-Gurion, January 6, 1961. Buber Archives, Ms. Var. 350/I A85.

28. *Ma'ariv*, January 10, 1961.

29. Maurice Friedman, *Martin Buber's Life and Work* (Detroit: Wayne State University Press, 1988), vol. 3, p. 286.

30. *Ma'ariv*, January 12, 1961.

31. Ibid.

32. *Ha'aretz*, January 15, 1961.

33. *Ma'ariv*, January 27, 1961. Buber also quoted Kant to the effect that politicians must heed the advice of philosophers.

34. *Pi Ha'aton*, February 19, 1961.

35. *Ha'aretz*, February 17, 1961. See also *Ma'ariv*, January 16, 18, 1961; *Lamerhav*, February 8, 1961.

36. *Lamerhav*, February 20, 1961.

37. From the professors' first statement. *Ha'aretz*, December 30, 1960.

38. *Pi Ha'aton*, February 19, 1961.

39. *Ma'ariv*, January 12, 1961.

40. Before the Mapai central committee. *Ma'ariv*, February 5, 1961.

41. Ibid., November 2, 1960.

42. *Pi Ha'aton*, February 19, 1961. For the discussions that the instructors conducted with their students, see *Ha'aretz*, February 7, 1961; Amos Oz, "Between the Razor's Edge and the Canopy of Peace," *Yediot Aharonot*, May 29, 1990; Kafkafi, *Lavon*, p. 404.

43. *Pi Ha'aton*, February 19, 1961. Student Union Chairman Dan Bitan and *Pi Ha'aton* Editor Yigal Eilam and Deputy Editor Shlomo Rosner all appeared at student rallies on January 18 and February 13, in opposition to Ben-Gurion, along with various others among the newspaper's staff. See Yigal Eilam, interviewed in Yona Hadari-Ramage, *Stopping to Think: Conversations on Public Thought in Israel* (Ramat Efal: Yad Tabenkin, 1994), p. 411 [Hebrew].

44. *Ma'ariv*, January 18, 19, 29, February 12, 16, 20, 21, 22, 1961. *Ha'aretz*, February 6, 1961. The first advertisement by the students against Ben-Gurion seems to have appeared in *Ha'aretz* on February 8.

45. Yosef Almogi, *The Struggle for Ben Gurion* (Tel-Aviv: Yediot Aharonot, 1988), p. 239 [Hebrew].

46. Nurit Gertz, *Amos Oz: A Monograph* (Tel Aviv: Sifriyat Poalim, 1981), pp. 27–28 [Hebrew]. On the hatred of Ben-Gurion's "totalitarianism" as expressed by Oz and other students of his generation, see Gershon Shaked, interviewed in Hadari-Ramage, *Stopping to Think*, pp. 647, 649, 661.

47. Gertz, *Amos Oz*, pp. 28–29. Compare Dan Miron's contemptuous dismissal of Labor Zionist poet Nathan Alterman and his "cult of the heroic dead": "In poetry by Alterman and his students, the living-dead stood out in their importance, which far excelled that of those who were simply alive." Dan Miron, "From Creators and Builders to the Homeless," *Igra* 2 (1985–1986), p. 123.

48. Shaika Ben-Porat, *Conversations with Yossi Sarid* (Tel-Aviv: Sifriyat Poalim, 1997), pp. 38, 51 [Hebrew]. Many of the other academics who later headed the Hebrew University were followers of the professors in the efforts against Ben-Gurion, including Moshe Lissak, Uriel Tal, Yehoshua Arieli, Israeli Kolatt, Shmuel Almog, and Shlomo Avineri. Kafkafi, *Lavon,* p. 404.

49. *Ma'ariv*, February 5, 1961.

50. Ibid.

51. *Ha'aretz*, February 5, 1961.

52. Ibid., February 7, 1961.

53. *Davar*, February 26, 1961.

54. Almogi indicates that the attacks of the professors weighed heavily on the minds of the various Labor leaders. Almogi, *Struggle*, pp. 220–222, 234.

55. In mid-February 1961, after the parties of the left had accepted the "prohibition" on forming a government headed by Ben-Gurion, the prime minister turned to the National Religious Party, whose ties to the professors were very limited. Indeed, MK Yitzhak Rafael felt constrained to stress to the members of the NRP executive that the moral theories of the professors are not generally considered decisive in religious circles—a statement that probably reveals the strong impression that the stand of the professors had in fact made more than anything else. *Yediot Aharonot*, February 21, 1961; *Ma'ariv*, February 21, 1961. Interior Minister Shapira also attacked the professors, pointing out that they had been silent when the state had collaborated with injustices toward religious immigrants, such as forcing them to attend secular schools and shaving the sidecurls from the heads of immigrant childrens' heads. *Ha'aretz*, February 17, 1961; *Hatzofeh*, February 17, 1961.

56. The observation that the religious youth had been pulled along by the attitudes of the secular students who had followed the professors was given voice repeatedly within Religious-Zionist circles. One column in *Hatzofeh* commented: "At last the National Religious Party has merited having a youth of its own . . . Yet one gets the impression that our youth is only dragged along after the opinions of the secular youth." Ya'akov Meron, "Conscience, the Youth, and the Coalition," *Hatzofeh*, February 20, 1961. Similarly: "Our young people are very hurt when they are told that their whole awakening is the result of a desire to imitate others who are outside our camp. Nevertheless, it is difficult to free oneself from the impression that, in fact, such is the case." M. Glidai, "Democracy in Danger or Dangerous Democracy," *Hatzofeh*, February 23, 1961. Much the same view was expressed in the deliberations of the party executive by Eliezer Goelman. *Hatzofeh*, February 21, 1961.

57. The Religious Zionist leadership, and particularly the head of the NRP, Interior Minister Haim Moshe Shapira, were at first inclined to join a new, narrow-based government under Ben-Gurion, but even within the National Religious Party, the influence of the university grew as the days went by. Yavneh, the organization of religious

students, sent letters to their party's national leadership calling for the rejection of Ben-Gurion, and on February 20, religious students and other youth leaders mounted a day-long demonstration outside of NRP party headquarters in Jerusalem, where Ben-Gurion's offer to join the new government was being discussed. *Hatzofeh*, February 15, 1961; *Yediot Aharonot*, February 20, 21, 1961. This unprecedented "awakening" of the observant youth was received as a shock by the party leaders, at least one of whom, fearful of repercussions among the students, argued that the executive reject entry into Ben-Gurion's new government so as "not to disappoint them, for they are our future." Michael Hazani in *Hatzofeh*, February 17, 1961. Indeed, most of the contemporary journalistic accounts of the deliberations emphasized the impression made by the students on the party's executive committee. For example, eight days before the student demonstrations outside of NRP headquarters in Beit Meir, Ma'ariv reported: "In the National Religious Party, there is also pressure from 'below,' on the part of youth and intellectual circles, not to join a government headed by Ben-Gurion. This pressure, which has now spread to all parties, is the result of joint organization by the students and the professors [*anshei haruah*]." *Ma'ariv*, February 12, 1961. Similar reports, referring to the religious students or the party's "Youth Watch," consisting of students and recent graduates and their peers through their mid-thirties, appeared in *Ha'aretz*, February 13, 14, 1961. See also Hazani's speech before the NRP executive in *Hatzofeh*, February 17, 1961. Shapira himself confirmed that those present had been in no small measure influenced by the reaction of "the street"—which is to say, the student demonstrators. *Ma'ariv*, March 16, 1961; Almogi, *Struggle*, p. 250. Compare *Ha'aretz*'s report: "The negative vote in the party executive is being explained primarily as a consequence of the heavy pressure of the youth wing of the party. Even though this generation is not represented in the executive, its representatives nevertheless met with the heads of the party, and pressed on Mr. Shapira in particular with moral objections [to joining Ben-Gurion]. This pressure was felt very well at the meeting of the party executive." *Ha'aretz*, February 25, 1961.

58. Ben-Gurion held Mapam, under the leadership of Ya'ari, responsible for having spearheaded the political maneuvers to bring him down. *Ma'ariv*, October 17, 1961.

59. Ibid., August 29, September 8, 13, October 13, 1961; *Ha'aretz*, September 14, 15, 1961.

60. *Ma'ariv*, September 8, 1961.

61. Friedman, *Martin Buber's Life and Work*, vol. 3, p. 355.

Epilogue

1. Shlomo Avineri, "Israel in the Post-Ben Gurion Era: The Nemesis of Messianism," *Midstream* (September 1965), p. 16.

2. Ibid., p. 31.

3. Shaika Ben-Porat, *Conversations with Yossi Sarid* (Tel-Aviv: Sifriyat Poalim, 1997), pp. 59–60 [Hebrew].

4. Anita Shapira, "The Labor Movement and the Hebrew University," in Shaul Katz and Michael Heyd, eds., *The History of the Hebrew University in Jerusalem: Origins and Beginnings* (Jerusalem: Magnes Press, 1997), pp. 688–689 [Hebrew]. Today, the effects of this university-driven ethos are understood to be so great that former education minister Amnon Rubinstein has called for the drastic increase in university education in Israel as the most effective way of changing voting patterns. Amnon Rubinstein, "Education as a Political Factor," *Ha'aretz*, January 26, 1999.

5. Nathan Alterman, "At the Beginning of the Day," in Nathan Alterman, *Writings* (Tel Aviv: Devar, 1962), vol. 3, pp. 29–32 [Hebrew].

6. As reported by Yosef Harif, "The Poem That Induced Panic," *Ma'ariv*, May 19, 1967. Both Harif and professors at the Hebrew University say they remember the event but cannot recall the identity of the professor.

7. Michael Oren, "Did Israel Want the Six Day War?" *Azure* 7 (Spring 1999), pp. 56–57.

8. Michael Bar-Zohar, *Ben Gurion: A Biography*, Peretz Kidron, trans. (New York: Adama Books, 1986), pp. 312–314.

9. *Ha'aretz*, June 8, 1967.

10. Ceremony on the Mount of Olives, August 3, 1967. Reproduced in Moshe Dayan, *A New Map* (Tel Aviv: Ma'ariv, 1969), p. 173 [Hebrew].

11. Reuven Pedatzur, *The Victory of Confusion: Israeli Policy in the Territories After the Six-Day-War* (Tel Aviv: Betan, 1996), p. 229 [Hebrew].

12. Jacob Talmon, "Is Force Indeed an Answer to Everything?" *Dispersion and Unity* 17/18 (1973), p. 12; Jacob Talmon, "The Homeland Is in Danger," *Ha'aretz*, March 31, 1980; Yeshayahu Leibowitz, "Occupation and Terror," in *Judaism, Human Values, and the Jewish State*, Eliezer Goldman, ed. (Cambridge: Harvard University Press, 1992), pp. 237–240; Yeshayahu Leibowitz, "On the Territories, Peace and Security," *Ha'aretz*, November 3, 1972.

13. The most famous argument in favor of peace through strength in the Zionist canon was Jabotinsky's famous essay "The Iron Wall." First published in *Rasvyet*, November 4, 1923. Reprinted in Ze'ev Jabotinsky, *Selected Writings* (Jerusalem, Masada, 1946), vol. 3, pp. 6–11 [Hebrew]. Ben-Gurion was persuaded of the correctness of this approach at least as early as the 1930s. Anita Shapira, *The Sword of the Dove* (Tel Aviv: Am Oved, 1993), p. 288 [Hebrew].

14. For a similar account of the roles played by the 1967 and 1973 wars in the downfall of the public culture of Zionism, see Oz Almog, "From 'Our Right to the Land of Israel' to 'the Rights of Citizens,' and from 'a Jewish state' to 'a State of Law': The Judicial Revolution in Israel and Its Cultural Implications," *Alpaim* 18 (1999), pp. 84–98.

15. "The tradition has been handed down to us that there will be a spiritual revolt in the land of Israel and among the people Israel when the national revival is about to begin. . . . The ground for this revolt is the inclination to materialism that must arise among the entire nation in an extreme form after the passage of so many years when the entire nation lacked the need and possibility of material activity." R. Avraham Yitzhak Kook, *Orot*, p. 84, quoted in Ehud Luz, *Parallels Meet: Religion and Nationalism in the Early Zionist Movement (1882–1904)*, Lenn J. Schramm, trans. (Philadelphia: Jewish Publication Society, 1988), p. xiv.

16. On the ideological affinity between Labor Zionism and the religious neosettlement movement, see Ze'ev Sternhell, *The Founding Myths of Israel: Nationalism, Socialism, and the Making of the Jewish State*, David Maisel, trans. (Princeton: Princeton University Press, 1998), pp. 332–343; Anita Shapira, "People as Human Beings," in *Basha'ar*, April 14, 1999, p. 25; Meron Benvenisti, *Conflicts and Contradictions* (New York: Villard Books, 1986), p. 70.

17. Both settlements were founded in locations in which Jewish settlements had been destroyed after their inhabitants had been massacred: Hebron in 1929 (the remaining Jews were evacuated by the British in 1936) and Kfar Etzion by invading Jordanian forces in 1948.

18. Hagai Segal, *Dear Brothers: The West Bank Jewish Underground* (Jerusalem: Keter, 1987), p. 21 [Hebrew].

19. Ibid., p. 40.

20. Michael Keren, *Ben-Gurion and the Intellectuals: Power, Knowledge, and Charisma* (Dekalb: Northern Illinois University Press, 1983), p. 99.

21. Herzl to Baron Maurice de Hirsch, June 3, 1895. *Briefe und Tagebuecher* (Vienna: Propylaeen, 1983–1996), vol. 4, p. 46 [German].

22. Ahad Ha'am, "The Revival of the Spirit," *Hashiloah* 10 (December 1902), p. 487 [Hebrew].

23. Keren, *Ben-Gurion and the Intellectuals*, p. 94. See also Anita Shapira, "Ben-Gurion and the Bible: The Forging of an Historical Narrative?" *Middle Eastern Studies* (October 1997), pp. 663, 669.

24. As retold by S. Yizhar, interviewed in *Panim*, Summer 1999, p. 51.

25. *Ha'aretz*, June 11, 1954; Eli Shaltiel, ed., *Ben-Gurion, the First Prime Minister: Selected Documents (1847–1963)* (Jerusalem: Israel State Archives, 1996), p. 261 [Hebrew].

26. Avineri, "Nemesis," p. 29.

27. Amos Oz, "A Laden Wagon and an Empty Wagon? Reflections on the Culture of Israel," *Free Judaism* (October 1997), p. 5.

28. For further discussion, see Yoram Hazony, "Did Herzl Mean to Establish a 'Jewish State'?" *Azure* 9 (Spring 2000), pp. 24–49.

Index

Hazony, Yoram

The Jewish State -
the Struggle for Israel's Soul

800
Haz

DATE DUE
